*Conventional Forces and American Defense Policy*

REVISED EDITION

# *International Security* Readers

*Strategy and Nuclear Deterrence* (1984)

*Military Strategy and the Origins of the First World War* (1985)

*Conventional Forces and American Defense Policy* (1986)

*The Star Wars Controversy* (1986)

*Naval Strategy and National Security* (1988)

—published by Princeton University Press

*Soviet Military Policy* (1989)

*Conventional Forces and American Defense Policy*, revised edition (1989)

—published by The MIT Press

# Conventional Forces and American Defense Policy

AN *International Security* READER

REVISED EDITION

EDITED BY

*Steven E. Miller*

*and Sean M. Lynn-Jones*

THE MIT PRESS

CAMBRIDGE, MASSACHUSETTS

# Contents

# The Contributors

STEVEN E. MILLER is Co-editor of *International Security* and a Senior Research Fellow at the Stockholm International Peace Research Institute (SIPRI).

SEAN M. LYNN-JONES is Managing Editor of *International Security* and a Research Fellow at the Center for Science and International Affairs, Harvard University.

STEPHEN M. WALT is Associate Professor of Political Science at the University of Chicago.

STEVEN R. DAVID is Associate Professor in the Department of Political Science at The Johns Hopkins University.

GORDON ADAMS is Director of the Defense Budget Project at the Center for Budget and Policy Priorities in Washington, D.C.

STEPHEN ALEXIS CAIN is the Senior Budget Analyst at the Defense Budget Project.

BARRY R. POSEN is Associate Professor of Political Science at MIT and teaches in the Defense and Arms Control Studies Program there.

JOHN J. MEARSHEIMER is Professor in the Political Science Department at the University of Chicago.

ELIOT A. COHEN teaches in the Strategy Department of the U.S. Naval War College, where he is Secretary of the Navy Senior Research Fellow. He is spending 1989–90 as the Lynne and Harry Bradley Senior Research Fellow in Strategic Studies at the John M. Olin Institute of Strategic Studies, Center for International Affairs, Harvard University.

SAMUEL P. HUNTINGTON is Eaton Professor of the Science of Government and Director of the John M. Olin Institute of Strategic Studies at the Center for International Affairs, Harvard University.

ROBERT D. BLACKWILL is Director of European and Soviet Affairs at the National Security Council.

JACK SNYDER is Associate Professor in the Political Science Department and the Harriman Institute for the Advanced Study of the Soviet Union at Columbia University.

JOSHUA M. EPSTEIN is a Senior Fellow at the Brookings Institution and Visiting Lecturer in Public and International Affairs at the Woodrow Wilson School, Princeton University.

# Acknowledgments

The editors gratefully acknowledge the assistance that has made this book possible. A deep debt is owed to all those at the Center for Science and International Affairs, Harvard University, who have played an editorial role at *International Security*, including Paul Doty, Joseph S. Nye, Jr., Albert Carnesale, Michael Nacht, Ashton Carter, Derek Leebaert, Stephen Van Evera, Melissa Healy, Lisbeth Tarlow Bernstein, Lynn Page Whittaker, Teresa Pelton Johnson, Mary Ann Wells, and Maude Fish. Special thanks go to Ann Callahan and Lisa Grumbach for their skill and diligence in preparing the volume for publication.

# Preface
Steven E. Miller and
Sean M. Lynn-Jones

In the time since the first edition of this book was published, issues of conventional forces have acquired a new importance and urgency in the American defense debate. The indisputable dangers of nuclear war have understandably compelled continued attention to nuclear weapons, but neglected issues of conventional deterrence and force planning have now come to the fore.

There are at least three explanations for the growing interest in conventional forces. First, negotiation of the INF Treaty has drawn renewed attention to the state of NATO's conventional forces and the NATO–Warsaw Pact conventional balance in Central Europe. By removing an entire class of nuclear weapons from Europe, the INF Treaty has, in the eyes of many commentators, reduced the significance of nuclear deterrence of a Warsaw Pact invasion and forced NATO to place greater reliance on its conventional defenses.

Second, the United States and the Soviet Union have become more concerned about the resources that they devote to defense, and conventional forces account for the overwhelming majority of Soviet and U.S. military spending. Although calculations of the exact percentages vary and the numbers are not constant from year to year, over 80 percent of the U.S. defense budget is invested in conventional forces. As concern over the U.S. federal budget deficit grows, even greater attention will be devoted to finding ways to control military spending. In the Soviet Union, maintaining large conventional forces imposes a heavy burden on a faltering economy. General Secretary Gorbachev's "new thinking" thus includes a desire to reduce the defense burden and thus stimulate economic growth.

Third, and related to the impact of the INF Treaty and the economic burden of conventional forces, conventional arms control has emerged as a critical issue in Europe. The long-running and hopelessly stalled talks on Mutual and Balanced Force Reductions (MBFR) have been replaced by new negotiations on Conventional Forces in Europe (CFE). Few observers expect that progress will be easy or rapid, but the prospect of conventional arms control compels serious analyses of the current conventional balance and the impact of arms control proposals on stability in Europe.

In addition to these new reasons for devoting attention to problems of conventional forces, several reasons enumerated in the preface to the first edition of this book remain valid. Conventional forces are still more likely to be used in combat or for diplomatic purposes than nuclear weapons. Rough parity at the strategic nuclear level may mean that nuclear weapons are most useful in deterring nuclear attacks, requiring enhanced conventional forces for other contingencies. It is also widely agreed that any nuclear conflict would almost certainly be the result of escalation from conventional warfare.

It has thus become even more important to consider the questions and issues associated with the choice of conventional strategies, the acquisition of conventional forces, and the employment of conventional military power. The essays in this volume offer analyses of and perspectives on several major conventional problems in American defense policy.

The first section addresses the broad questions of overall military strategy and its impact on the U.S. defense effort. Strategy includes determining interests and allocating resources—means as well as ends—so problems of the U.S. defense budget are also considered here.

In "The Case for Finite Containment: Analyzing U.S. Grand Strategy," Stephen Walt offers his analysis of the basic strategic objectives of the United States and the military policies needed to achieve those goals. After reviewing several prominent perspectives on U.S. grand strategy, he argues that four critical issues must be addressed in formulating it: identifying key areas of vital interest; the offense-defense balance; Soviet intentions; and the causes of alignment. Walt's analysis of these questions leads to the conclusion that finite containment is the most appropriate grand strategy for the United States. This strategy, similar to those outlined by Walter Lippmann and George Kennan in the 1940s, would emphasize containing Soviet expansion on the Eurasian landmass. The United States would preserve its present alliances with Western Europe, Japan, and Korea, as well as a commitment to protect Western access to Persian Gulf oil. It would not, however, develop forces for large-scale interventions in the Third World or mount a global crusade against Marxism. Walt argues that such a strategy would enable the United States to reduce its military capabilities while continuing to defend vital interests.

Steven David, on the other hand, contends that the Third World is central to U.S. interests and makes the case for continuing U.S. involvement there. In "Why the Third World Matters," David recognizes that defending Western Europe and Japan is a key strategic objective of the United States, but he argues that the probability of combat and the potential threats to U.S. interests are also great—and perhaps greater—in the Third World. Many Third World regimes are unstable and most post-1945 conflicts have taken place in the Third World. U.S. economic stakes in the Third World are not limited to the Persian Gulf; strategic minerals are found in many other regions, and

U.S.–Third World trade continues to grow. Concerns such as terrorism and nuclear proliferation are paramount in the eyes of the American public and require an active U.S. policy toward the Third World. The United States, David concludes, should avoid protracted Vietnam-like wars, but must maintain the capability to launch a major intervention that can accomplish its goals quickly.

Any grand strategy adopted by the United States will have to come to terms with economic and budgetary realities. The defense buildup of the Reagan administration has left a troubling legacy, say Gordon Adams and Stephen Alexis Cain in "Defense Dilemmas in the 1990s." They point out that the Reagan administration's heavy investment in weapons procurement has created a vast backlog of obligatory outlays for new weapons systems. As the stockpile of complex weapons expands, funding requirements for operations and for support will also grow. Initial commitments to research and development on many systems have also opened the way to future increases, unless some of these programs are cancelled before entering production. All these pressures to increase military spending come at a time of mounting political and economic pressures to trim the defense budget. Adams and Cain conclude that the United States can meet military requirements without increasing defense spending, but only if budgetary priorities are established on the basis of a thorough review of U.S. commitments. In the absence of such steps, they argue, continuing the present course will lead to budgetary chaos and military disorganization.

The single most important nonnuclear issue in U.S. defense policy is the commitment to defend NATO Europe. In Central Europe, the United States and its allies most closely confront Soviet military power. Large Soviet conventional forces directly threaten U.S. interests. Not surprisingly, the defense of Western Europe consumes the lion's share of U.S. defense spending. Parts II and III of this collection accordingly focus on two crucial considerations in assessing U.S. participation in European defense: the NATO–Warsaw Pact conventional balance and alternative approaches to European security.

Perceptions of the conventional balance in Europe have pervasive implications for U.S. defense policy. Concerns about NATO inferiority have led the alliance to embrace doctrines of nuclear first-use to deter a Soviet attack or to thwart it should war come. These issues have been prominent in relations among NATO members, as the United States has steadily pressed its West European allies to bolster their defense efforts to enhance NATO's conventional (and nuclear) force postures. The new prominence of conventional arms control has made assessing the conventional balance even more important. Such assessments are necessary to determine whether arms control measures will increase or decrease stability and security in Central Europe. In sum, the United States' conventional force posture, its negotiating position in conventional arms control talks, its nuclear doctrine and requirements, and its relations with its allies are deeply, if not always directly, influenced by judgments about the two large and heavily armed forces that face one another in the center of Europe.

Assessing the conventional balance in Europe is thus a vitally important exercise. But evaluating conventional capabilities is notoriously difficult because effectiveness on the battlefield often turns on intangible factors such as weather, and because military forces may be procured, organized, deployed, and employed according to different strategies and doctrines in response to different security situations. As a consequence, crude comparisons of numbers of men and equipment—"bean counts"—are very close to meaningless, although unfortunately commonplace. All this guarantees that the process of evaluating the conventional balance in Europe is not merely important, but complex, and fraught with possibilities for dispute and subjective judgment.

The three essays in Part II discuss the complexities that are inevitably involved in serious assessments of the conventional balance. In "Measuring the European Conventional Balance: Coping with Complexity in Threat Assessment," Barry Posen provides an inventory of the key variables—buildup rates, exchange rates, attrition rates, movement rates, and so on—in a thorough balance assessment and discusses how to assign values to these variables on the basis of historical experience. Posen shows how these variables can be combined in the Attrition-FEBA Expansion Model, which captures some of the complexities missed in simplistic force comparisons. He argues that NATO and the Warsaw Pact procure military capability according to very different doctrines (with NATO investing much more heavily in command, control, logistics, and training) and shows that conclusions about the state of the military balance are directly related to assumptions about which doctrine is correct. If NATO forces are measured against Soviet doctrine, they appear to be inadequate. If, however, NATO is given credit for the different sorts of military investments it makes, then its military capability appears sufficient to hold its own against the Warsaw Pact in Central Europe.

Soviet doctrine for conventional conflict in Europe is generally seen as calling for a blitzkrieg attack that would aim for a quick and decisive victory.

An important measure of the adequacy of NATO's forces, therefore, is whether they are capable of thwarting such a Soviet blitzkrieg. This question is analyzed by John Mearsheimer in "Why the Soviets Can't Win Quickly in Central Europe." He takes issue with the conventional wisdom that the Red Army and its allies could rapidly overrun NATO's conventional forces in Central Europe, arguing that in fact NATO's chances of stopping a Soviet blitzkrieg are really quite good. He arrives at this conclusion by carefully examining the forces, the geography, the terrain, and the operational difficulties that would obtain in any large armored battle in Central Europe. Contending that the Soviets would find it extremely difficult to achieve in the key sectors the ratios of superiority necessary to successfully effect armored breakthroughs, he further suggests that the Soviet military is not well prepared to conduct such a campaign.

Eliot Cohen presents a different perspective in "Toward Better Net Assessment: Rethinking the European Conventional Balance," suggesting that many relatively optimistic assessments of the conventional balance, including those offered by Mearsheimer and Posen, suffer from serious methodological flaws. In particular, Cohen contends that analysts lack important data on Warsaw Pact forces and have used models that do not capture the complex reality of modern war. His analysis indicates that comprehensive assessments must consider how alliance politics would affect NATO's ability to fight, must treat Western intelligence capabilities as well as Soviet military capabilities realistically, and must use data and models more carefully. He concludes that the European balance is not only worse, but also far more complex, than has been suggested by many optimistic analyses.[1]

In Part III, we shift our attention from the adequacy of NATO forces to the question of alternative means for achieving security in Europe. The debate on NATO strategy in recent years has included proposals for new military strategies, as well as calls for greater reliance on arms control to reduce the threat posed by Soviet and Warsaw Pact forces.

The role of nuclear weapons in European defense has been a critical issue in debates over NATO strategy. The United States and West European mem-

---

1. Readers who wish to pursue these questions further should see the exchange of correspondence on "Reassssing Net Assessment" in *International Security*, Vol. 13, No. 4 (Spring 1989), pp. 128–179; the Policy Focus section, "The European Conventional Balance," *International Security*, Vol. 12, No. 4 (Spring 1988), pp. 152–202; and John J. Mearsheimer, "Assessing the Conventional Balance: The 3:1 Rule and its Critics," and Joshua M. Epstein, "The 3:1 Rule, the Adaptive Dynamic Model, and the Future of Security Studies," both in *International Security*, Vol. 13, No. 4 (Spring 1989), pp. 54–89 and 90–127.

bers of the alliances wrangled over these issues in the 1950s and 1960s before ultimately adopting the strategy of flexible response, which called for significant conventional forces as well as the threat of nuclear escalation. It is therefore not surprising that these questions reemerged in the 1980s. Antinuclear protests and calls for NATO to adopt a no first-use policy placed the issue firmly on the agenda on both sides of the Atlantic. The INF Treaty has been seen (with both hope and despair) as a possible precursor to the removal of additional categories of nuclear weapons from Europe or even the complete denuclearization of the continent.

John Mearsheimer addresses these issues in "Nuclear Weapons and Deterrence in Europe." He argues that the threat of nuclear escalation is a critical component of NATO's strategy of deterrence. Even if the probability of nuclear war is low, the costs are so high that nuclear weapons significantly enhance NATO's ability to deter a Warsaw Pact conventional attack. Removing nuclear weapons or adopting a no first-use policy would require NATO to judge its conventional forces by a higher standard. Mearsheimer reviews the many alternatives to NATO's current posture of forward defense that have been proposed—area defense, maneuver defense, a counteroffensive capability, arms control, increased force levels, and a new generation of sophisticated weapons—and finds them wanting when evaluated on political and military grounds. He concludes that reducing the role of nuclear weapons is not a viable answer to NATO's defense dilemmas.

In "Conventional Deterrence and Conventional Retaliation in Europe," Samuel Huntington proposes another alternative to NATO's strategy of flexible response and forward defense. He makes the case for a strategy based on a conventional retaliatory offensive, whereby NATO would respond to a Soviet conventional attack in Central Europe by itself striking into Eastern Europe. Doing so, he suggests, would threaten the Soviet Union's own offensive plans, requiring of the Soviet military the kind of wartime innovation unsuited to its rigid approach to war, would force the Warsaw Pact to divert some of its offensive forces to defensive tasks, and would increase the likelihood that the war would be protracted, thus producing the outcome that the Soviet Union hopes to avoid. Huntington argues, therefore, that such a conventional retaliatory threat would shore up NATO's ability to deter conventional attack and thereby help to compensate for the dwindling credibility of NATO's nuclear threats.

The INF Treaty and Gorbachev's attempts to restructure Soviet military doctrine have given conventional arms control negotiations unprecedented prominence on the European defense agenda. Mutual reductions in NATO and Warsaw Pact force may enable both alliances to achieve the same level of security at less cost. In a time of constraints on military spending, conventional arms control has obvious appeal. If combined with a restructuring of conventional force postures and doctrinal changes, arms control may not only save money but also produce greater stability by reducing fears of surprise attacks.

Conventional arms control is, however, far more complicated than strategic nuclear arms control. The lack of progress in the long-running MBFR talks suggests that it would be premature to be optimistic about a new round of negotiations. Many issues of stability, parity, and verification have yet to receive detailed analysis. And negotiations are bound to be complicated by the involvement of NATO and Warsaw Pact allies.

Robert Blackwill offers an overview of these complexities in "Conceptual Problems of Conventional Arms Control." Drawing on his experience as U.S. ambassador to the MBFR talks, he cautions against premature optimism about the chances for negotiating limits on conventional forces in Europe. He suggests that any negotiations will have to take into account the relationship between military force levels and the political future of Europe, the appropriate level and deterrent role of U.S. forces in Europe, and the difficulties of verifying any agreement. These problems, Blackwill concludes, will bedevil future negotiations and must be addressed in a comprehensive negotiating position.

In "Limiting Offensive Conventional Forces: Soviet Proposals and Western Options," Jack Snyder takes the view that potential changes in the Soviet military posture in Europe have created the possibility of negotiating limits on offensive conventional forces. The Soviet Union has displayed greater willingness to restructure its conventional forces to reduce offensive capabilities. NATO should take advantage of this opportunity to seek an agreement that includes asymmetric reductions in armored forces and the withdrawal of deep-strike missiles and aircraft from the European theater.

While the European contingency is usually seen as the most important on the agenda of conventional defense issues, defending U.S. interests in the Third World also raises many troublesome (and very different) problems. Indeed, some of the gravest difficulties that the United States has faced since World War II have resulted from involvement in conflict in the Third World, as manifested particularly in the brutal and frustrating war in Korea and in the nightmarish experience in Vietnam. Most recent U.S. military forays into the Third World—in Grenada, Lebanon, and the Persian Gulf—have generated casualties and controversy. Third World contingencies raise a host of potential troubles: U.S. interests are often not well defined, complicating decisions on where to fight; public support may be shaky or nonexistent, undermining the war effort as in the Vietnam conflict; U.S. forces may not be well prepared for the kind of war they have to fight; distances are often great and bases scarce, posing challenging logistical problems; host governments may be frail; enemies may be elusive and unwilling to fight the kind of war that the U.S. military would prefer. Despite these potential difficulties, the United States continues to have significant interests in the Third World, and conflicts there seem more likely to occur than does large-scale war between NATO and the Warsaw Pact. Part IV addresses this set of issues.

Eliot Cohen, in "Constraints on America's Conduct of Small Wars," argues that the most serious impediment to successful American participation in small wars is the unsuitability of U.S. military power to the conditions and requirements of such conflicts. To be sure, Cohen notes, political considerations—the state of public opinion, the role of allies, the power of Congress— must be taken into account in the conduct of small wars. But the larger problem, he believes, is that small wars have particular characteristics all their own, and U.S. military power, shaped as it is primarily to meet the special challenges of a large war in Europe, is inappropriate, not at all tailored to meet the special challenges of these conflicts. Cohen outlines the distinct nature of small wars and suggests that in almost every way—manpower, doctrine, equipment, and organization—the U.S. military is unprepared for such conflict.

Since the oil crises of the 1970s, the Persian Gulf has assumed special importance in American consideration of projecting military power in the Third World. The disruption, destruction, or capture of the oil-bearing regions of the Gulf by hostile forces has been feared as a potential disaster for the United States and its import-dependent industrial allies. While there are many potential threats to the oil fields of the Persian Gulf that might require a military response, the largest military threat is the possibility of Soviet intervention in the region. It is this scenario that Joshua Epstein analyzes in "Soviet Vulnerabilities in Iran and the RDF Deterrent." He carefully examines the likely nature of a Soviet invasion aimed at the oil fields in the southwestern region of Iran and the capability of the United States to deter or to defeat such an attack. This is, without doubt, one of the most difficult parts of the world in which to operate U.S. military forces because its distance from the United States is so great, the number of useful U.S. bases is so few, the climate is so severe, the logistics requirements are so substantial, and the government of Iran is so hostile. Nevertheless, Epstein notes that military operations in this area pose many daunting difficulties for the Soviet Union as well, and he points out that if the United States makes effective use of the warning time that would be available and if it devises a strategy that exploits Soviet vulnerabilities, then it is capable of mounting a quite formidable military capability in southern Iran—one that should serve as an effective deterrent to Soviet aggression.

The twelve essays collected in this volume do not, of course, exhaust the menu of nonnuclear issues in U.S. defense policy, nor do they even cover every aspect of the several major issues that are addressed. They do, however, provide a good indication of the kinds of issues, problems, and debates that arise in connection with three of the most important and enduring components of U.S. defense policy: its overall military strategy; its commitment to defend Western Europe; and its need to project military power in the Third World. These issues will not go away in the foreseeable future, and U.S. security will depend to a considerable extent on the ways in which the dilemmas and disputes that attend them are addressed and resolved. It is hoped that this volume will inspire greater attention to these subjects and will provoke efforts to enlarge and enrich the debate over the conventional military power of the United States.

*Part I:*
*Strategy, Spending, and*
*Defense Policy*

# The Case for Finite Containment

Stephen M. Walt

## Analyzing U.S. Grand Strategy

**S**ince the Second World War, the main objective of U.S. grand strategy has been to prevent territorial expansion by the Soviet Union while avoiding a major war. Although both ends and means have varied over time, the central elements of this strategy—commonly known as "containment"—have been military alliances with Western Europe and Japan and the deployment of U.S. armed forces in Europe and the Far East.[1] Despite initial misgivings and occasional flurries of criticism, the strategy has enjoyed substantial popular support, largely because it has worked so well.

In recent years, however, containment has come under increasing attack. Given the widespread belief that U.S. power has declined (at least in relative terms), and the possibility that domestic reforms in the Soviet Union imply a reduction in the Soviet threat, it is not surprising that the fundamental principles of U.S. grand strategy are now the subject of a growing debate.[2]

A slightly different version of this essay will appear in Daniel Kaufman, David Clark, and Kevin Sheehan, eds., *The Future of U.S. National Strategy*. Some portions draw upon my "Two Cheers for Containment: Probable Allied Responses to U.S. Isolationism," in Ted Galen Carpenter, ed., *Collective Defense or Strategic Independence? Alternative Strategies for the Future* (Lexington Books, 1989). I would like to thank Richard Betts, Ivo Daalder, Charles Glaser, Robert Johnson, Deborah Welch Larson, John Mearsheimer, Warner Schilling, Jack Snyder, and Kenneth Waltz for their comments on earlier drafts of this article. I am especially grateful to Stephen Van Evera, whose work on this subject has shaped my thinking considerably, and to the MacArthur Foundation and Princeton's Center of International Studies for financial support.

*Stephen M. Walt is Associate Professor of Political Science at the University of Chicago, and the author of* The Origins of Alliances *(Cornell University Press, 1987). This article was written while he was a Guest Scholar at the Brookings Institution in Washington, D.C.*

1. On the evolution of postwar U.S. grand strategy and the shifts in ends and means, see John Lewis Gaddis, *Strategies of Containment* (New York: Oxford University Press, 1982); and Gaddis, "Containment and the Logic of Strategy," *The National Interest*, No. 10 (Winter 1987–88), pp. 27–38.
2. The best-known discussion of U.S. decline is Paul M. Kennedy, *The Rise and Fall of the Great Powers: Economic Change and Military Conflict from 1500 to 2000* (New York: Random House, 1987), chaps. 7–8. For arguments questioning this trend, see Bruce Russett, "The Mysterious Case of Vanishing Hegemony; or, Is Mark Twain Really Dead?" *International Organization*, Vol. 39, No. 2 (Spring 1985), pp. 207–231; Kenneth N. Waltz, *Theory of International Politics* (Reading, Mass.: Addison-Wesley, 1979), chaps. 7–9; Joseph S. Nye, Jr., "Understating U.S. Strengths," *Foreign Policy*, No. 72 (Fall 1988), pp. 105–129; and Samuel P. Huntington, "The U.S.—Decline or Renewal?" *Foreign Affairs*, Vol. 67, No. 2 (Winter 1988/89), pp. 76–96.

*International Security*, Summer 1989 (Vol. 14, No. 1)
© 1989 by the President and Fellows of Harvard College and of the Massachusetts Institute of Technology.

Unfortunately, this debate has not been conducted in a systematic way. In particular, the beliefs and assumptions that support different prescriptions are rarely identified or evaluated. As a result, assessing the relative merits of the various alternatives is extremely difficult.

Accordingly, this essay has two main goals. First, it presents a way of analyzing U.S. grand strategy that may help participants in this debate organize their discourse more effectively. In the simplest terms, a state's grand strategy is its plan for making itself secure. Grand strategy identifies the objectives that must be achieved to produce security, and describes the political and military actions that are believed to lead to this goal.[3] Strategy is thus a set of "contingent predictions": if we do A, B, and C, the desired results X, Y, and Z should follow.[4] Ideally, a state's grand strategy should be based on empirically grounded hypotheses that explain why a particular set of actions will produce greater security. Thus, the best—indeed, the *only*—way to assess the merits of different strategies is to evaluate the competing hypotheses on which they are based. This article attempts to perform this task.

Second, by comparing the theoretical and empirical underpinnings of several alternative U.S. grand strategies, this essay will demonstrate the advantages of a strategy of *finite* containment. Before outlining this strategy in more detail, however, let us first consider the main alternatives.

ALTERNATIVES TO FINITE CONTAINMENT

At some risk of oversimplification, alternative U.S. grand strategies can be divided into several distinct schools of thought.[5] At one extreme are those who may be termed the *"world order idealists."* These writers argue that the

---

3. According to Barry Posen, grand strategy is a "political-military means-ends chain, a state's theory about how it can best 'cause' security for itself." See Barry R. Posen, *The Sources of Military Doctrine: France, Britain, and Germany between the World Wars* (Ithaca: Cornell University Press, 1984), p. 13. For similar conceptions, see Edward Mead Earle, "Introduction," in Edward Mead Earle, ed., *Makers of Modern Strategy* (Princeton: Princeton University Press, 1943), p. vii; Bernard Brodie, "Strategy as a Science," *World Politics*, Vol. 1, No. 4 (July 1949), pp. 467–488; B.H. Liddell Hart, *Strategy* (New York: Praeger, 1967), pp. 335–336; and Carl von Clausewitz, *On War*, trans. and ed. Michael Howard and Peter Paret (Princeton: Princeton University Press, 1976), pp. 142–144.
4. See Alexander L. George and Richard Smoke, "Theory for Policy in International Relations," in *Deterrence in American Foreign Policy: Theory and Practice* (New York: Columbia University Press, 1974), pp. 617–625.
5. For a similar but not identical taxonomy of alternative U.S. grand strategies, see Colin S. Gray, *The Geopolitics of Super Power* (Lexington: University of Kentucky Press, 1988), chaps. 10–13.

main threat to the United States arises not from other states but from collective global problems such as the threat of nuclear war, ecological decay, and poverty. Because they believe that a system of independent states cannot deal effectively with these issues, these writers seek a fundamental transformation of the existing state system. The United States, they argue, should direct its efforts toward the creation of a more humanitarian world order through disarmament, moral education, greater reliance on international law, and strengthened international institutions. In the unlikely event that this approach were adopted, military power and alliance commitments would be of minor importance.[6]

A second grand strategy is *"neo-isolationism."* This strategy assumes that the United States has few security interests beyond its borders, that threats to these interests are modest, and that very limited means (a small army, a coastal navy, and a modest nuclear deterrent) are sufficient to protect them. Neo-isolationists argue that U.S. allies are capable of defending themselves, that U.S. alliance commitments entail escalatory threats that lack credibility, and that current economic conditions require massive reductions in U.S. defense expenditures. Accordingly, these writers advocate the rapid dissolution of U.S. alliance commitments, a drastic reduction in U.S. defense spending, and a return to hemispheric or continental defense.[7]

A third school favors *disengagement* from the traditional U.S. commitment to Western Europe, although most of these writers do not want to eliminate

---

6. See, e.g., Richard A. Falk, *A Study of Future Worlds* (New York: The Free Press, 1975); Robert C. Johansen, *The National Interest and the Human Interest: An Analysis of U.S. Foreign Policy* (Princeton: Princeton University Press, 1980); and Randall Forsberg, "Confining the Military to Defense as a Route to Disarmament," *World Policy Journal*, Vol. 1, No. 2 (Winter 1984), pp. 285–318.

7. Advocates of this view include Earl Ravenal, *NATO: The Tides of Discontent* (Berkeley: Institute of International Studies, 1985); Ravenal, "Europe Without America: The Erosion of NATO," *Foreign Affairs*, Vol. 63, No. 5 (Summer 1985), pp. 1020–1035; Ravenal, "The Case for a Withdrawal of Our Forces," *New York Times Magazine*, March 6, 1983, pp. 58–75; Laurence Radway, "Let Europe Be Europe," *World Policy Journal*, Vol. 1, No. 1 (Fall 1983), pp. 23–43; Christopher Layne, "Ending the Alliance," *Journal of Contemporary Studies*, Vol. 6, No. 3 (1983), pp. 5–31; and Layne, "Atlanticism Without NATO," *Foreign Policy*, No. 67 (Summer 1987), pp. 22–45. Some supporters of withdrawal also argue for greater efforts to promote international economic coordination, a view that analysts like Ravenal would reject. See Jerry W. Sanders, "Security and Choice," *World Policy Journal*, Vol. 1, No. 4 (Summer 1984), pp. 698–707; Jerry W. Sanders and Sherle R. Schwenninger, "Foreign Policy for the Post-Reagan Era," *World Policy Journal*, Vol. 3, No. 3 (Summer 1986), pp. 369–418 and "A Third-World Policy for the Post-Reagan Era," Vol. 4, No. 1 (Winter 1986–87), pp. 1–50; and Richard J. Barnet, "The Four Pillars," *The New Yorker*, March 9, 1987, pp. 76–89. Also advocating a U.S. withdrawal is Melvyn Krauss, *How NATO Weakens the West* (New York: Simon and Schuster, 1986).

it entirely. Some favor reducing the U.S. role in Europe in order to devote greater effort to the Third World or the Pacific Rim, while others favor withdrawal in order to reduce the U.S. defense budget. Unlike the neo-isolationists, these writers acknowledge that Europe is still a vital U.S. interest and that the United States should play an active role in deterring Soviet expansion. However, they also believe that U.S. allies should do more for their own defense, thereby allowing the United States to reduce or redeploy its military forces.[8]

Although there are important differences between these various schools (and among different representatives of each one), these analysts generally favor reductions in the United States' global role. By contrast, a number of other writers advocate a strategy of *global containment*, which would maintain or expand present U.S. commitments. This strategy seeks to contain Soviet *or* communist expansion on a global basis, on the assumption that the emergence of pro-Soviet regimes anywhere in the world is a positive addition to Soviet power. Contemporary advocates of this strategy also argue that the United States faces a diverse and growing array of other threats (such as international terrorism) which can best be met by continued increases in U.S. military capabilities and by a greater willingness to use these forces.[9]

---

8. The best example of this view is David P. Calleo, *Beyond American Hegemony: The Future of the Western Alliance* (New York: Basic Books, 1987). For a proposal that the United States focus greater attention on the Western hemisphere and the Pacific, see James Chace, "A New Grand Strategy," *Foreign Policy*, No. 70 (Spring 1988), pp. 3–25. Strategists advocating a reduction in Europe in order to increase U.S. capabilities in the Third World include Jeffrey Record, *Revising U.S. Military Strategy: Tailoring Means to Ends* (Washington, D.C.: Pergamon-Brassey's, 1984); Eliot A. Cohen, "The Long-Term Crisis of the Alliance," *Foreign Affairs*, Vol. 61, No. 2 (Winter 1982/83), p. 342; and Zbigniew Brzezinski, *Game Plan: The Geostrategic Framework for the Conduct of the U.S.-Soviet Contest* (Boston: Atlantic Monthly Press, 1986), p. 181 and passim. Overall, Brzezinski's recommendations suggest that his views lie closer to "global containment." Similarly, although he is essentially a neo-isolationist, Christopher Layne has suggested that a U.S. withdrawal from Europe could permit "reallocating remaining defense resources to stress strategic mobility and naval power projection." See Layne, "Atlanticism Without NATO," p. 45.
9. See, e.g., Samuel P. Huntington, ed., *The Strategic Imperative: New Policies for American Security* (Cambridge, Mass.: Ballinger, 1982), especially Huntington's essay "The Renewal of Strategy," pp. 1–52; Aaron Wildavsky, ed., *Beyond Containment: Alternative American Policies Toward the Soviet Union* (San Francisco: Institute for Contemporary Studies, 1983); Fred C. Iklé and Albert Wohlstetter, *Discriminate Deterrence: Report of the Commission on Integrated Long-Term Strategy* (Washington, D.C.: U.S. Government Printing Office [U.S. GPO], January 1988); and Gray, *Geopolitics of Super Power*, chap. 11. The grand strategy of the Reagan administration reflected this view as well. See Barry R. Posen and Stephen Van Evera, "Reagan Administration Defense Policy: Departure from Containment," in Kenneth A. Oye, Robert J. Lieber, and Donald Rothchild, eds., *Eagle Resurgent? The Reagan Era in American Foreign Policy* (Boston: Little, Brown, 1987), pp. 89–98; and Richard Melanson, *Writing History and Making Policy: The Cold War, Vietnam, and Revisionism* (Lanham, Md.: University Press of America, 1983), pp. 200–204.

A final alternative is *rollback*, which seeks to eliminate communist influence worldwide. Although it resembles global containment, this strategy rests on ideological preferences rather than an overriding concern for military security. The objective of rollback is not simply the containment of Soviet or communist power (though that is important) but the elimination of Marxism as a significant political force. Thus, rollback also prescribes active U.S. support for anti-communist forces (such as the Nicaraguan *contras* or pro-U.S. dictatorships) even if U.S. security interests are not involved.[10]

FINITE CONTAINMENT

Finite containment resembles the grand strategy outlined by George F. Kennan, Hans J. Morgenthau, and Walter Lippmann, which focused on containing direct Soviet expansion on the Eurasian landmass.[11] In addition to maintaining a robust nuclear deterrent, this strategy would preserve present U.S. alliances with Western Europe, Japan, and Korea (at roughly the current level of ground and air forces), along with the U.S. commitment to protect Western access to Persian Gulf oil.[12]

Finite containment is not simply a continuation of the status quo, however. For most of the Cold War, U.S. grand strategy has leaned towards global

---

10. The classic statement of the rollback strategy is James Burnham, *Containment or Liberation? An Inquiry into the Aims of United States Foreign Policy* (New York: John Day, 1952). For more recent versions, see Joseph Churba, *Soviet Breakout: Strategies to Meet It* (Washington, D.C.: Pergamon-Brassey's, 1988); Irving Kristol, "Foreign Policy in an Age of Ideology," *The National Interest*, No. 1 (Fall 1985), pp. 6–15; Charles Krauthammer, "The Poverty of Realism," *The New Republic*, February 17, 1986, pp. 14–22; and Norman Podhoretz, *The Present Danger* (New York: Simon and Schuster, 1980).
11. The goal of preventing Soviet expansion reflects the traditional U.S. interest in preventing any single power from controlling the combined resources of the Eurasian landmass. See Gaddis, *Strategies of Containment*, chap. 2; George F. Kennan, *Realities of American Foreign Policy* (Princeton: Princeton University Press, 1954), pp. 63–65; Walter Lippmann, *U.S. Foreign Policy: Shield of the Republic* (Boston: Little, Brown, 1943), pp. 108–113 and passim; Hans J. Morgenthau, *In Defense of the National Interest* (Lanham, Md.: University Press of America, 1982 reprint of 1951 edition), pp. 5–7 and passim; and Nicholas Spykman, *America's Strategy in World Politics: The United States and the Balance of Power* (New York: Harcourt, Brace, and Co., 1942), part 1. These prescriptions were not always consistent; for example, Kennan supported U.S. entry into the Korean War and remained ambivalent about intervention in other peripheral areas. See Walter L. Hixson, "Containment on the Perimeter: George Kennan and Vietnam," *Diplomatic History*, Vol. 12, No. 2 (Spring 1988), pp. 149–163.
12. See Stephen Van Evera, "American Strategic Interests: Why Europe Matters, Why the Third World Doesn't," testimony prepared for hearings before the Panel on Defense Burdensharing, Committee on Armed Services, U.S. House of Representatives, March 2, 1988; and Posen and Van Evera, "Departure from Containment," pp. 75–114.

containment, with occasional attempts to roll back Soviet clients.[13] Unlike global containment, finite containment seeks to prevent Soviet expansion only in the areas Kennan identified as "key centers of industrial power" (Western Europe and Japan). Thus, with the partial exception of the Persian Gulf (upon whose oil the industrial world depends), finite containment rejects a substantial U.S. military role in the Third World. And unlike rollback, finite containment does not entail a global crusade against Marxism. The United States would remain a global military power under this strategy, which would nevertheless permit substantial reductions in U.S. military capabilities. Thus, this strategy would help alleviate current U.S. fiscal problems without jeopardizing vital U.S. interests.

KEY QUESTIONS

The remainder of this essay examines four issues that divide the different schools of thought on U.S. grand strategy. How one answers these questions will determine the interests the United States should defend, the scope of possible threats, and the best way to overcome these challenges.

The first issue is the identification of *key areas of vital interest*: apart from U.S. territory itself, which regions are critical to U.S. security and which states are most likely to threaten them? The second issue is the *offense-defense balance*: is conquest easy or difficult, particularly in the regions that matter? In general, if offense is relatively easy, then vital regions will be more difficult to defend, and U.S. military requirements will increase. Third, what are Soviet intentions: how large are Soviet aims and how difficult are they to deter? If Soviet intentions are extremely hostile and if the Soviets are willing to run large risks, then U.S. security is reduced and providing an adequate deterrent is more difficult. Lastly, what are the *causes of alignment*: what factors will determine the level of support that the United States can obtain from others? If other states support U.S. strategic objectives, then the United States can safely do less. But if other states are unreliable, or hostile, then the United States must do more either to preserve its allies' allegiance or to overcome the additional opposition.

---

13. Not only has the United States used military force in a variety of Third World countries (e.g., Vietnam, the Dominican Republic, Lebanon), but it sought to overthrow a number of leftist or Marxist regimes on several occasions (e.g., Cuba, Iran, Guatemala, and the current targets of the "Reagan Doctrine").

Each of these issues has been debated throughout the Cold War, although these disputes have rarely been conducted openly. Fortunately, we now have over forty years of experience upon which to base our assessments: at the very least, it should be possible to reduce the range of disagreement. Taken together, the available evidence on these issues supports the strategy of finite containment.

*Identifying Vital Interests*

When formulating a grand strategy, the first step is to identify the key regions that comprise U.S. vital interests. For strong states who can afford to worry about more than just the defense of their own territory, the identification of vital interests will depend primarily on the distribution of global power: Which regions contain important assets? Which states possess the means to threaten these regions?

DEFINING POWER

National power is usually seen as a function of material assets like size of territory, population, military power, industrial capacity, and resource endowments.[14] These factors are often related (e.g., modern military power is based largely on industrial capacity), and together they determine a state's capacity to defend its interests, especially in war.[15] Moreover, it is a state's *combined* capabilities that are important; states that lack critical elements of power will be more vulnerable than states that possess a diverse array of capabilities.[16] There is no precise formula for weighing the different elements of power (which lack leads to recurring disputes about the relative importance

---

14. On the importance and measurement of national power, Hans J. Morgenthau, *Politics Among Nations: The Struggle for Power and Peace*, 5th ed., rev. (New York: Alfred A. Knopf, 1978), part 3; E.H. Carr, *The Twenty Years' Crisis, 1919–1939* (New York: Harper Torchbooks, 1964), chap. 8; Waltz, *Theory of International Politics*, pp. 98, 129–31; and Klaus E. Knorr, *The Power of Nations: The Political Economy of International Relations* (New York: Basic Books, 1975), chaps. 3 and 4.
15. Because no supreme authority exists to protect states from each other, the capacity to wage war is the ultimate guarantee of independence and source of influence in the international system. See Carr, *Twenty Years' Crisis*, p. 109.
16. On this point, see Waltz, *Theory of International Politics*, pp. 129–131.

of different components),[17] but most writers on strategy agree that power rests on a state's material assets and capabilities.

This conception of power is not universally accepted, however. Both world order idealists and proponents of rollback tend to focus more on ideas and ideology than on the physical capabilities of different states. Because they believe that the United States and its allies are threatened more by global problems than by other states, world order theorists devote little attention to the relative capabilities of different nations. For them, the relative power of nations is less important than the power of ideas; as mankind learns new values and forms new loyalties, the dangers inherent in the present system will be ameliorated.[18]

At the other extreme, advocates of rollback view contemporary international politics as a quasi-religious conflict between communism and democracy. Ideology is more important than the physical elements of power; interests are identified not by comparing capabilities but by examining political beliefs. States that embrace U.S. values deserve support, states that do not are suspect, and Marxist states are especially objectionable.[19] Coexistence

---

17. Some prominent theorists of international politics have emphasized the growing importance of economic capabilities in contemporary international relations, although they are careful to acknowledge the continued role of military power in shaping the behavior of states. See, for example, Robert O. Keohane and Joseph S. Nye, Jr., *Power and Interdependence: World Politics in Transition* (Boston: Little, Brown, 1978), pp. 8, 16–17, 24–29, 227–229; Keohane and Nye, *"Power and Interdependence* Revisited," *International Organization*, Vol. 41, No. 4 (Autumn 1987), pp. 727–729; and Robert O. Keohane, *After Hegemony: Cooperation and Discord in the World Political Economy* (Princeton: Princeton University Press, 1984), especially pp. 40–41. Echoing this view (albeit in less sophisticated form), some writers on U.S. grand strategy argue that the United States should abandon containment and focus on promoting international economic cooperation. See Sanders, "Security and Choice," pp. 698–707; Barnet, "The Four Pillars," pp. 88–89; and Sanders and Schwenninger, "Foreign Policy for the Post-Reagan Era," pp. 375–382. This view understates the role that containment plays in facilitating cooperation among the advanced industrial countries. If the Soviet threat declined dramatically or the U.S. abandoned containment, the other industrial powers would worry more about their positions relative to one another. From this perspective, economic cooperation among the industrial powers has been facilitated by the fact that the Soviet threat and the strategy of containment created a stable security environment and strong incentives for political collaboration in the West. Thus, declining cooperation among the industrial powers may be due as much to decreased concern about the Soviet Union as to the erosion of U.S. economic primacy. See Robert Gilpin, *U.S. Power and the Multinational Corporation: The Political Economy of Foreign Direct Investment* (New York: Basic Books, 1975), pp. 104–109. For useful theoretical background, see Joseph M. Grieco, "Anarchy and the Limits of Cooperation: A Realist Critique of the Newest Liberal Institutionalism," *International Organization*, Vol. 42, No. 3 (Summer 1988), pp. 485–507.
18. See Falk, *A Study of Future Worlds*, chap. 5; and Johansen, *National Interest and Human Interest*, pp. 20–37.
19. Thus Norman Podhoretz criticized the U.S. rapprochement with communist China by lamenting "the loss of political clarity it inevitably entails. Playing one Communist power off

with communism is assumed to be impossible, which justifies active efforts to undermine leftist or Marxist regimes.[20]

Ignoring the material elements of power raises several problems for these two schools of thought. Even if various global problems pose a threat to all states, world order idealists tend to overlook the fact that states also still threaten each other. The record of past efforts to erect moral barriers against war is not encouraging, and the various norms these writers extol would have to command near-universal acceptance before the danger of war would be gone. As a result, these writers cannot tell us how to preserve peace or defend other interests while the new world order is being created.

For their part, advocates of rollback err by exaggerating the importance of ideology in international politics and by downplaying the role of national power. Historically, no ideology has ever attracted a universal following, and neither superpower shows signs of doing so today. Even more important, a state's ability to promote ideological principles is largely a function of its economic and military capabilities. Communist ideology would be irrelevant if Albania were its chief sponsor; it is Soviet power that makes communism seem dangerous to the United States, not the specific content of the ideology itself. Thus, even if ideological beliefs do matter in certain circumstances, the relative power of their proponents matters far more.

WHY CONTAINMENT?

More than anything else the distribution of power, defined in terms of relative capabilities, identifies the regions that are strategically significant. As a continent-sized state lying far from the other major centers of power, the United States can be seriously threatened only if a single state were able to control the combined resources of the Eurasian landmass. Such an accumulation of power would dwarf U.S. capabilities, thereby placing U.S. security in jeopardy.[21]

---

against another may be sound geopolitics, but it increases the difficulty of explaining to ourselves and our friends what we are fighting for and what we are fighting against." See *Present Danger*, p. 98. Similarly, Irving Kristol suggests that many U.S. allies are of little value because they do not support the "assertive American foreign policy" he favors. See "Foreign Policy in an Age of Ideology," p. 14.
20. See Burnham, *Containment or Liberation?* pp. 176–182; Kristol, "Foreign Policy in an Age of Ideology"; and Krauthammer, "Poverty of Realism."
21. See Morgenthau, *In Defense of the National Interest*, pp. 5–7 and passim; Lippmann, *U.S. Foreign Policy*, pp. 108–113; Spykman, *America's Strategy in World Politics*, Part I; and Gray, *Geopolitics of Super Power*, pp. 69–70.

The strategy of finite containment follows directly from this insight. In George F. Kennan's original formulation, containment was intended to prevent the Soviet Union from gaining control of the "key centers of industrial power" that lay outside its grasp. Apart from the United States itself, these "key centers" were Western Europe and Japan.[22] More recently, the United States has added the goal of preserving Western access to oil from the Persian Gulf, because oil is a critical commodity for the United States and its industrial allies. Thus, as originally conceived, containment was deliberately finite in scope; it applied only to regions whose domination by the Soviet Union might enable it to assemble greater economic and military capacity than the United States. The point is crucial and bears repeating: the fundamental rationale for containment is derived from the distribution of power, defined in terms of military and industrial capability.[23]

DOES CONTAINMENT STILL MAKE SENSE?
Four developments might justify abandoning containment. First, if the Soviet share of world power were to increase dramatically, the United States might be forced to take more aggressive measures in order to keep from falling too far behind. Second, if Soviet power declined substantially, then containment might be unnecessary (though the U.S. interest in keeping Eurasia divided would remain). Third, if the economic and military power of the United States were to erode significantly, maintaining its present commitments might be impossible. Finally, if other regions were to acquire greater strategic importance, then the traditional locus of containment might become obsolete. Because most analysts who advocate alternative grand strategies usually invoke one or more of these arguments, let us consider the merits of each of these claims.

---

22. For a summary and analysis of Kennan's reasoning, see Gaddis, *Strategies of Containment*, chap. 2.
23. This perspective helps explain why Lippmann and Morgenthau opposed U.S. intervention in places like Vietnam. Communist control of Southeast Asia could not affect the global balance of power, both because the unity of international communism was illusory and because this region did not contain any militarily significant assets. It was therefore foolish for the United States to squander its own capabilities to defend it. See Ronald Steel, *Walter Lippmann and the American Century* (Boston: Little, Brown, 1980), pp. 565–567 and passim; and Hans J. Morgenthau, *A New Foreign Policy for the United States* (New York: Praeger, 1969), pp. 129–156. Not surprisingly, the preeminent contemporary realist, Kenneth Waltz, opposed the war on essentially the same grounds. See Waltz, "The Politics of Peace," *International Studies Quarterly*, Vol. 11, No. 3 (September 1967), pp. 199–211.

THE MYTH OF SOVIET GEOPOLITICAL MOMENTUM. First, do increases in Soviet power and global influence suggest that containment has failed?[24] The answer is a resounding no. Not only do the United States and its major allies surpass the Soviet alliance network on the principal indices of national power, but this favorable imbalance of power has remained roughly constant for the past four decades. The Western Alliance leads the Soviet bloc by nearly 3:1 in gross national product (GNP), by over 2:1 in population, by roughly 20 percent in annual defense spending, and it has slightly more men under arms.[25] Whereas the Western Alliance includes virtually all of the world's strategically significant states, the Soviet Union's main allies suffer from serious internal problems, widespread regional opposition, or both.[26]

In addition, reports of "Soviet geopolitical momentum" have been wildly exaggerated. Contrary to right-wing mythology, Soviet influence in the developing world has probably declined since the 1950s. Soviet gains in countries like Ethiopia, Nicaragua, Angola, or South Yemen are more than offset by their setbacks in Indonesia, China, Egypt, Somalia, Zimbabwe, Mozambique, and most recently, Afghanistan.[27] Soviet ideology attracts few converts, and even most so-called radical states look primarily to the West for educational assistance and economic exchanges.[28] Most important of all, the United States has successfully prevented the Soviets from expanding into any of the "key centers" identified by Kennan four decades ago. In terms of the global balance of power, therefore, containment has worked quite well.

---

24. The danger of imminent Soviet military superiority or of "Soviet geopolitical momentum" has been invoked repeatedly to justify increased U.S. defense spending or greater overseas commitments. For examples of these arguments, along with useful critiques, see Robert H. Johnson, "Periods of Peril: The Window of Vulnerability and Other Myths," *Foreign Affairs*, Vol. 61, No. 4 (Spring 1983), pp. 950–970; and David T. Johnson and Stephen D. Goose, "Soviet Geopolitical Momentum: Myth or Menace? Trends of Soviet Influence Around the World From 1945 to 1986," *The Defense Monitor*, Vol. 15, No. 5 (Center for Defense Information, 1986).
25. For the data on which these figures are based, see Stephen M. Walt, *The Origins of Alliances* (Ithaca: Cornell University Press, 1987), pp. 263–265 and Appendix II.
26. On the burdens of the Soviet empire, see Valerie Bunce, "The Empire Strikes Back: The Evolution of the Eastern Bloc from a Soviet Asset to a Soviet Liability," *International Organization*, Vol. 39, No. 1 (Winter 1985), pp. 1–46.
27. A contrasting view is Charles Wolf's assertion that "the gains and extension of the Soviet empire have vastly exceeded its losses and retrenchments." Unfortunately, Wolf does not provide any evidence to support this far-reaching claim. See Wolf, "Extended Containment," in Wildavsky, *Beyond Containment*, p. 154; and also Churba, *Soviet Breakout*, pp. 8–9. The most systematic examination of this issue reaches the opposite conclusion. See Johnson and Goose, "Soviet Geopolitical Momentum."
28. See Richard Feinberg and Kenneth A. Oye, "After the Fall: U.S. Policy Towards Radical Regimes," *World Policy Journal*, Vol. 1, No. 1 (Fall 1983), pp. 199–215.

WHY CONTAINMENT IS STILL NECESSARY. Second, do the internal difficulties currently afflicting the Soviet Empire (e.g., economic stagnation, increasing ethnic tensions, declining health standards) mean that containment is no longer necessary? Such a conclusion is, at best, premature. The Soviet Union is still the world's second or third largest economy, and possesses abundant economic potential. Its military capabilities are still formidable—especially its ground and air forces—and lie close to the key centers of industrial power. Although Gorbachev has eschewed direct confrontations with the West, has shown a willingness to resolve a number of persistent regional conflicts, and clearly hopes to reduce Soviet defense burdens through arms control or unilateral reductions, there is no guarantee that this restraint will not give way to more adventurous policies in the future. Indeed, if the United States abandoned containment, Soviet leaders might be more inclined to address their internal problems through a more aggressive foreign policy, because the risks would be smaller and the prospects for success would be greater. Grand strategy must take both capabilities and intentions into account, and at present, reports of the Soviet Union's demise have been greatly exaggerated. Barring a more substantial reduction in Soviet capabilities, the basic rationale for containment remains intact.

WHY CONTAINMENT IS STILL POSSIBLE. Has the relative decline of U.S. power left it too weak to bear the burden of containment?[29] Once again, this conclusion is premature at best. In particular, the tendency to blame U.S. economic ills on "strategic over-extension" (i.e., its overseas military commitments and defense spending) greatly oversimplifies the source of U.S. economic problems.[30] For example, defense spending is not the sole (or even the most important) cause of the U.S. budget deficit; increased social services, the expansion of indexed entitlements, and a chronic unwillingness to levy adequate taxes are equally responsible.[31] Similarly, those who blame declining U.S. competitiveness on military expenditures tend to overlook the other

---

29. Representatives of this view include Calleo, *Beyond American Hegemony*, chaps. 6 and 7; Layne, "Atlanticism Without NATO," p. 43; Sanders, "Security and Choice," pp. 700–701; and Chace, "A New Grand Strategy," pp. 3, 12. For additional background, see Kennedy, *Rise and Fall of the Great Powers*, pp. 514–535.

30. For example, Earl Ravenal has argued that the costs of containment "will wreck our economy and warp our society," and David Calleo suggests that present U.S. military commitments have produced a "fiscal nightmare." See Ravenal, "The Case for a Withdrawal of Our Forces," p. 75; and Calleo, *Beyond American Hegemony*, p. 165 and passim.

31. See Peter G. Peterson, "The Morning After," *Atlantic Monthly*, October 1987, pp. 43–69.

factors that hinder U.S. productivity, such as the low rate of personal savings and the lack of a coherent industrial policy. The evidence that defense spending hurts economic performance is ambiguous at best; although *excessive* defense spending can hurt any economy, its overall effects depend heavily on specific macroeconomic circumstances.[32]

Most important of all, even if excessive defense spending has weakened the U.S. economy somewhat, the strategy of containment is not to blame. The United States alone controls more industrial power than the entire Warsaw Pact; with adequate allied support, mounting an effective and credible defense of the key centers of industrial power should not be beyond its means. Instead, problems emerge when the United States adopts goals beyond those of finite containment (as it did in Vietnam), or when it combines an extravagant and poorly managed defense buildup with fanciful fiscal policies like Reaganomics. As always, the real question is not whether the United States is capable of maintaining its present commitments, but whether they are worth the cost. And if a reduction in defense burdens is now advisable, the logical approach is to liquidate peripheral commitments while maintaining the essential ones. By focusing on the key centers of industrial power, finite containment does exactly that.

WHY U.S. VITAL INTERESTS HAVE NOT CHANGED. Finally, do changes in the distribution of power imply that the United States should reduce or redirect its overseas military commitments? Once again, the evidence suggests that this would be unwise. Although Japan, Korea, and the ASEAN nations (Association of South East Asian Nations) have achieved impressive growth rates over the past two decades, Western Europe remains the largest economic prize. Western Europe produces approximately 22 percent of gross world product, while the Far East (counting Japan but not China) produces only 12.5 percent.[33] Even more important, U.S. allies in the Far East do not

---

32. On these points, see Gordon Adams and David Gold, *Defense Spending and the Economy: Does the Defense Dollar Make a Difference?* (Washington, D.C.: Center for Budget and Policy Priorities, 1987), especially pp. 2, 6–11; Huntington, "The U.S.—Decline or Renewal?"; Nye, "Understating U.S. Strengths"; Francis M. Bator, "Must We Retrench?" *Foreign Affairs*, Vol. 68, No. 2 (Spring 1989), pp. 93–123; and Aaron L. Friedberg, "The Political Economy of American National Strategy," *World Politics*, Vol. 41, No. 3 (April 1989), pp. 381–406.

33. With the People's Republic of China included, the percentage reaches 14.7 percent of gross world product (GWP), still substantially less than Western Europe. These figures are based on data in U.S. Arms Control and Disarmament Agency (ACDA), *World Military Expenditures and Arms Transfers 1986* (Washington, D.C.: U.S. GPO, 1986).

face as great a threat. The bulk of Soviet military power is directed at Western Europe; as a result, the U.S. commitment in the Far East can remain relatively modest.[34]

Furthermore, the relative decline of U.S. power suggests that the case for a U.S. commitment to Europe (and to a lesser extent, to its allies in the Far East) may be even stronger today than it was immediately after World War II. At the beginning of the Cold War, the loss of Western Europe would have been serious but not disastrous; the U.S. controlled nearly 40 percent of gross world product in 1949 and Western Europe was just beginning its postwar recovery. Since then, however, the European contribution to NATO's economic and military strength has grown steadily while the U.S. share has declined.[35] If conquered and exploited, Europe's economic and military potential would increase Soviet warmaking capabilities far more now than it would have several decades ago. Thus, while the Western Alliance retains an impressive lead over its main adversary, the United States is increasingly dependent upon allied contributions to achieve this favorable result.[36] Advocates of isolationism or disengagement should consider how the world might look were these assets either absent from the equation or arrayed against us. The prospect is not comforting: Soviet control over Western Europe would provide the Soviet Union with an advantage of more than 2.5:1 over the United States in population and gross national product, to say nothing of tangible military assets. In other words, as the U.S. ability to defend Europe unilaterally has decreased, the U.S. interest in making sure that Europe remains independent has grown. Because Europe remains the

---

34. See International Institute for Strategic Studies (IISS), *The Military Balance 1988–89* (London: IISS, 1987), pp. 39–44.

35. From 1969 to 1979, for example, Western Europe's share of NATO's combined expenditures rose from 22.7 percent to almost 42 percent. The Reagan administration's rapid defense buildup reversed this trend, however, and Western Europe's share of NATO's combined expenditures had fallen to 32 percent by 1986. See Robert Art, "Fixing Transatlantic Bridges," *Foreign Policy*, No. 46 (Spring 1982), p. 70; and Gordon Adams and Eric Munz, *Fair Shares: Bearing the Burden of the NATO Alliance* (Washington, D.C.: Center for Budget and Policy Priorities, 1988), pp. 6, 18.

36. The United States produced 39 percent of gross world product in 1950, with Western Europe and Japan contributing a total of 17 percent. By 1984, the U.S. share had dropped to 26 percent while the allied share had grown to roughly 27 percent (NATO Europe plus Japan). In terms of military spending, the U.S. share of the global total declined from 51 percent in 1960 to 28 percent in 1984, while that of Europe and Japan had grown to more than 13 percent. See ACDA, *World Military Expenditures 1986*. Western Europe now contributes over 50 percent of NATO's active manpower, main battle tanks, and combat aircraft, roughly 45 percent of NATO artillery, and nearly 80 percent of NATO's trained reserves. See Adams and Munz, *Fair Shares*, pp. 26–28.

largest concentration of economic and military power (apart from the two superpowers) and because the Soviet Union poses a larger threat there than in the Far East, the United States should continue to devote its main military effort to NATO.[37]

WHY THE THIRD WORLD DOESN'T MATTER. By contrast, the case for a greater U.S. commitment in the Third World is extremely weak. Although several studies have recently proposed that the United States reduce its commitment to Europe in order to increase its capacity for Third World intervention, there is little or no strategic justification for such a shift.[38] With the exception of oil, U.S. interests in the Third World are minor at best. The entire Third World produces less than 20 percent of gross world product, scattered over more than 100 countries. Africa has a combined GNP less than that of Great Britain; all of Latin America has a combined GNP smaller than that of West Germany. Because modern military power rests primarily upon industrial might, the strategic importance of the Third World is small.[39]

Nor does the United States have critical economic interests there. Foreign trade is only 14 percent of U.S. GNP, and nearly two-thirds of all U.S. trade is with its industrial allies in Western Europe, Canada, and Japan. In 1986, U.S. trade with the entire Third World (including OPEC, the Organization of Petroleum Exporting Countries) was only 3.5 percent of U.S. GNP, spread across nearly 100 Third World trading partners.[40] The same is true for overseas investment: U.S. direct investment abroad is a small fraction of total U.S. wealth, and most of it is in Europe and Canada.[41] Because U.S. trade

---

37. See Van Evera, "American Strategic Interests," pp. 12–13; Posen and Van Evera, "Departure from Containment," p. 79; and Keith A. Dunn, "NATO's Enduring Value," Foreign Policy, No. 71 (Summer 1988), pp. 156–175.
38. See Cohen, "Long Term Crisis of the Alliance," p. 342; and Brzezinski, Game Plan, pp. 182–184. The authors of Discriminate Deterrence point out that "nearly all the armed conflicts of the past forty years have occurred . . . in the Third World," and conclude that "the United States will need to be better prepared to deal with conflict" in these regions. Yet they offer no evidence for why these events are vital to U.S. interests; the importance of the Third World is simply assumed. See Iklé and Wohlstetter, Discriminate Deterrence, pp. 13–22.
39. See Van Evera, "American Strategic Interests," p. 25; and Posen and Van Evera, "Departure from Containment," pp. 95–96.
40. Calculated from The State of the Economy: Report by the President 1987 (Washington, D.C.: U.S. GPO, 1987); and Direction of Trade Statistics Yearbook 1987 (Washington, D.C.: International Monetary Fund, 1987), pp. 404–406.
41. In 1986, total U.S. direct foreign investment (DFI) was $259.89 billion, equivalent to 6.5 percent of U.S. GNP for that year. Seventy-one percent of total U.S. DFI is invested in Canada, Western Europe, and Japan (nearly half in Western Europe alone). See Russell B. Scholl, "The International Investment Position of the United States in 1986," Survey of Current Business, June 1987, pp. 38–45.

relations and foreign investments are dispersed over many separate countries, the danger of a costly disruption is greatly reduced. In short, the United States has few economic interests to protect in the developing world.

Alarmists often point to alleged U.S. dependence on raw materials from the developing countries. According to this view, the U.S. economy requires reliable access to a wide variety of "critical strategic minerals" like cobalt, chromium, the platinum group, or manganese. Together with South Africa, several Third World countries are among the leading exporters of these minerals, which raises fears of a possible cutoff arising from Soviet penetration, leftist revolutions, or endemic political instability. Accordingly, some analysts argue that the United States must be prepared to intervene in order to preserve Western access to these raw materials, and to defend the sea lines of communication to these regions. Support for pro-Western mineral exporters (such as South Africa or Zaire) is often cited as a further consequence of alleged U.S. dependence.[42]

Fortunately, such fears rest largely on propaganda. Although the United States imports a large percentage of its annual consumption of certain raw materials, it does so because foreign suppliers are the least expensive, not because they are the only alternative. The magnitude of a state's imports does not determine its dependence on others; what is important is the cost of replacing existing sources of supply or doing without them entirely.[43] A lengthy embargo is a remote possibility—why would a poor Third World country cut off a major source of revenue?—and the United States can rely upon alternative suppliers, substitutes, and plentiful stockpiles.[44] An em-

---

42. For pessimistic appraisals of Western raw materials dependence, see Uri Ra'anan and Charles M. Perry, eds., *Strategic Minerals and International Security* (Washington, D.C.: Pergamon-Brassey's, 1985); Alan C. Brownfeld, "The Growing United States' Dependency on Imported Strategic Minerals," *Atlantic Community Quarterly*, Vol. 20, No. 1 (Spring 1982), pp. 62–67; Council on Economics and National Security, *Strategic Minerals: A Resource Crisis* (New Brunswick, N.J.: Transaction Books, 1980); Robert J. Hanks, *Southern Africa and Western Security* (Cambridge, Mass.: Institute for Foreign Policy Analysis, 1983), pp. 10–15, 53; and Secretary of Defense Caspar W. Weinberger, *Annual Report to the Congress*, FY 1984 (Washington, D.C.: U.S. GPO, 1983), p. 29. For other examples and a critique, see Richard E. Feinberg, *The Intemperate Zone: The Third World Challenge to U.S. Foreign Policy* (New York: Norton, 1983), chap. 2.
43. See Kenneth N. Waltz, "The Myth of National Interdependence," in Charles P. Kindleberger, ed., *The International Corporation* (Cambridge: MIT Press, 1970), pp. 205–223; and also Waltz, *Theory of International Politics*, chap. 7.
44. According to the Congressional Budget Office (CBO), "the United States has a considerable range of policy options to reduce its dependence on nonfuel imported minerals and limit the impact of any shortages that might result from such dependence." See CBO, "Strategic and Critical Nonfuel Minerals: Problems and Policy Alternatives" (Washington, D.C.: CBO, 1983), pp. xi–xii and passim. For other reassuring analyses on this issue, see Michael Shafer, "Mineral

bargo might have some modest economic effects, but not much more than that. In short, the danger of a "resource war" is minuscule.

There is a final argument for a greater U.S. role in the Third World. Third World countries are said to be important for geopolitical reasons, because they occupy "strategic real estate."[45] The fear is that these countries might provide military facilities to the Soviet Union in time of war, thereby allowing the Soviets to threaten critical lines of communication. Thus, even if these states lack meaningful capabilities of their own, their geographic positions may give them some modest strategic value.

Once again, the importance of this factor is exaggerated. Given the low intrinsic value of the Third World, military bases there are important only if they can be used to affect events in areas that do matter. With the possible exception of Cuba (which might be able to delay—though not prevent—U.S. reinforcement of Europe), the Soviet Union's Third World clients could not affect the outcome of a major war. And because the Soviet Union cannot easily defend these regimes, they are likely to opt for neutrality, knowing that they would be among the first targets of a U.S. counterattack.[46] In short, although a few Third World states may have some modest strategic value,

---

Myths," *Foreign Policy*, No. 47 (Summer 1982), pp. 154–171; Stephen D. Krasner, "Oil is the Exception," *Foreign Policy*, No. 14 (Spring 1974), pp. 68–84; Brian McCartan, "Resource Wars: The Myth of American Mineral Vulnerability," *The Defense Monitor*, Vol. 14, No. 9 (Center for Defense Information, 1985); Joel P. Clark and Frank R. Field III, et al., "How Critical Are Critical Materials?" *Technology Review*, Vol. 88, No. 6 (August/September 1985), pp. 39–46; and Jock A. Finlayson and David G. Haglund, "Whatever Happened to the Resource War?" *Survival*, Vol. 29, No. 5 (September/October 1987), pp. 403–415. Hanns Maull argues that Western raw materials dependence is substantial and should be taken seriously, but he notes that a variety of measures can minimize these risks rather easily. See Maull, *Energy, Minerals, and Western Security* (Baltimore: Johns Hopkins University Press, 1984), chap. 4; and Maull, "South Africa's Minerals: The Achilles Heel of Western Economic Security?" *International Affairs*, Vol. 62, No. 4 (Autumn 1986), pp. 619–626.

45. Obvious examples are states that border on major international waterways, such as Vietnam, Cuba, South Yemen, or Indonesia. See Robert E. Harkavy, "Soviet Conventional Power Projection and Containment," in Terry L. Deibel and John Lewis Gaddis, eds., *Containment: Concept and Policy*, Vol. II (Washington, D.C.: National Defense University Press, 1986), pp. 311–400; Gray, *Geopolitics of Super Power*, p. 101; Peter J. Duignan, "Africa Between East and West," in Dennis L. Bark, ed., *To Promote Peace: U.S. Foreign Policy in the Mid-1980s* (Stanford: Hoover Institution Press, 1984), p. 187; and Michael Gordon, "Reagan's 'Choke Points' Stretch from Sea to Sea," *New York Times*, February 13, 1986, p. A12.

46. If the United States lost a major war in Europe, it would be likely to seek revenge against states like Cuba or Nicaragua, particularly if they had aided the Soviet Union during the war. Such a defeat would also give the United States ample incentive to eliminate the threat of a Soviet "bridgehead" in the Western hemisphere. If the Soviets' Third World allies understand this (and U.S. leaders should make sure they do), they are unlikely to invite such an attack by supporting Moscow.

the overall strategic importance of the Third World remains small.[47] Those who would reallocate U.S. military assets toward the Third World have their priorities exactly backwards: they would weaken the U.S. position in the places that matter in order to stand guard in places that do not.

To summarize: the rationale for finite containment rests upon the current distribution of world power, defined in terms of economic and military capabilities. Although the balance of power has changed somewhat since the late 1940s, these trends in fact strengthen the case for finite containment.

### The Offense-Defense Balance: Is Conquest Easy or Difficult?

In recent years, a growing body of scholarship has suggested that the offense-defense balance plays a major role in the frequency and intensity of international conflict.[48] If offense is or is thought to be relatively easy (i.e., states can expand at low cost), then national leaders must worry more about security and do more to protect it. By contrast, when defense is easier (especially when it is easy to distinguish between offensive and defensive capabilities), states can protect their territory with greater confidence at lower cost. The probability of war declines because potential aggressors will realize that they will pay a high price for relatively small gains.[49] As one would expect, therefore, competing assessments about the ease of offense or defense lead to different prescriptions for U.S. grand strategy.

---

47. For an excellent analysis of this issue, see Robert H. Johnson, "Exaggerating America's Stakes in Third World Conflicts," *International Security*, Vol. 10, No. 3 (Winter 1985/86), pp. 32–68. On Latin America, see Lars Schoultz, *National Security and United States Policy Toward Latin America* (Princeton: Princeton University Press, 1986); and Jerome Slater, "Dominos in Central America: Will They Fall? Does it Matter?" *International Security*, Vol. 12, No. 2 (Fall 1987), pp. 105–134. For more pessimistic views, see Michael C. Desch, "Turning the Caribbean Flank," *Survival*, Vol. 29, No. 6 (November/December 1987), pp. 528–551; and Alvin H. Bernstein, "The Soviets in Cam Ranh Bay," *The National Interest*, No. 3 (Spring 1986), pp. 17–29.

48. On the effects of offensive and defensive advantages, see Robert Jervis, "Cooperation Under the Security Dilemma," *World Politics*, Vol. 30, No. 2 (January 1978), pp. 167–214; Stephen W. Van Evera, "Causes of War" (Ph.D. dissertation, University of California, Berkeley, 1984); and George Quester, *Offense and Defense in the International System* (New York: John Wiley, 1977). For a sympathetic critique of this literature, see Jack S. Levy, "The Offensive/Defensive Balance of Military Technology: A Theoretical and Historical Analysis," *International Studies Quarterly*, Vol. 28, No. 2 (June 1984), pp. 219–238.

49. When the offense has the advantage, states are more likely to: 1) spend more on military capabilities; 2) adopt offensive military doctrines; 3) seek to acquire territory because it is both easy to do and because territory is more valuable; and 4) engage in a more aggressive foreign policy (including preemptive or preventive wars). See Jervis, "Cooperation Under the Security Dilemma"; and Van Evera, "Causes of War."

In general, those who endorse strategies of rollback or global containment believe that offensive action is easy, and that the United States and its allies are thus extremely vulnerable to attack by the Soviet Union or by other hostile forces. Some also assume that the United States can score significant gains through offensive actions of its own. By contrast, those who favor isolationism, disengagement, or finite containment usually stress the relative advantage of defense. Even if the Soviet Union is extremely aggressive and U.S. interests are extensive, these writers see protecting U.S. interests as a relatively easy task. By the same logic, these writers see inherent limits in what the United States can accomplish; efforts to expand U.S. influence through force or subversion are likely to be difficult and costly.

This general debate appears in many guises, corresponding to the different ways that states can threaten one another.[50] Throughout the Cold War, for example, communist subversion has been seen as an offensive threat that required and justified an expanded U.S. commitment to distant regions.[51] Advocates of rollback have also argued that the Soviet empire is vulnerable to subversion, propaganda, and other forms of "political warfare."[52] Taking this belief a step further, writers like James Burnham claimed that rollback was necesssary because the United States and the Soviet Union represented antithetical political values whose very existence threatened each other's legitimacy.[53] By this logic, both superpowers were vulnerable to ideological subversion, so it was rational for the United States to undermine communist regimes before their subversive efforts could succeed.

---

50. In addition to direct military action, states can also threaten each other by subversion or propaganda. However, such campaigns rarely succeed, even against relatively weak governments, because the targets usually respond quickly to attempts by foreign powers to mobilize domestic discontent. For evidence and further discussion, see Walt, *Origins of Alliances*, pp. 242–251.

51. When seeking congressional support for aid to Greece and Turkey, for example, Dean Acheson warned that "a highly possible Soviet breakthrough might open three continents to Soviet penetration. Like apples in a barrel infected by one rotten one, the corruption of Greece would infect Iran and all to the east. It would also carry infection to Africa . . . , and to Europe through Italy and France. . . . The Soviet Union was playing one of the greatest gambles in history at minimal cost." See Dean Acheson, *Present at the Creation: My Years in the State Department* (New York: Norton, 1969), p. 293. For a more recent version of this argument, see "President Reagan's Speech Urging Support for Nicaraguan Contra Rebels," *Facts on File*, March 21, 1986, p. 180.

52. See Burnham, *Containment or Liberation?* chaps. 9–11; Aaron Wildavsky, "Containment Plus Pluralization," and Max Singer, "Dynamic Containment," in Wildavsky, *Beyond Containment*; and Churba, *Soviet Breakout*, pp. 130–132.

53. This theme is echoed by neo-conservative writers like Irving Kristol. See Kristol, "Foreign Policy in an Age of Ideology," pp. 7–9. See also Churba, *Soviet Breakout*.

Advocates of global containment also stress the offensive nature of Soviet military forces and suggest that it would be relatively easy for them to conquer Western Europe, the Persian Gulf, or the Middle East.[54] Predictably, these writers assume that contemporary politico-military conditions favor the attacker.[55] By contrast, those who downplay the danger of Soviet expansion generally believe that defenders enjoy a substantial advantage over attacking forces, at least when fighting from prepared positions.[56]

This dispute also reflects differing views on the impact of nuclear weapons. On one side, advocates of rollback and global containment almost always favor continued increases in U.S. counterforce capabilities. To justify this recommendation, they suggest that nuclear weapons make conquest easier by inhibiting the U.S. ability to resist conventional aggression or diplomatic pressure. In the 1970s, for example, Paul Nitze and others suggested that the *theoretical* vulnerability of U.S. land-based ICBMs could enable the USSR to extract major political concessions from the United States without firing a

---

54. Recent analyses stressing the danger of a Soviet offensive in Europe include James A. Thomson, "An Unfavorable Situation: NATO and the Conventional Balance," N-2842-FF/RC (Santa Monica: RAND Corporation, 1988); "An Exclusive AFJ Interview with: Phillip A. Karber," *Armed Forces Journal International*, Vol. 124, No. 11 (June 1987), pp. 112–117; Eliot A. Cohen, "Toward Better Net Assessment: Rethinking the European Conventional Balance," *International Security*, Vol. 13, No. 1 (Summer 1988), pp. 50–89; and Huntington, "Renewal of Strategy," pp. 22–23. With respect to the Persian Gulf, Huntington writes that "if the Soviets were free to concentrate their forces on Southwest Asia, they clearly could overrun any force that the Western allies and Japan might deploy in a reasonable amount of time." See "Renewal of Strategy," p. 27. For an especially dire view on the Gulf, see Churba, *Soviet Breakout*, chap. 7.

55. As Huntington puts it: "the great advantage to the offensive is that the attacker chooses the point [of attack] and hence can concentrate his forces there." Huntington believes that NATO's forces are weaker than those of the Warsaw Pact, but he suggests that "history is full of successful offensives by forces that lacked numerical superiority." Thus, NATO's forces cannot defend their own territory but are somehow strong enough to conduct a "prompt retaliatory counteroffensive" into Eastern Europe. A clearer example of the belief in offense dominance would be hard to find. See Huntington, "The Renewal of Strategy," pp. 29–30; and Huntington, "Conventional Deterrence and Conventional Retaliation in Europe," *International Security*, Vol. 8, No. 3 (Winter 1983/84), pp. 46–47. For a similar appraisal, see Iklé and Wohlstetter, *Discriminate Deterrence*, pp. 27–28.

56. For relatively optimistic appraisals of the balance in Europe, see Barry R. Posen, "Measuring the European Conventional Balance: Coping with Complexity in Threat Assessment," *International Security*, Vol. 9, No. 3 (Winter 1984/85), pp. 47–88; and Posen, "Is NATO Decisively Outnumbered?" *International Security*, Vol. 12, No. 4 (Spring 1988), pp. 186–202; Joshua M. Epstein, "Dynamic Analysis and the Conventional Balance in Europe," *International Security*, Vol. 12, No. 4 (Spring 1988), pp. 154–165; John J. Mearsheimer, "Why the Soviets Can't Win Quickly in Central Europe," *International Security*, Vol. 7, No. 1 (Summer 1982), pp. 3–39; and Mearsheimer, "Numbers, Strategy, and the European Balance," *International Security*, Vol. 12, No. 4 (Spring 1988), pp. 174–185. All of these writers assume that defenders have a tactical advantage in a European battle.

shot.[57] Similarly, other writers argue that an effective deterrent requires U.S. nuclear superiority, because threats to use nuclear weapons will not be credible unless the United States possesses "escalation dominance." Rather than reducing U.S. defense requirements, in short, nuclear weapons make the requirements of deterrence even more demanding. Writers who endorse this view call for the United States to regain meaningful strategic superiority through increased counterforce capabilities and "defensive" weapons programs like the Strategic Defense Initiative (SDI).[58]

By contrast, advocates of isolationism, disengagement, or finite containment usually claim that nuclear weapons make defense easier. In this view, the physical characteristics of nuclear explosives make it impossible for either superpower to escape the world of Mutual Assured Destruction.[59] Crises thus become contests of will; it is the balance of commitment and interests, not the balance of forces, that determines the outcome. Because the side defending the status quo should possess greater resolve, nuclear weapons aid defenders, irrespective of force levels. In this view, the imposing deterrent effects of nuclear weapons increase each side's ability to defend its vital interests.[60]

---

57. See Paul H. Nitze, "Assuring Strategic Stability in an Era of Détente," *Foreign Affairs*, Vol. 54, No. 2 (January 1976), pp. 207–232; and Nitze, "Deterring Our Deterrent," *Foreign Policy*, No. 25 (Winter 1976–77), pp. 195–210. For an even more far-reaching version, see Churba, *Soviet Breakout*, chap. 5. For critiques, see John Steinbruner and Thomas Garwin, "Strategic Vulnerability: The Balance between Prudence and Paranoia," *International Security*, Vol. 1, No. 1 (Summer 1976), pp. 138–181; Albert Carnesale and Charles Glaser, "ICBM Vulnerability: The Cures Are Worse Than the Disease," *International Security*, Vol. 7, No. 1 (Summer 1982), pp. 76–78; and Jan M. Lodal, "Assuring Strategic Stability: An Alternate View," *Foreign Affairs*, Vol. 54, No. 3 (April 1976), pp. 462–481.
58. For representative examples, see Huntington, "Renewal of Strategy," pp. 32–40; Colin S. Gray, "Nuclear Strategy: The Case for a Theory of Victory," *International Security*, Vol. 4, No. 1 (Summer 1979), pp. 54–87; Iklé and Wohlstetter, *Discriminate Deterrence*, pp. 35–37; Brzezinski, *Game Plan*, pp. 159–168; and Churba, *Soviet Breakout*, pp. 108–111, 120–122.
59. Both superpowers would have thousands of warheads and hundreds of equivalent megatons left after the *best* first strike that the other could inflict. See Michael A. Salman, Kevin J. Sullivan, and Stephen Van Evera, "Analysis or Propaganda? Measuring American Strategic Nuclear Capability, 1969–1988," in Lynn Eden and Steven E. Miller, eds., *Nuclear Arguments: Understanding the Strategic Nuclear Arms and Arms Control Debates* (Ithaca: Cornell University Press, 1989); and Joshua M. Epstein, *The 1988 Defense Budget* (Washington, D.C.: Brookings, 1987), pp. 21–27. Another recent study concludes that even drastic arms reductions would not confer a first-strike capability on either superpower and would not reduce civilian casualties significantly in a nuclear war. See Michael M. May, George F. Bing, and John D. Steinbruner, *Strategic Arms Reductions* (Washington, D.C.: Brookings, 1988).
60. See Robert Jervis, *The Illogic of American Nuclear Strategy* (Ithaca: Cornell University Press, 1984); and Kenneth N. Waltz, *The Spread of Nuclear Weapons: More May Be Better*, Adelphi Paper No. 171 (London: IISS, Autumn 1981).

Finally, world order idealists adopt a somewhat different view of the offense-defense balance. On the one hand, they agree that defensive strategies are desirable and feasible, and they support a variety of schemes for territorial and "non-offensive" defense.[61] On the other hand, they reject reliance upon nuclear deterrence, arguing that the risks of a nuclear war outweigh the stabilizing effects of these weapons. Instead, these writers favor far-reaching efforts at nuclear and conventional disarmament, leading to the rapid and total elimination of all nuclear weapons.[62]

In short, competing appraisals of the offense-defense balance exert a powerful impact on the assessment of military requirements and the development of grand strategy. If offense is easy, then U.S. strategic requirements increase significantly. Strategies of rollback or global containment become more attractive under these conditions. If expansion is hard, however, then U.S. leaders can take a more relaxed view of potential threats and adopt less demanding goals. The question, therefore, is which of these views provides the best guidance for U.S. grand strategy today?

WHY DEFENSE HAS THE ADVANTAGE
The available evidence suggests that defense enjoys a major advantage in the contemporary world. This may not be true for all states in all circumstances, but in general, and especially with respect to key U.S. interests, conquest has become particularly difficult.

This condition results from four key developments. First, the spread of nationalism has increased the costs of expansion and foreign occupation. The British experience in India, the French and American experience in Vietnam, the Soviet experience in Afghanistan, and Israel's occupation of Lebanon all support this conclusion: native populations enjoy superior knowledge of local conditions and are usually willing to bear greater costs than foreign invaders, which makes conquering and holding foreign territory often more expensive than it is worth.[63] Similarly, the growth of modern

---

61. See Dietrich Fischer, *Preventing War in the Nuclear Age* (Totowa, N.J.: Rowman and Allanheld, 1984); Forsberg, "Confining the Military to Defense," esp. p. 310; and the symposium on "Nonoffensive Defense," in *Bulletin of the Atomic Scientists*, Vol. 44, No. 7 (September 1988), pp. 12–54. For a summary and critique of some of these ideas, see David Gates, "Area Defense Concepts: The West German Debate," *Survival*, Vol. 29, No. 4 (July/August 1987), pp. 301–317.
62. See, for example, Forsberg, "Confining the Military to Defense."
63. As Ho Chi Minh told a French diplomat in 1945: "You will kill ten of our men, but we will kill one of yours and it is you who will finish by wearing yourself out." Quoted in John T. McAlister, Jr., *Viet Nam: The Origins of Revolution* (New York: Alfred A. Knopf, 1969), p. 296.

nationalism makes it more likely that efforts to acquire and manipulate clients through subversion or covert penetration will backfire.[64]

Second, this trend is enhanced by the increased availability of modern weapons, especially small arms.[65] During the heyday of European expansion, the colonial powers enjoyed enormous technological superiority over their opponents. In the modern era, however, resistance movements can readily obtain the military means of inflicting protracted costs on a foreign invader, as the conflicts in Afghanistan, Indochina, and Lebanon illustrate.

Third, despite the creative efforts of some writers to plead the offensive implications of nuclear arms, they are overwhelmingly an advantage to the defender. Not only do nuclear weapons make a direct attack on the United States virtually unthinkable, but they deter threats to other interests as well. Although the historical record is not definitive, the evidence suggests that political leaders in all nuclear states have been reluctant to challenge each other's vital interests in the face of even weak nuclear threats. One cannot *prove* that nuclear weapons have helped keep the peace and inhibit expansion, but the record of the past four decades is extremely persuasive.[66]

Fourth, U.S. security is enhanced by the fact that its vital interests are relatively easy to defend. In particular, the Central Front in Europe provides an excellent setting for a prepared defense against armored attack.[67] Defend-

---

See also Andrew Mack, "Why Big Nations Lose Small Wars: The Politics of Asymmetric Conflict," *World Politics*, Vol. 27, No. 2 (January 1975), pp. 175–200.

64. Such tactics might include supporting a coup by a dissident faction, or attempting to influence emerging elites through military or educational assistance. Because impeccable nationalist credentials remain an important qualification for leadership in most states, however, leaders who are perceived as foreign puppets are unlikely to reach positions of power or to remain in them for long. For further discussion, see Walt, *Origins of Alliances*, pp. 244–251.

65. For surveys of the global arms market, see Anthony Sampson, *The Arms Bazaar: From Lebanon to Lockheed* (New York: Viking Press, 1977); Stephanie G. Neuman and Robert E. Harkavy, eds., *Arms Transfers in the Modern World* (New York: Praeger, 1979); and Andrew Pierre, *The Global Politics of Arms Sales* (Princeton: Princeton University Press, 1982).

66. Virtually all scholarly studies of the impact of nuclear weapons on diplomacy suggest that national leaders believed these weapons greatly inhibited their freedom of action, irrespective of the precise state of the nuclear balance. See Marc Trachtenberg, "The Influence of Nuclear Weapons in the Cuban Missile Crisis," *International Security*, Vol. 10, No. 1 (Summer 1985), pp. 137–163; Richard K. Betts, *Nuclear Blackmail and Nuclear Balance* (Washington, D.C.: Brookings, 1987); McGeorge Bundy, *Danger and Survival: Choices About the Bomb in the First Fifty Years* (New York: Random House, 1988), pp. 378–382, 445–453, 589–597; and Barry M. Blechman and Stephen S. Kaplan, *Force Without War: U.S. Military Forces as a Political Instrument* (Washington, D.C.: Brookings, 1978), pp. 127–129. For a provocative argument that nuclear weapons have had little impact on stability, see John Mueller, "The Essential Irrelevance of Nuclear Weapons: Stability in the Postwar World," *International Security*, Vol. 13, No. 2 (Fall 1988), pp. 55–79.

67. Among other things, attack routes in Central Europe are heavily congested, forcing an

ers enjoy considerable advantage in this type of warfare, because they can fight from prepared positions and exact a favorable casualty-exchange ratio on the attacking forces. Similarly, a Soviet attempt to seize the Persian Gulf oil fields would be a risky and difficult operation. Not only is Iran likely to mount a fierce resistance, but the oil fields lie roughly 1000 kilometers from the Soviet border. The terrain is inhospitable and road networks are primitive; thus Soviet armored forces would be extremely vulnerable to air interdiction. These factors do not guarantee that a Soviet attack would fail, but they suggest that deterring or defeating a Soviet attack is not beyond present U.S. capabilities.[68]

In sum, obstacles to large-scale aggression may be greater now than at any time in modern history. This does not mean that expansion is impossible, of course, but since World War II, successful examples are few in number and involved substantially greater costs than were originally anticipated.[69] Those who believe that offensive advantages render U.S. security especially precarious have yet to present strong evidence for their position. Indeed, the evidence strongly supports the opposite view.

Are these defensive advantages so great as to permit the United States to reduce its overseas commitments? Advocates of isolationism or disengagement tend to believe that they are, in part by assuming that nuclear weapons render the traditional focus on industrial power obsolete. In this view, even if the Soviet Union were able to seize Western Europe, it would be unable to exploit Europe's industrial potential and would still be deterred by the threat of nuclear retaliation from attacking the United States directly.[70] Sim-

---

attacker into narrow and well-defined attack routes. See Paul Bracken, "Urban Sprawl and NATO Defence," *Survival*, Vol. 18, No. 6 (November/December 1976), pp. 254–260.

68. On the obstacles to a Soviet invasion, see Joshua M. Epstein, "Soviet Vulnerabilities in Iran and the RDF Deterrent," *International Security*, Vol. 6, No. 2 (Fall 1981), pp. 126–158; and Keith Dunn, "Constraints on the USSR in Southwest Asia: A Military Analysis," *Orbis*, Vol. 25, No. 3 (Fall 1981), pp. 607–629.

69. Examples of successful expansion include Israel's conquest of the Golan Heights and West Bank, India's seizure of Kashmir, Sikkim, and Goa, China's conquest of Tibet, North Vietnam's expansion into South Vietnam and Cambodia, Libya's occupation of the Aouzo Strip, Morocco's seizure of the Western Sahara, Turkey's occupation of Cyprus, and Indonesia's conquest of East Timor. Perhaps only Kashmir, Goa, Sikkim, and East Timor are not being actively contested at the present time.

70. See Ravenal, *NATO: The Tides of Discontent*; Richard J. Barnet, *Real Security: Restoring American Power in a Dangerous Decade* (New York: Simon and Schuster, 1981), pp. 90–98; Layne, "Atlanticism Without NATO," pp. 27–28; Sanders and Schwenninger, "Foreign Policy for the Post-Reagan Era"; Sanders, "Security and Choice," p. 710; Calleo, *Beyond American Hegemony*, chap. 9; and Chace, "A New Grand Strategy," pp. 12–16.

ilarly, analysts with great confidence in the credibility of extended deterrence have suggested that the United States could deploy just a "trip-wire" force in Europe or the Persian Gulf and rely primarily upon the threat of escalation to deter an attack.[71] In either case, the advantage currently enjoyed by defenders is used to justify bringing U.S. forces back to the United States.

These arguments are not without some basis, but the conclusion should be rejected for at least three reasons. First, the current condition of defense dominance is not independent of U.S. policy; the U.S. commitment to oppose Soviet expansion raises the obstacles to such actions considerably.[72] Europe would still be difficult to conquer if the United States withdrew, but it would certainly be easier. Thus, the U.S. commitment provides a valuable insurance policy against a remote but very important contingency.[73] Second, although the United States can easily maintain its second-strike capability today, an arms race with a Eurasian hegemon with the combined technological and industrial assets of the Soviet Union, Western Europe, and Japan (and more than twice the U.S. GNP) would be a daunting prospect. Third, although nuclear weapons enhance the defender's advantage through deterrence, this advantage is not as great in third areas as it is when deterring direct attacks against one's homeland. A "trip-wire" strategy might work, but in the absence of large U.S. conventional forces, the Soviets could more easily convince themselves that the strategy was a bluff. By contrast, maintaining a substantial U.S. presence in Europe offers a convincing demonstration of its importance to the United States and provides a credible capacity to respond to a Soviet conventional assault. Given the costs and risks of *any* war in Europe and the fact that NATO is far wealthier than the Warsaw Pact, the deployment of U.S. ground and air forces on the continent seems well worth continuing.[74]

All things considered, the prevailing state of defense dominance supports a strategy of finite containment. Preventing Soviet expansion is the central

---

71. Among those advocating a "trip-wire" force is Kenneth N. Waltz, in "A Strategy for the Rapid Deployment Force," *International Security*, Vol. 5, No. 4 (Spring 1981), pp. 49–73; and Waltz, "Spread of Nuclear Weapons," p. 7.
72. For example, the resistance movement in Afghanistan was greatly strengthened by the U.S. decision to provide ground-to-air missiles and other military supplies.
73. Some writers complain that the U.S. commitment to Europe is an expensive burden directed at a low-probability event. This view ignores the fact that the U.S. commitment is part of the reason why such an event is so unlikely.
74. It is also in the U.S. interest to ensure that it retains the dominant influence in NATO decisions regarding the deployment and use of nuclear weapons. Maintaining a large conventional commitment to Europe is probably the best way to do this.

goal of this strategy; the fact that conquest is difficult makes it feasible and affordable. U.S. commitments in Europe and the Far East increase the obstacles to aggression and should be maintained for precisely this reason. Finally, defense-dominance cuts both ways: the same factors that make it easy to defend U.S. interests make U.S. efforts to seize key *Soviet* interests both costly and extremely risky. For all of these reasons, therefore, arguments for rollback, isolationism, or disengagement are not persuasive.

*What Are Soviet Intentions?*

One's view of the merits of alternative grand strategies is also influenced by one's image of the adversary. Obviously, states that are strongly motivated to alter the status quo pose a greater threat than those that seek only to defend their own territory. When facing a highly expansionist regime, therefore, states will seek additional allies and increased military capabilities in order to improve their chances of deterring or defeating an attack.

Not surprisingly, then, disagreements about U.S. grand strategy are shaped by differing views about Soviet intentions.[75] Rollback and global containment rest on the assumption that the Soviet Union is highly expansionist. Writers who favor these strategies tend to portray the Soviet Union as equivalent to Nazi Germany; for them, it is a ruthless totalitarian power driven to relentless expansion by ideological convictions or domestic political requirements. Efforts at appeasement are doomed to fail; deterring Soviet expansion or reversing Soviet gains requires superior military power and unquestionable U.S. resolve.[76] By contrast, isolationist or idealist writers

---

75. On this general point, the classic analysis is Robert Jervis, *Perception and Misperception in International Politics* (Princeton: Princeton University Press, 1976), chap. 3. See also Richard Herrmann, *Perceptions and Behavior in Soviet Foreign Policy* (Pittsburgh: University of Pittsburgh Press, 1985), chap. 1; Robert E. Osgood, et al., *Containment, Soviet Behavior, and Grand Strategy* (Berkeley: Institute of International Studies, 1981), pp. 8–15; and Barry R. Posen, "Competing Images of the Soviet Union," *World Politics*, Vol. 39, No. 4 (July 1987), pp. 579–597.
76. This view goes back at least as far as NSC 68. For other examples, see Burnham, *Containment or Liberation?*; Podhoretz, *Present Danger*, pp. 91–95; Churba, *Soviet Breakout*, chap. 2; Wildavsky, "Containment Plus Pluralization," in Wildavsky, *Beyond Containment*; Gray, *Geopolitics of Super Power*, chap. 9, especially pp. 95–96; Committee on the Present Danger, "What Is the Soviet Union Up To?" and "Is America Becoming Number 2?" reprinted in Charles Tyroler II, ed., *Alerting America: The Papers of the Committee on the Present Danger* (Washington, D.C.: Pergamon-Brassey's, 1984), pp. 10–14, 39–40; H. Joachim Maitre, "Soviet Military Power," in Bark, *To Promote Peace*, pp. 215–230; and Iklé and Wohlstetter, *Discriminate Deterrence*, p. 63. Harsh assessments of Soviet intentions often portray the Soviet Union as a "paper tiger" that will back down if confronted. As Richard Herrmann points out, this image is impossible to falsify because

often assume that the Soviet Union is a highly insecure status quo power. This view implies that deterrence is unnecessary and that the United States should concentrate on alleviating Soviet fears through cooperative diplomacy.[77] Finally, those who favor limited forms of containment tend to see Soviet foreign policy as reflecting both insecurity and ambition. They conclude that a combination of deterrent threats and positive inducements, corresponding to shifts in Soviet behavior, offers the greatest chance of protecting U.S. interests.[78] Each of these prescriptions follows directly from an assessment of Soviet intentions.

At the onset of the Cold War, there was considerable uncertainty regarding the scope of Soviet aims and Soviet willingness to take risks to achieve them. After forty years, however, we have considerable experience upon which to base this appraisal. The evidence is not definitive, of course, because aggressors that have been successfully deterred behave much like status quo powers. Nor does it provide a perfect guide to future conduct. Nonetheless, the experience of the past four decades should not be ignored.[79]

The historical record does not support an image of the Soviet Union as either a highly aggressive power or an insecure status quo state. Unlike the great expansionist states of the past (revolutionary France, Wilhelmine and Nazi Germany, Imperial Japan, etc.), the Soviet Union has yet to engage in a direct test of military strength with any of its major adversaries.[80] Nor has

---

"proponents . . . can interpret evidence inconsistent with the expansionist proposition as evidence of Soviet restraint in the face of U.S. strength; the USSR was simply 'compelled to behave'." See Herrmann, *Perceptions and Behavior*, p. 12.

77. The most extreme version of this approach is the revisionist school of Cold War historiography, which places primary responsibility for the Cold War on the United States. Contemporary writers who take a benign view of Soviet intentions include Radway, "Let Europe Be Europe," pp. 34–38; Richard J. Barnet, "Why Trust the Soviets?" *World Policy Journal*, Vol. 1, No. 3 (Spring 1984), pp. 461–482, and Barnet, "The Four Pillars," p. 80; Forsberg, "Confining the Military to Defense," pp. 292–293; and Sanders, "Security and Choice," pp. 709–710.

78. This view formed the basis for George Kennan's original prescription for containment. See "X" [Kennan], "The Sources of Soviet Conduct," *Foreign Affairs*, Vol. 25, No. 4 (July 1947), pp. 566–582. For more recent versions, see Posen, "Competing Images of the Soviet Union"; Kenneth N. Waltz, "Another Gap?" in Osgood, et al., *Containment, Soviet Behavior, and Grand Strategy*, pp. 79–80; John Lewis Gaddis, "Containment: Its Past and Future," *International Security*, Vol. 5, No. 4 (Spring 1981), pp. 74–102; and Ernst B. Haas, "On Hedging Our Bets: Selective Engagement with the Soviet Union," in Wildavsky, *Beyond Containment*, pp. 93–124.

79. For a summary of these different images, combined with a careful attempt to test their relative validity, see Herrmann, *Perceptions and Behavior*. For an earlier assessment of Western views, see William Welch, *American Images of Soviet Foreign Policy: An Inquiry into Recent Appraisals from the Academic Community* (New Haven: Yale University Press, 1970).

80. Among other things, this behavior casts grave doubt on the belief that Soviet leaders would risk the lives of millions of Soviet citizens in a nuclear confrontation, even if their own survival

Soviet foreign policy been significantly more aggressive than that of the United States; Soviet interventions in Eastern Europe and support for Third World clients mirror the U.S. role in Latin America, the CIA's assorted covert action campaigns, and U.S. support for its own array of Third World allies. Furthermore, the Soviet's most aggressive postwar action—the invasion of Afghanistan in 1979—occurred in an area that the United States had long indicated was of minor interest at best. Even the deployment of missiles to Cuba in 1962 is most accurately seen as a defensive act, given the strategic situation facing the Soviet Union at that time and its resemblance to the U.S. deployment of nuclear missiles in Turkey.[81] Finally, the Soviet Union has shown a capacity to reverse course when costs and risks outweighed benefits, as it is now doing in Afghanistan.[82] Although testing motivations is inherently difficult and the available evidence is incomplete, an image of the Soviet Union as an ambitious but cautious great power is probably closest to the truth.[83]

Does the "Gorbachev revolution" justify altering this conclusion? In particular, does the Soviet Union's recent interest in defensive military doctrines, together with its recent offers to withdraw thousands of troops and tanks from Eastern Europe and to reduce total Soviet military manpower by 500,000 troops, suggest that the United States should adopt a new grand strategy?[84]

---

were assured. For examples of this belief: Richard Pipes, "Why the Soviet Union Believes It Can Fight and Win a Nuclear War," *Commentary*, Vol. 64, No. 1 (1977), pp. 21–34; and Seymour Weiss, "Labyrinth Under Moscow," *Washington Post*, May 25, 1988, p. A19.

81. Given the small size of the Soviet strategic arsenal and its vulnerability to surprise attack, the United States may have been close to a first-strike capability in the early 1960s. The decision to deploy missiles in Cuba was thus a "quick fix" for the strategic balance and possibly an attempt to deter U.S. efforts to overthrow Castro. See Raymond L. Garthoff, "Intelligence Assessment and Policymaking: A Decision Point in the Kennedy Administration," Staff Paper (Washington, D.C.: Brookings, 1984), pp. 29–31; and Garthoff, "Cuban Missile Crisis: The Soviet Story," *Foreign Policy*, No. 72 (Fall 1988), pp. 63–66; Bundy, *Danger and Survival*, pp. 415–420; and James G. Blight and David Welch, *On the Brink: Americans and Soviets Reexamine the Missile Crisis* (New York: Hill and Wang, 1989), pp. 228–244.

82. On declining Soviet interest in the Third World, see Elizabeth K. Valkenier, "Revolutionary Change in the Third World: Recent Soviet Assessments," *World Politics*, Vol. 38, No. 3 (April 1986), pp. 415–434; Jack Snyder, "The Gorbachev Revolution: A Waning of Soviet Expansionism?" *International Security*, Vol. 12, No. 3 (Winter 1987/88), pp. 93–131; and Francis Fukuyama, *Moscow's Post-Brezhnev Reassessment of the Third World*, R-3337-USDP (Santa Monica: RAND, 1986).

83. See Hannes Adomeit, *Soviet Risk-taking and Crisis Behavior: A Theoretical and Empirical Analysis* (London: Allen and Unwin, 1982).

84. These proposals were originally announced in Gorbachev's speech to the United Nations on December 7, 1988. See the *New York Times*, December 8, 1988, p. A1. The Soviets proposed further reductions in May 1989, as part of the conventional arms control negotiations that began in March 1989.

The answer is no. Although these reforms may lead to a reduction in Soviet military capabilities (thereby reducing U.S. force requirements), it does not justify abandoning the fundamental premises of containment. Gorbachev's efforts to "restructure" Soviet society have been only partially successful thus far, and they have yet to make a significant dent in Soviet military power. Even more important, the belief that *perestroika* (restructuring) and *glasnost* (openness) imply a permanent reduction in the Soviet threat rests on the widespread but unproven hope that a more open Soviet society will be less inclined to expand.[85] This conclusion may be too optimistic: the Soviet Union will remain an authoritarian regime, and if *perestroika* succeeds in reinvigorating the Soviet economy and increasing the Soviet Union's relative power, the West could face a more formidable adversary in the future than it does today. Furthermore, the domestic tensions unleashed by *perestroika* (such as the resurgence of ethnic nationalism) may have unpredictable effects on Soviet foreign policy. Thus, there is little reason to abandon the basic tenets of containment at present.

These warnings do not mean that the United States and its allies should ignore the hopeful prospects raised by Gorbachev's reforms. The West should continue to seek a more durable détente—both for its own sake and to prevent Gorbachev's diplomatic initiatives from undermining Western cohesion. So long as the Soviet Union remains the most threatening Eurasian power, however, the fundamental rationale for containment remains intact. As the threat declines (through reductions in Soviet forces or a more defensively oriented military posture), the United States and its allies can reduce their own military preparations as well.[86] In short, Gorbachev's recent initiatives do not alter the case for finite containment, but they may allow this strategy to be implemented at lower cost.

All things considered, the available evidence suggests that deterring Soviet expansion does not require the extraordinary efforts proposed by advocates of rollback or global containment. At the same time, Soviet capabilities are still potent and one cannot be sure that the Soviets would not exploit op-

---

85. For a sophisticated presentation of this view, see Snyder, "The Gorbachev Revolution." For an alternative appraisal, Stephen M. Meyer, "The Sources and Prospects of Gorbachev's New Political Thinking on Security," *International Security*, Vol. 13, No. 2 (Fall 1988), pp. 124–163.
86. An obvious example is President Bush's recent proposal that the United States withdraw 30,000 U.S. troops from Europe as part of a conventional arms control agreement. This proposal was endorsed at a NATO summit meeting in Brussels on May 29–30, 1989, and reflects an awareness that substantial decreases in Soviet military power can reduce—though not eliminate—the need for U.S. troops in Europe.

portunities when they arise. In terms of grand strategy, therefore, isolationism and disengagement run the risk of encouraging Soviet expansion, but rollback and global containment are both provocative and largely unnecessary. Finally, although the United States should welcome Gorbachev's efforts to reform the Soviet domestic order, U.S. leaders should not exaggerate their ability to influence this process or to predict its impact on foreign policy. For all of these reasons, finite containment remains the best alternative for the foreseeable future.

*What Are the Causes of Alignment?*

When formulating a grand strategy, national leaders must also consider the forces that will lead other states to join forces with them or to unite in opposition.[87] As a result, debates about foreign policy and grand strategy also turn on disputes about the causes of alignment. In general, advocates of rollback and global containment argue that U.S. allies are likely to "bandwagon" with the Soviet Union should U.S. power or credibility begin to wane.[88] Since the beginning of the Cold War, this fear has been invoked repeatedly to justify military buildups or overseas intervention.[89] This argument is still popular: when seeking support for the Nicaraguan *contras* in 1983, for example, President Reagan predicted that "if we cannot win in Central America, our credibility will collapse and our alliance will crumble."[90] These writers often maintain that ideology is a powerful cause of alignment as well, which implies that leftist or Marxist states will be strongly inclined to ally with the Soviet Union. If these hypotheses are true, the United States

---

87. The discussion in this section draws heavily upon Walt, *Origins of Alliances*.
88. Examples of this belief include Iklé and Wohlstetter, *Discriminate Deterrence*, pp. 13–14; Aaron Wildavsky, "Dilemmas of American Foreign Policy," in Wildavsky, *Beyond Containment*, p. 13; Podhoretz, *Present Danger*, pp. 40–41, 58–60; Burnham, *Containment or Liberation?* pp. 245–247; and Churba, *Soviet Breakout*, pp. 42–45, 70–71.
89. See "U.S. Objectives and Programs for National Security" (NSC 68), reprinted in Thomas H. Etzold and John Lewis Gaddis, eds., *Containment: Documents on American Policy and Strategy, 1945–1950* (New York: Columbia University Press, 1978), pp. 404, 414, 418, 4343. On the impact of U.S. leaders' concerns about credibility in motivating Third World intervention, see Bruce W. Jentleson, "American Commitments in the Third World: Theory vs. Practice," *International Organization*, Vol. 41, No. 4 (Autumn 1987), pp. 667–704.
90. See "Speech to a Joint Session of Congress on Central America," *New York Times*, April 28, 1983, p. A12. For other examples of bandwagoning logic, see Walt, *Origins of Alliances*, pp. 3–4, 19–20; and Deborah Welch Larson, "The Bandwagon Metaphor and the Role of Institutions," in Robert Jervis and Jack Snyder, eds., *Dominoes and Bandwagons: Strategic Beliefs and Superpower Competition in the Eurasian Rimland* (New York: Oxford University Press, forthcoming).

must act to prevent Marxist regimes from coming to power or must attempt to overthrow them if they do.[91]

By contrast, less ambitious strategies—including finite containment—reflect precisely the opposite view. These strategies assume that states are more likely to balance against threats rather than bandwagon with them; in this view, Soviet efforts to expand will trigger increased opposition from other powerful states. Similarly, finite containment assumes that ideology is a rather weak force for alignment. Although U.S. leaders may prefer democracy, this strategy assumes that U.S. security is not endangered by ideological diversity.[92]

Which of these competing beliefs is correct? The available evidence overwhelmingly supports the latter view. First, as I have argued at length elsewhere, balancing behavior predominates in international politics. This tendency defeated the various attempts to achieve hegemony in the European great power system and helps explain why the U.S. defeat in Indochina led to increased cooperation among the ASEAN countries and accelerated the Sino-American rapprochement. These cases are hardly isolated examples; similar behavior is characteristic of international politics in the Middle East and South Asia as well.[93] Second, as the history of international communism reveals (e.g., the quarrels between Stalin and Tito, Khrushchev and Mao, and the fratricidal conflict between Kampuchea, Vietnam, and China), Marxist ideology has been a relatively weak motive for alignment. Indeed, centralized ideological movements (such as international communism or pan-Arabism) are especially prone to ideological divisions, just as George Kennan once predicted.[94]

These results expose the poverty of much of the justification for U.S. foreign policy since World War II. Contrary to the prescriptions of finite

---

91. For a recent statement of this view, which also attempts to resurrect the "domino theory," see Singer, "Dynamic Containment," in Wildavsky, *Beyond Containment*, p. 173.
92. Disagreements about the importance of ideology divide those who advocate finite containment (which focuses on containing *Soviet* power) from those who advocate either rollback or global containment (which seeks to contain or eliminate *communist* power). On this point, see Morgenthau, *In Defense of the National Interest*, chap. 3.
93. See Walt, *Origins of Alliances*, chap. 5; Walt, "Alliance Formation and the Balance of World Power," *International Security*, Vol. 9, No. 4 (Spring 1985), pp. 3–43; and Walt, "Testing Theories of Alliance Formation: The Case of Southwest Asia," *International Organization*, Vol. 42, No. 2 (Spring 1988), pp. 275–316.
94. See Kennan's memo, "U.S. Objectives with Respect to Russia," in Etzold and Gaddis, *Containment*, pp. 186–187; and Gaddis, *Strategies of Containment*, pp. 43–45. On the impact of ideology more generally, see Walt, *Origins of Alliances*, chap. 6.

containment, the United States has consistently sought commitments beyond the defense of the "key centers of industrial power" and has occasionally tried to reverse leftist revolutions in the Third World. In other words, the United States has for the most part adopted the strategy of global containment, with occasional efforts at rollback. This strategy was justified in part by the fear that allies would bandwagon or by the belief that leftist forces in the Third World would inevitably be drawn towards alignment with Moscow.[95]

In retrospect, however, neither fear was well-founded. Although a number of Third World countries have chosen to ally with Moscow, this is primarily because they faced serious internal and external threats (often including the United States) and could not obtain other allies. Soviet military power was confined to Eurasia, and the Soviet Union was publicly sympathetic to Third World nationalism. By contrast, the United States denounced neutralism as "immoral" and intervened directly in a number of developing countries. Thus, Soviet power threatened the industrial powers but not the former colonies; American power did just the opposite. Given this fundamental difference, it is not surprising that the United States has been closely allied with the industrial powers of Europe and Asia while the USSR has done relatively better (although not especially well) in the Third World.

We may draw several lessons from these results. The forces that create international alliances make finite containment relatively easy to accomplish; in particular, the United States does not need to intervene in peripheral areas in order to maintain the alliances that matter.[96] The Soviet Union's geographic proximity and military power make it the main threat to Europe and Japan; because states tend to balance, virtually all of the world's strategically significant nations are inclined to ally with the United States. By the same logic, strategies of rollback or global containment should be rejected. Adopting these strategies would require the United States to use force more often and in more places, thereby increasing the likelihood that other states will unite against it.

---

95. The fear of bandwagoning explains why some early proponents of containment (including Kennan) supported U.S. intervention in Korea and were reluctant to advocate an early withdrawal from Vietnam. See Hixson, "Containment on the Perimeter," pp. 149, 159.

96. It is worth noting that most U.S. allies opposed U.S. involvement in the Vietnam War, just as most opposed U.S. support for the Nicaraguan *contras*.

WILL U.S. ALLIES BALANCE IF THE UNITED STATES WITHDRAWS?
As noted above, writers who favor a reduced U.S. role tend to invoke the logic of balancing in order to justify this recommendation. After accusing U.S. allies of "free-riding," advocates of isolationism or disengagement argue that Europe and Japan would balance a U.S. withdrawal by greatly increasing their own defense efforts. Instead of letting its allies "free-ride," in short, the United States should start "free-riding" on them.[97]

The tendency for states to balance means that a reduction in U.S. support is unlikely to trigger a stampede towards the Soviet bloc. Moreover, U.S. allies will probably do more if the United States does less. Yet the conclusion that the United States can substantially reduce its commitment to Europe should be rejected for at least five reasons.

First, the claim that a U.S. withdrawal is justified by allied free-riding greatly oversimplifies the issue of burden-sharing within the alliance. Although its allies spend a smaller percentage of GNP on defense than the United States does (measured in terms of annual defense budgets), focusing solely on percentages of GNP ignores or understates the full range of allied contributions.[98] Moreover, when comparing budget figures or shares of GNP, U.S. defense costs are inflated by its reliance on an all-volunteer force rather than conscription.[99] Most important of all, the disproportionate burden borne by the United States may be due less to free-riding than to differing percep-

---

97. See Chace, "A New Grand Strategy," pp. 12–13; Kristol, "What's Wrong with NATO?" p. 71, and Kristol, "Foreign Policy in an Age of Ideology," p. 14; Layne, "Atlanticism Without NATO," p. 32, 38–39; Ravenal, "NATO: The Tides of Discontent," pp. 86–88; Krauss, *How NATO Weakens the West*; and Calleo, *Beyond American Hegemony*, pp. 165–171.
98. According to a recent study of NATO burdensharing, "Data that count military equipment and personnel show that the large and small member states make a significant contribution to NATO's military capability, well beyond their shares of the alliance's economic resources or defense spending." The authors conclude that "it cannot be said that the NATO allies have obtained a 'free ride' in the alliance since it was created." See Adams and Munz, *Fair Shares*, pp. 7, 17, 25–30. See also Klaus E. Knorr, "Burden-Sharing in NATO: Aspects of U.S. Policy," *Orbis*, Vol. 29, No. 3 (Fall 1985), pp. 517–536; CBO, "Alliance Burdensharing: A Review of the Data," Staff Working Paper (Washington, D.C.: U.S. GPO, 1987); James Steinberg, "Rethinking the Debate on Burden-sharing," *Survival*, Vol. 29, No. 1 (January/February 1987), pp. 56–78; and Dunn, "NATO's Enduring Value," pp. 164–165.
99. According to several rough estimates, abandoning conscription might raise European defense expenditures by as much as 20 percent. Given their sensitivity to fluctuating exchange rates and differences between European and U.S. labor markets, these figures should be used with caution. See Ruth Leger Sivard, *World Military and Social Expenditures 1981* (Leesburg, Va.: World Priorities, 1981), p. 37; Knorr, "Burden-Sharing in NATO," pp. 529–530; CBO, "Alliance Burdensharing," p. 12; and Adams and Munz, *Fair Shares*, pp. 18–20.

tions of the threat. Because U.S. allies do not believe that the Soviet Union is as dangerous as the United States does and because they do not share the U.S. fear of leftist forces in the developing world, they do not spend as much to counter either threat. Thus the United States spends more because its leaders (and taxpayers) have accepted a more pessimistic view of the threat and have adopted more ambitious goals for dealing with it, not because U.S. allies are lazy or decadent.[100]

Second, advocates of withdrawal take the logic of balancing to an illogical extreme. The real question is not whether its allies will do more if the United States withdraws; it is whether they will do *enough*. To replace the U.S. commitment, the rest of NATO would have to mobilize at least 500,000 more troops along with the associated military hardware.[101] Given present demographic trends in Europe, that is an unlikely event.[102] Those who call for a U.S. withdrawal have yet to provide a detailed analysis of what an independent European force would look like, what it would cost, and how effectively it could fight or deter.[103] In this respect, the suggestion that the United States withdraw within four or five years—as Melvyn Krauss and Christopher Layne have proposed—reveals a worrisome disregard of basic military realities.[104]

Furthermore, the "logic of collective action" would still operate after a U.S. withdrawal. Because security is a collective good, the separate European states would inevitably try to pass the burden of deterring the Soviets onto each other.[105] Even if Europe did balance by building up after a U.S. with-

---

100. If one excludes non-NATO U.S. expenditures, the U.S. share of NATO's combined defense spending falls from 68.8 percent to 56.8 percent in 1986 (for comparison: U.S. GNP is 53.6 percent of the alliance total GNP). This figure probably understates the total U.S. contribution, but it does suggest that U.S. defense burdens are greater in part because U.S. strategic objectives are more ambitious than those of its allies. See Adams and Munz, *Fair Shares*, pp. 72–73; and Van Evera, "American Strategic Interests," pp. 16–18.

101. This figure includes both U.S. forces currently deployed in Europe and designated reinforcements based in the United States. According to Keith Dunn, if the U.S. were to remove 100,000 troops, the allies would have to increase their defense spending by 18 to 30 percent over two years to offset it. See Dunn, "NATO's Enduring Value," p. 170.

102. For example, the number of West German males between the ages of 17 and 30 will decline by more than 30 percent by 1999. Similar trends apply to France and Britain as well. See IISS, *The Military Balance 1983–84* (London: IISS, 1983), pp. 145–147.

103. The best attempt is Calleo, *Beyond American Hegemony*, chap. 9. Calleo argues that Europe can easily match the Warsaw Pact through greater reliance on reserves, but he does not provide an adequate description of the force he envisions or its likely effectiveness against the Pact.

104. See Krauss, *How NATO Weakens the West*, p. 237; and Layne, "Atlanticism Without NATO," p. 33.

105. The classic analysis of the "collective goods" problem in alliances remains Mancur Olson

drawal, the effort would still be weaker than it is with the United States included.

Third, advocates of withdrawal overlook the stabilizing effects of the U.S. presence in Europe and the Far East. America's global presence helps safeguard its allies from one another; they can concentrate on balancing the Soviet Union because they do not need to worry about other threats. Although the Soviet Union would remain the principal adversary in the short term, rivalries within Europe would be more frequent and more intense if the U.S. withdrew. This possibility may appear far-fetched after forty years of peace, but it should not if one recalls the four centuries of conflict that preceded them.[106] This problem could be even more serious in the Far East, where a U.S. withdrawal would encourage renewed regional tensions.[107] And even if U.S. allies balanced after a U.S. withdrawal, they might do so in ways the United States would soon regret. Withdrawal would encourage Britain and France to increase their nuclear capabilities, it would tempt West Germany to acquire a nuclear force of its own, and it would probably encourage a *rapprochement* between the Soviet Union and either China or a militarily resurgent Japan, depending on how regional relations in the Far East evolved.

Fourth, even if U.S. allies increased their defense efforts considerably, a U.S. withdrawal from Europe would still weaken deterrence. With the United States firmly committed, the Soviets face a coalition possessing vastly greater combined capabilities. But if the U.S. withdraws its forces, Soviet decisionmakers could more plausibly expect a blitzkrieg to succeed.[108] Students of history will recognize that this situation resembles the deterrence failures that produced World Wars I and II.[109] The U.S. presence in Europe helps

---

and Richard Zeckhauser, "An Economic Theory of Alliances," *Review of Economics and Statistics*, Vol. 48, No. 3 (August 1966), pp. 266–279. A recent review of this literature is Wallace J. Thies, "Alliances and Collective Goods: A Reappraisal," *Journal of Conflict Resolution*, Vol. 31, No. 2 (June 1987), pp. 298–332.

106. See Josef Joffe, "Europe's American Pacifier," *Foreign Policy*, No. 54 (Spring 1984), pp. 64–82; and Dunn, "NATO's Enduring Value," pp. 171–172.

107. This point is nicely made in Henry A. Kissinger, "The Rearming of Japan—and the Rest of Asia," *Washington Post*, January 29, 1987, p. A25.

108. On the conditions for successful conventional deterrence, see John J. Mearsheimer, *Conventional Deterrence* (Ithaca: Cornell University Press, 1983).

109. Because Britain did not make its commitment to France clear in 1914, Germany's leaders concluded that Britain would not fight. Because Hitler doubted the Allied commitment to Poland in 1939, he ignored Britain and French warnings. And had Germany's leaders known that they would eventually face the United States, both wars might have been avoided.

prevent a similar miscalculation today, because it provides a potent reminder that the Soviet Union cannot attack Western Europe without directly engaging the bulk of U.S. ground forces, backed by U.S. nuclear weapons.

Finally, it is unwise to assume—as some isolationists do—that the United States could easily stay out of a major war on the Eurasian landmass.[110] Despite its isolationist traditions and modest military assets, the United States was eventually drawn into three of the last four major European wars.[111] The United States is better off with its present policy, which reduces the likelihood that the United States will be forced to fight *any* war in Europe.

In short, although balancing is much more common than bandwagoning, this tendency does not mean that the United States would be better off leaving the defense of Eurasia to others. The neo-isolationists are correct to discount the danger of "Finlandization," but their confidence that Europe and Japan would fully compensate for a U.S. demobilization is too optimistic.

*Alternative Perspectives on U.S. Grand Strategy: A Summary*

As Table 1 reveals, there is a marked tendency for a given analyst's views about U.S. grand strategy to display a self-reinforcing consistency—i.e., each to support the same general conclusion—even when the different issues appear to be logically unrelated.[112] For example, those who favor either rollback or global containment tend to believe that the United States has

---

110. This view is most evident in the writings of Earl Ravenal. See his "NATO: The Tides of Discontent," pp. 60–63, 72–75.

111. A "major war" is defined here as involving more than two great powers and lasting at least two years. The United States eventually entered the Napoleonic Wars (the War of 1812) and World Wars I and II; the Crimean War is the exception. As Stephen Van Evera notes: "History warns that in the past, [the United States] got into great European wars by staying out of Europe—not by being in." See Van Evera, "American Strategic Interests," p. 20.

112. The tendency for an analyst's beliefs to reinforce each other is often attributed either to irrational cognitive consistency or to efforts to assemble convincing arguments during a political debate. On the role of cognitive psychology, see Jervis, *Perception and Misperception*, pp. 128–142, and Jervis, "Beliefs About Soviet Behavior," in Osgood, et al., *Containment, Soviet Behavior, and Grand Strategy*, pp. 57–58. It should be noted, however, that logical connections do link different issues. For example, beliefs about the offense/defense balance are related to inferences about an adversary's intentions: if offense is easy, then aggressors are more likely to conclude that an attack might succeed. Similarly, when offense has the advantage, bandwagoning may be more likely because weak states fear being conquered before allies can come to their aid. And if national leaders believe war is likely, then the need for reliable access to raw materials will grow, expanding the scope of vital interests. Thus, the tendency for a strategist's beliefs to reinforce each other may be due less to psychological distortions than to the logical connections between different elements of grand strategy.

**Table 1. Alternative U.S. Grand Strategies.**

| STRATEGY | Main Objectives | Areas of Vital Interest | Expansion Easy or Hard | Soviet Intentions | Causes of Alignment |
|---|---|---|---|---|---|
| World Order Idealism *Falk, Johansen, Forsberg* | Promote new world order, solve collective global problems | None | Very hard | Benign | Irrelevant |
| Neo-Isolationism *Ravenal, Layne, Sanders, Barnet* | War-avoidance, promote economic prosperity | U.S. territory | Very hard | Probably benign and may not matter | Balancing; allies will do more |
| Disengagement *Chace, Calleo* | Deter Soviet expansion; restore U.S. "solvency" | Varies: Western hemisphere, Far East, etc. | Hard | Hostile but very cautious | Balancing; allies may do more |
| Finite Containment *Early Kennan, Lippmann, Morgenthau, Posen, Van Evera, Walt, Waltz* | Deter Soviet expansion in industrial Eurasia | Key centers of industrial power (W. Europe, Japan and Persian Gulf) | Hard but not impossible | Hostile but easy to deter | Balancing |
| Global Containment *Weinberger, Brzezinski, Huntington, Iklé, Wildavsky, Wohlstetter* | Prevent Soviet or Marxist expansion, terrorism, etc. | Entire world | Easy | Hostile, difficult to deter | Bandwagoning; also ideological solidarity |
| Rollback *Burnham, Churba, Kristol, Krauthammer, Podhoretz* | Eliminate communism; promote democracy | Entire world | Very easy, via military action or subversion | Very hostile; will conduct relentless political warfare | Bandwagoning; ideological solidarity very powerful |

NOTE: Placement of authors by category is approximate; individual authors may not share all of the beliefs associated with each strategy.

critical economic and security interests in all parts of the globe, that the Soviet Union is extremely aggressive, that conquest is relatively easy, that bandwagoning is commonplace, and that communist ideology is both a powerful force for alignment and a potent weapon of subversion. By contrast, advocates of isolationism or disengagement tend to believe that U.S. interests are extremely limited, that Soviet intentions are benevolent and would be worsened by U.S. pressure, that expansion is virtually impossible irrespective of U.S. policy, and that current U.S. allies are certain to balance effectively if the United States withdraws. Finally, proponents of finite containment tend to believe that U.S. interests are confined to a few critical regions, that conquest is difficult provided that the United States remains committed to opposing Soviet expansion, that the Soviet Union is a cautious but potentially dangerous rival, and that other states will tend to balance against whichever superpower appears most threatening.

The analysis in the preceding pages suggests that a strategy of "finite containment" remains the best choice for the United States. The other strategies examined here fail on one or more grounds; by contast, finite containment is most consistent with the present state of the international system. Of course, if further research were to reveal that my assessment of these different factors was wrong, then different conclusions might be in order. This possibility suggests that additional research on the four questions examined above should be part of further efforts to refine U.S. grand strategy.

There is a final rationale for finite containment, however. In international politics, large changes are usually dangerous; national leaders are more likely to miscalculate when facing novel circumstances. After World War II, the United States and its allies devised a geopolitical formula for peace that has proven to be remarkably durable. Following the precept that "if it ain't broke, don't fix it," the United States should be reluctant to discard arrangements that have worked so well thus far. Although circumstances do change and strategy must eventually adapt, the burden of proof should remain with those who now seek to abandon a successful strategy. They have yet to make an adequate case.

*Implementing Finite Containment*

Finite containment would be a modest, but important departure from the expansive form of containment that the United States has followed since 1950. As a result, implementing this strategy would entail a number of adjustments in U.S. foreign and defense policy. Although a detailed description of its implications is beyond the scope of this essay, the central elements of the strategy can be sketched briefly.

OBJECTIVES AND CAPABILITIES

First, and most importantly, finite containment strategy would maintain the present United States commitment of ground and air forces in Western Europe and the Far East. These forces are the best symbol of the U.S. interest in preserving the independence of these regions. Because the main threat in Europe is the Soviets' powerful land army, U.S. ground and air forces are also the most valuable contribution that the United States can make to the defense of Europe in time of war. Contrary to much of the conventional wisdom, the prospects for a successful defense in Europe are reasonably good, provided that the United States does not withdraw the bulk of its forces.[113] To improve its chances even more, NATO should spend less on improving its offensive capabilities—such as deep-strike aircraft for so-called Follow-on Forces Attack (FOFA)—and spend more on defensive measures designed to thwart a Soviet armored assault.[114]

Second, finite containment would drastically reduce U.S. preparations for intervention in the Third World. During the 1980s, the Reagan administration conducted a major buildup in U.S. naval forces and increased U.S. intervention capabilities by creating "light divisions" in the army, by increasing U.S. amphibious warfare and air- and sea-lift capacity, and by establishing a separate Special Operations Command responsible for "low intensity conflict." Under finite containment, these programs could be eliminated. Of the twenty-one active U.S. Army and Marine divisions, only sixteen are assigned to missions in Europe, the Far East, or the Persian Gulf. The remaining five divisions (including three "light divisions" and one Marine division) should be viewed as intervention forces; among other things, these forces would be

---

113. For optimistic appraisals of the conventional balance, see the references in footnote 56. More pessimistic views can be found in Kim R. Holmes, "Measuring the Conventional Balance in Europe," *International Security*, Vol. 12, No. 4 (Spring 1988), pp. 166–173; Andrew Hamilton, "Redressing the Conventional Balance: NATO's Reserve Military Manpower," *International Security*, Vol. 10, No. 1 (Summer 1985), pp. 111–136; Cohen, "Toward Better Net Assessment"; and Thomson, "An Unfavorable Situation."

114. For example, close support aircraft like the A-10 are preferable to high-priced items like the F-15 or Tornado, because the deep interdiction mission performed by the latter is both more difficult and less important to a successful defense. Greater attention to terrain preparation and other types of fixed defenses would slow a Pact advance and improve exchange ratios as well.

of little value against the Soviet army. Because the United States has few economic or strategic interests in the Third World, it can eliminate some or all of these intervention forces, along with most of its special forces and covert action capabilities.[115]

Third, finite containment would maintain the U.S. commitment to protect Western oil supplies in the Persian Gulf. As noted earlier, pessimism about this mission is excessive: the impressive barriers to a Soviet invasion of the Gulf and the likelihood that regional powers would actively oppose Soviet aggression give the United States a good chance of deterring or defeating a Soviet attack.[116] Thus, finite containment would call for maintaining the U.S. Central Command at roughly its present size.[117]

Fourth, because finite containment focuses U.S. commitments on the key centers of industrial power, the obvious target for reductions is the U.S. Navy. In a major war, the navy's main mission would be to defend the sea lines of communication (SLOCs) between the United States and its European and Far Eastern allies.[118] The main threats to the SLOCs are Soviet land-based aircraft and Soviet attack submarines. Primary defenses against these forces are NATO's own submarines, its ASW (anti–submarine warfare) ships and patrol aircraft, and land-based interceptors, in a strategy of "defensive sea control."[119] Although U.S. aircraft carriers can play a role in SLOC de-

---

115. After these reductions, the United States would still possess an adequate intervention capability (e.g., the 82nd Airborne and 101st Air Assault divisions, as well as the remaining Marine forces). Because these units are assigned missions in the Persian Gulf, the U.S. ability to intervene in the Third World would be limited in the early stages of a global war. But in the event of a major war in Europe or the Gulf, intervention elsewhere in the Third World would be of little concern.

116. See Epstein, "Soviet Vulnerabilities," and Dunn, "Constraints on the USSR." For a more pessimistic assessment, see Jeffrey Record, The Rapid Deployment Force and U.S. Military Intervention in the Persian Gulf (Cambridge, Mass.: Institute for Foreign Policy Analysis, 1981).

117. The U.S. Central Command is assigned 4⅓ Army divisions, 1⅓ Marine divisions, 3 carrier battle groups, 7 tactical fighter wings, and a variety of special forces and support units. See John D. Mayer, Jr., Rapid Deployment Forces: Policy and Budgetary Implications (Washington, D.C.: Congressional Budget Office, 1983), p. xv; and Weinberger, Annual Report to the Congress, Fiscal Year 1984, p. 195.

118. The rationale for and primacy of this mission is explained in John J. Mearsheimer, "A Strategic Misstep: The Maritime Strategy and Deterrence in Europe," International Security, Vol. 11, No. 2 (Fall 1986), pp. 3–57.

119. A defensive sea control strategy would establish barriers across "choke points" like the Sea of Japan, and the Greenland–Iceland–United Kingdom (GIUK) gap. The Soviet Navy is unlikely to challenge these barriers, because its main mission is to defend Soviet SSBNs in the Arctic Sea. If it did attack the SLOCs, however, these barriers would pose a highly effective defense. See William W. Kaufmann, A Thoroughly Efficient Navy (Washington, D.C.: Brookings, 1987), chap. 7, especially pp. 79–81.

fense, other forces will bear the major responsibility for this mission.[120] Aircraft carriers are primarily useful for "power projection" in the Third World, but with the exception of the Persian Gulf, this mission is of minor importance. Moreover, land-based aircraft can perform the "power projection" mission more efficiently in many cases. The United States should therefore abandon the misguided "Maritime Strategy" (intended primarily to justify an expensive 600-ship fleet), because it is infeasible, potentially destablizing, and unnecessary.[121] Instead of the fifteen carrier battle groups currently deployed, a force of eight to ten carrier battle groups could easily fulfill the requirements of finite containment.[122]

Fifth, finite containment would also permit reductions in U.S. strategic nuclear forces. Whereas rollback strategies require strategic superiority (i.e., a first-strike capability), containment requires only that the United States maintain a robust second-strike force. This requirement is easy to meet; according to one recent estimate, the United States would have over 4000 warheads (totaling over 1000 equivalent megatons) left after a *successful* Soviet

---

120. Although aircraft carriers have their own anti-submarine and anti-aircraft capabilities, the United States "can operate patrol aircraft and fighters from land bases more efficiently than from the more costly and vulnerable carrier battle groups." See Kaufmann, *A Thoroughly Efficient Navy*, p. 83.
121. The Maritime Strategy is *infeasible* because carrier battle groups are an inefficient means of projecting power (a battle group devotes most of its capabilities to defending itself), yet the strategy calls for direct naval attacks on heavily defended Soviet bases (e.g., the Kola Peninsula). The strategy is *destabilizing* because it includes attacks on Soviet SSBNs, thereby threatening the Soviets' second-strike capability and tempting them to escalate. Finally, the strategy is *unnecessary* because it would have little or no effect on the critical ground war in Europe. On these points, see Epstein, *1988 Defense Budget*, pp. 45–55; Kaufmann, *A Thoroughly Efficient Navy*, pp. 12–21 and passim; Mearsheimer, "A Strategic Misstep"; and Barry R. Posen, "Inadvertent Nuclear War? Escalation and NATO's Northern Flank," *International Security*, Vol. 7, No. 2 (Fall 1982), pp. 28–54. For arguments in favor of the Maritime Strategy, see Admiral James D. Watkins, "The Maritime Strategy," Supplement, *U.S. Naval Institute Proceedings*, Vol. 112, No. 1 (January 1986) pp. 2–17; Linton F. Brooks, "Naval Power and National Security: The Case for the Maritime Strategy," *International Security*, Vol. 11, No. 2 (Fall 1986), pp. 58–88; and Bradford Dismukes, "Strategic ASW and the Conventional Defense of Europe," Professional Paper No. 453 (Alexandria, Va.: Center for Naval Analyses, April 1987).
122. Assuming two carriers are in overhaul at any time, a total of eight carriers would permit wartime deployment of three in the Persian Gulf (as currently assigned to Central Command), two in the Atlantic, and one in the Pacific. This force would be more than enough in a global war and would provide ample naval muscle for lesser contingencies. On the limited value of carriers for SLOC defense, see Epstein, *1988 Defense Budget*, pp. 49–50; and Mearsheimer, "A Strategic Misstep," p. 55. Using extremely conservative assumptions, William Kaufmann suggests that 12 carrier battle groups would satisfy U.S. naval requirements in a major war with the Soviet Union. See Kaufmann, *A Thoroughly Efficient Navy*, pp. 84–99. All three authors agree that the current fleet is unjustified and extravagant.

first strike.[123] Much the same situation applies in reverse, of course, and because both superpowers have second-strike forces that are far larger than they need to destroy each other, both are deterred.[124] Recognizing the durable reality of Mutual Assured Destruction, finite containment would entail abandoning the costly and futile search for strategic superiority. Specifically, the United States could cancel the B-1B and B-2 bombers, the Trident D-5, the Midgetman and MX missiles, and various schemes for land-mobile ICBMs, and still possess an overwhelming deterrent.[125] The U.S. SSBN fleet would be modernized as needed, along with the current ICBM force and an expanded cruise missile arsenal (possibly incorporating stealth technology). The Strategic Defense Initiative (SDI) can be canceled as well: the available evidence suggests it will not work, and it would be undesirable even if it did. A modest research program should continue as a hedge against future breakthroughs, but plans for testing and deployment should be abandoned.[126]

Sixth, finite containment does not require the United States to sacrifice its moral commitment to personal freedom and human rights. However, this strategy recognizes the inherent limits of an ideologically-based foreign policy and adopts a realistic set of goals. Specifically, U.S. leaders should realize that: 1) efforts to "promote democracy" via military force will place the United States at odds with most of the world (including its major allies); 2) the "freedom fighters" that the United States now supports are unlikely to establish democratic regimes if they win; 3) we lack an adequate theory explaining how states achieve stable democracy and thus cannot be confident of the U.S. ability to create democracy in these settings; 4) the record of past

123. See Salman, Sullivan, and Van Evera, "Analysis or Propaganda"; and Epstein, *1988 Defense Budget*, pp. 21–27.
124. One recent estimate shows that 100 one-megaton airbursts would kill 45–77 million Soviet citizens and cause 73–93 million lethal and nonlethal injuries. See Barbara G. Levi, Frank N. von Hippel, and William H. Daugherty, "Civilian Casualties from 'Limited' Nuclear Attacks on the Soviet Union," *International Security*, Vol. 12, No. 3 (Winter 1987/88), pp. 168–169.
125. On U.S. retaliatory capabilities after these reductions, see Epstein, *1988 Defense Budget*, pp. 21–32.
126. For studies challenging the feasibility of SDI, see Kurt Gottfried, "The Physicists Size Up SDI," *Arms Control Today*, Vol. 17, No. 6 (July/August 1987), pp. 28–32; John Tirman, *Empty Promise: The Growing Case Against Star Wars* (Boston: Beacon Press, 1986); and Sidney D. Drell, David Holloway, and Philip J. Farley, "Preserving the ABM Treaty: A Critique of the Reagan Strategic Defense Initiative," *International Security*, Vol. 9, No. 2 (Fall 1984), pp. 51–91. For analyses suggesting that SDI would be undesirable even if it were possible, see Charles Glaser, "Why Even Good Defenses May Be Bad," *International Security*, Vol. 9, No. 2 (Fall 1984), pp. 92–123; and Glaser, "Do We Want the Missile Defenses We Can Build?" *International Security*, Vol. 10, No. 1 (Summer 1985), pp. 25–57.

efforts (in Panama, Nicaragua, Guatemala, Vietnam, Cuba, Lebanon, El Salvador, etc.) is not encouraging; 5) the rare successes (such as Germany and Japan after World War II) suggest that lengthy occupation and radical social reform would be necessary; and 6) crusades to promote American values usually require abandoning the very ideals that such campaigns claim to be defending.[127] Because U.S. security interests are not at stake in most of these situations, more modest but unambiguous objectives would be appropriate.[128] In addition to public support for the United Nations Declaration on Basic Human Rights, the United States should actively oppose all governments that engage in the systematic murder of unarmed opposition.[129] This criterion ignores what foreign leaders profess to believe and focuses on what they actually do. How U.S. leaders chose to respond to such regimes will vary on a case-by-case basis, but this general criterion is likely to command widespread support at home and abroad.

Adopting the strategy of finite containment would go a long way toward alleviating the fiscal pressures that the United States will face in the 1990s. It would concentrate U.S. defense capabilities in the places that matter and reverse the policies that have undermined U.S. prestige elsewhere in the world. It would also help correct the perception that Europe and Japan were "free-riding" on the United States. In effect, finite containment would bring U.S. grand strategy closer to its allies' perspective, which focuses on the main threat (the Soviet Union), and downgrades the importance of the Third World and the futile quest for strategic superiority. Finally, the reduction in U.S. naval forces implied by finite containment would encourage Japan to continue expanding its responsibilities for sea and air defense in the Far East. And if the United States maintains a tangible presence in East Asia (such as

---

127. For example, the U.S. effort to "promote democracy" in Nicaragua has claimed over 20,000 civilian lives, led to the condemnation of the United States by the World Court, inspired a series of illegal arms shipments, and involved a carefully orchestrated U.S. government disinformation campaign intended to deceive U.S. citizens about the conflict in Central America. See Robert Parry and Peter Kornbluh, "Iran-Contra's Untold Story," *Foreign Policy*, No. 72 (Fall 1988), pp. 3–30.
128. Even some of the most fervent advocates of the "Reagan Doctrine" admit that U.S. security interests are not at stake in the Third World. For example, Charles Krauthammer has written that "if the security of the United States is the only goal of American foreign policy, all that is needed is a minimal deterrent arsenal, a small navy, a border patrol, and hardly any foreign policy at all." See Krauthammer, "The Poverty of Realism," p. 16. This view implies that the United States should spend over $200 billion each year on defense and promote civil war against Marxist regimes solely in order to get other countries to adopt the U.S. vision of the ideal political order.
129. On these points, see Van Evera, "American Strategic Interests," pp. 33–37.

its ground and air forces in Japan and Korea), increases in Japan's naval and air force capabilities are less likely to alarm other states in this region.

Of course, implementing finite containment would face impressive domestic obstacles. Because finite containment would reduce or eliminate several entrenched but unnecessary missions, service interests (e.g., the Navy) and defense contractors are certain to resist its adoption.[130] In order to succeed, a campaign to implement finite containment would require aggressive presidential leadership and a persistent and well-orchestrated effort to explain its rationale. The foremost task of this campaign would be to educate U.S. citizens on the finite scope of U.S. security interests and the limited means that are necessary to protect them.

Because they do not have entrenched interests to defend, experts outside official circles—in universities, foundations, independent "think tanks" and the media—must take a leading role in this "war of ideas." By participating actively in the debate on U.S. grand strategy, and in particular, by performing rigorous and critical analysis of the assumptions that underlie competing proposals, independent analysts can provide the intellectual ammunition that meaningful reform will require. Without a lively and serious debate, the United States is likely to repeat past errors, postpone the necessary adjustments, or adopt misguided and excessive reforms. But if the debate on grand strategy attains reasonable standards of scholarship and rigor, then U.S. strategy in the 1990s is more likely to be consistent with U.S. interests and better suited to the evolving international system.

*Conclusion*

After four decades, the changing patterns of world power have led many to question the central premises of U.S. grand strategy. By provoking a rigorous reassessment, the recent wave of writings on U.S. grand strategy has made a valuable contribution to this debate. Unfortunately, many of the solutions that have been proposed—especially the growing interest in isolationism or disengagement—are too extreme. Where adjustments should be made, they call for radical surgery. But if their predictions are wrong—and the weight

---

130. On the political forces that distort the development of strategy, see Stephen M. Walt, "The Search for a Science of Strategy: A Review Essay on *Makers of Modern Strategy*," *International Security*, Vol. 12, No. 1 (Summer 1987), especially pp. 146–160.

of the evidence is against them—their prescriptions could have catastrophic results.

At the other exteme, those who believe that U.S. security can be enhanced by repeating past extravagances or by a renewed ideological offensive are equally misguided. A strategy of global containment will increase U.S. defense burdens in areas of little strategic value and will further tarnish the U.S. image in the eyes of its principal allies. Similarly, an ideological crusade to export U.S. ideals is more likely to compromise these principles than to convert other nations to democracy. At best, these programs waste U.S. wealth and other peoples' lives. At worst, they fan the flames of regional conflict and increase the danger of a larger war.

The essential elements of containment were identified four decades ago. They have never been implemented correctly, because America's dominant global position allowed it to indulge in a variety of excesses without incurring immediate penalties. For good or ill, this is no longer the case. By returning U.S. grand strategy to the original prescription for containment—*finite* containment—the United States can begin to ease its present fiscal worries without jeopardizing its vital interests. The essential elements of containment have worked remarkably well thus far; its main failures have occurred when the United States tried to extend containment beyond its original sphere of application. The strategy of containment has brought forty years of great power peace, and the key ingredients of that recipe should not be casually discarded. Although modest amendments are now in order, this strategy remains America's best choice.

# Why the Third World Matters

$\mathbf{T}$he Third World has been and will remain central to U.S. interests.[1] The risks of superpower confrontation, of the use of nuclear weapons, and of American or Soviet soldiers engaging in combat are all greater in the Third World than in Europe or Japan. Economic disaster to the United States and its allies is more likely to arise from developments in the Third World than anywhere else. It is in the Third World that the broader receptivity to American goals and values will be determined. In short, the instability and ferment characteristic of the Third World will continue to engage American interests with an urgency and unpredictability unmatched by its so-called "vital" allies.

Nevertheless, there is a growing literature arguing that the United Sates exaggerates the importance of the Third World to its interests. Although disputes exist among adherents to this view, there is agreement on several fundamental points. Proponents of this view claim that the Third World does not pose a threat to the vital interests of the United States (defined as the preservation of American security, economic well-being, and core values). Any threat to the limited U.S. interests in the Third World is not so much from the Soviet Union or radical revolutionaries, they argue, but from misguided American policies. By pursuing an aggressive, activist policy the United States will drive Third World regimes into the arms of the Soviets, thus bringing about the outcome it is most seeking to avoid. They argue that the best way for the United States to maintain its interests in the Third World is to pursue an accommodationist policy that recognizes its inability to control Third World developments. Above all, the United States must avoid the trap

---

Of the many who provided advice, I would like especially to thank Aaron Friedberg, Stephen Van Evera, Eric Nordlinger, John Mearsheimer, and *International Security*'s anonymous reviewers for their detailed comments.

---

*Steven R. David is an Associate Professor in the Department of Political Science at The Johns Hopkins University.*

---

1. I have defined the "Third World" to include all countries *except* the USSR, the United States, Canada, Japan, Australia, New Zealand, South Africa, the European states, and the People's Republic of China.

---

*International Security*, Summer 1989 (Vol. 14, No. 1)

of squandering scarce resources on peripheral Third World interests while truly vital concerns receive inadequate attention.[2]

These analysts, whom I will call "hyper-realists," have provided a service in forcing the explicit consideration of just what is and is not important in the Third World, and how American policy can best secure U.S. interests.[3] Moreover, the hyper-realists are correct in arguing that the United States must give top priority to its own protection and the protection of its Western European and Japanese allies. But this does not require an abandonment of American interests and commitments in the Third World such as the hyper-realist approach would bring about. This is all the more true because an engaged American policy in the Third World can be carried out at a reasonable cost without requiring the protracted use of American personnel abroad. The United States cannot allow fears of threats that almost certainly will never materialize to prevent us from dealing with Third World threats that already exist, and the far more serious challenges to American interests that are likely to develop in the future.

My argument is put forth in three parts. First, I review some of the principal assertions of those who believe the United States exaggerates the importance of the Third World and should play a less active role in trying to determine the outcome of developments there. Second, I explain why their assertions are incorrect or are themselves exaggerated, and why the United States needs to be actively involved in attempting to influence the course of Third World

---

2. The "school" of thought that this article addresses is derived principally from the following pieces of work: Robert H. Johnson, "Exaggerating America's Stakes in Third World Conflicts," *International Security*, Vol. 10, No. 3 (Winter 1984/85), pp. 32–68; Richard E. Feinberg and Kenneth A. Oye, "After the Fall: U.S. Policy Toward Radical Regimes," *World Policy Journal*, Vol. 1, No. 1 (Fall 1983), pp. 201–215; Jerome Slater, "Dominos in Central America: Will They Fall? Does It Matter?" *International Security*, Vol. 12, No. 2 (Fall 1987), pp. 105–134; Barry R. Posen and Stephen W. Van Evera, "Reagan Administration Defense Policy: Departure From Containment," in Kenneth A. Oye, Robert J. Lieber, and Donald Rothchild, eds., *Eagle Resurgent? The Reagan Era in American Foreign Policy* (Boston: Little, Brown, 1987), pp. 75–114; Stephen M. Walt, *The Origins of Alliances* (Ithaca: Cornell University Press, 1987); and Richard E. Feinberg, *The Intemperate Zone: The Third World Challenge to U.S. Foreign Policy* (New York: Norton, 1983). For a concise statement of the hyper-realist position, see Stephen Van Evera, "American Strategic Interests: Why Europe Matters, Why the Third World Doesn't," testimony prepared for hearings before the Panel on Defense Burdensharing, Committee on Armed Services, U.S. House of Representatives, March 2, 1988.
3. The term "hyper-realists" was chosen because of the strong adherence of these authors to the "realist" school of international politics, especially as practiced by George Kennan, Walter Lippmann and, to a lesser extent, Hans Morgenthau. The "hyper" prefix stems from their taking the emphasis of Kennan and others on material, objective factors (as compared to other factors such as ideology) to its illogical extreme. I am indebted to Aaron Friedberg for the use of the term "hyper-realists" to describe this school of thought.

events. Finally, I briefly discuss the approach the United States ought to take towards the Third World.

*The Threats to American Interests from the Third World*

The Third World threats to American interests can be broadly divided into three categories: They are the threats to American strategic-military interests, the threats to American economic interests, and the threats to American political-ideological interests.

THE STRATEGIC-MILITARY THREAT POSED BY THE THIRD WORLD
A major tenet of the hyper-realist argument is that the Third World poses only a negligible threat to U.S. security interests: The United States need not fear even Soviet control of Third World groups and countries because in the hyper-realist view, the USSR will never achieve the kind of domination of the Third World necessary to enhance Soviet power. In part, this belief rests on the hyper-realist judgment that the Soviet Union has historically not done well in the Third World, with Soviet losses (e.g., Egypt) outweighing gains.[4] More important, the hyper-realists argue that the Soviet Union lacks the capability and will to make significant inroads in the Third World in the future.

For the hyper-realists, the Soviet Union has little to offer Third World states. Economically, it accounts for only two percent of Third World trade while contributing negligible amounts of aid. With decolonization virtually complete, the appeal of Soviet ideology has diminished. Even in the area of military assistance—clearly the USSR's strong suit—Moscow does not have a durable instrument of influence, as evidenced by its setbacks in states such as Egypt, Sudan, and Somalia where the Soviet Union had been the chief arms supplier.[5]

The hyper-realists also emphasize that Gorbachev recognizes the limita-tions of the Soviet appeal in the Third World, and is disappointed with the

4. Stephen D. Goose, "Soviet Geopolitical Momentum: Myth or Menace? Trends of Soviet Influence Around the World From 1945 to 1980," *The Defense Monitor*, Vol. 11, No. 1 (Center for Defense Information, 1980); and Feinberg and Oye, "After the Fall," p. 207.
5. Feinberg, *The Intemperate Zone*, pp. 136, 173.

high costs and meager gains of previous Soviet Third World policy.[6] The Soviet decision to withdraw from Afghanistan and encouragement of the Cuban withdrawal from Angola are seen as tangible support for the view that Gorbachev is serious about downgrading Soviet involvement in the Third World as part of his "new political thinking."

Even if the Soviets adopted an activist policy in the Third World, the hyper-realists reassure us that nationalism and better indigenous security forces are making Third World regimes increasingly difficult to control.[7] Barry Posen and Stephen Van Evera argue that, "Ultimately this serves American interests, since America's chief purpose is not to establish world dominion but rather to keep the world free from Soviet dominion."[8] Similarly, the tendency of states to "balance" (by aligning against an aggressive power) will prevent the USSR from reaping the benefits of a threatening posture.[9] Nor, say the hyper-realists, need the United States fear that successful communist revolutions can be exported to other Third World states.[10]

Finally, the hyper-realists assert, even if the Soviets succeeded in establishing bases throughout the Third World, America's security would not be threatened. The United States can mitigate the impact of Soviet bases, for example by deploying new forces.[11] More important, Soviet bases in the Third World do not matter because of the existence of nuclear weapons. Inasmuch as "any direct prolonged superpower war would likely become nuclear," fear of Soviet bases in "strategic" locations, such as the Gulf of Mexico, is an example of outdated thinking that employs a pre-1945 mentality to a world transformed by the nuclear revolution.[12] In sum, the hyper-realists

---

6. On Soviet disappointment with the Third World and how it may change future Soviet policy, see Francis Fukuyama, "Soviet Strategy in the Third World," in Andrzej Korbonski and Francis Fukuyama, eds., *The Soviet Union and the Third World: The Last Three Decades* (Ithaca: Cornell University Press, 1987), especially pp. 37–42; Elizabeth Kridl Valkenier, "New Soviet Thinking About the Third World," *World Policy Journal*, Vol. 4, No. 1 (Fall 1987), pp. 651–674; Graham E. Fuller, "The Case for Optimism," *The National Interest*, Number 12 (Summer 1988), pp. 73–82; and Jerry Hough, *The Struggle for the Third World: Soviet Debates and American Options* (Washington, D.C.: Brookings, 1986). Although their views support some of the hyper-realist positions, these authors are not necessary hyper-realists themselves.
7. Feinberg and Oye, "After the Fall," p. 208.
8. Posen and Van Evera, "Departure From Containment," p. 97.
9. This is one of the principal findings in Walt, *The Origins of Alliances*. See also Feinberg, *The Intemperate Zone*, p. 175; Feinberg and Oye, "After the Fall," p. 202.
10. For example, see Slater, "Dominos in Central America," p. 113.
11. Slater, "Dominos in Central America," p. 124; Posen and Van Evera, "Departure From Containment," p. 196. The deployment of new forces would presumably be less costly than maintaining an activist policy in the Third World.
12. Quotation is from Slater, "Dominos in Central America," p. 124. See also Johnson, "Exag-

THE THREAT TO AMERICAN ECONOMIC INTERESTS POSED BY THE THIRD WORLD

The hyper-realist view that the Third World does not pose a significant economic threat to the United States rests on two arguments. First, they assert, the Third World lacks the ability to hurt the United States through economic means. The aggregate gross national product (GNP) of the entire Third World is less than three-quarters of Western Europe and only one-half that of Western Europe plus Japan.[13] Thus Soviet domination of the Third World would not grant Moscow the military potential that control of more important industrial regions (Europe and Japan) would give them. Even the control of raw materials by Third World states is not cause for concern, because these states are supposed to be unable to form OPEC-like cartels that could embargo the West.[14] Should a cutoff nevertheless occur, the hyper-realists allege that the availability of alternative suppliers and stockpiles would mitigate its effects.[15]

Second, even when it is acknowledged that the Third World does possess significant economic instruments, the hyper-realists assert that self-interest dictates it will not use them. Regardless of their ideology or degree of pro-Soviet orientation, all Third World states, it is argued, recognize the necessity to participate in the Western-dominated international economy. As Richard Feinberg writes, "Whether they are neoliberals, populists, social democrats, or Marxists, most Third World leaders desperately want to participate in this new international system."[16]

Thus, insofar as American trade and investment with the Third World is important to the United States, the hyper-realists allege that it has little to fear so long as it does not needlessly antagonize Third World states by trying to determine the character of their regimes.[17] Similarly, the hyper-realists argue that the United States need not fear a boycott by strategic mineral-

13. Posen and Van Evera, "Departure From Containment," p. 95.
14. For an analysis that has stood the test of time on why oil is different from other commodities, see Stephen S. Krasner, "Oil is the Exception," *Foreign Policy*, No. 14 (Spring 1974), pp. 68–83. See also Feinberg, *The Intemperate Zone*, p. 119.
15. For more on this point, see Johnson, "Exaggerating America's Stakes," pp. 37–38; Michael Shafer, "Mineral Myths," *Foreign Policy*, No. 48 (Summer 1982), pp. 154–171; Congressional Research Service, *Imports of Minerals from South Africa by the United States and the OECD Countries* (Washington, D.C.: U.S. Government Printing Office [U.S. GPO], 1980).
16. Feinberg, *The Intemperate Zone*, p. 109.
17. Feinberg, *The Intemperate Zone*, pp. 24, 113, 192; Slater, "Dominos in Central America," pp. 121–122; Feinberg and Oye, "After the Fall," pp. 203–204.

producing states because such an action would hurt their own fragile economies far more than it would the United States.[18]

THE THIRD WORLD THREAT TO AMERICAN POLITICAL-IDEOLOGICAL INTERESTS
For the hyper-realists, American political-ideological interests (e.g., maintaining freedom and democracy) in the Third World are of only marginal concern. While it would be gratifying if Third World states embraced American values, it is not necessary that they do so. Few Americans are even aware of Third World political systems. If Third World leaders opt for Marxism, the hyper-realists assert, it would have little or no effect on the strength of the American political system. American democracy simply does not depend on the existence of democracies elsewhere, particularly in the Third World. The only threat to our values posed by the Third World is the tendency of the United States to claim that those values are at stake in Third World conflicts, when in fact they are not.[19]

THE HYPER-REALIST APPROACH TO THE THIRD WORLD
The hyper-realists see America's chief concerns in the world as protecting its allies in Europe and Japan, and preserving the security of the United States. In both of these areas, the Third World (with the possible exception of the Persian Gulf) plays a marginal role at best. Those few interests that the United States does maintain in the Third World are not seriously threatened and can easily be safeguarded without U.S. involvement in Third World conflicts.

The United States has more to lose in the Third World, they argue, by acting than by not acting. The inability of the United States to control events in the Third World is not a cause for concern to the hyper-realists, because they believe that regional powers and nationalism, rather than the Soviet Union, will fill any gap left by the decline of American influence.[20] So long as revolutionary states do not launch armed attacks on the "truly vital" interests of the United States, a policy of non-intervention will prove more beneficial to American interests than attempts to topple unfriendly regimes.[21]

---

18. Feinberg, *The Intemperate Zone*, p. 118; Johnson, "Exaggerating America's Stakes," p. 38.
19. Johnson, "Exaggerating America's Stakes," pp. 44–46; Feinberg, *The Intemperate Zone*, pp. 193–194.
20. Feinberg, *The Intemperate Zone*, p. 25.
21. Slater, "Dominos in Central America," p. 129.

As for the prospect of the Soviet Union extending its influence in the Third World, "the best response to a Soviet inroad may be to give the Soviets time to make their own mistakes."[22]

Most important, as Stephen Walt argues, because we live in a "balancing" world (in which states will resist aggressors) rather than a "bandwagoning" world (in which states appease aggressors), forceful policies by the USSR (or anyone else) will not succeed in attracting allies. Therefore the United States, a status quo power, can be complacent about most international developments.[23]

The hyper-realists also emphasize the limits of U.S. power, and argue that the United States must avoid wasting scarce resources in the Third World.[24] This means spending far less than the United States is presently doing for Third World contingencies. The hyper-realists want the United States to scale down Third World interventionary forces, cut back on American commitments throughout the Third World, and lessen its reliance on security instruments to accomplish American objectives.[25] These steps will not only save money, they say, but also lessen the prospect of another disastrous intervention such as occurred in Vietnam.

*Responding to the Hyper-Realists*

Before challenging the specifics of the hyper-realist position, it will be useful to confront the basic premise of the argument, namely that the Third World contains few, if any, threats to the vital interests of the United States. The hyper-realists err by failing to define what they mean by "vital," and by an undifferentiated lumping together of all Third World states. It is unarguably true that the Third World threatens few "vital" interests, if that means the preservation of American security, economic well-being, and core values. But

22. Feinberg, *The Intemperate Zone*, p. 240.
23. Walt, *The Origins of Alliances*. See esp. p. 282.
24. This view is likely to gain additional credibility as a result of Paul Kennedy's argument that the United States (like other great powers before it) may be on the road to decline due to "imperial overstretch," i.e., having more interests than the ability to defend them. See Paul M. Kennedy, *The Rise and Fall of the Great Powers: Economic Change and Military Conflict from 1500 to 2000* (New York: Random House, 1987). For the realist defense of this view, see Hans J. Morgenthau, "Another Great Debate: The National Interest of the United States," *American Political Science Review*, Vol. 46, No. 4 (December 1952), pp. 961–988; and Robert W. Tucker, "The Purposes of American Power," *Foreign Affairs*, Vol. 59, No. 2 (Winter 1980/81), pp. 241–275.
25. See, for example, Posen and Van Evera, "Departure from Containment," pp. 93–98.

such a standard also means that the United States faces few threats to its vital interests anywhere in the world. Many of the key arguments used to demonstrate the lack of importance of the Third World could be employed to justify a policy of non-involvement in Europe. Such a result is especially disturbing in that it does not appear that any of the hyper-realists would approve of such a policy.

Militarily, the arguments of the hyper-realists would also support an American withdrawal from Western Europe. Since we supposedly live in a world of balancing, the West Europeans (whose combined GNP is larger than the Soviet GNP) would simply take it on themselves to resist the Soviet Union. Nor, according to the logic of some of the hyper-realists, would the United States have to fear Western Europe's industrial power falling to the Soviets. If nuclear war makes protracted conventional war virtually impossible, Soviet control of Europe's industrial potential does not enhance the Soviet threat to American security, since any major conflict would be over long before Europe's economic strength could play a role.

Economically, the arguments of the hyper-realists suggest that the United States need not fear domination of Western Europe by the Soviet Union or by radical governments. After all, if ideology does not determine trading partners, it does not matter what kind of regime is in power. With all governments seeking to participate in the international economy, a communist Western Europe should be just as reliable and valuable a trading partner as the Western Europe of today. The idea that a communist Europe would trade freely with the United States, and would contribute little to the military threat posed against it, also calls into question the view that industrial power is the best gauge of strategic importance.

In terms of the threat to American political-ideological interests, as conceived by the hyper-realists, Europe is also expendable. If the survival of American democracy does not depend on the internal characteristics of other governments, it is difficult to label such characteristics as "vital." To do so stretches the meaning of the word so far as to cloud its meaning. But, for those who accept the principle that American democracy depends on democracy elsewhere, the existence of democratic governments in the Third World should be no less vital than their counterparts in Western Europe.[26]

---

26. For an argument that the United States needs to ensure democracy only in Europe and Japan, see Robert S. Tucker, "Isolation and Intervention," *The National Interest*, No. 1 (Fall 1985),

The point of this comparison with Europe is not that the Third World is as important as Europe, or that policy-makers should not make distinctions among interests. Rather, the United States is fortunate that its vital interests (the preservation of American security, economic well-being, and core values) are not under serious threat from any quarter. The hard choices come not in determining what is vital, but in deciding which non-vital interests are worth defending and how to do so. By utilizing the standard of vital interests to direct American policy in the Third World (while applying it much more loosely to Europe), the hyper-realists are led to dismiss countries as unimportant simply because they are not vital. Such an approach will lead to isolationism whether or not that is the intention of its adherents.

Furthermore, it is misleading to assert that our interests in Europe are somehow vital while those in the Third World are not, without making distinctions among individual countries. An outbreak of civil war in Mexico would threaten American interests more than a similar occurrence in Spain. The ascension to power of a Marxist-Leninist regime in South Korea would arguably be more damaging to the United States than a similar regime taking power in Portugal. U.S. interests in the Third World, as elsewhere, must be judged on their individual merits. This precludes the simple division of the world between the "vital" interests of Europe and the "non-vital" interests of the Third World.

Broadly speaking, just how important are American interests in the Third World? First, it is difficult to identify far in advance which interests and countries are likely to be important. When Secretary of State Dean Acheson excluded South Korea from the range of American vital interests, he did so because South Korea lacked intrinsic importance to the United States. The subsequent invasion by North Korea (probably encouraged by Acheson's action) demonstrated that countries of seemingly small significance can gain in importance when threatened (even indirectly) by Soviet power because the threat calls into question America's credibility as an ally. In the 1960s, few predicted that Saudi Arabia would assume the significance it did scarcely a decade later. Chad viewed in isolation is almost stereotypical of a Third World country without importance to the United States. Yet when it was threatened by Libya, Chad became important as a symbol of American re-

pp. 16–25. For an opposing view, see Charles Krauthammer, "Isolationism, Left and Right," *The New Republic*, March 4, 1985; and Krauthammer, Isolationism: A Riposte," *The National Interest*, No. 2 (Winter 1985/86), pp. 115–118.

solve to help protect countries from Qadhafi's expansionist designs. Whether the specific policies applied to these countries were justified is the subject of legitimate dispute, but it is impossible to determine *a priori* where American policy will next be engaged.

Second, the United States needs to devote more diplomatic and military attention to Third World contingencies, not because vital interests are at stake, but because U.S. interests there are more *likely* to be threatened. The United States has focused its efforts on interests of high intrinsic worth that confront relatively small risks: defending Western Europe and avoiding nuclear war. Third World interests cannot match these in importance, but there is a far greater probability that they will be threatened. When deciding how to spend the marginal dollar, the greater likelihood of risk to American interests from the Third World must be given weight.

The United States must be especially concerned about the Third World, because that is where it stands the greatest chance of becoming embroiled in some violent conflict. Nearly all the armed conflicts since World War II (including civil wars) have occurred in the Third World. All the wars in which the United States was involved have been wars in the Third World.[27] Insofar as any large-scale conflict has the potential to bring about U.S. involvement, the mitigation of such conflict is in American interests.

Moreover, even if by some "objective" standard, reasons can be offered why the United States should stay out of Third World conflicts, domestic politics ensure that the potential will remain for American involvement. The American public worries more about threats from the Third World than from any other source; whether objectively correct or not, this fact makes dealing with those threats a matter of political survival for any administration.[28] It

27. U.S. Department of Defense, *Commitment to Freedom: Security Assistance as a U.S. Policy Instrument in the Third World* (Washington, D.C.: U.S. GPO, May 1988) p. 1. See also John Mueller, "The Essential Irrelevance of Nuclear Weapons: Stability in the Postwar World," *International Security*, Vol. 13, No. 2 (Fall 1988), p. 78.

28. A recent study by the Public Agenda Foundation and Brown University's Center for Foreign Policy Development listed the top three foreign policy concerns of Americans as terrorism, Third World conflicts, and the spread of nuclear weapons. It is noteworthy that all three concerns originate in the Third World. *Newsweek*, March 21, 1988, p. 7. When asked to pick the area most likely to draw the U.S. and the USSR into a war, 67 percent picked the Middle East/Persian Gulf, 41 percent picked Central America, and only 7 percent chose Europe. When asked the most likely way a nuclear war would start, 52 percent identified the escalation of a Third World conflict, 21 percent said through its use by terrorists, while only 15 percent chose a Soviet invasion of Europe. Public Agenda Foundation and the Center for Foreign Policy Development, Brown University, *U.S. Soviet Relations in the Year 2010: Americans Look to the Future* (New York: Public Agenda Foundation; Providence: Center for Foreign Policy Development, 1988), Technical Appendix by Stephen Immerwahr, esp. Tables 1, 2, 56.

can be argued, for example, that terrorism does not play a central role in threatening the interests of the United States.[29] Nevertheless, when terrorism becomes an overriding concern to the American public it also becomes important to those politicians seeking or wishing to retain office. Objectively, the Third World might not be important enough to justify the worsening of U.S.-Soviet relations or the derailing of arms control treaties, but it has historically done just that.[30] Objectively, Third World interests might not warrant superpower interventions (such as Vietnam and Afghanistan) and nuclear alerts (such as occurred during the 1973 Middle East war), but experience demonstrates their potential to reoccur.[31]

The hyper-realists, of course, put forth their arguments in an attempt to prevent these very developments from arising in the future. Nevertheless, they should recognize that factors such as the domestic political environment will ensure that their views will never be fully accepted. Instead they should accept that there is a good chance that Americans will become involved if there is trouble in the Third World; hence the United States should try to keep order there, since it probably will not have the self-restraint to stay out if order breaks down.[32] Consequently, as "meaningless" as Third World reverses might be, their likely (even if misguided) impact on U.S. policy must be taken into account, giving the Third World a significance that an "objective" analysis might miss.

THE STRATEGIC-MILITARY THREAT POSED BY THE THIRD WORLD
The Third World matters because of the strategic-military threat from the Soviet Union and, more importantly, because of the threat from the Third

---

29. See, for example, Walter Laqueur, "Reflections on Terrorism," *Foreign Affairs*, Vol. 65, No. 1 (Fall 1986), pp. 86–100. Laqueur sees terrorism as a "nuisance" but with the potential to get much worse.

30. As Zbigniew Brzezinski noted, "SALT lies buried in the sands of the Ogaden." See Zbigniew Brzezinski, *Power and Principle: Memoirs of the National Security Adviser, 1977–1981* (New York: Farrar, Straus, and Giroux, 1983), p. 189. See also Gloria Duffy, "Crisis Mangling and the Cuban Brigade," *International Security*, Vol. 8, No. 1 (Summer 1983), pp. 67–87. One of the best accounts of how U.S.-Soviet relations have been hurt by Third World developments reviews occurrences in Angola, the Horn of Africa, the Yemens, Zaire, and the Middle East, see Raymond L. Garthoff, *Détente and Confrontation: American-Soviet Relations from Nixon to Reagan* (Washington, D.C.: Brookings, 1985), esp. chaps. 15, 19, and 24.

31. It is noteworthy that Third World crises (e.g., in Cuba, the Middle East, the Taiwan Straits, Korea, the Persian Gulf) provoked the overwhelming number of occasions in which the threat to use nuclear weapons was employed to coerce an opponent. See Richard K. Betts, *Nuclear Blackmail and Nuclear Balance* (Washington, D.C.: Brookings, 1987).

32. I am indebted to Stephen Van Evera for clarifying this point.

World states themselves. The hyper-realists underestimate the former and virtually ignore the latter.

THE SOVIET THREAT IN THE THIRD WORLD. Despite a weak economy and diminishing ideological appeal, the Soviet Union retains the tools to gain substantial influence in the Third World. The Soviets are unequalled at getting people into power and keeping them there. Soviet clients are rarely overthrown by coups, insurgencies, or invasions. For would-be and actual Third World leaders, this asset is most important in a patron. Third World leaders generally face a far greater number of more serious threats than leaders elsewhere, and loss of power often means execution. Thus they place a high premium on securing a patron who can help counter the threats to their regimes.

For Third World regimes needing large amounts of arms, Soviet advantages in speed of delivery (averaging twice as fast as the United States), flexibility in whom to sell, large stockpiles, good prices, easy to maintain weapons, and availability of proxies has made them the supplier of choice. Consequently, the Soviet Union has emerged as the leading supplier of arms to the Third World in the 1980s.[33] Compared to the United States, the Soviet Union in the Third World has thirty times more military advisers, trains twice the military personnel, and provides three times the military aid (in dollar terms).[34] To help deal with internal threats, the Soviet Union places security "cocoons" of East German advisers or Cuban bodyguards around leaders of such Third World countries as Angola, Ethiopia, Mozambique, Zambia, South Yemen, and Libya. As a result, no pro-Soviet regime afforded Moscow's protection has been forcibly replaced by a pro-Western regime since the 1960s, despite the prevalence of coups in the Third World.[35]

The security cocoon used to protect pro-Soviet leaders from coups can also serve to intimidate those same leaders from realigning. The leader of Ethiopia, Mengistu Haile Mariam, may one day decide that his best interests lie

---

33. Mark N. Kramer, "Soviet Arms Transfers to the Third World," *Problems of Communism*, Vol. 36, No. 5 (September–October 1987) pp. 63–64. Kramer also makes the point that the USSR has supplied more arms to the Third World than the U.S. has in every category but subsonic aircraft; ibid. p. 56.
34. Fred C. Iklé and Albert Wohlstetter, *Discriminate Deterrence: Report of the Commission on Integrated Long-Term Strategy* (Washington, D.C.: U.S. GPO, January 1988), p. 19; *Supporting U.S. Strategy for Third World Conflict* (Washington, D.C.: U.S. Department of Defense, June 1988), p. 9.
35. For more on the Soviet use of security "cocoons," see Steven R. David, *Third World Coups d'Etat and International Security* (Baltimore: Johns Hopkins University Press, 1987), pp. 79–82.

with a turn to the West. But with a secret service trained by East Germans and several thousand Cuban troops based near the capital, he may recognize that such a move could prove fatal. Even when the Soviets are expelled by Third World clients, U.S. interests may be damaged. The Soviets were indeed evicted from Egypt, but only after twenty-five years in which they actively supported and helped bring about four wars against Israel. Should the United States accept a similar Soviet presence in Saudi Arabia with equanimity?

Neither can the United States afford to be complacent about future Soviet actions in the Third World. Gorbachev has indeed downgraded the overall importance of the Third World, but his leadership or his policies might be superseded. There is already evidence of a renewed Soviet emphasis on some areas of the Third World. The Soviet Union is courting major Third World states such as the Association of South East Asian Nations (ASEAN), Mexico, and the Persian Gulf countries with renewed vigor. It is pursuing closer ties with former enemies such as Israel. Military aid to radical clients has increased under Gorbachev and, in part due to the need for hard currency, arms transfers are likely to rise in the future.[36] Historically, the Soviet Union has consistently escalated the means it employs to gain influence among Third World states—from arms transfers to proxies, to direct intervention. Despite Gorbachev's rhetoric, one cannot be confident that this pattern will be reversed.[37]

Moscow has experienced losses as well as gains in the Third World, but in 1952 the Soviet Union counted only North Korea as a Third World ally. Today, countries firmly in the Soviet camp or leaning to the Soviet Union

---

36. On increase of aid to radical clients, see Peter W. Rodman, "The Case for Skepticism," *The National Interest*, No. 12 (Summer 1988), p. 85; Stephen Sestanovich, "Gorbachev's Foreign Policy: A Diplomacy of Decline," *Problems of Communism*, Vol. 37, No. 1 (January–February 1988), pp. 12–13. On the projected increase in arms sales for economic profit and levels of Soviet security assistance to the Third World, see Mark Kramer, "Soviet Arms Transfers to the Third World," esp. pp. 58, 62. For views that acknowledge the possibility of a continuing or increased role for the USSR in the Third World under Gorbachev, see Francis Fukuyama, "Patterns of Soviet Third World Policy," *Problems of Communism*, Vol. 36, No. 5 (September–October 1987), pp. 1–13; and Robert S. Litwak and S. Neil MacFarlane, "Soviet Activism in the Third World," *Survival*, Vol. 29, No. 1 (January–February 1987), pp. 21–39, esp. p. 33.
37. For an illustration of how the USSR has escalated its use of force in Third World conflicts, see Bruce Porter, *The USSR in Third World Conflicts: Soviet Arms and Diplomacy in Local Wars, 1945–1980* (Cambridge: Cambridge University Press, 1984). The Soviet withdrawal from Afghanistan may, of course, affect Moscow's future behavior in the Third World. Nevertheless, it is at least as likely to galvanize the Soviets to act more aggressively to preserve their credibility as a global power, as to signal a more general retreat.

include Cuba, Vietnam, Laos, Cambodia, Nicaragua, Benin, Mozambique, Ethiopia, South Yemen, the Congo, Libya, and Syria, as well as North Korea. Moreover, the effects of the Soviet influence cannot be accounted for just by listing countries "won" and "lost." The Soviet Union maintains considerable influence in the nonaligned movement, the United Nations, and with non-governmental actors such as the Palestine Liberation Organization. Undoubtedly, new setbacks will occur, but it is incontrovertible that the Soviet Union has emerged as a major power in the Third World.

The hyper-realists are wrong to assert that American security interests will not be threatened by a Soviet surge in the Third World because of the difficulty Moscow has in controlling its Third World clients.[38] The Soviet Union, like the United States, cannot "control" most of its Third World allies. But this standard is too demanding as a measure of Soviet success. Instead of forcing countries to do its bidding, Moscow will achieve much of what it wants if it can secure the cooperation of Third World states to achieve joint ends. These ends may be diplomatic support of Soviet goals or, more important from the American perspective, Soviet access to military facilities.

Mirroring its overall record in the Third World, the Soviet Union has had mixed success in securing and maintaining access to military facilities among Third World states.[39] Despite several setbacks, the Soviet Union presently makes use of military facilities throughout the Third World, including Angola, Ethiopia, South Yemen, Vietnam, Cuba, and most recently Syria. These facilities assist the Soviet Union in force projection (especially for the navy), provide staging areas for Soviet reconnaissance flights, facilitate intervention in other Third World conflicts, and (especially in Cuba) permit intelligence collection including the monitoring of U.S. communications.[40] The Soviet

---

38. Two valuable discussions of Soviet–Third World influence that are skeptical about its value can be found in Rajan Menon, *Soviet Power and the Third World* (New Haven: Yale University Press, 1986), pp. 214–235; and Alvin Z. Rubinstein, ed., *Chinese and Soviet Influence in the Third World* (New York: Praeger, 1975), "Introduction."

39. I am using the term "facilities" to include bases. For differences between facilities and bases, see Menon, *Soviet Power and the Third World*, pp. 228–229.

40. For more on Soviet access to military facilities, see Robert E. Harkavy, *Great Power Competition for Overseas Bases: The Geopolitics of Access Diplomacy* (New York: Pergamon, 1982), esp. chap. 5; Menon, *Soviet Power and the Third World*, pp. 228–235; Richard Remnek, "The Politics of Soviet Access to Naval Support Facilities in the Mediterranean," in Bradford Dismukes and James M. McConnell, eds., *Soviet Naval Diplomacy* (New York: Pergamon, 1979), pp. 357–392; and "U.S. Says Soviets are Expanding Base for Warships on Syrian Coast," *New York Times*, August 28, 1988.

military presence in these countries may not endanger "vital" American interests, but it poses substantial costs. For example, Soviet bases (especially in strategically significant areas such as Central America) hurt American interests by increasing the ability of the Soviet Union to extend its influence and power with fewer forces. The existence of Soviet bases also drives the United States to expend scarce resources to neutralize their impact, thus reducing the American ability to defend other interests.[41]

Most important, access to Third World military facilities matters because they could play a decisive role in the event of a major conventional war between the United States and the Soviet Union. There is a remarkable consensus among Western scholars that the Soviet Union believes that any major conflict with the United States would most likely be conventional, and that Moscow believes its interest lies in preventing any escalation to the nuclear level. Although there is some dispute as to exactly when Soviet priorities shifted from preparing for nuclear war to preparing for conventional war, there is virtually no dispute that it predated Gorbachev and has continued under his rule. In support of this position, scholars representing diverse political views point to Soviet writings, the unilateral Soviet declaration of "No First Use" in 1982, and the tremendous accumulation of Soviet conventional weaponry over the past twenty years.[42]

The growing irrelevance of nuclear weapons (except to deter other nuclear weapons) is seen on the United States side as well.[43] As Edward Luttwak persuasively argues, changes in public and elite perceptions have made it increasingly unlikely that the United States would use nuclear weapons

---

41. *Report of the President's National Bipartisan Commission on Central America* (New York: Macmillan, 1984), p. 111; see also Michael C. Desch, "Turning the Caribbean Flank: Sea Lane Vulnerability During a European War," *Survival*, Vol. 29, No. 6 (November/December 1987), p. 533.

42. Some of the scholars who argue that the USSR gives priority to preparing to fight a conventional war are: Michael MccGwire, *Military Objectives in Soviet Foreign Policy* (Washington, D.C.: Brookings, 1987), pp. 3, 36–49, 213–231; Raymond L. Garthoff, "New Thinking in Soviet Military Doctrine," *Washington Quarterly*, Vol. 11, No. 3 (Summer 1988), p. 133; James M. McConnell, "Shifts in Soviet Views on the Proper Focus of Military Development," *World Politics*, Vol. 37, No. 3 (April 1985), pp. 317–343; Andrew C. Goldberg, "The Present Turbulence in Soviet Military Doctrine," *Washington Quarterly*, Vol. 11, No. 3 (Summer 1988), pp. 159–170; and Charles Bluth, "The Evolution of Soviet Military Doctrine," *Survival*, Volume 30, No. 2 (March–April 1988), pp. 149–162. For views emphasizing the Soviet desire to fight a nuclear war, see Richard Pipes, "Why the Soviet Union Thinks It Could Fight and Win a Nuclear War," *Commentary*, July 1977, pp. 21–34; Joseph Douglass, Jr., and Amoretta M. Hoeber, *Soviet Strategy For Nuclear War* (Stanford: Hoover Institution Press, 1979).

43. For a view that nuclear weapons have made little difference in international affairs since World War II, see Mueller, "The Essential Irrelevance of Nuclear Weapons," pp. 55–79.

against nonnuclear threats. In earlier years, the United States could credibly threaten to use nuclear weapons to defend South Korea, or Taiwan's offshore islands of Quemoy and Matsu. Now, it is difficult for the United States to threaten their use credibly even for the defense of Europe.[44]

Preparing for a protracted conventional war dramatically increases the importance of some Third World states by heightening the relevance of traditional concepts of strategy. The likelihood of a major conventional war (at least compared to that of a nuclear war) means that the United States must be concerned about choke points, strategic waterways, land bridges, and sea lines of communication (SLOCs). Consequently, Third World states such as Morocco, Panama, Oman, and the Philippines acquire special importance. Of particular significance is the U.S. ability to secure access to military facilities in time of war while denying them to the Soviet Union. According to one analyst, the threat to sea lines of communication posed by Cuba, and potentially by Nicaragua, could cause the United States to lose a war in Europe.[45] Preparing to neutralize these threats and forestalling additional Soviet footholds consequently become a pressing American concern. Moreover, it is critical that the United States be able to project forces into Third World areas that the Soviet Union deems critical for the successful prosecution of a conventional war. In a conventional war, the Soviet Union would probably attempt to maintain a defense perimeter that included Europe, southwest Asia and northern Africa.[46] By making it clear to the Soviet Union that these objectives would be denied them in the event of war (by, for example, maintaining U.S. access to military facilities in the relevant regions), American deterrence is enhanced.

BALANCING AND BANDWAGONING. The argument made by Stephen Walt that, because we live in a "balancing" world, threatening U.S. (or Soviet) policies will drive countries to the adversary, is dangerously misguided. The argument (which is supported by traditional balance of power theory) is an important one because the hyper-realists rely heavily on their analyses of balancing behavior to justify their recommendations that the United States should remain essentially aloof from the security concerns of the Third World.

---

44. Edward N. Luttwak, "An Emerging Postnuclear Era?" *Washington Quarterly*, Vol. 11, No. 1 (Winter 1988), pp. 11–13. See also Robert S. McNamara, "The Military Role of Nuclear Weapons: Perceptions and Misperceptions," *Foreign Affairs*, Vol. 62, No. 1 (Fall 1983), pp. 59–80.
45. Desch, "Turning the Caribbean Flank," p. 524; Desch believes that Soviet use of Nicaragua to interdict American shipping would double the threat now posed by Cuba.
46. MccGwire, *Military Objectives in Soviet Foreign Policy*, pp. 48–49, 213–231.

After all, if aggressive involvement will simply force countries to the other side, the United States need not actively counter Soviet threats in the Third World since the threatened states will flock to the United States on their own.

There are several problems with this argument. Determining that states *tend* to balance does not tell us much about the prospects for a specific country. It is foolhardy to assume complacently that balancing will occur in a given situation simply because it predominated in another context. The concept of balancing might not be relevant to many countries in the Third World. As Walt acknowledges, "bandwagoning" (or appeasing an aggressor) will occur when states are weak and when useful allies are not available.[47] These are important qualifications that would seem to make many Third World countries susceptible to bandwagoning. Moreover, if states will bandwagon when they cannot count on outside help, an aloof American posture in the Third World might undermine tendencies to balance Soviet aggression.

Most important, the nature of the Third World does not lend itself to simple "balancing versus bandwagoning" formulas in which a threatening superpower drives balancing states into the other camp. Third World leaders typically face a multiplicity of threats. In order to survive in power, Third World leaders will attempt to defeat (or balance against) the most pressing threats. In some cases, this will indeed mean turning against the superpower that backs a threat against it. In many other cases, however, Third World leaders will turn toward (bandwagon with) the superpower backing a threat against it, as the best means of defeating that threat. The Third World leadership does this in the belief that the superpower backing the threat against it is also in the best position to undermine that threat (by, for example, suspending its arms supplies or applying political pressure on its client). Moreover, by bandwagoning with a superpower that backs the threat and not with the country or group that directly poses the threat, the Third World regime does not place its survival in the hands of its greatest enemy.

Equally significant, the great majority of threats against Third World leaders are internal (a point virtually ignored by Walt). As such, Third World leaders seeking outside support to survive in power are at least as likely to align with countries that will protect them from insurgencies, revolutions, and coups as they are to align with those that will protect them from other

---

47. Walt, *The Origins of Alliances*, pp. 173, 175.

threatening states. The concepts of balancing and bandwagoning employed by the hyper-realists ignore this critical domestic dimension and are thus not very helpful in understanding Third World alignment decisions.

Egypt's Sadat and Ethiopia's Mengistu are examples of Third World leaders bandwagoning with superpowers in order to defeat the principal internal and external threats to their rule. In Egypt, despite record levels of Soviet support, President Anwar Sadat became convinced that the only way to neutralize the Israeli threat and deal with mounting difficulties at home was to turn away from Moscow and realign with the United States, his adversary's chief backer. Sadat recognized that while the Soviet Union could supply him with weapons, only a huge increase in Soviet military assistance (perhaps even the intervention of Soviet forces) could enable him to defeat the Israelis. Sadat knew that the Soviet Union would never agree to provide him with such a capability because an Egyptian defeat of Israel risked a Soviet confrontation with the United States. On the other hand, the United States, by virtue of its support of Israel, needed only to apply political pressure on Jerusalem to achieve Sadat's objectives. Moreover, the United States was willing and able to provide Egypt with the economic assistance that it so desperately needed. Correctly realizing that it was far more likely to secure American diplomatic and economic support than a massive escalation in Soviet military involvement, Sadat turned to Washington.[48]

In Ethiopia, the new government emerging after the 1974 overthrow of Haile Selassie faced many internal threats as well as a major external threat from Somalia. The principal threats had in common direct or indirect Soviet backing. By turning to the Soviets for support, the Ethiopian regime implicitly acknowledged that the Soviet backing of these threats placed Moscow in the best position to undermine them and thus guarantee the survival of the new government. That the new regime was also ideologically disposed toward the Soviet Union (a factor usually overlooked by the hyper-realists) also contributed to the realignment.[49]

---

48. Some of the many studies of the Soviet role in Egypt include: Anwar al-Sadat, *In Search of Identity* (New York: Harper and Row, 1977); Robert O. Freedman, *Soviet Policy Toward the Middle East Since 1970*, rev. ed. (New York: Praeger, 1978); Alvin Z. Rubinstein, *Red Star on the Nile: The Soviet-Egyptian Influence Relationship Since the June War* (Princeton: Princeton University Press, 1977). In addition to demonstrating that balancing cannot always be relied upon, the Egyptian case also shows that an aloof U.S. stance would have made Sadat's switch impossible.
49. Accounts of the Ethiopian realignment can be found in: Colin Legum and Bill Lee, *The Horn of Africa in Continuing Crisis* (New York: Africana Publishing Company, 1979); Marina Ottaway, *Soviet and American Influence in the Horn of Africa* (New York: Praeger, 1982); David Korn, *Ethiopia, the United States, and the Soviet Union* (Carbondale: Southern Illinois University Press, 1986).

Even if Third World leaders would choose to balance against American threats by intensifying their alignment with the Soviet Union, the presence of an American-sponsored threat may deprive them of that option by foreclosing Soviet support. After all, Third World states cannot align with the Soviet Union if Moscow refuses to back them. American assistance to groups seeking the overthrow of pro-Soviet regimes (the "Reagan Doctrine") has raised the cost to Moscow of its Third World empire and has helped bring about the downgrading of some Third World states in Soviet priorities so ballyhooed by the hyper-realists.[50] In Africa, American and South African aid to the rebel group UNITA (Union for Total Independence of Angola) convinced the Soviet Union that its hold on Angola had become increasingly expensive to maintain. By denying the Soviet Union and its allies a military victory, the United States helped induce Moscow to apply pressure on its Cuban and Angolan clients to reach a diplomatic settlement.[51] Most significant, American efforts in Afghanistan have helped bring about a Soviet withdrawal, which may result in the first-ever success of an insurgency against a Marxist-Leninist government.

None of this is meant to suggest that threatening states is the most effective way for an outside power to secure influence in the Third World. Rather, the complexity of the Third World is such that it is misleading to draw sweeping conclusions about how outside powers should approach the Third World based on abstract notions of balancing and bandwagoning. In attempting to assess how Third World states will react to threats, each situation must be judged on its own merits and special attention must be devoted to the role of internal threats. Since Third World leaders (as leaders anywhere) will turn to the state most likely to keep them in power, policies of benign neglect stand little prospect of attracting many friends.

Finally, the hyper-realists are especially misleading in their assertions that when Third World regimes turn to the Soviet Union, they are usually "driven" by hostile American policies.[52] These arguments reflect a disregard for

---

50. On this point, see Rodman, "The Case for Skepticism"; see also Litwak and MacFarlane, "Soviet Activism in the Third World," p. 30.
51. Similarly, an increase in Soviet and Cuban support to Angola convinced South Africa that it could not impose a military settlement. This helped bring about a settlement calling for independence for the territory of Namibia (presently under South African control) in exchange for a Cuban withdrawal from Angola.
52. See, for example, Oye and Feinberg, "After the Fall," pp. 208–209.

the ideological beliefs of Third World leaders and the real value (both domestic and external) that Soviet support can offer. In their enthusiasm to blame the United States for whatever happens, the hyper-realists ignore the fact that many Third World leaders are intent on a pro-Soviet alignment whatever Washington does. For example, the United States stretched tolerance to the limit in dealing with the Ethiopian regime that took power in 1974. It assured the leaders of the new Marxist government that it would not interfere with their revolution, provided record levels of economic and military aid, and initially overlooked horrendous human rights abuses. Nevertheless, these American efforts did not deter the Ethiopian leadership from seeking Soviet support.[53]

THIRD WORLD THREATS WITHOUT SOVIET INVOLVEMENT. Even if the Soviet Union were to remove itself totally from the Third World, the United States would still face major threats to its interests from Third World countries and groups. In their zeal to debunk the Soviet threat and promote American non-involvement, the hyper-realists have placed little emphasis on these threats. Foremost among them is the specter of nuclear proliferation. At present, it is believed that India, Israel, and Pakistan either have nuclear weapons or are very close to developing nuclear weapons capability. Several other countries (such as Libya, Argentina, Brazil, and Iraq) are suspected of attempting to buy or develop nuclear weapons.[54] The threat of nuclear proliferation is especially alarming when Third World countries are involved. In contrast to the relatively stable U.S.-Soviet balance, Third World countries embroiled in intense conflicts might develop vulnerable nuclear forces without sophisticated command and control. The possibility of accidental or deliberate use of nuclear weapons would thus be far greater than has ever existed between the superpowers. Can anyone doubt that the possession of nuclear weapons by Iran or Iraq would have led to their use during their conflict? If nuclear

---

53. For an argument that there was little the United States could have done, once Mengistu achieved power, to prevent Ethiopia's realignment to the Soviet Union, see Korn, *Ethiopia, the United States, and the Soviet Union*.
54. Israel is reliably reported to have a large nuclear stockpile. India exploded a nuclear "device" in 1974 and either maintains a stockpile of weapons or could amass one quickly. Pakistan possesses the capability to make nuclear weapons, and has already done so or could do so quickly. Brazil and Argentina could each possibly manufacture a nuclear weapon on its own in several years. Libya and Iraq would need outside help before they could acquire nuclear weapons. For a contemporary assessment of proliferation prospects, see Leonard S. Spector, *Going Nuclear* (Cambridge, Mass.: Ballinger, 1987).

weapons are used, the United States or its allies face the possibility of being dragged into a Third World nuclear conflict, perhaps in confrontation with the Soviet Union, or even being the target of a nuclear strike itself.[55]

In addition to the threat posed by proliferation, Third World states are gaining access to other weapons that threaten the security interests of the United States and its allies. At least fifteen Third World countries now possess ballistic missiles; seven maintain active indigenous development programs.[56] The greatest danger posed by ballistic missiles is that they will be used to deliver nuclear weapons, but it is not the only threat. Their speed, combined with the absence of defenses against them, makes ballistic missiles ideal for use in surprise or terror attacks even without nuclear warheads. This is especially the case, given increasing improvements in accuracy and range for Third World ballistic missiles. Moreover, the fact that Iran and Iraq launched over 500 ballistic missiles in early 1988 is likely to lessen any taboo against their use in future wars.[57] Although the Western countries formally agreed in 1987 to limit the spread of technology for ballistic missiles, indigenous development and the actions of countries outside that agreement (e.g., the Soviet Union, China, Argentina, and Brazil) raise the prospects of their likely proliferation throughout the Third World. This in turn places American allies (e.g., Israel, Pakistan, South Korea) at risk, and increases the chances that an irresponsible leadership or terrorist element may gain control of these weapons and endanger the United States directly.[58]

Along with ballistic missiles, other weapons enhance the threat posed by Third World states to American security interests. At present, the Central

---

55. For a view that nuclear proliferation might not be so threatening, see Kenneth N. Waltz, *The Spread of Nuclear Weapons: More May be Better*, Adelphi Paper No. 171 (London: International Institute for Strategic Studies [IISS], 1981).

56. Aaron Karp lists, *inter alia*, Taiwan, Israel, Algeria, Egypt, North Korea, South Korea, Kuwait, India, Iraq, Libya, South Yemen, Turkey, and Syria. See Aaron Karp, "Ballistic Missiles in the Third World," *International Security*, Vol. 9, No. 3 (Winter 1984/85), p. 176; and W. Seth Carus, "Missiles in the Middle East: A New Threat to Stability," Washington Institute for Near East Policy, *Policy Focus*, No. 6 (June 1988). Carus's list also includes Iran and Saudi Arabia. Active missile development programs exist in Brazil, Argentina, Israel, India, Taiwan, Korea, and Pakistan. See *Supporting U.S. Strategy for Third World Conflict*, p. 13.

57. Carus, "Missiles in the Middle East," pp. 1, 2.

58. There is some disagreement about the extent to which ballistic missiles without nuclear weapons pose a risk. Aaron Karp tends to downgrade the importance of nonnuclear ballistic missiles, while Seth Carus argues that their use, especially with chemical weapons, dramatically enhances the capabilities of the countries that possess them while increasing the likelihood of war. See Karp, "Ballistic Missiles in the Third World," esp. pp. 167–173; and Carus, "Missiles in the Middle East," pp. 2–5, 6–9.

Intelligence Agency estimates that fourteen Third World states have chemical weapons, while an additional ten are trying to make them.[59] Chemical weapons are especially frightening because small amounts can quickly kill large numbers of people (especially unprotected civilians). Iraq has already used chemical weapons in its war with Iran and against its own Kurdish population. The effectiveness of the Iraqi attacks in blunting Iranian offensives, forcing the evacuation of much of Tehran, and promoting the expulsion of the Kurds, combined with a lack of international condemnation, is likely to make similar attacks by other Third World states more probable in the future.[60] As an indication of American concern over chemical attacks, the United States in early 1989 refused to rule out launching a pre-emptive strike on a suspected Libyan chemical plant. Like nuclear weapons, chemical weapons are especially frightening when carried by ballistic missiles. Syria has reportedly already developed a chemical weapon filled with nerve gas for its Scud-B missiles; the Libyans may have the capability to do the same. More ominously, Syria and Iraq (among others) are believed to be developing biological weapons.[61]

Even without exotic weapons, Third World states pose a significant and increasing threat to American security interests. The emergence of well-armed, socially mobilized populations enables Third World states to confront the United States without Soviet support. The ascension to power in Iran of Ayatollah Khomeini, for example, dramatically hurt U.S. interests, particularly by endangering American allies and shipping in the Gulf. The growing strength of Third World militaries, some of which (e.g., Iraq and Syria) have military forces larger and better equipped than most European countries, is also cause for deep concern.[62] Their strength endangers American allies (e.g.,

59. *Newsweek*, September 19, 1988, p. 30. The list includes Iraq, which is confirmed to have chemical weapons, and Egypt, Syria, Libya, Israel, Ethiopia, Burma, Thailand, North Korea, Cuba, Iran, Vietnam, Taiwan, and South Korea, which are believed to have them. The People's Republic of China and South Africa (not usually categorized as Third World states) are also included on the list of countries suspected of having chemical weapons.
60. See, for example, "U.S. Asserts Iraq Used Poison Gas Against the Kurds," *New York Times*, September 9, 1988, p. A1.
61. Carus, "Missiles in the Middle East," p. 5. See also "Panel of Scientists Fears Biological Arms Race," *New York Times*, January 18, 1989, p. A7. The article notes that as many as ten countries are believed to be developing biological weapons.
62. For example, Iraq, with 1,000,000 active duty troops, has larger forces than any of the NATO states except the United States. Syria has more tanks (4,050 including those in storage and in static positions) than any of the NATO states except the United States and West Germany. IISS, *The Military Balance 1988–89* (London: IISS, 1988), pp. 101, 110.

Israel, the ASEAN countries) and could deter American involvement or retaliation in response to attacks on United States interests.[63] Moreover, even the weakest of Third World states can threaten American interests by threatening the lives of United States citizens traveling or living in their countries. The Reagan administration invoked just such a threat (to American medical students) to justify its invasion of Grenada.

The greatest threat to U.S. bases in the Third World comes not from the Soviet Union, but from indigenous forces. American bases in the Philippines are threatened by a communist insurgency that receives little support from Moscow, while the security of the Panama Canal may be endangered more by an erratic Panamanian leadership than by any Soviet threat. In addition, while terrorism is not yet a major threat to American interests, the destruction of the U.S. Marine barracks in Beirut provides ample warning of how even primitive technology can damage American security interests. Should terrorists gain control of more devastating weapons (e.g., precision guided munitions or, most horribly, nuclear arms), the threat they pose to U.S. security would increase accordingly.

The Third World also threatens American interests in ways that are not usually thought of in terms of security. As evidenced by a secret presidential directive in 1986, the massive drug trafficking to the United States (most of which originates in the Third World) has become a national security threat.[64] Drugs threaten the security interests of the United States by draining an estimated $300 billion a year away from legitimate American business to groups of which some are hostile to the United States; by destabilizing democratic governments friendly to the United States (e.g., Colombia, Peru, Bolivia, Panama); and by diverting the military from its traditional security mission to drug interdiction.[65] Emigration from the Third World to the United States is also increasingly being seen as cause for concern. From 1977 to 1986, about one million people came to the United States each year. This is three

---

63. For example, although it is generally acknowledged that Syria is involved with international terrorism at least as much as Libya, the United States did not retaliate against Syria (as it did with Libya), perhaps due to concern over the casualties the Syrian military would have exacted.
64. "U.S. Security Interests Thwart War on the Narcotics Trade," *New York Times*, April 10, 1988, p. A10. The article also reports on a poll in which the American people overwhelmingly (48 percent) believe that drug traffic is a more important international problem than Central America (22 percent), Palestinian unrest (4 percent), terrorism (9 percent), or arms control (13 percent).
65. *Supporting U.S. Strategy for Third World Conflict*, pp. 12, 64–71.

times the annual rate in the years from 1925–65. Most of the recent immigrants are Third World refugees fleeing conflicts in Central America and Asia. Large, uncontrolled influxes of populations have strained the resources of local communities, producing bitterness and occasionally violence.[66] The prospect of internal instability in Mexico will make this problem many times worse. If the United States is to deal with this issue humanely, mitigating the frequency and causes of Third World conflict will be essential.[67] Finally, the Third World affects American security through its impact on the global environment. There is increasing concern that the burning of tropical forests contributes to the "greenhouse effect," whereby the climate of the earth is substantially warmed (the fires create a buildup of carbon dioxide that traps solar heat in the atmosphere, warming the earth). It is not yet clear how serious this problem is. Nevertheless, if the warnings of many of the scientific community are accurate, then all countries (including the United States) will be affected. Since virtually all of the tropical forests are in Third World countries, getting the leaders of these countries not to burn their forests can become a pressing interest of the United States.[68]

THE THIRD WORLD THREAT TO AMERICAN ECONOMIC INTERESTS

Many hyper-realists argue that economic factors determine the worth of a country to the United States, and that the Third World is economically insignificant. But the Third World is of substantial and increasing importance, especially when specific countries are considered. The Third World portion of the gross world product (GWP) grew from 11.1 percent in 1960, to 12.3 percent in 1970, to 14.8 percent in 1980. These figures are dwarfed by the share of the developed states (66.5 percent in 1960, 65.7 percent in 1970, and 62.7 percent in 1980) but nevertheless represent a sizeable and growing share of the world economy.[69] U.S. trade with the Third World has also shown

---

66. See for example, "Disorder Erupts Again in Miami On 2nd Night After Fatal Shooting," *New York Times*, January 18, 1989, p. A1. The article reported that a major underlying cause of the riots was the belief by blacks that Hispanic immigrants had taken over the city.
67. U.S. Department of Defense, *Commitment to Freedom*, p. 19.
68. For a description of what the United States can do to persuade Third World leaders not to burn their tropical forests, see Peter P. Swire, "Tropical Chic," *The New Republic*, January 30, 1989, pp. 18–21.
69. Percentages are based on figures from U.S. Central Intelligence Agency, National Foreign Assessment Center, *Handbook of Economic Statistics, 1981* (Washington, D.C.: U.S. GPO, 1981), Table 9. Percentages were calculated by Kenneth A. Oye and can be found in Oye, "Constrained Confidence and the Evolution of Reagan Foreign Policy," in Oye, et al., *Eagle Resurgent?* p. 10.

modest growth, with Third World countries consistently buying over one-third of American exports and providing over one-third of American imports. During the 1970s, American trade with even the non-OPEC states of the Third World grew faster than American trade with the developed world.[70] As a result, the Third World's share of U.S. imports grew from 26 percent in 1970 to 48 percent in 1980, and the percentage of U.S. exports going to the Third World grew from 30 percent in 1970 to 37 percent in 1980. Although the portion of trade with the Third World has declined slightly in the 1980s (due in part to the lower price of oil), it continued to make up more than a third of American trading activity through the middle of the decade (see Table 1). Similarly, the share of American direct investment in the Third World (which does not count bank loans to Third World countries) has declined slightly since 1970, but still accounts for roughly one-quarter of the United States total.[71]

**Table 1.  U.S. Exports Going to and U.S. Imports Coming from the Third World.**

|  | Percentage of U.S. Exports That Go to Third World | Percentage of U.S. Imports That Come from Third World |
|---|---|---|
| 1960 | 35% | 41% |
| 1970 | 30% | 26% |
| 1980 | 37% | 48% |
| 1985 | 34% | 34% |

SOURCE: U.S. Bureau of the Census, *Statistical Abstract of the United States: 1973*, 93rd ed. (Washington, D.C.: U.S. GPO), Table No. 1292, "Exports and Imports of Merchandise by Continent, Area, and Country: 1960–1972"; *Statistical Abstract of the United States: 1987*, 107th ed., Table No. 1406, "Exports, Imports and Merchandise Trade Balance by Continents, Areas, and Countries, 1975–1985."

70. John Mathieson, *U.S. Trade with the Third World: The American Stake*, The Stanley Foundation, Occasional Paper 28 (Muscatine, Iowa: The Stanley Foundation, January 1982), pp. 8–10. Average annual growth rate of U.S. exports was 20 percent for non-OPEC Third World states, and 17 percent for industrialized states. The growth rate of U.S. imports was 22 percent for non-OPEC Third World states and 17 percent for industrialized states.
71. U.S. direct investment in the Third World as a percentage of total U.S. direct investment has gone from 25 percent in 1970 to 21 percent in 1975, to 23 percent in 1980, to 25 percent in 1985. Percentages calculated from Table 1395 in U.S. Bureau of the Census, *Statistical Abstract of the United States: 1987*, 107th ed. (Washington, D.C.: U.S. GPO, 1986).

Even if the economic importance of the Third World as a whole to the United States can be debated, the economic importance of individual Third World countries is indisputable. Of particular significance are the East Asian newly industrializing countries (NICs): Taiwan, Hong Kong, South Korea, and Singapore. U.S. trade with them has exploded in the 1980s to the extent that, in 1987, U.S. imports from these countries were more than two-thirds as large as those from the European Economic Community (EEC) and Japan. For each dollar of GNP, the East Asian NICs' exports to the United States are three times greater than those of the EEC. Moreover the United States now obtains more high-tech imports from the East Asian NICs than it does from the EEC.[72] Taiwan, South Korea, and Hong Kong were among the top ten exporters to the United States, with Taiwan serving as the fourth largest source of U.S. imports—larger than any European country except West Germany.[73]

Other Third World states are also growing in economic importance. Mexico buys more exports from the United States than does any European country (it ranks third in the world behind Canada and Japan), and is a greater source of imports to the United States than any European country except West Germany (it ranks fifth behind Japan, Canada, West Germany, and Taiwan).[74] Other countries such as Brazil play an increasingly important role in the U.S. economy. If present trends continue, by the year 2010 India's GNP will be nearly equal to that of France, and Brazil's will be about the same as that of Great Britain.[75] In economics, as with strategic concerns, it is misleading to try to draw a distinction between the "important" states (Western Europe and Japan) and the "unimportant" states of the Third World.

The economic strength of the Third World, particularly of certain states, has a direct bearing on the economic well-being of the United States. As the world's largest debtor nation, the United States must increase its exports of good and services. As the Mexican example demonstrates, some Third World states have assumed central importance as trading partners for the United States. If these Third World states become unwilling or unable to buy American goods, the U.S. economy will suffer.

---

72. U.S. Department of Commerce, *United States Trade Performance in 1987 and Outlook* (Washington, D.C.: U.S. GPO, June 1988), pp. 38, 39, 42.
73. *U.S. Trade Performance in 1987*, pp. 35, 38, 39, 42.
74. *U.S. Trade Performance in 1987*, p. 35.
75. U.S. Department of Defense, *Sources of Change in the Future Security Environment* (Washington, D.C.: U.S. GPO, April 1988), p. 4.

Ironically, it is the economic weakness of some Third World states that makes them a source of concern for the United States. Nowhere is this more apparent than on the issue of Third World debt. From $2.1 billion in 1950, Third World debt has mushroomed to $1,080 billion in 1987.[76] At the very least, the huge debt impedes economic growth and threatens the stability of countries important to the United States such as Brazil and Mexico, by forcing drastic cuts in domestic consumption. Moreover, the inability of many of the countries ever to repay the debt threatens the viability of Western banks, many of them in the United States. A major default reverberating through the banking system could even seriously damage the world economy.[77]

Some hyper-realists acknowledge the growing economic importance of the Third World to the United States, but they wrongly suggest that the economic self-interest of the Third World states will ensure that American economic interests in the Third World will not be threatened.[78] It is a fundamental tenet of realism that security concerns will override economic factors in determining a country's policies. A Third World leadership beset by internal and external threats may not choose, or may not be able to choose, policies that maximize wealth when its survival is at stake. The United States cannot expect its Third World trading partners to continue policies that benefit the United States if their economic interests are superseded by concerns for basic security. In addition, Third World leaders may be motivated by political or ideological interests to pursue policies that are not in their economic self-interest. That many Third World leaders (e.g., Nicaragua's Ortega, or Ethiopia's Mengistu) choose to maintain ruinous communist systems does not give confidence that economic gain will be their primary goal in dealing with other states. These concerns are especially acute when one considers American dependence on oil and other raw materials.

The United States and its allies remain dependent on foreign oil, much of it from the Persian Gulf. At present, imports make up one-third of American

---

76. Robert Girling, *Multinational Institutions and the Third World: Management, Debt, and Trade Conflict in the International Economic Order* (New York: Praeger, 1985), p. 21; U.S. Senate, Committee on Banking, Housing and Urban Affairs, Subcommittee on International Finance and Monetary Policy, *Exchange Rates and Third World Debt*, 100th Cong., 1st sess., 1987, p. 35.

77. For a chart detailing the exposure of American banks as a result of Third World debt, see U.S. Senate, *Exchange Rates and Third World Debt*, p. 40.

78. Feinberg departs from many of the other hyper-realists in arguing that the United States has a significant economic stake in the Third World. He agrees with the other hyper-realists, however, in arguing that the Third World is in no position to threaten American economic interests. See Feinberg, *The Intemperate Zone*, pp. 24, 117–122, 127–129.

requirements, more than 60 percent of West European requirements, and virtually all of Japan's needs.[79] All indications are that import requirements of the United States and its Western allies will grow in the next ten years, while the existing excess production capacity (of ten million barrels per day) is expected to shrink. A major part of the shortfall will have to be made up by the Persian Gulf states who possess nearly 70 percent of the world's current excess production capacity and two-thirds of the world's known reserves.[80] Consequently, it is virtually assured that Western dependence on Persian Gulf oil will become greater in the next decade.

Although the United States is not as dependent on Persian Gulf oil as are its allies, an oil cutoff could severely damage American interests. As a member of the International Energy Agency (IEA), the United States is obligated to share oil with its allies in the event of a worldwide shortage. Should such a shortage come about, there would be greater competition for alternative suppliers of oil, increases in the price of oil, and possibly shortages in the United States itself.[81] The creation of the IEA and maintenance of larger stocks of oil have placed the Western states in a better position to deal with a cutoff than they were 1973. Nevertheless, the projected greater need for foreign oil in the next decade could still provoke an "everyone for himself" scramble, producing divisive consequences similar to those that occurred in 1973 within the Western alliance.[82] Even if the IEA and stockpiles prove effective, a major disruption would cause economic hardship for the United States (including inflation and unemployment) and might hurt America's ability to conduct a protracted conventional war.[83]

American allies in Japan and Western Europe are threatened far more by developments in the Persian Gulf than by any direct threat against these allies themselves. There have been fifteen oil supply disruptions since 1950,

---

79. United States Department of Energy (DOE), *Energy Security: A Report to the President of the United States* (Washington, D.C.: U.S. GPO, March 1987). For more detailed statistics on American imports of foreign oil, see Energy Information Administration, *Petroleum Supply Annual 1987*, Vol. 2 (Washington, D.C.: U.S. GPO, June 2, 1988), esp. pp. 172–230 (Table 15).
80. U.S. DOE, *Energy Security*, pp. 3, 25, 27, 36. The remaining 30 percent of world excess production capacity is held almost entirely by other members of OPEC.
81. Energy Information Administration, *Annual Energy Review, 1983* (Washington, D.C.: U.S. GPO, 1984). For a discussion of the range of possible price increases, see U.S. DOE, *Energy Security*, pp. 28–30.
82. For the effects of the 1973 crisis on the NATO alliance, see Raymond Vernon, ed., *The Oil Crisis* (New York: Norton, 1976), esp. Part 3.
83. U.S. DOE, *Energy Security*, p. 10.

and possibilities exist for many more.[84] Saudi Arabia, which alone possesses 27 percent of the free world's total proven reserves, like the rest of the Persian Gulf states, faces vulnerabilities that simply do not exist among America's more developed allies. Fundamentalist religious groups, such as the one that seized Mecca's Grand Mosque in 1979, could take over the government and sharply curtail oil sales to prevent what they see as drift into Western decadence. A pro-Soviet group could seize power and then request Soviet assistance and military advisers. Palestinian nationalists living in Saudi Arabia, civil war between Saudi clans, military officers unhappy with rising levels of corruption, and a dissatisfied Saudi Shi'ite minority are all potential threats to Saudi stability.[85] The apparent end of the Iran-Iraq war has not removed the threat of an external attack, most probably from Iran. Another oil embargo stemming from another Arab-Israeli war also cannot be discounted, especially as Western dependence on the Gulf increases.

The United States cannot hope to end all of these threats. Nevertheless, American involvement could prove critical in the event of protracted internal instability, external aggression or even in reversing an anti-American coup. It is not probable that the United States will ever have to play such a role. It is, however, far more likely that any call upon the United States to defend its interests in Western Europe and Japan will be in response to threats in the Persian Gulf, rather than to a Soviet invasion of its allies.

Western dependence on other raw materials, while not as critical as oil, is cause for concern. The United States imports more than 90 percent of its domestic consumption of manganese (for steel manufacturing), chromium (for jet engine parts), cobalt (for high-strength steel alloys) and platinum (used for refining and communication equipment).[86] The United States depends on a handful of states in southern Africa for these minerals. Neither substitutes nor alternative suppliers are readily available.[87]

---

84. U.S. DOE, *Energy Security*, p. 231.
85. For some of the threats confronting the Saudi regime, see Samuel P. Huntington, "The Renewal of Strategy," in Samuel P. Huntington, ed., *The Strategic Imperative: New Policies for American Security* (Cambridge, Mass.: Ballinger, 1982), p. 46.
86. Shafer, "Mineral Myths," pp. 156–157.
87. On the extent and strategic importance of U.S. reliance on southern African sources see U.S. Senate, *Imports of Minerals from South Africa*; and *South Africa: Time Running Out*, Report of the Study Commission on U.S. Policy Toward Southern Africa (Berkeley: University of California, 1981), esp. pp. 310–318.

Although steps such as stockpiling would ameliorate the damage to the United States, it is clear that a cutoff could seriously hurt the United States and its allies. The immediate impact would be higher inflation and economic disruptions resulting from production cutbacks among the OECD (Organization for Economic Cooperation and Development) states. In the medium term (five to ten years), failure to adapt to new technologies could result in major dislocations in the production of stainless and other types of steel. Over the long term, there is no alternative to some of the minerals, such as chromium.[88]

Far more likely than an intentional embargo is the possibility that widespread instability might prevent the export of strategic minerals. Zaire and Zimbabwe, for example, are major producers of chromium, cobalt and manganese. Both countries have experienced severe internal strife and regional conflict. Given the staggering array of threats faced by the southern African states and their dependence on primitive transportation facilities to export their products, events in the region might bring about a de facto cutoff that would seriously damage American interests. It is this prospect of chaos, rather than Soviet or other hostile control of strategic minerals, that presents the greatest threat to American interests.[89] Some of the hyper-realists acknowledge this possibility,[90] but in their zeal to debunk the Soviet threat and emphasize the logic of the marketplace, they do not afford it much attention.

It is beyond the scope of this work to detail how the United States should deal with the possibility of chaos threatening the supply of strategic minerals. Even under the best of circumstances American leverage will be limited. Nevertheless, it is clear that reliance on the laws of economic rationality will not in itself be sufficient. Only an American policy that is engaged in helping bring order and stability to southern Africa and other regions can be relied upon to mitigate this threat.

Just as the hyper-realists exaggerate the role of economic factors in determining a Third World country's interests, they also exaggerate the role of these factors in American interests. This focus on economic factors is con-

---

88. U.S. Senate, *Imports of Minerals from South Africa*, p. xv. Although the potential effects of an embargo are great, the study concludes that a long-lasting and total cutoff of South African minerals is very unlikely. See p. xvi.
89. See U.S. Senate, *Imports of Minerals from South Africa*, p. 22, for a brief discussion of the impact of revolutionary violence in South Africa.
90. Johnson, "Exaggerating America's Stakes," p. 38; Feinberg, *The Intemperate Zone*, pp. 118–119.

venient for the hyper-realists, since they are largely correct that most Third World countries, regardless of ideology, will trade with the United States. Consequently they can argue that no Third World countries, even radical, pro-Soviet ones, threaten the United States. This view ignores Third World countries that can be supportive of the U.S. economy and yet threaten a more important set of interests. That Angola is good for the Gulf Oil company does not change the fact that for ideological and strategic reasons the United States may not wish to see a Marxist-Leninist government in control of an important southern African country. Similarly, just because American companies have profitable investments in Libya and South Africa does not mean that the United States does not have an interest in seeing the regimes of those countries undergo fundamental change. It is precisely because big business does not control American policy, and interests other than economic are relevant to American behavior in the Third World, that countries can be excellent trading partners and still be hostile to broader American interests.[91]

THE THIRD WORLD THREAT TO AMERICAN POLITICAL-IDEOLOGICAL INTERESTS
The Third World matters because the effort to spread American values matters. The hyper-realists tend to denigrate the importance of ideology; because they believe ideology *should* not matter, they argue that it *does* not matter. One cannot calculate the value of a country to the United States in terms of the character of its government, in the same way that one can assess its value by virtue of its GNP or military forces. Nevertheless, promoting American values in the Third World is and should remain a critical component of United States foreign policy.

It is important for the United States to promote freedom and democracy in the Third World because Americans believe this to be the best way of life. The Third World encompasses most of the world's people. With Western Europe and Japan already democratic and essentially secure, the Third World stands out as one of the arenas for the extension of American values. If attempting to spread freedom and democracy is good in its own right,

---

91. It is interesting to remember that revisionist critics have long decried the undue influence of big business on American foreign policy. See for example, Gabriel Kolko, *The Roots of American Foreign Policy: An Analysis for Power and Purpose* (Boston: Beacon Press, 1969). It is ironic that the hyper-realists today invoke the benefits to big business when trying to convince Washington that certain regimes are not damaging to American concerns.

ignoring how most of the world's people are ruled simply because they live in countries lacking some objective measure of power is simply wrong.[92]

Extending American values to the Third World is also important in that it can enhance other American interests. None of the democratic countries (with the possible exceptions of Finland and India) are aligned with the Soviet Union. The fact that democratic states rarely if ever go to war with one another supports the American interest in stability.[93] Democracies also make better allies: since democratic governments usually do not assert control over other states, they avoid the disputes common to alliances with trans-national ideologies such as pan-Arabism or communism.[94] The spread of democracy in the Third World is also important because it can weaken the Soviet Union. The Third World is the last remaining area where Marxist-Leninist ideology is still afforded respect. The lack of receptivity to Marxism-Leninism in the Third World would clearly signal the obsolescence of Soviet ideology, diminishing any contribution it makes to the power of the Soviet Union.[95]

The promotion of American values in the Third World also matters as a component of American policy because it is likely to persist: As Robert Tucker argues, all great powers seek to spread their ideologies to other states to make certain that their ways of life and institutions are not isolated from the rest of the world.[96] There is no reason to believe that the United States will be an exception. Moreover, as even some of the hyper-realists acknowledge, the American people have never been driven by narrow conceptions of the national interest or *realpolitik*.[97] Instead, the public is concerned with the nature of regimes in the Third World and ways of bringing them more into

---

92. For an articulate exposition of this argument, see Krauthammer, "Isolationism: A Riposte," p. 118.
93. Michael Doyle, "Kant, Liberal Legacies and Foreign Affairs," *Philosophy and Public Affairs*, Vol. 12, Nos. 3 and 4 (Summer/Fall 1983), pp. 205–235, 323–353. This American interest in stability, however, does not extend to unfriendly regimes that the United States, under the Reagan Doctrine, seeks to topple.
94. Stephen Walt, "Alliance Formation and the Balance of Power," *International Security*, Vol. 9, No. 4 (Spring 1985), p. 23.
95. For a discussion of the ideological importance to the USSR of winning Third World converts, see Adam B. Ulam, *Dangerous Relations: The Soviet Union in World Politics, 1970–1982* (New York: Oxford University Press, 1983), pp. 153–154, 311–312.
96. Robert Tucker does not, however, believe that it is necessary for the United States to spread its values to the Third World. See for example, Tucker, "The Purposes of American Power," *Foreign Affairs*, Vol. 59, No. 2 (Winter 1980–81), pp. 241–274.
97. Feinberg, *The Intemperate Zone*, p. 194.

conformity with U.S. values.[98] The competition with the Soviet Union in the Third World also guarantees continuing American attention to the promotion of its values. So long as the United States and the Soviet Union remain the two dominant powers, each will attempt to demonstrate to the rest of the world that its way of life is superior, regardless of any hopes for tangible gains.

*A Truly Realistic Approach to the Third World*

American interests threatened by developments in the Third World are too important and too numerous to ignore. Instead of abandoning the Third World, the United States needs a modulated policy that recognizes the limits of its power, but also does not shrink from involvement where the United States can do some good. Preparations to protect U.S. interests from Third World threats need not be massive or expensive. By employing prudent policies that are sensitive to Third World conditions, the United States can safeguard its interests from actual and potential Third World threats at an acceptable cost and risk.

A successful American policy in the Third World must first focus on the security concerns of Third World leaders. These leaders typically face a multiplicity of internal and external threats that endanger their hold on power and personal survival. To turn to the outside state that is most likely to ensure their hold on power is as prudent as it is predictable. The hyper-realists are right to point out the increasingly important role played by economics in the affairs of Third World states; economic aid and trade should remain significant American instruments of influence. But economic interests will not predominate in an environment of insecurity. As seen by the pro-Soviet alignments of Angola and Ethiopia, the potential benefits of long-term economic gains will mean little to Third World leaders facing short-term security threats. There is no substitute for employing military instruments such as arms transfers and advisers to meet the security needs of Third World leaders. Whether to defend or to threaten, the use of these instruments

---

98. Seventy-six percent of Americans believe that the United States should foster reforms in the Third World by linking human rights to foreign assistance. Sixty-six percent believe that the United States should withhold assistance from countries ruled by dictators. Overseas Development Council, *What Americans Think: Views on Development and U.S.–Third World Relations*, Report prepared by Christine E. Contee (Washington, D.C.: Overseas Development Council, 1987), p. 7. The survey has a margin of error of 2.8 percent.

by the United States must be aimed at persuading the leaders of Third World states that their security needs are best met by policies that do not jeopardize American interests.

U.S. policies must increasingly deal with Third World challenges that have little or no connection to the Soviet Union, prominent among them Third World revolutions. The United States should not rush to accommodate apparent Third World revolutions. Before a movement seeks power, the United States must determine whether it truly represents a mass-based movement for social change, or if it is a narrowly supported insurgency. If the former, there is little the United States can do at an acceptable cost. If the latter, and if the regime emerging from the upheaval is likely to pursue policies against American interests, assisting groups attempting to repress the insurgency may very well be the correct policy. The success to date of containing the El Salvador insurgency demonstrates the fallacy of prematurely assuming that a guerrilla movement represents an "inevitable" revolution.

Nor should the United States rush to appease hostile groups that have assumed power. If these regimes attack American interests and violate American values, it makes little sense to support them. Economic aid and trade might be extended if there are prospects that a hostile regime might moderate its behavior; the United States should make sure that it is not pushing regimes into the hands of the Soviets or creating hostility where none exists. But once it is determined that the regime (be it on the right or left) is implacably opposed to American interests regardless of U.S. attempts at conciliation (as was the case with Ethiopia, for example), Washington need not apologize for opposing it. Appeasement would not work, and furthermore it must be remembered that there is much to lose in accommodating regimes whose practices and goals are repugnant to the American people. The American experience with Panama under General Manuel Noriega is a case in point.

In the Third World, as elsewhere, the United States must set priorities. The hyper-realists are certainly correct in arguing that, given limited resources, the United States cannot pursue all interests with equal vigor. Moreover, the United States must avoid the danger of spending scarce human and financial capital on peripheral interests. The hyper-realists' fear of another Vietnam, however, has prevented them from realizing that an activist, involved U.S. policy to safeguard U.S. interests in the Third World can be pursued at a reasonable cost.

Such a policy would begin with the assumption that no interest in the Third World is worth another protracted, Vietnam-like war. Instead, the

United States must be prepared to protect vital interests, such as in the Persian Gulf, by maintaining the ability to launch a major intervention that can accomplish its goals quickly. On the other end of the spectrum, the United States must also be able to mount low-level operations and provide economic and military assistance so that the vast majority of its other interests in the Third World can be safeguarded as well. This is not a formula for a "resurgent" America but for an engaged one.

On the U.S. need to be able to intervene in the Persian Gulf, there is little dispute. There is some disagreement as to just what kind of capability is needed, but the hyper-realists accept the premise that some such capability is necessary. There is no reason why the interventionary capability developed primarily for the Gulf could not be used for other Third World contingencies as well. The United States thus has a requirement to maintain forces capable of intervening in the Third World, whether one believes they are needed outside the Gulf or not.

It is on the question of what to do about the great number of non-vital interests that the hyper-realists focus their criticism. This is somewhat curious, as the United States can protect its less-than-vital Third World interests at a relatively low cost. Although numerous and potentially serious, the vast majority of the threats to American interests in the Third World can be defeated without direct American intervention or the expenditure of large sums. As the *Report of the Commission on Integrated Long-Term Strategy* states, a program to deal with low-intensity Third World threats that included increased security assistance for friendly states and support for anti-communist insurgencies would cost only four percent of the U.S. defense budget, resulting in expenditures of $12 billion per year.[99] Even for non-vital Third World interests, this sum can hardly be considered excessive, nor would it leave the United States unable to confront more important challenges. If Washington is serious about reducing its defense budget, it must look not to the Third World, but to Europe where the bulk of the defense dollar is spent.

In the final analysis, the preceding debate is less about costs or even tactics than it is about the attitude one should adopt toward the Third World. It is indisputable that the United States must give priority to protecting itself and its allies in Western Europe and Japan. But the United States also needs to

---

99. Iklé and Wohlstetter, *Discriminate Deterrence*, p. 16.

recognize that, in large part due to American efforts, the prospect of a Soviet invasion of Europe or a nuclear war between the superpowers has become extremely remote. In the meantime, the great majority of the world's states and peoples possess new levels of power at the same time they are beset by increasing instability. To ignore the threat they pose and will continue to pose to American interests would be the most unrealistic policy of all.

# Defense Dilemmas in the 1990s

*Gordon Adams and Stephen Alexis Cain*

$T$he new administration has inherited a troubling defense legacy. The Reagan administration left behind a defense program that cannot be enacted without significant real growth in defense budgets and spending during the first half of the 1990s, but there is little prospect for such growth. It is more likely that defense budgets will not grow at all for several years, and they may even fail to keep pace with inflation.

It should be possible to meet U.S. national security requirements without any growth in defense spending. Defense spending has grown 40 percent after inflation since Fiscal Year (FY) 1980, reaching unprecedented peacetime levels. If spending were to decline as much as three percent after inflation each year until FY 1994, it would still be higher, in constant dollars, than in any peacetime year prior to FY 1983.

High spending levels alone, however, will not guarantee a strong defense. Security needs will be better served by sound defense policies and a long-term plan that matches programs to realistic projections of resources. In the absence of such planning, U.S. defense capabilities could erode, even with a continuation of high levels of defense spending. If the new administration simply tries to proceed with the program that it has inherited, a growing share of the defense budget will be consumed by expensive new weapons that will not be purchased in adequate amounts, while force structure contracts, and readiness and sustainability decline.

If the United States is to achieve military security at lower cost in the 1990s, tough choices must be made. Some programs will have to be cancelled or deferred, while less expensive solutions to military problems are sought. A proper balance must be struck among the size of military forces, their level of readiness and sustainability, and the rate at which military hardware is modernized. Choices must be guided by a reexamination of global U.S. security policies and commitments, especially towards the Soviet Union and Western Europe.

---

*Gordon Adams is the director of the Defense Budget Project, a non-partisan, non-profit research organization in Washington, D.C. Stephen Alexis Cain is the senior budget analyst at the Project.*

---

*International Security*, Spring 1989 (Vol. 13, No. 4)

*The Fiscal Legacy of the 1980s Defense Buildup*

The Reagan administration's emphasis on military hardware has left a legacy of high defense spending and pressures for further spending growth. Commitments made to a large number of weapons programs in the 1980s have created a "stern wave" of defense spending in the latter part of the decade, which will persist into the early 1990s. Commitments to the next generation of weaponry threaten to create a "bow wave" in the 1990s, pushing defense spending still higher.[1]

This fiscal dilemma results from the shift in the composition of the defense budget since FY 1980 from "consumption" to "investment."[2] Between FY 1980 and FY 1985, funds for Department of Defense (DoD) investment grew 104 percent after inflation, while budgets for operations and maintenance (up 37 percent) and for military personnel (up only 8 percent) grew far more slowly. This rapid growth pushed the investment share of the defense budget from 38 percent in FY 1980 to a peak of 48 percent in FY 1985.

When defense investment funding grows rapidly, actual spending (outlays) lags behind budget authority, creating a backlog of appropriated but unspent funds.[3] This backlog results because Congress "fully funds" weapons programs in a single appropriation, but contractors receive these funds in incremental "progress payments" during the several years that it takes to build a system or to complete a contract. While overall DoD budget authority doubled (including inflation) between FY 1980 and FY 1988, the backlog of unexpended funds grew 188 percent, from $92 billion to an estimated $266 billion. Approximately 80 percent of this backlog is already obligated to contracts.

Because the spending that flows from these obligations is virtually automatic, the share of defense outlays considered "relatively uncontrollable"

---

1. The term "stern wave" reflects the fact that spending commitments already made are pushing up levels of defense spending "from behind." The term "bow wave" refers to increased weapons procurement funding brought on by the movement of several weapons programs from the research and development (R&D) stage to the production stage.
2. By "investment," the Department of Defense (DoD) means spending on weapons procurement, research and development, and military construction. The term "consumption" as used here covers the elements of the defense budget devoted largely to people and consumables: the military personnel and operations and maintenance accounts.
3. Defense *funding* (budget authority) is the authority, appropriated by Congress, to spend money (make outlays). Funding is not necessarily spent in the year it was appropriated. The defense *spending* of each year results partly from that year's funding and partly from the funding of prior years.

(due to prior-year contracts) rose from 20 percent in FY 1976 and 27 percent in FY 1980, to an estimated 40 percent by FY 1987, according to Office of Management and Budget (OMB) data. This fiscal "stern wave" places severe limits on the new administration's ability to stabilize or reduce defense spending. Adding the approximately 45 percent of defense spending allocated to payroll and pensions, roughly 85 percent of defense spending will be essentially beyond the control of the new Secretary of Defense, unless he cancels already-signed contracts or cuts personnel.

Reflecting the growing uncontrollability of spending, outlays rose six percent after inflation in FY 1986 and one percent after inflation in FY 1987, even though Congress cut defense budget authority in both years. Even in FY 1988, defense outlays kept pace with inflation and, if Congressional Budget Office (CBO) estimates are accurate, FY 1989 outlays will fall only marginally below the rate of inflation.

The investment buildup has also increased the requirement for operations and support funding.[4] As the stockpile of weapons grows more expensive and technologically complex, the cost of operating and supporting military forces also grows, even if the number of weapons does not increase. While the Army and Air Force have not expanded in the 1980s, the number of ships and sailors has increased significantly; more importantly, each service procured increasingly complex and expensive weapons.[5]

Operations and support (O&S) funding needs will continue to grow in the 1990s, largely because of weapons that have been funded but have yet to be delivered. If the relationship between the cost of acquiring weapons and the cost of operating and supporting them holds true for the next generation of military hardware, O&S funding requirements will increase 2.3 percent to 5.5 percent per year in the early 1990s, according to CBO.[6]

Furthermore, growth in the research and development (R&D) budget has created pressure for a "bow wave" of weapons procurement funding in the 1990s. Defense Department R&D funding grew 92 percent after inflation from FY 1980 to FY 1989, more than any other category during the same

---

4. Operations and support funding includes the budgets for operations and maintenance and military personnel. It can also include funds for the procurement of readiness-related items like ammunition and spare parts.
5. Congressional Budget Office (CBO), *Operations and Support Costs for the Department of Defense* (Washington, D.C.: CBO, July 1988).
6. Ibid., pp. 16–20. The impetus behind this cost growth seems to be the increasing technological complexity of new weapons systems. Complex weapons tend to require more expensive maintenance, spare parts, and diagnostic equipment than do simpler ones.

period. Nearly all of this increase was devoted to the development of military hardware, rather than to basic research.

Despite its relatively small 10-to-15 percent share of any given year's defense budget, research and development drives future requirements for defense funding. Although no two weapons are alike, the life-cycle costs for a "typical" major program are: three percent for advanced development, 12 percent for full-scale engineering development, 35 percent for procurement, and 50 percent for operations and support. Significant growth in R&D funding leads the way to future increases in defense funding as a whole, unless weapons programs are cancelled before entering production. As a result of the rapid growth in R&D funding in the 1980s, a large number of programs are approaching the production stage, creating strong pressures for rapid increases in procurement funding in the 1990s.[7]

*The Gap Between Plans and Resources*

The defense budget buildup ended in FY 1986. Actual defense appropriations have declined in constant dollars every year beginning in FY 1986; at $298.8 billion in FY 1989, they are ten percent below the FY 1985 level in constant dollars. Few analysts or politicians expect that real growth will resume in the coming years, given the powerful pressures for deficit reduction created by the Gramm-Rudmann-Hollings law, public opposition to further defense spending increases, and the growing demand for federal spending on neglected social and economic needs.

Despite this dramatic change in the fiscal outlook, DoD plans continue to anticipate real dollar budget growth. Through the Reagan administration's FY 1990–91 budget request,[8] each year's budget has been approached as a one-year exercise, trimming the necessary amounts through program stretch-outs (reductions in production rates below planned levels), cuts in the excess

---

7. The major weapons systems expected to reach production in the near future include: the Army's Tactical Missile System (ATACMS) and Forward Area Air Defense Systems (FAADS), the Navy's Advanced Tactical Aircraft (ATA), V-22 Osprey tilt-rotor aircraft and SSN-21 attack submarine, and the Air Force's C-17 transport jet, Stealth bomber, Tacit Rainbow anti-radiation missile, Midgetman missile, Short Range Attack Missile (SRAM II), and new rail garrison basing mode for the MX missile. Advanced development programs moving to the engineering development stage, and then on to production in the 1990s include the Strategic Defense Initiative (SDI), the National Aerospace Plane Program, the Army's LHX helicopter and Advanced Antitank Weapon System, the Navy's Advanced Air-to-Air missile, and the Air Force's Advanced Tactical Fight (ATF).
8. President Bush's revisions to President Reagan's final budget were unavailable when this article was written.

funds that resulted from overestimates of inflation, and reductions in funds for readiness and sustainability.

These short-term strategies have now lost most of their efficacy. After several years of cutting planned production rates, fewer major weapons can now be stretched out without major losses in efficiency and, at best, marginal short-term savings.[9] Most of the excess funds from overpricing of weapon programs and overestimates of inflation in the early 1980s have dried up, and more realistic inflation estimates are being used in current DoD planning.[10] Operations and support funding has been reduced since FY 1985, leading to growing depot maintenance backlogs and reductions in training tempos. Further cuts could reduce military readiness and sustainability to unacceptable levels.

In the current fiscal year, major changes in defense programs were avoided, even after a Capitol Hill White House deficit reduction agreement imposed $33 billion in cuts from the original FY 1989 defense budget request. Instead, Secretary Frank Carlucci's budget proposal cut funds for readiness and sustainability and reduced the size of the force structure slightly, but made few significant changes in planned weapons acquisitions.[11] The FY 1990–91 budget request also cuts funds for readiness and sustainability, while stretching out on-going production programs and preserving funds for new weapons.

As a result of this short-sighted approach, there is now a sizeable gap between the resources required to fund fully the defense program left by the Reagan administration and the resources that Congress is likely to appropriate. According to the CBO, the Reagan program (excluding deployment of the Strategic Defense Initiative and acquisition of the Midgetman missile) will require annual real growth of between three and four percent from FY

---

9. The defense plan for FY 1988 through FY 1992 forecast that more than half of a sample of 25 weapons would fail to achieve minimum economic rates of production, and only five would approach the maximum rate. On the problem of stretch-outs, see CBO, *Effects of Weapons Procurement Stretch-outs on Costs and Schedules* (Washington, D.C.: CBO, November 1987).

10. For detailed analysis of the inflation dividend, see General Accounting Office (GAO), *Potential for Excess Funds in DOD*, GAO/NSIAD-85-145 (Washington, D.C.: GAO, September 3, 1985); ibid., *March 1986 Update*, GAO/NSIAD-86-76 (Washington, D.C.: GAO, March 1986); and CBO, *Budgeting for Defense Inflation* (Washington, D.C.: CBO, January 1986).

11. Program cancellations accounted for only $4.8 billion (less than 15 percent) of DoD's FY 1989 reductions, $2 billion of which would result from the proposed cancellation of the Midgetman missile, which may yet be preserved. While several small programs were cancelled, the only major programs cancelled were the A-6F aircraft and the anti-satellite (ASAT) missile. DoD's proposed cancellations, excepting the Midgetman, would save only an estimated $12 billion in FY 1989 and future years. Calculated from figures in Department of Defense, "News Release: Amended FY 1988/FY 1989 Department of Defense Budget" (Washington, D.C.: Office of Assistant Secretary of Defense for Public Affairs, February 18, 1988).

1990 to FY 1994.[12] The gap between this spending path and one that would merely keep pace with inflation is approximately $180 billion from FY 1990 to FY 1994, and about $65 billion in FY 1994 alone. If spending does not keep pace with inflation but remains constant, the gap would be approximately $310 billion, and would be over $100 billion in FY 1994 alone.[13]

Significant changes in programs will be required to bring the projected five-year plan in line with fiscal realities. For example, CBO has calculated the impact of reducing aircraft carrier purchases by two in the 1990s; cutting annual production of new C-17 airlift planes and Advanced Tactical Fighters by one-third; cutting production of DDG-51 guided missile destroyers by one-half; and delaying initial procurement of the B-2 bomber from 1989 to 1993 and the Anti-tank Guided Missile from 1992 to 1995. Even this scaled-down program would require real spending growth of one to two percent per year.

*Commitments, Force Structure, and Budgets: The Need for a Policy Review*

The choices for the 1990s are difficult; the politically easy methods for reducing defense budgets no longer suffice. Today, U.S. strategies and commitments must be reevaluated in connection with more realistic defense budget planning. While the need for a link between strategy and budget planning seems obvious, military strategy played only a small role in the formulation of defense budgets in the 1980s. Budgets were determined primarily by fiscal opportunity and the perceived need to demonstrate U.S. resolve through funding growth.

The new administration has inherited a nearly unlimited agenda of military missions, including: the development of a space-based strategic defense against a Soviet nuclear strike; deterrence of such an attack through the ability to strike hardened Soviet military targets promptly with strategic nuclear weapons; maintenance of a capability to defend Europe with nuclear and conventional forces, while opening second military fronts in Asia and

---

12. CBO, *Costs of Supporting and Modernizing Current Military Forces (Briefing Summary)* (Washington, D.C.: CBO, September 1988). These calculations assume that SDI funding grows only three percent annually and that the Midgetman missile is cancelled.
13. William W. Kaufmann estimates that Defense Secretary Caspar Weinberger's defense budget projections for FY 1990 through FY 1994 were $475 billion higher than a nominal freeze, which is a likely path for the defense budget. Kaufmann, "Restructuring Defense," *Brookings Review*, Vol. 7, No. 1 (Winter 1988/89), p. 64.

attacking Soviet home ports; development of a nonnuclear capability to attack second-echelon Warsaw Pact forces; defense of the Middle East with naval and land forces; control over the high seas worldwide; projection of military power abroad with amphibious and airborne forces, battleships, and naval air; and intervention in the developing countries through special operations forces. These missions must be reexamined in the light of the budget crunch, and can be redefined given the evolving relationship with the Soviet Union and new prospects for strategic and conventional arms control.

STRATEGIC NUCLEAR POLICY AND ARMS CONTROL

Funds for strategic nuclear forces have grown more rapidly than the defense budget as a whole during the 1980s, and are currently projected to expand even further as a large number of new strategic weapons reach the production stage in the early 1990s. DoD currently plans to proceed with all of these modernization programs, with the possible exception of the Midgetman missile, even if a strategic arms reduction talks (START) treaty is reached. The United States would comply with treaty limits by simply dismantling older weapons.

Consideration should be given instead to cancelling new strategic hardware programs or deferring their production, pending the negotiation of a new START agreement. A START treaty that limits modernization on both sides may be achievable, leaving each with strategic forces consisting largely of weapons now deployed or already in the pipeline. Even in the absence of progress on START, the need for and cost-effectiveness of programs such as the B-2 bomber, rail garrison–based MX missiles, and the refit of currently-deployed Trident submarines to carry the D-5 missile should be reviewed.

The Strategic Defense Initiative needs particularly close scrutiny, for fiscal and policy reasons. The program currently concentrates on technologies and hardware that could be acquired in the mid-to-late 1990s for a "Phase One" system costing an estimated $69 billion to acquire, with an additional $45 billion in basic research and development. There would also be substantial further costs for the development of Phases Two and Three of SDI for deployment in the next century.

There is considerable doubt about whether such a strategic defense system would be militarily effective, and some concern that it could prompt a costly offensive-defensive arms race between the superpowers. Although it would be prudent to continue a long-term research program on strategic defenses, which would require roughly $2 billion per year, DoD could achieve considerable budget savings by foregoing a rush toward deployment.

DETERRENCE IN EUROPE

A review of security policy in Europe, conducted in concert with the NATO allies, should define defense options that are less expensive than the current posture, while providing equivalent or greater security. Such a review could help specify the force upgrades that are truly necessary and clarify how they might fit with a potential conventional arms reduction agreement.

Current U.S. defense plans include new and costly upgrades of remaining tactical nuclear forces in Europe and the acquisition of nonnuclear "deep strike" weapons.[14] These systems may not provide cost-effective deterrence in Europe when compared with options such as increased sustainability and sealift capacity, improved close air support, and barrier defenses such as mines and tank traps.[15] Moreover, offensively-oriented technologies and tactics may not be desirable, given their possible impact on crisis stability in Europe and on NATO's defensive mission.

The military options for Europe also need to be evaluated in light of the unilateral Soviet conventional force cuts and the opportunities for multilateral reduction. Although negotiations with the Warsaw Pact are bound to be lengthy and difficult, the Soviets have shown a new willingness to consider such previously non-negotiable items as asymmetrical reductions and intrusive verification.[16] Progress on such a treaty could enhance regional stability while allowing a phased reduction in the U.S. and Soviet military presence in Europe, providing significant budgetary savings by the late 1990s.

---

14. The new tactical nuclear programs include more artillery-fired atomic projectiles, a nuclear version of the Army Tactical Missile System (as a follow-on to the Lance), a new air-to-surface nuclear missile, and new dual-capable fighter aircraft. The conventional deep-strike technologies include new intelligence and communications systems to assist in processing combat information and targeting adversary forces, and longer-range conventional missiles to target second-echelon adversary forces and supplies. See Office of Technology Assessment (OTA), *New Technology for NATO: Implementing Follow-On Forces Attack*, OTA-ISC-309 (Washington, D.C.: U.S. Government Printing Office [U.S. GPO], June 1987).

15. For a discussion of the high value and low cost of barrier defenses, see CBO, *U.S. Ground Forces and the Conventional Balance in Europe* (Washington, D.C.: U.S. GPO, June 1988), pp. 38–43.

16. Jonathan Dean, "Will Negotiated Force Reductions Build Down the NATO–Warsaw Pact Confrontation?" *The Washington Quarterly*, Vol. 11, No. 2 (Spring 1988), pp. 69–84.

POWER PROJECTION FORCES

The global deployment of U.S. forces in the Persian Gulf, Indian Ocean, East Asia, the Pacific, and Central America also needs review. It is increasingly clear that the Navy's goal of 600 deployed combatant ships will be unobtainable for fiscal reasons. It is time to reexamine the justification for such a large fleet and the missions to which it is committed. The plan to increase the number of carrier battle groups to 15 should be reconsidered given its link to the unachievable "Maritime Strategy,"[17] which even the Navy has begun to reconsider. Early retirement of older carriers or termination of plans to build additional new carriers in the 1990s could save considerable sums, given the costs of both the carriers themselves and their support ships and aircraft.

*The Need to Set Budgetary Priorities*

The new administration needs to implement its policies through its budgets. It must decide whether to favor preservation of the force structure, protection of readiness and sustainability, or modernization of military hardware.

It is especially important for the new administration and Congress to reconsider weapons modernization plans. Scarce resources might be better devoted to producing current weapon programs at efficient rates than to undertaking all of the new starts now planned. In many cases, DoD would be wise to upgrade current weaponry rather than produce entirely new systems. While it is unnecessary to forego the entire list of "bow wave" programs, priorities must be set. DoD should cancel some new programs and postpone decisions on production or engineering development for others.

Given the limits on resources, the current push for new starts will force DoD to sacrifice current modernization programs, terminating them prematurely or stretching them out at extremely inefficient rates. For example, the Air Force and the Navy are each planning a new, advanced tactical aircraft,

17. This strategy included a requirement for carrier capabilities that would make it possible to attack Soviet European home ports. See William W. Kaufmann, *A Thoroughly Efficient Navy* (Washington, D.C.: Brookings, 1987); John J. Mearsheimer, "A Strategic Misstep: The Maritime Strategy and Deterrence in Europe," *International Security*, Vol. 11, No. 2 (Fall 1986), pp. 3–57; and CBO, *Future Budget Requirements for the 600-Ship Navy* (Washington, D.C.: CBO, September 1985).

while production rates for current fighter programs have already been stretched out to accommodate the funding requirements of these new programs. A less costly alternative would be to defer acquisition of the new planes while buying F-16s and modified A-6s at efficient rates. The Navy faces the same issue with nuclear attack submarines, and the Army with helicopters. Current weapon programs would give the services a better chance of buying sufficient amounts of equipment, since, as a rule, they are less expensive than new programs and their costs are more stable. In addition, the capabilities of current programs are known, while new programs may promise more than they ultimately deliver.

In some instances, advances in military technology may be desirable. However, it would be more fiscally responsible to consider upgrading existing programs, thus avoiding the risks of escalating cost and disappointing performance, than to jump ahead to new ones. Upgrades would provide new capabilities in Navy attack aircraft and Army helicopters less expensively than new systems.

Deferring or cancelling low-priority new starts, such as the Air Force stealth bomber, Navy A-12, or Army LHX (light helicopter experimental), could free resources for higher priority programs, such as anti-tank munitions or air defense. It could also allow the new administration to start some programs that were low on the Reagan administration's list of priorities, such as new sealift ships and close air support aircraft.

Unless current weapon modernization plans are reined in, there is a risk that military readiness and sustainability will bear the brunt of budget cuts. There is some evidence that this began to occur in FY 1986, creating the danger of a growing imbalance between investment and readiness. As the new administration and Congress seek to close the gap between plans and resources, they should protect funding levels for depot maintenance, education and training, sailing days, training days, and flying hours, all of which bear directly on the readiness of the armed forces. In addition, attention needs to be devoted to maintaining and improving munitions levels for all of the services and to coping with shortfalls in funding for spare parts and support equipment.

An additional advantage of giving budgetary priority to readiness and sustainability over modernization is that it helps bring the budget under control. A continued weapons buildup will put pressure on future budget plans by increasing the requirement for future operations and support funding. Slower modernization reduces the need for increases in operations and support funding.

Slowing the modernization program would also reduce the budgetary pressure for the sort of ill-considered cuts in force structure that were made in the FY 1989 budget request. Reductions in the force structure (e.g., carrier battle groups, air wings, and divisions) should be contemplated, but only if they match a revised agenda of military missions and strategies reached after careful study.

*Conclusion*

The fiscal pressures on national defense pose a serious problem for the new administration. The Defense Department has failed to set budgetary priorities or to make the choices necessary to hold back waves of new spending, while deficit reduction requirements block further budget growth. Continuing on the present course will lead to budgetary chaos and military disorganization. Military readiness and sustainability will decline, ill-considered cuts in force structure may occur, and the services will be top-heavy in new weaponry that they cannot adequately operate or support. At the same time, because of the fiscal requirements of the "bow wave," defense budgets will remain high and difficult to control.

The new administration can provide adequate military security within budgetary constraints only by facing up to the long-term problem of the mismatch between programs and likely budgets. It must make politically difficult decisions, starting with the FY 1990 budget. "Trimming the fat" from the defense program cannot solve the budget dilemma. The time is ripe for a fundamental rethinking of defense priorities, programs, and policies.

*Part II:*
*Assessing the*
*Conventional Balance*

# Measuring the European Conventional Balance

### Coping with Complexity in Threat Assessment

Barry R. Posen

$\mathbf{I}$f NATO is to invest its
scarce resources wisely in the coming years, if it is to choose intelligently
from the menu of possible conventional improvements,[1] it must begin with
a careful assessment of the current NATO–Warsaw Pact military balance in
Central Europe. Such assessments can only provide useful program guidance

This article is a substantially revised version of "Competing Views of the Center Region Conventional Balance," in Keith A. Dunn and William O. Staudenmaier, eds., *Alternative Military Strategies for the Future* (Boulder, Colo.: Westview Press, forthcoming). The author wishes to thank all of the friends and colleagues who provided comments on various drafts of this essay. He also wishes to thank the Council on Foreign Relations and the Rockefeller Foundation for their financial support. The author alone is responsible for the content of this essay.

*Barry Posen is an Assistant Professor in the Department of Politics and the Woodrow Wilson School at Princeton University and the author of* The Sources of Military Doctrine: France, Britain, and Germany between the World Wars *(Ithaca: Cornell University Press, 1984).*

1. The wide range of possible improvements may be loosely grouped into three categories: those of the "military reformers," who advocate a host of tactical, organizational, and hardware changes that would improve conventional capabilities without major spending increases; those of the NATO (and Pentagon) bureaucracy, which has made a battery of proposals (such as the Long Term Defense Plan) simply to buy a lot more of what we have been buying; and those of a group of technology-minded individuals who advocate investments in "new" technologies (usually called "emerging technologies" or "E.T."). For a critical discussion of the possible tactical implications of the military reformers' prescriptions for ground warfare, see John J. Mearsheimer, "Maneuver, Mobile Defense, and the NATO Central Front," *International Security*, Vol. 6, No. 3 (Winter 1981/82), pp. 104–122. For the best example of how the reformers' ideas have crept into official U.S. Army doctrine, see U.S. Army, *FM 100-5, Operations* (August 20, 1982). The reformers are also keenly concerned about weapons design. Their principal criticism of current U.S. weapons design philosophy is that it strives for technological parameters that are too far removed from the actual circumstances of *both* peacetime and wartime military practice. For a useful reform perspective on the technology of ground warfare, see Steven Canby, *The Alliance and Europe: Part IV, Military Doctrine and Technology*, Adelphi Paper No. 109 (London: International Institute for Strategic Studies, 1974/75), pp. 34–41. On aerial technology, see Jack N. Merritt and Pierre M. Sprey, "Negative Marginal Returns in Weapons Acquisition," in Richard G. Head and Ervin J. Rokke, eds., *American Defense Policy*, 3rd ed. (Baltimore: Johns Hopkins University Press, 1973), pp. 486–495. On the Long Term Defense Plan, see Harold Brown, *Annual Report of the Department of Defense, Fiscal Year 1981* (Washington, D.C.: U.S. Government Printing Office, 1980), pp. 47–49, 215. For arguments in favor of "emerging technologies," see *Strengthening Conventional Deterrence in Europe*, Report of the European Security Study (New York: St. Martin's Press, 1983).

*International Security*, Winter 1984/85 (Vol. 9, No. 3) 0162-2889/84/030047-42 $02.50/1
© Barry R. Posen.

if they focus on the most dangerous threats faced by the Alliance, and capture as fully as possible the efforts NATO has already made to deal with those threats. Most assessments, unfortunately, are too simplistic, relying heavily on simple "bean counts" and failing to take adequate account of the many other variables involved. This analysis will explain what some of these other variables are and how they may be combined into a model that will provide a more realistic balance assessment and a basis for evaluating possible improvements.

*The Problem*

The distinctive characteristic of military competition in Central Europe is the large concentration of mechanized ground forces on both sides, supported by substantial numbers of attack helicopters and fighter aircraft. Most assessments give the Warsaw Pact credit for quantitative superiority in these assets. These are the same kinds of forces that are associated with the major blitzkrieg operations of the last half-century: the German invasions of Poland, France, and the Soviet Union in World War II; the Israeli victory over the Arabs in 1967; and the Israeli counterattack across the Suez Canal in 1973. Western scholars and political leaders have tended to fixate on the powerful offensive potential of Soviet armored forces, thus creating fears that a convential war in Europe could end in a quick NATO defeat. If the Soviets believe that they can achieve victory with conventional forces alone, then overall deterrence of Soviet aggression is surely undermined. As John Mearsheimer has pointed out, in the world of *conventional* deterrence, it is confidence in quick, cheap victory that causes the aggressor to attack.[2] In NATO's case, Soviet confidence in a speedy conventional victory may also undermine the deterrent effect of the Alliance's nuclear weapons, providing hope to the Pact that NATO could be overrun before a decision to use nuclear weapons were taken.

In spite of the prevailing fears and perceptions, however, not all of the military history of the last fifty years confirms the hypothesis that armored forces enhance the offense's chances of success. Individual battles such as Kursk and the Bulge in the Second World War and the Israeli defense of the Golan Heights in 1973 all suggest that armored assaults can be stopped—

---

2. John J. Mearsheimer, *Conventional Deterrence* (Ithaca: Cornell University Press, 1983), pp. 23–66.

that mechanized *defenders* can also turn in impressive performances. Indeed, the German army's overall performance during the second half of World War II, when it was substantially outnumbered, is testimony to the defensive potential of even *partially* mechanized forces.

A survey of the history of armored warfare also suggests that the place to begin any assessment of the current NATO–Warsaw Pact military balance is the so-called "breakthrough" battle. Armored attackers customarily have concentrated their best resources on narrow sectors of their enemy's front, hoping to achieve a degree of quantitative superiority that could cause a major rupture in the defense line. Such ruptures permit the deep exploitations associated with the classical German, and Israeli, practice of blitzkrieg, and the encirclements associated with German and Soviet operations on the Eastern Front during World War II. This essay, however, does not deal explicitly with the exploitation phase, but focuses on NATO's initial capability to keep it from arising.[3]

Most analyses of warfare in the Central Region of Europe correctly assume a front of roughly 750 kilometers (km) and further assume that the Soviets will attempt to break through in a small number of areas where the terrain and the road net are particularly suitable for armored warfare. The map of the Central Region in Figure 1 shows the four most attractive breakthrough sectors. Most analysts agree that the Pact will mount at least one major attack in the North German plain, considered to be the best corridor. One will almost surely be launched in the Fulda Gap, if only to tie down the powerful U.S. V Corps. The Göttingen corridor running through the German III Corps sector just north of the Fulda Gap is somewhat more attractive as a third choice than the Hof corridor. Each of these corridors is roughly 50 km wide.

In spite of the often cited Soviet numerical superiority in Europe, most analyses of potential Soviet attacks expect that the Pact will have to concentrate its efforts on these three or four rather well-defined breakthrough sectors since the Pact's quantitative advantage over NATO is not great enough to permit it to greatly outnumber Western forces everywhere. Thus, the successful breakthrough battle is the key to a quick Pact victory, and thwarting Pact breakthrough efforts becomes NATO's primary conventional

---

3. If breakthroughs do occur, operational reserves are necessary to combat the adversary's exploitation or encirclement efforts. NATO should, therefore, maintain sufficient "operational reserves" to counterattack in the event that the adversary manages to achieve a clean breakthrough.

**Figure 1.   Most Likely Axes of Advance in a Warsaw Pact Attack Against NATO**

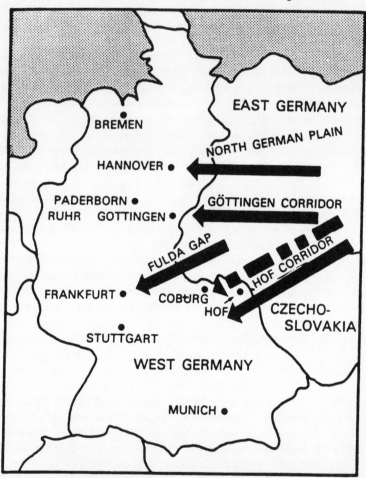

SOURCE: John J. Mearsheimer, "Why the Soviets Can't Win Quickly in Central Europe," *International Security,* vol. 7, no. 1 (Summer 1982), p. 21.

military task. If NATO can achieve this in war, it may ultimately be able to mobilize its superior economic power against the Pact. If the Soviet Union can be made to believe in peacetime that NATO has this capability, then overall deterrence is enhanced. This analysis, therefore, concentrates upon the relative ability of NATO and the Warsaw Pact to cope with the demands imposed by multiple breakthrough battles.

*NATO vs. Pact Doctrine*

How does the breakthrough battle figure in each side's general war plans? Every military organization, explicitly or implicitly, has a theory of victory, a notion of the combination of human and material resources and tactics that it believes is most likely to produce success on the battlefield. This theory of victory is the organization's military doctrine.

The Warsaw Pact's and NATO's military doctrines, which determine how each alliance builds and organizes its military forces, are quite different from each other. At the most *general* level, the Pact prefers large numbers of major weapons and formations (often called "tooth") over training, the experience of military personnel, logistics, and the command, control, communications, and intelligence ($C^3I$) functions broadly defined. (Logistics and $C^3I$ are often referred to as "tail.") Additionally, it prefers ground forces to tactical aviation, although the Soviet Union does have substantial tactical air capability. NATO, on the other hand, prefers a more balanced mix of tooth and tail, shows greater interest in the training and experience of its personnel, and places greater emphasis on tactical airpower.

In terms of military operations, Pact doctrine tends to extol the advantages of the offense. This is fairly explicit in Soviet military writings. On the other hand, partly as a function of the Alliance's political orientation but also because of the lessons it has drawn from the school of military experience, NATO tends towards a more balanced view of the relative advantages of defensive and offensive tactics. This view is more implicit than explicit in NATO doctrine, which as a whole tends to be less formal than that of the Pact. Particularly at the level of the small unit engagement, Western military thinkers have long held that the defense has a substantial advantage—one that can be turned into an overall strategic defensive advantage through careful planning and the skillful conduct of military operations.[4]

---

4. On the defender's tactical advantage, see John J. Mearsheimer, "Why the Soviets Can't Win Quickly in Central Europe," *International Security*, Vol. 7, No. 1 (Summer 1982), pp. 15–20, especially footnote 30. The now superseded July 1976 version of the U.S. Army's basic field manual, *FM 100-5, Operations*, included some explicit statements on the extent of numerical inferiority that the defender could accept and still expect to hold successfully. In describing the tasks of a defending general, it asserts, "As a rule of thumb, they should seek not to be

The net result of these differences is that the Warsaw Pact generates military forces that, at least at first glance, look substantially more formidable than those of NATO. Although official comparisons of NATO and Warsaw Pact defense spending have consistently shown NATO outspending the Pact by varying degrees ($360 billion vs. $320 billion in 1982 according to a recent Department of Defense estimate[5]), the tendency in both official and unofficial balance assessments has been to highlight Pact advantages in tanks, guns, planes, or divisions. The possibility that NATO's higher spending might be generating less visible, but equally important, elements of military capability seldom receives much consideration. Instead, NATO's superiority in the spending comparisons and apparent equality or near-equality in manpower[6] are ignored, or explained away with relatively cursory arguments.[7]

---

outweighed more than 3:1 in terms of combat power. With very heavy air and field artillery support on favorable terrain, it may be possible to defend at a numerical disadvantage of something like 5:1 for short periods of time" (p. 5-3). Somewhat ambiguously, these ratios are said to apply "at the point and time of decision" (p. 3-5). The document also holds that on the offense, U.S. generals should strive for "concentrated combat power of about 6:1 superiority" (p. 3-5). In general, then, the Field Manual seems to hold that defenders can fight successfully if outnumbered 3:1, and may be able to do so if outnumbered as much as 5:1. The new version of the Field Manual is silent on these numerical ratios. It does, however, seem to imply that, given certain tactical advantages held by the defender, the attacker must muster numerical superiority at a small number of times and places of his choosing. See *FM 100-5* (1982), pp. 8-5, 8-6, 10-3, 10-4.

5. U.S. Department of Defense, *The FY 1984 DOD Program for Research, Development and Acquisitions*, Statement by the Honorable Richard DeLauer, Undersecretary of Defense for Research and Engineering, 98th Congress, 1st session (March 2, 1983), p. I-7.

6. International Institute for Strategic Studies, *The Military Balance 1983–84* (London: IISS, 1983), pp. 125–126. According to the IISS counting rules employed in the preceding editions, the Warsaw Pact fields 4.7 million men to NATO's 5.4 million. In 1983, IISS credits the Soviet Union with an additional 1.5 million men, bringing the Pact total to 6.2 million. The manpower ratio is thus either 1.15:1 in the Pact's favor, or 1.15:1 in NATO's favor. Unfortunately, IISS offers no explanation for why it has changed its counting rules.

7. Richard DeLauer argues that the Soviet Union somehow has a lower cost of doing business than the United States or NATO. This argument is almost certainly based on the Central Intelligence Agency (CIA) dollar model which prices Soviet activities at the rate that it would cost the United States to accomplish them in exactly the same way that the Soviets do. Pact manpower is largely valued according to U.S. wages and maintenance costs for individuals of equal rank and experience. If Soviet manpower costs in dollars appear lower than NATO's, it should be a function of the relatively smaller professional non-commissioned officer and officer cadre in the mass conscription Pact militaries, not of greater Soviet efficiency. Moreover, what is publicly known about Soviet maintenance practices, for instance, suggests that they are less efficient than those of the West. When priced according to the dollar model, these inefficiencies emerge as a higher cost of doing business, making the Pact effort appear to be greater than it would if it allocated its resources more efficiently. See DoD, *The FY 1984 DOD Program for Research, Development and Acquisitions*, pp. 1–9. On the CIA methodology, see Central Intelligence Agency, National Foreign Assessment Center, *Soviet and US Defense Activities, 1970–79: A Dollar Cost Comparison* (Washington, D.C.: Central Intelligence Agency, 1980).

Although the investment (i.e., major procurement) spending of NATO compared to the Pact

In effect, then, NATO tends to buy military forces according to its own theory of victory, its own military doctrine. Analysts, however, have tended to assess the military balance according to a different—the Soviet—theory of victory. Adopting Soviet criteria for measuring the balance will always make the West look bad in comparison to the Pact, short of very substantial increases in NATO defense spending and manpower, because NATO organizes and procures its forces according to quite different criteria. Indeed, if NATO were to try to build a military force that would redress the imbalance portrayed by its current assessments, yet build that force according to its own military doctrine, it would have to increase its spending lead over the Pact still further, and probably keep even more men under arms. The fact that the Reagan Administration's substantial increases in defense spending have done very little, and will do very little, to change the numbers of tanks, guns, and planes in military units that have provided the basis for so many pessimistic assessments of the balance in Europe supports this judgment.

NATO's political and military leaders consistently have allocated scarce economic and demographic resources according to a particular military doctrine. In spite of assaults by dedicated military reformers, this pattern of resource allocation continues.[8] The only conclusion that can be drawn from

---

is only somewhat lower (roughly 113 to 135 billion dollars in 1981), the argument is often advanced that NATO's procurement spending is less efficient than the Pact's. Caspar W. Weinberger, *Annual Report of the Department of Defense, Fiscal Year 1984* (Washington, D.C.: U.S. Government Printing Office, 1983), pp. 21–23. (I have crudely estimated Japan's investment spending and subtracted it from the "NATO plus Japan" figure offered by Weinberger.) These Pact investment figures are probably a little high, as the CIA recently concluded that its previous estimates in this area were wrong, and that Soviet procurement spending did not grow very much from 1976 to 1984. See "Soviets Seen Slowing Pace of Arming," *The Washington Post*, November 20, 1983, p. A-14. The efficiency argument has an element of plausibility, since more Pact production is concentrated in big Soviet plants than NATO production is in any plants. Still, more than a sentence is required. The Pact, indeed the Soviet Union itself, tends to produce several different types of the same weapon simultaneously. For instance, somewhere in the Pact, three or four medium tanks (T-55, 62, 64, and 72) have been in production over the last several years. Moreover, the Pact seems to have as much difficulty as NATO does in writing off unsuccessful weapons. The SU-7 and 9 fighters have never seemed particularly impressive, for instance. Finally, it has long been believed that the Soviet Union is less efficient than the West in most areas of industrial production. Why should the advantages of scale economies totally wipe out the West's historical advantages in managerial skills and production efficiency? If arguments to the effect that NATO's spending superiority is virtually irrelevant to the military balance, indeed that it produces a net military inferiority of substantial proportions, are to be taken seriously, then proponents must make their arguments more thoroughly than they have.
8. Canby, *The Alliance and Europe*, pp. 15–41, offers the clearest critique. Recent events illustrate that not much has actually changed. In the mid-1970s, Senator Sam Nunn of Georgia succeeded in getting the Seventh Army in Europe to trade off some support for combat assets—creating two new combat brigades in Europe. Since then, the U.S. Army has effectively reversed the Senator's reforms. The "Division '86" reorganization has reduced the number of maneuver

this situation is that NATO planners believe that their theory of military outcomes is correct. It may be prudent planning to ask what *could* happen if most of NATO's fundamental decisions about the allocation of its military resources proved to be wrong, and to buy some insurance against this possibility. Absent *convincing* arguments that *most* of NATO's military decisions have been wrong (and I believe that the arguments that have been made fall well short of this standard), these "worst-case" analytical exercises should never stand alone. Rather, they should accompany analyses that capture the expected positive military impact of the fundamental doctrinal assumptions that guide NATO's defense decisions. If they do not, they portray such pessimistic outcomes of a NATO–Pact conflict that they make improvements in conventional capabilities seem pointless, and, if believed by NATO's adversaries, may undermine the conventional component of its deterrent posture. Therefore, estimating the consequences for NATO if its current military doctrine is correct is as important to a comprehensive assessment of the military balance as assessments that assume the superiority of Pact doctrine. Moreover, by disaggregating NATO's relatively inexplicit military doctrine into subcomponents directly related to military outcomes, critical attention can be better focused upon them. Such attention will permit clearer thinking about the adequacy of NATO's current doctrine and may reveal that some aspects seem less plausible than others.

*Factors in Thorough Balance Assessment*

Public discussion of the conventional balance in Europe often focuses on simple force comparisons that fail to include factors that will be vital to the outcome of any real battle. The Secretary of Defense's current Annual Report, for example, asserts that: "Measures of total combat potential, which take into account both numbers and quality of weapons, show that Warsaw Pact forces in the Central Region of Europe have improved by more than 90% from 1965 to the present, while NATO forces advanced by less than 40%. . . . Overall, the shift in the conventional balance has posed new challenges

---

battalions in the European-based divisions from eleven or twelve each, down to ten. Recently, the Army has announced its intention to disband one of the independent brigades based in Europe. The net loss is at least seven maneuver battalions, more than the six battalions contained in the Nunn brigades. Meanwhile, total Army manpower in Germany has risen by nearly 20,000 men.

to our ability to offset the Soviets' quantitative superiority with our qualitative superiority, and has raised serious questions about our ability to halt a Soviet advance."[9] Such simplistic analysis represents only the beginning of a complete threat assessment. At least six other variables must be taken into account before we arrive at a reasonable appraisal of relative battlefield capabilities. Analyses that exclude these factors are incomplete and unrevealing, and provide no meaningful basis for NATO planning. These variables are:

1) RELATIVE MILITARY CAPABILITIES OVER TIME. At what rate can both sides move military forces into the battle area along the inter-German and Czech–West German border? What is the likely combat capability of these forces when training, maintenance, command and control, leadership, and quantity and quality of weaponry are taken into account?

2) THE EFFECT OF TACTICAL AIR FORCES ON THE GROUND BATTLE. Many public assessments of the balance simply leave out "tacair,"[10] and official assessments often give each side equal credit for tactical air effectiveness. In either case, possible advantages that NATO might hold in this area are unaccounted for.

3) FORCE-TO-SPACE (AND HENCE FORCE-TO-FORCE) RATIOS. Implicitly, or explicitly, the adversary is often given credit for an ability not only to close his many divisions to the battle area quickly, but to actually concentrate them on small segments of the front to achieve the very high local offense-to-defense force ratios that could produce breakthroughs. Yet, historically, armies have found that there is a limit to how much force can be concentrated in a given space. If NATO can achieve some level of density of its ground forces across the front, then it should be difficult for the Pact, even with more forces overall, to achieve very high ratios in selected breakthrough sectors.

4) ATTRITION RATES. At what "pace" or "level of violence" will the battle proceed? What kinds of casualties is the adversary willing to take? Does "friction" place some limits on the pace at which the battle can be forced? Historically, short periods of very intense combat can be identified in which

---

9. Caspar W. Weinberger, *Annual Report of the Department of Defense, Fiscal Year 1985* (Washington, D.C.: U.S. Government Printing Office, 1984), p. 24.
10. See, for example, Pat Hillier and Nora Slatkin, *US Ground Forces: Design and Cost Alternatives for NATO and Non-NATO Contingencies* (Washington, D.C.: Congressional Budget Office, 1980), pp. 25–26.

one side or both suffered 10 percent or worse attrition to armored fighting vehicles per day. On the other hand, rarely are battles of this intensity sustained for more than a few days.

5) EXCHANGE RATES. How many destroyed armored fighting vehicles must NATO suffer in order to kill a Pact vehicle? Given the Pact superiority in numbers of major weapons, NATO must achieve favorable exchange rates in order to defeat the Pact. If the exchange rate is not in the 2:1 range in NATO's favor, then the Alliance could find itself in trouble. Favorable exchange rates are not uncommon for defenders fighting on their own ground, particularly if that ground has been prepared with field fortifications, obstacles, and mines. Indeed, an often quoted rule of thumb suggests that the defender can hold at an engaged force ratio of 3:1 in favor of the offense. This would be consistent with a 3:1 exchange rate.

6) ADVANCE RATES. There is a tendency to assign fairly fast advance rates to Pact forces, several tens of kilometers per day in some cases. Some of this tendency can be attributed to Soviet military literature, which *calls for* very high advance rates. There has also been a tendency to simply assume that the high advance rates characteristic of armored warfare's headier historical successes would be replicated by the Soviets. Finally, crediting the Pact with very large forces and very high force ratios in breakthrough sectors tends to produce relatively fast forward movement according to some widely employed dynamic analytical techniques, such as the Lanchester square laws. On the other hand, even with armor pitted against armor, and often with high force ratios, modern mechanized armies have frequently found forward movement against determined defenders to be very difficult.

These six variables can be combined into a model that provides a more realistic approach to comparing forces, for it will include quantitative and other factors in precisely the way the one-dimensional comparisons do not. One such model, known as the "Attrition–FEBA Expansion Model," provides the framework for the subsequent analysis.[11]

This model (a noncomputerized analytical framework) assumes that, at the outset of war, NATO populates the front evenly and tries to hold what forces it can in reserve. The Pact similarly populates the less important sectors of

---

11. The Attrition–FEBA Expansion Model illustrates the stresses imposed on Pact and NATO forces depending on the values assigned to these six variables. FEBA is an acronym for "Forward Edge of the Battle Area." I am deeply indebted to Dr. Richard Kugler, who devised this model, for explaining it to me. The uses to which it has been put in this essay are my responsibility alone.

the front, but concentrates to the extent that it can in the three breakthrough sectors. Also, it is assumed that, as the Pact's breakthrough effort begins to move in NATO's direction, each side tries to move forces into the flanks of the penetrating salient at a density equal to that achieved on the nonbreakthrough parts of the front (see Figure 2).

The model tests the adequacy of each side's forces to meet the demands of these multiple breakthrough battles. Once some assumptions are made about attrition, exchange rates, the role of "tacair," movement rates, and force-to-space ratios, a curve can be generated that shows each side's military requirements starting out with the first day of the war, then rising with the accumulated consequences of daily attrition and the need to populate a FEBA that expands as a function of the forward movement of the breakthrough salients. This requirements curve for each side can be compared to each side's mobilization curve to test the adequacy of its forces. At some point, if the defending forces are inadequate to fulfill their requirements, the defense finds itself having to defend with an ever-shrinking force-to-space ratio—that is, fewer and fewer defensive forces are available to hold the line. The

**Figure 2. Simple Model of a Warsaw Pact Breakthrough Effort**

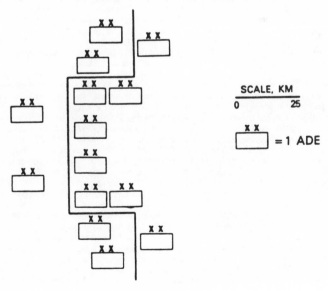

consequence is that the attacker can muster the large local force ratios in his favor that could produce a clean breakthrough. If the defender has not already ordered a general withdrawal to "shorten the front," he may soon suffer a catastrophic rupture of the line, followed by a classical armored exploitation. Since the defender's reserves have been exhausted by the requirement of defending an expanded FEBA, he is not in a position to combat the exploitation. The offense, on the other hand, may find his breakthrough effort stalling as a function of insufficient reserves to sustain high intensity combat at the front of his penetrating salients or to defend the flanks of those salients from the defender's likely counterattacks.[12]

12. The Attrition–FEBA Expansion Model uses Armored Division Equivalents (ADEs) as the common basic unit for comparison: "The ADE is a relative measure of effectiveness of ground forces based on quantity and quality of major weapons. This measure—which is widely used within DOD for ground force comparisons—is an improvement over simple counts of combat units and weapons; however, it does not take into account such factors as ammunition availability, logistical support, training, communications, and morale." Caspar W. Weinberger, *Report on Allied Contributions to the Common Defense* (Washington, D.C.: U.S. Government Printing Office, 1983), p. 36. The ADE scoring system used in this essay is summarized in Mako, *U.S. Ground Forces*, Appendix A, pp. 105–125. For example, a U.S. armored division based in Germany is worth nearly 1.1 ADEs, an average German armored division .72 ADEs, and a Soviet armored division in East Germany .9 ADEs. In terms of real divisions, roughly 110 Soviet and East European formations are included in Figures 3, 4, and 6. Independent regiments, brigades, and divisions equivalent to nearly 50 U.S. or West German divisions are included for NATO. NATO's forces look a little stronger relative to the Pact when forces are measured in ADEs than when selected weapons categories, such as numbers of tanks, are compared. This is because NATO tends to buy a different mix of weapons than the Pact, weapons that receive less attention in public comparisons. It is also worth noting that infantry soldiers do not contribute much to a formation's ADE score. Yet, NATO armies "buy" proportionally more infantry than Pact armies. Infantry soldiers are expensive for Western armies, where manpower is often scarce. Thus, the NATO choice to invest in this area would seem to reflect a different judgment about the importance of infantry to mechanized combat than that of the Pact. This difference may simply be a function of tradition, but it may also reflect a tactical insight. Whatever the reason, much of NATO's combat manpower is not contributing as much to the ADE score as the Pact's manpower. Thus, the ADE system may still fail to capture fully NATO's alternative view of the appropriate mix of weaponry for mechanized formations. See Mako, *U.S. Ground Forces*, p. 37, for an estimate of the length of front an ADE should be able to cover with confidence.

The "Force Needs" curves are derived as follows. In Figure 3, NATO needs one ADE per 25 km of front to establish a defensive line. The Pact needs one ADE per 25 km to tie down NATO's forces in the nonbreakthrough sectors. The Pact manages to concentrate two ADEs per 25 km in each of three 50-km breakthrough sectors for a total of twelve ADEs involved in breakthrough operations. Thus, for 750 km of front, NATO needs thirty ADEs to start; the Pact needs thirty-six to start. If twelve Pact ADEs on breakthrough sectors are willing to accept 10 percent attrition per day, they lose 1.2 ADEs. If the Pact-to-NATO exchange rate is 1.5:1, NATO loses .8 of an ADE to destroy the Pact forces. To generate the total demand for additional forces imposed by the day's action, the forces needed to populate the "expanding FEBA" must be calculated. Here, it is assumed that the Pact manages to advance 5 km per day, producing 30 km of additional FEBA (i.e., two flanks, 5 km long, for each of three penetrations). Both NATO and the Pact need another 1.2 ADEs to populate the flanks of the penetrating sectors. Thus,

This model of hypothetical military confrontation in Central Europe will be used to illustrate the sensitivity of the outcome of such a battle to assumptions that are either consistent with the caricature of Soviet doctrine often used for balance assessments (referred to here as the "Soviet" doctrine) or with the very different military doctrine that appears to guide the way NATO builds its forces (referred to here as the "NATO" doctrine). This model highlights the interrelated effects of several aspects of combat between NATO and the Pact about which there is substantial uncertainty. If we resolve all these uncertainties in favor of the Pact's military doctrine, we can produce the pessimistic portrayal of the outcome of a conventional clash in Europe that has been common over the last decade. On the other hand, if we resolve these uncertainties in favor of NATO's military doctrine, the Alliance appears to be capable of preventing a successful Pact breakthrough.

*Limitations of Model-Building*

Before turning to an analysis of what we learn about the NATO–Warsaw Pact balance by employing the "Attrition–FEBA Expansion" model, it is necessary to note the limitations of this or any model that attempts to approximate the vast and unpredictable complexities of the battlefield.

First, like all models, this one does not generate predictions for the outcome of a war in the Central Region. There are simply too many uncertainties for any model to capture, certainly too many for a model to capture with high confidence. This model illustrates the adequacy of forces of a given capability to cope with particular sets of military demands. The values assigned to the six variables discussed above determine the demands imposed and the amount of capability present to deal with those demands. Thus, the model does not portray a particular battlefield outcome in terms of forces destroyed or territory lost. Rather, it says, "Depending on how well the adversary performs in combat in the likely breakthrough sectors, NATO should or

---

the Pact's total additional force requirement after a day of combat is 2.4 ADEs. NATO's is 2 ADEs. Each side's demand for forces rises at this constant daily rate, producing the slope of the "Force Needs" curves. This same basic procedure is applied in Figure 4. Aside from changing the attrition, exchange, and movement rates, the major change is the factoring in of armored vehicles killed by "tacair." NATO's estimated average daily number of "tacair" armored vehicle kills is converted to an ADE score and subtracted from the total daily attrition that the Pact is willing to accept. NATO must pay to kill the rest of the Pact's ground force loss for the day in the coin of its own ground forces. The damage done by Pact "tacair" is added to this attrition to arrive at NATO's daily loss rate.

should not be able to forestall a catastrophic rupture of its defense line with or without a major withdrawal across the front."

Several additional caveats are in order. The model is a substantial abstraction from reality. Breakthrough sectors are not exactly 50 km wide; attrition does not occur at a steady rate; the offense does not move forward at a steady rate; all offensive efforts are not equally successful, or necessarily successful at all. Moreover, in real combat, divisions do not "fight to the finish" as assumed here; rather, they fight until they are down to 50–70 percent of their initial strength and then they are pulled out of the line for rest and refitting. Additionally, not all the attrition is taken in breakthrough sectors; some occurs on "quiet" sectors of the front. Finally, this model does not make any complicated tactical assumptions. As any student of armored warfare knows, defenders and attackers do not merely attempt to populate the flanks of penetrations. Rather, the defender tries to counterattack into the flanks of the penetration to pinch it off, while the attacker tries to widen the hole in the enemy line.

The model also does not deal well with the fluid warfare that would probably characterize a Pact attack after only a few days of mobilization, one that would likely catch most NATO forces before they were able to form a coherent defense line—in other words, a surprise attack. Such an attack would pit about three dozen Soviet and East German divisions against various U.S., West German, French, and other NATO forces, equivalent in strength to roughly two dozen U.S. mechanized divisions. This fighting would, at least initially, take the form of mobile warfare, in which NATO's small, ready, forward-deployed, covering forces (equivalent to a few armored brigades), supported by some portion of NATO's tactical aircraft, would fight a running battle of delay to enable the rest of NATO's standing forces to form a rough defense line several tens of kilometers back from the inter-German border. The model would only become useful as an analytical tool if and when such a line were established. NATO's forces might also try to mount some quick, sizable counterattacks during this covering force battle, in order to exploit some of the coordination and logistics problems that would surely attend the Pact's efforts to mount an attack with such little preparation time.[13]

---

13. While it is true that, if Polish and Czech Category I divisions joined the Soviet and East German attack, the Pact could outnumber NATO in firepower assets (ADEs) by as much as 2:1, both sides would experience problems getting into action with only a few days of mobilization.

*Assigning Values in the Attrition–FEBA Expansion Model*

These caveats aside, the Attrition–FEBA Expansion Model illustrates the effects of various assumptions about NATO–Warsaw Pact military capabilities and the course of combat on NATO's ability to forestall a Pact breakthrough. But how are we to assign specific values to the variables captured by the model? In principle, one could assign values based upon a historical survey of many battles; or upon an intensive examination of a few battles that one believes to be sufficiently similar to a NATO–Warsaw Pact clash to be instructive; or upon the application of dynamic models; or upon the use of military rules of thumb or planning factors. To some extent, the analysis presented here relies upon all of these methods.

The values of the variables that place demands on the forces—buildup rates, tactical air power, force-to-space ratios, attrition rates, exchange rates, and advance rates—can be set by the user as he or she sees fit. The only

---

To assess relative performance under these circumstances, a thorough comparative assessment of the peacetime readiness for combat of each side's ground and tactical air forces is essential, as well as an assessment of how many days would be required for each to overcome its deficiencies. The circumstantial evidence is that NATO's standing forces are substantially readier for combat than those of the Pact, but data available in the public domain do not permit a high-confidence judgment.

Several pieces of evidence are suggestive, however. Since NATO outspends the Pact, but the Pact "out-invests" NATO, it follows that NATO outspends the Pact on people, operations, training, maintenance, and the like. In 1981, NATO roughly outspent the Pact by 35 percent in these areas, using the CIA dollar model (see footnote 7). Since the Pact is credited with more major items of equipment in active inventory than the West, it follows that its "readiness" spending per unit of equipment is a good deal lower. What is known about Soviet maintenance and training practices supports this judgment. Similarly, assigning NATO some military credit for its greater peacetime manpower committed to the command and support area suggests an initial *capabilities* ratio less favorable to the Pact than is commonly supposed. As Figure 3 illustrates, under this assumption the Pact-to-NATO capabilities ratio after seven days of Pact mobilization and no NATO mobilization is little better than 1.3:1. These points lead one to suspect that NATO is "readier" for combat on a day-to-day basis than the Pact and has already built some cushion into its military structure against the possibility that the Pact will have a seven-day mobilization lead.

In the net, however, the available data tell us little about the speed with which each side could transition to combat. A balance assessment that compares relative NATO and Warsaw Pact peacetime readiness for combat would be an essential tool for testing the Alliance's vulnerability to surprise attack. Short of such a comprehensive assessment, one can only venture the judgment that the facts available do not suggest that the Pact should have high confidence that a short-preparation attack, aimed at suprising NATO, would produce decisive results.

On the readiness of Pact units for short warning attacks, see William W. Kaufmann, "Defense Policy," in Joseph A. Pechman, ed., *Setting National Priorities: Agenda for the 1980s* (Washington, D.C.: Brookings, 1980), p. 300; and William W. Kaufmann, "Nonnuclear Deterrence," in John D. Steinbruner and Leon V. Sigal, eds., *Alliance Security: NATO and the No-First-Use Question* (Washington, D.C.: Brookings, 1983), pp. 59, 70.

requirement is that the reasons for the user's judgments on these matters be explicit. Since these variables affect one another, the user should also work out plausible relationships among them. For instance, it seems unlikely that low attrition rates and high offense-defense exchange rates would produce much retreat by the defender.[14] In applying the model, variables were set according to the two different doctrines employed by the Alliance: the "Soviet" doctrine often used for balance assessment, and the "NATO" doctrine that in fact seems to drive NATO's force planning.

BUILDUP RATES

Estimates of relative Pact and NATO military buildup rates include two areas of uncertainty that strongly affect possible military outcomes. For the Pact, the major question is the speed with which partially manned, low-readiness Soviet and East European divisions can be mobilized, brought to a standard of training that will permit them to operate effectively in combat, and moved to the front. For NATO, the major question is whether or not the Alliance's propensity to allocate greater manpower to command and support than the Pact produces any military benefit.

The standard Pact buildup curve usually employed in public analyses was first published by the Department of Defense (DoD) in 1976.[15] Although the published chart contained no actual numbers on its time and force axes, subsequent published information can be used to reconstruct those numbers. This information is provided in Figure 3. Adding this to knowledge of how the ADE scoring system worked at that time allows one to estimate which Pact divisions were included by the DoD.[16] Unless the DoD curve included

---

14. This is in sharp contrast to the most widely used dynamic analytical technique—the Lanchester Square Law. The equations that capture the Law do explicitly relate force ratios and attrition rates, once some assumptions are made about the number of forces engaged in a battle and their effectiveness. An exchange rate can be derived from the calculation. Analysts have also derived movement equations consistent with the Law. It is important to note, however, that those who use the equations must make several judgments about the values assigned to the key variables—particularly the forces included in the engagement, their effectiveness, and the relationship between the attrition suffered by the defender and his propensity to withdraw. In that sense, the Lanchester technique is nearly as dependent upon the analyst's "military judgment" as is the model suggested here. For a clear explanation of the Lanchester Laws and how to use them, see William W. Kaufmann, "The Arithmetic of Force Planning," in Steinbruner and Sigal, eds., *Alliance Security*, pp. 208–216.
15. U.S. Department of Defense, *A Report to Congress on U.S. Conventional Reinforcements to NATO* (Washington, D.C.: U.S. Government Printing Office, 1976), Chart IV-1, p. IV-3, cited in Richard K. Betts, *Surprise Attack: Lessons for Defense Planning* (Washington, D.C.: Brookings, 1982), p. 182.
16. William P. Mako, *U.S. Ground Forces and the Defense of Central Europe* (Washington, D.C.: Brookings, 1983), pp. 108–125.

**Figure 3. A NATO Defeat: NATO/Warsaw Pact Military Capabilities and Requirements Over Time if NATO's Doctrine Is Incorrect**

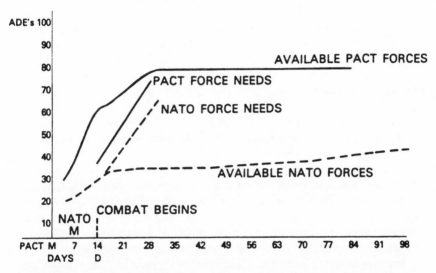

SOURCE: Derived from US Department of Defense, OSD, "A Report to Congress on U.S. Conventional Reinforcements to NATO" (June, 1976), chart IV-1 (cited in Richard K. Betts, *Surprise Attack: Lessons For Defense Planning* [Washington: The Brookings Institution, 1982], p. 182); William Mako, *U.S. Ground Forces and the Defense of Central Europe* (Washington: The Brookings Institution, 1983), pp. 42, 134; and author's estimates.

Assumptions Summary:
— No Pact build-up delay for post-mobilization training
— No NATO credit for greater command and support efforts
— One ADE per twenty-five km for NATO; Pact puts one ADE per twenty-five km in minor sectors, two ADEs per twenty-five km in breakthrough sectors. NATO needs thirty ADEs to start; Pact needs thirty-six to start
— Daily Pact attrition in breakthrough sectors—10 percent
— Daily NATO attrition in breakthrough sectors—13 percent
— Exchange Rate - - Pact:NATO 1.5:1
— Pact advance rate in breakthrough sectors, five km/day
— Each side's tactical air force and ground based air defenses neutralize the effectiveness of the other's air force on the ground battle

Category I divisions from the Far East (not often done to my knowledge), this estimate projected the arrival of roughly nineteen Category II divisions to the battle area by M+14 and thirteen to fourteen Category III divisions by M+21. Nine low-readiness Czech and Polish Category III divisions were considered available by M+7. While the assembly and delivery of these forces in such a short time is plausible, most public assessments of the combat capability of these divisions under conditions of rapid mobilization and deployment suggest that they would not be particularly effective. Yet, assigning these divisions equivalent combat capability to Category I divisions is common practice in many analyses of the NATO–Pact balance.[17]

Published estimates indicate that the Soviets (and their East European allies) would likely subject these mobilized divisions to intensive refresher training before committing them to combat: thirty to forty-five days for Category IIs, ninety days or more for Category IIIs.[18] There are two major reasons for such estimates. First, Soviet Category II and III divisions are manned at "cadre" strength, perhaps an average of 50 percent for the former and 25 percent for the latter. The cadre of these divisions are not all seasoned professionals. Perhaps one-half or more are themselves conscripts, serving their obligatory two-year term of service. Some are in their first six months of service and, like many Soviet conscripts, receive basic training in their combat units. Since these divisions have quite a bit of equipment, much conscript time is spent in basic vehicle maintenance, not in field training. Similarly, because the divisions are only partially manned, thorough training of officers and enlisted men at all levels is not always possible.

Second, upon mobilization, these divisions would be "fleshed out" with reservists that have completed their two-year term of service and returned to civilian life. Unlike U.S. National Guard or Israeli reservists, these people do not know each other. Most receive no annual refresher training. Because of the many generations of equipment in the Soviet inventory, mobilized reservists may receive equipment different from that with which they originally trained. Category II and III divisions seldom call up large numbers of conscripts for major exercises.[19] This is in sharp contrast to U.S. or Israeli reservists who receive thirty to forty-five days of individual and unit training

---

17. This is effectively what was done in the DoD 1976 buildup curve and in the CBO buildup estimates in 1980. It is also the implication of most of the public "bean-count" comparisons of NATO and Warsaw Pact holdings of various kinds of military equipment. The 1982 edition of the Luns Report is a good example: Joseph Luns, Secretary General of NATO, *NATO and the Warsaw Pact: Force Comparisons* (Brussels: NATO, 1982).
18. Irving Heymont and Melvin Rosen, "Foreign Army Reserve Systems," *Military Review*, Vol. 53, No. 3 (March 1973), pp. 84–85; David C. Isby, *Weapons and Tactics of the Soviet Army* (London: Jane's, 1981), p. 28; Jeffrey Record, *Sizing Up the Soviet Army* (Washington, D.C.: Brookings, 1975), pp. 21–22.
19. On the peacetime organization and training of low-readiness Category II and III divisions, see testimony of the Defense Intelligence Agency in U.S. Congress, Joint Economic Committee, *Allocation of Resources in the Soviet Union and China—1981*, Hearings before the Subcommittee on International Trade, Finance, and Security Economics, 97th Congress, 1st session, part 7, 1982, p. 199.

per year with the people and the units that they will accompany into battle. It is worth noting that, even given this level of annual activity, Israeli reservists were not particularly effective during the first few days of the 1973 war. Moreover, close observers of the Guard and U.S. Army Reserve suggest that a month or more of postmobilization refresher training is required.[20] The long postmobilization training periods suggested above reflect these shortcomings.

My estimate of Soviet postmobilization training is more favorable to the Soviet Union than those cited above. The mobilization curve in Figure 4 gives the Category IIs thirty days of training and the Category IIIs sixty days. It appears that the DoD mobilization curve does not bring U.S. National Guard divisions to the front until M+60. Allowing thirty days for mobilization and shipment to Europe, these troops could have thirty days to train, if arrangements had been made in advance to facilitate this, so that they would not be further delayed.[21]

This slow Pact buildup stands in sharp contrast to the curves published by DoD in 1976 and used in several subsequent studies. These projections of a relatively fast Soviet buildup rate are consistent with a "Soviet theory" of victory, i.e., the collection of hardware is what counts, not the human organization. Moreover, the standard Pact buildup models seem to credit the Soviets with a willingness to expend lives with great profligacy. This may be true, but credit should then be taken for greater Western effectiveness against these divisions. Finally, fast buildup rates for low-readiness Soviet divisions often cloak a hidden assumption: the Pact does in fact take a month or more to retrain these divisions, but Western intelligence misses this extraordinary activity, Western leaders prove too frightened to take any military response to such actions, or consensus takes too long to build. Given the tremendous publicity that attended Soviet efforts to ready *some* divisions for action against Poland in 1981 and the recent public disclosures of the amount of technical warning Western intelligence had of Soviet preparations for the

20. Mako, *U.S. Ground Forces*, p. 83, quotes Martin Binkin's estimate of fourteen weeks to prepare a U.S. reserve division for combat, but judges this estimate to be pessimistic.
21. I have not added any delay for roundout battalions and brigades assigned to fill out active U.S. Army divisions. Nor has any special delay been factored in for refresher training for German Territorial Army Units, which are somewhat similar to U.S. Guard and Reserve units. Since the Pact is not in a position to attack before M+30 and the Germans are fighting at home, these units would probably have time for some refresher training before commitment to battle. Finally, the Army's XVIIIth Airborne Corps, effectively three divisions and their support units worth roughly 3.4 ADEs, are assumed to be tied up in a non-European contingency. See Mako, *U.S. Ground Forces*, p. 133.

**Figure 4.** A Successful NATO Defense: NATO/Warsaw Pact Military Capabilities and Requirements Over Time if NATO's Doctrine Is Correct

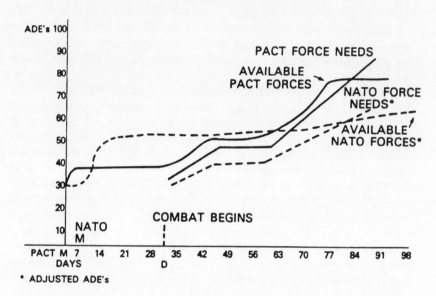

\* ADJUSTED ADE's

SOURCE: Derived from US Department of Defense, OSD, "A Report to Congress on U.S. Conventional Reinforcements to NATO" (June, 1976), chart IV-1, p. IV-3 (cited in Richard K. Betts, *Surprise Attack: Lessons For Defense Planning* [Washington: The Brookings Institution, 1982], p. 182); William Mako, *U.S. Ground Forces and the Defense of Central Europe* (Washington: The Brookings Institution, 1983), pp. 42, 134; and author's estimates.

Assumptions Summary:
— Category II divisions delayed an additional thirty days, Category III divisions sixty days for post-mobilization training
— NATO ADE strength is multiplied by 1.5 for command and support efforts
— One adjusted ADE per twenty-five km for NATO; Pact puts one ADE per twenty-five km on minor sectors, 1.5 ADE per twenty-five km on breakthrough sectors. NATO needs thirty adjusted ADEs to start (twenty real ADEs). Pact needs thirty-three to start.
— Daily attrition, Phase I—Breakthrough Sectors
  Pact 7.5 percent; 57 percent of casualties caused by NATO tacair
  NATO\* 4.3 percent; 45 percent of casualties caused by Pact tacair
— Daily attrition, Phase 2—Breakthrough Sectors
  Pact 7.5 percent; 27 percent of casualties caused by NATO tacair
  NATO\* 5.8 percent; 29 percent of casualties caused by Pact tacair
— Pact: NATO exchange rate 2:1
— Pact advance rate 2km/day
\*NATO attrition is assessed against the adjusted ADE score

invasion of Czechoslovakia in 1968 and the Afghan invasion of 1979 (both smaller affairs than that projected here), the argument that NATO leaders will not know about Soviet preparations seems suspect.[22] If American and European planners believe that the West could lose a war because its political leaders are likely to be too concerned with provocation to order mobilization or too militarily ill-informed to understand that NATO must compete with Soviet partial mobilization efforts (i.e., refresher training for Category IIs and IIIs), then the task is to educate the leaders. Finally, it may be possible to design partial mobilization efforts for NATO that would be sufficiently unprovocative to win political approval.

My NATO buildup curves, both the standard and adjusted versions, rely heavily on the buildup schedule developed by William Mako,[23] whose schedule is roughly consistent with the curve published by DoD in 1976. The major difference between the two is that DoD's criteria for readiness seem to be less stringent than Mako's. Like DoD and unlike Mako, I assume that all forward-based NATO forces are effectively "ready" on M-Day, even though this clearly simplifies what must surely be more complicated reasoning on the part of DoD. The principal change, however, has been to assign an effectiveness multiplier to the NATO ADE score. This multiplier is not assigned for weapons quality, which is ostensibly handled in the ADE methodology, nor for personnel quality, which is difficult to measure. The multiplier is simply applied for greater numbers of people performing command, intelligence-reconnaissance, maintenance, and supply functions.

Nearly ten years ago, in an essay that remains one of the more useful primers on differences between NATO and Warsaw Pact strategy, tactics, and organization, Steven Canby highlighted NATO's emphasis on the command and support areas.[24] He devised a system for comparing the total number of combat, combat support, and combat service support people, inside and outside the divisional organization, needed to generate a fighting force of a given size. While his numbers are somewhat dated, they are good enough for our purposes here. Using an average West European division as base, Canby estimated that the NATO allies needed roughly 40,000 men to field and support a given number of individuals in front-line combat roles in

---

22. Kaufmann, "Defense Policy," in Pechman, ed., *Setting National Priorities*, p. 300, estimates that it takes the Soviets months, rather than weeks, even to organize a small military operation.
23. Mako, *U.S. Ground Forces*, p. 134.
24. Canby, *The Alliance and Europe*, pp. 3–4, 10, and footnote 10.

wartime. Given prevailing Soviet practices, the Pact would have only allocated 21,500 people to the same task. A similar comparison was made for peacetime U.S. and Soviet divisions, which yielded 41,000 for the United States and 21,500 for the Soviets. Thus, on the average, it took NATO roughly twice as many people to field a front-line force of a given size as it did the Pact. Because Canby's methodology is a bit opaque, it is worth looking at the current figures in a somewhat different way as a check. Adapting figures from the *Military Balance 1983–84*, we see that the United States now allocates roughly 34,000 men *per ADE* in Germany, the German Army 31,000, and the Soviet Army 24,000 per ADE deployed in Eastern Europe. This yields an average peacetime NATO superiority of 1.33:1. The wartime superiority would probably grow in the direction suggested by Canby, since much of the American and German reserve structure is devoted to support. Given the large number of divisions that the Soviets are said to man on mobilization, it seems unlikely that their support-to-combat ratio would grow at quite the same rate. Finally, a comparison of the organizational charts of current first-class Soviet and U.S. divisions shows that *within* the divisional organization, the United States allocates about 1.5 times as many people to command and support per ADE as the Pact. These numbers and ratios are all, of course, quite rough, but they are indicative of how NATO allocates its personnel and its financial resources.[25]

Canby, of course, argues that whatever the difference, the West should receive no special credit for these assets. Rather, by organizing their forces to achieve greater initial firepower, the Pact will simply swamp NATO's smaller forces before these support assets become useful. In this formulation, these support assets are seen primarily as "long-war" capabilities. In spite of Canby's arguments and substantial pressure from such reformers as Senator Sam Nunn, little has changed in the Central Region since Canby's analysis. Instead, the U.S. Army has managed to reverse many of the "tooth-to-tail" reforms imposed on it by the Nunn amendment, and NATO's military leaders remain committed to rich command and support assets. Since most public assessments of the military outcome of an East–West war do not project a particularly long NATO effort, one can only deduce that NATO's military leaders believe that these command and support assets would play a signif-

---

25. See Kaufmann, "Nonnuclear Deterrence," pp. 55–58. On Soviet and U.S. divisions, see Defense Intelligence Agency, *Soviet Divisional Organizational Guide* (Washington, 1982); and U.S. Army Armor School, *U.S. Army Armor Reference Data*, Vols. I and III (Fort Knox, Ky., 1981).

icant role in a short war as well. A careful examination of the history of armored warfare does reveal that the supply and maintenance of mechanized forces have been a consistent problem, although historical accounts do not reveal much about the details of the appropriate combat-to-support ratio.

In sum, as a function of NATO's efforts in the command and support areas, a multiplier of 1.5 is applied to NATO's ADE score to take into account the increased combat effectiveness that NATO's military leaders presumably expect from their efforts.[26] (The median between the high ratio of 2:1 and the low of 1.35:1 would be 1.67:1. Thus, a 1.5 effectiveness multiplier seems a conservative way to take credit for NATO's greater support efforts.) Balance assessments that do not try to account for these factors are implicitly admitting the correctness of Canby's arguments. If this is true, then NATO must ask itself whether it can afford to compete with the Soviet Union if it does not make efforts to change its structure. Consistent with the respect for Soviet organization implicit in balance assessments that do not take credit for NATO's support and command efforts, NATO should imitate its adversary. If, however, NATO's military professionals remain committed to doing

---

26. The Lanchester Square Law provides an argument for taking some credit for NATO's superior personnel investment in the command and support areas. The law captures, arithmetically, the effect of concentration on military outcomes. Put simply, as most military commanders have long realized, the side that manages to *concentrate* more forces on the actual battle will achieve a substantial advantage. The question is not who has more, which some users of the law seem to believe, but who concentrates more. Concentration should depend not merely on the availability of weapons, but also on the ability to find the places where they can best be employed and get forces there in fighting shape. Achieving concentration should, in short, depend on an appropriate balance between "concentrators" and "concentratees." NATO views about this balance clearly differ from Soviet views. If NATO is right, then it should be able to make the Lanchester process work better for its "smaller" force than the Pact should for its larger force.

Taking credit for support assets provides an avenue for including NATO's war reserve stocks, equipment held outside of units to replace damaged vehicles that cannot be repaired in the forward areas. NATO tries to keep its divisions in combat at full strength in contrast to the Pact intention of pulling out and replacing the whole division. While the European allies do not have large war reserve stocks, U.S. stocks, particularly of tanks, seem to be quite large. The U.S. Army is currently credited with roughly 12,000 usable tanks in its inventory. Harold Brown, *Annual Report of the Department of Defense, Fiscal Year 1982* (Washington, D.C.: U.S. Government Printing Office, 1981). Yet, by a generous counting procedure, there are barely enough armored units in the Army to swallow up 7,000 of them, leaving 5,000 as war reserve stocks. These 5,000 tanks are worth nearly six ADEs and are never counted in balance assessments. One of the purposes of the U.S. support structure is to keep these tanks flowing into units so that they can remain near their designated strength and to keep damaged tanks flowing to the rear where they can be fixed. It is difficult to predict how long this stockpile would last in war. The average Israeli "total loss" rate in 1973 (tanks utterly destroyed) was about a half percent per day of the total original force. At this rate, the U.S. stockpile could keep its nominal 7,000 tank operational force at full strength for four months of relatively serious combat.

business in their traditional fashion, then they should be asked to explain and to take account of the benefits that they derive that the Soviets do not.

THE EFFECTIVENESS OF TACTICAL AIR POWER
Frequently, public assessments of the Central Region military balance do not account for the possible influence of NATO's tactical air forces ("tacair") on the ground battle.[27] NATO, however, allocates substantial funds to aircraft with ground attack capability and to special ground attack ordnance. My analysis takes credit for NATO's tactical air investments in a simple and straightforward way, not to show how well they *will* do, but to show the kinds of outcomes that might be produced if they do as well as NATO's persistent investments in the area seem to imply.

While public comparisons of relative NATO and Pact "tacair" investments are not available, one may deduce from several facts that NATO probably makes a greater effort than the Pact. American spending on "tacair" has nearly equaled the Soviets' over the last ten years.[28] U.S. allies, who themselves seem to spend a good deal on "tacair," contribute substantially more to NATO's total defense spending than the East European states do to Pact total spending.[29] As Joshua Epstein has argued, Pact efforts in the training and support of its "tacair" assets are significantly less than those of the United States.[30] It seems unlikely that a different pattern would prevail in overall NATO–Pact comparisons.

NATO has made a substantial financial effort to produce aircraft and weapons devoted specifically to close air support (CAS). With the exception of the still small number of "Frogfoot" aircraft, Pact tactical fighter-bombers are not well suited to this mission. Moreover, the Pact seems more concerned with attacking NATO's tactical nuclear assets and airbases than with using "tacair" to affect the ground battle. Moreover, Epstein demonstrates that, even given assumptions about Soviet Frontal Aviation's performance that

---

27. See Hillier and Slatkin, *U.S. Ground Forces*; Mako, *U.S. Ground Forces*; and Dan Gans, "Fight Outnumbered and Win," Part 1, *Military Review*, Vol. 60, No. 12 (December 1980), pp. 31–45.
28. Central Intelligence Agency, National Foreign Assessment Center, *Soviet and US Defense Activities, 1970–79: A Dollar Cost Comparison*, SR 80-1000J (Washington, D.C., January 1980), p. 10.
29. IISS, *Military Balance, 1983–1984*, pp. 125–126; and U.S. Department of Defense, *The FY 1984 DOD Program for Research, Development and Acquisitions*, Statement by Honorable Richard De-Lauer, Undersecretary of Defense for Research and Engineering, 98th Congress, 1st session, March 2, 1983.
30. Joshua Epstein, *Measuring Military Power: The Soviet Air Threat to Europe* (Princeton: Princeton University Press, 1984), pp. 96–98.

are relatively favorable to the Warsaw Pact (e.g., three sorties per day), the Pact would probably only complete 44 percent of its counternuclear, counterairfield missions before virtually exhausting itself in the middle of the sixth day of combat. A recent Brookings study offers a similar estimate of the Pact's likely performance.[31]

My assessment of relative NATO–Warsaw Pact tactical air influence on the ground battle jumps off from the preceding two assessments. Simply put, NATO and the Pact are given credit for their known CAS assets—attack helicopters and fighter aircraft specifically configured for antiarmor operations in close proximity to friendly ground forces.[32] Thus, this analysis is conservative in that it does not try to account for the contribution that hundreds of other NATO aircraft configured for bombing missions could make to the ground battle. Effectiveness, sortie rate, and attrition rate values are assigned to these aircraft, to produce an estimate of how many armored vehicle kills each side could achieve in Phase I and Phase II of the "NATO doctrine" case.[33] (See Table 1.) The principal tactical assumption is that both sides allocate all their CAS assets to the breakthrough sectors. This is unlikely to be fully achieved in practice, but it is a sensible way to use the aircraft.

For the first phase of the conflict, NATO is given credit for U.S. reinforcing aircraft. Neither the Pact nor NATO is given credit for reinforcing attack helicopters, since unclassified numbers on attack helicopters are not very reliable.[34]

---

31. Ibid., Appendix C, pp. 243–245, especially Table C-9, p. 245; Kaufmann, "Nonnuclear Deterrence," pp. 76–77.
32. For NATO, I count 300 A10s, 100 A7s (with GE 30mm gun pods), 100 German Alphajets, and 400-odd armed helicopters. For the Pact, I count 800-odd armed helicopters; see footnote 34. The rest of NATO and Pact aircraft are presumed to be absorbed in a hugh air battle consisting of air-to-air, airfield suppression, and SAM suppression activities. The sum total of all these efforts allows each side's CAS assets to operate at the relatively high attrition and low effectiveness assumed in this analysis. It is my judgment that these assumptions are favorable to the Pact.
33. The "tacair" formula is straightforward. For each sortie the total number of aircraft leaving base is multiplied by .95 (i.e., 5 percent attrition) and then by the kill rate to come up with a total kill per sortie. Those aircraft that have survived the sortie (i.e., 95 percent) are run through the equation for the next sortie. Second sortie survivors are run through the third, etc.
34. The numbers used are drawn from the Luns Report (1982) and include combat helicopters in the region in peacetime. The numbers are somewhat favorable to the Pact; the report is favorable to the Pact across the board. See Luns, *NATO and the Warsaw Pact (1982)*, Figure 2. This report assigns 400 attack helicopters to NATO and 700 to the Pact in peacetime. IISS, *Military Balance, 1983–84*, p. 139, assigns 805 to NATO and 786 to the Pact. IISS includes French assets, while the Luns Report does not. Which Pact helicopters are being counted in both sources is unclear. I have given NATO credit for only 400 armed helicopters and the Pact 800 for the sake of conservatism.

**Table 1.  The Tactical Air Efforts**

|  | Phase I | | Phase II | |
|---|---|---|---|---|
|  | **NATO** | **Pact** | **NATO** | **Pact** |
| **Aircraft** | | | | |
| **Fixed Wing** | 500 | 0 | 350 | 0 |
| **Helicopter** | 400 | 800 | 250 | 800 |
| **Total** | 900 | 800 | 600 | 800 |
| **Attrition** | 5% | 5% | 5% | 5% |
| **Kills/Sortie** | .5 | .25 | .5 | .25 |
| **Sortie Rate Per Day** | 2 | 1 | 1.5 | 1 |

In the second phase of the battle, the Pact is permitted to replace all losses incurred during the first phase (400 helicopters), and NATO is allowed to replace two-thirds (400 helicopters and fighters) of its Phase I losses of 600 aircraft. On the NATO side, this would be achieved by bringing in some of the remaining 500 attack helicopters in U.S. operational units, by stripping helicopters and aircraft from the training base and maintenance pipeline (currently planned), and by battle-damage repair.[35]

The 5 percent attrition per sortie assumed here is high by historical standards for Western air forces.[36] One-quarter to one-half a vehicle killed per sortie is in the historical range of performance. The West has been assigned a higher kill rate primarily on the grounds of superior weaponry. The General

---

35. This level of replacement is consistent with the number of CAS aircraft candidates remaining in both sides' inventories. For example, although the United States has 476 A10s and 700 Cobra attack helicopters in units, it appears to have roughly 687 A10s and 1,000 Cobras in inventory. See relevant sections of *Annual Report of the Department of Defense*, Fiscal Years 1978, 1982, 1983, and 1984 for the sources of these numbers. The difference between what is in units and what is in the inventory is presumably used for training or is in the maintenance pipeline. Plans exist to tap these sources in wartime. The Pact is permitted its level of replacement to account, at least in part, for the very large number of "armed" helicopter assets credited to them by several sources. For instance, although IISS only seems to count the Soviet Union's 800-odd MI24s of all kinds as attack helicopters, it also suggests that some portion of the 1,500 MI8 troop transports assigned to the Soviet Air Force should be considered as armed. This is consistent with *Jane's All the World's Aircraft, 1982–83* (London: Jane's, 1983) entries for both helicopters.

36. Congressional Budget Office, *Navy Budget Issues for FY 1980* (Washington, D.C.: Congressional Budget Office, 1979), pp. 98, 102–103. U.S. Navy attrition over North Vietnam between 1965 and 1973 was .1 percent. Israeli Air Force attrition during the 1973 war was .8 percent. Israeli A4s, whose missions most closely approximated NATO's CAS missions, suffered 1.5 percent. Historically, U.S. air commanders were willing to accept sustained 5 percent attrition during World War II and Korea, if the mission was perceived to be important.

Electric 30mm antiarmor cannon on U.S. fixed wing aircraft and the TOW antitank guided missile on U.S. attack helicopters should be more effective than the Swatter missile which most Soviet attack helicopters still carry according to public sources.[37] Finally, NATO is assigned a higher sortie rate on the grounds of greater maintenance efforts and greater ruggedness of aircraft over helicopters. During the battle's second phase, NATO's sortie rate is lowered on the assumption that spare parts inventories will be reduced, and wear and tear on the aircraft will have made them more subject to failure. The Pact's sortie rate remains constant.

The damage in armored fighting vehicles destroyed can be calculated and converted to an average number of ADEs destroyed per day for a fourteen-day campaign in Phase I and a twenty-one-day campaign in Phase II of the battle. (An ADE equals roughly 1,200 combat vehicles, including self-propelled and towed artillery weapons.) For ease of comparison, the total number of ADEs destroyed in the campaign is divided by the total number of days in the campaign to come up with an average number. (See Table 2.) This obscures the fact that "tacair" would probably do better early in the campaign than later, when high aircraft losses will have cut the number of sorties being flown per day.

Taking credit for NATO's investments in CAS aircraft and armaments as well as training and maintenance suggests that these assets could make a substantial contribution to stopping Pact breakthrough efforts, if properly employed. NATO's "tacair" destroys roughly nine Pact ADEs in five weeks of combat, while Pact "tacair" gets credit for destroying roughly four NATO ADEs. Put another way, NATO "tacair" destroys Pact ground forces equivalent to nearly one-half of all Soviet forces stationed in East Germany in peacetime.

**Table 2. The Tactical Air Contribution**

|  | Phase I | | Phase II | |
|---|---|---|---|---|
|  | **NATO** | **Pact** | **NATO** | **Pact** |
| **Sorties Flown** | 13,000 | 7,000 | 9,200 | 10,000 |
| **AFVs Killed** | 6,500 | 1,950 | 4,600 | 2,500 |
| **ADEs Killed** | 5.4 | 1.6 | 3.8 | 2.1 |
| **Average Enemy Killed Per Day** | .4 | .12 | .18 | .1 |

37. *Jane's All the World's Aircraft*, MI8 and MI24 entries.

FORCE-TO-SPACE RATIOS

How much force does a defender require to hold a given sector? How much force can the attacker concentrate in a given breakthrough sector? The "Soviet" and "NATO" cases illustrate different assumptions about these values. A close examination of the admittedly sparse information on these questions turns up an important insight. Simply put, given the number of forces that NATO already has, it may be extremely difficult for the Pact to achieve the high offense-to-defense ratios (greater than 3:1) that experience suggests are necessary to achieve breakthroughs.

Among those who have discussed the preferred defensive force-to-space ratio, the prevailing assumption seems to be that roughly one ADE is required to hold every 25 km of front. Mako settles on this figure, although he quotes some retired U.S. officers to the effect that a U.S. armored or mechanized division, armed with modern weaponry (worth perhaps 1.1–1.3 ADEs), should be able to hold 30 to 60 km of front (i.e., as little as .5 or as much as one ADE could be needed to defend 25 km).[38] If William Kaufmann's methodology for assessing divisional firepower is converted to ADEs, he appears to assume that between .75 and one ADE would be required to hold 25 km of front.[39] David Isby suggests that the Soviets would assign one Motor Rifle Division (.66–.76 ADE) to defend 25 km of front.[40] The appropriate "conservative figure" would then appear to be one ADE per 25 km of front.

Because NATO has only thirty real ADEs at Pact M+14 (Pact D-Day), a literal application of this conservative planning factor plays into the hands of the Pact armored offensive, as many students of armored warfare have observed. In effect, many NATO forces would be pinned down, "conservatively" defending sectors that are not the victims of major breakthrough efforts, while those that are the victims would find themselves short of the tactical and operational reserves that might stop a breakthrough from happening or restore the situation if it occurred.

---

38. Mako, *U.S. Ground Forces*, pp. 36–37, especially footnote 18. See, also, the most widely quoted discussion of the defender's force-to-space requirements: B.H. Liddell Hart, *Deterrent or Defense: A Fresh Look at the West's Military Position* (New York: Praeger, 1960), pp. 97–109. Liddell Hart observed that the defender's force-to-space requirement, measured in manpower in divisions, has been dropping in this century. He also observed that the level of quantitative superiority that the attacker must enjoy if he is to achieve a successful breakthrough has been rising. Citing U.S. and British experience in World War II, he noted that superiorities between 3:1 and 5:1 were required, with some attacks failing at ratios of 10:1.
39. Kaufmann, "Nonnuclear Deterrence," pp. 62, 210.
40. Isby, *Weapons and Tactics of the Soviet Army*, pp. 20, 38.

In the "NATO" case, operational reserves become available as a function of the effectiveness multiplier assigned to NATO ADEs. This case assumes one *adjusted* ADE per 25 km, .66 of the real ADE.[41] The command, reconnaissance, and logistics assets assigned to NATO forces should affect the amount of space that they can control. For example, the ammunition-handling capability of an average U.S. or West German division permits a far greater daily ammunition expenditure than that of a comparable Soviet division. Supply and maintenance assets should also affect the overall attrition that NATO divisions suffer, since these assets should provide NATO a superior capability to repair damaged vehicles or replace them from war reserve stocks.

This assumption leaves NATO defending within the one-half to one ADE per 25 km range cited above and is consistent with Isby's estimates for Soviet defending forces. Thus, NATO puts two-thirds of its forces in the line (with each division in the line holding a small tactical reserve), and one-third of its forces in operational reserve. This is lower than Liddell Hart's prescription that one-half of the defender's forces be held in reserve, higher than the one-fourth that appears to be NATO's intention, and equal to the one-third figure attributed to Canby.[42]

There is even less in the open literature on the question of appropriate *offensive* force-to-space ratios. How much force can the attacker pack into a given segment of the front in his efforts to achieve the very high force-to-force ratios that are often thought to be the key to the successful armored breakthrough? In general, the impression has been created that the achievement of very high force-to-space ratios is relatively simple and that the adversary certainly intends to do so.

---

41. This force-to-space ratio is substantially higher than that enjoyed by the Israeli 7th armored brigade in 1973, which successfully defended roughly 20 km of front on the Golan Heights with less than one-quarter of an ADE, no major reserves (other than the brigade's organic reserve), and virtually no CAS. This brigade was outnumbered 4:1 or worse. This was not, of course, a comfortable position, and Colonel Janush Ben-Gal (now Major General retired) was aided by prepared positions and Syrian unimaginativeness. Even with these advantages, the brigade was nearly exhausted after 2.5 days. Its performance, however, is exemplary of the impressive defensive potential of modern armored forces. At least 300 tanks plus other armored fighting vehicles were damaged, destroyed, or captured by the 7th Brigade. See Trevor N. Dupuy, *Elusive Victory: The Arab-Israeli Wars, 1947–1974* (New York: Harper and Row, 1978), pp. 437–461. By comparison to the 7th Brigade, the standard suggested here would leave a U.S. or West German division with two brigades forward, each on 19 km fronts, backed by one brigade in reserve. In the breakthrough sectors, such a force would receive substantial air support and could be reinforced rather quickly by reserves that are withheld in the "NATO" case.
42. Mako, *U.S. Ground Forces*, pp. 37–38.

While it is true that Soviet doctrinal literature calls for very high offense-to-defense ratios in breakthrough sectors, on the order of 4–6:1 in tanks and artillery, the available evidence on how the Pact would set up a breakthrough attack casts doubt on its ability to achieve such ratios easily. These high ratios may be achievable, but they will likely occur on only a few very small 4 or 5 km segments of the front.[43] Thus, successful attacks in these sectors would take the form of narrow "wedges" driven into the NATO line. Whether or not these "wedges" would produce a catastrophic failure of the defense line depends upon the defending division commander's ability to bring tactical reserves quickly to bear on the engagement. He has these reserves available, so the question may ultimately be one of competent leadership.

Figure 5 illustrates the kinds of major efforts the Soviets seem to envision. It appears that a four-division Soviet or Pact Army and some attached Army and Front artillery would be tasked against a 50 km breakthrough sector, like that assumed in the model. Apparently, the Soviets would put two divisions forward and hold two in reserve. Other estimates suggest either slightly wider Army sectors; three divisions forward, and only one in reserve; or a five-division Army. To capture the full potential utility attributed to the divisions in reserve, the "Soviet" case factors this entire force into the battle for every day of combat, roughly four ADEs.

In the "NATO" case, the Pact is assumed to be slightly less successful at concentration than assumed above; it achieves only three ADEs in engaged combat power on any 50 km of front. This partially reflects the Soviets' apparent intention to hold a substantial part of its force in reserve. It also reflects the difficulty of managing such a high concentration of capabilities in such a small area. For instance, during November of 1944, in its attempt to reach the Roer River, the U.S. XIX Corps attempted a concentration similar to that assumed by the Soviet case. The commanders on the scene found their position to be very cramped, and it was necessary to withhold one-half of the armored division for several days until more space could be opened by the Corps' advance. It is also worth remembering that this concentration was achieved under conditions of total air superiority, and against an enemy that was short of ammunition and thus could afford little harassing artillery fire.[44]

---

43. See, for example, Isby, *Weapons and Tactics of the Soviet Army*, p. 38.
44. While one example is scarcely definitive, the XIX Corps' attempt to concentrate one armored and two infantry divisions plus fifteen-odd nondivisional artillery batteries on a 16 km front is

**Figure 5. Breakthrough Attack Deployments (Tank Units)**

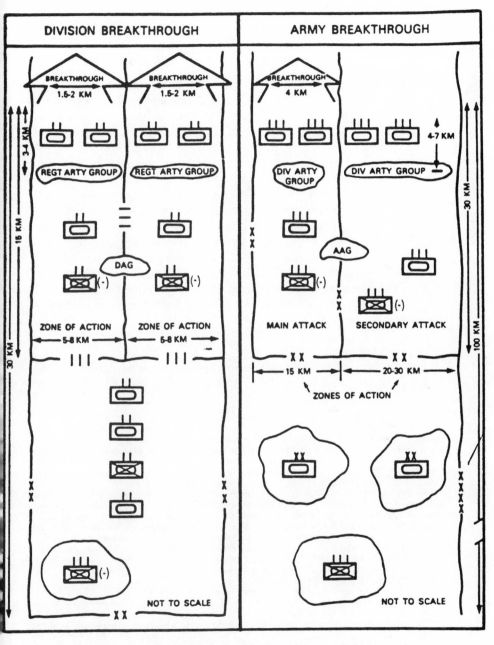

SOURCE: US Army, FM 71-2; *The Tank and Mechanized Infantry Battalion Task Force* (June 30, 1977), p. 5–12.

NATO's existing ability to cover the front at densities that permit an effective defense, coupled with real world constraints on the ability of the Pact to concentrate large forces in small breakthrough sectors, suggests that the Pact will, *at least initially*, have difficulty achieving high offensive-to-defensive force ratios in *either* the "Soviet" or the "NATO" case.

Thus, in the "Soviet" case, a force ratio of 2:1 is produced in the breakthrough sectors. In the "NATO" case, a ground force ratio in real ADEs of 2.25:1 is produced, although in adjusted ADEs the force ratio remains 1.5:1. NATO and Pact "tacair" should also be factored into the force ratio, however.[45] Using a very simple formula, NATO and Pact "tacair" can be converted into an ADE score and added to the breakthrough sectors. This would produce a "real" force ratio on the order of 2:1. If this procedure were adopted for the adjusted ADE score, the ratio drops to 1.4:1. It is worth noting that none of these force-to-space ratios produce force-to-force ratios near the 3:1 rule of thumb at which a defender has generally been thought to be capable of holding.

ATTRITION RATES

Attrition rates in the breakthrough sectors are a key variable in the Attrition–FEBA Expansion Model. The daily attrition rate that the Pact is willing to

---

instructive. These three divisions had, at minimum, 6,500 vehicles of all types and probably more. Actual combat vehicles, however, probably added up to no more than 1,500–2,000, worth between one and one-and-a-half ADEs. Additionally, two infantry divisions and a cavalry group were waiting "in the wings" on the Corps' left flank. The Official History reports that the commanders found the situation extremely cramped. The 2nd Armored division had to withhold half its strength from the battle for several days. This level of concentration is roughly consistent with that attributed to the Pact in the "Soviet" case, and thus one ADE per 12.5 km would seem a good theoretical maximum. On the XIX Corps assault, see Charles B. MacDonald, *The Siegfried Line Campaign* (Washington, D.C.: U.S. Government Printing Office, 1963), pp. 521–522. At first glance, it appears that a higher force-to-space ratio was achieved by the British in their GOOD-WOOD offensive out of the Normandy perimeter. A close examination of the forces involved and the course of battle, however, suggests that the British were unable to commit their third division to the fray and were forced to engage their first two armored divisions sequentially. Once spread out and engaged, these two divisions (with roughly 1,200 fighting vehicles or an ADE) took up about 12 km of front. See John Keegan, *Six Armies in Normandy* (New York: Viking, 1982), pp. 183–219, especially p. 218.

45. For purposes of aggregation, I simply treat these aircraft as tanks, since helicopters armed with anti-tank guided missiles and cannon-equipped aircraft are basically just very mobile direct-fire weapons. I multiply my average-sorties-per-day figure (derived from Table 1) by the ADE system's defensive weighting for tanks (55). I multiply that by a weapons effectiveness factor to come up with a weighted value that can then be converted to an ADE score. As a function of the different kill rates that I assign the two CAS fleets, NATO's effectiveness score is one and the Pact's is .5. Sorties are scored, rather than aircraft, because actual battlefield presence is the output to be measured.

suffer ultimately is a key determinant of NATO's daily ground force needs. Varying the attrition rate is a way of representing how much Pact commanders and their troops are willing to suffer on a sustained basis. Additionally, it is a way of representing the effects of "friction" on the Pact offensive. How much can the attacker suffer, even if he wants to? I have chosen two values for the sustained breakthrough sector attrition rate: 10 percent for the "Soviet" case and 7.5 percent for the "NATO" case.

Tank attrition rates provide a useful starting point for estimating overall ADE attrition rates. Tanks make up one-half of the ADE score for NATO divisions and one-half or more for Pact divisions. Three sources of data for sustained, front-wide, tank attrition are employed: two from real wars and one from a recent unclassified projection of tank attrition in a NATO/Pact war. Table 3 compares these attrition rates with those of the "NATO" and "Soviet" cases from the Attrition–FEBA Expansion Model. To arrive at the front-wide attrition figure, breakthrough sector casualties are added to an estimate of the casualties taken in the minor sectors: 1 percent per day.

**Table 3. Frontwide Attrition Rates[a]**

| Source | Victim | Daily Rate | Comments |
|---|---|---|---|
| U.S. Army Official History[b] | U.S. | 2% | Tanks, Battle of the Bulge, First and Third Armies, 14 days |
| Author's Estimate[c] | Israel | 2% | 20-Day War, 1973, tanks, one-half reparable |
| Author's Estimate | Arabs | 3% | 20-Day War, 1973, tanks |
| Cordesman[d] | Pact | 3.3% | D + 12–32, tanks |
|  | NATO | 2.77% | D + 12–32, tanks |
| "Soviet" Case | Pact | 4% | ADEs |
| "Soviet" Case | NATO | 3.5% | ADEs |
| "NATO" Case | Pact | 2.8% | ADEs |
| "NATO" Case | NATO | 1.7% | Adjusted ADEs, Phase I |

[a] Percent of engaged/committed forces at original strength.
[b] Hugh Cole, *The Ardennes: Battle of the Bulge* (Washington, D.C.: U.S. Government Printing Office, 1965), p. 664.
[c] These estimates are based on Trevor N. Dupuy, *Elusive Victory: The Arab–Israeli Wars, 1947–1948* (New York: Harper and Row, 1978), p. 609; Shlomo Gazit, "Arab Forces Two Years After the Yom Kippur War," in Louis Williams, ed., *Military Aspects of the Israeli–Arab Conflict* (Tel Aviv: University Publishing Projects, 1975), pp. 188, 194.
[d] Daniel Gans, "Fight Outnumbered and Win," pp. 24–33, as cited by Anthony H. Cordesman, "The NATO Central Region and the Balance of Uncertainty," *Armed Forces Journal International,* July 1983, pp. 36–37, Table Six.

The "Soviet" case assumes higher front-wide attrition rates than those experienced by the Israelis or the Arabs in the 1973 war, which was viewed at the time as a very high-attrition war by historical standards. The "NATO" case applies slightly lower values to the "attacker" and the "defender" than those prevailing in the 1973 war. It seems plausible that, in the 1973 war, Arab and Israeli attrition rates were partly driven by the need for Middle East belligerents to achieve their military objectives with great speed, in order to beat the truce usually imposed by the superpowers. Neither NATO nor the Pact would be under such pressure. On the other hand, of course, weaponry has improved since that war, and some would argue that the Soviets will press the pace of the war in order to somehow forestall NATO's resort to nuclear escalation. The attrition suffered by the Alliance in the "NATO" case is a good deal lower than Anthony Cordesman's estimates, but it is consistent with U.S. Army experience during an intense World War II battle against a competent adversary at the Battle of the Bulge. Several Pentagon experts on armored vehicle attrition were skeptical that attackers would accept *sustained* 10 percent attrition in breakthrough sectors. Some simply doubt that the battle could be forced at such a pace on a sustained basis.

EXCHANGE RATES

Exchange rates are an equally difficult problem to discuss. As noted earlier, given Pact superiority in numbers of weapons, NATO must achieve favorable exhange rates if it is not simply to be worn down into defeat. There seems to be general agreement, however, that the defender should enjoy favorable exchange rates. Table 4 represents a range of possible exchange rates derived from experience and from the judgments of professional defense analysts.

None of these values can be taken as definitive. Factors of troop quality, leadership, terrain, and terrain preparation would all figure in determining the exchange rate of an actual battle. Nevertheless, consistent with the view that Soviet doctrine is superior to NATO's and the view that offense is somehow a "better" posture than defense implicit in that doctrine, a relatively gentle 1.5:1 exchange rate is imposed on the Soviets in the "Soviet" case. This still assumes some advantage for the tactical defender, although not very much.

The "NATO" case assumes a slightly more favorable exchange rate, 2:1. This is still a good deal less than the Israelis enjoyed in 1973 and a good deal less than many professional estimates available.

Table 4. Exchange Rates

| Source | Exchange Rate | Comments |
|--------|---------------|----------|
| Author's Estimate[a] | Arab–Israeli, 3:1 | 1973 War, tanks, Israel outnumbered 2:1, Israel on both defense and offense. |
| Author's Estimate[b] | Syria–Israel, 4.5:1 | Golan Heights, 1973, tanks, 1st five days, Israel outnumbered by at least 3:1 for much of the fighting, Israel mainly on defense. |
| Cordesman[c] | Pact–NATO, 3.2:1 | Tanks, Pact outnumbers NATO 2.7:1, theater-wide. |
| Dunnigan[d] | Offense–Defense, 4–6:1 | Offense outnumbers defense 2–3:1, tactical engagement. |
| Interviews | Offense–Defense, 3–6:1 | Consistent with the view that the defender, armed with modern weaponry, can hold outnumbered 3–6:1. |

[a] These estimates are based on Trevor N. Dupuy, *Elusive Victory: The Arab–Israeli Wars, 1947–1948* (New York: Harper and Row, 1978), p. 609; Shlomo Gazit, "Arab Forces Two Years After the Yom Kippur War," in Louis Williams, ed., *Military Aspects of the Israeli–Arab Conflict* (Tel Aviv: University Publishing Projects, 1975), pp. 188, 194.
[b] This estimate is based on Dupuy, *Elusive Victory,* pp. 437–461; and Chaim Herzog, *The War of Atonement: October 1973* (Boston: Little, Brown, 1975), pp. 55–127. Both accounts agree that by the end of the fourth day of combat, the two Israeli armored brigades that had withstood the initial Syrian attacks were left with less than two dozen operable tanks. This would imply that roughly 200 tanks had suffered enough damage to be viewed as casualties. Not all of these were seriously damaged, and some tanks from reinforcing brigades were also casualties, but 200 seems a good rough estimate of losses for this phase of the battle. Herzog reports that, for one reason or another, the Syrians left nearly 900 tanks on the Golan Heights in their retreat. Some of these had been abandoned in operable condition (p. 127). Thus a 4.5:1 exchange rate for this phase of the battle would seem a fair estimate.
[c] Anthony H. Cordesman, "The NATO Central Region and the Balance of Uncertainty," *Armed Forces Journal International,* July 1983, pp. 36–37.
[d] James F. Dunnigan, *How To Make War* (New York: William Morrow, 1982), pp. 39–40.

ADVANCE RATES

Advance rates during breakthrough operations have also not received a thorough public discussion, although one analyst has compared historical advance rates with those found in published Soviet writing. Perhaps the most definitive conclusion that can be gleaned from a quick historical survey is that sustained advances of 15–20 km per day are possible against a disorganized, erratic, and uncoordinated defense.[46] This estimate, however, is in

46. Jeffrey Record's dated, but still useful, examination of historical armored advance rates notes that some Soviet guidelines call for sustained advances of over 100 km per day. "Armored

sharp contrast to the 100 km or more per day found in some Soviet literature. Since the Attrition–FEBA Expansion Model tests NATO's ability to prevent breakthroughs during stressful assaults, the question is: what is a reasonable rate of advance for a determined breakthrough effort?

Jeffrey Record notes that during the breakthrough battle at Sedan in 1940, it took the German XIX Panzer Corps (1st, 2nd, and 10th Panzer divisions) some four days to crack the French defense line near Sedan for an average daily advance of about 6 km per day.[47] The "Soviet" case assumes a 5 km daily rate of advance. Such an assumption would be consistent with the hypothesis that a NATO–Pact quantitative and qualitative gap similar to that which existed between the best-armed and best-trained mechanized formations of the German army and a mixed bag of largely unmechanized, active and reserve, French infantry divisions will prevail in the breakthrough sectors. This would seem a pessimistic assessment of the quality and quantity of NATO's military forces.

The "NATO" case makes movement rate assumptions more consistent with the tougher defensive actions of World War II. The U.S. First and Ninth Armies' efforts to reach the Roer River, after the Siegfried Line had been partially breached, may be taken as representative of such actions. The area opposite the Ninth Army's XIX Corps was rolling, open country, dotted with small villages. The Germans had taken three weeks to prepare the area with earthworks and belts of mines. This sector would be similar to the more topographically attractive breakthrough sectors along the inter-German border. Since the "Soviet" case assumes that at least a month is required for the Pact to train and move forward the Category II divisions needed to support a big attack, NATO would have as much time to prepare the terrain for defense as the Germans did. Although the Allies enjoyed complete air superiority, reasonably good (though not great) flying weather, outnumbered the Germans by at least 5:1, and had a very high offensive force-to-space ratio, the advance rate for the XIX Corps was barely one km per day, for a three-week period.[48] Low rates of advance also prevailed in the First Army sectors, especially in the highly defensible Hurtgen forest. Similarly, low advance rates and high attrition rates were experienced by the U.S. and

---

Advance Rates: A Historical Inquiry," *Military Review*, Vol. 53, No. 9 (September 1973), p. 63. For advance rates against scattered opposition, see pp. 65–66.

47. Ibid., p. 64.

48. MacDonald, *The Siegfried Line Campaign*, pp. 397, 409–410, 520, 577, Maps VII and VIII.

British forces in their efforts to break out of the Normandy bridgehead in early to mid-July 1944.[49]

In order not to appear excessively optimistic, despite these historical examples, the Soviets are given credit in the "NATO" case for a sustained 2 km rate of advance—this with a real force ratio, including "tacair," below 2:1, and an adjusted force ratio below 1.5:1. Both of these ratios are in stark contrast to the 3:1 offense-defense superiority traditionally cited as acceptable to the defense, the 4–6:1 ratio that I have encountered among experts, and the 5:1 force ratios that U.S. and British forces usually needed to dislodge the Germans in World War II. Thus, allowing the Pact a *sustained* forward movement rate of 2 km per day in all three breakthrough sectors is not a particularly optimistic assumption from NATO's perspective.

*Lessons of the Model*

In sum, using standard military judgments and historical analogies, it is possible to estimate some plausible alternative values for the seven variables discussed here. Each of these variables is, for a variety of reasons, very difficult to gauge with confidence. The analysis above describes one possible way of using these variables to model an assessment of the Warsaw Pact

---

49. Martin Blumenson, *Breakout and Pursuit* (Washington, D.C.: U.S. Government Printing Office, 1961), pp. 175–176, 194. Extrapolation from past military engagements to possible future battles between NATO and the Warsaw Pact is an exercise that requires much care. In general, I have chosen to examine recent battles in the Middle East and World War II battles on the Western Front because both involve most of the same basic kinds of ground and air forces that would be employed in a NATO–Pact war.

Middle East combat is especially interesting because the belligerents employ virtually the same weapons and much of the same tactics and organization as are found in Central Europe today. One must, of course, be sure to account for the great qualitative disparity that seems to prevail between Israeli officers and enlisted men and those of that country's Arab adversaries.

Careful study of World War II battles in Western Europe between Anglo–American forces and those of Germany offers somewhat different advantages and disadvantages. Clearly, the equipment was a good deal more primitive than that which we field today, but all the basic elements of current military forces were present. Combat in Europe in 1944 occurred on nearly as large a scale as would prevail today. By 1944, as a function of the casualties that Germany had suffered and the experience that the British and Americans had accrued, the qualitative disparity between the officers and enlisted men of the German army and those of the Allies was probably the smallest that has prevailed between mechanized armies anywhere. Historians do seem to agree, however, that the Germans still enjoyed a meaningful degree of superior military leadership. Much of the terrain fought over in 1944 is quite similar to that along the inter-German border today. In gross terms, the Allies enjoyed a substantial materiel superiority over the Germans, which far exceeded the level of superiority attributed to the Pact today. Thus, it is my judgment that German defensive successes against the Allies are quite relevant to assessing the course of future conflict between NATO and Warsaw Pact.

conventional threat to Europe. Using a similar model, one could have used numbers different from those chosen here, but for the purposes of illustration, these numbers seem to represent sound choices.

Using these explicit judgments for the reasons explained in the preceding sections, what do we learn about the NATO–Warsaw Pact balance?

Figures 3 and 4 (pp. 63, 66) portray the results of applying "Pact" and "NATO" military doctrine respectively to assessing NATO's ability to cope with a conflict in the Central Region today. Figure 3 illustrates the application of Soviet doctrine and is broadly consistent with more pessimistic assessments of the balance. The figure shows the rapid development of a rather dangerous situation for NATO, one that would ultimately lead either to the loss of Germany or to nuclear escalation. The Pact manages to close its low-readiness Category II and III divisions to the battle area in short order. They are assigned full credit for their assigned weaponry, without reference to combat readiness or supportability. I do assume, however, that the Pact would need at least two full weeks to ready itself for an attack of this magnitude. NATO mobilizes seven days after the Pact, and receives no credit for the larger command and support apparatus with which it manages, maintains, and supplies its combat equipment. The Pact concentrates large forces and imposes a sustained, violent battle in the key breakthrough sectors, effectively neutralizes NATO tactical air capabilities, and prevents NATO from achieving a particularly favorable exchange rate. Additionally, the Pact achieves fairly high rates of advance in the breakthrough sectors.

Under these circumstances, after two weeks of combat, NATO finds itself trying to hold 45 km sectors with each remaining ADE of firepower.[50] The Pact, on the other hand, still has enough forces left to populate the whole front and the flanks of each salient at one ADE per 25 km, and has two ADEs per 25 km poised for a fresh effort in each breakthrough sector. Given this situation, NATO is clearly in trouble. Either it will have already ordered a general withdrawal to shorten the total defense line (i.e., eliminate the shoulders of the major penetrations), or it will have suffered, or be on the verge of suffering, a breach in the line. Such a breach could produce disruptive, deep, blitzkrieg-style penetrations into NATO's rear areas. More con-

---

50. This is in sharp contrast to the 25 km per ADE that some analysts view as a conservative average strength that NATO should try to achieve along the Central Front. See, for example, Mako, *U.S. Ground Forces*, p. 37, based on his interview with analysts in the Office of the Secretary of Defense.

servatively, the Pact could aim for envelopments of major NATO formations and their subsequent annihilation. In either case, NATO would face disaster. Thus, NATO would likely opt for early withdrawal across the front, allowing a general Pact advance that could ultimately result in the loss of Germany. As such a process unfolded, some NATO military leaders would no doubt request authorization for the use of nuclear weapons.

Figure 4 illustrates a very different outcome. In my view, this seems a more accurate portrayal of the pattern of conflict than does the preceding case. Here, as a consequence of the relative unreadiness of Pact Category II and III divisions, and as a function of taking some credit for NATO's efforts in the areas of command and support (i.e., NATO's ADE score is multiplied by 1.5 in order to represent the increased effectiveness that should result from greater efforts in these areas), the overall capabilities ratio over time looks very different from what the conventional wisdom would suggest. Figure 6 illustrates the conventional view of the capabilities balance over time and an adjusted view. Figure 4 also credits NATO's tactical aircraft with markedly greater success against Pact ground forces than Pact aircraft enjoy

**Figure 6. Pact/NATO Capability Ratios Over Time; Mobilization Only–No Attrition**

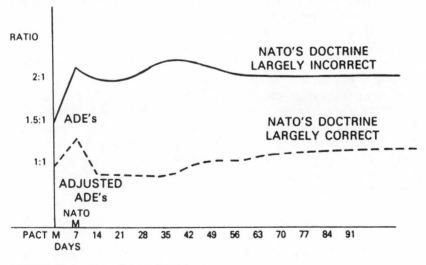

SOURCE: Derived from Figures 3 and 4

against NATO's ground forces. Reflecting available information on Pact intentions and historical experience, the Pact is credited with a lower offensive concentration in the breakthrough sectors. A more favorable exchange rate, reflecting the advantages often credited to the defense by military planners and commentators, is also assumed. Consistent with all of the preceding assumptions, and with a good deal of American and British experience fighting the Germans in World War II, a slower advance rate in the breakthrough sectors is factored into the model.

With these assumptions, NATO appears capable of coping successfully with Pact efforts to achieve catastrophic breakthroughs. The Pact is capable of mounting a good-sized attack at M+30, which it could sustain for roughly two weeks before it would find itself short of reserves. NATO's mobilization lags the Pact's by seven days, but the Alliance would possess sufficient reserves to cope with the Pact advance without having to initiate a general withdrawal. The Pact would resume the offensive two weeks later once its Category III divisions were ready for action, but NATO forces would still be strong enough to deal with the penetrations without resorting to a general withdrawal. As a result, NATO should not be particularly vulnerable to a major rupture of the line. In this second phase of the battle, as a function of unreplaced aircraft attrition and lower sortie rates, NATO ground forces would have to work harder and take more casualties than they did in the first phase of the battle. Both the Pact and NATO would begin running short of forces to sustain this pace of battle after three weeks, and it seems likely that a period of reduced activity would set in. Finally, the outcome portrayed here is a little artificial, since NATO's reserves in the first phase of the battle would probably allow it to counterattack successfully and thus hold the Pact to an even slower rate of advance than that assumed. Similarly, the "surplus" of NATO's available forces over its needs for most of the battle suggests that, even if the Pact somehow managed to convert one of its salients into a clean breakthrough, NATO would have operational reserves to throw against the Pact's exploitation effort. Several uncommitted ADEs would remain to NATO until the last week of heavy fighting, when the Pact itself would begin to run short of forces.

*Conclusion*

Figures 3 and 4 portray the very different implications for NATO in the Central Region that arise from a comprehensive application of Pact and

NATO doctrine. If assumptions consistent with the notion that most of the Pact's allocation decisions are right and most of NATO's are wrong are factored into a balance assessment, one can produce a very pessimistic portrayal of NATO's military prospects. If, however, assumptions consistent with NATO's pattern of resource allocation are factored into a balance assessment, things look better (see Figure 4). If these assumptions are further combined with an assessment of the constraints that would govern the employment of Pact forces, a conservative application of military rules of thumb, and some inferences from Western military experience, NATO's prospects seem much brighter.

Under relatively conservative assumptions, NATO's forces appear adequate to prevent the Pact from making a clean armored breakthrough. The ground forces of the Alliance seem large enough to hold the Pact to breakthrough-sector force ratios that are much lower than those that soldiers and military commentators have thought necessary to produce success. If the Pact is given credit for an ability to make NATO withdraw at a slow pace that is consistent with the low force ratio, *and* Pact units are forced to pay a relatively modest price to do so (i.e., a two-to-one exchange rate), NATO still appears capable of containing the penetrations and preventing breakthroughs. Moreover, as was noted earlier, NATO still would have sizable uncommitted reserves for much of the battle, which could counterattack a successful breakthrough if it occurred.

Clearly, if NATO's doctrine is correct (and I have tried to show that this is at least plausible), its forces are much more likely to defend successfully than is widely perceived to be the case. The question then is whether NATO has chosen the correct doctrine. If not, then huge new investments spent the same old way cannot rectify whatever defense problems the Alliance may actually have. If the doctrine is correct, then major new investments in capabilities may not be necessary. Rather, investments should be carefully directed towards buying more insurance in the areas of greatest uncertainty.[51]

The practice of building forces according to a theory of victory that NATO's military planners apparently believe and then assessing their capabilities

---

51. For some specific recommendations for improving NATO's conventional forces, see, for example, Barry R. Posen and Stephen Van Evera, "Defense Policy and the Reagan Administration: Departure from Containment," *International Security*, Vol. 8, No. 1 (Summer 1983), pp. 39–42; and Barry R. Posen, "Competing Views of the Center Region Conventional Balance," in Keith A. Dunn and William O. Staudenmaier, eds., *Alternative Military Strategies for the Future* (Boulder, Colo.: Westview Press, forthcoming).

according to a very different theory of victory can only confuse NATO's political leaders and publics about the state of the military balance and what should be done to improve it. The principal result of this practice is that NATO's current position in conventional forces is made to appear very poor and the investments needed to repair the situation are made to appear very great. While this behavior might help promote some extra investments that could ultimately provide a useful margin of military safety, they may also obscure the progress that NATO has already made, and make modest improvements that lie within the realm of political and economic feasibility appear pointless to those who must find the resources. Similarly, the practice also inhibits clear thinking about NATO's future military efforts. Pessimistic portrayals of the military balance may divert scarce political and economic resources to speculative military ventures that promise quick and easy solutions to NATO's seemingly insurmountable difficulties. To some extent, NATO is already falling victim to these pitfalls.

Finally, one-sided portrayals of the conventional balance may have a pernicious effect in political crises. It is surely true that, if the Pact mobilizes, trains, and assembles its Category II and III divisions and NATO does not respond in some fashion, then the Alliance will shortly find itself in a very dangerous military situation. If, however, NATO's political leaders are convinced that no amount of mobilization will make the Alliance competitive with the Pact, then they will be more inclined to delay in a crisis, out of fear that any military action will not only appear provocative, but will not improve NATO's chances in war anyway. In short, whatever the motives, failure to account fully for the Alliance's current military effort in a NATO–Pact balance assessment has costs. These costs are not always immediately visible, nor are they necessarily incurred by those who engage in such assessments, but they are real—and they may be high.

# Why the Soviets Can't Win Quickly in Central Europe

*John J. Mearsheimer*

In light of the emergence of strategic parity and NATO's manifest lack of enthusiasm for tactical nuclear weapons, the importance of the balance of conventional forces in Central Europe has increased significantly in the past decade.[1] Regarding that balance, the conventional wisdom is clearly that the Warsaw Pact enjoys an overwhelming advantage. In the event of a conventional war, the Soviets are expected to launch a *blitzkrieg* that will lead to a quick and decisive victory.

The implications of this specter of a hopelessly outgunned NATO are significant. Certainly, NATO's behavior in a major crisis would be influenced by its view of the conventional balance. Furthermore, one's perception of the conventional balance directly affects his or her view of the importance of both strategic and tactical nuclear weapons for deterrence in Europe. *The New York Times*, for example, endorsed the controversial neutron bomb as a means to counter NATO's perceived inferiority at the conventional level.[2]

The fact of the matter is that the balance of conventional forces is nowhere near as unfavorable as it is so often portrayed to be. In fact, NATO's prospects for thwarting a Soviet offensive are actually quite good.[3] Certainly, NATO

The author wishes to thank the following people for their helpful comments on earlier drafts of this essay: Robert Art, Mary Mearsheimer, Stephen Meyer, Barry Posen, and Jack Snyder.

*John J. Mearsheimer is a Research Associate at Harvard University's Center for International Affairs. This article is based on a chapter in his forthcoming book,* The Theory and Practice of Conventional Deterrence.

1. Recognition of this is clearly reflected in the annual *Posture Statements* of the Secretaries of Defense for the past ten years. Also see: Helmut Schmidt's October 1977 speech before the International Institute for Strategic Studies, a copy of which can be found in *Survival*, Vol. 20, No. 1 (January/February 1978), pp. 2–10; and *White Paper 1979: The Security of the Federal Republic of Germany and the Development of the Federal Armed Forces* (Bonn: Federal Minister of Defence, September 4, 1979), p. 112, hereinafter cited as *1979 German White Paper*. Very importantly, the Soviets have also shown increased interest in the possibility of a conventional war in Europe. See Colonel Graham D. Vernon, *Soviet Options For War In Europe: Nuclear or Conventional?* National Security Affairs Monograph 79–1 (Washington D.C.: National Defense University, January 1979).
2. "The Virtues of the Neutron Bomb," Editorial, *The New York Times*, March 30, 1978, p. 32.
3. It should be noted that since the early 1960s there have been a handful of studies which have concluded that NATO has the capability to defend itself against a conventional attack by the

*International Security*, Summer 1982 (Vol. 7, No. 1) 0162-2889/82/010003-37 $02.50/0

does not have the capability to *win* a conventional war on the continent against the Soviets. NATO does have, however, the wherewithal to *deny* the Soviets a quick victory and then to turn the conflict into a lengthy war of attrition, where NATO's advantage in population and GNP would not bode well for the Soviets.[4]

The aim of this article is to examine closely the Soviets' prospects for effecting a *blitzkrieg* against NATO. In analyzing this matter, two closely related issues must be addressed. First, one must determine whether the Soviets have the force structure, the doctrine, and the raw ability to implement this strategy. In other words, do the Soviets, when viewed in isolation, have the capacity to effect a *blitzkrieg*? Secondly, when NATO's defense capabilities and the theater's terrain are considered, what then are the prospects for Soviet success? It may very well be that the Soviet military is well-primed to launch a *blitzkrieg*, but that NATO in turn has the capability to thwart it.[5]

Any assessment of the NATO–Pact balance is dependent on certain as-

---

Warsaw Pact. See, for example, Alain C. Enthoven and K. Wayne Smith, *How Much Is Enough?* (New York: Harper and Row, 1971), chapter 4. In 1973, the *Washington Post* reported that "a major new Pentagon study," which had been "two years in the making," concluded that NATO could defend itself. See Michael Getler, "Study Insists NATO Can Defend Itself," *Washington Post*, June 7, 1973, pp. 1, 20. Since NATO has spent considerably more money on defense than has the Pact since 1973 (see former Secretary of Defense Harold Brown's *FY 1982 Posture Statement*, Appendix C-12, which is entitled "Comparison of NATO and Warsaw Pact Total Defense Costs") and since there have been no significant changes in the force levels of each side since 1973, there is no reason to believe that the conclusions of this study are outdated. Actually, Harold Brown's four *Posture Statements* (FY 1979–FY 1982) describe a situation where NATO stands a reasonable chance of thwarting a Warsaw Pact offensive without resorting to nuclear weapons. Such a viewpoint, however, is hardly commonplace.

4. There are a variety of other reasons why the Soviets would want to avoid a war of attrition. Obviously, they would not want to suffer the tremendous costs associated with a lengthy conventional war. Second, the Soviet Army is not configured for a long war. Although the Soviets could remedy this problem, the fact remains that they have not. Third, because of the Sino-Soviet split, the Soviets must consider the possibility of a war on two fronts. Even if there was not an imminent threat of war with China, a war of attrition in the West would threaten to weaken the Soviets to the point where they might think themselves vulnerable to a Chinese attack. Fourth, there is the real threat of unrest among the non-Soviet armies as well as the populations of the East European states, should the Pact find itself engaged in a bloody war. (See A. Ross Johnson et al., "The Armies of the Warsaw Pact Northern Tier," *Survival*, Vol. 23, No. 4 [July/August 1981], pp. 174–182.) Finally, there is the danger that nuclear weapons will be used if the Soviets do not win a quick and decisive victory. Also see fn. 65.

5. This study does not consider the impact of air forces on the balance. Although it is possible that NATO's airpower will not have the decisive influence on the land battle that many expect, it is clear that the air balance, when qualitative and quantitative factors are considered, does not favor the Pact. See Carnegie Panel on U.S. Security and the Future of Arms Control, *Challenges for U.S. National Security, Assessing the Balance: Defense Spending and Conventional Forces*, A Preliminary Report, Part II (Washington D.C.: Carnegie Endowment for International Peace, 1981), pp. 69–73.

sumptions made about the preparatory moves both sides take before the war starts. Among the many that might be considered, three scenarios are most often posited. The first of these is the "standing start" attack,[6] in which the Soviets launch an attack after hardly any mobilization and deliver a knock-out blow against an unsuspecting NATO.[7] This is not, however, a likely eventuality. First of all, without significantly improving the readiness of their standing forces, the Soviets would not have the capability to score a decisive victory. Instead, they would have to settle for capturing a portion of West German territory. Such a limited victory is hardly an attractive option.[8] Secondly, for a war in Europe to become a realistic possibility, there would have to be a significant deterioration in East–West relations. Given such a development, it is very likely that both sides will take some steps, however limited, to increase the readiness of their forces. It is difficult to imagine a scenario where an alert Pact catches NATO completely unprepared.

---

6. The two most prominent examples of this viewpoint are General Robert Close, *Europe Without Defense?* (New York: Pergamon, 1979) and U.S., Congress, Senate Armed Services Committee, *NATO and the New Soviet Threat*, report by Senators Sam Nunn and Dewey F. Bartlett, 95th Cong., 1st Sess. (Washington D.C.: GPO, January 24, 1977), hereinafter cited as *Nunn-Bartlett Report*. For the best critique of this scenario, see Les Aspin, "A Surprise Attack On NATO: Refocusing the Debate," a copy of which can be found in *Congressional Record*, February 7, 1977, pp. H911–H914.

7. It should be emphasized that, given NATO's intelligence-gathering capabilities, the Pact would not be able to mobilize its forces in any significant way without being detected—thus taking away the element of surprise. Therefore, the notion of "an immense blitzkrieg preceded by little warning" (*Nunn-Bartlett Report*, p. 16) or a "gigantic operation [that] would have the advantage of complete surprise" (Robert Close, "The Feasibility of a Surprise Attack Against Western Europe," study prepared for the NATO Defense College, February 24, 1975) is unrealistic. A massive surprise attack is a contradiction in terms.

8. With an attack from a standing start, the Soviets would not be able to employ all of the Pact's 57⅓ standing divisions. Undoubtedly, they would rely on the 19 Soviet divisions stationed in East Germany and the 5 Soviet divisions stationed in Czechoslovakia. However, they probably would not upgrade these divisions significantly prior to an attack for fear that this would tip off NATO. Given that non-Soviet divisions in the Pact are three-quarters or less manned and that alerting them of a forthcoming offensive might lead to a security breach, it is highly unlikely that these forces would be used for a surprise attack. This would leave the Pact with 24 Soviet divisions, which would be striking against NATO's 28 divisions. The 24:28 ratio would shrink even further if translated into either armored division equivalents or divisional manpower. Although NATO's forces would not be in their forward positions in this scenario, the Pact would still have to defeat these forces to gain a decisive victory. This is hardly likely given the balance of forces that attend this scenario and the fact that the Pact would not overrun NATO's forces *at the outset* of this conflict. Instead, a majority of NATO's forces would be located behind their forward defensive positions, where they would have ample time to identify the Pact's main thrusts. A number of analysts point out that such a short-warning attack will invariably result in a limited victory. See, for example, Aspin, "A Surprise Attack On NATO," pp. H912–H913; Alain Enthoven, "U.S. Forces In Europe: How Many? Doing What?" *Foreign Affairs*, Vol. 53, No. 3 (April 1975), pp. 517–518; and General James H. Polk, "The North German Plain Attack Scenario: Threat or Illusion?" *Strategic Review*, Vol. 8, No. 3 (Summer 1980), pp. 60–66.

The second scenario is a more realistic and more dangerous one. Here, in the midst of a crisis, NATO detects a Pact mobilization, but does not mobilize its forces for a fear of triggering a Soviet attack.[9] Surely, if NATO fails to respond quickly to a Pact mobilization as posited in this second scenario, the Pact would soon be in a position to inflict a decisive defeat on NATO.

In the third scenario, NATO's mobilization begins immediately after the Pact starts to mobilize. Here, the Pact does not gain an overwhelming force advantage as a result of NATO's failure to mobilize. It is with this third scenario that I shall concern myself in the present essay. The focus will thus be on a conflict in which both sides are alerted and where neither enjoys an advantage as a result of the other's failure to mobilize.

This is not to deny that strategic warning and especially the political decision to mobilize are important issues. They certainly are and they will have a significant influence on the outcome of any future conflict in Europe. The assumption on which I base the following analysis is that strategic warning and mobilization are acted upon by NATO; the raw capabilities of the opposing forces will thus be examined under those clearly defined conditions.

Before directly assessing Soviet prospects for launching a successful *blitzkrieg*, we must examine briefly the balance of forces on the Central Front and the doctrines of the two sides.

*The Balance of Forces on the Central Front*

The Pact has 57⅓ divisions located in Central Europe, while NATO has 28⅓, giving the Pact slightly more than a 2:1 advantage in divisions.[10] Comparing

---

9. For an excellent discussion of this matter, see Richard K. Betts, "Surprise Attack: NATO's Political Vulnerability," *International Security*, Vol. 5, No. 4 (Spring 1981), pp. 117–149. Also see his "Hedging Against Surprise Attack," *Survival*, Vol. 23, No. 4 (July/August 1981), pp. 146–156.

10. These figures are taken from Robert L. Fischer, *Defending the Central Front: The Balance of Forces*, Adelphi Paper No. 127 (London: IISS, 1976), p. 8. Fischer's calculations are based on the assumption that the Pact has 58⅓ divisions in Central Europe. Actually, the Soviets recently removed a division from East Germany, leaving 57⅓ divisions. Since the Soviets have increased the size of their remaining divisions somewhat and since my argument does not rest on precise calculations (see fn. 20), this minor discrepancy raises no problems. Regarding the balance of divisions on the Central Front, also see James Blaker and Andrew Hamilton, *Assessing the NATO/Warsaw Pact Military Balance* (Washington D.C.: Congressional Budget Office, December 1977) and *The Military Balance, 1980–1981* (London: IISS, 1980). Although the Fischer and Blaker/Hamilton studies are somewhat dated, there have been no shifts in the force levels on either side which would alter the figures in these studies in any significant way. It should be noted

numbers of divisions, however, gives a distorted view of the balance, since this measure does not account for the significant differences, both qualitative and quantitative, among each nation's divisions. There are generally two alternative ways of assessing the balance. One is to focus on the manpower on each side, while the other is to compare weaponry.[11]

MANPOWER

Robert Lucas Fischer, in his 1976 study of the conventional balance in Europe (which is, unfortunately, one of the few comprehensive studies done on that subject), notes that NATO has 414,000 men in its divisions, while the Pact has 564,000.[12] With this measure of divisional manpower, the Soviet advantage shrinks to 1.36:1. Fischer calculates that when overall manpower levels on the Central Front are considered, the Pact's advantage shrinks even further to 1.09:1. This is because NATO has traditionally had more men assigned to combat units which are not organic to divisions. Since the study was issued, the Pact has added approximately 50,000 men, raising the overall advantage in manpower to 1.15:1—hardly an alarming figure.[13] In the British Government's recent *Statement on Defence Estimates, 1981*, the Soviets are given an advantage in overall manpower of 1.2:1.[14] Under the category of "soldiers in fighting units," the Soviets are again given a 1.2:1 advantage. These figures are clear evidence that NATO is not hopelessly outnumbered.[15]

---

that throughout this article, French forces are counted in the NATO totals. Regarding this assumption, see *1979 German White Paper*, p. 118.

11. It should be emphasized that the available data base on the conventional balance is a relatively primitive one. Certainly, there are a number of simple assessments where, for example, numbers of tanks or numbers of divisions are counted. There are, however, very few comprehensive studies of the balance in which analysts attempt to examine the balance of forces in a detailed manner. This is especially true with regard to weaponry. There is an acute need for studies which attempt to look at all the weapon systems on each side, and at all of the various indexes by which their effectiveness is measured, and then make some overall judgment about the balance. This article will not attempt such a net assessment of forces on the European front. Its purposes are, rather, more limited: to rebut on their own terms the many critics who claim that NATO's numerical inferiority has made it hopelessly vulnerable to defeat by a Soviet *blitzkrieg*.

12. See Fischer, *Defending the Central Front*, pp. 10–15.

13. This increase has been reflected in the annual *Military Balance*. Also see Robert Shishko, *The European Conventional Balance: A Primer*, P–6707 (Santa Monica, Calif.: Rand Corporation, November 24, 1981), p. 18.

14. Quoted in Shishko, *ibid.*, p. 18.

15. It should be noted that if the entire French Army were counted, instead of just the French forces stationed in West Germany, NATO forces *would* outnumber Pact forces. See Blaker and Hamilton, *Assessing the NATO/Warsaw Pact Military Balance*, p. 11.

Perhaps the most important problem with comparing manpower levels, however, is that it does not account for weaponry.

## WEAPONS

It is not difficult to compare numbers of specific weapons on each side. For example, the Pact has approximately a 2.5:1 advantage in tanks and about a 2.8:1 advantage in artillery.[16] Such comparisons, however, do not take into account qualitative differences within the same category of weapons (i.e., NATO's artillery is significantly better than Pact artillery); nor do they deal with the problem of comparing different categories of weapons (i.e., tanks vs. artillery). To counter this problem, the Defense Department has devised a system of weighing weapons within the same category as well as across different categories.[17] Three principal characteristics of each weapon are considered: mobility, survivability, and firepower. Using this system, the Defense Department weighs all the weaponry in every division on the Central Front and then arrives at a composite figure, known as armored division equivalents (ADEs), for both NATO and the Warsaw Pact. Unfortunately, the number of armored division equivalents on each side is classified. Very importantly, however, the ratio is not. Looking at standing forces, the Pact has a 1.2:1 advantage.[18] Again, it is clear that NATO is not hopelessly outnumbered.

## REINFORCEMENT AND MOBILIZATION

Now, consider the critical matter of comparative reinforcement capabilities. Although NATO's reinforcement capability is not as great as the Soviets' in an absolute sense, NATO has the potential to keep the overall ratio of forces very close to the pre-mobilization ratio. The notion that the Soviets can rely

---

16. These figures are from Shishko, *The European Conventional Balance*, p. 18.
17. For further discussion of the concept of armored division equivalents, see Blaker and Hamilton, *Assessing the NATO/Warsaw Pact Military Balance*; and U.S. Army Concepts Analysis Agency, *Weapon Effectiveness Indicies/Weighted Unit Values (WEI/WUV)*, Study Report CAA–SR–73–18 (Bethesda, Maryland: U.S. Army Concepts Analysis Agency, April 1974).
18. Regarding the balance of armored division equivalents, see Pat Hillier, *Strengthening NATO: Pomcus and Other Approaches* (Washington D.C.: Congressional Budget Office, February 1979), pp. 53–57; and Pat Hillier and Nora Slatkin, *U.S. Ground Forces: Design and Cost Alternatives for NATO and Non-NATO Contingencies* (Washington D.C.: Congressional Budget Office, December 1980), pp. 23–24. It should be noted that this figure was calculated on the basis of 58⅓ Pact divisions and not 57⅓ divisions (see fn. 10). Also, it is not possible to ascertain whether NATO and Pact non-divisional assets have been incorporated into this 1.2:1 ratio. If not, the ratio would shift further in NATO's favor when they were added to the balance.

on some massive second echelon that NATO cannot match is a false one. However, the ratio of forces in any future mobilization will be heavily influenced by the timeliness with which each side starts to mobilize. If NATO begins mobilizing its forces before the Pact does, or simultaneously with the Pact, then the force ratios will remain close to the 1.2:1 (in armored division equivalents) and 1.36:1 (in divisional manpower), the ratios which obtained before mobilization.[19] If NATO starts mobilizing a few days after the Pact, then the balance of forces should approach but not exceed a 2:1 ratio in the very early days of mobilization and then fall to a level close to the pre-mobilization ratios. But once the gap in mobilization starting times reaches seven days (in the Pact's favor), NATO begins to face serious problems, problems which become even more pronounced as the mobilization gap widens further. As noted, the assumption here is that NATO starts mobilizing immediately after the Pact, thus ensuring that the overall force ratios never reach 2:1, and, in fact, remain reasonably close to the pre-mobilization ratios.

NUMBERS AND STRATEGY: THE CRITICAL CONNECTION

It should be emphasized that there are definite limits to the utility of measuring force levels. After all, even a cursory study of military history would show that it is impossible to explain the outcome of many important military campaigns by simply comparing the number of forces on each side. Nevertheless, it is clear that if one side has an overwhelming advantage in forces, that glaring asymmetry is very likely to lead to a decisive victory. In essence, the larger force will simply overwhelm the smaller one as, for example, the Germans did against the Poles in September 1939. The previous analysis of the balance of forces in Europe indicates that the Soviets do not enjoy such an overwhelming advantage. They do not have the numerical superiority to simply crush NATO. In a conventional war in Europe, whether or not the Soviets prevail will depend on how they employ their forces against NATO's defenses. In other words, success will be a function of strategy, not overwhelming numbers. This is not to deny that the Soviets would be better

---

19. See Fischer, *Defending the Central Front*, pp. 20–25 and Hillier, *Strengthening NATO*, pp. 53–57. Also see Hillier's more recent study (*U.S. Ground Forces*), where he makes the highly questionable assumption that the Soviets will have 120 divisions in Central Europe after 30 days. Even then, the overall ratio of armored division equivalents never exceeds 2:1 (see p. 24 of his study). In fact, at its peak, the ratio for the 120 division figure is 1.7:1.

served with an overall advantage in armored division equivalents of 1.8:1 rather than, say, 1.2:1. But regardless of which ratio obtains, ultimate success will turn on the issue of strategy. More specifically, success will depend on the Soviets' capability to effect a *blitzkrieg*.[20]

*Doctrine*

NATO's forces are divided into eight corps sectors which are aligned in layer-cake fashion along the inter-German border (see Figure 1).[21] There are four corps sectors each in Northern Army Group (NORTHAG) and Central Army Group (CENTAG). There are also German and Danish forces located in Schleswig-Holstein, which is adjacent to the northern portion of the Central Front.

NATO's forces are arrayed to support a strategy of forward defense. In other words, to meet a Pact offensive, the forces in each of NATO's corps sectors are deployed very close to the border between the two Germanies. The objective is to meet and thwart an attack right at this boundary. Political as well as military considerations dictate the choice of this strategy. A number of defense analysts in the West, however, argue that NATO's chances of thwarting a Pact attack are negligible as long as NATO employs a forward defense. They claim that the Soviets can mass their forces at points of their choosing along NATO's extended front, achieve overwhelming force ratios, and then blast through NATO's forward defense. It would then be very easy to effect deep strategic penetrations, since NATO has few reserves which could be used to check the Soviets' armored spearheads. These analysts favor a maneuver-oriented defense.[22] The subsequent discussion will address the charge that NATO's strategy of forward defense is fundamentally flawed.

---

20. This discussion of the importance of strategy highlights the key point that my argument does not depend on precise calculations about the balance of forces. In other words, whether or not the balance of armored division equivalents is 1.2:1 or 1.3:1 is not, in and of itself, of great consequence. Of course, there is no doubt, as just noted in the text, that there is an important difference between a balance of 1.2:1 and 1.8:1. See the discussion in fns. 33 and 61.
21. A corps normally controls from 2–3 divisions as well as a number of non-divisional assets. In NATO, corps are comprised of forces from only one nation.
22. For a discussion of the views of the maneuver advocates, see my "Maneuver, Mobile Defense, and the NATO Central Front," *International Security*, Vol. 6, No. 3 (Winter 1981/1982), pp. 104–122.

**Figure 1. NATO Corps Sectors West Germany**

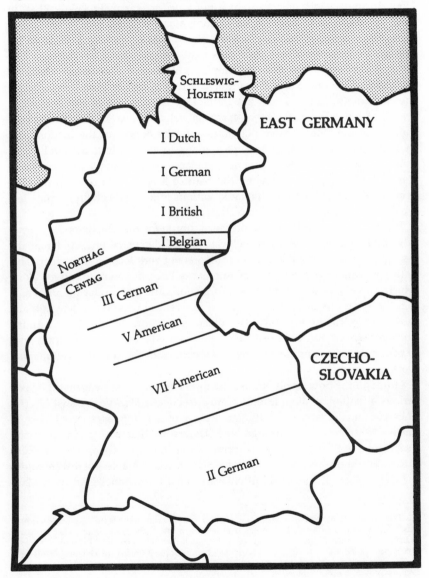

SOVIET BLITZKRIEG STRATEGY

How do the Soviets plan to fight a non-nuclear war in Europe? What, in other words, is their doctrine for fighting a conventional war? Western analysts often assume that the Soviets have a neatly packaged doctrine for fighting a conventional war. As will become evident, this is not the case. The assumption here is that they will employ a *blitzkrieg*.[23] This strategy calls for the attacker to concentrate his armored forces at one or more points along the defender's front, pierce that front, and race deep into the defender's rear. The aim is to avoid a broad frontal attack and, instead, to drive a small number of powerful armored columns into the depths of the defense. Although it may be necessary to engage in a set-piece battle to accomplish the initial breakthrough, a high premium is placed on avoiding further battles of this sort and, instead, following the path of least resistance deep into the opponent's rear. Of course, the tank, with its inherent flexibility, is the ideal weapon for implementing such a strategy.

The *blitzkrieg* is predicated upon the assumptions that the defender's army is geared to fighting along a well-established defensive line, and that the defender has a vulnerable communications network located in its rear. This network would be comprised of numerous lines of communication, along which move supplies as well as information, and key nodal points which join these various lines. Destruction of this central nervous system is tantamount to destroying the army. The attacker, therefore, attempts to pierce the defender's front and then drive *deep* into the defender's rear, severing lines of communication and destroying key junctures in the communications network as he proceeds.

Although the Soviets do not use the term *blitzkrieg*, it is clear that they pay serious attention to the question of how to effect a *blitzkrieg* against NATO. They continually emphasize the importance of massing large tank forces on narrow fronts, breaking through NATO's forward defenses, and then racing deep into NATO's rear so as to bring about the rapid collapse of NATO's forces. Furthermore, the Soviets have shown considerable interest in studying the lessons of their 1945 offensive against the Japanese Army in Man-

---

23. Despite the frequency with which the term *blitzkrieg* is used, there is no systematic study of this military strategy. It will be discussed at length in my forthcoming book, *The Theory and Practice of Conventional Deterrence*. Also see B.H. Liddell Hart, *Memoirs*, Vol. 1 (London: Cassell, 1967), pp. 64–65; *HDv 100/100, Command and Control* (Bonn: Ministry of Defence, September 1973), chapter 27; and Edward N. Luttwak, "The Operational Level of War," *International Security*, Vol. 5, No. 3 (Winter 1980/1981), pp. 67–73.

churia.[24] That operation was a classic *blitzkrieg*. Although the focus here is on the Soviets' capability to effect a *blitzkrieg*, there *is* an alternative strategy that the Soviets might employ. They could employ their forces as they did against the Germans on the Eastern Front in World War II.[25] Instead of relying on deep strategic penetrations to bring about the collapse of the German Army, Soviet strategy called for wearing the German Army down by slowly pushing it back along a broad front. Massive firepower is the key ingredient in this strategy of attrition.

There is no doubt that the Soviets want to use a *blitzkrieg* strategy in any future war in Europe. There is, however, growing doubt in the Soviet Union as to whether this is possible on the modern battlefield.[26] This matter has been debated at length in Soviet military journals. Despite such attention, apparently no clear consensus has emerged on this issue. The important question, which will be addressed later, is: what effect does this doctrinal uncertainty have on the Soviets' ability to effect a *blitzkrieg*?

*Soviet Prospects for Effecting a Blitzkrieg in Central Europe*

By choosing a forward defense strategy, NATO has effectively determined that a war in Europe will be won or lost along the inter-German border. It is thus imperative that NATO thwart the Pact in those initial battles along the border. This point is clearly reflected on the opening page of *FM 100-5*, which spells out basic U.S. Army doctrine: "the first battle of our next war

---

24. See John Despres, Lilita Dzirkals, and Barton Whaley, *Timely Lessons of History: The Manchurian Model for Soviet Strategy,* R–1825–NA (Santa Monica, Calif.: Rand Corporation, July 1976); Lilita I. Dzirkals, *"Lightning War" In Manchuria: Soviet Military Analysis Of The 1945 Far East Campaign,* P–5589 (Santa Monica, Calif.: Rand Corporation, January 1976); and Peter Vigor and Christopher Donnelly, "The Manchurian Campaign and Its Relevance to Modern Strategy," *Comparative Strategy,* Vol. 2, No. 2 (1980), pp. 159–178.
25. For a good description of Soviet strategy against Germany, see Erich von Manstein, "The Development of the Red Army, 1942–1945," in *The Soviet Army,* ed. B.H. Liddell Hart (London: Weidenfeld and Nicolson, 1956), pp. 140–152.
26. See Christopher N. Donnelly's *very important* article, "Tactical Problems Facing the Soviet Army: Recent Debates in the Soviet Military Press," *International Defense Review,* Vol. 11, No. 9 (1978), pp. 1405–1412. This article challenges the widely held belief that the Soviets have developed a well-knit strategy for defeating NATO (see the sources cited in fn. 79 for evidence of this belief). Also see A. A. Grechko, *The Armed Forces Of The Soviet Union,* trans. Yuri Sviridov (Moscow: Progress Publishers, 1977), p. 160; Phillip A. Karber, "The Soviet Anti-Tank Debate," *Survival,* Vol. 18, No. 3 (May/June 1976), pp. 105–111; V. Kulikov, "Soviet Military Science Today," *Strategic Review,* Vol. 5, No. 1 (Winter 1977), pp. 127–134; and Vigor and Donnelly, "The Manchurian Campaign."

could well be its last battle. . . . the U.S. Army must, above all else, *prepare to win the first battle of the next war.*" [27] If the Soviets win those initial battles and penetrate with large armored forces deep into NATO's rear, NATO's fate is sealed, since it has neither the reserve strength necessary to counter such penetrations, nor the strategic depth which would allow for retreat and the establishment of a new front.

To determine whether the Soviets can successfully launch a *blitzkrieg* against NATO's forward defense, two key questions must be answered. First, can the Soviets achieve the necessary force ratios on their main axes of advance so that they can then open gateways into NATO's rear? In other words, given the deployment of NATO's forces as well as the terrain, how likely is it that the Soviets will be able to repeat the German achievement opposite the Ardennes Forest in 1940? Is it true, as advocates of a maneuver-oriented defense claim, that the Pact can choose any point on the NATO front and achieve the superiority of forces necessary to effect a breakthrough? The answer to these questions will largely be determined by matching NATO's deployment pattern, which is well known, against those deployment patterns which would most likely be used as part of a Soviet *blitzkrieg.*

Second, if the Soviets are able to tear open a hole or two in NATO's defensive front, will the Soviets be able to exploit those openings and penetrate into the depths of the NATO defense before NATO has a chance to shift forces and slow the penetrating spearheads? Effecting a deep strategic penetration in the "fog of war," when the defender is doing everything possible to seal off the gaps in his defense, is difficult and requires a first-rate army. How capable is the Soviet Army of accomplishing this difficult task? Although it is not possible to provide definitive answers to these questions, there is good reason to believe that NATO is capable of thwarting a Soviet *blitzkrieg* and turning the conflict into a war of attrition.

THE INITIAL DEPLOYMENT PATTERNS

When considering Soviet deployment patterns for a conventional European war, the most basic question is: how will the Soviets apportion their forces across the front? More specifically, will the Soviets disperse their forces rather evenly across the front, mounting attacks along numerous axes, or will they concentrate their forces at one, two, or three points along the inter-German

---

27. *FM 100-5: Operations* (Washington D.C.: Department of the Army, July 1, 1976), p. 1-1.

border? In many of the accounts by Western analysts, it is assumed that a Soviet offensive will be a multi-pronged one. For example, John Erickson expects that they will attempt "eight to ten breakthrough operations."[28] In effect, NATO will be faced with numerous attacks across its entire front. Equally important, it is frequently assumed that the Soviets will achieve overwhelming superiority in forces on *each* of these avenues of attack.

It is possible that the Soviets might choose to launch an offensive along multiple axes of advance. This would be consistent with their doctrine for fighting a nuclear war in Europe, where the emphasis is on keeping the attacking forces widely dispersed so that they are not vulnerable to nuclear attacks. However, such a deployment pattern would hardly facilitate employment of a *blitzkrieg*, simply because it would be virtually impossible for the Soviets, given the present overall balance of forces, to achieve overwhelming force ratios on any of the axes. This can be demonstrated by looking at a *hypothetical* but realistic model of the Central Front.

Let us assume that the Pact has 64 armored division equivalents while NATO has 32; in other words, the Pact has a 2:1 force advantage across the front.[29] Furthermore, assume that the Soviets plan to employ a multi-pronged attack, aiming to strike along six main axes. In keeping with the dictates of a forward defense, NATO divides its 32 divisions evenly among its eight corps sectors (see Figure 2). It is usually assumed that to overwhelm the defense, an attacking force needs more than a 3:1 advantage in forces on the main axes of advance; assume, then, in the first instance, that the Soviets decide that they require a 5:1 advantage.[30] They would therefore need 20

28. John Erickson, "Soviet Breakthrough Operations: Resources and Restraints," *Journal of the Royal United Services Institute*, Vol. 121, No. 3 (September 1976), p. 75. Also see the scenario described by John Hackett et al., *The Third World War: A Future History* (London: Sidgwick and Jackson, 1978), p. 127.

29. It should be emphasized that in light of the balance of standing forces in Central Europe (1.2:1 in terms of armored division equivalents) and the fact that NATO has the capability to match the Pact as it brings in reinforcements, this 2:1 force advantage is a conservative figure. Unless otherwise specified, the unit of measurement in all subsequent discussion of force ratios is armored division equivalents.

30. The Soviets emphasize the importance of achieving overwhelming superiority on the main axes of advance in a conventional war. See V. Ye. Savkin, *The Basic Principles of Operational Art and Tactics* (Moscow, 1972), trans. U.S. Air Force (Washington D.C.: GPO, 1976), pp. 119–152, 201–229 and A.A. Sidorenko, *The Offensive: A Soviet View* (Moscow, 1970), trans. U.S. Air Force (Washington D.C.: GPO, 1976), chapter 1. Based on the lessons of World War II, the Soviets estimate that "a decisive superiority . . . [is] 3–5 times for infantry, 6–8 times for artillery, 3–4 times for tanks and self-propelled artillery, and 5–10 times for aircraft." Sidorenko, p. 82. These ratios are consistent with the American Army's view on the matter. See *FM 100-5*, p. 3-4.

**Figure 2. Initial Distribution of NATO Divisions**

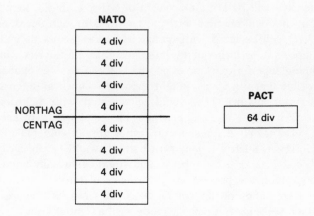

divisions per axis, which would allow them only three main axes of advance[31] (see Figure 3). Moreover, they would be quite vulnerable to NATO in the remaining five corps sectors.

If we assume that the Soviets require only a 4:1 advantage on the main axes, they would then need 16 divisions per axis. This would allow them only four main axes; however, they would not have any forces left with which to defend the remaining corps sectors (see Figure 4). If the Soviets were to aim for the projected six axes, they would be able to place approximately ten divisions on each main axis (see Figure 5). This would give them a force ratio on each axis of 2.5:1, which is hardly satisfactory in light of the widely recognized assumption that an attack requires more than a 3:1 ad-

---

31. This *hypothetical* model is based on the important assumption that the Soviets can only place one main axis in each corps sector. As will become evident in the subsequent discussion, the terrain features along the inter-German border force the attacker to think in terms of a single axis per corps sector. Moreover, in light of the length of the various NATO corps sectors and the length of front the Soviets allot their attacking divisions and armies, it is most likely that the Soviets would locate only one axis in each corps sector. For a discussion of Soviet attack frontages, see Christopher Donnelly, "The Soviet Ground Forces," in *The Soviet War Machine*, ed. Ray Bonds (New York: Chartwell, 1976), pp. 166–170; John Erickson, "Soviet Theatre-Warfare Capability: Doctrines, Deployments and Capabilities," in *The Future of Soviet Military Power*, ed. Lawrence L. Whetten (New York: Crane, Russak, 1976), p. 148; and fn. 58 and the attendant text of this article.

**Figure 3. Distribution of Forces When Soviets Desire 5:1 Advantage**

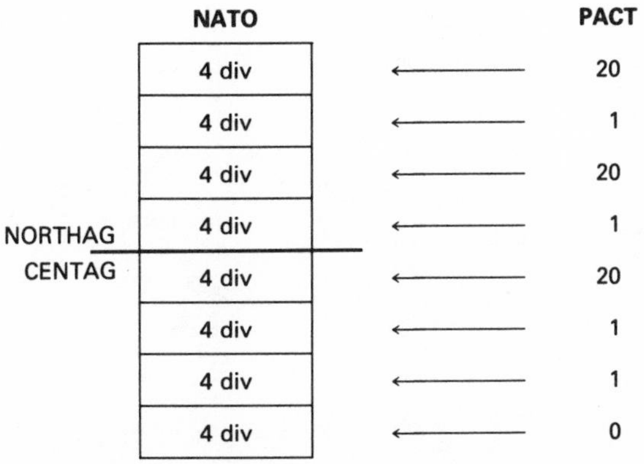

| | NATO | | PACT |
|---|---|---|---|
| | 4 div | ← | 20 |
| | 4 div | ← | 1 |
| | 4 div | ← | 20 |
| NORTHAG | 4 div | ← | 1 |
| CENTAG | 4 div | ← | 20 |
| | 4 div | ← | 1 |
| | 4 div | ← | 1 |
| | 4 div | ← | 0 |

vantage on each main axis to succeed. Obviously, the more axes you have, the smaller the advantage you achieve on each axis. Finally, the point is reached, in this case with eight main axes of advance, where the distribution of forces on each axis is the same as the overall 2:1 ratio (see Figure 6).

It is apparent from this *hypothetical* model that as long as NATO keeps the overall force ratio under 2:1, it is impossible for the Soviets to have 6–10 axes

**Figure 4. Distribution of Forces When Soviets Desire 4:1 Advantage**

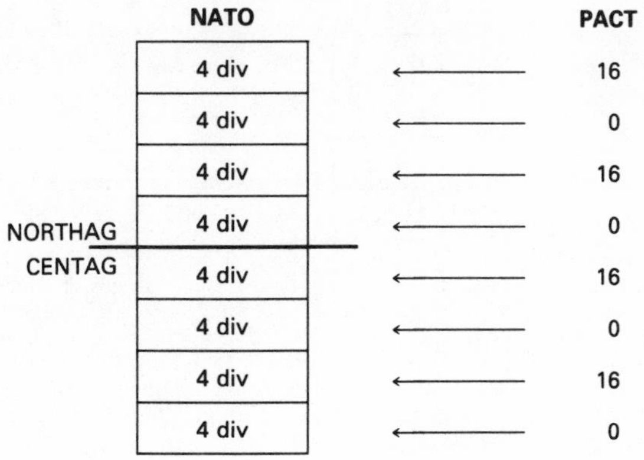

| | NATO | | PACT |
|---|---|---|---|
| | 4 div | ← | 16 |
| | 4 div | ← | 0 |
| | 4 div | ← | 16 |
| NORTHAG | 4 div | ← | 0 |
| CENTAG | 4 div | ← | 16 |
| | 4 div | ← | 0 |
| | 4 div | ← | 16 |
| | 4 div | ← | 0 |

**Figure 5. Distribution of Forces When Soviets Aim for 6 Main Axes**

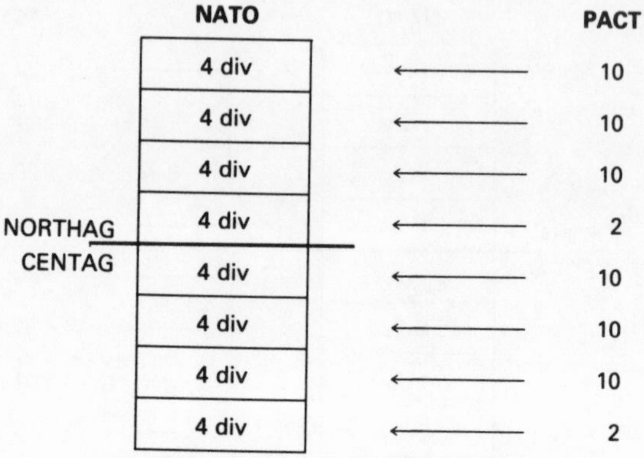

| | NATO | | PACT |
|---|---|---|---|
| | 4 div | ← | 10 |
| | 4 div | ← | 10 |
| | 4 div | ← | 10 |
| NORTHAG | 4 div | ← | 2 |
| CENTAG | 4 div | ← | 10 |
| | 4 div | ← | 10 |
| | 4 div | ← | 10 |
| | 4 div | ← | 2 |

of advance and at the same time have an overwhelming advantage in forces on each axis (i.e., a ratio of 4:1 or more). They just do not have a great enough overall force advantage to allow them to spread out their forces on numerous widely dispersed axes. The matter of force ratios aside, from NATO's viewpoint, a multi-pronged attack is the most desirable Pact deployment pattern. Then, NATO, whose forces are evenly spread out along

**Figure 6. Distribution of Forces When Soviets Aim for 8 Main Axes**

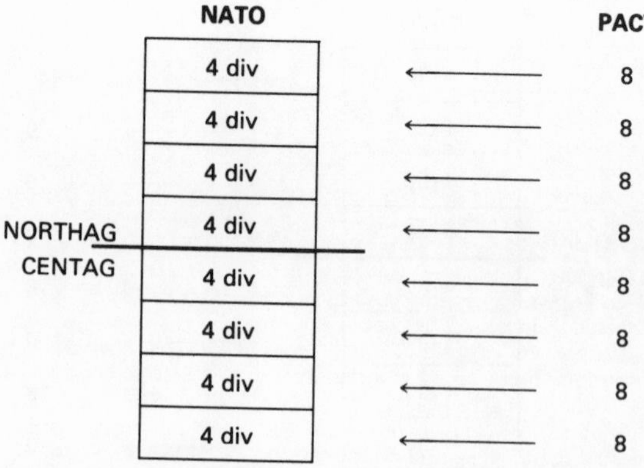

| | NATO | | PACT |
|---|---|---|---|
| | 4 div | ← | 8 |
| | 4 div | ← | 8 |
| | 4 div | ← | 8 |
| NORTHAG | 4 div | ← | 8 |
| CENTAG | 4 div | ← | 8 |
| | 4 div | ← | 8 |
| | 4 div | ← | 8 |
| | 4 div | ← | 8 |

a wide front, does not have to concern itself with shifting forces to counter massive concentrations of force by the Pact. From NATO's perspective, a multi-pronged attack results in a propitious meshing of the offensive and defensive deployment patterns.[32]

If the Pact does choose to employ a multi-pronged attack, it will, at best, end up pushing NATO back across a broad front, similar to the way the Soviets pushed the Germans westward across Europe in World War II. This is not a *blitzkrieg*, but a strategy of attrition. If the Soviets hope to defeat NATO with a *blitzkrieg*, they will have to concentrate massive amounts of armor on one, two or, at most, three major axes of advance. This raises the obvious questions: where are those axes likely to be? and how well-positioned is NATO to deal with the most likely Pact deployment patterns? More specifically, are NATO's forces positioned so that they can: first, stymie the initial onslaughts on the various potential axes of advance; and secondly, provide the time for NATO to move reinforcements to threatened positions, and, in effect, erase the temporary superiority in forces that the Pact has achieved by massing its forces at specific points?[33] These questions are best answered by closely examining, corps sector by corps sector, both the terrain and the deployment of NATO's forces.

---

32. Frequently, the claim is made that the Soviets will monitor progress along the various axes and move second-echelon armies (those forces moving up from the Western Soviet Union) onto the axes where they are making the most progress. This is hardly conducive to effecting a *blitzkrieg*. First, NATO will also be moving its reinforcements onto those same axes since that is where the Pact is threatening a breakthrough. Moreover, it takes time to move second-echelon forces into an attacking position, time during which NATO will make important adjustments. A *blitzkrieg*, by effecting a rapid breakthrough and then immediately exploiting it, seeks to deny the defender the time to make such adjustments. Finally, the divisions in the Pact's second-echelon armies will not be the Pact's most capable divisions. The 26 divisions in Central Europe, and specifically the 19 Soviet divisions in East Germany, are the best divisions in the Pact. They will have to make the key breakthroughs and conduct the deep strategic penetrations. The second-echelon armies may be of crucial importance in a war of attrition, but they will not play a major role in a *blitzkrieg*.
33. The assumption here is that, even if the Pact has only a small overall force advantage, it can still establish a significant superiority on at least one axis. NATO must then shift its forces so as to re-establish the overall balance at the points of main attack before the Pact is able to effect a deep strategic penetration. When one considers that it is widely accepted that the attacking forces need more than a 3:1 advantage at the points of main attack (see fn. 30 and the attendant text), and that the overall balance will be significantly less than 3:1, one sees that NATO will be in excellent shape if it has the capability to stop the initial onslaughts and then shift NATO forces to threatened points. Some analysts argue that, if the overall balance of forces is greater than 1.5:1, NATO's chances of accomplishing this task will be slim. See Hillier, *Strengthening NATO*; Hillier and Slatkin, *U.S. Ground Forces*, chapter 2; and James Schlesinger's *FY 1976 and 197T Posture Statement*, p. III-15. See also the discussion of this matter in fn. 61.

It is most unlikely that the Pact would place a major axis of advance in either the far north or the far south of the NATO front. In the south, this would preclude a major attack against II German Corps, simply because it would not result in a decisive victory. The Allies could afford to lose almost the entire corps sector, reaching back to the French border, and they would still be able to continue the war. Moreover, the mountainous terrain in this part of Germany is not conducive to the movement of large armored forces. In the north, a major offensive against Schleswig-Holstein is unlikely. Although the terrain is not mountainous in this sector there are still enough obstacles (bogs, rivers, urban sprawl around Hamburg) to hinder the movement of a large armored force. Furthermore, a Pact success in this region would not constitute a mortal blow to NATO. The main body of NATO's forces would still be intact and capable of conducting a vigorous defense.

CHANNELING FORCES: THE PACT'S AXES OF ATTACK IN CENTAG
The Soviets are most likely to locate their main attacks along the front stretching from the I Dutch Corps Sector in the north to the VII American Corps Sector in the south. Let us first consider the three key corps sectors in CENTAG (III German, V U.S., and VII U.S.). Generally, the terrain in the CENTAG area is very obstacle-ridden. Besides being a mountainous region, it has numerous rivers and forests. Consequently, there are a small number of natural avenues of attack in CENTAG. Actually, there are three potential axes on which the Soviets are likely to attack.

The most threatening of the three possibilities would be an attack from the Thuringian Bulge through the Fulda Gap, aimed at Frankfurt (see Figure 7). Except for the Fulda River, the terrain on this axis should not greatly hinder the movement of large armored forces. Importantly, this axis cuts across the "wasp-waist" or the narrowest section of Germany. The distance from the inter-German border to Frankfurt is a mere 100 km. Frankfurt, because of its central location in Germany's communications network, would be a most attractive target. Capturing Frankfurt would effectively cut Germany in half, and given the importance of north-south lines of communication, would leave NATO's forces in southern Germany isolated.

The second potential axis of advance is located in the sector covered by the III German Corps. The attacking forces would move through the Göttingen Corridor, just south of the Harz Mountains. The industrialized Ruhr is located due west of Göttingen. Although the terrain on the western half of this axis (between Paderborn and the Ruhr) is suitable for the large-

**Figure 7. Most Likely Axes of Advance in a Warsaw Pact Attack Against NATO**

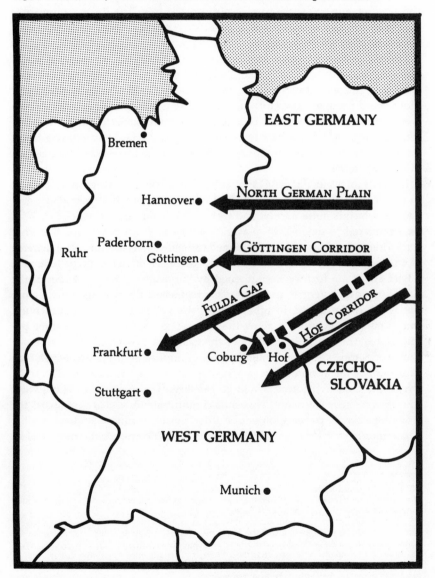

scale employment of tanks, the terrain on the eastern half of the axis, which the attacker must traverse first, is not obstacle-free. There are a number of forests in the region, and the attacking forces would have to cross the Leine River and then the Weser River.

There is a third potential axis of advance in CENTAG, although it is less attractive than the axes which run through the Fulda Gap and the Göttingen Corridor. This axis runs from Bohemia through the area around the city of Hof toward Stuttgart: the Hof Corridor.[34] The terrain that an attacking force would have to traverse there is considerably more obstacle-ridden than the terrain along the other axes. Moreover, Stuttgart is a far less attractive target than either Frankfurt or the Ruhr. Aside from these three axes, there are no attractive alternatives.

NATO's forces in CENTAG should be able to contain a major Soviet attack in this region. There are only a limited number of potential axes of advance, each of which is quite narrow and well defined and each of which NATO is well prepared to defend. Moreover, NATO has contingency plans to shift forces to combat Soviet efforts designed to achieve overwhelming force ratios at the points of main attack.[35] NATO's prospect of successfully halting a Soviet attack are further strengthened by the terrain, which not only limits the number of potential axes, but also channels the attacking forces across the width of Germany. In other words, the potential axes of advance are rather narrow and do not allow the attacker to spread his forces after the initial breakthrough.[36] In 1940, once the Germans crossed the Meuse River, they came upon the open, rolling plains of northeastern France, which was ideal terrain for armored forces. This would not be the case in CENTAG, where the attacking forces would be canalized by terrain throughout their movement across Germany. This should contribute to NATO's prospects for stopping a Soviet penetration before a decisive blow can be landed.

Another reason for optimism is that the NATO corps sectors in CENTAG

---

34. This axis could be shifted somewhat by moving the axis of advance 50 km to the west of Hof, toward the city of Coburg. Therefore, one could argue that there are actually two potential axes of advance in the U.S. VII Corps Sector.
35. Furthermore, given the sophisticated intelligence-gathering devices in the service of NATO forces, it should be possible to locate the Pact's main forces as they move to concentrate for the attack. Certainly, NATO should know where to look for Soviet troop concentrations.
36. It should be noted, however, that the Göttingen Corridor only covers the eastern half of West Germany. (It is approximately 100 km in length.) To the west of Paderborn, the terrain is open and generally well suited for armored warfare.

are manned by German and American Forces, which are the best in NATO.[37] Furthermore, there are reinforcements in CENTAG. The United States has pre-positioned materiel for two divisions in CENTAG's rear.[38] Also, French and Canadian forces (three small French armored divisions and one Canadian brigade) are located in CENTAG and can serve as an operational reserve for this half of NATO's defense.[39]

THE NORTH GERMAN PLAIN: OPEN ROAD FOR A PACT ADVANCE?

Now, consider NATO's prospects for containing a Soviet attack directed against NORTHAG. It is widely held that NATO is more vulnerable in this region than in CENTAG. The terrain in NORTHAG, because it is not mountainous and covered with forests, is generally held to be more favorable to the movement of large armored formations. Frequent reference is made to the suitability of the North German Plain for a *blitzkrieg*.[40] Secondly, there are doubts about whether the Dutch and the Belgians, and even the British, have the capability to withstand a Soviet attack. There is only one German Corps Sector in NORTHAG and there is no U.S. Corps Sector, although pre-positioned materiel for a U.S. Corps, which will serve as an operational reserve for NORTHAG, is being deployed near Bremen.[41] Notwithstanding

---

37. In terms of the quality of the fighting forces, it is widely recognized among NATO military leaders that the German Army is the best in Europe, the Soviets included. Regarding equipment, the German and American Armies are the best equipped in NATO.

38. This equipment for U.S. forces is commonly referred to as POMCUS (pre-positioned materiel configured to unit sets). In a crisis, the United States will fly the designated units (only the troops) to Europe, where the necessary equipment will be waiting for them. POMCUS solves the difficult problem of rapidly transporting a unit's equipment across the Atlantic. A POMCUS division is expected to be ready to fight 10 days after mobilization. For a discussion of POMCUS, see Hillier, *Strengthening NATO*.

39. It should be noted that the Germans are in the process of significantly upgrading the fighting capability of their Territorial Army. The core of this force is six armored infantry brigades, although there are numerous other units (including six more armored infantry brigades) which are being upgraded. See *1979 German White Paper*, pp. 154–156.

40. For example, see Close, *Europe Without Defense?*, p. 172; John M. Collins, *U.S.–Soviet Military Balance* (New York: McGraw-Hill, 1980), pp. 312–314; Hackett et al., pp. 101–102; and Richard D. Lawrence and Jeffrey Record, *U.S. Force Structure in NATO* (Washington D.C.: The Brookings Institution, 1974), p. 28. For an excellent discussion of this matter, which directly challenges this view, see Polk, "The North German Plain Attack Scenario."

41. This corps will comprise three divisions. It is important to note that only two brigades will actually be stationed in Europe. These two brigades will serve as forward elements for two of the divisions, the remainder of which will be flown in from the U.S. All of the third division will be stationed in the United States. The POMCUS (see fn. 38) for one of these three divisions is in place. The POMCUS for the remaining two is presently being deployed (see *FY 1983 Posture Statement*, pp. III-96–III-97). The presence of these three POMCUS divisions in NORTHAG, plus

that NATO is more vulnerable in this region than in CENTAG, the prospects for thwarting a major Soviet attack in NORTHAG are quite good. The terrain is not obstacle-free by any means and, as will become clear, the Belgian and Dutch Corps Sectors are not the weak links that they are often said to be.

NORTHAG covers a front of only 225 km while CENTAG defends a front that is more than two times as long (500 km).[42] Appropriately, the corps sectors in NORTHAG are smaller than those in CENTAG. The I Belgian Corps occupies the southernmost and smallest sector in NORTHAG, measuring only 35 km. Approximately one-third of the front is covered by the Harz Mountains, while the terrain throughout the depth of the corps sector is laden with obstacles. Belgium's two divisions, small as they are, are adequate for defending this short front in the initial stages of an attack.[43] Although it is unlikely that the Pact would place a main axis through this corps sector, if it did, forces from the III German Corps, immediately to the south, could be moved north to reinforce the Belgians, and forces from the U.S. Corps in reserve could be moved forward.

The North German Plain, above the Belgian Corps Sector, is covered by the I British and I German Corps. There is widespread agreement that the Pact will place a single main axis against NORTHAG and that that axis will be located on the North German Plain. Although there are no mountains and few forests in this region, there are obstacles in both the German and British Corps Sectors. In the British Corps Sector, there is significant urban sprawl centered on Hannover, which is located in the heart of this corps sector.[44] Armored forces simply will not be able to move rapidly through those urban

---

the two POMCUS divisions in CENTAG, highlights how important it is that NATO begin mobilizing its forces immediately in a crisis.

42. Polk, "The North German Plain Attack Scenario," p. 61. It is somewhat difficult to reach a precise agreement on these distances because one can measure either: the actual contour of the inter-German border; the straight-line distance of the corps sector front; or some combination of the two.

43. The matter of force-to-space ratios will be discussed later in greater detail. It is generally agreed that a brigade can hold a front of 7–15 km (see fn. 52 and the attendant text). Since the Belgians have four brigades in their corps sector (a good portion of which is covered by the Harz Mountains), they should be able to hold 35 km of front long enough for NATO to bring in reinforcements.

44. See Paul Bracken, "Urban Sprawl and NATO Defence," *Survival*, Vol. 18, No. 6 (November/December 1976), p. 256; and *FM 100-5*, p. 14-17. The Soviets are fully cognizant of the difficulties of conducting offensive operations in urban areas. See C.N. Donnelly, "Soviet Techniques for Combat in Built up Areas," *International Defense Review*, Vol. 10, No. 2 (1977), pp. 238–242. For a general discussion of the terrain in NORTHAG, see Polk, "The North German Plain Attack Scenario," pp. 61–62.

areas that NATO chooses to defend. Since urbanization continues in this area, it will become increasingly difficult, if not impossible, to avoid large-scale urban fighting in the event of war. There are also a number of rivers in the British sector. The terrain in the I German Corps Sector, on the other hand, is covered, in large part, by the Lüneberger Heath, which is a formidable impediment to the rapid movement of masses of armor. It is for this reason that the North German Plain is usually identified with the British Corps Sector.

The British Army of the Rhine (BAOR) is comprised of four small divisions, a force that is adequate for covering the 70 km corps sector front.[45] There are, however, 13 brigades—or four and one-third formidable divisions—in the I German Corps Sector.[46] Aside from the fact that these German forces are more than adequate for defending their assigned corps sector, they can be rapidly moved to the south to augment the BAOR and, of course, they can also move northward to help the Dutch. This contingent in the I German Corps Sector represents the largest concentration of forces in all of the sectors. Given its central location in NORTHAG as well as the excellent north-south lines of communication in that region, this force is a formidable instrument for thwarting a Pact attack across the North German Plain.[47] Furthermore, there will be an American Corps, part of which is already deployed, in NORTHAG's rear.[48] In sum, NATO *has* the wherewithal to deal with a Pact attack across the North German Plain.

Finally, there is the Dutch Corps Sector, which is manned by two Dutch divisions. Should the Soviets place a main axis through this sector, the Dutch

---

45. There are the equivalent of seven brigades in the BAOR. Assuming that a brigade can cover a front of 7–15 km (see fn. 52 and the attendant text), the BAOR should be able to hold its front long enough for NATO to bring in reinforcements.
46. Furthermore, those 13 brigades are ten percent "over strength." Daniel Schorr, "The Red Threat And NATO Today," *Norfolk Virginian-Pilot*, October 2, 1978, section 1, p. 19. Also see Polk, "The North German Plain Attack Scenario," p. 61.
47. The German forces are divided among three corps sectors and Schleswig-Holstein. None of these sectors are adjacent to each other (see Figure 1), which means that the Germans, by bumping forces up or down the line, can move German brigades into every non-German corps sector on the front. When an attacking force executes a *blitzkrieg*, the attacker's flanks are usually vulnerable. The Soviets would have to keep in mind that if they penetrate into the rear of a non-German corps, the Germans will undoubtedly drive into their exposed flanks, attempting to sever the penetrating forces from their base.
48. Furthermore, German units from CENTAG can be moved to NORTHAG. See Ulrich de Mazière, *Rational Deployment of Forces on the Central Front*, Study Prepared for the Western Economic Union, April 2, 1975, p. 40. There are also the forces in the German Territorial Army (see fn. 39), a portion of which will undoubtedly be assigned to NORTHAG in a conflict.

forces, like their British and Belgian counterparts, should be capable of defending their front in the initial stages of the conflict. Then, forces from the adjacent I German Corps can be moved north to assist the Dutch. Moreover, the American Corps will be located directly to the rear of the Dutch Sector. The terrain within the Dutch Corps Sector is not conducive to the rapid movement of armored forces. In addition to the Elbe River, which forms the inter-German border in this sector, a number of other rivers, canals, and bogs are liberally sprinkled throughout this sector. The Lüneberger Heath, which is such a prominent feature in the adjacent I German Corps Sector, extends northward across the Dutch Sector. To add to the woes of the attacker, there is significant urban sprawl around Bremen and Bremerhaven.[49] Finally, even if the attacking forces were able to penetrate through this sector rapidly, it is unlikely that NATO would be mortally wounded. Certainly, NATO would feel the loss of the ports in northern Germany. However, since the attacking forces would exit Germany into the northern part of the Netherlands, NATO would still have access to the most important Belgian and Dutch ports.

FORCE-TO-SPACE RATIOS

There are a number of additional points concerning Soviet and NATO deployment patterns that merit attention. The discussion has so far focused on the matter of the Pact's achieving overwhelming superiority on specific axes of advance. However, when examining prospects for a breakthrough at the point of main attack, one cannot simply focus on the *balance* of forces. It is also necessary to consider *force-to-space ratios*, or the number of divisions that the defender requires to *hold* a specific sector of territory.[50] If a defender can comfortably hold 100 km with four divisions, then even if the attacker has 24 divisions, that attacker will have to sacrifice a significant number of his 24 divisions before he finally wears the defender down to the point where he can effect a penetration. Obviously, this would be a time-consuming as well as a costly process, during which the defender can bring in reinforcements. There is an important factor which complicates the attacker's task in such a situation: the "crossing the T" phenomenon.[51] Simply put, there is not

---

49. See Bracken, "Urban Sprawl and NATO Defence," p. 256 and *FM 100-5*, p. 14-17.
50. For an excellent discussion of this concept, see B. H. Liddell Hart, *Deterrent or Defense* (New York: Praeger, 1960), chapter 10.
51. Although originally a naval concept (see George Quester, *Offense and Defense in the International System* [New York: John Wiley, 1977], p. 92), "crossing the T" also applies to land warfare.

enough room for the attacker to place all of his 24 divisions at the point of attack. He must therefore locate a portion of his divisions in subsequent echelons behind the attacking forces, where their impact on the battlefield will be minimal while the first echelon is engaged. In essence, the defender is in the enviable position of being able to deal with the attacker's forces on a piecemeal basis. How do these abstract considerations relate to the European Central Front?

It is generally agreed that a brigade can hold a front approximately 7–15 km long.[52] With 7 km, which is obviously the more desirable figure, a brigade should be able to hold its position for an extended period of time before it needs reinforcement. As the figure approaches 15 km, the defender should be able to cope with the initial onslaughts without any problem. However, it will be necessary to bring in reinforcements after a day or so since the attacker's forces will have begun to wear down the defender by then. Since the length of the NORTHAG front is 225 km, if one assumes that each brigade could hold 15 km, then a minimum of 15 brigades would be needed to cover the front. There are actually 30 brigades within the four NORTHAG corps sectors.[53] Given that there are 30 brigades and a 225 km front, this means that each brigade will have to cover 7.5 km, which is extremely close to the most desirable force-to-space ratio for a brigade.

Now, let us assume that NATO deploys its 30 brigades along the NORTHAG front in the traditional "two brigades up, one back" configuration. This would leave 20 brigades to cover 225 km (each brigade would have to cover 11 km), with 10 brigades in immediate reserve. This leaves NATO in very good shape. Two other important points are in order. First, because there are a number of obstacles along the NORTHAG front, NATO would

---

52. Regarding the optimum number of km which a brigade can hold, it is difficult to come up with an exact figure. This is because such a force-to-space ratio varies according to the size and quality of the forces on each side as well as the nature of the terrain. Recognizing that this problem exists, it is generally estimated that a brigade can hold 7–15 km of front. These figures are based on discussions with American, German, and Israeli military officers as well as: J. R. Angolia and Donald B. Vought, "The United States Army," in *The U.S. War Machine*, ed. Ray Bonds (New York: Crown, 1978), p. 74; Hillier and Slatkin, *U.S. Ground Forces*, p. 25; Liddell Hart, *Deterrent or Defense*, chapter 10; Hans-Joachim Löser, "Vorneverteidigung der Bundesrepublik Deutschland?" *Österreichische Militärische Zeitschrift*, Vol. 18, No. 2 (March/April 1980), p. 121; and U.S. Army Training and Doctrine Command, *Division Restructuring Study*, Phase 1 Report, Executive Summary, Vol. 1, Fort Monroe, VA, March 1, 1977, p. 3.

53. There are: 6 brigades in the I Dutch Corps Sector; 13 brigades in the I German Corps Sector; the equivalent of 7 brigades in the I British Corps Sector; and 4 brigades in the I Belgian Corps Sector. These figures are from de Mazière, "Rational Deployment of Forces," pp. 11–12.

not have to worry about covering every section of the 225 km front. Second, the American Corps in NORTHAG's rear, when fully operational, will provide an additional nine brigades. Also, there are at least six armored infantry brigades in the German Territorial Army that could be assigned to NORTHAG.[54] In short, NORTHAG does not have force-to-space problems.[55]

The length of the CENTAG front is 500 km. Assuming 15 km per brigade, 33 brigades would be required to cover this front. NATO has 33 brigades in the four CENTAG corps sectors, a figure which is hardly alarming in light of the obstacle-ridden terrain along this portion of the NATO front and the fact that the brigades in these corps sectors are the heaviest in NATO and therefore will have the least amount of trouble covering 15 km of front.[56] Furthermore, there are 21 brigades (including the French, but not including the German territorials) available for reinforcement in CENTAG's rear.[57]

"CROSSING THE T" IN EUROPE

Consider briefly the "crossing the T" phenomenon, which further highlights the problems that the Soviets will have breaking through NATO's forward positions. In one of the U.S. Army's standard scenarios for a major Soviet attack against one of the two U.S. Corps Sectors in CENTAG, a Soviet force of five divisions is pitted against two American divisions.[58] In the opening battle, three Soviet divisions attack across about 40 to 50 km of front against

---

54. See the discussion of the German Territorial Army in fn. 39.
55. It should be noted that after a lengthy mobilization involving both sides, NATO's position, regardless of what the overall balance of forces looked like, would be extremely favorable on force-to-space ratio grounds. In other words, with regard to having adequate forces to cover the entire front, NATO's position, which is favorable before mobilizing, improves even more as large numbers of additional forces are moved to the Central Front.
56. There are: 7 brigades in the III German Corps Sector; 7 brigades in the V U.S. Corps Sector; 7 brigades in the VII U.S. Corps Sector; and 12 brigades in the II German Corps Sector. These figures are from de Mazière, *ibid.*, pp. 12–13.
57. Also, given the nature of the terrain along the inter-German border in CENTAG, NATO would not have to be very concerned with protecting sizeable segments of the front. The 21 brigades include a Canadian brigade and 3 French divisions (6 brigades) stationed in West Germany as well as 2 American-based divisions (6 brigades) with POMCUS in CENTAG and 4 French divisions (8 brigades) stationed in France.
58. See U.S., Congress, Senate Armed Services Committe, *Hearings on Department of Defense Authorization for Appropriations for Fiscal Year 1981 (Part 5)*, 96th Cong., 2nd Sess. (Washington D.C.: GPO, 1980), pp. 3053–3078. It should be noted that the Americans would actually have two and one-third divisions, not two divisions, in each of their corps sectors. This discrepancy is a result of the fact that the armored cavalry regiment that would be in each corps sector is not counted in this scenario.

two U.S. divisions.[59] The remaining two Soviet divisions are held in immediate reserve. Thus, in that opening battle the ratio of forces directly engaged
is 3:2 in the Pact's favor, not 5:2. (It should be noted that these ratios would
be even more favorable to NATO if they were translated into armored division equivalents.) Of course, the key question is: can those three Soviet
divisions so weaken the two American divisions that the remaining two
Soviet divisions will be able to effect a breakthrough? In this regard, the
matter of force-to-space ratios is of crucial importance. Since two divisions,
or six brigades, are defending 40–50 km, each of these powerful American
brigades will be holding approximately 7 km. Without a doubt, the Soviets
would have a great deal of difficulty penetrating that American front.

Now, let us assume that the Soviets start with ten or even fifteen divisions,
instead of the five employed in the above scenario. Only a very few of these
additional divisions could be placed at the point of main attack, simply
because there would be limited room on the front to accommodate them.
They would have to be located *behind* the attacking forces, where they would
have little impact on the initial battles.[60] Certainly, the forces in each NATO
corps sector should be capable of blunting the initial Soviet attack and providing adequate time for NATO to shift forces from other corps sectors and
its operational reserves to threatened points along the front.[61]

---

59. It should be noted that these three attacking divisions would not be spread out evenly
across the 40–50 km of front. They would concentrate at specific points along that front.
60. The Soviets could attempt to spread their forces out and attack across a broad front.
However, this would lead to serious problems. First of all, the terrain along the inter-German
border is such that the natural avenues of attack are relatively narrow and well defined. Second,
and more importantly, once the attacking forces are spread out, the key principle of concentrating forces on narrow fronts to effect a breakthrough is violated. Not surprisingly, all evidence
indicates that the Soviets intend to concentrate their attacking forces on narrow fronts, placing
large numbers of their divisions in echelons behind the main body of attacking divisions. (See
the sources cited in fns. 31 and 72.) It should be noted that over the past decade the United
States has devoted considerable attention to developing weaponry specifically designed to attack
second and third echelon forces. (See, for example, the discussion in the document cited in fn.
58.)
61. It was noted in fn. 33 that a number of defense analysts argue that NATO must prevent the
overall ratio of forces on the Central Front from exceeding 1.5:1 in the Pact's favor. Once this
occurs, it becomes easier for the Pact to achieve overwhelming force advantages at specific
points along the front. Although it is certainly desirable to keep that overall ratio at 1.5:1 or less,
it seems clear from the foregoing discussion that even if the overall ratio reaches 2:1 (which is
*certainly* a worst case assumption, with NATO mobilizing immediately after the Pact) and the
Pact thus achieves overwhelming superiority on two or three axes, NATO should be able to
hold at those points of main attack long enough to allow NATO to shift its forces and establish
ratios at these points that reflect the overall 2:1 ratio. However, it is clear that NATO would

In sum, given the initial deployment patterns of both NATO and the Pact, it appears that NATO is reasonably well deployed to meet a Soviet *blitzkrieg*. Although both Pact and NATO deployment patterns have been examined, attention has been focused, for the most part, on examining *NATO*'s capability to thwart a *blitzkrieg*. Now let us shift the focus and examine, in detail, *Soviet* capabilities.

*Soviet Capabilities for Blitzkrieg Warfare*

To ascertain whether the Soviet Army has the capacity to effect a *blitzkrieg*, it is necessary to examine that Army on three levels. First, one must consider how the Soviet Army is organized. In other words, are the forces structured to facilitate a *blitzkrieg*? Second, it is necessary to consider doctrine, a subject that has already received some attention. Finally, there is the matter of raw skill. Assuming that the problems with force structure and doctrine are minimal, is the Soviet Army capable of performing the assigned task? There are, of course, no simple answers to these questions. They are nonetheless extremely important questions which have received little serious attention in the West, where it is all too often assumed that the Soviets have only strengths and no weaknesses.

Since almost all the Pact divisions that would be used in a European war are either armored or mechanized infantry, it seems reasonable to assume that the Pact is appropriately organized to launch a *blitzkrieg*. On close inspection, however, there are potential trouble spots in the Pact's force structure. Over the past decade, Soviet divisions have become extremely heavy units. Western analysts pay a great deal of attention to the large and growing number of tanks, infantry fighting vehicles, artillery pieces, rocket launchers, surface-to-air missiles, air defense guns, anti-tank guided missiles (ATGMs), and assorted other weapons that are found in Soviet as well as other Pact divisions.[62] Past a certain point, however, there is an inverse relationship between the mass and the velocity of an attacking force. As the size of the attacking force increases, the logistical problems as well as the command and control problems increase proportionately. Then, it becomes very difficult to

---

have significant problems should the overall ratio surpass 2:1. See *FY 1982 Posture Statement*, p. 74.
62. See, for example, Richard Burt, "Soviet Said To Add To Its Bloc Troops," *The New York Times*, June 8, 1980, section 1, p. 4.

move that force rapidly—an *essential* requirement for a *blitzkrieg*, where the attacker is seeking to strike deep into the defender's rear before the defender can shift forces to deal with the penetrating forces. Although the notion is perhaps counterintuitive, bigger divisions are not necessarily better divisions when an attacking force is attempting to effect a *blitzkrieg*.[63]

Consider now the matter of doctrine. As noted earlier, it is not possible to determine exactly how the Soviets plan to fight a conventional war in Europe. This is because the Soviets themselves are not sure; there is presently doctrinal uncertainty in their military circles. Certainly, they continue to emphasize the necessity of rapidly defeating NATO, should a war in Europe break out. The Soviets recognize, however, that it is becoming increasingly difficult to do this, especially because of the proliferation of ATGMs.[64] Moreover, they are well aware of how these organizational problems compound their task. They realize that it will be difficult to effect deep strategic penetrations against prepared defenses.[65] Although there has been a considerable effort to find a solution to this problem, if anything, the Soviets appear to be moving closer to a strategy of attrition. This is reflected in their growing reliance on artillery and dismounted infantry.[66] There is no evidence that the Soviets have made a conscious decision to fight a war of attrition. Instead, it appears that they are being inexorably drawn in this direction by their

---

63. See the comments of the former German General Balck on this matter in General William E. DePuy, *Generals Balck and von Mellenthin On Tactics: Implications For NATO Military Doctrine*, BDM/W–81–077–TR (McLean, VA: The BDM Corporation, December 19, 1980), pp. 46–48.
64. See the sources cited in fn. 26, especially Donnelly's "Tactical Problems," which examines in detail Soviet thinking on strategy and tactics in a European land war. Also see his "Soviet Tactics for Overcoming NATO Anti-Tank Defenses," *International Defense Review*, Vol. 12, No. 7 (1979), pp. 1099–1106. For a general discussion of ATGMs and the *blitzkrieg*, see my "Precision-guided Munitions and Conventional Deterrence," *Survival*, Vol. 21, No. 2 (March/April 1979), pp. 68–76.
65. Christopher Donnelly writes, "[I]f the victory is not achieved quickly, the Russians believe, no meaningful victory can be achieved at all. It is not surprising, therefore, that Soviet officers have applied themselves to the problem of how to ensure their rapid rate of advance in war. . . . What is of particular interest is that no single straightforward answer to this problem has yet emerged and that it is still the subject of intense discussion." Donnelly, "Tactics for Overcoming," p. 1099. He then goes on to say that, "In general, their identification and dissection of the problem is excellent. Their suggestions as to what should be done usually appear quite sound, but are often tinged with lack of confidence or an excess of bland enthusiasm, hiding uncertainty. Sometimes they are contradictory in detail." *Ibid.*, p. 1100.
66. See Christopher Donnelly, "Modern Soviet Artillery," *NATO's Fifteen Nations*, Vol. 24, No. 3 (June–July 1979), pp. 48–54; Donnelly, "Tactical Problems"; Donnelly, "Tactics for Overcoming"; and Karber, "Anti-Tank Debate."

efforts to neutralize the growing firepower, both ground-based and air-delivered, available to NATO.

BLITZKRIEG AND THE NUCLEAR BATTLEFIELD
The Soviets continue to pay serious attention to the possibility that NATO will use nuclear weapons. Thus, they devote much time to training for a nuclear war which, by their own admission, would be fundamentally different from a conventional war and would require a different doctrine. For example, unlike a *blitzkrieg*, where the armor is concentrated in massive formations, the armor would be widely dispersed across the front so as not to present NATO with lucrative targets for her nuclear weapons.[67] Moreover, given the firepower provided by nuclear weapons, piercing NATO's front would not *require* the high concentration of forces that is necessary to achieve that objective in a conventional conflict. This highlights the point that the role of artillery would be greatly diminished on a nuclear battlefield. The upshot of this is that the time and resources the Soviets spend on preparing their forces to fight a nuclear war are time and resources that could be spent training those forces to fight a conventional war. In a crisis, the Soviets will be faced with an acute dilemma: whether to prepare their forces for a nuclear war or a conventional war. In this regard, NATO's plethora of tactical nuclear weapons serves a valuable purpose. The nuclear-conventional dichotomy aside, the Soviets still have not found a satisfactory strategy for fighting a conventional war. As long as they are not confident that they have a sound doctrine for inflicting a rapid and decisive defeat on NATO, the Soviets are not likely to initiate conflict in a crisis.

SOVIET TRAINING AND INITIATIVE
Finally, there is the question of whether the Soviet Army has the necessary raw skills. An army that intends to implement a *blitzkrieg* must have a highly flexible command structure as well as officers and NCOs at every level of the chain of command who are capable of exercising initiative.[68] A *blitzkrieg* is

---

67. See Savkin, *The Basic Principles of Operational Art and Tactics*, chapter 3. Also see V.D. Sokolovskiy, *Soviet Military Strategy*, ed. Harriet Fast Scott, 3rd ed. (New York: Crane, Russak, 1968).
68. These distinguishing characteristics are readily apparent in both the Israeli and German armies. See Dan Horowitz, "Flexible Responsiveness and Military Strategy: The Case of the Israeli Army," *Policy Sciences*, Vol. 1, No. 2 (Summer 1970), pp. 191–205; DePuy, *Generals Balck*

not a steamroller: success is ultimately a consequence of able commanders making rapid-fire decisions in the "fog of battle" which enable the attacking forces to make the crucial deep strategic penetrations. Should the Soviets attack NATO, there is a chance that the Soviets will open a hole or holes in the NATO front. Naturally, NATO will try to close those holes and seal off any penetrations as quickly as possible. The key question is: can the Soviets exploit such opportunities before NATO, which is well prepared for such an eventuality, shuts the door? In this battle, the crucial determinant will not be how much firepower the Soviets have amassed for the breakthrough; success will be largely the result of highly skilled officers and NCOs making the decisions that will enable the armored spearheads to outrun NATO's defenses. A *blitzkrieg* depends on split-second timing since opportunity on the battlefield is so fleeting.

There is substantial evidence that Soviet officers and NCOs are sadly lacking in individual initiative and, furthermore, that the Soviet command structure is rigid. Christopher Donnelly notes:

It is hard for a western officer to appreciate what a difficult concept [initiative] this is to reconcile with a normal Soviet upbringing. There has never been a native Russian word for initiative. The idea of an individual initiating unilateral action is anathema to the Soviet system. The Soviet army has always considered as one of its strengths its iron discipline and high-level, centralised command system combined with a universal tactical doctrine. The run-of-the-mill officer, particularly a sub-unit officer, has never had to do other than obey orders.[69]

The Soviets are keenly aware of the need for initiative and flexibility, and they go to great lengths to stress the importance of these qualities in their military journals.[70] These are not, however, attributes which can be willed into existence. Their absence is largely the result of powerful historical forces.[71] Fundamental structural change in Soviet society and the Soviet

---

*and von Mellenthin on Tactics*, pp. 16–23, 54–55; Erich Von Manstein, *Lost Victories* (Chicago: Regnery, 1958), pp. 63, 284; and *HDv 100/100* (especially p. 10-2).
69. Christopher Donnelly, "The Soviet Soldier: Behavior, Performance, Effectiveness," in *Soviet Military Power and Performance*, ed. John Erickson and E.J. Feuchtwanger (Hamden, Conn.: Archon Books, 1979), p. 115. Also see Joshua M. Epstein, "Soviet Confidence and Conventional Deterrence in Europe," *Orbis*, Vol. 26, No. 4 (Spring 1982).
70. Interestingly, Donnelly notes that when the Soviets discuss the problem of achieving a quick victory on the battlefield, "Not infrequently, the panacea of 'initiative' is invoked as a *deus ex machina*." Donnelly, "Tactics for Overcoming," p. 1100.
71. See Norman Stone, "The Historical Background of the Red Army," in Erickson and Feuchtwanger, *Soviet Military Power and Performance*, pp. 3–17.

military would be necessary before there would be any significant increase in flexibility and initiative.

Certainly analysts in the West argue that the Soviets have obviated this problem by relying on "steamroller tactics at the divisional level." Steven Canby, one of the leading proponents of this view, writes:

Steamroller tactics, at the divisional level, are characterized by a relatively inflexible command system and a rigid system of echeloned forces. . . . As formations are exhausted by fighting they are replaced rapidly by other echelons. . . . By maintaining momentum with large numbers of formations, Soviet forces plan to saturate enemy defences and offset the need for flexibility and initiative at the company level, where their tactics tend to be rigid. Having large numbers available gives higher commanders considerable flexibility.

Combat divisions and *even armies* can be used like drill tips on a high-speed drill—to be ground down and replaced until penetration occurs. [Emphasis mine][72]

There are major problems with this approach. First, the Pact does not have the overall superiority in forces needed for such "steamroller tactics." The notion that the Pact has an overwhelming superiority of forces which would allow it to expend forces in such a manner does not square with reality.[73] Secondly, the process of removing shattered divisions from the front and replacing them with fresh divisions is a complex and time-consuming task. Thirdly, even if such "steamroller tactics" enable the Pact to open a hole in NATO's front in the initial stages of the conflict, the Pact forces still must effect a deep strategic penetration while NATO is moving forces into its path. This is a most demanding task and requires both flexibility and initiative. Continued use of "steamroller tactics" after the breakthrough battle will not suffice.[74]

---

72. Steven Canby, *The Alliance and Europe: Part IV, Military Doctrine and Technology*, Adelphi Paper No. 109 (London: IISS, 1974/5), pp. 10–11. Also see John Erickson, "Soviet Ground Forces and the Conventional Mode of Operations," *Journal of the Royal United Services Institute*, Vol. 121, No. 2 (June 1976), p. 46.
73. This is reflected in the overall force ratios presented in this study.
74. What is particularly ironic about Canby's views on a Soviet offensive is that he criticizes NATO for preparing for a firepower-oriented battlefield while the Pact "is oriented towards an armoured-style conflict based on manoeuvre." He goes on to say, "[T]his means the United States fights battles to wear down opponents. The Soviet Union fights battles to *avoid* further battles." Steven Canby, "NATO: Reassessing the Conventional Wisdoms," *Survival*, Vol. 19, No. 4 (July/August 1977), p. 165. This view of Soviet strategy hardly squares with his discussion on using divisions and *even armies* in support of "steamroller tactics."

Other deficiencies in the Soviet Army cast doubt on the Soviets' capacity to launch a successful *blitzkrieg*. For example, the Soviets have significant problems with training.[75] Overreliance on training aids and simulators is a factor often cited, and there is widespread feeling that the training process does not satisfactorily approximate actual combat conditions. Training is of special importance for the Soviets since their army is comprised largely of conscripts who serve a mere two years. Moreover, since new conscripts are trained in actual combat units, more than half of the troops in the 19 Soviet divisions in East Germany are soldiers with less than two years of experience. At any one time, a significant number of those troops is either untrained or partially trained. It should also be noted that Soviet soldiers are deficient in map reading, a skill which is of much importance for an army attempting to launch a *blitzkrieg*.[76]

Finally, one must consider the capabilities of the non-Soviet divisions, which comprise approximately half of the Pact's 57⅓ standing divisions. Although the Soviet divisions will certainly perform the critical tasks in any offensive, the non-Soviet divisions will have to play a role in the operation. Otherwise, the size of the offensive would have to be scaled down significantly. One cannot say with any degree of certainty that the East Europeans would be militarily incapable of performing their assigned task or that they would not commit themselves politically to supporting a Soviet-led offensive. The Soviets, however, would have to give serious consideration to the reliability of the East Europeans.[77] If the Soviets indeed pay such careful attention to the lessons of the Great Patriotic War as is widely claimed, they recall what happened opposite Stalingrad in 1942 when the Soviets were able to inflict a stunning defeat on the Germans by ripping through those sectors of the front covered by the Rumanians, the Hungarians, and the Italians.[78]

---

75. See Donnelly, "Soviet Soldier," pp. 117–120; Keith A. Dunn, "Soviet Military Weaknesses and Vulnerabilities: A Critique Of The Short War Advocates," memorandum prepared for Strategic Studies Institute, U.S. Army War College, Carlisle Barracks, PA, July 31, 1978, pp. 15–16; Herbert Goldhamer, *Soviet Military Management at the Troop Level*, R–1513–PR (Santa Monica, Calif.: Rand Corporation, May 1974), chapters 2–4; Leon Gouré and Michael J. Deane, "The Soviet Strategic View," *Strategic Review*, Vol. 8, No. 1 (Winter 1980), pp. 84–85; and Karber, "Anti-Tank Debate," p. 108.
76. Dunn, "Soviet Military Weaknesses," pp. 16–17.
77. See Johnson et al., "The Armies of the Warsaw Pact" and Dale R. Herspring and Ivan Volgyes, "Political Reliability in the Eastern European Warsaw Pact Armies," *Armed Forces and Society*, Vol. 6, No. 2 (Winter 1980), pp. 270–296.
78. As John Erickson notes, it is very unlikely "that any non-Soviet national force would be alloted an independent operational role on any scale." Erickson, "Soviet Military Capabilities in

Although the Soviet Army has important deficiencies, it would still be a formidable opponent in a war in Europe; the Soviet Army is not by any means a hapless giant. Neither, however, is it an army which is well prepared to defeat NATO with a *blitzkrieg*. The shortcomings noted in the foregoing cast extreme doubt on the claim that the Soviets have the capability to launch a *blitzkrieg* with confidence of success. The Soviet Army is definitely not a finely tuned instrument capable of overrunning NATO at a moment's notice. To claim, then, that the Soviets have "adopted and improved the German *blitzkrieg* concept"[79] has a hollow ring. Most importantly, the evidence indicates that the Soviets recognize these shortcomings and their implications for winning a quick victory.

*Conclusion*

Even if one were to discount these weaknesses of the Soviet Army, the task of quickly overrunning NATO's defenses would be a very formidable one. A Pact offensive would have to traverse the obstacle-ridden terrain which covers almost all of Germany and restricts the movement of large armored units. Moreover, there is good reason to believe that NATO has the wherewithal to thwart such an offensive. In short, NATO is in relatively good shape at the conventional level. The conventional wisdom which claims otherwise on this matter is a distortion of reality. Since, as former Defense Secretary Donald Rumsfeld noted, "the burden of deterrence has once again fallen on the conventional forces," this is welcome news.[80]

Two very important caveats, however, are in order. First, NATO must provide for the continuation of ongoing improvements in its force structure. There is no evidence that the Soviet effort to modernize her forces in Central Europe is slowing down. Therefore, NATO must continue to make improvements if it is to maintain the present balance. It is absolutely essential, for example, that deployment of the American Corps in NORTHAG be com-

---

Europe," *Journal of the Royal United Services Institute*, Vol. 120, No. 1 (March 1975), p. 66. This could lead to problems for the Soviets because it forces them to disperse their own divisions, thus limiting the number available for the principal attacks.
79. Canby, *The Alliance and Europe*, p. 9. This view is also reflected in: Eugene D. Bétit, "Soviet Tactical Doctrine And Capabilities And NATO's Strategic Defense," *Strategic Review*, Vol. 4, No. 4 (Fall 1976), p. 96; Erickson, "Soviet Ground Forces," p. 46; and Daniel Gouré and Gordon McCormick, "PGM: No Panacea," *Survival*, Vol. 22, No. 1 (January/February 1980), p. 16.
80. *FY 1978 Posture Statement*, p. 85.

pleted. It is also imperative that the Belgians, the British, and the Dutch continue to modernize and upgrade their conventional forces. More specifically, these forces, especially the British, must increase the firepower of their individual brigades. The Germans, for their part, must maintain their commitment to developing a formidable Territorial Army. At a more general level, NATO should make a greater effort to prepare the terrain in West Germany so as to further compound the attacker's problems. And, the Allies need to place more emphasis on improving the sustainability of their forces.

Although none of these improvements require significant increases in defense spending, there is cause for concern over their implementation. The various policy disputes that have plagued the Alliance over the past few years (neutron bomb, TNF modernization, Afghanistan, and Poland) have markedly weakened Alliance cohesion. Once again there is serious talk in the United States about greatly reducing the American commitment to Europe.[81] And although there is no direct evidence yet that the Reagan Administration wants to scale back the American commitment to Europe, it is apparent from the Administration's first *Posture Statement* that it is primarily interested in spending defense dollars on strategic weaponry and the Navy.[82] Even in the American Army, which was very much a Europe-oriented force in the 1970s, there is growing interest in preparing for contingencies outside of Europe.[83] If the Administration has to cut back projected defense spending for the next five years, it is likely that the NATO portion of the budget will come under attack.

Of course, there are danger signs on the other side of the Atlantic as well. Given the state of Britain's economy and her decision to purchase the expensive Trident missile, one cannot help but wonder if the British Army will not suffer in the future allocation of scarce resources.[84] Unfortunately, the

---

81. See for examples: David S. Broder, "Rising Isolationism," *Washington Post*, January 13, 1982, p. 23; Morton M. Kondracke, "Talking Ourselves Into Breaking Up the Alliance?" *Wall Street Journal*, January 7, 1982, p. 21; Ronald C. Nairn, "Should the U.S. Pull Out of NATO?" *Wall Street Journal*, December 15, 1981, p. 30; and Stansfield Turner, "A New Strategy for NATO," *New York Times Magazine*, December 13, 1981, pp. 42–49, 134–136.
82. See *FY 1983 Posture Statement*.
83. See, for example, General Edward Meyer's (the Army Chief of Staff) comments in Richard Halloran, "$40 Billion Is Urged To Modernize Army," *The New York Times*, November 30, 1980, p. 33.
84. For an excellent discussion of the problems the British face as a result of a weak economy and the purchase of Trident missiles, see Lawrence Freedman, "Britain: The First Ex-Nuclear Power?" *International Security*, Vol. 6, No. 2 (Fall 1981), pp. 80–104.

British economy is not the only European economy that has fallen on hard times. Even in Germany, defense spending has been curtailed because of economic considerations.[85]

It seems reasonable to assume that in the next few years, NATO will have some difficulty holding the line against attempts to cut back spending for the conventional defense of Europe. If such efforts were to succeed, NATO's present capability to defend against a Soviet offensive would be seriously eroded. Given the widespread recognition that parity obtains at all levels of the nuclear equation, and given the need for a conventional deterrent which flows from nuclear parity, such a development would be a mistake of grand proportions. What is particularly ironic about this threat of lost momentum at the conventional level is that it is due, in part, to the popular misconception that Western forces are hopelessly outnumbered at the conventional level. The reason is simple: if one believes that the disparity in conventional forces is very great, then what is the point of continuing to spend precious resources on a hopeless cause? Those Allied leaders who continually denigrate NATO's substantial conventional capability are, in effect, undermining popular support for continued spending on NATO's conventional forces.[86]

Two other points regarding this popular misconception about the conventional balance in Europe bear mentioning. First, for the purposes of deterring a Soviet attack in some future crisis, it makes absolutely no sense to emphasize that should the Soviets attack, an easy victory would await them. Second, should there be a war in Europe, that message will not help and may very well threaten the resolve of NATO's fighting forces. As Senator Sam Nunn once remarked, "If our American fighting men ever conclude that high levels of this Government have them deployed on a strategy that is inevitable failure, then nothing could destroy military morale of our country quicker."[87] No one wants to die for a lost cause. Fortunately, the conventional wisdom is wrong; NATO presently has the capability to thwart a Soviet attack. Unfortunately, too few people recognize this.

The second caveat concerns warning time and mobilization. Given NATO's

---

85. For a pessimistic assessment of the future of the German military, see John Vinocur, "Study by Bonn Foresees Trouble for the Military," *The New York Times*, February 9, 1982, p. 12.
86. This is not to deny that NATO has legitimate deficiencies which Allied leaders have a responsibility to point out and to rectify.
87. See U.S., Congress, Subcommittee on Manpower and Personnel of the Senate Armed Services Committee, *Hearings on NATO Posture And Initiatives*, 95th Cong., 1st Sess. (Washington D.C.: GPO, August 3, 1977), p. 20.

present intelligence capabilities and the Pact's force structure, there is little doubt that NATO would detect a full-scale Pact mobilization almost immediately. Obviously, NATO must ensure that it maintains this capability. Problems arise, however, in circumstances where the Pact pursues a limited mobilization which is somewhat difficult to gauge. Although there are real limits as to how much mobilization the Soviets can achieve before tipping their hand, NATO needs to be especially sensitive to such an eventuality. Moreover, NATO must be prepared to respond to a limited mobilization, even if the evidence of such a mobilization is somewhat ambiguous. This leads to the critical problem of mobilization.

This article highlights how important it is that NATO mobilize its forces immediately after the Pact begins its mobilization. A favorable balance of forces in a crisis will be a function of political as well as military factors. As Richard Betts notes in his very important article on this subject, "Even if intelligence monitoring can ensure warning, it cannot ensure authorization to respond to it."[88] Therefore, it is essential that NATO's political and military leaders carefully consider the various mobilization scenarios that they may face in a crisis. The real danger is that NATO's leaders will not agree to mobilize in a crisis for fear that such a move might provoke a Soviet attack. The risk of pushing the Soviets to preempt can be reduced, however, by avoiding certain provocative moves and by clearly communicating one's intentions to the other side. Nevertheless, the risk of provoking a Soviet attack by initiating NATO mobilization can never be completely erased. That risk, however, must be weighed against the far greater danger that if NATO does not mobilize, the capability to defend against a Pact attack will be lost. Moreover, once the Pact achieves a decisive superiority because of NATO's failure to mobilize, it would be not only difficult, but very dangerous for NATO to attempt to redress the balance with a tardy mobilization. Seeing that process set into motion, the Pact would have a very strong incentive to attack before NATO erased its advantage. In short, it is essential that NATO plan for ways to mobilize that do not provoke a Soviet attack, but, at the same time, ensure that NATO does not lose its present capability to defend itself effectively against a Soviet offensive.

---

88. Betts, "Surprise Attack," p. 118.

# Toward Better Net Assessment

*Eliot A. Cohen*

## Rethinking the European Conventional Balance

$\mathbf{O}$ver the past six years, a curious split has opened among those who study and worry about the NATO–Warsaw Pact conventional military balance. On the one hand, we see grim assessments such as those given by the recently retired Supreme Allied Commander Europe (SACEUR), General Bernard Rogers:

If attacked conventionally today, NATO would be forced fairly quickly to decide whether it should escalate to the non-strategic nuclear level. (The alternative would be to accept defeat).[1]

At the same time, however, a group of analysts in universities and policy research institutes have come up with markedly more favorable assessments of the balance.[2] These authors conclude that the Soviets, as one author's title

---

I am grateful to many friends and colleagues for comments on earlier drafts of this manuscript and for many helpful leads and suggestions. In particular, I would like to thank Alvin Bernstein, Richard Betts, Judith Cohen, William Fuller, Samuel Huntington, Robert Jervis, Jeffrey McKitrick, Stephen Meyer, David Petraeus, Stephen Rosen, Steven Ross, Kevin Sokolski, Henry Sokolski, and Barry Watts for their help. I owe a very great intellectual debt to Andrew Marshall in regard to the general subject of net assessment. I take sole responsibility, however, for the data and arguments presented herein.

---

*Eliot A. Cohen teaches in the Strategy Department of the U.S. Naval War College, where he is Secretary of the Navy Senior Research Fellow. This paper represents the views of the author only, and not necessarily those of the Naval War College or any other government agency.*

---

1. Bernard Rogers, "NATO's Conventional Defense Improvement Initiative," *NATO's Sixteen Nations*, Vol. 31, No. 4 (July 1986), p. 18. See also "Gen. Rogers: Time to Say 'Time Out,'" *Army*, September 1983, p. 27. For similar judgments see Andrew J. Goodpaster, et al., *Strengthening Conventional Deterrence in Europe: A Program for the 1980's* (ESECS II) (Boulder, Colo.: Westview, 1985); H.J. Neuman, ed., *Conventional Balance in Europe: Problems, Strategies, and Technologies* (Zoetermeer: Netherlands Institute of International Relations, 1984); Harold Brown, *Thinking About National Security: Defense and Foreign Policy in a Dangerous World* (Boulder, Colo.: Westview, 1983), p. 102. Recently, the current SACEUR, General John R. Galvin, declared that he could guarantee "only that we can defend ourselves for two weeks against an all-out Warsaw Pact attack—then we will have to use nuclear weapons." "NATO," he said, "has never had sufficient capabilities for conventional deterrence." Henry van Loon, "An Exclusive AFJ Interview with General John R. Galvin, Supreme Allied Commander Europe," *Armed Forces Journal International*, Vol. 125, No. 8 (March 1988), pp. 50–57.
2. See, for example, William W. Kaufmann, "Who is Conning the Alliance?" *Brookings Review*, Vol. 5, No. 4 (Fall 1987), pp. 10–17; Kaufmann, "Nonnuclear Deterrence," in John D. Steinbruner and Leon V. Sigal, eds., *Alliance Security: NATO and the No-First-Use Question* (Washington, D.C.:

---

*International Security*, Summer 1988 (Vol. 13, No. 1)
© 1988 by the President and Fellows of Harvard College and of the Massachusetts Institute of Technology.

has it, "can't win quickly in Central Europe," and, more generally, that NATO faces an acceptable conventional balance in Europe. Some of these authors— let us call them the Optimists, for short—have high confidence in their conclusions. One of them declares:

In short, the prevalent pessimistic view is a myth that is unsupported by scholarship, analysis, or sound professional opinion. How this gloomy view gained such broad currency, especially among members of the press corps, is a puzzle.[3]

This discrepancy between the views of many senior statesmen and military commanders on the one hand and those of some academic analysts on the other is, at the very least, striking and would seem to require explanation. But the reasons for examining the Optimists' arguments extend beyond a desire to reconcile mere divergences of opinion. Particularly in the wake of the INF agreement, NATO nations must look with renewed interest—some would say anxiety—at the state of their conventional defense. Moreover, although the Optimists' view of the military balance has not gained wide acceptance in government, it has achieved a great deal of credence in the academic world.[4] For this reason as well, the Optimists' views, like any other prominent academic theory, deserve scrutiny.

---

Brookings, 1983), pp. 43–90; Joshua M. Epstein, *Measuring Military Power: The Soviet Air Threat to Europe* (Princeton: Princeton University Press, 1984); Epstein, *The 1988 Defense Budget* (Washington, D.C.: Brookings, 1987); Epstein, "Dynamic Analysis and the Conventional Balance in Europe," *International Security*, Vol. 12, No. 4 (Spring 1988), pp. 154–165; Barry R. Posen, "Measuring the European Conventional Balance: Coping with Complexity in Threat Assessment," *International Security*, Vol. 9, No. 3 (Winter 1984/1985), pp. 47–88; Posen, "Is NATO Decisively Outnumbered?" *International Security*, Vol. 12, No. 4 (Spring 1988), pp. 186–202; John J. Mearsheimer, "Why the Soviets Can't Win Quickly in Central Europe," *International Security*, Vol. 7, No. 2 (Summer 1982), pp. 3–39; Mearsheimer, "Maneuver, Mobile Defense, and the NATO Central Front," *International Security*, Vol. 6, No. 3 (Winter 1981/82), pp. 104–122; Mearsheimer, "Nuclear Weapons and Deterrence in Europe," *International Security*, Vol. 9, No. 3 (Winter 1984/85), pp. 19–46; Mearsheimer, "Numbers, Strategy, and the European Balance," *International Security*, Vol. 12, No. 4 (Spring 1988), pp. 174–185. My citations to Mearsheimer's "Why the Soviets Can't Win Quickly" and "Maneuver," and to Posen's "Measuring" refer to the versions reprinted in Steven E. Miller, ed., *Conventional Forces and American Defense Policy* (Princeton: Princeton University Press, 1986).
3. Mearsheimer, "Numbers, Strategy, and the European Balance," p. 180 n. 8.
4. These views have been criticized before, however. See Richard K. Betts, "Conventional Deterrence: Predictive Uncertainty and Policy Confidence," *World Politics*, Vol. 37, No. 2 (January 1985), pp. 153–179. For introductory accounts, see "NATO's Central Front," *The Economist*, August 30, 1986; International Institute for Strategic Studies (IISS), *The Military Balance 1987–1988* (London: IISS, 1987), pp. 226–231; Roger L.L. Facer, *Conventional Forces and the NATO Strategy of Flexible Response*, R-3209-FF (Santa Monica, Calif.: RAND, 1985). The best overall historical surveys of the NATO/Warsaw Pact balance, though limited by age and an excessively

These analysts deserve full credit for raising and exploring an interesting set of issues concerned with the problem of net assessment: the weighing of opposing military forces. Moreover, one should not let the label "Optimists" conceal the fact of important internal disagreements among them with respect to both method and conclusions.[5] For that reason, this article deals primarily with the arguments offered by two prominent Optimists, John Mearsheimer and Barry Posen. Space constraints do not allow a full rendition here of their arguments: for that, readers should refer to sources cited in the notes. Briefly, the Optimists concede that NATO has substantially fewer weapons—tanks, artillery pieces, attack helicopters, and the like—than does the Warsaw Pact.[6] They argue, however, that these so-called static indicators do not tell us how well NATO would perform against a Warsaw Pact attack. Rather, by looking at more complex measures, and in particular armored division equivalents (ADEs), one comes to a truer estimate of the balance.[7] Their study of the ADE balance after various periods of mobilization by both sides suggests that NATO can hold a line close to the inter-German border, for at least four reasons: (1) the inherent advantages of the defense; (2) the force-to-space

narrow focus, are Phillip A. Karber, "To Lose an Arms Race: The Competition in Conventional Forces Deployed in Central Europe, 1965–1980," and "The Battle of Unengaged Military Strategies," both in Uwe Nerlich, ed., *The Soviet Asset: Military Power in the Competition Over Europe*, Vol. 1 (Cambridge, Mass.: Ballinger, 1983), pp. 31–88, 207–232. Karber updates his data in an essay that will appear in *NATO at Forty*, a volume edited by several members of the Social Sciences faculty at West Point, and which will appear in 1989. Useful data is also available in Supreme Headquarters Allied Powers Europe (SHAPE), *NATO and Warsaw Pact Force Comparisons, 1973–1986*, (Brussels: SHAPE, 1987), and Heinz Schulte, "NATO/Warsaw Pact Balance: A West German Survey," *Jane's Defence Weekly*, August 15, 1987. A still useful discussion of how various assumptions can shape one's assessment of the balance appears in James Blaker and Andrew Hamilton, *Assessing the NATO/Warsaw Pact Military Balance* (Washington, D.C.: Congressional Budget Office [CBO], 1977), in particular pp. 27–38.
5. See the recent articles in *International Security*, Vol. 12, No. 4 (Spring 1988), pp. 154–202, and in particular Epstein, "Dynamic Analysis." Despite Epstein's critique, however, Posen declares, "I find myself in broad agreement with Epstein and Mearsheimer on the essentials of how to do a thorough assessment of the conventional balance in central Europe." Posen, "Is NATO Decisively Outnumbered?" p. 187 n. 6.
6. From the Atlantic to the Urals the ratios are roughly 2.35:1 for tanks, 3.3:1 for artillery pieces, and 2.1:1 for armed helicopters. These ratios are suggestive, and depend on a variety of uncertainties and assumptions, which may favor either side. *The Military Balance 1987–1988*, p. 231.
7. Posen and Mearsheimer rely most heavily on the ADE methodology, which is briefly explained in Posen, "Is NATO Decisively Outnumbered?" p. 190 n. 12. Epstein argues forcefully for a different methodology of his own devising, which makes a greater effort to capture the interaction of military forces. See chiefly his *Strategy and Force Planning: The Case of the Persian Gulf* (Washington, D.C.: Brookings, 1987), pp. 117–125. However, this methodology does use WEI/WUV (Weapons Effectiveness Indices/Weighted Unit Value) inputs, i.e., the building blocks of the ADE system.

ratio problem, that is, the impossibility of the Soviets usefully massing very large forces in a given sector of the front; (3) the limited avenues of approach from Eastern Europe into West Germany; (4) the qualitative superiority of NATO forces in a number of areas. Most of the Optimists concede that a large inferiority in ADE scores (3:1 or even 2:1 in favor of the Warsaw Pact) would leave NATO in poor shape.[8] But they believe that even using conservative assessments the ratios would remain manageable, i.e., around 1.2:1 or better. The Optimists oppose reliance on a purely conventional defense of Western Europe, but they conclude that the West can block a Soviet quick win without resort to nuclear weapons: "NATO has strong conventional forces that stand a *good* chance of thwarting a Soviet blitzkrieg."[9]

*Six Problems*

This article is *not* about "why the Soviets *would* win quickly in Europe." Rather, it discusses problems of net assessment and uses as its point of departure a critique of important views about the conventional balance in Europe. The Optimists *do* share, despite their internal disagreements, a mind-set and set of techniques common to American defense analysts for over two decades.[10] This approach, whether in the hands of Optimists or Pessimists, has deficiencies. In particular, the analysis that follows will discuss six flaws in the Optimists' arguments: (1) failure to weave political analysis into assessments of the conventional balance; (2) erroneous assumptions about intelligence, particularly with respect to order of battle and warning; (3) inaccurate depictions of Soviet military doctrine; (4) a linear conception of battle which bears little resemblance to real war; (5) misstatements and distortions of quantitative data and relationships; (6) the use of models that rest on problematic *a priori* assumptions. The critique that follows does not take the Optimists to task for arguments that have been overtaken by events. Rather, it deals with fundamental problems of method, and with questions

---

8. Again, it should be noted that Epstein very largely rejects this approach.
9. Mearsheimer, "Nuclear Weapons," p. 26. Emphasis in the original.
10. For a preliminary critique see Eliot A. Cohen, "Guessing Game: A Reappraisal of Systems Analysis," in Samuel P. Huntington, ed., *The Strategic Imperative* (Cambridge, Mass.: Ballinger, 1982), pp. 163–191. These methods can be applied by a more pessimistic author; see Andrew Hamilton, "Redressing the Conventional Balance: NATO's Reserve Military Manpower," *International Security*, Vol. 10, No. 1 (Summer 1985), pp. 111–136. Obviously, parts of my critique of the Optimists (e.g., concerning the handling of outdated information) apply to them alone, and not necessarily to all efforts of this kind.

of evidence that should have been addressed at the time any given article or book was published.

WAR WITHOUT POLITICS

Most of the Optimists are political scientists, but they define their studies as military ones. In footnotes and introductory or concluding remarks they assert the importance of political considerations such as obtaining a prompt NATO decision to mobilize. Their analyses, however, focus on military matters. They do not discuss at length how a war in Europe might break out, what goals the opposing states and coalitions might seek, or how internal political considerations would shape mobilization and other prewar activities. They categorize such issues as "political problem[s, having] little to do with the military balance *per se*, which is the focus of our attention here."[11] Their theoretical premise—that military assessments can proceed in at least partial isolation from political ones—is questionable.

Interestingly enough, the Soviets reject such a bifurcated approach to net assessment, relying instead on the more comprehensive notion of the "correlation of forces," which treats political and military calculations as a whole. The Deputy Chief of the Soviet General Staff has recently written that "war is generally politics through and through," and adds that "on the eve and at the start of a war its political aspects are even more prevalent."[12] Net assessments, the Soviets believe, must be *political*-military in character, for no purely "military" balance exists. A war that starts over a collapse of Soviet rule in Eastern Europe will look completely different from a war that begins as a premeditated grab for hegemony on the Continent. A NATO in internal

---

11. Mearsheimer, "Numbers, Strategy," p. 181 n. 10. Posen, "Measuring," p. 99, declares that the problem of NATO mobilization boils down to one of educating the political leadership. For a historical critique of the consequences of such a bifurcated style of analysis—politics in one compartment, military matters in another—see Hans Delbrueck's indictment of the German High Command in World War I in Albrecht Philipp, ed., *Die Ursachen des Deutschen Zusammenbruches im Jahre 1918*, Vol. 3 (Berlin: Deutsche Verlagsgesellschaft fuer Politik und Geschichte, 1928), pp. 239–373.

12. M.A. Gareev, *M.V. Frunze, Military Theorist* (Moscow: Voyenizdat, 1985; Washington, D.C.: Pergamon-Brassey's, 1988), p. 218. Clausewitz, too, observes that "war is only a branch of political activity: it is in no sense autonomous." Carl von Clausewitz, *On War*, Michael Howard and Peter Paret, trans. (Princeton: Princeton University Press, 1976), Book 8, ch. 6B, p. 605. Emphasis in the original. I am grateful to John Hines and William Fuller for calling Gareev's work to my attention. Despite its title it treats contemporary problems in depth, and is particularly instructive about Soviet views of future war. See also S.P. Ivanov et al., *The Initial Period of War*, Soviet Military Thought Series No. 20 (Moscow: Voyenizdat, 1974; Washington, D.C.: U.S. Government Printing Office [U.S.G.P.O.], 1986).

disarray presents a far different military problem to the Warsaw Pact than a NATO that agrees on the nature of a proper response to a threat from the East.

In this, as in other cases, Western analysts can learn from Soviet-style analysis. "Political" problems do not necessarily have purely "political" solutions, and many nominally "military" problems are in fact politico-military in character. If, for example, one believes that in a crisis European states will mobilize their own reserves but will refuse to allow an influx of American reinforcements, NATO nations—including the United States—should put their resources into building up European reserve systems. If, on the other hand, neither a prompt reserve mobilization nor a call for American help appears likely, NATO should invest in standing forces that require few sticky political decisions to prepare for war.[13]

The problem of mobilization is one of the most important political aspects of the balance, but by no means the only one. Analysts must incorporate in their studies of the balance problems of wartime coalition cohesion as well, gauging among other things the likely impact of strategies designed to exploit fissures in an opponent's camp. Scrutiny of such issues forces one to look at fundamental asymmetries between West and East with respect to coalition unity and purpose. Some of those asymmetries surely favor NATO, particularly with regard to the dubious loyalty of East European populations to the Soviet Union: NATO should, in fact, do everything it can to exploit Soviet vulnerabilities in this regard. But explicit and careful analysis is required here. It is probably incorrect, for example, to say that "non-Soviet Warsaw Pact forces could be relied on fully only if they were persuaded that a threat to their countries was developing in NATO."[14] Defections and mutinies are most likely to occur if NATO looks to be *victorious*—if, for example, American forces have battered their way into the East.[15] Historically, disgruntled and

---

13. There are grounds for concern about the willingness of NATO nations to implement serious military precautions during a crisis with the East. During the Czechoslovak crisis in 1968, for example, the commander of NATO's Central Army Group had orders not to increase "air patrols or undertake any sort of activity that might be interpreted as inflammatory." James H. Polk, "Reflections on the Czechoslovakian Invasion, 1968," *Strategic Review*, Vol. 5, No. 1 (Winter 1977), p. 33. See also Richard K. Betts, *Surprise Attack* (Washington, D.C.: Brookings, 1982), pp. 81–86.
14. Kaufmann, "Nonnuclear Deterrence," p. 55.
15. On this see Samuel P. Huntington, "Conventional Deterrence and Conventional Retaliation in Europe," *International Security*, Vol. 8, No. 3 (Winter 1983/1984), pp. 32–56, reprinted in Miller, ed., *Conventional Forces*, pp. 251–275, especially 261–262; and Stephen P. Rosen, "Mutiny and the Warsaw Pact," *The National Interest*, No. 2 (Winter 1985/86), pp. 74–82.

oppressed client states have indeed turned on despotic patrons, but rarely have they done so unless that ally faced defeat *and* the other side could offer immediate succor. The Prussians deserted Napoleon after the retreat from Moscow, not when the Grande Armée plunged over the Russian border; the Italians joined the Allies after the invasion of Sicily, not while Rommel pounded on the gates of Egypt.

In a number of important respects NATO suffers from serious disadvantages with respect to coalition warfare. Unlike the Soviet Union, the United States cannot dictate to its allies the fact, let alone the timing, of their mobilization, nor their choice of arms and doctrine. NATO, unlike the Warsaw Pact, constitutes an alliance of sixteen free states, and although that freedom makes NATO worth defending, it also creates a real impediment to military efficiency.[16] In no war has an alliance of *independent* states gone to war in lock-step. Invariably some partners drag their heels or even attempt to dodge their responsibilities: each pursues unique and often divergent aims. This held true even during the Second World War, when the United States and Great Britain operated in closer harmony than any other alliance in history—and in that case the Anglo-Americans submitted to very little of the cumbersome multilateral decision-making required by NATO. Churchill's warning to the House of Commons on January 17, 1942 is all too relevant to NATO's predicament:

To hear some people talk, however, one would think that the way to win the war is to make sure that every Power contributing armed forces and every branch of these armed forces is represented on all the councils and organisations which have to be set up, and that everybody is fully consulted before anything is done. That is, in fact, the most sure way to lose a war.[17]

If, for example, some of NATO's smaller states—Belgium, Denmark, or the Netherlands—mobilize tardily or not at all, weaknesses will appear in NATO's front line which could open the way for Soviet breakthroughs in the Northern Army Group (NORTHAG) region. This could unhinge NATO defenses in the Baltic, threaten NATO's ability to draw in American reinforcements through Rotterdam, and endanger NATO air bases and rear

---

16. For a comparison of NATO and Warsaw Pact command structures see John G. Hines and Phillip A. Petersen, "Is NATO Thinking Too Small? A Comparison of Command Structures," *International Defense Review*, Vol. 19, No. 5 (1986), pp. 563–572.
17. Robert Rhodes James, ed., *Winston S. Churchill: His Speeches, 1897–1963*, Vol. 6 (London: Chelsea House, 1974), p. 6565.

areas—no matter how solid the line held by the Germans and the Americans in the Central Army Group (CENTAG) region.

A failure to make a discussion of the politics of a NATO/Warsaw Pact war part of one's assessments will distort them. This problem becomes particularly acute if an analyst concludes that the conventional balance in Europe is adequate on the basis of a single scenario resting on highly questionable political premises. The case to which Mearsheimer gives most of his attention, for example, proceeds from the implausible assumption that "NATO's mobilization begins *immediately* after the Pact starts to mobilize."[18] Other more cautious analysts usually assume a lag of up to a week between Warsaw Pact and NATO mobilization, to allow time for intelligence analysis and a politically difficult decision to react.[19] But even this convention smacks of artificiality. A far better approach would examine a variety of scenarios involving *heterogeneous* mobilization—some nations mobilizing swiftly and fully, others mobilizing slowly or partially—depending on the origins of the conflict. A war that begins in the Persian Gulf will resonate differently in European capitals than would one that commences over Berlin.

The Soviets incorporate coalitional politics not only into their analyses of the balance in Europe, but their strategic planning as well.[20] Western analysts should pay heed to this aspect of Soviet military art and study the ways in which the Soviets target their opponents' coalitional weaknesses and manipulate their decision-making.[21] Throughout a war, but particularly in its early phases, the Soviets would probably try very hard to split off some of America's allies from the NATO coalition. And should war ever come, Soviet ability to bribe, bully, or cajole a NATO nation into quiescence could make

---

18. Mearsheimer, "Why the Soviets Can't Win Quickly," p. 124. Emphasis added. Mearsheimer even refers to the possibility of NATO mobilizing *before* the Pact does (p. 127).
19. For example, Robert Lucas Fischer, *Defending the Central Front: The Balance of Forces*, Adelphi Paper No. 127 (London: International Institute for Strategic Studies, 1976), pp. 16ff.
20. See John J. Yurechko, *Coalitional Warfare: The Soviet Approach* (Cologne: Bundesinstitut fuer ostwissenschaftliche und internationale Studien, 1986); Yurechko, "Command and Control for Coalitional Warfare: The Soviet Approach," *Signal*, Vol. 40, No. 4 (December 1985), pp. 31–44; John Erickson, "Koalitsionnaya Voina: Coalition Warfare in Soviet Military Theory, Planning and Performance," in Keith Neilson and Roy A. Prete, eds., *Coalition Warfare: An Uneasy Accord* (Waterloo, Ont.: Wilfrid Laurier University Press, 1983), pp. 81–122; Christopher N. Donnelly and Phillip A. Petersen, "Soviet Strategists Target Denmark," *International Defense Review*, Vol. 19, No. 8 (1986), pp. 1047–1051.
21. See P.H. Vigor, *Soviet Blitzkrieg Theory* (New York: St. Martin's, 1983), pp. 131–143; Jiri Valenta, "From Prague to Kabul: The Soviet Style of Invasion," *International Security*, Vol. 5, No. 2 (Fall 1980), pp. 130–136; Alex R. Alexeiev, "The Soviet Campaign Against INF," *Orbis*, Vol. 29, No. 2 (Summer 1985), pp. 319–350.

as real a difference to the outcome of a Battle of Europe as any tank army rumbling through the Fulda Gap.[22]

PERFECT INTELLIGENCE

Implicitly, the Optimists assume that they have at their disposal reliable and extensive open source information about the size, composition, equipment and location of Soviet-bloc forces, what is known in intelligence jargon as "order of battle." Their writings do not suggest that uncertainty about such information makes their conclusions tentative or provisional. Explicitly, moreover, the Optimists declare that NATO would have reliable warning of Soviet mobilization and attack: "there is little doubt that NATO would detect a full-scale Pact mobilization almost immediately."[23] Are these assumptions with regard to order of battle and warning intelligence correct, and if not, what consequences does this have for analysis?

The problem of reliable order of battle intelligence is by no means trivial. Even standard reference works contain occasional glaring inconsistencies or lacunae in their descriptions of Soviet forces.[24] An accumulation of such uncertainties can give way to much larger ones, and not just in the private sector. In early 1980, for example, the Secretary of Defense informed Congress that the North Korean Army had 600,000 men, rather than 450,000 men, as reported the previous year.[25] The IISS *Military Balance* listed the North Korean Army with twenty infantry divisions in its 1978 edition, but

---

22. Referring to World War I Churchill made a similar point: "The distinction between politics and strategy diminishes as the point of view is raised. At the summit true politics and strategy are one. The maneuver which gains an important strategic point may be less valuable than that which placates or overawes a dangerous neutral." Winston S. Churchill, *The World Crisis*, Vol. 2, *1915* (New York: Charles Scribner's Sons, 1923), p. 6.

23. Mearsheimer, "Why the Soviets Can't Win Quickly," p. 157. The term "full scale" may constitute an escape clause; if other kinds of mobilization would be less detectable, however, it is reasonable to think that the Soviets would choose them. Yet Mearsheimer does not consider scenarios of this kind; ibid., pp. 122–124.

24. The most recent version of one authoritative source, the International Institute for Strategic Studies' *Military Balance*, contains some interesting anomalies. In one place the 1987–1988 edition estimates Soviet holdings of T-80 tanks (the latest and presumably the best in the Soviet arsenal) to be 1,400, in another 2,300. It tentatively identifies two new Soviet Army corps, but cannot decide whether these forces serve as the nuclei for Operational Maneuver Groups (OMGs, large scale raiding forces designed to penetrate NATO rear areas early in a war) or are simply upgraded reserve units. *Military Balance 1987–1988*, pp. 27, 35, 234.

25. Harold Brown, *Annual Report of the Secretary of Defense, FY 1981* (Washington, D.C.: U.S.G.P.O., 1980), p. 50. It should be noted that North Korea is a country subject to intense scrutiny by the United States and its chief ally in the region, the Republic of Korea, because of the proven bellicosity of the North Korean regime.

*thirty-five* the next year. In 1980, twenty-two North Korean special forces or commando brigades—each numbering several thousand men—suddenly appeared in the accounts. During this time the IISS's inventory of North Korean tanks increased 25%, artillery 30%, and rocket launchers 50%.

This episode reveals the intrinsic difficulty of collecting information against a totalitarian society. When the Wehrmacht invaded the Soviet Union, the German General Staff underestimated the number of Soviet divisions opposing them by a factor of two—and knew nothing of the existence of the superior T-34 tank. A more recent demonstration of Western underestimates of Soviet strength appeared in the negotiations leading up to the signing of the INF treaty. The Soviets revealed that they had some one hundred launchers for the 500 km–range SS-23; Western open sources had previously estimated that they had only twenty.[26]

First rate net assessment requires the use of highly classified information. This is not because the "real" numbers exist in government—some do, some do not—but because analysts need to know how particular items of intelligence have been gathered in order to assess the reliability of those estimates. Moreover, certain kinds of information about Soviet methods of operation can only be derived from highly classified sources.[27] Of course, academic

---

26. *Military Balance 1987–1988*, pp. 35, 203. The Soviets reported having an average of two per launcher SS-23s and five  per launcher of the longer range SS-12s. According to one source, in July 1987 the Central Intelligence Agency (CIA) and State Department estimated that the Soviet Union had 550 SS-20 missiles—versus an estimate by the Defense Intelligence Agency of 1,200 missiles. In the INF agreement, the Soviets confirmed the existence of 405 deployed and 245 non-deployed SS-20s, for a total of 650. In December 1987, CIA and State were reported to agree with those numbers, but the relevant National Intelligence Estimate declared that the Soviets had 950. "Crimson Whales, Contd." *Wall Street Journal*, February 3, 1988, p. 22; "Memorandum of Understanding regarding the establishment of the database for the Treaty between the United States of America and the Union of Soviet Socialist Republics on the elimination of their intermediate and shorter-range missiles." See "Documentation: The INF Treaty," *Survival*, Vol. 30, No. 2 (March/April 1988), pp. 163–180, esp. p. 180. Both *Military Balance 1987–1988* and the Department of Defense, *Soviet Military Power 1987* (Washington, D.C.: U.S.G.P.O., 1987), p. 34, estimated that the Soviets had 441 SS-20 launchers; in the INF treaty, the Soviets confirmed the existence of 523. On past U.S. estimates of Soviet forces see David S. Sullivan, "Evaluating U.S. Intelligence Estimates," in Roy Godson, ed., *Intelligence Requirements for the 1980's*, Vol. 2, *Analysis and Estimates* (Washington, D.C.: National Strategy Information Center, 1980), pp. 49–84; Albert Wohlstetter, "Is There a Strategic Arms Race?" *Foreign Policy*, No. 15 (Summer 1974) pp. 3–20; idem, "Rivals, But No 'Race'," *Foreign Policy*, No. 16 (Fall 1974), pp. 48–81; idem, "How to Confuse Ourselves," *Foreign Policy*, No. 20 (Fall 1975) pp. 170–198.

27. A historical case illustrates this point. U.S. Navy communications intelligence in the early 1930s provided insights, otherwise unobtainable, into Japanese operational concepts and capabilities. See two papers by Laurance F. Safford, "A Brief History of Communications Intelligence in the United States," and "The Undeclared War, 'History of R.I.' [radio intelligence]," SRH-149 and SRH-305 respectively, in Record Group 457, Records of the National Security Agency, National Archives.

analysts have no choice but to work with the data available to them. The fundamental uncertainty of this data, however, should induce considerable modesty about their conclusions.

The matter of warning is also far from clear cut. One Optimist declares that in view of NATO's ample warning of the invasion of Czechoslovakia (and other crises), "the argument that NATO leaders will not know about Soviet preparations seems suspect."[28] But the Commander of U.S. Army Europe learned about the 1968 invasion from an Associated Press dispatch out of Prague: "To say that we were surprised by the timing and intensity of the invasion," he later wrote, "is a plain statement of fact."[29] The record of poor U.S. prediction of the Soviet invasion of Czechoslovakia in 1968 or the botched Israeli assessment in 1973 of the likelihood of an Egyptian attack suggests caution. So too does the steady Soviet effort to reduce NATO warning time by building up forward logistics and peacetime command nets, thus complicating the problem of warning.[30] Indeed, even clear warning often fails to evoke adequate preparation: As Richard Betts wisely observes, the causes of warning failure are "deeply embedded: human psychology, political uncertainty, military complexity and organizational viscosity."[31] Warning is not, in other words, a simple matter of having raw data in the intelligence system: in retrospect, bits and pieces of information adequate for a sound judgment were present in most cases of intelligence failure.

The Soviets seek to deny their opponents reliable order of battle information and warning of an attack in Europe, in large part because they assign a very high value to surprise in warfare.[32] The historical record, from World

28. Posen, "Measuring," p. 67.
29. Polk, "Reflections," pp. 30–31.
30. John Erickson, "The Soviets: More Isn't Always Better," *Military Logistics Forum*, Vol. 1, No. 2 (September/October 1984), pp. 60–61. See also Carl-Friedrich Dwinger, "Warning Time and Forward Defence," National Security Series 2/84 (Kingston, Ont.: Queen's University Centre for International Relations, 1984), especially pp. 55–62. Soviet emphasis on the attack from the march (rather than from pre-arranged areas of concentration) is important in this regard. See V.G. Reznichenko, ed., *Tactics*, Soviet Military Thought Series No. 21 (Moscow: Voyenizdat, 1984; Washington, D.C.: U.S.G.P.O., 1987), pp. 69–70.
31. Betts, *Surprise Attack*, p. 309. The case of Israeli and U.S. intelligence before the October 6, 1973 Arab attack is particularly important for students of surprise. See Hanoch Bar Tov, *Daddo: 48 Shanim v'od 20 Yom*, Vol. 1 (Tel Aviv: Ma'ariv Book Guild, 1978), pp. 240ff.; Vol. 2, pp. 9–47. More generally, see Betts, *Surprise Attack*.
32. See P.T. Kunitskiy, "Achieving Surprise From the Experience of the Great Patriotic War," *Voyenno-Istoricheskiy Zhurnal*, No. 10 (October 1985), pp. 24–30, trans., Joint Publications Research Service (JPRS), JPRS-UMA-86-014, 27 February 1986, pp. 25–33; Reznichenko, *Tactics*, pp. 44–46. More generally see Michael I. Handel, "Technological Surprise in War," *Intelligence and National Security*, Vol. 2, No. 1 (January 1987), pp. 5–53.

War II to the present, suggests that they devote tremendous physical and intellectual resources to *maskirovka*—camouflage, concealment, and deception in all of their many forms—and have achieved considerable successes in this field.[33] They fully understand that the West's intelligence apparatus can detect many things, including troop movements and the technical characteristics of some weapons. Indeed, their considerable successes in penetrating Western intelligence organizations—think of the Prime, Lee-Boyce, Kampiles, Pelton, and Walker cases—may have given them an excellent picture of what those organizations can and cannot do.[34]

In any event, the Soviets understand that less than total surprise can still have enormous military value. It will suffice to mislead an opponent about the size, location, timing, or direction of an attack, or about the numbers or technical parameters of key weapon systems.[35] Moreover, the Soviets believe that under modern conditions, surprise can "be achieved through the manipulation of the enemy's interpretation of the activity that is observed."[36] They might, for example, "explain" mobilization as mere exercises (the ploy used successfully in Czechoslovakia in 1968), upgrade readiness incrementally, or attack after a crisis has been resolved. In all cases they will seek to mislead NATO about the nature of such an attack.

33. See, for example, P.M. Simchenkov, "Achieving Covertness," *Voyenno-Istoricheskiy Zhurnal*, No. 6 (June 1986), pp. 17–24, trans., JPRS-UMA-86-063, 14 November 1986, pp. 10–19; Brian D. Dailey and Patrick J. Parker, eds., *Soviet Strategic Deception* (Lexington, Mass.: D.C. Heath, 1987), particularly Notra Trulock, "The Role of Deception in Soviet Military Planning," pp. 275–292; Michael Handel, ed., *Intelligence and National Security*, Vol. 2, No. 3 (July 1987), "Special Issue on Strategic and Operational Deception in the Second World War," in particular David M. Glantz's article, "The Red Mask: The Nature and Legacy of Soviet Military Deception in the Second World War," pp. 175–259. In June 1944 the Germans estimated that the Soviet forces opposite them in the Central sector of the front had between 400 and 1,100 tanks. The Soviets had 5,000. Ibid., p. 222.
34. On the relationship between intelligence coups of this kind and deception operations, see Michael Handel, "Introduction: Strategic and Operational Deception in Historical Perspective," *Intelligence and National Security*, Vol. 2, No. 3 (July 1987), pp. 1–91. Also, by the same author, "Intelligence and the Problem of Strategic Surprise," *Journal of Strategic Studies*, Vol. 7, No. 3 (September 1984), pp. 229–281. Allied penetration of German ciphers—and particularly of the *Abwehr's* radio traffic—allowed Anglo/American deceivers to monitor and calibrate their own deception efforts. A brief recent summary of the contemporary American counterintelligence problem is John Walcott, "War of the Spies," *Wall Street Journal*, November 27, 1987, pp. 1, 8.
35. See Kunitskiy, "Achieving Surprise," pp. 24–30.
36. John G. Hines and Phillip A. Petersen, "The Soviet Conventional Offensive in Europe," *Military Review*, Vol. 64, No. 4 (April 1984), p. 18. See also V. Meshcheryakov, "Strategic Disinformation in Achievement of Surprise," *Voyenno-Istoricheskiy Zhurnal*, No. 2 (February 1985), pp. 74–80, trans., JPRS-UMA-85-039, 24 June 1985, pp. 53–59; Clifford Reid, "Reflexive Control in Soviet Military Planning," in Dailey and Parker, eds., *Soviet Strategic Deception*, pp. 293–312.

Many analysts, including the Optimists, tend to separate intelligence uncertainties from issues of force planning, or measurements of military sufficiency. Here too, however, such a distinction is artificial and inappropriate. A country with high confidence in its intelligence assessments can afford to skimp on its standing forces, fortifications, and operational readiness. The events of October 6, 1973, when the Israeli Defense Forces found their promised warning time reduced from 48 hours to fewer than twelve, taught the Israelis a bitter lesson about the perils of excessive confidence in one's ability to see through an opponent. After 1973, changes in Israeli force structure—not merely intelligence organization—followed. NATO nations must measure the sufficiency of their forces on the basis of a realistic assessment of their own abilities to react to warning and gauge accurately many facets of a Soviet attack. The problem is not easily treated using open sources; it may not even be that much more amenable to assessment within government, but neither consideration makes it any less serious a problem.

MISREADING THE SOVIETS

The Optimists set forth stereotyped, generally disparaging and occasionally quite inaccurate assessments of Soviet operational capabilities. In some cases, to be sure, they correctly point to undeniable afflictions.[37] But aside from broad generalizations about rigidity and lack of initiative, they do not investigate the Soviet way of war closely. They believe that the Soviet military's limited operational abilities would lead it to adopt a strategy similar to that used:

against the Germans on the Eastern Front in World War II. Instead of relying on deep strategic penetrations to bring about the collapse of the German Army, Soviet strategy called for wearing the German Army down by slowly pushing it back along a broad front.[38]

---

37. For example, Mearsheimer points to the multilingual character of Soviet forces. "Why the Soviets Can't Win Quickly," pp. 148–154; and 1987 testimony before the Subcommittee on Conventional Forces and Alliance Defense of the U.S. Senate Committee on Armed Services. Mearsheimer has made a similar observation about NATO in a different context: "NATO's variegated structure is a mighty impediment to good command and control. The language problem alone would present great difficulties." Mearsheimer, "Maneuver," p. 114.
38. Mearsheimer, "Why the Soviets Can't Win Quickly," p. 131. For a quick look at the Soviet view, see V.V. Giurkin and M.I. Golovnin, "On the Question of Strategic Operations in the Great Patriotic War," *Voyenno-Istoricheskiy Zhurnal*, No. 10 (October 1985), pp. 10–23, trans., JPRS-UMA-86-014, 27 February 1986, pp. 10–24.

This view is contradicted by Soviet operations such as the destruction of German Army Group Center (June/July 1944), a campaign in which the Red Army penetrated 400 km in three weeks and inflicted 350,000 casualties on the Wehrmacht, including the annihilation of 28 German divisions. The Vistula/Oder operation of January/February 1945 similarly brought Soviet forces 550 to 600 km forward in three weeks.[39]

In the same vein, the Optimists' declaration that "the Soviets were only able to defeat the Germans in the Second World War by overwhelming them with superior numbers"[40] requires qualification. First, Soviet superiority obtained most heavily in selected areas of equipment (tanks and artillery in particular)—those "bean counts" deprecated by the Optimists. Second, the overwhelming odds behind most Soviet breakthroughs in the East resulted in part from shrewd concentration of forces at particular points, as well as across-the-board strength. Third, even when the Soviets had slight odds on their side, they achieved some remarkable successes. At Stalingrad, for example, with force ratios of only 1.4:1 in tanks and motorized artillery, 1.3:1 in field guns and mortars, and only slightly better than parity in fighter aircraft and overall manpower, the Soviets encircled and ultimately annihilated a force numbering a third of a million men.[41] By 1944, according to David Glantz, "Soviet mastery of sound strategic, operational, and to some extent tactical military techniques deprived the Germans of the ability they had previously possessed of being able to deal with a more numerous but somewhat artless foe."[42] By then, the Germans had begun to notice adroit Soviet use of combined arms forces striking deep and relying heavily on concentrated fires rather than massed infantry attacks.[43] Repeatedly during the last years of World War II, the Soviets penetrated well-defended positions and struck deep, even in unfavorable terrain.

---

39. See, for example, the 1984, 1985, and 1986 "Art of War Symposia" conducted by the Center for Land Warfare, U.S. Army War College. These symposia reviewed in great detail Soviet operations from December 1942 to March 1945. See also the special section on the Vistula/Oder operation in *Voyenno-Istoricheskiy Zhurnal*, No. 1 (January 1985), pp. 11–52, trans., JPRS-UMA-85-033, 20 May 1985, pp. 11–53.
40. Mearsheimer, "Nuclear Weapons," p. 33.
41. Mikhail Heller and Aleksandr M. Nekrich, trans. Phyllis B. Carlos, *Utopia in Power: The History of the Soviet Union from 1917 to the Present* (New York: Summit Books, 1986), p. 393. See also the discussion of force ratios, pp. 372, 414.
42. 1985 Art of War Symposium, "From the Dnepr to the Vistula: Soviet Offensive Operations— November 1943–August 1944. A Transcript of Proceedings" (Carlisle Barracks, Pa.: U.S. Army War College, Center for Land Warfare, 1985), p. 542. See more generally pp. 540–563.
43. Ibid., p. 547. This volume and the other two in the series are of particular interest because these symposia included many German veterans and historians.

The latter point is important, since much of the Optimists' analysis rests on the supposedly few and confined axes of advance available to the Soviets in Western Europe.[44] But the history of armored warfare is, as Stephen Rosen has put it, the story of tanks going where they are not supposed to be able to go: desert sands (North Africa, 1941–1942, Sinai, 1967); hilly forests (the Ardennes, 1940 *and* 1944); jungle (Burma, 1945); cities (Beirut, 1982); and mud (Southern Russia, February/March 1944). NATO planners would not be the first to underestimate Soviet abilities when matched against formidable terrain obstacles. In 1945 one and a half million Soviet troops advanced 500 to 950 km into Manchuria in nine days, defeating a force of some 700,000 Japanese troops:

Soviet units routinely crossed terrain the Japanese considered unpassable, leaving it virtually undefended. . . . Perhaps most unexpected for the Japanese was Soviet reliance on forward detachments to probe Japanese defenses, bypass them, and attack deep into the Japanese operational rear. The Soviet commanders' display of initiative at all levels did not fit Japanese preconceptions of Soviet performance.[45]

Perhaps the Soviets could not duplicate today such operations as this or the Vistula/Oder operation, which occurred under conditions of greater Soviet material superiority than obtain in Western Europe today and after several years of battlefield hardening. We should study these operations nonetheless, and not merely out of regard for scholarly accuracy, but because they tell us something about Soviet methods and capacities. The Soviets, for their part, study the Eastern Front in World War II with tremendous seriousness, and use it as a base for their military art. In addition, a dispassionate study of Soviet operations in World War II should inoculate us against any tendency to deprecate unduly the skill, determination, and ingenuity of our chief opponents.[46]

---

44. Mearsheimer, "Why the Soviets Can't Win Quickly," pp. 138–144. But see P.T. Kunitskiy, "Choosing Sectors of the Main Thrust in Campaigns and Strategic Operations," *Voyenno-Istoricheskiy Zhurnal*, No. 7 (July 1986), pp. 29–40, trans., JPRS-UMA-87-003, 13 January 1987, pp. 20–33, which emphasizes the importance of selecting *un*favorable terrain for avenues of approach. See by the same author, "Massing of Forces in Sector of Main Thrust," *Voyenno-Istoricheskiy Zhurnal*, No. 4 (April 1987), pp. 11–21, trans., JPRS-UMJ-87-003, 9 September 1987, pp. 1–14.
45. Glantz, "Red Mask," p. 237.
46. The Optimists draw freely on details of World War II Western Front experience to support their analyses, but rarely mention and never examine at comparable length Soviet offensive operations on the Eastern Front. See Posen, "Measuring," pp. 111–115, for example, which relies heavily on the experience of Anglo-American forces fighting the Germans in 1944–45.

In a number of cases, the Optimists narrow Soviet options without explanation or justification. For example, their analysis does not allow for Soviet attack other than across the inter-German border, i.e., thrusts through neutral Austria and weakly defended Denmark. Combined arms attacks through those countries offer the Soviets attractive possibilities to achieve large scale encirclements of NATO forces. The search for such encirclements characterizes Soviet military thought today as it did Soviet military practice in World War II.[47]

At times, the Optimists misstate Soviet views. Thus, we have the proposition that "the Soviets probably rate the non-German forces [in NATO] quite highly as well," when in fact the Soviets have recently suggested that Dutch units may require as little as half the artillery pounding needed for operations against American or German divisions.[48] Assertions that the Soviets would attempt only three or four breakthroughs in the Central Front region, or that the Soviets would launch only one army-sized assault per 70 km NATO corps sector, bear no resemblance to Soviet operational practices. According to one study of Soviet doctrine, for example, army breakthrough sectors could be as narrow as ten kilometers, easily allowing for two such efforts in a seventy kilometer NATO corps sector.[49] The Optimists' treatments of Soviet air power in a NATO/Warsaw Pact war do not discuss how the Soviets conceive of the "initial air operation" of a war against the West. Although Soviet doctrine suggests the use of different kinds of forces to strike at Western nuclear

---

Such studies, though useful, reflect the operations of forces unwilling casually to spend tens of thousands of lives to achieve breakthroughs, an important characteristic of Soviet commands on the Eastern Front.

47. P. Lashchenko, "Army General Lashchenko on Technique of Encircling Large Groups," *Voyenno-Istoricheskiy Zhurnal*, No. 2 (February 1985), pp. 21–31, trans., JPRS-UMA-85-039, 24 June 1985, pp. 8–20. See as well Donnelly and Petersen, "Soviet Strategists Target Denmark," and Michael Sadykiewicz, *Soviet–Warsaw Pact Western Theater of Military Operations: Organizations and Missions*, N-2596-AF (Santa Monica: RAND, 1987), pp. 33–36.

48. Mearsheimer, "Nuclear Weapons," p. 32; John G. Hines, "Soviet Front Operations in Europe—Planning for Encirclement," *Spotlight on the Soviet Union* (Oslo: Alumni Association of the Norwegian Defense College, 1986), p. 92. For the dangers of such an approach see Wesley K. Wark in *The Ultimate Enemy: British Intelligence and Nazi Germany* (Ithaca, N.Y.: Cornell University Press, 1985). For a thoughtful view of the Soviet military see Christopher N. Donnelly, "The Human Factor in Soviet Military Policy," *Military Review*, Vol. 65, No. 3 (March 1985), pp. 12–22.

49. Army breakthrough sectors could range from ten to thirty kilometers and Front sectors from thirty to seventy kilometers, depending on the amount of mobilization time. Sadykiewicz, *Soviet–Warsaw Pact Western Theater of Military Operations*, p. 78. A combined arms army can number from three to seven divisions, a tank army from two to six. See also Hines, "Soviet Front Operations," p. 86, which discusses *Front*-level operations as narrow as twenty kilometers. A Front consists of several Armies.

targets and air fields, the Optimists treat the "air balance" as if it had nothing to do with forces other than tactical aviation.[50] The Soviet Union, particularly in the last two decades, has developed a relentlessly integrated, combined-arms approach to warfare, and studies military problems accordingly.[51] This holistic approach has shaped systematic improvements in Soviet forces over the last twenty years.

Further, the Optimists pay little or no attention to unconventional Soviet weapons or tactics, including chemicals, blinding lasers, and special operations forces. This seems particularly unwarranted given overwhelming evidence that the Soviets train extensively with (and may indeed have used) chemicals, and given growing indications of the use of lasers to blind American and other countries' pilots and military personnel.[52] It is reasonable to exclude nuclear weapons from an assessment of the conventional balance. It is not, however, appropriate to exclude weapons and forces that the Soviets might very well use in a nominally "conventional" war.

THE LINEAR BATTLEFIELD

On the whole, the Optimists take a literally one-dimensional view of the front lines in Europe. Mearsheimer simply excludes air power from his analysis, looking only at a line-up of armored division equivalents (ADEs) along the border.[53] Those who do take air power into account do so in an extremely narrow fashion, ignoring air defenses and Soviet concepts of operations, and making simplistic—and favorable—assumptions for the West. Posen, for example, looks not at how well NATO's tactical air forces *"will* do, but [at] the kinds of outcomes that might be produced if they do as well as NATO's persistent investments in the area seem to imply."[54] He assumes,

---

50. Benjamin S. Lambeth, review of Joshua M. Epstein, *Measuring Soviet Military Power,* in *American Political Science Review,* Vol. 80, No. 3 (September 1986), pp. 1064–1066.

51. For example, Sadykiewicz, *Soviet–Warsaw Pact Western Theater of Military Operations,* pp. 158–163, discusses how the Soviets might integrate military intelligence (GRU) agents, electronic countermeasures, surface-to-surface missile (SSM) strikes, fighter-bomber strikes, and heliborne raids in attacks on NATO command posts.

52. See, for example, Benjamin F. Schemmer, "U.S. Army Debates Battlefield Laser Need; Soviets May Have Two Systems Deployed," *Armed Forces Journal International,* June 1987, pp. 24–26; *Soviet Military Power 1987,* pp. 89–91, 109–112.

53. Mearsheimer, "Why the Soviets Can't Win Quickly," p. 122. This one-dimensional approach does not even necessarily favor the Optimists' arguments: certain weaknesses in the Warsaw Pact rear—in particular, the Pact's dependence on railroads for forward movement of its forces—offer interesting opportunities for Western deep-strike forces.

54. Posen, "Measuring," p. 102. Emphasis in the original.

among other things, five percent attrition of NATO aircraft flying against Warsaw Pact air defenses (the densest in the world), twice as many NATO as Warsaw Pact sorties, three times as many hits on Warsaw Pact as on NATO vehicles, and above all no Soviet preemptive attack on NATO airfields to disrupt operations in the first few days of the war.[55]

In either case, however, the Optimists regard air power as a mere increment—important or not—to what happens along the Forward Edge of the Battle Area (FEBA), the front line of a war in Europe. Their central concept, despite their several qualifications, is essentially linear, and seeks to establish whether the struggling forces will sway the FEBA this way or that. The Optimists, like many other analysts, convert NATO and Warsaw Pact forces to ADEs. In the Optimists' models, Soviet ADEs only move straight ahead, butting against NATO ADEs. The Optimists' analysis, however, neglects both Soviet doctrine and tactical reality, for in the real world, Soviet forces can mass artillery and rocket fire from neighboring sectors and supporting units against key sectors of the NATO front. (See Figure 1.) And contemporary Soviet military doctrine assigns as much or more importance to massed fire as it does to massed ground forces (that is, tanks and mechanized infantry): "Concentrating men and weapons on the crucial sector requires clarification and adjustment under the new conditions. It should be carried out not by the method of moving up a large number of troops to the selected sector, *but chiefly by massing the weapons.*"[56]

The Optimists assert that one NATO brigade can hold from seven to eleven kilometers of front and that, moreover, the Soviets will find it difficult, if not physically impossible, to cram forces into such sectors that will tip the ratio

---

55. Ibid., pp. 102–105. Soviet doctrine suggests that that is precisely how they *would* begin an attack on the West. Not surprisingly, Posen comes to the conclusion that NATO tactical air forces would destroy Warsaw Pact ground forces "equivalent to nearly one half of all Soviet forces stationed in East Germany in peacetime." Posen's attrition estimates may be too low: American forces attacking Schweinfurt in 1943, for example, lost nineteen percent of the forces that made it to the target, as well as large numbers damaged. And their own air bases were not under attack, as would be the case in a war in Europe. Posen takes his five percent figure from attrition rates over long campaigns: what counts here, however, is the clash of attacking forces against heavy and sophisticated defenses in the first few days of a war, for which Schweinfurt is not a bad analogy. The Israeli Air Force took half of its heavy losses in 1973 (102 airplanes in all, a third or more of its force) in the first three days of battle, when it could not stop Egyptian forces from seizing their initial objectives. Chaim Herzog, *The War of Atonement* (Boston: Little, Brown, 1975), pp. 256–261. See also John Terraine, *The Right of the Line: The Royal Air Force in the European War, 1939–1945* (London: Hodder and Stoughton, 1985), pp. 545–558.
56. Gareev, *Frunze*, p. 217. Emphasis added. See also Reznichenko, *Tactics*, pp. 88–97.

FIGURE 1.

## THE BATTLEFIELD

### OPTIMISTS' MODEL — THE LINEAR BATTLEFIELD

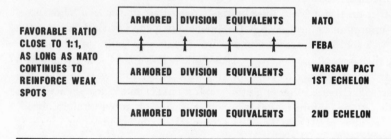

FAVORABLE RATIO
CLOSE TO 1:1,
AS LONG AS NATO
CONTINUES TO
REINFORCE WEAK
SPOTS

### SOVIET DOCTRINE — "DEEP OPERATIONS"

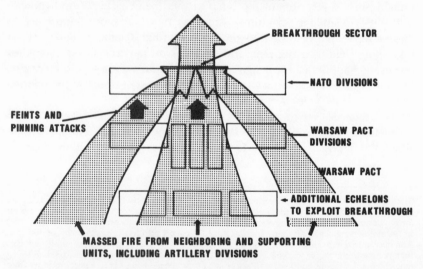

NOTE: FIRE STRIKES OCCUR IN <u>CONCENTRATION</u> AND IN <u>DEPTH</u>.
MULTIPLE BREAKTHROUGHS BY HIGHLY CONCENTRATED FORCES
ARE SUPPORTED BY RAIDING AND HELIBORNE UNITS.

as high as two to one, much less three to one in their favor.[57] Ignore, for the moment, the question of massed fires: Would it be impossible, as the Optimists say, for the Soviets to get 2:1 or better odds in *ground forces alone* opposite NATO brigades? An American military observer (one generally sympathetic to the Optimists' views) of *Druzhba '86*, a recent Warsaw Pact exercise in Czechoslovakia, at first thought that massed Soviet forces would simply offer a lot of targets,

but then I thought about the typical widths that we talk about in our doctrine about a rifle company's sector of defense, and then suddenly I thought about the fog rolling in. You now have somewhere on the order of 325 to 350 armored vehicles in these two regiments, three kilometers wide, pouring through a rifle company armed with M-113s, .50 caliber weapons, and so forth . . . and I concluded very rapidly that a breakthrough was very much a potential if the Russians want to pay the price, because in fact they can mass a superior amount of force on a very narrow forward line of troops; that's a *lot of* combat power coming at you very quickly.[58]

In other words, in this exercise a Soviet force twice the size of a NATO brigade attacked a sector a third or a quarter as wide as that held by such a brigade. Soviet doctrine allows, in fact, for main attack sectors as narrow as four kilometers for a division and two kilometers for a motorized rifle regiment (the equivalent of a NATO brigade).[59] Thus, contrary to the assertions of the Optimists,[60] the Soviets could easily create ground force ratios better than 2:1 opposite NATO brigades—*not counting supporting fires.*

Posen and Mearsheimer declare that a Soviet army—a formation rather larger than a NATO corps—could attack only on a fifty kilometer break-

---

57. For the most recent assertion of this, see Mearsheimer, "Numbers, Strategy," pp. 178–179.
58. Scott D. Dean and Benjamin F. Schemmer, "Warsaw Pact Success Would Hinge on Blitzkrieg, U.S. Army Observer Says," *Armed Forces Journal International*, November 1987, pp. 32, 36. Emphasis in the original. As well as fog one may reasonably expect smoke, a commodity which the Soviets use heavily.
59. John Erickson, Lynn Hansen, and William Schneider, *Soviet Ground Forces: An Operational Assessment* (Boulder, Colo.: Westview, 1986), pp. 162–164.
60. On Mearsheimer, see note 57. Posen says that the Soviets could achieve high breakthrough ratios of 4–6:1 "on only a few very small 4 or 5 km segments of the front. Thus, successful attacks in these sectors would take the form of narrow 'wedges' driven into the NATO line." "Measuring," p. 108. In support of these contentions he cites David C. Isby, *Weapons and Tactics of the Soviet Army* (London: Jane's, 1981), p. 38. In fact, however, Isby neither says nor implies that the Soviets could achieve such force ratios on "only a few very small segments" of the front, and in no way suggests that these attacks would consist of mere "narrow wedges." Rather, he merely observes that the Soviets concentrate their divisions on 4–5 km attack sectors. Posen's model of force ratios at the NATO corps sector level, however, keeps the Soviets at bare 2:1 odds. "Measuring," pp. 90–91.

through sector. Only one Soviet army, therefore, could attack any given NATO corps, which has something like one hundred thousand men and defends, on average, seventy kilometers or more of front. We have seen that this assertion runs counter to Soviet doctrine, which envisions breakthrough efforts by army-sized forces in sectors as narrow as a fifth the width assigned them by the Optimists. Posen offered no direct evidence to support his choice of the fifty kilometer sector, but in 1982 Mearsheimer cited two sources published in 1976 in support of this assessment.[61] Only one of these sources, however, could conceivably be construed as supporting the Optimists, since it described Soviet army breakthrough sectors of *"up to* fifty kilometers.[62] This source did, however, leave open the possibility of considerably *narrower* attack sectors, which would allow the Soviets to direct two or more armies against a NATO corps. The second source cited by Mearsheimer actually contradicted him. In it, Christopher Donnelly stated that a Soviet army's attack sector would be twenty to thirty kilometers wide, in principle allowing for two or three Soviet armies attacking a given NATO corps sector.[63] Both sources, moreover, discussed operations involving tactical nuclear weapons, and hence were irrelevant to the Optimists' discussion of a conventional attack on Western Europe. Purely conventional operations allow for far narrower axes of advance than do those involving nuclear weapons, as Donnelly noted.[64] Furthermore, had either Optimist consulted a more up-to-date source—for example, the 1980 version of Donnelly's essay—they would have

---

61. Posen's 1984/85 article did, however, reproduce a diagram from U.S. Army FM 71-2, *The Tank and Mechanized Infantry Battalion Task Force* (June 30, 1977). Posen, "Measuring," p. 109. This diagram—which is badly dated, and appears to reflect the problems discussed below— shows a division massing to a width of only four km for a breakthrough. And yet, in Posen's model the Soviets can bring only 1.5 ADEs to bear in a twenty-five km sector. Posen, "Measuring," pp. 90–92, 98; "Is NATO Decisively Outnumbered?" pp. 199ff; Mearsheimer, "Why the Soviets Can't Win Quickly," p. 134; "Numbers, Strategy," p. 183. Neither Posen nor Mearsheimer offers sources for the fifty km convention in the 1988 *International Security* articles.
62. John Erickson, "Soviet Theatre-Warfare Capability: Doctrines, Deployments, and Capabilities," in Lawrence L. Whetten, ed., *The Future of Soviet Military Power* (New York: Crane, Russak, 1976), p. 148, citing a 1972 Soviet manual. Emphasis added. In 1982, Mearsheimer nominally accepted Erickson's ten-year-old data on breakthrough frontages but rejected Erickson's description (p. 148) of eight to ten such breakthrough efforts. Instead, Mearsheimer (again, like Posen) declared that only two or three—four at the outside—could occur.
63. Christopher Donnelly, "The Soviet Ground Forces," in Ray Bonds, ed., *The Soviet War Machine* (New York: Chartwell, 1976), p. 169.
64. "In conventional conditions, greater concentration is possible than in conditions where nuclear weapons might be used." Ibid., p. 170.

found discussion of Soviet army breakthrough sectors as narrow as ten kilometers.[65]

Analyses that only look at ADEs fighting along a line ignore the host of deep operations which could paralyze a NATO response, particularly the timely movement of reserves forward. A surprise attack against NATO air bases and air defenses—using surface-to-surface missiles, special forces, airborne and heliborne units, as well as aircraft—could inaugurate several days of deep Soviet strikes against NATO command posts, mobilization centers and the like.[66] The "initial air operation" would draw not only on aircraft but on long range missiles and unconventional forces. The Soviets have at their disposal large and sophisticated special forces units (*Spetsnaz*), some of which may already be in place in Western Europe.[67] These, together with air assault battalions and brigades which the Soviets have developed since the 1970s, may disrupt NATO rear areas through sabotage and raids. All of this would serve the Soviet concept of "deep operations," which integrates a variety of strikes throughout the entire depth of an enemy position, coupled with breakthroughs at various points and deep armored penetrations. This concept of deep operations has a long lineage, going back to the 1930s at least, and informs Soviet doctrine today.[68]

The core paradigm of the Optimists looks to the clash of opposing ADEs along a generally stationary line in Central Europe. They calculate only

65. Christopher Donnelly, "The Modern Soviet Ground Forces," in Ray Bonds, ed., *The Illustrated Encyclopedia of the Strategy, Tactics, and Weapons of Russian Military Power* (New York: St. Martin's, 1980), p. 155.
66. See, inter alia, John G. Hines, "Soviet Front Operations in Europe," and Phillip A. Petersen, "Soviet Planning for Strategic Operation Against NATO," in *Spotlight on the Soviet Union*, pp. 74–125; Dennis M. Gormley, "A New Dimension to Soviet Theater Strategy," *Orbis*, Vol. 29, No. 3 (Fall 1985), pp. 537–569; Phillip A. Petersen and John G. Hines, "The Conventional Offensive in Soviet Theater Strategy," *Orbis*, Vol. 27, No. 3 (Fall 1983), pp. 695–739.
67. See Viktor Suvorov, "Spetsnaz: The Soviet Union's Special Forces," *International Defense Review*, Vol. 16, No. 9 (September 1983), pp. 1209–1216; Victoria Pope, "Soviet-Bloc Troops Prowl in West Europe," *Wall Street Journal*, March 7, 1988, p. 14.
68. See Kurt S. Schultz, "Vladimir K. Triandafillov and the Development of Soviet 'Deep Operations'," in David R. Jones, ed., *Soviet Armed Forces Review Annual 1984/1985*, Vol. 9 (Gulf Breeze, Fla.: Academic International Press, 1986), pp. 233–244; see also an article as significant for its authorship as its substance, N. V. Ogarkov, "Glubokaia operatsiia [The Deep Operation]," *Sovetskaia voennaia entsiklopedia* [Soviet Military Encyclopedia], Vol. 2 (Moscow: Voyenizdat, 1976), p. 578 (excerpt translated by William Fuller): Among other things, former Chief of the Soviet General Staff Ogarkov describes how postwar developments have "significantly increased the prospects for simultaneously acting against the entire depth of the enemy's formation, breaking through his defenses at high tempos and rapidly developing success."

uninterrupted reinforcement and mobilization rates.[69] In truth, however, a NATO/Warsaw Pact war would more likely begin with a confused and turbulent battle, conducted throughout the depths of the Western position in Europe. Reinforcements and reserves would move forward fitfully and in fragments, in the midst of indescribable confusion. Panicked mobs of civilian refugees, air raids, heliborne assaults, and a wide variety of commando-type operations could clog up NATO's rear areas in these circumstances.[70]

DATA TRAPS

Much of the discussion thus far has concentrated on what one might call intangible elements of the balance—politics, intelligence, Soviet concepts of operations, and the like. Yet even with respect to "hard" data, careful examination of the Optimists' writings reveals that substantial errors can occur. These problems have, furthermore, nothing to do with the vagaries of order of battle information discussed above.

One kind of errancy proceeds from the use of out-of-date statistics. For example, Mearsheimer recently avowed that the ADE ratio between Warsaw Pact and NATO standing forces on the Central Front is 1.2:1.[71] He did not give a source for this ratio, but one may infer that he derived it from his 1982 study.[72] At that time, he derived the figure from two Congressional Budget Office studies, one completed in 1979, the other in 1980.[73] When one checks those sources, it transpires that they in turn derived the 1.2:1 ratio from a Department of Defense (DoD) study issued in 1976.[74]

The 1.2:1 ADE ratio is highly questionable. A recent DoD assessment suggests that, depending on a variety of assumptions, the ratio ranges be-

---

69. Thus, it is critically important that NATO can "shift forces from other Corps sectors and its operational reserves to threatened points along the front." Mearsheimer, "Why the Soviets Can't Win Quickly," p. 147. Curiously, Mearsheimer has also declared that "there is no doubt that NATO's forces do not have *strategic* mobility. By and large, they are restricted to fighting in specific areas of the NATO front." (Emphasis in the original.) Mearsheimer, "Maneuver," p. 106.
70. The campaign of France, May/June 1940 is instructive in this regard. One should note that independent political directives to national corps commanders may worsen the problem.
71. Mearsheimer, "Numbers, Strategy," p. 180.
72. Mearsheimer, "Why the Soviets Can't Win Quickly," p. 126.
73. Pat Hillier, *Strengthening NATO: POMCUS and Other Approaches* (Washington, D.C.: CBO, February 1979), pp. 53–57; and Pat Hillier and Nora Slatkin, *U.S. Ground Forces: Design and Cost Alternatives for NATO and Non-NATO Contingencies* (Washington, D.C.: CBO, December 1980), pp. 23–24. Cited in Mearsheimer, "Why the Soviets Can't Win Quickly," p. 124 n. 10.
74. Office of the Secretary of Defense, "A Report to Congress on U.S. Conventional Reinforcements to NATO," (Washington, D.C.: Department of Defense, June 1976).

tween 1.5:1 and 2:1.[75] Just as striking, however, as the discrepancy between Mearsheimer's and DoD's assessments of the ratio in 1988, is his use in 1982 of statistics at least six years old, and in 1988 at least twelve years old. Yet Mearsheimer declared in 1982 that the basic balance between NATO and the Warsaw Pact had remained stable even longer than that: "there have been no significant changes in the force levels of each side since 1973."[76]

The only way he could have come to this conclusion would have been by confining his comparison to the number of standing tank and mechanized divisions in Western and Eastern Europe, excluding those in the Soviet Union itself. But this completely avoids the heart of the force level issue—the size of those divisions, the number and type of their weapons, and the number and strength of various "non-divisional" units. Here the story is very different, as the DoD assessment of combat ratios suggests. Consider only evidence available when Mearsheimer wrote his 1982 article. The previous year, a standard reference work on the Soviet military stated that between 1970 and 1980, first-line Soviet motorized rifle divisions (the kind stationed in East Germany) had gone from a strength of 10,000 men and 188 tanks to a strength of 13,000 men and 266 tanks, while Soviet tank divisions had gone from 8,500 men and 316 tanks to 11,000 men and 325 tanks.[77] Similarly, a quick perusal of the IISS *Military Balance* would have revealed steady increases in the numbers of Soviet forces stationed in East Europe. Not only did absolute force levels change: so too did force ratios. In some cases—with respect to manpower and numbers of divisions—NATO's relative position slipped only slightly. With respect to quantities of weaponry and the firepower they could deliver, the ratio deteriorated more sharply from the Western point of view, as the DoD analysis suggests. The Soviets have steadily increased the quantity and quality of their firepower by adding heavier calibers of artillery, increasing the proportion of self-propelled guns and howitzers, introducing attack helicopters, and modernizing their tanks. These qualitative improvements, in addition to quantitative increases, account for the deterioration since the 1970s of the ADE ratios and similar measures of the balance.[78]

---

75. Frank C. Carlucci, *Annual Report of the Secretary of Defense, FY 1989* (Washington, D.C.: U.S. Government Printing Office, 1988), p. 31. See also Caspar W. Weinberger, *Annual Report of the Secretary of Defense, FY 1988/FY 1989* (Washington, D.C.: U.S.G.P.O., 1987), p. 30.
76. Mearsheimer, "Why the Soviets Can't Win Quickly," p. 122, n. 3.
77. David R. Jones, ed., *Soviet Armed Forces Review Annual*, Vol. 4, *1980* (Gulf Breeze, Fla.: Academic International Press, 1980), p. 91.
78. For a vivid sense of the "bean count" changes, see Supreme Headquarters Allied Powers Europe, "NATO and the Warsaw Pact Force Comparisons, 1973–1986."

Another kind of error results from the Optimists' counting rules. In 1982, for example, Mearsheimer examined the chance of a "bolt-from-the-blue" attack, and declared that 24 Warsaw Pact divisions would have to hurl themselves against 28 NATO divisions, a very favorable ratio for NATO. Those 24 divisions, moreover, could not reach full strength in such an attack, because a mobilization of Warsaw Pact reservists would give warning of an invasion from the East.[79] How did he come to the 24:28 ratio?

For the Warsaw Pact number Mearsheimer counted only the nineteen Soviet tank and motorized rifle divisions in East Germany and their five Soviet counterparts in Czechoslovakia. He allowed no East European divisions (even the generally reliable East Germans) to participate, because they would require a partial reserve mobilization to become operational. He did not explain why the Soviets would use *their* divisions without a mobilization, but not East European divisions manned at nearly the same level.[80] Moreover, he excluded from consideration the four Soviet divisions stationed in Hungary, presumably because they would have to attack through neutral Austria to come into play. If so, he should have explained why the Soviets would willingly ignite World War III while scrupulously avoiding an infringement of Austrian neutrality. Mearsheimer derived the 28-division figure for NATO from a 1976 study.[81] If one turns to that study, one finds that it included over two French divisions (although the French are not part of NATO's integrated military structure) and a variety of forces (nearly four Danish and Dutch divisions, for example) that require substantial reserve callups to reach their nominal strength.[82] Thus, Mearsheimer not only undercounted the Warsaw Pact forces, but inflated NATO strength by postulating a scenario in which an unmobilized Warsaw Pact attacks a partially mobilized NATO.

This sort of skewed counting shows up in other places as well, for example in Mearsheimer's assertion that if one were to add "non-divisional assets" to assessments of the balance (i.e., fighting units separate from formally organized infantry and armor divisions), "the ratio would shift further in NATO's favor."[83] In fact, the Warsaw Pact has more of these "non-divisional assets"

---

79. Mearsheimer, "Why the Soviets Can't Win Quickly," p. 123 n. 8.
80. According to the most up-to-date source available when Mearsheimer wrote, East European Category I divisions were manned at up to 3/4 strength, and Soviet Category I divisions were manned at 3/4 strength or better. IISS, *Military Balance 1981–1982*, pp. 12, 18.
81. Ibid., p. 124, n. 10. The study in question was Fischer's *Defending the Central Front*.
82. Fischer, *Defending the Central Front*, p. 8.
83. Mearsheimer, "Why the Soviets Can't Win Quickly," p. 126 n. 18.

than does NATO, and has been adding them to its force structure at a greater rate.[84] Included here are units for which no Western analogue exists, such as an entire artillery division in East Germany in addition to other units which have their analogues in type, if not quantity, in the West. Today, for example, the IISS assesses that those Soviet forces in East Germany alone would receive support from an artillery division, an air assault brigade, five artillery brigades, and five attack helicopter regiments.

Another example of biased counting appears in Posen's assessment of Soviet command and control as inferior to NATO's, an important part of his analysis. He adduces as evidence the view that the Soviets have fewer headquarters per division than do their American counterparts. He can say this because he does not count Soviet battalion headquarters and support forces (numbering 150 men) as "major" headquarters. These headquarters are, in his view, "tiny" relative to a comparable U.S. headquarters only twice the size.[85] Posen advances no operational reason why Soviet battalion headquarters should not count as such, nor does he examine the logic by which the more clerks one places in a command post the more effective the headquarters becomes. It is worth remembering in this connection that some forces with "tiny" operational headquarters have proved formidable indeed.[86] Moreover, Posen takes no account in his assessment of the importance of echelons above division—including Army, Front, Theater of Strategic Military

---

84. In 1982, for example, the IISS *Military Balance* listed for the Soviet Union 8 air assault brigades and 14 artillery divisions. The most recent *Military Balance* lists 2 additional air assault brigades, 2 additional artillery divisions, and 20 attack helicopter regiments. This last number reflects, in part, a growth in the number of Soviet helicopters from fewer than 3500 in 1982 to 4,300 or more today. *Military Balance 1982–1983*, pp. 14–17; *Military Balance 1987–1988*, pp. 22–27. By way of contrast, NATO force structure in Europe has remained stable during this time, with minor changes (up and down), usually at the battalion level. *Military Balance 1982–1983*, pp. 4–10, 24–44; *Military Balance 1987–1988*, pp. 11–26, 54–82.
85. Posen, "Is NATO Decisively Outnumbered?" p. 197 n. 26. These 150 men amount to fully a third the complement of such a Soviet battalion's strength. Moreover, in both the American and the Soviet cases Posen appears to count specialized combat units as "support."
86. This was particularly true of the Wehrmacht during World War II. General Heinz Gaedke, a distinguished German commander and chief of staff to General Hermann Balck, said: "When I see the enormous staff apparatus that we [the Bundeswehr] have now constructed, partly under your [American] influence, I often ask, 'My God, how is this going to work?' Here is how we controlled our divisions in both the West and East in WWII: My division commander and I would sit together in a half-track vehicle with the maps on our laps, exchange opinions, 'Should we go to the left or to the right, should we do it tonight or tomorrow at dawn?'—then we'd scribble our instructions, give them to the driver next to us, and he'd pass the orders along to a couple of radio operators in the back of our vehicle." "Translation of Taped Conversation with Lieutenant General Heinz Gaedke," Contract No. DAAK 40-78-C-0004 (Columbus, Ohio: Battelle Columbus Laboratories, 1979), pp. 36–37.

Action (TVD), and higher—in which Soviet command and control looks considerably better than NATO's.[87]

A third kind of error consists of seemingly factual but unsupported assertions such as, "NATO's artillery is significantly better than Pact artillery."[88] This reflects a technical judgment, since the author concedes the superior quantity of Soviet guns, mortars, howitzers, and rocket launchers. Leaving aside the Soviet proverb that "quantity has a quality all its own," the truth would appear to be far more complicated. Sources available at the time Mearsheimer made his assertion suggested that, in many respects, Soviet artillery pieces matched and in some cases overmatched those in Western inventories.[89] A British expert recently declared that, "the Russian artillery has always had equipment as good as any, and often better."[90]

Openly introduced alterations of statistics often have no better foundation. Consider for example, Posen's "Measuring the European Conventional Balance," an article widely cited by other Optimists (most notably Mearsheimer) as providing the analytic base for their assessments. Posen obtains a relatively favorable ADE ratio for NATO (only slightly worse than 1:1, or comparable to the Stalingrad case) rather than the more usually cited 1.5 or 2:1 ADE ratio theater-wide. He does this in part by assigning a multiplier of 1.5 to NATO ADEs "to take into account the increased combat effectiveness that NATO's military leaders *presumably* expect from their efforts."[91] Posen refers to NATO's relatively high investment in support forces, "tail," compared with that of the Warsaw Pact. In the tail, Posen includes some areas (e.g., intelligence) in which it is very difficult to believe that the Soviets do not invest every bit as heavily as does the West, if not more so. But NATO forces have

---

87. See Hines and Petersen, "Is NATO Thinking Too Small?"
88. Mearsheimer, "Why the Soviets Can't Win Quickly," p. 126.
89. The Soviet M-1946 130mm gun (27 km range) outdistanced the heaviest American piece coming into service, the M-110 203mm howitzer (17 km range). Range makes a critical difference for these heavy artillery pieces, which have the vital task of long-range counterbattery fire. In 1981 the standard U.S. M-109 self-propelled 155mm howitzer fired an explosive weighing 43 kg a distance of 15 km. Its Soviet counterpart, the self-propelled 152mm howitzer, was assessed to fire a 48 kg round 18 km. One could extend this comparison across a range of guns (we have picked the best on the Western side, not comparing Soviet artillery, for example, with the self-propelled 105mm howitzers of the British artillery), with similar or even more startling results. Shelford Bidwell, ed., *Brassey's Artillery of the World*, 2nd ed. (London: Brassey's, 1981). Ranges refer to standard projectiles rather than the RAP (rocket-assisted-projectile) rounds possessed by both sides; warhead weights refer to a standard high explosive round.
90. Chris Bellamy, *Red God of War: Soviet Artillery and Rocket Forces* (London: Brassey's, 1986), p. 216.
91. Posen, "Measuring," p. 69. Emphasis added.

heavy tails for a host of reasons, including the considerable demand for creature comforts in Western armed forces, and the duplication and waste caused by the existence of loosely integrated national military organizations. NATO's heavy tail does not result merely from unconstrained choice, as Posen implies; it comes from a host of organizational routines as well as from doctrinal preferences. The merits of NATO's logistical and organizational practices require discussion, not an assumption that the West's practices are invariably correct, and certainly not an increase of NATO firepower scores by fifty percent. Furthermore, an optimum solution—logistical or otherwise—to every military problem does not necessarily exist. It is quite possible that one set of logistical arrangements will serve Soviet purposes, given Soviet strategy, culture, and operational style, and that a very different set answers the West's needs.

A final kind of error comes from the misapplication of a rule of thumb such as that which states that odds of better than 3:1 are required by an attacker to overwhelm a defender.[92] One Optimist, citing U.S. Army Field Manual 100-5 (Operations), uses this ratio to analyze breakthrough attempts directed against NATO *corps* (forces on the order of one hundred thousand men holding, it will be remembered, a 70 km or wider front). An examination of the Field Manual in question, however, reveals that it discusses this ratio in the context of combat involving *battalions* and *brigades* (forces between a thousand and four thousand strong).[93] The Optimists took a (questionable) *tactical* dictum and applied it to an *operational* problem.

LIMITATIONS OF MODELS

The basic model that underlies analysis of some Optimists runs something as follows: in order to achieve a breakthrough in a sector, an attacker needs odds of at least 3:1. So long as NATO can prevent the Soviets from achieving those kinds of odds in a competitive game of reinforcement, the front will

---

92. Mearsheimer, "Why the Soviets Can't Win Quickly," p. 133. See also Posen, "Measuring," pp. 83–84, 88.
93. *U.S. Army Field Manual 100-5, Operations* (Washington, D.C.: Department of the Army, 1976), pp. 3–4ff. On one occasion only (p. 5-3) does the manual appear to apply the 3:1 rule to divisional combat (fifteen to twenty thousand men holding a twenty-five km front), and then only to suggest that the odds are pretty nearly hopeless. It should also be noted that this manual had been largely repudiated by the Army in 1982, in part because of its reliance on the mechanistic application of firepower ratios. See Kevin P. Sheehan, "Preparing for Imaginary War: Examining Peacetime Functions and Changes of Army Doctrine," Ch. 5, "AirLand Battle," (unpublished dissertation, Harvard University, 1988).

probably hold. We have already seen weaknesses in this analysis—for example, the assumptions about reinforcement rates envisage a smooth process quite distant from the real world, and the assertions about force ratios do not hold up.[94]

The Optimists have explicitly presented some but not all of their mathematical models.[95] In all cases, however, several serious internal problems deserve note. The first and most pressing of these is that many of the Optimists have not applied their models to historical cases comparable to the situation on the Central Front: they have not validated their a priori assertions. Such studies—though tricky and laborious—are possible, and have in fact been run. The most interesting of these applied the ADE methodology to the Battle of France in 1940.[96] The Director of Net Assessment of the Department of Defense, who commissioned that study, summarized its findings:

German forces in a reconstruction of armored division equivalent measures were about 5 to 10 percent inferior to the combined French, British, Belgian, and Dutch forces. We all know the result. This does not make me feel very comfortable when someone tells me that we have now moved up to a comfortable armored division equivalent (ADE) ratio in which the Warsaw Pact is only 50 percent greater than NATO and therefore far from being at the canonical threefold advantage that attackers require.[97]

He concluded that confidence "that we currently have the analytic capabilities needed to assess military balances is undue."[98]

---

94. This is particularly true of Mearsheimer's 3:1 breakthrough model, which contains numerous flaws, as discussed above. Analytic models which rely on Lanchester equations, particularly those used by William Kaufmann, have received devastating treatment in John W.R. Lepingwell, "The Laws of Combat? Lanchester Reexamined," *International Security* Vol. 12, No. 1 (Summer 1987), pp. 89–134. See also Joshua M. Epstein, *The Calculus of Conventional War: Dynamic Analysis without Lanchester Equations* (Washington, D.C.: Brookings, 1985).

95. Epstein has, but Posen has not. In neither "Measuring" nor his 1988 *International Security* article does Posen present more than his assumptions and the "output" of his model, i.e., a graph. Its actual workings remain somewhat mysterious. It should be noted that not all Optimists use mathematical models, although they do use conceptual ones (Mearsheimer, for example). For a general critique of formal defense modeling see U.S. Congress, General Accounting Office, "Models, Data, and War: a Critique of the Foundations for Defense Analyses," PAD-80-21 (Washington, D.C.: U.S.G.P.O, 1980).

96. Phillip A. Karber, Grant Whitley, Mark Herman, and Douglas Komer, "Assessing the Correlation of Forces: France 1940," DNA-001-78-C-0114 (McLean, Va.: BDM Corporation, 1979).

97. Andrew W. Marshall, "Arms Competitions: The Status of Analysis," in Nerlich, ed., *The Western Panacea*, p. 13.

98. Ibid., p. 15.

Consider one staple of analysis, the armored division equivalent (ADE) methodology itself, which measures the firepower of any unit, relying on the Weapons Effectiveness Indices/Weighted Unit Value (WEI/WUV) scoring system. The ADE system is used by many Optimists, and indeed most analysts.[99] Upon taking a close look we again find the use of out-of-date information (the original WEI/WUV system was devised in the early 1970s, and reflects judgments, information, and tables of organization current at the time).[100] But beyond these problems we should question the wisdom of using the ADE measure as the *prime* indicator of relative combat effectiveness because it compares incommensurables.

No sensible composer or conductor would attempt to evaluate the instruments in an orchestra according to a common index of musical effectiveness.[101] Yet the ADE enforces just this kind of absurdity. In one standard version of the ADE system, for example, forty of the Soviets' thirty-year-old T-55 tanks count for almost twice as much in the attack as do a similar number of their BM-21 multiple rocket launchers or M-1946 long-range artillery pieces.[102] But the three kinds of weapons have completely different tasks. Rocket launchers and towed artillery cannot storm a defended position; tanks cannot lay down a curtain of poison gas or knock out enemy artillery batteries from a distance of 30 kilometers. And the ADE system says nothing about tactical efficiency, doctrine, and the like.

The ADE does indeed have its usefulness as an accounting measure—a look at ADE scores over time provides some useful information about the development of opposing forces in peacetime. It may serve as one—but only one—input into an assessment of relative combat effectiveness. The problem arises when analysts use it as the brick out of which to build supposedly definitive models. And the problems of the Optimists' model do not end here.

---

99. Posen, "Is NATO Decisively Outnumbered?" p. 190 n. 12, briefly describes this methodology.
100. Most of the Optimists base their ADE numbers on the work of William P. Mako, *U.S. Ground Forces and the Defense of Central Europe* (Washington, D.C.: Brookings, 1983), pp. 105–134. Mako relies heavily on a 1974 U.S. Army report (U.S. Army Concepts Analysis Agency, *Weapons Effectiveness Indices/Weighted Unit Values*) which he modifies in obscure ways. His tables do not reflect current equipment; for example; his listing of the tanks in a U.S. armored division includes only the M-60A1 tank, two generations behind the equipment in the Army inventory in 1983.
101. The analogy between an army and an orchestra is not a fanciful one, as a great commander in World War II noted. William Slim, *Defeat Into Victory* (New York: David McKay, 1961), p. 3.
102. Mako, *U.S. Ground Forces*, p. 125.

Posen explicitly describes many of the assumptions of his model, some of which are questionable: units are assumed to fight until annihilated, instead of collapsing or being withdrawn; the model does not deal with the peculiar problems of surprise; units can only advance a maximum of five kilometers a day. Such aggregated (even if acknowledged) unreality, however, leads one to wonder about the usefulness of his model in the first place. Furthermore, many models have assumptions and use variables that drive their conclusions in particular directions.[103] For example, Posen runs his model out over four months, during which time Pact forces can *never* advance more than five kilometers a day (and in another variant, two kilometers a day), even if NATO forces collapse at any point along the front. In other words his model creates a rubberized battle line which can stretch but never break. That an analyst makes such assumptions explicitly does not necessarily make it realistic or appropriate to do so.

So-called dynamic analysis—particularly when it involves computer modeling—appears at once more sophisticated and more realistic than mere "bean counting." In some respects it may be so. But it has its own perils because of the very seductiveness of simulations, their mathematical elegance and their supposed resemblance to warfare in the real world. Most entrancing of all, they seem to offer the student of war the possibility of representing enormously complicated relationships in a single book or even article. But these attempts to capture the course of World War III in Central Europe represent a highly questionable departure from the precursor of contemporary modeling, the operations research effort of World War II. Not only did operations researchers study far narrower problems than the totality of a NATO/Warsaw Pact war in Europe: in those days, analysts considered *first-hand observation of an ongoing war* essential to build sound models.[104] Obviously, we have nothing resembling first-hand (or, for that matter, second-hand) information on what a war in Europe might look like. At best, analysts

---

103. These assumptions include the 50 km attack sectors and 1.5 NATO ADE multiplier discussed above, allowing the Soviets only three or four attack sectors, full French participation in the war from the first day, greatly superior NATO air power, and prompt mobilization.

104. "Second-hand contact with operations obtained by talking to people who once were engaged in these operations or to people who have talked to people so engaged now, is too tenuous a contact upon which to base operational research." Philip M. Morse, "Comments on the Organization of Operations Research," n.d. (1942?) *Tenth Fleet Records*, Anti-Submarine Measures Division, Box 24, Operational Archives, Washington Navy Yard, p. 3. More generally, see Clayton J. Thomas, "Models and Wartime Combat Operations Research," in Wayne P. Hughes, ed., *Military Modeling* (Alexandria, Va.: Military Operations Research Society, 1984), pp. 55–93.

can glean shreds of evidence from testing grounds and the odd fracas in the Third World—hardly reliable substitutes for a prolonged and close look at the real thing.

We may have little choice, in some cases, but to make efforts to reduce war to algebra (as Clausewitz put it). We should not, however, lose sight of the essential futility of attempts to reduce to a few equations as titanic and complex a process as a coalition war fought by millions of men with scores of novel weapons over hundreds of thousands of square kilometers. To succumb to such an intellectual *folie de grandeur* is to delude not only one's readers but oneself.

## The Soviet Calculus

The preceding criticisms do *not* necessarily imply that in every case the Soviets would win a crushing and instantaneous victory in Europe were war to break out tomorrow. Many important factors have not been addressed: the absolutely critical issue of war stocks, for example, or the complex question of Soviet ability to implement their demanding doctrine. Much would depend on warning and mobilization, and even more on the incalculable clash of vast forces whose equipment and doctrine have not been tested and refined in combat. Under some conditions one could imagine a quick Soviet win: under others a more protracted battle, although probably one unfavorable for the West. It is hard to see how, in any case, NATO could avoid losing (temporarily, at least) large chunks of the Federal Republic of Germany. But if this more pessimistic assessment holds true, what has kept the Soviets from invading Western Europe?

There are two broad explanations. Richard Betts argues that is one thing to have reasonably good hopes of victory, and quite another to accept the hazards of war on the basis of those hopes.[105] This is plausible, but rather cold comfort, since many nations have launched enormously destructive wars with opening campaigns that they knew to be far more risky—the Japanese attack on Pearl Harbor is a case in point. A more convincing set of explanations comes from an attempt to understand the Soviet calculus of war.

Most of the Optimists do not proceed this way, because they hold to an abstract doctrine of deterrence, that is, one that operates on the basis of

---

105. This, I take it, is partly the point of Betts' subtitle to "Conventional Deterrence: Predictive Uncertainty and Policy Confidence."

principles generalizable across regime and culture, geographical configuration and historical circumstance. Implicitly, they reject the Clausewitzian notion that "war is not waged against an abstract enemy, but against a real one who must always be kept in mind."[106] In the Optimists' view, "the best way to prevent war is to ensure that it would have devastating consequences for all the participants,"[107] or "in the world of *conventional* deterrence, it is confidence in quick, cheap victory that causes the aggressor to attack."[108] The laws of deterrence operate independently, in this view, of the characteristics and predicaments of particular countries or leaders.

The Soviets view this understanding of deterrence as dangerous folly. Their terms for deterrence suggest not *mutual* devastation but constraint of a particular opponent—making sure that *he* will lose, and that he *understands* that he will lose.[109] Here again the Soviets judge rightly: we must seek to deter not generic opponents, but unique ones. American and West European defense planners must ask, "what will deter the *Soviets* from an attack on NATO nations?" Why then, if General Rogers is correct in his assessment of the balance, have the Soviets not attempted to overrun Western Europe?

The first and most obvious answer is that they have had no overwhelming reason to try to do so. No pressing threat resides west of the Iron Curtain, and certainly none that merits the costs of war. By and large the Soviets have shown themselves quite conservative about using force, although far from compunction-ridden about doing so. But more importantly, the Soviet assessment of the balance may very well differ from both the Optimists' position of confidence and the more pessimistic views presented by General Rogers. For one thing, the Soviets may think their chances of a quick win to be poor: they may see more of NATO's strengths and fewer of their own. It is difficult to find precise Soviet judgments on these matters. Some larger aspects of the Soviet assessment do, however, appear in their open literature. For one thing, the view of the conventional balance as something entirely distinct from the question of nuclear weapons does not hold in the East. Soviet military authors do discuss the possibility of conventional operations— even lengthy conventional operations—under the threat of the use of nuclear

---

106. Clausewitz, *On War*, Book II, Chapter 5, p. 161.
107. Mearsheimer, "Nuclear Weapons," p. 21.
108. Posen, "Measuring," p. 80. Emphasis in the original.
109. The Soviets have two words for deterrent, "*sredstvo ustrasheniia*" or "means of frightening," and "*sderzhivaeuschee sredstvo*" or "means of restraining." (Translation by William Fuller.) The former seems to come closest to American concepts of deterrence, the latter to the Soviets'.

weapons. The Soviets do not believe, however (again, for sound common sense reasons), that either side can completely lift the shadow of nuclear weapons from consideration of war in Europe, and they understand full well how grim a nuclear war could be.

A second sobering consideration for the Soviets comes from their awareness of the costliness of any campaign—even a successful one—to seize sections of Europe. One should not confuse a *quick* campaign with a *cheap* one. The Soviets judge that, in World War II, between two-thirds and four-fifths of their armies' losses in offensive operations occurred during the penetration phases of a breakthrough.[110] Even the German blitzkrieg in France in May 1940—an operation which went considerably more smoothly and cheaply than would a Soviet attack on Western Europe—paid a heavy price. A third of all German tanks and over a quarter of all German aircraft were destroyed in what remains a model of lightning war.[111] Even in the most pessimistic assessment of the balance, NATO forces are, on an absolute scale, large and effective enough to inflict very heavy damage on a Soviet attacker, even if they could not deny him victory in the initial campaign. A Europe reduced to flame and rubble, awash with refugees and the debris of catastrophic battles, has far less to offer the Soviets than the Europe of today, or a Europe detached from the United States tomorrow.

This leads in turn to another consideration, perhaps the definitive one in the minds of Soviet planners. The conquest of most or all of the Federal Republic of Germany would not necessarily mean the Soviet occupation of all of Europe, and certainly not the termination of a war. Although the Soviets have devoted a great deal of attention to problems of winning a war in its "initial period," they also recognize that a successful blitzkrieg does not foreordain the outcome of the war.

A number of the first campaigns [of World War II] showed that a blitzkrieg victory could be achieved in the initial period only over a militarily and economically weak enemy with limited territory and lacking high morale, political unity, and the will to fight until the end. When large nations (or

---

110. Phillip Petersen, "Soviet Offensive Operations," *NATO's Sixteen Nations*, Vol. 32, No. 5 (August 1987), pp. 26–33.
111. Hans Umbreit, "Der Kampf um die Vormachtstellung in Westeuropa," in Klaus A. Maier et al., *Das Deutsche Reich und der zweite Weltkrieg*, Vol. 2, *Die Errichtung der Hegemonie auf dem Europaeischen Kontinent* (Stuttgart: Deutsche Verlags-Anstalt, 1979), pp. 283, 294, 307; Williamson Murray, *Luftwaffe* (London: Allen & Unwin, 1985), p. 44. According to Murray's figures some 28% of the German Air Force—over a thousand aircraft—were destroyed on operations during the Battle of France, and 36% damaged.

coalitions of nations) with great military and economic potential, vast territory, and especially important, tremendous morale and political potential entered the war against the aggressor, blitzkrieg warfare failed entirely, even when the aggressor achieved important strategic results in the initial period.[112]

Today, the Soviets seem to expect that a war with the West would, in fact, mean war against a large and wealthy coalition; moreover, they appreciate (more systematically than do their counterparts in the West) the quantum increases in weapons ranges and lethalities since World War II. They paint a picture of a global war of unparalleled ferocity, enormously destructive even in its conventional stages, and quite possibly prolonged.[113]

In other words, even if the Optimists are wrong, and the Soviets could, under particular conditions, overrun West Germany and the Benelux countries, what would they have gained? By their own estimates they would have suffered heavily in the process, and conquered nations devastated by war. NATO armies, navies, and air forces might well continue the battle from the periphery—Britain, France, Norway, Spain, Turkey, and Italy, for example—and the economic potential of the United States would remain untouched. The longer the war continued, the greater the likelihood that new actors—China perhaps, or in the longer run, a hastily rearmed Japan—would join the fray. And on top of all of this, the threat of a large scale nuclear exchange would remain. The uncertainties of such a war might well seem more daunting than the challenges of overwhelming NATO's forces in the Central Region. We cannot, then, understand the conventional balance if we do not look beyond it.

*How Should We Think About the Balance?*

One may question the methods the Optimists use to reach their conclusions, but in turn it is fair to ask: "What alternative approach should analysts take?" A full and complete assessment of the conventional balance in Europe would

---

112. Ivanov, *The Initial Period of War*, p. 308. "It is essential to be ready for a protracted, stubborn, and fierce struggle." Gareev, *Frunze*, p. 217.
113. See Gareev, *Frunze*, especially pp. 213–222. A brief summary of the views of one of the Soviet Union's most thoughtful soldiers is Dale R. Herspring, "Nikolay Ogarkov and the Scientific-Technical Revolution in Soviet Military Affairs," *Comparative Strategy*, Vol. 6, No. 1 (1987), pp. 29–59, especially pp. 48–51. See also N.V. Ogarkov, *History Teaches Vigilance* (Moscow: Voyenizdat, 1985).

require far more space than this or any article could provide. Indeed, a multivolumed work—and access to the most highly classified information—would be required to do it properly. Quite possibly a team of analysts rather than an individual would have to develop it. Nonetheless, one can sketch a framework for analysis which would aid in such an endeavor. In part, what follows simply reflects the obverse of the criticisms leveled at the Optimists; it also, however, suggests a different approach that has some precedent in this kind of work.[114] This approach has five components.

POLITICS FIRST

Political assessments must begin, end, and pervade an analysis of the balance. The origins of a war in Europe will shape many elements of relative strength: the composition of the coalitions, the unity of purpose and firmness of will on the part of decision-makers, the military resources available to either side, the tempo of mobilization and operations, and the location and purpose of particular campaigns. One can imagine very different kinds of wars emerging from such scenarios as: a confrontation that spreads from the Persian Gulf following U.S. and Soviet clashes there and in the Middle East; a lunge of desperation by a Soviet Union which sees its East European empire crumbling and the Iron Curtain dissolving; an assertion of Soviet hegemony in the Balkans (including Rumania, Yugoslavia, and Albania) in the face of fissiparous tendencies there. Depending upon the scenario, optimistic or pessimistic conclusions may be in order. In addition to making judgments about what a war would be about and whence it would come—no mean task—we must consider the internal configurations of the allied and neutral states now and in the event of such a war. Such an evaluation must deal with the fundamental fact germane to our problem, that is, the division of Europe between communist and democratic states, the former coordinated and militarized but poor and failing, the latter prosperous and purse-conscious in matters of defense, but fractious and only intermittently cooperative.

---

114. See in particular two articles by Andrew W. Marshall in addition to "Arms Competitions," cited above: "Problems of Estimating Military Power," P-3417 (Santa Monica: RAND, 1966) and "A Program to Improve Analytic Methods related to Strategic Forces," *Policy Sciences*, No. 15 (1982). What follows, however, seems to me to depart from Marshall's views in a number of respects. This section of this article builds on work done by the author and Stephen P. Rosen in *Net Assessment and Strategic Planning* (New York: The Free Press, forthcoming).

TRENDS

Net assessment has a number of functions. It gives us a sense of what might occur should war in fact break out: it should also help us to understand peacetime processes of competition. In some cases the two purposes overlap. Often we cannot know with any precision how well particular opposing forces will perform against one another, but we may have a sense of whether the situation has improved or deteriorated. A study of long term developments also helps build a picture of the opponent's modus operandi, and perhaps even of his assessment of the balance. Trend analysis can and should take many forms. It is here that measures such as the ADE have their greatest value—as units of account, not instruments of divination. Even the humble "bean count" has its merit, provided we handle it carefully.

CONCEPTS OF OPERATIONS

Implicit in this essay's critique of the Optimists is the view that we must study Soviet concepts of operations and Soviet practices at all levels of war. Careful sifting of a very rich open Soviet military literature can contribute greatly to this.[115] Senior Soviet officers, in far larger numbers than their Western counterparts, write reams of history and contemporary military analysis. Despite the stultifying and false character of their ideological framework, which makes these works tiresome to read and frequently hard to accept, they merit study. This injunction holds true in particular for generalists in the field of strategic studies, who have tended to leave such browsing to professional Sovietologists.

ASYMMETRIES

From the foregoing should proceed a careful comparison of Western and Eastern methods of war, including approaches to organization and to methods of command and control, as well as tactics and technology. A serious net assessment of the opposing sides becomes possible only when we understand the complex differences between them. For example, commanders of NATO battalions, brigades, and perhaps even divisions and corps may have far greater flexibility and discretion than their Warsaw Pact counterparts. Battalion for battalion, NATO troops will most likely outfight Warsaw

---

115. Exemplary are the very fine work of Christopher Donnelly and his colleagues at Sandhurst and Stephen M. Meyer's *Soviet Theatre Nuclear Forces*, Adelphi Papers Nos. 187, 188 (London: International Institute for Strategic Studies, 1983/1984).

Pact forces. At the level of High Command, however, the Soviet Front and higher-level commands will have far greater control over their forces and far greater flexibility than their Western counterparts.

But an attempt to describe asymmetries should go further. It should address what is, perhaps, the largest difference between the two sides, and one accepted but rarely discussed by virtually all analysts: the assumption that the war can only begin with a Warsaw Pact attack, never with a NATO preemptive blow, much less with a premeditated attack. Despite the strengths of the defensive—some real, some merely assumed—the advantage of initiative in an East-West war will be large. It will include the ability to choose the time, place, manner and weight of an attack. It will mean, almost inevitably, a certain degree of tactical surprise, if only of a few hours—no mean advantage if one looks at the "initial air operation." In war as in chess, the initiative provides a valuable if not always a decisive edge, and for good or bad reasons NATO has foregone it.

Analysis of asymmetries should direct force planners' attention to those measures or remedies that have the greatest leverage in dissipating or counterbalancing Soviet advantages. If it is indeed true, for example, that the Soviets assess NATO aircraft to provide fifty percent or more of NATO firepower (even if nuclear weapons are not used), it may pay to devote scarce resources to shielding those forces by improving airbase defense, building new airbases, or otherwise dispersing Western air power.[116] This brings up, however, a dilemma that no method of net assessment can answer: should we build forces that will affect Soviet perception of the balance, or should we act on the "Western" assessment instead? Either approach, however, offers more promising results than the questions: "What does the balance look like if all of our implicit doctrinal choices are correct?" and "What conditions prevent a generic attacker from pouncing on a generic defender?"

SCENARIOS

*The* balance does not exist—many do. Accordingly, we should look at many different possible prewar situations, not just one or two analytically convenient but practically implausible ones. Scenarios, particularly in war games, should deal with campaigns in which the political considerations discussed above have their effects—in which, for example, one or several NATO nations

---

116. The fifty percent figure comes from Donnelly and Petersen, "Soviet Strategists Target Denmark," p. 1049.

delay their mobilizations considerably. War gaming, like any other analytical method, has its peculiar perils, and in particular a verisimilitude even more misleading than that of simulations. Analysts must use war games as a tool for inquiry, not tests of what would happen if a war broke out.[117] Obviously, war games that do make politically realistic assumptions are themselves politically sensitive, particularly if performed by official analysts. For that reason one suspects that they occur very rarely or very secretly. Nonetheless, it is precisely these kinds of war games that can make the greatest contributions to understanding the problem before us.

*Conclusion*

The requirements of defense and deterrence in Europe will change over time, as the Soviets adjust to our defensive measures by seeking new ways to restore or increase their military advantages. The net assessment approach laid out here calls attention to the dialectic of move and countermove which constitutes the reality of political-military competition. By way of contrast, the "snapshot" method of the Optimists and other conventional analysts provides a distorted—because perspectiveless—picture. Rather than finding in one model the solution to understanding the balance, practitioners of net assessment must commit themselves to analytic eclecticism. This requires a willingness to factor in not only many varieties of academic analysis but reasoned and intuitive judgments made by men like General Rogers. We must seek many windows into an intellectual and practical problem of staggering complexity and obscurity.

The means suggested here for addressing the conventional balance on the Central Front are indeed complicated, iterative, and often (although by no means always) unquantifiable. The analytic approach I have described—call it Clausewitzian, since it has its intellectual roots in the teachings of *On War*—addresses directly, if imperfectly, the political, the interactive, and the other intangible elements of strategy. Undoubtedly, the Optimists' method

---

117. David A. Rosenberg, "Being Red: The Challenge of Taking the Soviet Side in Wargames at the Naval War College," *Naval War College Review*, Vol. 41, No. 1 (Winter 1988), pp. 81–93.

offers analytic manageability, but it purchases intellectual ease at the price of a deceptive and unwarranted certainty. In its place this article offers a method that will provide only flashes of insight. It has neither the simplicity nor the charm of the Optimists' seemingly-scientific analyses: that, however, reflects not the primitiveness of the approach, but the intractability of the problem.

*Part III:*
*Alternative Approaches*
*to European Security*

# Nuclear Weapons and Deterrence in Europe

The famous "gang of four" article in *Foreign Affairs* and voices in the American antinuclear movement have forcefully opened an important strategic debate by recommending that NATO adopt a "no first use" (NFU) policy for nuclear weapons in Europe.[1] Advocates of NFU maintain that NATO should declare that it will not initiate the use of nuclear weapons. Specifically, if NATO's conventional forces fail to contain a Warsaw Pact offensive, NATO should accept defeat rather than turn to nuclear weapons. As NFU advocates recognize, an NFU declaration would also require changes in NATO's force posture to give it practical meaning and effect. Some advocates of NFU would create a limited nuclear free zone in Central Europe, although a meaningful NFU policy would seem to require larger changes, probably including the removal of nuclear weapons from continental Europe. Proponents of NFU also recognize that to compensate for the removal of the threat of nuclear escalation, NATO must improve markedly its conventional defenses before an NFU policy can be adopted.[2] Thus, NFU incorporates both doctrinal and force posture adjustments.

---

John Mearsheimer is an Associate Professor in the Political Science Department at the University of Chicago and the author of Conventional Deterrence *(Ithaca: Cornell University Press, 1983), which won the 1983 Edgar S. Furniss, Jr., Award.*

---

1. See McGeorge Bundy, George F. Kennan, Robert S. McNamara, and Gerard Smith, "Nuclear Weapons and the Atlantic Alliance," *Foreign Affairs*, Vol. 60, No. 4 (Spring 1982), pp. 753–768. Also see: McGeorge Bundy, "'No First Use' Needs Careful Study," *Bulletin of the Atomic Scientists*, Vol. 38, No. 6 (June 1982), pp. 6–8; "The Debate Over No First Use," *Foreign Affairs*, Vol. 60, No. 5 (Summer 1982), pp. 1171–1180; Kurt Gottfried, Henry W. Kendall, and John M. Lee, "'No First Use' of Nuclear Weapons," *Scientific American*, Vol. 250, No. 3 (March 1984), pp. 33–41; Robert S. McNamara, "The Military Role of Nuclear Weapons: Perceptions and Misperceptions," *Foreign Affairs*, Vol. 62, No. 1 (Fall 1983), pp. 59–80; and *No First Use*, A Report Prepared by the Union of Concerned Scientists (Cambridge, Mass.: Union of Concerned Scientists, February 1, 1983). There have been surprisingly few articles written on the other side of this debate. Two exceptions are Karl Kaiser, Georg Leber, Alois Mertes, and Franz-Josef Schulze, "Nuclear Weapons and the Preservation of Peace," *Foreign Affairs*, Vol. 60, No. 5 (Summer 1982), pp. 1157–1170; and Colin S. Gray, "NATO's Nuclear Dilemma," *Policy Review*, No. 22 (Fall 1982), pp. 97–116. For essays on various aspects of the NFU question, see John D. Steinbruner and Leon V. Sigal, eds., *Alliance Security: NATO and the No-First-Use Question* (Washington, D.C.: Brookings, · 1983).
2. The principal American advocates of NFU subscribe to the notion that NATO will have to improve the conventional balance before it is possible to adopt an NFU policy. See, for example, George Kennan, Letter, *The New York Times*, May 23, 1982, Sec. 4, p. 22. Despite this rhetorical

---

International Security, Winter 1984/85 (Vol. 9, No. 3) 0162-2889/84/030019-28 $02.50/0
© 1984 by the President and Fellows of Harvard College and of the Massachusetts Institute of Technology.

Although there is a certain intuitive attraction to NFU, the argument of this essay is that NFU is a flawed idea. First, the threat of nuclear escalation is a key element in the NATO deterrent equation which cannot be fully replaced by a significant improvement in NATO's conventional forces. Nuclear weapons, because of the horror associated with their use, really are the ultimate deterrent. Formidable conventional forces simply do not have and can never have the deterrent value of nuclear weapons. Therefore, the possibility of war breaking out in Europe would increase if NATO were to adopt an NFU policy which actually persuaded the Soviet Union that NATO would not use nuclear weapons first. Second, if the full burden of deterrence were shifted to the conventional forces, they would then have to be judged against a higher standard than obtains with nuclear weapons in the deterrence equation. Although NATO's conventional forces are certainly stronger than most commentators suggest and would stand a good chance of defeating a Pact offensive, they do not measure up to such a standard today. An NFU policy would require a more formidable conventional deterrent; however, there is no reason to believe that NATO is going to improve significantly its conventional forces. Indeed, NATO's conventional forces will probably grow weaker relative to those of the Pact, *not* stronger, making an NFU policy even less appropriate in the future than it is today.

*The Deterrent Value of Nuclear Weapons*

Deterrence, at its root, is a function of both political and military considerations.[3] Decision-makers must weigh the perceived political consequences of military action against the military risks and costs of going to war. In a crisis, political considerations are likely to place significant pressures on decision-makers to go to war. Generally, deterrence is most likely to hold when the

---

support for increasing NATO's conventional forces, it is not very likely that support for increased defense spending (which certainly would be necessary to improve the conventional balance) will be generated among those elements of American society who advocate NFU. In the German case, NFU proponents are opposed in principle to increasing conventional forces to compensate for NFU. See Gert Krell, Thomas Risse-Kappen, and Hans-Joachim Schmidt, "The No-First-Use Question in West Germany," in Steinbruner and Sigal, eds., *Alliance Security*, p. 169; and James M. Markham, "Bonn Opposition Affirms NATO Tie," *The New York Times*, May 20, 1984, p. 7.
3. For a more detailed discussion of how political and military factors interact to affect deterrence, see John J. Mearsheimer, *Conventional Deterrence* (Ithaca: Cornell University Press, 1983), pp. 60–66, 208–212. Also see Richard K. Betts, *Surprise Attack: Lessons for Defense Planning* (Washington, D.C.: Brookings, 1982), chapter 5; Michael E. Brown, *Deterrence Failures and Deterrence Strategies*, Rand Paper P-5842 (Santa Monica, Calif.: Rand, March 1977); and Richard N.

risks and costs of military action are very high. In certain cases, however, decision-makers might still opt for war even when the risks of military action are very high—simply because the political pressures for war are so great that pursuing a risk-laden military policy may be preferable to the status quo. The risks of doing nothing in those situations may seem greater than the risks of military action. The two classic cases of deterrence failure that follow this logic are the Japanese decision to strike against the United States in 1941 and the Egyptian decision to strike against Israel in 1973.[4] In both cases, the attacker recognized that he would be undertaking a high-risk military operation. Nevertheless, given the unacceptability of the political status quo and the fact that there was some hope of a favorable military outcome, offensives were launched.

Not all crises fit this description, but policymakers must prepare for these worst case scenarios. A prudent planner will ultimately gauge the worth of his deterrent posture by considering the prospects for deterrence in those cases where the political pressures for war are great. The best way to maximize those prospects is to ensure that the military risks are extremely high— so that the opponent's decision-makers see virtually no chance of achieving success by going to war. In short, deterrence is best served when decision-makers think that a war will be a ghastly and destructive experience. If, for example, policymakers in Europe before World War I could have foreseen the carnage that lay ahead, it is likely that the Great War could have been averted. That war did start, however, because it was widely believed that the war would be relatively short and not too costly. We see here that disturbing paradox of deterrence theory: the best way to prevent war is to ensure that it would have devastating consequences for all the participants.

The threat to use nuclear weapons is an excellent deterrent because it so greatly increases the risks and costs associated with war. The potential consequences of using nuclear weapons are so grave that it is very difficult to conceive of achieving a meaningful victory in a nuclear war. It is the fear of these consequences, of course, that motivates the NFU movement; it is, however, the utter horror we associate with these weapons that makes them so dissuasive. There is little doubt that the presence of thousands of nuclear

---

Rosecrance, "Deterrence and Vulnerability in the Pre-Nuclear Era," in *The Future of Strategic Deterrence, Part I*, Adelphi Paper No. 160 (London: International Institute for Strategic Studies, 1980), pp. 24–30.

4. For a discussion of the Japanese case, see Robert J.C. Butow, *Tojo and the Coming of War* (Stanford: Stanford University Press, 1961); and for a discussion of the Egyptian case, see Mearsheimer, *Conventional Deterrence*, pp. 155–162, 210–211.

weapons in Europe coupled with a declaratory policy of first use significantly enhances deterrence.

Nuclear weapons not only work to shore up deterrence in specific crises, but they also condition the way the superpowers think about dealing with each other. In a nuclear world, the danger associated with *any* war between the superpowers is so great that it becomes difficult for them to think in terms of achieving political objectives by going to war against each other. Napoleon or Hitler could use their military forces to attempt to win control of the European continent. Neither the Soviets nor NATO can afford to think in those terms because of the catastrophic risks of nuclear war.

It is not uncommon to hear the argument that nuclear weapons no longer have much deterrent value because the threat to use them is not credible.[5] Although the probability that NATO would employ nuclear weapons has lessened over the past twenty-five years, claims that NATO has what amounts to a de facto NFU policy are greatly exaggerated.[6] The deterrent value of a weapon is a function of the costs and risks of using that weapon as well as the probability that it will be used. Given the consequences of using these horrible weapons, it is not necessary for the likelihood of use to be very high. It is only necessary for there to be some reasonable chance that they will be used. Earl Ravenal has captured the essence of this point with his assertion that "even the whiff of American nuclear retaliation is probably enough to keep the Soviet Union from invading Western Europe."[7]

There are many reasons why the Soviets should expect more than a whiff of possible use. First, there is considerable evidence that many key officials in the Reagan Administration believe that nuclear weapons have at least some military utility.[8] This is not to say that they would be anxious to use them in a crisis, but only to point out that it would not be unthinkable for

---

5. This belief is subscribed to by many individuals who are not advocates of NFU. See, for example: Samuel P. Huntington, "Conventional Deterrence and Conventional Retaliation in Europe," *International Security*, Vòl. 8, No. 3 (Winter 1983–1984), pp. 32–34; Fred Charles Iklé, "NATO's 'First Nuclear Use': A Deepening Trap?," *Strategic Review*, Vol. 8, No. 1 (Winter 1980), pp. 18–23; Henry A. Kissinger, "The Future of NATO," in Kenneth A. Myers, ed., *NATO: The Next Thirty Years* (Boulder, Colo.: Westview Press, 1980), pp. 3–19; and Irving Kristol, "What's Wrong With NATO?," *The New York Times Magazine*, September 25, 1983, pp. 64–71.
6. Among NFU advocates, this claim is most clearly articulated by Robert McNamara in "The Military Role of Nuclear Weapons."
7. Earl C. Ravenal, "Counterforce and Alliance: The Ultimate Connection," *International Security*, Vol. 6, No. 4 (Spring 1982), p. 36.
8. See, for example, Richard Halloran, "Pentagon Draws Up First Strategy for Fighting a Long Nuclear War," *The New York Times*, May 30, 1982, pp. 1, 12.

them to turn to nuclear weapons if NATO's conventional forces failed to contain a Soviet offensive.[9] Second, the United States has devoted considerable resources to develop the capability to use its strategic nuclear forces for defending Europe. Each American administration since the beginning of the Cold War has paid serious attention to the concept of extended deterrence.[10] Third, NATO has contingency plans for using its theater nuclear weapons, and these plans enjoy support among NATO military planners, who do not regard them as mere pro forma preparations.[11] Some analysts dismiss the importance of such plans by arguing that NATO would not in fact resort to its nuclear weapons because doing so would not give NATO any tactical advantage on the battlefield, and would be tantamount to suicide. These analysts usually assume that NATO plans to seek a victory on the battlefield by using nuclear weapons to destroy enemy front-line units, much as artillery and tactical aircraft were employed in World War II. NATO

---

9. General Bernard Rogers, the present NATO commander, has publicly stated, for example, that he would use nuclear weapons to defend Europe. See David Mason, "If Worse Comes to Worse: How NATO Would Pull the Nuclear Trigger," *Philadelphia Inquirer*, November 24, 1983, p. 14.

10. For a good discussion of how the NATO commitment has affected American strategic nuclear posture, see Ravenal, "Counterforce and Alliance," pp. 26–43; and Earl C. Ravenal, "No First Use: A View from the United States," *The Bulletin of the Atomic Scientists*, Vol. 39, No. 4 (April 1983), pp. 11–16. It is important to note that the McNamara "no cities" doctrine enunciated in Athens and Ann Arbor (1962), the Schlesinger doctrine (1974), and the Carter Administration's PD-59 (1980) were all heavily influenced by the need to reassure the Europeans and convince the Soviets that the American strategic nuclear deterrent is coupled with NATO. See Anthony H. Cordesman, *Deterrence in the 1980s: Part I*, Adelphi Paper No. 175 (London: International Institute for Strategic Studies, 1982); David N. Schwartz, *NATO's Nuclear Dilemmas* (Washington, D.C.: Brookings, 1983), pp. 156–165; U.S. Congress, Senate, Committee on Foreign Relations, *U.S.–U.S.S.R. Strategic Policies*, 93rd Congress, 2nd Session (Washington, D.C.: U.S. Government Printing Office, March 4, 1974); U.S. Congress, Senate, Committee on Foreign Relations, *Briefing on Counterforce Attacks*, 93rd Congress, 2nd Session (Washington, D.C.: U.S. Government Printing Office, September 11, 1974); and Walter Slocombe, "The Countervailing Strategy," *International Security*, Vol. 5, No. 4 (Spring 1981), pp. 18–27. This effort to maintain a credible extended deterrent is often obscured in the public debate about nuclear strategy because of the popular myth that the United States eschewed counterforce capabilities in the late 1960s and adopted a simple strategy of Mutual Assured Destruction (MAD). In fact, the United States has maintained very significant counterforce capabilities for the past thirty years. For a debunking of the MAD myth, see Desmond Ball, *Déjà Vu: The Return to Counterforce in the Nixon Administration* (Santa Monica, Calif.: California Seminar on Arms Control and Foreign Policy, December 1974); Aaron L. Friedberg, "A History of U.S. Strategic 'Doctrine'—1945 to 1980," *The Journal of Strategic Studies*, Vol. 3, No. 3 (December 1980), pp. 37–71; and Henry S. Rowen, "The Evolution of Strategic Nuclear Doctrine," in Laurence Martin, ed., *Strategic Thought in the Nuclear Age* (Baltimore: Johns Hopkins University Press, 1979), pp. 131–156.

11. For an excellent discussion of NATO thinking about the actual employment of nuclear weapons, see J. Michael Legge, *Theater Nuclear Weapons and the NATO Strategy of Flexible Response*, Rand Report R-2964-FF (Santa Monica, Calif.: Rand, April 1983), chapter 2.

planners, however, do not envision using nuclear weapons to achieve victory on the battlefield. Instead, they would use nuclear weapons to signal NATO's seriousness, and to introduce greater risk of an all-out nuclear exchange should the Soviets continue to exploit their conventional successes. Recognition of this possibility should be enough, so proponents argue, to stop the Soviet offensive. In short, the objective is not to use nuclear weapons to reverse NATO's fortunes on the battlefield but, instead, to end the war as quickly as possible on politically acceptable terms.

This discussion about signalling NATO's seriousness leads to a fourth point: the loss of Western Europe would have devastating consequences for the United States.[12] Soviet control of the Eurasian heartland would result in a decisive shift in the distribution of world power against the United States.[13] Is it not possible that NATO would use nuclear weapons to try to prevent the Soviets from conquering Western Europe? The United States' traditional commitment to Europe as an interest vital to its own security would certainly support that possibility in the minds of Soviet leaders. Finally, nuclear weapons might be used by accident or as the unintended consequence of conventional moves. For example, Barry Posen has shown how conventional operations on NATO's northern flank could threaten Soviet strategic nuclear

---

12. Of course, the consequences of losing Western Europe would not be as devastating to the United States as would a general thermonuclear exchange. These are not, however, the only two alternatives that U.S. decision-makers would face in a crisis. The initial use of nuclear weapons, although fraught with the possibility of escalation, would be very selective and designed to avoid escalation. The aim, as emphasized earlier, would be to send a signal to the Soviets about the danger of continuing their attack.

13. For the classic statement of this view, see Nicholas J. Spykman, *America's Strategy in World Politics: The United States and the Balance of Power* (1942; reprint ed., Hamden, Conn.: Archon, 1970). There has been considerable talk in the United States recently about pulling American forces out of Europe. A key assumption in this debate, sometimes explicit but more often implicit, is that Europe is really not of great importance for American security. In other words, the United States can afford to withdraw from Europe without too much concern for what impact this would have on the global balance of power. This line of thinking complements the widespread belief that the United States would not use nuclear weapons to defend Europe. (It should be stressed, however, that the authors of the 1982 *Foreign Affairs* piece do *not* advocate any lessening of U.S. commitment to Europe.) After all, if maintaining American interests in Europe is really not that important for American security, why use nuclear weapons to protect those interests? This view is wrongheaded, not to mention dangerous. The loss of Western Europe to the Soviet Union would be a blow of staggering proportions to the United States. Europe's important geographical position, not to mention those raw power assets like manpower and GNP that it controls, makes it hard to see how one can separate European security from American security. Although some Americans have lost sight of this reality, one can be quite confident that in a crisis, where the loss of Europe is a possibility, the dimensions of the disaster that could lie ahead will become abundantly clear. Undoubtedly, those individuals will then, at the very least, give some consideration to using nuclear weapons to stabilize the situation.

assets, thus pushing the Soviets to use their nuclear weapons.[14] The important point here is that neither side can ever be sure that nuclear weapons will not be used accidentally or that a conventional war will not, at some point, impinge on the strategic nuclear balance.[15]

These considerations substantiate the fact that there *is* a reasonable chance that NATO will use nuclear weapons in the event its conventional forces crumble. As long as that remains the case, NATO's nuclear forces will continue to have great deterrent value.

Excising nuclear weapons from the European deterrence equation, therefore, would significantly reduce the costs and risks of a NATO–Pact conflict and weaken deterrence. Conventional war, deadly as it may be, cannot duplicate the horror associated with nuclear weapons. More specifically, without the threat of nuclear escalation, the superpowers would be able to contemplate fighting a war in Central Europe with little risk of their own homelands being destroyed. It is vastly more alarming to contemplate the destruction of one's society than to envision the failure to gain a victory on a conventional battlefield. If the Soviets believed that NATO really would not use nuclear weapons first, an NFU policy would drop the downside risk to the Soviets from the former to the latter—from total catastrophe to mere frustration. This would represent a major change in the Soviet calculus, a shift from unthinkable to thinkable consequences. In short, NATO would lose an important deterrent capability, thus making war more likely in some future crisis. NATO can obviate this problem to a considerable extent by maintaining very formidable conventional forces; after all, there are significant risks associated with conventional war. A pure conventional deterrent, nevertheless, would not be as formidable a deterrent as one based on powerful conventional forces plus nuclear weapons.

Indeed, it seems at least questionable as to whether peace could have been

14. Barry R. Posen, "Inadvertent Nuclear War? Escalation and NATO's Northern Flank," *International Security*, Vol. 7, No. 2 (Fall 1982), pp. 28–54. Also see Paul Bracken, *The Command and Control of Nuclear Forces* (New Haven: Yale University Press, 1983), chapter 5.

15. McGeorge Bundy, writing before he became an advocate of NFU, stated this point nicely: "Now, of course, no one *knows* that a major engagement in Europe would escalate to the strategic nuclear level. But the essential point is the opposite; no one can possibly know it would not." Bundy, "Strategic Deterrence Thirty Years Later: What Has Changed?," in *The Future of Strategic Deterrence, Part I*, p. 11. It is also worth quoting Bundy's views on extended deterrence: "I believe the effectiveness of this American [strategic nuclear] guarantee is likely to be just as great in the future as in the past. It has worked, after all, through 30 years, and as we have seen, 20 of those years have been a time of underlying parity in mutual destructive power." Ibid.

maintained in Europe for the past forty years without the threat of nuclear escalation. Two large and powerfully armed militaries have stood face to face in Central Europe since the early days of the Cold War. There has been much bitter hostility between the two sides during this period—especially between the superpowers. There have been, however, very few crises in Europe that directly involved both superpowers, and only the Berlin crisis came even close to escalating into a major war.[16] Given the hostility between the two blocs and the level of armaments on each side, it is quite remarkable that there has been no war and that there seems to be so little chance of war in the future. Leslie Gelb was undoubtedly correct when he recently noted, "Were it not for the fear of nuclear war, chances are that Moscow and Washington would have clashed many times."[17] If it were possible to remove that threat of escalation, as proponents of NFU would like to do, it would be more likely that war would return to Europe.

*The Prospects for Improving the Conventional Balance*

It has been the accepted wisdom since the early days of the Cold War that the Warsaw Pact enjoys great superiority over NATO in conventional forces. As I have argued elsewhere, this is not the case.[18] NATO has strong conventional forces that stand a *good* chance of thwarting a Soviet blitzkrieg. This optimistic assessment is actually not as iconoclastic a view as it was three or more years ago. Numerous studies of the conventional balance in Europe have appeared over the past two years, and a significant number describe a somewhat hopeful situation.[19] Certainly, the level of optimism varies from study to study. Nevertheless, if NATO were to excise nuclear

---

16. See Jack M. Schick, *The Berlin Crisis, 1958–1962* (Philadelphia: University of Pennsylvania Press, 1971); and Robert M. Slusser, "The Berlin Crises of 1958–59 and 1961," in Barry M. Blechman and Stephen S. Kaplan, eds., *Force Without War* (Washington, D.C.: Brookings, 1978), chapter 9.
17. Leslie H. Gelb, "Is the Nuclear Threat Manageable?," *The New York Times Magazine*, March 4, 1984, p. 28.
18. See John J. Mearsheimer, "Why the Soviets Can't Win Quickly in Central Europe," *International Security*, Vol. 7, No. 1 (Summer 1982), pp. 3–39.
19. See, for example: Paul Bracken, "The NATO Defense Problem," *Orbis*, Vol. 27, No. 1 (Spring 1983), pp. 83–105; Otto P. Chaney, Jr., "The Soviet Threat to Europe: Prospects for the 1980's," *Parameters*, Vol. 13, No. 3 (September 1983), pp. 2–22; William W. Kaufmann, "Nonnuclear Deterrence," in Steinbruner and Sigal, eds., *Alliance Security*, pp. 43–90; Christian Krause, *The Balance Between Conventional Forces in Europe* (Bonn: Friedrich Ebert Stiftung, 1982); William P. Mako, *U.S. Ground Forces and the Defense of Central Europe* (Washington, D.C.: Brookings, 1983); F.W. von Mellenthin and R.H.S. Stolfi with E. Sobik, *NATO Under Attack* (Durham, N.C.: Duke University Press, 1984); Barry R. Posen, "Measuring the European Conventional Balance: Coping

weapons from the deterrence equation and rely on a pure conventional deterrent, its conventional forces would have to measure up to a significantly higher standard. Prudence would dictate that NATO then have an *extremely high* probability of battlefield success. It is for this reason that no serious analyst argues that NATO's present conventional forces are robust enough to allow nuclear weapons to be removed from the deterrent posture. Thus, NATO would have to improve markedly the balance in Europe before it could move to an NFU policy.

There is actually much talk today about the encouraging prospects for developing a robust conventional deterrent. This rhetoric notwithstanding, it is *very* unlikely that the balance will shift in NATO's favor in the decade ahead. In fact, it is going to be difficult for NATO to prevent the present balance from deteriorating.

Four ways of strengthening NATO's conventional defense are now being seriously discussed in Western defense circles.[20] First, NATO can alter its strategy for meeting a Pact offensive, the key assumption being that a better strategy will serve as a force multiplier. Second, NATO can attempt to change the balance through arms control. Neither of these options requires increased NATO spending and, in fact, it is reasonable to assume that the arms control option might mean slight reductions in spending. The third approach requires NATO to increase significantly defense outlays for the purpose of expanding the size and strength of its ground and air forces. In other words, NATO would attempt to beef up its existing force structure. The final option—the technological solution—calls for NATO to increase spending to procure highly sophisticated weaponry that represents a quantum leap in capabilities over existing systems. Let us consider each option.

STRATEGY

NATO presently employs a forward defense strategy: the majority of its forces on the Central Front are to be deployed in a crisis in linear fashion

---

with Complexity in Threat Assessment," *International Security*, Vol. 9, No. 3 (Winter 1984–85), pp. 47–88; and Union of Concerned Scientists, *No First Use*, part 2. There are also some key policymakers whose assessments of NATO's capabilities are somewhat optimistic. In March 1983, for example, the Commander of the U.S. Army in Europe told an interviewer, "It disappoints me to hear people talk about the overwhelming Soviet conventional military strength. We can defend the borders of Western Europe with what we have. I've never asked for a larger force. I do not think that conventional defense is anywhere near hopeless." Charles W. Corddry, "General Says NATO Is Able to Defend Europe," *The Baltimore Sun*, March 6, 1983, p. 7.
20. Many of the individuals linked to the proposals for improving the conventional balance discussed in this section do *not* advocate an NFU policy.

along the intra-German and Czech–German borders; the remaining forces are held as reserves. The aim is to defeat a Pact offensive before a significant amount of West German territory is lost. Some defense analysts are dissatisfied with forward defense and have proposed alternate strategies that they believe will significantly improve NATO's chances of thwarting a Pact attack. These proposed strategies can be divided into two categories: offensive and defensive.

Among the defensive strategies, two are most prominent. The first is commonly referred to as "area defense," and it is especially popular with the political Left in Germany.[21] Instead of placing the majority of NATO's forces in large armored units along the intra-German border, the forces would be deployed in relatively small units throughout the depth of Germany. The key assumption is that the defender would be able to wear down attacking forces as they move westward—thus preventing the attacker from delivering the decisive blow. In effect, the defense would act as a large "attrition sponge." Great emphasis is placed on using infantrymen with precision-guided munitions (PGMs) to thwart a Soviet armored attack. Proponents of area defense believe that the introduction of "high tech" weaponry like PGMs has, to quote a prominent advocate of area defense, "altered the character of warfare and the whole basis of strategy."[22] Specifically, they believe that a defender can now rely almost exclusively on small groups of PGM-armed infantrymen to defeat an armored offensive; tanks are no longer necessary to stop attacking tanks. This strategy is particularly attractive to many on the political Left, where there is strong opposition to maintaining forces with any offensive potential, since it is difficult, if not impossible, to launch an offensive with dispersed bands of infantrymen. There are, of course, somewhat different variations of this strategy. Some proponents, for example, believe that it is necessary to have some mobile armored units that can be moved about the battlefield to aid those defensive positions that are engaging the attacker's main forces.[23]

---

21. See Frank Barnaby and Egbert Boeker, "Non-provocative, Non-nuclear Defense of Western Europe," *ADIU Report*, Vol. 5, No. 1 (January–February 1983), pp. 5–10; Lt. Col. Norbert Hanning, "The Defense of Western Europe with Conventional Weapons," *International Defense Review*, Vol. 14 (1981), pp. 1439–1443; Maj. Gen. Jochen Löser, "The Security Policy Options for Non-Communist Europe," *Armada International*, March–April 1982, pp. 66–70, 72, 74–75; and R. Levine et al., *A Survey of NATO Defense Concepts*, Rand Note N-1871-AF (Santa Monica, Calif.: Rand, June 1982), pp. 45–47, 68–69.
22. Löser, "Security Policy Options," p. 67.
23. Ibid., pp. 66–70.

The second proposed defensive strategy, which emanates from the self-styled "military reform movement," calls for NATO to place greater reliance on maneuver instead of emphasizing firepower, which it now does with its forward defense.[24] The maneuver advocates have not clearly defined how a maneuver strategy would work. It appears, however, that they are calling for NATO to adopt a classical mobile defense. Here, the majority of NATO's forces, instead of being placed along the intra-German border, would be located in powerful operational reserves, while a small "screening force" would be placed along the intra-German border to detect and slow the Pact's main forces. No attempt would be made to prevent the Pact from striking into the depths of Germany; in fact, such a development would be welcomed. The key assumption is that the attacking forces will have an Achilles' heel—vulnerable flanks, which, when struck by the defender's powerful operational reserves, will lead to the collapse of the attack. In essence, the defender is betting that he can find and strike the attacker's flanks before the attacker can deliver the decisive blow against the defender.

In addition to these defensive strategies, calls for NATO to adopt an offensive capability are being heard. Few have gone so far as to call for an all-out offensive strategy, although one can find hints about developing such a capability in the writings of the maneuver advocates as well as in the U.S. Army's new AirLand Battle doctrine.[25] The most articulate and forthright case for developing an offensive strategy has been made by Samuel Huntington.[26] He calls for launching a "retaliatory offensive" into Eastern Europe

---

24. For a detailed discussion of the proposed maneuver strategy, see John J. Mearsheimer, "Maneuver, Mobile Defense, and the NATO Central Front," *International Security*, Vol. 6, No. 3 (Winter 1981–82), pp. 104–122.

25. For information on AirLand Battle, see Lt. Col. Huba Wass de Czege and Lt. Col. L.D. Holder, "The New FM 100-5," *Military Review*, Vol. 62, No. 7 (July 1982), pp. 53–70; U.S. Army, *Operations: FM 100-5* (Washington, D.C.: Department of the Army, August 20, 1982); *The AirLand Battle and Corps 86*, TRADOC Pamphlet No. 525-5 (Fort Monroe, Va.: U.S. Army Training and Doctrine Command, March 25, 1981); and Michael R. Gordon, "The Army's 'Air-Land Battle' Doctrine Worries Allies, Upsets the Air Force," *National Journal*, June 18, 1983, pp. 1274–1277.

26. See Samuel P. Huntington, "The Renewal of Strategy," in Samuel P. Huntington, ed., *The Strategic Imperative: New Policies for American Security* (Cambridge, Mass.: Ballinger, 1982), pp. 1–52; Samuel P. Huntington, "Broadening the Strategic Focus," in *Defence and Consensus: The Domestic Aspects of Western Security, Part III*, Adelphi Paper No. 184 (London: International Institute for Strategic Studies, 1983), pp. 27–32; Samuel P. Huntington, "Correspondence," *International Security*, Vol. 9, No. 1 (Summer 1984), pp. 210–217; and especially Huntington, "Conventional Deterrence and Conventional Retaliation." Also see Kristol, "What's Wrong with NATO?," p. 67.

almost immediately after the Pact begins its attack.[27] There is no explicit discussion in any of the writings of these offensive-minded strategists of launching a preemptive strike into Eastern Europe, although there are hints of this; and certainly the capability would exist if NATO had a counteroffensive strategy. One could argue, somewhat tongue-in-cheek, that an offensive strategy is a real "forward defense" and thus should be very attractive to the West Germans, whose territory would then be spared in a conventional war.

A thorough examination of each of these alternative strategies would show them to be militarily unattractive. It is not necessary for our purposes here, however, to consider them so carefully, since two political factors make it extremely unlikely that they will be adopted in the foreseeable future. Regarding the two defensive strategies, successive West German governments have made it unequivocally clear that they will reject any strategy that requires NATO to surrender territory, however temporary it may be, and to fight major battles in the heart of West Germany. For this reason, the Germans have remained firmly committed to forward defense and have dismissed outright alternative defensive strategies like the two described here.[28] Concerning an offensive strategy, it is very clear that the Europeans, and especially the Germans, are adamantly opposed to any talk of NATO's purposely developing an offensive capability.[29] Since they believe that such a capability would be provocative, would further increase East–West tensions, and would increase the risk of war, Europeans go to great lengths to emphasize that NATO is a defensively oriented alliance with no offensive inclinations. In sum, the Germans are not going to tolerate abandonment of forward defense. Any attempt to force them to do so will only lead to a severe crisis in the Alliance.

---

27. Huntington, "Conventional Deterrence and Conventional Retaliation," p. 44.
28. Regarding the German commitment to forward defense, see Commission on Long-term Planning for the Federal Armed Forces, *Final Report* (Bonn: Federal Minister of Defence, June 21, 1982), pp. 25, 106; and *White Paper 1983: The Security of the Federal Republic of Germany and the Development of the Federal Armed Forces* (Bonn: Federal Minister of Defence, 1983), pp. 83, 127, 142–145, 158–162.
29. See Joseph Joffe, "Can Europe Live With its Defense?," in Lawrence Freedman, ed., *The Troubled Alliance* (London: Heinemann, 1983), p. 133. Here, it is interesting to note that General Rogers (the NATO commander), well aware of the offensive overtones in the U.S. Army's new doctrine (AirLand Battle), has made it clear that NATO has not adopted that doctrine and that NATO forces will be employed in accordance with Alliance doctrine—"not under that of any individual nation." Elizabeth Pond, "NATO's Rogers Says Euromissiles Are Effective Deterrent," *The Christian Science Monitor*, April 27, 1984, p. 8.

ARMS CONTROL

NATO and the Pact have conducted arms control negotiations concerning the conventional balance since the early 1970s. No successes have been achieved at these Mutual and Balanced Force Reduction (MBFR) talks.[30] NATO's stated aim has been to reduce the number of troops on each side so as to achieve parity in manpower on the Central Front. The question is whether NATO can convince the Soviets to agree to shift the balance so that the Pact's present force advantage is eliminated. For a variety of reasons, this is very unlikely to happen.

It is difficult to imagine the Soviets' gratuitously giving up their force advantage. Experience in other arms control negotiations has shown them to be tough bargainers who exact a price for every concession they make. Second, the Soviets undoubtedly are concerned about a NATO attack, and they almost certainly believe that deterrence is best served by the present balance, rather than one that eliminates their present advantage.[31] Third, the Soviets must be concerned about the reliability of the East European armies. And there is reason for the Soviets to have serious doubts about their allies' loyalty.[32] The Pact's numerical advantage takes on a different light when one considers that slightly more than half of the Pact's standing divisions in Central Europe are non-Soviet. This is not to say with certainty that Soviet allies will not fight, but that the Soviets must seriously consider this possibility. This discussion leads to a fourth point. It is generally assumed in

---

30. For a good discussion of this matter, see Jonathan Dean, "MBFR: From Apathy to Accord," *International Security*, Vol. 7, No. 4 (Spring 1983), pp. 116–139. Also see John G. Keliher, *The Negotiations on Mutual and Balanced Force Reductions* (New York: Pergamon, 1980); Lothar Ruehl, "The Slippery Road of MBFR," *Strategic Review*, Vol. 8, No. 1 (Winter 1980), pp. 24–35; Lothar Ruehl, *MBFR: Lessons and Problems*, Adelphi Paper No. 176 (London: International Institute for Strategic Studies, 1982); Jane M.O. Sharp, "Is European Security Negotiable?," in Derek Leebaert, ed., *European Security: Prospects for the 1980s* (Lexington, Mass.: Lexington Books, D.C. Heath, 1979), pp. 261–296; and U.S. Congress, House of Representatives, Committee on Foreign Affairs, *Report on East–West Troop Reductions in Europe: Is Agreement Possible?*, 98th Congress, 1st Session (Washington, D.C.: U.S. Government Printing Office, 1983).
31. The discussion of NATO's developing a counteroffensive capability certainly contributes to this fear.
32. See Robert W. Clawson and Lawrence S. Kaplan, eds., *The Warsaw Pact: Political Purpose and Military Means* (Wilmington, Del.: Scholarly Resources, 1982), passim; Dale R. Herspring and Ivan Volgyes, "Political Reliability in the Eastern European Warsaw Pact Armies," *Armed Forces and Society*, Vol. 6, No. 2 (Winter 1980), pp. 270–296; David Holloway and Jane M.O. Sharp, eds., *The Warsaw Pact: Alliance in Transition?* (Ithaca: Cornell University Press, 1984), passim; and A. Ross Johnson, Robert W. Dean, and Alexander Alexiev, "The Armies of the Warsaw Pact Northern Tier," *Survival*, Vol. 23, No. 4 (July–August 1981), pp. 174–182.

discussions of the military balance that Pact forces are concerned exclusively with the NATO threat. This is not the case. They must also maintain order in Eastern Europe.[33] In 1968, for example, the Soviets placed three new divisions in Czechoslovakia to deal with the severe turmoil in that country. This mission undoubtedly influences Soviet force requirements, since they almost surely consider the possibility that an uprising in Eastern Europe will divert Soviet divisions in a crisis with the West. Moreover, the Soviets must consider the political signal that a troop withdrawal would send to the East Europeans. After the recent unrest in Poland and given the likelihood that there will *not* be significant improvement in relations between the Soviets and the East Europeans, the Soviets probably do not want to take a step that might be interpreted as a loosening of their grip. A troop withdrawal is likely to be seen as sending just such a message.

Finally, efforts to achieve numerical parity do not account for qualitative differences between the two sides. Although Western analysts frequently describe the Soviet military as a finely tuned organization, the Soviet army is plagued with significant problems that reduce its fighting power.[34] This fact, which is recognized by Soviet military leaders, does *not* mean that the Soviet army is a "paper tiger," likely to collapse in the first days of combat. It does mean, however, that Soviet leaders will have cause to doubt the capabilities of their own soldiers, as well as the reliability of the numerous non-Soviet divisions. As for their opponents, it is not easy to determine what Soviet leaders think about the fighting power of NATO. One would think that they would have high regard for the German army, since there is much respect for that army in the West and the German army was a most formidable foe for the Soviets in two world wars. Given the tendency of military leaders to err on the side of prudence when judging an opponent's capabilities, the Soviets probably rate the non-German forces in NATO quite highly as well. In short, it seems reasonable to assume that Soviet leaders believe

---

33. See Christopher D. Jones, *Soviet Influence in Eastern Europe* (New York: Praeger, 1981).
34. See Alexander Cockburn, *The Threat: Inside the Soviet Military Machine* (New York: Random House, 1983); Christopher Donnelly, "Tactical Problems Facing the Soviet Army: Recent Debates in the Soviet Military Press," *International Defense Review*, Vol. 11 (1978), pp. 1405–1412; Christopher Donnelly, "Soviet Tactics for Overcoming NATO Anti-Tank Defenses," *International Defense Review*, Vol. 12 (1979), pp. 1099–1106; Coit D. Blacker, "Military Forces," in Robert F. Byrnes, ed., *After Brezhnev* (Bloomington: Indiana University Press, 1983), pp. 125–185; and Peter H. Vigor, "Doubts and Difficulties Confronting a Would-be Soviet Attacker," *Journal of the Royal United Services Institute*, Vol. 125, No. 2 (June 1980), pp. 32–38.

that the Pact will always require numerical superiority to offset the West's qualitative advantages.

This may appear to belittle Soviet capabilities, but after all, the Soviets were only able to defeat the Germans in the Second World War by overwhelming them with superior numbers. Furthermore, the Russians have historically relied on superior numbers as a guarantor of battlefield success.[35] This consideration is thus likely to work against an agreement which aims to achieve a straightforward numerical balance.

In sum, there is little reason to be sanguine about the prospects for concluding an MBFR agreement that eliminates the existing asymmetry in force levels.

INCREASING NUMBERS

NATO could attempt to improve the balance by increasing its number of combat units. This would require raising additional manpower and spending more money, but would not guarantee that the balance would shift in NATO's favor, since the state of the balance is a function of Pact as well as of NATO measures. If NATO were to increase its numbers significantly, the Pact would probably attempt to offset that increase.[36] Here, however, I will examine the likelihood of NATO's increasing the size of its forces, while largely setting aside the matter of a Soviet response.[37]

NATO is not likely to increase the number of men under arms. In fact,

---

35. See, for example, John Erickson, "The Soviet Military System: Doctrine, Technology and 'Style'," in John Erickson and E.J. Feuchtwanger, eds., *Soviet Military Power and Performance* (Hamden, Conn.: Archon, 1979), pp. 18–43.
36. This discussion presupposes that, when discussing force levels, NATO's prospects for battlefield success are essentially a function of the *relative* balance of forces. This is not the case. NATO must also be concerned about the *absolute* number of forces that it needs to execute a strategy of forward defense. In other words, in addition to considering the overall balance of forces, it is essential to recognize that there is an optimum number of units that NATO needs to cover its front in the initial stages of a conflict. More specifically, NATO must be concerned with "force-to-space ratios." For a discussion of this matter, see Mearsheimer, *Conventional Deterrence*, pp. 44, 47, 181–183. Therefore, although the Pact might offset NATO's efforts to change the relative balance of power, NATO would still benefit from increasing its force levels because, on the absolute dimension, it would have additional forces with which to execute its strategy of forward defense. Thus, an increase in the size of NATO's forces is to be welcomed— even if the Soviets move to prevent a change in the relative balance. Unfortunately, as I argue in this section, NATO is hardly likely to increase its force levels in the years ahead.
37. The previous discussion about why the Soviets are so unlikely to bargain away their quantitative force advantage points up why the Soviets are likely to attempt to offset an increase in the size of NATO's forces.

the Germans and the Americans, who form the nucleus of the Alliance, will be hard pressed to maintain their present force levels. The principal reason in the German case is demography.[38] Germany will begin experiencing serious manpower problems in 1987, which will become even more severe as time passes. Given the existing system of conscription, the strength of the German armed forces will drop to 290,000 in the mid-1990s from its present level of 495,000. This is a consequence of the drop in the German birth rate that began in the mid-1960s. There are a variety of measures that the Germans can take to maintain a standing force of 495,000 men. This would include: increasing the proportion of short-term volunteers, while lengthening their term of enlistment; extending the 15-month term of conscript service; reducing exemptions from military service; and expanding the roles of women and of non-German residents. It will be politically and economically difficult to implement many of these measures, although the Germans might succeed in doing enough to maintain present manpower levels. It is not easy to imagine circumstances, however, short of a war in Europe, in which the Germans would actually increase the present size of their armed forces.

The demographic situation is somewhat better in the United States. Here, however, the problem is exacerbated by a volunteer military. It is going to be difficult for the United States to maintain present force levels in the decade ahead, much less expand the military, without resorting to conscription.[39] Furthermore, there is pressure in the United States to reduce the size of the American commitment to Europe. This pressure is the result of anti-European sentiment, as well as the fact that the United States has other commitments that compete with NATO for scarce resources.[40] It is thus difficult to imagine

38. Gilbert Kutscher, "The Impact of Population Development on Military Manpower Problems: An International Comparison," *Armed Forces and Society*, Vol. 9, No. 2 (Winter 1983), pp. 265–273. For a detailed discussion of this matter, see Commission on Long-term Planning for the Federal Armed Forces, *Final Report*. Also see John Vinocur, "Study by Bonn Foresees Trouble for the Military," *The New York Times*, February 9, 1982, p. 12; and Wolfram von Raven, "A Grim Perspective for the Bundeswehr: Manpower Problems Created by the Pill," *German Comments: Review of Politics and Culture*, No. 1 (April 1983), pp. 25–31.
39. See Martin Binkin, *America's Volunteer Military: Progress and Prospects* (Washington, D.C.: Brookings, 1984); and Michael R. Gordon, "If Reagan Wants to Expand the Military, He May Also Have to Revive the Draft," *National Journal*, August 22, 1981, pp. 1501–1505.
40. For an excellent discussion of how the mission of defending the Persian Gulf threatens the American commitment to defend Europe, see John D. Mayer, Jr., *Rapid Deployment Forces: Policy and Budgetary Implications* (Washington, D.C.: Congressional Budget Office, February 1983). Regarding anti-European sentiment in the United States, a sign of the depth of that sentiment can be found in the reaction to Senator Sam Nunn's June 1984 proposal to remove a portion of

the United States *increasing* the number of American units stationed in Europe.

There is little chance, either, that the other NATO members with forces in West Germany (Britain, Belgium, Canada, France, and the Netherlands) will increase the size of their contingents in any meaningful way.[41] In fact, there will be pressure in each case to decrease present force levels. In short, it is most unlikely that NATO manpower on the Central Front will increase significantly in the foreseeable future. In effect, this means that there will not be an increase in the number of active units assigned to NATO.[42]

One could argue, on the other hand, that although NATO is not likely to increase its number of combat units, it could do much to improve the balance by deploying greater numbers of existing weapons. NATO could seek, for example, to reduce the Soviets' advantage in such categories of weaponry as tanks and artillery. This argument is not very convincing: it is actually very unlikely that NATO will alter the balance of weapons in a significant way.

One reason is cost. NATO will certainly have to spend a great deal more money if it hopes to shift the balance of weapons. All available evidence points to no marked increase in defense spending among the Europeans. The United States, of course, has significantly increased defense spending over the past five years. It remains to be seen, however, whether American defense spending can be kept at present levels. Even if it can, it does not appear that NATO's conventional capabilities will be affected in any significant way since the emphasis in the Reagan Administration's defense program has been on strategic nuclear forces, the Navy, and the rapid deployment

---

U.S. forces from Europe if America's allies do not do more to improve their conventional forces. Although the proposal was defeated in the Senate (by a vote of 55–41), the Reagan Administration had to go to considerable lengths to ensure that outcome.

41. The French are actually reducing the size of their conventional forces. See John Vinocur, "France Plans Cut in Armed Forces," *The New York Times*, December 7, 1982, p. 5; and John Vinocur, "More French Plans for Military Cuts Reported," *The New York Times*, December 8, 1982, p. 15. There are also danger signs in Britain. For a discussion of Britain's most recent Defense White Paper, which highlights these dangers, see "The Ships, but Not the Men," *The Economist*, May 19, 1984, pp. 65–66. In Britain, especially after the Falklands conflict, there is considerable sentiment for reducing the size of Britain's commitment to NATO and developing instead intervention forces for contingencies outside Europe. For an example of this thinking, see Lord Cameron et al., *Diminishing the Nuclear Threat: NATO's Defense and Technology*, Report prepared for the British Atlantic Committee (London, 1984), pp. 20–21, 44–45, 52–55.

42. NATO could, of course, reorganize its forces into smaller units, thus increasing the total number of units. There is no evidence, however, that this is likely to happen and it is not clear that such a move would improve NATO's overall position.

force.[43] Although the Administration has not been opposed to spending money for European security, no effort is being made or is likely to be made to improve the balance by unilateral American measures.[44]

It is very difficult at this point to envision NATO's spending significantly more money on defense. The NATO members committed themselves in 1978 to increase defense spending by 3 percent per year in real terms, and General Rogers, the NATO commander, has argued that NATO can develop a formidable conventional deterrent by increasing spending by 4 percent per year in real terms. These are unlikely but nevertheless not unrealizable goals, given some improvement in the international economy and in European attitudes towards defense spending.[45] Increased spending on the order of 3 to 4 percent, however, is not going to lead to a significant shift in the balance of weaponry.

Leaving aside the matter of a Soviet response, those increases in spending will undoubtedly be absorbed in part by the increasing cost of both manpower and technology. For example, the commission which the German government established to study the manpower problem makes it clear that in order to maintain the present force level (495,000), additional expenditures of money will be necessary.[46] The situation is equally grim in the United States, where an improved economy will undoubtedly dampen recruiting efforts and force the services to increase salaries and benefits so that they can compete in the labor market. The escalating cost of weaponry is a more familiar but no less acute problem. Jacques Gansler, for example, reports that "the generation-to-generation increase in the cost of weapons systems has

---

43. See Richard Halloran, "Reagan Selling Navy Budget as Heart of Military Mission," *The New York Times*, April 11, 1982, p. 1; Caspar W. Weinberger, *Annual Report to the Congress, Fiscal Year 1983* (Washington, D.C.: U.S. Government Printing Office, 1982) and *Annual Report to the Congress, Fiscal Year 1984* (Washington, D.C.: U.S. Government Printing Office, 1983); Robert W. Komer, "Maritime Strategy vs. Coalition Defense," *Foreign Affairs*, Vol. 60, No. 5 (Summer 1982), pp. 1124–1144; Drew Middleton, "Shortage of Arms, Troops and Funds Complicates Job Ahead for the Army," *The New York Times*, April 22, 1982, p. B-17; James Coates, "Training, Nuclear Arms Get Pentagon Priority in Face of Cuts," *Chicago Tribune*, August 1, 1983, p. 4; and Richard Halloran, "Planning Memos Stress U.S. Show of Armed Force," *The New York Times*, September 20, 1983, p. 1.
44. It is important to note that the U.S. Congress has not been sympathetic to increased spending for the NATO commitment. See Robert W. Komer, "Congress Lets NATO Down Hard," *The Los Angeles Times*, December 8, 1982, p. 11.
45. For a sobering account of how NATO countries have performed since making that commitment, see Caspar W. Weinberger, *Report on Allied Contributions to the Common Defense*, A Report to the U.S. Congress from the Secretary of Defense, March 1984.
46. Commission on Long-term Planning, *Final Report*, pp. 40, 93–98.

been consistently rising by 5–6 per cent every year, after adjusting for inflation and annual variations in the number of weapons purchased."[47] Such
increases alone leave little hope that NATO can procure significant numbers
of additional weapons with a 3 or 4 percent increase in spending.

There is a second major obstacle to improving the balance of weaponry.
In each NATO unit, be it a brigade or a division, there is an optimum number
of tanks, artillery pieces, infantry fighting vehicles, etc., that are needed for
battlefield success. Once that unit has the necessary number of weapons, it
is pointless, if not counterproductive, to add more weapons. No one would
seriously argue that NATO should pursue such a policy merely to increase
its total number of tanks or artillery pieces.[48] There is presently no shortage
of major weapons systems in the German and American units on the Central
Front. NATO's two largest contingents are also its best-equipped forces. It
is clear, however, that there is a need to increase somewhat the number of
weapons, especially artillery, in the Belgian, British, and Dutch forces. Defense spending increases on the order of 3 to 4 percent per year in each of
these nations should provide the wherewithal to procure the needed weaponry. These additions, however, would not shift the overall balance of weapons very much. If NATO wants to increase significantly its number of tanks
and other major weapons, it will have to introduce new units to the Central
Front. There simply is not much opportunity to increase numbers within the
existing force structure. NATO is unlikely, however, to increase its number
of units because of manpower constraints and American reluctance to commit
more forces to Europe.[49]

---

47. Jacques S. Gansler, "We Can Afford Security," *Foreign Policy*, No. 51 (Summer 1983), p. 67.
It should also be emphasized that there are fundamental deficiencies in the American weapons
acquisition process that will undoubtedly work to complicate the Reagan Administration's efforts
to purchase increased numbers of weapons in an efficient manner. See Jacques S. Gansler, "Can
the Defense Industry Respond to the Reagan Initiatives?," *International Security*, Vol. 6, No. 4
(Spring 1982), pp. 102–121; Michael R. Gordon, "Pentagon Cost Overruns, a Venerable Tradition,
Survive Reagan's 'Reforms'," *National Journal*, January 8, 1983, pp. 56–60; and the sources cited
in note 53.
48. This discussion points up the very important fact that the Pact and NATO build and organize
their divisions in quite different ways, with the Pact maintaining a higher ratio of weapons to
manpower in its divisions. Thus, the Pact's advantage in different categories of weaponry is
greater than its advantage in manpower and division equivalents. See Krause, *The Balance Between
Conventional Forces in Europe*, pp. 7–18; and Posen, "Measuring the European Conventional
Balance," pp. 51–54.
49. It is not surprising in light of this discussion that General Rogers, in his call for 4 percent
spending increases, has not emphasized the need to shift the overall balance of the more
traditional weapons, but instead has emphasized the need to develop sophisticated new weaponry (see the following discussion of "The Technological Solution").

THE TECHNOLOGICAL SOLUTION

Other analysts recommend strengthening NATO's conventional forces by technological remedies. The most fashionable of these proposals, frequently labelled the "Deep Strike" solution, relies on sophisticated new weapons which allegedly could reach far behind the battle front to destroy Warsaw Pact "second echelon" forces.[50] Proponents of this solution assume that weapons with this capability can be successfully developed and deployed and that, by destroying the Pact's second echelon, NATO will destroy a critical element of the invasion force. Specifically, the key to success is to deny the Pact the reinforcements they will need to exploit their initial victories along the forward edge of the battle area. Thus, while other analysts emphasize improving the quantitative balance of existing weapons, the emphasis here is on introducing new weaponry. The key assumption is that while NATO *cannot* match the Pact in raw numbers, NATO *can* offset Pact numerical superiority with new technologies.

There is no doubt that NATO has benefitted in the past from the qualitative superiority of Western weaponry, and it should surely seek to maintain and exploit this technical edge. Also, NATO can indeed improve its position on the battlefield by destroying elements of the Pact's second echelon—something which NATO air forces have in fact long been structured to do. However, it seems unlikely that the proposed technological solution can shift the conventional balance markedly in NATO's favor.

There are a number of reasons for skepticism.[51] First, many of the weapons

---

50. For examples of the enthusiasm this solution has generated, see, *inter alia*: *Strengthening Conventional Deterrence in Europe: Proposals for the 1980s*, Report of the European Security Study (New York: St. Martin's Press, 1983); "How Pave Movers and WASPS Will Help to Hold the NATO Line," *The Economist*, December 11, 1982, pp. 41–42; "Defending NATO," Editorial, *The Wall Street Journal*, November 19, 1982, p. 29; Lord Cameron et al., *Diminishing the Nuclear Threat*; and Manfred Woerner and Peter-Kurt Wurzbach, "NATO's New 'Conventional Option'," *The Wall Street Journal*, November 19, 1982, p. 30. For a description of the weapons that are being developed to support this strategy, see Benjamin F. Schemmer, "NATO's New Strategy: Defend Forward, but Strike Deep," *Armed Forces Journal International*, November 1982, pp. 50–68; Benjamin F. Schemmer, "Defend Forward, but Strike Deep—Part II," *Armed Forces Journal International*, December 1982, pp. 68–73, 92; and Benjamin F. Schemmer, "Defend Forward, but Strike Deep—Part III," *Armed Forces Journal International*, January 1983, pp. 48–54.
51. There is a growing body of literature which is highly critical of this technological solution. See, for example: Steven L. Canby, "The Conventional Defense of Europe: The Operational Limits of Emerging Technology," Wilson Center Working Paper No. 55 (Washington, D.C.: The Wilson Center, April 1984); Matthew A. Evangelista, "Offense or Defense: A Tale of Two Commissions," *World Policy Journal*, Vol. 1, No. 1 (Fall 1983), pp. 45–69; Daniel Gouré and Jeffrey R. Cooper, "Conventional Deep Strike: A Critical Look," *Comparative Strategy*, Vol. 4, No. 3 (1984), pp. 215–248; Fen Osler Hampson, "Groping for Technical Panaceas: The European

have not yet been developed and deployed. Moreover, some of the weapons have experienced significant problems in the development process.[52] Given American experiences with developing sophisticated weaponry over the past three decades, it seems reasonable to assume that a number of the proposed systems will not be deployed and that most, if not all of those that are deployed, will fall short of initial expectations.[53] Second, the cost of this solution is unclear. Given the escalating costs of sophisticated weaponry and the fact that some portion of that 3 to 4 percent increase will have to be spent on replacing and modernizing more traditional weapons, it remains to be seen whether NATO can afford such a solution. More specifically, it is not clear whether America's allies will be capable of or will be interested in procuring the weaponry to support this strategy. The United States has been the principal proponent up to this point. Unless the allies actively participate, this solution is flawed.

Third, it is not clear that the second echelon forces are the most important targets. In the classical blitzkrieg operations of the past, the breakthrough and the exploitation that produced the decisive victory were both conducted by the same first echelon forces.[54] The second echelon forces played a pe-

---

Conventional Balance and Nuclear Stability," *International Security*, Vol. 8, No. 3 (Winter 1983–84), pp. 57–82; Jeffrey Record, "NATO's Forward Defense and Striking Deep," *Armed Forces Journal International*, November 1983, pp. 42–44, 46–48; Phil Williams and William Wallace, "Emerging Technologies and European Security," *Survival*, Vol. 26, No. 2 (March–April 1984), pp. 70–78; and Joel Wit, "Deep Strike: NATO's New Defense Concept and Its Implications for Arms Control," *Arms Control Today*, Vol. 13, No. 10 (November 1983), pp. 1, 4–7, 9.

52. See, for example, Mark Hewish, "The Assault Breaker Program: U.S. Stand-off Weapon Technology of the Future," *International Defense Review*, Vol. 15 (1982), pp. 1207–1211; Fred Hiatt, "Conventional Weapon May Go Nuclear," *The Washington Post*, November 25, 1983, p. 1; Charles Mohr, "Antitank Testing Unrealistic, Some Officials Say," *The New York Times*, May 22, 1984, p. 21; "Pentagon Study Doubts Value of Antitank System," *The New York Times*, September 20, 1983, p. 13; and Wit, "Deep Strike," pp. 4–6. Regarding policymakers' doubts about this strategy, see Richard Halloran, "Pentagon Debating Commitment to Complex Computerized Arms," *The New York Times*, August 23, 1983, p. 1.

53. For three of the best studies on this subject, see: Merton J. Peck and Frederic M. Scherer, *The Weapons Acquisition Process* (Boston: Harvard University Business School, 1962); J.R. Fox, *Arming America: How the U.S. Buys Weapons* (Cambridge: Harvard University Press, 1974); and Robert L. Perry et al., *System Acquisition Strategies*, Rand Report R-733-PR/ARPA (Santa Monica, Calif.: Rand, June 1971). There is another reason to doubt the claim that we are about to witness a technological revolution that will markedly alter the balance in Europe. As Karl Lautenschläger makes clear in his excellent study of the evolution of naval technology, weapons developments tend to be evolutionary rather than revolutionary. Lautenschläger, "Technology and the Evolution of Naval Warfare," *International Security*, Vol. 8, No. 2 (Fall 1983), pp. 3–51. There is much evidence that developments in the realm of so-called Deep Strike technologies are following the path described by Lautenschläger.

54. For a discussion of how a classical blitzkrieg works (which draws heavily upon German and

ripheral role. If the Soviets are going to score a quick and decisive victory in Europe, which is certainly going to be their objective, it will have to be accomplished by those divisions that are massed at the breakthrough points. These are the first echelon forces, and NATO should be primarily concerned with thwarting them.

Fourth, the historical record on deep interdiction operations is not encouraging.[55] This is a difficult mission, even when one has overwhelming air superiority, and this is not likely to be the case in the critical first weeks of a European conflict. This brings us to the final point: the Soviets will undoubtedly make a concerted effort to develop the appropriate countermeasures. Although it is impossible to predict how successful they will be, it is safe to assume that there would be some degradation of those new NATO capabilities. In short, there is presently little reason to believe that NATO can markedly improve the balance with the proposed technological solution.

FUTURE PROSPECTS

This pessimistic prognosis notwithstanding, the balance could shift markedly in the decade ahead if there were to be a fundamental change in the general political and economic environment. For example, if the West were to undergo a sustained and robust economic recovery in the next few years and, concomitantly, the Soviet economy were to continue to deteriorate, this would make it much easier for NATO to increase defense spending and very difficult for the Pact to continue its spending pattern of the past decade. If, at the same time, the Soviets were forced to intervene directly in Poland or another Eastern European country, the NATO nations would undoubtedly

---

Israeli experiences), see Mearsheimer, *Conventional Deterrence*, pp. 35–43. Also see Trevor N. Dupuy, "The Soviet Second Echelon: Is This a Red Herring?," *Armed Forces Journal International*, August 1982, pp. 60–64.
55. One can gain an appreciation of the difficulties and complexities of the deep interdiction mission from, *inter alia*: Gregory A. Carter, *Some Historical Notes on Air Interdiction in Korea*, Rand Paper P-3452 (Santa Monica, Calif.: Rand, September 1966); Wesley F. Craven and James L. Cate, eds., *The Army Air Forces in World War II* (Chicago: University of Chicago Press, 1951), Vol. 3, parts 1–3; Edmund Dews and Felix Kozaczka, *Air Interdiction: Lessons from Past Campaigns*, Rand Note N-1743-PA&E (Santa Monica, Calif.: Rand, September 1981); Edmund Dews, *NATO Inland Transport As A Potential Rear-Area Target System: Lessons from Germany's Experience in World War II*, Rand Note N-1522-PA&E (Santa Monica, Calif.: Rand, June 1980); W.W. Rostow, *Pre-Invasion Bombing Strategy: General Eisenhower's Decision of March 25, 1944* (Austin: University of Texas Press, 1981); F.M. Sallagar, *Operation "Strangle" (Italy, Spring 1944): A Case Study of Tactical Air Interdiction*, Rand Report R-851-PR (Santa Monica, Calif.: Rand, February 1972); *The Senator Gravel Edition, The Pentagon Papers* (Boston: Beacon Press, 1971), Vol. 4, pp. 1–276; John Slessor, *The Central Blue: Recollections and Reflections* (New York: Praeger, 1957), chapter 20.

be galvanized into spending more of their newly available resources on defense. No one would argue that this is a likely scenario. In fact, one can think of a number of more pessimistic scenarios, which appear more realistic than the one described above. The important point, however, is that the balance is only likely to shift significantly if there are marked changes in the economic and political environment. National security policymakers have little direct control over such developments.[56]

Although this discussion has focused on proposals to improve the present balance, it is evident that it is going to be very difficult just to maintain the present balance. There are numerous danger signs on the horizon: the continuing economic problems in Europe, especially Britain and France; the German demographic problem; the French decision to emphasize nuclear forces at the expense of conventional forces; the escalating costs of Britain's Trident and its need for a surface navy, both of which are likely to rob resources from the British Army of the Rhine; and growing sentiment in America to remove some forces from Europe. Surely the Soviets will have their share of problems.[57] Still, this does not detract from the fact that NATO is going to need skillful political leadership just to maintain the present balance.

*Further Reasons for Skepticism about NFU*

There are three other problems with an NFU policy that merit discussion. First, if NATO significantly improves its conventional forces, it will have an improved offensive capability.[58] This is not to say that NATO will automat-

---

56. This point is reflected in the Reagan Administration's defense buildup. Despite the Administration's success at getting its way with Congress and despite the rhetoric about how much the overall U.S.–Soviet balance has improved since 1980, a close examination of the record shows very clearly that, although the balance is now somewhat more favorable in certain areas, there has been no marked shift in the overall balance.

57. The Soviets, for example, have significant demographic problems of their own. See Alexander Alexiev and S. Enders Wimbush, *The Ethnic Factor in the Soviet Armed Forces: Historical Experience, Current Practices, and Implications for the Future—An Executive Summary*, Rand Report R-2930/1 (Santa Monica, Calif.: Rand, August 1983); and Edmund Brunner, Jr., *Soviet Demographic Trends and the Ethnic Composition of Draft-Age Males, 1980–1995*, Rand Note N-1654-NA (Santa Monica, Calif.: Rand, February 1981).

58. This would certainly be the case if NATO were to improve the raw balance of forces. The technological solution, with its emphasis on weaponry that could be used for preemptive strikes, would also push NATO in the direction of an offensive capability. Regarding the proposed alternative strategies, this tendency towards offense is manifest in the maneuver-oriented strategy, not to mention the writings of those who call for NATO to develop an offensive or

ically develop an offensive strategy in such circumstances; nevertheless, those forces will undoubtedly have more offensive capability than do the present ones. Given that militaries traditionally tend to prefer offense over defense, it is likely that there will be much pressure to exploit that offensive potential.[59] Even if NATO resists that pressure and maintains its commitment to a defensive strategy, those force improvements may well seem offensive in nature to the Soviets. What is offensive and what is defensive are all in the eye of the beholder. Consider, for example, what might happen if NATO increased the size and quality of its forces but still retained its strategy of forward defense. That strategy, although a defensive one, requires NATO to move the majority of its forces right up to the intra-German border. NATO might claim that executing this strategy in a crisis is a defensive move. The Soviets, however, are likely to see the movement of those strengthened NATO forces to the intra-German border as the final preparatory step for launching an offensive into East Germany. Given Soviet thinking on the advantages of striking first in a war, there would undoubtedly be much pressure on the Soviets to launch a preemptive strike. Of course, there is good reason to expect that NATO leaders would be subjected to similar pressure.

In short, significant improvements in NATO's conventional force structure would undoubtedly produce a situation in which the Pact, whose doctrine and force structure are already oriented towards offense, directly faces a NATO with significant offensive capability. This situation would obtain in a world in which decision-makers believe that it is possible, thanks to NFU, to fight a conventional war in Europe. As we know from 1914, this is a prescription for disaster.[60]

Second, NFU is likely to create a false illusion that is considerably more dangerous than the current reality. One point to recognize is that it is impossible to guarantee, even with an NFU policy, that nuclear weapons will not be used in a European conflict. The difficulty is greatest as long as nuclear

---

counteroffensive strategy. Only area defense, which is explicitly designed to prevent NATO from having any offensive capability, avoids this problem.

59. See, for example, Jack L. Snyder, *The Ideology of the Offensive: Military Decision-Making and the Disasters of 1914* (Ithaca: Cornell University Press, 1984). Also see Snyder's "Civil–Military Relations and the Cult of the Offensive, 1914 and 1984," *International Security*, Vol. 9, No. 1 (Summer 1984), pp. 108–146; and Stephen Van Evera, "Causes of War" (Ph.D. dissertation, University of California, Berkeley, 1984), chapter 7.

60. See Stephen Van Evera, "The Cult of the Offensive and the Origins of the First World War," *International Security*, Vol. 9, No. 1 (Summer 1984), pp. 58–107.

weapons remain in Europe, although the problem does not disappear when they are removed—since they could be reintroduced in a crisis or the super-powers could turn to their strategic retaliatory forces. Another point to rec-ognize is that there are two good reasons why NATO might use nuclear weapons first, despite the fact that NATO had in good faith adopted an NFU policy: 1) when American decision-makers are *actually* confronted with the prospect of the Soviets conquering Western Europe, they might reassess their NFU policy and decide to use nuclear weapons. Interests sometimes crystalize or change in the heat of conflict; moreover, nations are sometimes willing to take risks in crises that they would have otherwise considered unacceptable. How the United States might react to a cataclysmic event like the loss of Western Europe cannot be easily predicted and certainly cannot be guaranteed by an NFU policy. So, it is possible that NATO, even with an NFU policy, might purposely turn to nuclear weapons in a crisis. And, 2) as noted, a conventional war might inadvertently turn into a nuclear conflict.

This discussion points to the fact that, as long as the superpowers have nuclear weapons, one should never feel confident that they will not be used in a war. An NFU policy, however, is tantamount to saying that a purely conventional war could be fought in Europe. If policymakers believe that such is the case, war will become more likely in a crisis—simply because it will be less horrible than a nuclear war. In reality, though, not that much will have changed since it still remains possible that nuclear weapons will be used. In effect, one has the worst of both worlds: the possibility of war occurring is more likely because decision-makers believe that it will be less horrible; and the war may actually be just as deadly as before because nuclear weapons may still be used. Accordingly, unless nuclear weapons can be eliminated altogether or at least radically reduced in number and certainly eliminated from Europe, an NFU policy is positively dangerous.

If there is a great risk of nuclear escalation in any European conventional war, it is best to make this explicit in NATO's declaratory policy. Otherwise NATO's leaders risk deluding the Soviets into underestimating the risks of aggression, while moreover denying themselves the deterrent effect that comes from recognizing that risk of escalation.

A third additional problem with adopting an NFU policy is that it would cause severe political problems within the Alliance. It is not widely under-stood in the United States that within the different national security estab-lishments in Western Europe there is a long-standing concern with main-taining a strong emphasis on the nuclear part of the NATO deterrent equation. Throughout the early 1960s, for example, both the French and the Germans engaged in a bitter dispute with the United States over the latter's insistence on increasing reliance on conventional forces.[61] The Europeans did not want to abandon massive retaliation and adopt flexible response. The Europeans, and particularly the Germans, who have no nuclear weapons of their own, constantly worry that the United States will remove its nuclear umbrella from over their heads. Since an NFU policy does just that, it is not surprising that there is strong opposition in Europe to that policy proposal. This sentiment is reflected in the *Foreign Affairs* article that was written in response to the original "gang of four" piece.[62] That response, which categorically rejected NFU, was written by four Germans representing different positions on the political spectrum. One can point to numerous other examples of European opposition to NFU as well as strong opposition to any public questioning of American willingness to use nuclear weapons to defend Europe.[63]

There is little doubt that, as a consequence of the uproar surrounding the deployment of Pershing IIs and GLCMs, European, and especially German, elites have been reluctant to speak frankly in public about the need for maintaining a strong nuclear element in the NATO deterrence equation. It is also true that a small portion of the European elite has moved away from the above-described position. The fact remains, however, that within the different national security communities in Europe, there remains widespread, although somewhat muted, opposition to NFU. Consequently, any attempt by the United States to force an NFU policy on its reluctant Allies will meet great resistance and will do serious damage to the Alliance.

---

61. See Catherine Kelleher, *Germany and the Politics of Nuclear Weapons* (New York: Columbia University Press, 1975), chapters 6–11; Wilfrid Kohl, *French Nuclear Diplomacy* (Princeton: Princeton University Press, 1971), chapter 6; and Schwartz, *NATO's Nuclear Dilemmas*, chapter 6.

62. Kaiser et al., "Nuclear Weapons and the Preservation of Peace." Moreover, there is evidence that former Secretary of State Alexander Haig's denunciation of the Bundy et al. piece days before its publication was prompted by European concern about the article. See Bundy, "'No First Use' Needs Careful Study," p. 6. For a copy of Haig's speech, see "Haig's Speech on American Nuclear Strategy and the Role of Arms Control," *The New York Times*, April 7, 1982, p. 8. Also see John Vinocur, "Bonn Aide Upholds Atom-Arms Policy," *The New York Times*, April 16, 1982, p. 7.

63. Consider, for example, the sharp rebukes that former Canadian Prime Minister Pierre Trudeau recently received for publicly expressing doubts about the American nuclear guarantee. See Michael T. Kaufman, "Trudeau Assailed for Remarks on NATO," *The New York Times*, February 2, 1984, p. 3.

*Conclusion*

NATO would lose a very important deterrent capability if it adopted an NFU policy. Policymakers then might *think* that Europe is safe for conventional war. Although NATO could build very formidable conventional forces, they simply would not have the deterrent value of nuclear weapons. Thus, an NFU policy would mean that the possibility of war breaking out in a future crisis would increase. Moreover, although NFU is likely to lead policymakers to think that there is little prospect that nuclear weapons would be used in a conventional conflict, a real risk of nuclear escalation would remain. Regardless, there is no reason to believe that NATO is going to improve significantly its conventional forces. In fact, it is going to be very difficult just to maintain the existing balance in the decades ahead.

The irony of the present controversy over NATO's deterrent posture is that, despite claims that it is fundamentally flawed, NATO has a formidable deterrent posture. The conventional balance is nowhere near as unfavorable as the popular wisdom has it. In fact, NATO's prospects for thwarting a Soviet blitzkrieg are quite good. NATO should be able to deny the Soviets a quick and decisive victory and then turn the conflict into a lengthy war of attrition—in which the Soviets could not be confident of ultimate victory. When one considers the risks that the Soviets would face in a conventional conflict against a formidable opponent like NATO, as well as the great risks associated with the presence of thousands of nuclear weapons, there is good reason to be very confident about NATO's deterrent posture.

All this is not to say that NATO cannot improve its posture or that any change in the present posture is necessarily bad. In fact, it has been widely recognized for years that NATO's nuclear forces suffer important deficiencies; for example, some are too vulnerable to surprise attack and the NATO nuclear arsenal overall is bigger than necessary. Not surprisingly, therefore, NATO is in the process of markedly altering the composition of its nuclear arsenal.[64] The real challenge in the decades ahead, however, will be to preserve the existing conventional balance. It is ironic that there is so much talk these days about improving the conventional balance when, in fact,

---

64. Approximately 2400 out of a total of 7000 nuclear warheads have been or shortly will be removed from Europe. Also, more weapons will be removed to make way for the Pershings and ground-launched cruise missiles now being deployed.

there is little prospect of doing that. Although NATO should be encouraged to exploit technological developments and maintain its qualitative advantage over the Pact, it is chimerical to think that esoteric technology can compensate for a deterioration in the balance of fighting units. NATO must make every effort to prevent unilateral cutbacks in the size of its fighting forces.

Unfortunately, a concerted effort to foist NFU on the United States' European allies is very likely to stymie efforts to maintain the existing conventional balance. European policymakers have always been reluctant to improve the conventional balance because of their fear that it would lead to the decoupling of America's strategic nuclear forces. This, of course, is what NFU is specifically designed to do. European policymakers are hardly likely to accommodate NFU advocates on this count. Thus, if the case for NFU were to begin winning converts in the United States, it is almost certain that the Europeans would not make the sacrifices that will be necessary to maintain the present balance. There is only one way to gain European support for maintaining a formidable conventional deterrent and that is by convincing them that the United States remains committed to the principle that strong conventional forces *complement* the nuclear deterrent. Increased interest in NFU will make that a difficult task.

# Conventional Deterrence and Conventional Retaliation in Europe

*Samuel P. Huntington*

$\mathbf{F}$or a quarter century the slow but continuing trend in NATO strategy—and in thinking about NATO strategy—has been from emphasis on nuclear deterrence to emphasis on conventional deterrence. When it became clear that the famous Lisbon force goals of 1952, embodied in MC 14/1, had no hope of realization, NATO strategy appropriately stressed the deterrent role of nuclear weapons, in terms of both massive retaliation by U.S. strategic forces and the early use of tactical nuclear weapons in Western Europe. This strategy was codified in MC 14/2 in 1957. Shortly thereafter, however, the development of Soviet strategic nuclear capabilities and, more particularly, the massive deployment by the Soviets of theater nuclear weapons raised serious questions as to the desirability of NATO's relying overwhelmingly on early use of nuclear weapons to deter Soviet attack. In the following years, the emphasis shifted to the need for stronger conventional forces capable of mounting a forward defense of Germany for a period of time and to a strategy of flexible response, in which, if deterrence failed and if conventional defenses did not hold, NATO would have the options of resorting to tactical, theater, and eventually strategic nuclear weapons. In 1967 this strategy became official NATO policy in MC 14/3.

The past several years have seen increasing support for shifting the deterrent emphasis even further in the conventional direction. This perceived

This paper, prepared for a conference at the U.S. Army War College, Strategic Studies Institute, Carlisle Barracks, Pennsylvania, July 29–30, 1983, will be published in William O. Staudenmaier and Keith Dunn, eds., *Strategy in Transition: Defense and Deterrence in the 1980s*. It elaborates in more refined and detailed form arguments which I originally set forth in "The Renewal of Strategy," in Huntington, ed., *The Strategic Imperative: New Policies for American Security* (Cambridge, Mass.: Ballinger, 1982), pp. 21–32, and in "Broadening the Strategic Focus," in *Defense and Consensus: The Domestic Aspects of Western Security, Part III*, Adelphi Paper No. 184 (London: International Institute for Strategic Studies, 1983), pp. 27–32. In a few spots in this essay I have shamelessly plagiarized these earlier writings. I am grateful to Richard K. Betts and Eliot Cohen for their helpful critical comments.

*Samuel P. Huntington is the Eaton Professor of the Science of Government and Director of the Center for International Affairs, Harvard University.*

*International Security*, Winter 1983/84 (Vol. 8, No. 3) 0162-2889/84/030032-25 $02.50/0

need derives, of course, from the facts of strategic parity between the U.S. and the Soviet Union, Soviet achievement of substantial predominance in theater nuclear forces, and a continued and, in some respects, enhanced Soviet superiority in conventional forces. In these circumstances, in the event of a successful Soviet conventional advance into Western Europe, how credible would be the threat of a nuclear response? In the face of Soviet superiority at that level, why would NATO resort to theater nuclear weapons, with all the destruction to both sides that would entail? Even more significantly, why would the United States use or even threaten to use its strategic nuclear forces, if that would ensure massive Soviet retaliation against North America? The concerns which DeGaulle articulated (even if he may not have believed them) in the early 1960s had by the early 1980s come to be first believed and then articulated by a broad spectrum of statesmen and strategists. The standard reassurances of the validity of the American nuclear guarantee, as Henry Kissinger put it in 1979, "cannot be true" and "it is absurd to base the strategy of the West on the credibility of the threat of mutual suicide."[1] Even McGeorge Bundy, who immediately countered Kissinger's statement with an argument for the continued efficacy of nuclear deterrence in Europe, dramatically abandoned that position three years later.[2]

Current NATO strategy also has little support among Western publics. In 1981 in the four major Western European countries, for instance, overwhelming majorities (66 percent in Germany, 71 percent in Britain, 76 percent in France, 81 percent in Italy) favored either no NATO use of nuclear weapons "under any circumstances" or NATO use only if the Soviet Union "uses them first in attacking Western Europe." In all four countries only small minorities (12 percent in Italy, 17 percent in France and Germany, 19 percent in Britain) supported existing NATO strategy that "NATO should use nuclear weapons

---

1. Henry A. Kissinger, "The Future of NATO," in Kenneth A. Myers, ed., *NATO: The Next Thirty Years* (Boulder, Colo.: Westview Press, 1980), p. 7.
2. McGeorge Bundy, "Strategic Deterrence Thirty Years Later—What Has Changed?", in *The Future of Strategic Deterrence, Part I*, Adelphi Paper No. 160 (London: International Institute for Strategic Studies, 1980), pp. 10–11: ". . . the strategic protection of Europe is as strong or as weak as the American strategic guarantee. . . . the effectiveness of this American guarantee is likely to be just as great in the future as in the past." Cf. McGeorge Bundy, George F. Kennan, Robert S. McNamara, and Gerard Smith, "Nuclear Weapons and the Atlantic Alliance," *Foreign Affairs*, Vol. 60, No. 4 (Spring 1982), pp. 754, 765: U.S. "willingness to be the first . . . to use nuclear weapons to defend against aggression in Europe . . . needs reexamination now. Both its cost to the coherence of the Alliance and its threat to the safety of the world are rising while its deterrent credibility declines. . . . [T]he present unbalanced reliance on nuclear weapons, if long continued, might produce [some deeply destabilizing] political change."

to defend itself if a Soviet attack by conventional forces threatened to overwhelm NATO forces."[3] Somewhat similarly, in the United States, public opinion generally opposed a "no first use" declaration but also by an overwhelming margin (62 percent) answered "no" to the question as to whether the United States "would *ever* be justified in using nuclear weapons first during a war against another country."[4] In democratic societies, expert opinion and public opinion often differ on nuclear weapons issues. In the West today, however, they agree in rejecting reliance on the use of nuclear weapons to respond to conventional attack. In its current formulation, flexible response is seen as inadequate by the strategists, unsupportable by the public, and, one must assume, increasingly incredible by the Soviets.

The conclusion almost universally drawn from this perceived deteriorating credibility of the nuclear deterrent to Soviet conventional attack in Western Europe is the need to strengthen NATO conventional forces. The desirability of doing this is broadly supported by conservative, liberal, and, in Europe, socialist politicians. It has been endorsed in one form or another by a wide variety of military experts and strategists, including General Bernard Rogers, Professor Michael Howard, Senator Sam Nunn, the Union of Concerned Scientists study group, the No First Use "Gang of Four," the American Academy of Arts and Sciences European Security Study, informed Social Democratic Party (SPD) analysts, the Reagan Administration, and, so far as one can gather, those Democratic presidential aspirants who have addressed the issue.[5] The conventional wisdom is, in short, that stronger conventional forces are needed to enhance conventional deterrence and thus compensate for the declining effectiveness of nuclear deterrence.

---

3. Leo P. Crespi, "West European Perceptions of the U.S.," Paper presented at the International Society of Political Psychology convention, June 1982, Table 4, quoted in Bruce Russett and Donald R. Deluca, "Theater Nuclear Forces: Public Opinion in Western Europe," *Political Science Quarterly*, Vol. 98 (Summer 1983), p. 194.

4. CBS/*New York Times* poll, May 1982, cited in "Opinion Roundup," *Public Opinion*, Vol. 5 (August–September 1982), p. 38.

5. General Bernard W. Rogers, "Greater Flexibility for NATO's Flexible Response," *Strategic Review*, Vol. 11 (Spring 1983), pp. 11–19; Michael Howard, "Reassurance and Deterrence: Western Defense in the 1980s," *Foreign Affairs*, Vol. 61, No. 3 (Winter 1982–83), pp. 309–343; Senator Sam Nunn, "NATO: Can the Alliance Be Saved?", Report to the Committee on the Armed Services, United States Senate, 97th Congress, 2d Session, May 13, 1982; *The Washington Post*, February 2, 1983, p. 10; *Strengthening Conventional Deterrence in Europe: Proposals for the 1980s*, Report of the European Security Study (New York: St. Martin's Press, 1983); Bundy et al., "Nuclear Weapons and the Atlantic Alliance," pp. 753–768; Eckhard Lübkemeier, "Problems, Prerequisites, and Prospects of Conventionalizing NATO's Strategy," Unpublished paper, Bonn, Friedrich-Ebert-Stiftung, February 1983; English version, July 1983, pp. 3 and *passim*.

## The Requirements of Conventional Deterrence

The conventional wisdom suffers from two significant weaknesses.

First, NATO countries are unlikely to commit the resources necessary to achieve the required strengthening of NATO defenses. Ever since the Lisbon conference, various efforts have been made to bolster NATO's conventional capabilities so as to decrease reliance on nuclear retaliation. Except for a brief period in the mid-1960s, these efforts have not been notably successful. After a quarter of a century, deterrence by conventional forces remains appealing, but it also remains an unreality. For understandable reasons, European governments and publics have been unwilling to appropriate the funds and make the sacrifices that would be required to make it effective. This pattern continues. In 1978 the Alliance committed itself to the Long Term Defense Program requiring 3 percent annual increases in defense spending by its member countries. Apart from the United States, however, the members of NATO have, with occasional exceptions, generally failed to meet that goal. General Rogers now argues that an effective conventional defense for NATO can be achieved if its members increase their military spending by 4 percent annually. The European Security Study comes to a similar conclusion. But if NATO countries have failed to achieve a sustained 3 percent increase, how realistic is it to talk of 4 percent increases? The attitudes of European publics and governments do not seem to be more favorable to voting larger defense budgets than they have been in the past, and economic conditions for such increases are at present far less propitious. This does not mean that no increases in NATO conventional defense capability will occur. Clearly they will. The budget increases are likely, however, to be no more than 2.0–2.5 percent, and hence they will not achieve the levels thought necessary by those who see increased conventional capability as the solution to the problem of deterrence. Thus, while nuclear deterrence of a Soviet conventional attack on Western Europe suffers from a lack of credibility, conventional deterrence of such an attack suffers from a lack of capability.

The second problem with the strengthening-conventional-forces approach is more serious. It concerns not inadequate resources but erroneous, if generally unarticulated, assumptions. It would still be present in some form even if NATO defense spending did increase by 4 percent a year. It is much more salient if that goal is not achieved. It involves the requirements of deterrence.

Military forces can contribute to deterrence in three ways. First, they may deter simply by being in place and thus increasing the uncertainties and potential costs to an aggressor, even though they could not mount an effective defense. Allied forces in Berlin have performed this role for years, and the argument for being able to move airborne forces and Marines rapidly to the Persian Gulf, in the event of a Soviet invasion of Iran, rests on a similar premise. Simply the presence of American forces in Khuzistan might deter the Soviets from moving in on the oil fields. Second, military forces can deter by raising the possibility of a successful defense and hence forcing the aggressor to risk defeat in his effort or to pay additional costs for success. This has been the traditional deterrent role assigned to NATO forces in Germany. Third, military forces can deter by threatening retaliation against assets highly valued by the potential aggressor. This, of course, has been the classic role of strategic nuclear forces. Unlike deterrence by presence or deterrence by defense, however, this form of deterrence is not effective simply because the requisite military capabilities exist; it requires a conscious choice by the defender to retaliate; and hence the aggressor has to calculate not only the defender's capabilities to implement a retaliatory threat but also the credibility of that threat.

One of the striking characteristics of the new conventional wisdom is the extent to which stronger conventional defenses are identified with a stronger conventional deterrent. If only NATO can enhance its military defenses, Soviet aggression will be deterred: this assumption is implicit in most of the arguments for stronger NATO forces and it is at the heart of the report by the European Security Study. That report, indeed, treats conventional defense and conventional deterrence as virtually interchangeable concepts. The title of the report is "Strengthening Conventional Deterrence in Europe"; the central sections of the report deal with "The Specific Requirements for Effective NATO Conventional Defense" and "The Means for Enhancing NATO's Conventional Defensive Capability"; throughout it is assumed that improved conventional defenses mean improved conventional deterrence.

To a limited degree, this assumption is, of course, justified. The stronger NATO forces are, the greater the investment the Soviets would have to make to achieve a given set of goals in Western Europe. Yet the easy identification of deterrence with defense flies in the face of logic and in the face of long-standing traditions in strategic thought. One of the landmark works on this subject (still valuable after twenty years), *Deterrence and Defense* by Glenn Snyder, is. indeed, based on the opposition between defense and deterrence and the extent to which strategies and forces appropriate to serve one goal may not be suited to achievement of the other. In addition, deterrence itself, that is, the effort to influence enemy intentions, may be pursued through both "denial capabilities—typically, conventional ground, sea, and tactical air forces" and "punishment capabilities—typically, strategic nuclear power for either massive or limited retaliation."[6] In the years since Snyder, strategists have generally tended to make the same identification. In the process, concern with the distinction between nuclear and conventional capabilities has tended to obscure the equally important distinction between defensive and retaliatory capabilities. In current NATO planning, nuclear and conventional capabilities can both be used for defensive purposes; only nuclear capabilities can be used for retaliatory purposes. Eliminating or drastically downgrading nuclear forces means eliminating or drastically downgrading the retaliatory component that has always been present in NATO strategy. Those who argue for conventional defense are, in effect, arguing for deterrence without retaliation. This is a fundamental change in NATO strategy, at least as significant in terms of deterrence as the shift from nuclear to conventional forces. For as both logic and experience make clear, a purely denial strategy inherently is a much weaker deterrent than one which combines both denial and retaliation.

For a prospective attacker, the major difference between denial and retaliation concerns the certainty and controllability of the costs he may incur. If faced simply with a denial deterrent, he can estimate how much effort he will have to make and what his probable losses will be in order to defeat the enemy forces and achieve his objective. He can then balance these costs against the gains he will achieve. He may choose zero costs and zero gains; he may decide to limit his gains to what can be achieved by a given level of costs; he may decide to incur whatever costs are necessary to achieve the gains he desires. The choice is his. If, however, he is confronted with a retaliatory deterrent, he may well be able to secure the gains he wants with relatively little effort, but he does not know the total costs he will have to pay, and those costs are in large measure beyond his control. The Soviet general staff can give the Politburo reasonably accurate estimates as to what forces it will require and what losses it will probably suffer to defeat NATO forces in Germany and extend Soviet control to the Rhine. For years, however, it could not predict with any assurance whether U.S. nuclear retaliation to such a move would be directed to battlefield targets, military targets in

---

6. Glenn H. Snyder, *Deterrence and Defense: Toward a Theory of National Security* (Princeton, N.J.: Princeton University Press, 1961), pp. 4, 14–16.

Eastern Europe and/or the Soviet Union, or industrial and population centers in the Soviet Union. Precisely this uncertainty and absence of control made the threat of retaliation a strong deterrent. If these problems of uncertainty and uncontrollability are eliminated or greatly reduced, the effectiveness of the deterrent is seriously weakened.

The difficulties of relying on deterrence by defensive means have long been emphasized in the strategic field. No defense system—antiaircraft, ABM, or civil defense—deployable now or in the foreseeable future could prevent some nuclear weapons from reaching their targets and causing un-precedented destruction. Hence deterrence of an attack must depend upon the ability to retaliate after absorbing the attack. Much the same is true at the conventional level. In the past, conventional deterrence has usually meant deterrence-by-denial, and the frequency of wars in history suggests that this conventional-denial deterrence was not often effective. Nor has it been effective in the modern era. In a careful survey, John Mearsheimer identified twelve major instances of conventional deterrence between 1938 and 1979. In two of these cases, deterrence worked; in ten, deterrence failed.[7] This 83.3 percent failure rate for deterrence by conventional defense after 1938 contrasts rather markedly with the zero failure rate for deterrence by nuclear retaliation for a quarter century after 1945.

An initial offensive by a strong and determined attacker, particularly if accompanied by surprise, inevitably will score some gains. As Saadia Amiel summed up the lessons of the 1973 Arab–Israeli war and the implications of precision guided munitions (PGMs): "without very clear offensive options, a merely passive or responsive defensive strategy, which is based on fire-power and fighting on friendly territory, cannot withstand an offensive strat-egy of an aggressor who possesses a relatively large, well-prepared standing offensive military force."[8] This is certainly the case in central Europe. Given NATO's current conventional defenses and any likely improvements in them, a Soviet conventional offensive in Europe is, inevitably, going to be at least a partial success. The Soviets may not reach the Pyrenees, or the English Channel, or even the Rhine. They may or may not occupy Frankfurt, Ham-burg, or Munich. Inevitably they will, however, score some gains. They may

---

7. John J. Mearsheimer, *Conventional Deterrence* (Ithaca, N.Y.: Cornell University Press, 1983), pp. 19–20. Mearsheimer identifies six additional possible cases of conventional deterrence, in five of which deterrence failed.
8. Saadia Amiel, "Deterrence by Conventional Forces," *Survival*, Vol. 20 (March–April 1978), p. 59.

pay a substantial price in losses of men and equipment, but they will still occupy West German territory and conquer West German population and industry. That is a certainty produced by geography and any realistically conceivable balance of conventional forces in central Europe. Given the nature of existing forces and strategies, these gains could well be substantial, but that is not necessary for the argument.

Assume that the Soviet offensive does grind to a halt after Soviet forces have occupied a greater or a lesser portion of West Germany. What then? In theory, the Allies should bring in their reinforcements from North America and put together a counteroffensive to drive the Soviets back. This would, however, be an extraordinarily difficult military and logistical undertaking. Inevitably the pressures would be on all parties to attempt to negotiate a cease-fire and a resolution of the conflict. With their armies ensconced in Hesse, Lower Saxony, and Bavaria and the differing interests of the Allies manifesting themselves, the Soviets would clearly have the upper hand in such negotiations. It takes little imagination to think of the types of appeals the Soviets would make to West German authorities and political groups to accept some degree of demilitarization or neutralization in order to secure Soviet withdrawal and to avoid the replay of World War II in their country.

A Soviet invasion of West Germany that ended with the neutralization and/or demilitarization of all or part of that country would be a tremendous success from the Soviet point of view. It would decisively alter the balance of power in Europe and in the world. Its costs, in terms of losses of men and equipment, would have to be very substantial to outweigh these political, military, and diplomatic gains. In 1939 and in 1941, once they had devised means to neutralize possible Allied retaliation by bomber attacks on cities, Hitler and the Japanese launched their offensives into Poland and southeast Asia expecting, not entirely unreasonably, that their democratic opponents would lack the staying power to deprive them of their initial territorial conquests.[9] In the absence of a credible retaliatory threat against valued

---

9. For analyses in depth of the failure of pre-World War II deterrence, see Mearsheimer, *Conventional Deterrence*, esp. chapters 3, 4, and Scott D. Sagan, "Deterrence and Decision: An Historical Critique of Modern Deterrence Theory" (Ph.D. dissertation, Harvard University, 1983), chapters 4–7. The bomber introduced the possibility of more effective deterrence by retaliation and compelled aggressors to take countermeasures. Both Hitler and the Japanese were deeply worried about retaliatory air attacks on their cities. Hitler guarded against this by mutual deterrence through an informal understanding with the Allies that neither side would target population; Japan guarded against it by a disarming first strike. Neither Axis power was deterred by Allied defensive measures, including the Maginot Line.

Soviet assets, the Allies would be tempting fate to assume that the Soviets would not be tempted to make a comparable move into Western Europe sometime in the next decade or two.

In sum, a substantial increase in NATO conventional forces is unfeasible politically. Even if it could be achieved, it would not compensate for the decline in the credibility of nuclear retaliation as a deterrent. To be effective, deterrence has to move beyond the possibility of defense and include the probability of retaliation. Conventional deterrence requires not just an increase in conventional forces; it also requires a reconstitution of conventional strategy.

*The Role of Conventional Retaliation*

The new element required in NATO strategy is conventional retaliation. NATO has four possible means of deterring Soviet aggression: defense with conventional or nuclear forces and retaliation by conventional or nuclear forces. Under MC 14/3, NATO relied on a sequence of three responses, conventional defense, nuclear defense, nuclear retaliation (Figure 1). The decreasing credibility of NATO use of nuclear weapons, however, has loosened the connections between these responses (indicated by the dotted lines in Figure 2). As a result, both nuclear and retaliatory deterrence are weakened. The problem is to restore the latter without resorting to the former. The need, in short, is to add some form of conventional retaliation to NATO strategy (Figure 3). That retaliatory component can best take the form of provision for, in the case of a Soviet attack, a prompt conventional retaliatory offensive into Eastern Europe.

For the threat of retaliation to be an effective deterrent it must (a) be directed against a target that is highly valued by the potential aggressor and (b) have a high degree of probability it will be implemented. It is reasonable to assume that the Soviet elite values, next to the security of the Soviet Union itself, the security of its satellite regimes in Eastern Europe. If the threat of nuclear attacks against the Soviet Union has lost its credibility, the next most effective threat NATO can pose surely is the possibility of a conventional retaliatory offensive directed against the Soviet empire in Eastern Europe. In addition, as Snyder observed, the credibility of the threat of retaliation to "a large-scale Soviet ground attack on Western Europe depends on convincing the enemy that we would gain more by carrying out this threat than we

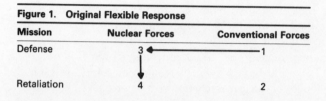

Figure 1.  Original Flexible Response

| Mission | Nuclear Forces | Conventional Forces |
|---|---|---|
| Defense | 3 | 1 |
| Retaliation | 4 | 2 |

Figure 2.  Deteriorated Flexible Response

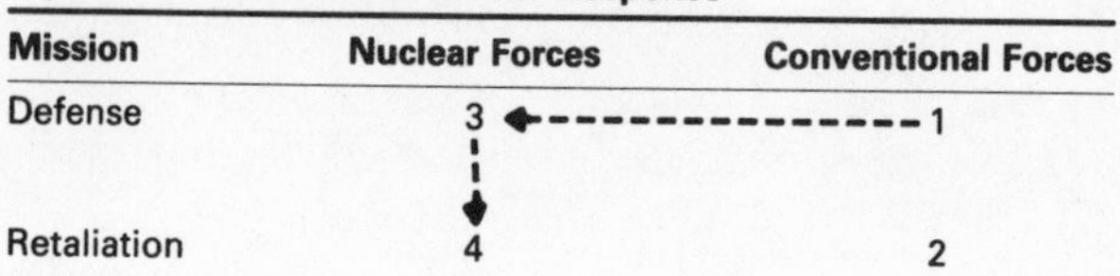

| Mission | Nuclear Forces | Conventional Forces |
|---|---|---|
| Defense | 3 | 1 |
| Retaliation | 4 | 2 |

Figure 3.  Reconstituted Flexible Response

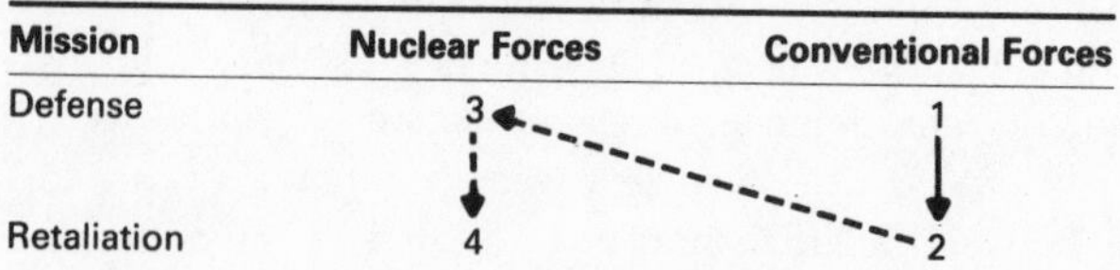

| Mission | Nuclear Forces | Conventional Forces |
|---|---|---|
| Defense | 3 | 1 |
| Retaliation | 4 | 2 |

would lose."[10] Precisely because this condition is no longer met, the threat of nuclear retaliation has lost its credibility. No such problem arises, however, by the threat of a conventional retaliatory offensive into Eastern Europe.

Almost every other form of retaliation against conventional attack involves escalation, either vertical, as in NATO doctrine, or, conceivably, horizontal. A conventional offensive into Eastern Europe, in contrast, is retaliation in kind, at the same level and in the same theater as the initial attack. It thus has unimpeachable credibility. Just as the Soviets have to believe that the United States would retaliate in kind against a strategic attack on American cities or a theater nuclear attack on Western Europe, they would also have to believe that the United States and its allies would retaliate in kind against a conventional attack on West Germany. Deterrence without retaliation is weak; retaliation through escalation is risky. Conventional retaliation strengthens the one without risking the other.

10. Snyder, *Defense and Deterrence*, p. 79.

Strategy should exploit enemy weaknesses. A deterrent strategy that included provision for conventional retaliation would do this in two ways. First, it would capitalize on the uncertainties and fears that the Soviets have concerning the reliability of their Eastern European allies, and the uncertainties and fears that the governments of those countries have concerning the reliability of their own peoples. It would put at potential risk the system of controls over Eastern Europe that the Soviets have developed over thirty years and which they consider critical to their own security. The deterrent impact of the threat of conventional retaliation would be further enhanced by prior Allied assurances to Eastern European governments that their countries would not be invaded if they abstained from the conflict and did not cooperate in the Soviet attack on the West. At the very least, such an invitation would create uneasiness, uncertainty, and divisiveness within satellite governments, and hence arouse concerns among the Soviets as to their reliability. In practice, the Allied offensive would have to be accompanied with carefully composed political-psychological warfare appeals to the peoples of Eastern Europe stressing that the Allies were not fighting them but the Soviets and urging them to cooperate with the advancing forces and to rally to the liberation of their countries from Soviet military occupation and political control. A conventional retaliatory strategy is based on the assumption that the West German reserves, territorial army, and populace will put up a more unified, comprehensive, and determined resistance to occupation by Soviet armies than the East German, Czech, Polish, and Hungarian forces and populations will to liberation from Soviet armies. (If this assumption is unwarranted, the foundations of not only a conventional retaliatory strategy but also of NATO would be in question.) Politically speaking, the Soviet Union has more to lose from Allied armies invading Eastern Europe than NATO has to lose from Soviet armies invading Western Europe. The Soviet Union should, consequently, give higher priority to preventing an Allied offensive into Eastern Europe than to pushing a Soviet offensive into Western Europe.

If the satellites did fight, the extent of their participation in a war, it is generally recognized, would depend on the scope and speed of Soviet success in the conflict. So long as the Soviets are moving westward, they are more likely to have complacent and cooperative allies. If, however, they are stalemated or turned back, disaffection is likely to appear within the Warsaw Pact. A prompt Allied offensive into Eastern Europe would stimulate that disaffection at the very start of the conflict. Neither the Soviets nor, more importantly, the satellite governments could view with equanimity West German tanks on the road to Leipzig and Berlin and American divisions heading for Prague and Cracow. From the viewpoint of deterrence, such a prospect would tremendously enhance the undesirability of war for the governments of these satellite countries. Those governments, which provide more than one-third of the Warsaw Pact combat forces on the central front, would lose more than anyone else in such a war and hence would become a puissant lobby urging their Soviet partner not to initiate war.

A conventional offensive into Eastern Europe would thus threaten the Soviets where they are politically weak. It would also be aimed at Soviet military weakness. Both Western observers and Soviet military leaders agree that Soviet officers and NCOs are much better at implementing a carefully detailed plan of attack than they are at adjusting to rapidly changing circumstances. A conventional offensive into Eastern Europe would confront the Soviets with just exactly the situation their doctrine and strategy attempt to avoid: one in which they do not have control of developments and in which they face a high probability of uncertainty and surprise. It would put a premium on flexibility and adaptability, qualities in which the Soviets recognize themselves to be deficient. One knowledgeable observer has even argued that, "If the Soviet Union were poised to launch an offensive, and were preempted in this by a NATO spoiling attack, there is little doubt that, in their own eyes, the Soviets reckon that *they* stand a good chance of collapse."[11]

A prompt Allied offensive into Eastern Europe would also greatly increase the probability of a protracted war. Soviet planning, however, is in large part directed toward a short-war scenario in which the Soviets score a breakthrough, occupy a substantial portion of West Germany, and then negotiate a cease-fire from a position of strength. With a retaliatory strategy, Soviet armies might be in West Germany but Allied armies would also be in East Europe, and driving them out would require more time for mobilization and organization of a counteroffensive.

The basic point, moreover, is deterrence. The prospects for the sustained success of the Allied offensive into Eastern Europe do not have to be 100

11. Christopher N. Donnelly, "Soviet Operational Concepts in the 1980s," in European Security Study, *Strengthening Conventional Deterrence*, p. 135. See also the report of the Steering Group of this study, p. 18, and Joshua M. Epstein, "Soviet Confidence and Conventional Deterrence in Europe," Unpublished paper, Harvard University, Center for International Affairs, 1982.

percent. They simply have to be sufficiently better than zero and to raise sufficient unpleasant uncertainties to increase significantly the potential costs and risks to the Soviets of starting a war.

Current NATO strategy already contemplates the possibility of a counter-offensive. It would occur after the enemy's offensive forces have penetrated NATO territory and then been slowed or brought to a halt and NATO forces have been reinforced. A counteroffensive follows sequentially after the enemy's offensive and is directed to retrieving the initiative and recovering occupied territory.[12] A retaliatory offensive, in contrast, occurs simultaneously with the enemy's offensive. Its primary purpose is not to strike the enemy where he has furthest advanced, as is usually the case with a counteroffensive; rather it is to attack him in an entirely different sector. It thus would have a very different impact on Soviet force planning. The threat of a counteroffensive will lead the Soviets to make their offensive drive as strong as possible in order to advance as far as they can and do as much damage as they can to NATO's defensive forces and thus to postpone or blunt NATO's counteroffensive possibilities. The threat of a retaliatory offensive, on the other hand, will lead the Soviets to worry about their defensive capabilities and hence to deploy their forces more evenly across the entire front. A counteroffensive threat, in short, will lead the Soviets to strengthen their offense; a retaliatory offensive threat will lead them to weaken it.

NATO adoption of a conventional retaliatory option would thus pose a new problem to the Soviets. The Soviet military forces in Europe are now almost entirely offensively oriented. Soviet doctrine places overwhelming emphasis on the importance of the offensive and, in particular, on the need for both speed and surprise so as to achieve Soviet objectives before NATO reinforcements arrive and NATO decides to use nuclear weapons. At present the Soviets are free to develop their plans and forces for a lightning and overpowering offensive into Western Europe without having to worry about any defensive needs, other than air defense. The Soviets, as Richard Burt has observed, "have designed and trained a force to attack, not to defend. Whatever their ultimate plans, the Soviets have deployed their forces to seize territory, not to hold it."[13] They have been able to do this, however, only

---

12. See, for example, Richard B. Remnek, "A Possible Fallback Counteroffensive Option in a European War," Unpublished paper, Airpower Research Institute, Air University, Maxwell Air Force Base, Alabama, 1983.
13. Richard Burt, "The Alliance at a Crossroad," Address, Friedrich-Ebert-Stiftung, Bonn, December 2, 1981. See also European Security Study, *Strengthening Conventional Deterrence*, p. 55.

because NATO has permitted them to do so. NATO strategy has given the Soviet offensive a free ride. If, however, the Soviets also had to consider the possibility of a prompt NATO conventional offensive, they would either have to reallocate forces from offensive to defensive missions or to devote still more scarce resources to military purposes to meet this need.

The purpose of a conventional retaliatory option is to deter Soviet attack on Western Europe. The capability to exercise that option, however, could also contribute to the deterrence of Soviet aggressive moves in other parts of the world. At present the Soviets know that they could advance in force into the Persian Gulf area without having to worry about the security of their flank in central Europe. Their position is, in this respect, similar to that of Hitler in the 1930s. Although France had various commitments to Poland and the Little Entente, which presupposed, as DeGaulle argued, an offensively oriented army, it could not in fact pose any deterrent threat against Hitler's moving eastward because it had adopted a purely defensive strategy, symbolized by the Maginot Line. French military strategy left Hitler free to do what he wanted in Eastern Europe. In similar fashion, NATO forces do not now pose even a theoretical restraint on Soviet moves elsewhere. If, however, NATO were prepared to launch a military offensive into Eastern Europe, the Soviets would have to assure themselves as to the adequacy of their defenses there and as to the loyalty of their allies before they could take the offensive against Iran, Pakistan, China, Japan, or any other neighboring state.[14]

The point is sometimes made that NATO is a defensive alliance and that a defensive alliance requires a defensive strategy. This argument has no basis in logic or history. NATO is a defensive alliance politically, which means that its purpose is to protect its members against Soviet attack through deterrence if possible and through defense if necessary. There is, however, no reason why a politically defensive alliance cannot have a militarily offensive strategy. Such a strategy may, indeed, be essential to securing the deterrent purposes of the alliance. For two decades NATO did in fact pursue its purposes primarily through the threat of launching a strategic nuclear offensive against the Soviet Union. If a nuclear offensive is compatible with the defensive purposes of the Alliance, certainly a conventional offensive should be also. Given long-standing NATO reliance on the possible first use

---

14. For elaboration of this point, see Huntington, "Renewal of Strategy," in Huntington, ed., *Strategic Imperative*, pp. 24–29.

of tactical nuclear weapons and, if necessary, strategic retaliation against the Soviet Union itself, it would be rather anomalous for its members to find something unduly abhorrent about a conventional offensive into Eastern Europe. On moral and political grounds, surely it is far more desirable to deter by threatening to liberate Eastern Europeans than by threatening to incinerate Russians.

*The Military Feasibility of Conventional Retaliation*

At this point, the reader may well be saying to himself: "Your argument is all wonderful in theory, *but* (a) as you've pointed out, NATO is not meeting its own already-established conventional buildup goals, and (b) the strategy you advocate would require a buildup far larger than anything NATO has contemplated. Conventional retaliation just is not practical." The question is: What are the military requirements of a conventional retaliatory offensive?

The answer is not as great as one might think.

First, it is necessary to clear away the popular cliché that the offensive requires a three-to-one overall superiority. If this were the case, NATO's problems would be over. Under no circumstances, given the current balance and probable rates of mobilization on each side, could the Warsaw Pact achieve an overall three-to-one superiority over NATO. Most scenarios do not deviate much from Fischer's 1976 estimate that Pact superiority in men in combat units would peak at about 2:1 two weeks after Pact mobilization began, assuming NATO mobilization lagged one week.[15] Unfortunately, however, 3:1 overall superiority is not what is required to attack. It is instead what may be required at the exact point of attack. Achieving that superiority is the product not of overall superiority in numbers but rather of superiority in mobility, concentration of forces, deception, and surprise.

Second, while the Soviets clearly do have a significant conventional superiority in Europe in numerical terms, that superiority is not enough, in itself, to give them a decisive advantage. In 1981, Pact superiority in divisional manpower was roughly 1.36:1, but in terms of overall manpower there was almost equality, with a ratio of 1.09:1. The Pact had many more tanks than NATO, but NATO was better off in attack aircraft. In terms of armored

---

15. Robert Lucas Fischer, *Defending the Central Front: The Balance of Forces*, Adelphi Paper No. 127 (London: International Institute for Strategic Studies, 1976), pp. 24–25.

division equivalents (ADEs), perhaps the single most useful measure, the ratio was 1.2:1. Overall the Pact wins the numerical bean count, but it does not have an advantage which would guarantee victory in war.[16] If a high probability currently exists of the Soviets' achieving substantial success in a central European war, that stems as much from their strategy as from their numbers. They are planning to concentrate their forces and use them offensively in the most militarily effective manner possible, while NATO has, for a variety of understandable reasons, been committed to a defensive strategy which almost ensures military defeat.

Third, a force which is inferior in overall strength can still pursue an offensive strategy. History is full of successful examples. The German offensive into France in 1940 and the North Vietnamese offensive in 1975 are two such cases. As U.S. Army FM 100-5 points out, other examples are the Third Army's attack through France in 1944, the U.S. offensive in Korea in 1951, and the Israeli Sinai campaign of 1967. In these cases, as in Grant's Vicksburg campaign (cited at length in FM 100-5 as a model offensive), the attackers succeeded "by massing unexpectedly where they could achieve a brief local superiority and by preserving their initial advantage through relentless exploitation."[17]

Obviously, stronger forces are more desirable than weaker ones. Implementing a strategy that includes conventional retaliation, however, requires more changes in the NATO military mind-set than it does in NATO military forces. For thirty years NATO has thought about conventional warfare exclusively in defensive terms. It has assumed that all the ground war and the bulk of the war generally would be fought in West Germany. It has pursued a strategy of forward defense, entirely defensible and necessary in terms of German interests, that leaves NATO forces strung out along the entire eastern border of the Federal Republic and hence highly vulnerable to an overpowering Soviet concentration of offensive forces. It has, moreover, done this without being able, also for understandable political reasons, to construct major fortifications that could slow down and greatly complicate a Soviet

---

16. For two excellent analyses emphasizing the uncertainties on the Central Front, see John J. Mearsheimer, "Why the Soviets Can't Win Quickly in Central Europe," *International Security*, Vol. 7, No. 1 (Summer 1982), pp. 5–39, and Anthony H. Cordesman, "The NATO Central Front and the Balance of Uncertainty," *Armed Forces Journal International*, Vol. 120 (July 1983), pp. 18–58.
17. U.S. Army, *FM 100-5 Operations* (20 August 1982), p. 8-5.

attack. NATO developed, as *The Economist* put it, "a Maginot-line mentality without the Maginot line."[18]

Fortunately there are signs that this mentality may be changing. SHAPE is developing plans for the deep interdiction of Warsaw Pact second-echelon forces. The aim is to locate Pact follow-on forces through improved intelligence and to attack them with long-range conventional means before they reach the battle zone, while at the same time NATO forces are holding the forward defense line against Pact first-echelon forces. It is, as General Rogers said, a way of adding "depth to the battlefield by extending the area of NATO's operations into the *enemy's* rear area."[19] A conventional retaliatory offensive as proposed here is compatible with and would supplement this emphasis on deep interdiction. It would involve NATO operations into the enemy's rear at the operational rather than simply the tactical level. It would employ not just conventional PGMs and missiles but the full range of conventional combined arms, and it would also serve to disrupt enemy logistics and reinforcements. Similarly, a retaliatory offensive is highly compatible with U.S. Army AirLand Battle doctrine, with its emphasis on the initiative, deep attack, and maneuver: "*Initiative*, the ability to set the terms of the battle by action, *is the greatest advantage in war.* . . . The offense is the decisive form of war, the commander's only means of attaining a positive goal or of completely destroying the enemy force."[20] There are at least some signs that German military thinking may be moving in a similar direction.[21]

A strategy with an offensive component would better capitalize on the current capabilities of NATO forces in Europe than does a purely defensive strategy. By and large, these forces are heavy forces; two-thirds of the Allied divisions in Germany are armor divisions; most of the rest are mechanized infantry. It is often said, of course, that these forces will enable NATO to have a mobile defense and to launch counteroffensives. That is true, and the

---

18. "Thrust counter-thrust," *The Economist*, May 9, 1981, p. 15: "Nato . . . should plan an armoured counter-thrust towards the Warsaw pact's rear areas from the part of the front that is not under communist attack. The knowledge that such a counter-offensive was part of Nato's strategy would, at the very least, complicate the Soviet plan of attack. It could even prevent the attack from happening. The Warsaw pact should not have the luxury of thinking that attack is its monopoly."
19. Rogers, "Greater Flexibility for NATO's Flexible Response," p. 17.
20. U.S. Army, *FM 100-5*, pp. 7-2, 8-1.
21. See K.-Peter Stratmann, "Prospective Tasks and Capabilities Required for NATO's Conventional Forces," in European Security Study, *Strengthening Conventional Deterrence*, p. 163.

same qualities also make them suited for a retaliatory offense. It is a misuse of expensive resources to consign these heavy forces primarily to a defensive role. In addition, NATO's forward defense strategy has always caused problems with respect to how Allied forces in the various sectors could reinforce each other. If the Soviets, for instance, launch their principal attack across the North German plain, what role could the substantial American and German forces in southern Germany play in bringing that advance to a halt? To move those forces laterally, that is parallel to the front, would be a logistical nightmare and could leave Bavaria open to a secondary Soviet attack. Not to move those forces northward, on the other hand, would greatly facilitate the Soviets' overwhelming the NATO forces in the north. The most efficient use of any substantial Allied forces not close to the Soviet attack corridors is to carry the war to the enemy.

The solution to NATO's deterrence problem is not to be found in any particular technological or doctrinal gimmick. It requires a diversified effort including more resources, qualitative improvements, and strategic innovations. Preparing for a retaliatory offensive will not do it alone, but it cannot be done without preparing for a retaliatory offensive.

In practical terms, what might a retaliatory offensive look like?

If the threat of such an offensive is to serve its deterrent purpose, the Soviets must have good reason to believe that an offensive is possible and little knowledge as to exactly where and when it might occur. NATO military planning for such an offensive would have to encompass a variety of alternative scenarios and possible options reflecting:

a. Warsaw Pact deployments and axes of advance;
b. NATO force capabilities and deployments;
c. East European politics, which might dictate withholding or limiting NATO offensive actions.

It is clearly not possible to spell out in this paper detailed plans for a NATO offensive. Many different possibilities exist. To give some idea as to what could be involved, however, it might be desirable briefly to elaborate what is undoubtedly the most obvious scenario for both Soviet and NATO planners. Because it is the most obvious scenario, it could also be one which is unlikely to be realized in practice.

Three of the most probable Soviet invasion routes are across the North German plain to Hannover and then northward towards Bremen and Hamburg, through the Göttingen corridor towards the Ruhr, and through the

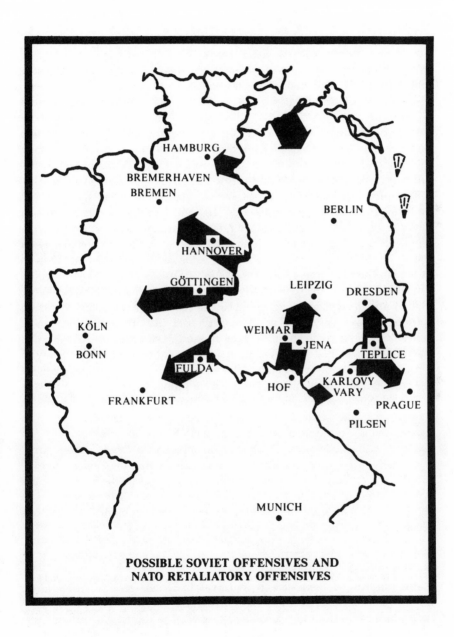

**POSSIBLE SOVIET OFFENSIVES AND
NATO RETALIATORY OFFENSIVES**

Fulda Gap towards Frankfurt. These attacks would be led by the powerful Third Shock Army (which includes 4 tank divisions and one motorized rifle [MR] division) in the center of the front and the 2nd Guards Tank Army (1 tank and 2 MR divisions) to the north.[22] They would engage the Dutch, German, British, and Belgian forces in NORTHAG and the III German and V American Corps in CENTAG. In these circumstances, the most appropriate retaliatory offensive would be by the VII American and II German Corps plus the 12th Panzer Division from the III German Corps. These are among the strongest and best equipped Allied forces in Central Europe; their Leopard II and Abrams tanks would provide the heart of the offensive thrust.

The offensive could well consist of two prongs. The major thrust would be through the Hof corridor towards Jena and Leipzig. Its primary axis of advance would not be west-east but rather south-north, and hence the problem of river barriers would be minimized. The Soviet forces immediately on the scene include the three motorized rifle divisions and one tank division of the 8th Guards Army, headquartered in Weimar. Such an offensive would threaten the most direct Soviet supply routes supporting their forces in the Fulda Gap. The second prong would be launched in a more easterly direction towards Karlovy Vary and Teplice in Czechoslovakia. The immediate Soviet resistance would come from a single division deployed north of Pilsen. If this advance reached the Elbe, it could then either swing north towards Dresden or south towards Prague. The second prong would also help protect the southern and eastern flanks of the main prong.

The Allied forces engaged in these offensive moves would be superior in manpower, tanks, and ADEs to the Soviet forces immediately deployed against them. To the north and east of the 8th Guards Army, however, is the 1st Guards Tank Army. It is roughly comparable to the 3rd Shock Army and clearly is designed to make a major contribution to the Soviet offensive into West Germany. If it joined that offensive, however, the Soviets would have to face the possibility of the Allies' overrunning their other forces in the south. If they used the 1st Guards Tank Army to blunt the Allied offensive, they would risk not achieving their breakthrough in the north. The

22. Information on the deployments and strengths of Soviet and Allied forces comes from: Fischer, *Defending the Central Front*; Cordesman, "The NATO Central Front," pp. 18ff.; and John Erickson, *Soviet–Warsaw Pact Force Levels* (Washington: United States Strategic Institute, Report 76-2, 1976). For simplicity's sake, the discussion here is couched purely in terms of deployed forces, without reference to the reinforcements possible on both sides. In addition, the data used are meant to be illustrative, not necessarily definitively accurate.

purpose of a retaliatory offensive is to confront them with precisely that sort of dilemma.

Allied military dispositions should supplement political and diplomatic measures in helping to minimize the enthusiasm of satellite forces for the Soviet cause. The Allied offensive should be directed at Soviet forces. The thrust into East Germany should be primarily by German forces and that into Czechoslovakia exclusively by American ones. At present the deployment of Allied forces in Bavaria is not the most satisfactory from this point of view, although it would not necessarily prevent Allied forces from being used in this manner. The movement of Allied divisions into East Germany and Czechoslovakia could also be supplemented by the infiltration by sea and air into Poland and Hungary of specially trained Special Forces units to encourage disaffection and resistance in those countries.

For many years NATO strategists have bemoaned the deployment of Allied forces in Germany, a legacy of the occupation, which left U.S. forces in the south, some distance from the highly probable Soviet axis of advance across the North German Plain. This deployment is, however, made to order for a retaliatory offensive. It places U.S. forces as well as German forces in a favorable location for a move into the heart of East Germany which would be highly threatening to Soviet lines of communication (LOCs). In addition, the French forces in southern Germany constitute a reserve which could reinforce Allied forces in the Frankfurt area or respond to any Soviet counteroffensive against Germany, e.g., through Austria.

How successful would be a retaliatory offensive such as this? That clearly would depend, among other things, on:

—the size, character, and leadership of the NATO forces committed to the offensive;
—the strength and readiness of the opposing Warsaw Pact forces;
—the degree of surprise NATO achieved; and
—the extent to which non-Soviet Warsaw Pact forces fought vigorously alongside their Soviet allies.

Just how these factors would play out is impossible to predict in advance. At one extreme, it is conceivable although unlikely that NATO forces could sweep north towards the Baltic and join up with amphibious forces in a giant pincer movement cutting East Germany in half and isolating Soviet forces to the west. At the other extreme, they might penetrate only a few kilometers into East Germany and Czechoslovakia. The point is that neither side could know for sure in advance, and that uncertainty is precisely what is required to reinforce deterrence. The Soviets would only know that, if they went to war under these circumstances, they would be putting at risk far more of great value than they would be at present.

Some changes in NATO forces are desirable to enhance the feasibility of a conventional offensive. These would not necessarily involve expansion in force levels. They would, however, require:

a. redeployment of German forces in II Corps to positions closer to the inter-German border and compensating movement of some U.S. forces to positions on the Czech border;
b. major improvements, already called for in NATO plans, in stockpiles of fuel, ammunition, spare parts, equipment, and other supplies necessary to sustain an offensive movement; and
c. emphasis in weapons procurement on those items most relevant to offensive needs, e.g., attack aircraft, attack helicopters, long-range PGMs.

In addition to these actions, it would also be highly desirable to strengthen NATO defensive capabilities through the construction of fortifications and improvement in West German reserves and territorial forces. At present NATO follows a forward defense strategy but lacks forward fortifications. The principal reason for this has been the reluctance of the West German government to create a major fortified line that would give concrete embodiment to a permanent division of Germany. If, however, NATO strategy included provision for the invasion and liberation of at least portions of East Germany, a fortified line along the inter-German border would no longer have the symbolism that the Bonn government fears. The construction of such a line would, of course, make it possible to release additional Allied forces to offensive missions. The same result will also be achieved to the extent that territorial army units play a larger role in area defense.[23]

The special requirements for a conventional offensive capability will obviously compete with other claims on the modest and only slowly growing

---

23. See, for example, the supportive but contrasting views of Steven L. Canby, "Territorial Defense in Central Europe," *Armed Forces and Society*, Vol. 7 (Fall 1980), pp. 51–67, and Waldo L. Freeman, Jr., *NATO Central Region Forward Defense: Correcting the Strategy/Force Mismatch* (Washington, D.C.: National Defense University Research Directorate, National Security Affairs Issue Paper Series 81-3, 1981).

NATO resources. The central criterion for allocating resources among these competing claims, however, should be the extent to which they contribute to deterrence. Improvements in NATO defensive capabilities strengthen deterrence, but only marginally so. At the most they simply require the Soviets to invest comparable additional resources in their forces so as to maintain the same probability of success. Enhancement of NATO offensive capabilities, on the other hand, confronts the Soviets with an entirely new danger in terms of Allied penetration into and disruption of their Eastern European empire. It thus forces them to set this risk off against the advantages of attacking NATO and to mobilize or to divert resources from other sources if they are to meet that threat. A given increase in NATO offensive capabilities, in short, will produce a considerably higher return in terms of deterrence than the same investment in defensive capabilities. As a result, this addition to NATO strategy will also lower the total new resources NATO needs to invest to achieve effective deterrence. It could make conventional deterrence not only more credible but also cheaper than it would otherwise be.

## The Politics of Conventional Retaliation

If conventional retaliation is strategically desirable and militarily feasible, the final question is whether it is politically possible. Will the Alliance agree to this amendment to the long-standing strategic doctrines set forth in MC 14/3?

Some may say that this proposal involves a fundamental change in NATO strategy for which it will be difficult if not impossible to mobilize support within the Alliance. In fact, however, incorporation of a conventional retaliatory offensive into NATO's strategy would, in many respects, be less a change in strategy than an effort to prevent a change in strategy. As it is, flexible response is inexorably becoming a dead letter. NATO strategy is changing fundamentally from a multi-pronged flexible response to a single-prong conventional defense. The addition of a conventional retaliatory option would, as the figures on p. 41 indicate, simply restore some element of flexibility to a strategy that is rapidly becoming inflexible. It would pose new uncertainties for the Soviet Union. It would adapt flexible response to the conditions of the 1980s. In similar fashion, a retaliatory offensive is not incompatible with the idea of forward defense. The latter is a necessary and appropriate response to German concern that as little of their country as possible become the locus of battle and subject to Soviet occupation. A retaliatory offensive would move at least some of the battle from West Germany to East Germany and Czechoslovakia. It is thus not a substitute for a strategy of flexible response and forward defense, broadly conceived, but rather a fleshing out of that strategy in changed circumstances. It would, in effect, make flexible response more flexible and forward defense more forward.

Adoption of a conventional retaliatory option would reinvigorate flexible response through conscious choice. Inevitably, the political feasibility of making such a conscious choice is a function of time and circumstance. In democratic societies, no new policy suggestion is immediately feasible. Every new proposal has to go through a process of discussion, consideration, analysis, amendment, and often initial rejection before it becomes reality. This is true in military policy as well as domestic policy, and it is doubly true in *alliance* military policy. The changes in NATO strategy in the mid-1950s and in the mid-1960s each required about five years to be implemented. There is no reason to think that the time required for change in the mid-1980s will be much different, nor to think that such change will not occur.

A broad consensus already exists on the need to enhance conventional deterrence. The political support of NATO governments and peoples for moving in this direction will in due course emerge, as is true of any new policy, from consideration of the unpalatability of the alternatives. In this instance, there are, broadly speaking, two such alternatives. One is to acquiesce in a greatly weakened deterrent, as the credibility of a U.S. nuclear response declines. This is, in terms of short-range politics, unquestionably the easiest way out, but it is one which also will have its political costs in terms of both heightened Soviet influence over alliance members and heightened political tensions among alliance members. The other alternative to effective conventional deterrence is to recreate a credible nuclear deterrent. Nuclear deterrence of a conventional attack is most credible—and, indeed, may *only* be credible—when the national existence of the deterring state is at risk. No one doubts that an Israeli government would use nuclear weapons to prevent Arab armies from overrunning Tel Aviv. A similar rationale furnishes the explicit justification for the French nuclear force and the implicit justification for the British one. Nuclear deterrence could be restored in central Europe if an independent, invulnerable, modest-sized German nuclear force were brought into being. The Soviets would have to believe that such a force would be used in the event of a Soviet attack on the Federal Republic. The political problems involved in the creation of such a force, however, dwarf those that arise from adoption of a conventional retaliation strategy.[24]

The strategic environment in the United States is increasingly favorable towards conventional retaliation becoming a NATO option. The other key locus of decision-making is the Federal Republic. One would think that German leaders would endorse a military strategy that, in comparison to the alternatives, promised to produce stronger deterrence at lower cost, to reduce the probability that nuclear weapons would be used in the territory of the Federal Republic, and to shift at least some of the fighting, if war did occur, from the Federal Republic to East Germany and Czechoslovakia. It is hard to see why it might be good politics in West Germany to oppose such a move. If, after the normal debate necessary for policy innovation in any democratic country, the West German government was unwilling to support such a change, the United States would clearly have to reconsider its commitment of forces to a strategy and posture that is doomed to be found wanting. "For deterrence to be credible," as General Rogers has said, "it requires capabilities adequate for successful defense and effective retaliation."[25] Effective retaliation means credible retaliation, and, in today's world, credible retaliation means conventional retaliation. That is the inescapable logic that will drive NATO's strategic choices in this decade.

---

24. For further discussion of this option, see Huntington, "Broadening the Strategic Focus."
25. Rogers, "Greater Flexibility for NATO's Flexible Response," p. 15.

# Conceptual Problems of Conventional Arms Control

*Robert D. Blackwill*

$A$fter fourteen years of stalemate in the Conference on Mutual and Balanced Force Reductions (MBFR), a new phase of conventional arms control efforts in Europe is underway.[1] The twenty-three members of NATO and the Warsaw Pact are preparing in Vienna a mandate for new talks to begin this year on conventional force reductions and limitations in all of Europe from the Atlantic to the Urals.[2] Conceptual complexities bedeviled MBFR and its Central European focus. These same difficulties will hinder even more future arms control attempts dealing with the larger area.

These conceptual problems can be divided into five categories: (1) the difficulty in both the West and perhaps recently in the East of integrating conventional arms control proposals into a coherent political vision of the future of Europe; (2) the question of the proper size and shape of U.S. forces in Europe and their relationship to extended deterrence; (3) the exacting challenge of analyzing the conventional military balance in Europe, especially its qualitative and geographic aspects; (4) the role of conventional forces in NATO's deterrent strategy and the reliability of conventional deterrence; and (5) the extraordinary technical feat of verifying a conventional arms control agreement, particularly given the Soviet Union's probable resistance to the intrusive measures required.

The author would like to thank the National Security Program at the Kennedy School of Government and the Ford Foundation for supporting the preparation of this article.

*Robert D. Blackwill was U.S. Ambassador to the Mutual and Balanced Force Reduction (MBFR) negotiations in Vienna from 1985 to 1987, and is now on the faculty of the Kennedy School of Government, Harvard University. Associate Dean of the Kennedy School in 1983–85, he has held several senior national security positions at the State Department and the White House.*

1. Informed treatments of the MBFR negotiations are found in William B. Prendergast, *Mutual and Balanced Force Reduction: Issues and Prospects* (Washington, D.C.: American Enterprise Institute for Public Policy Research, 1978); John G. Keliher, *The Negotiations on Mutual and Balanced Force Reductions: The Search for Arms Control in Central Europe* (New York: Pergamon, 1980); and Jonathan Dean, *Watershed in Europe: Dismantling the East-West Military Confrontation* (Lexington, Mass.: Lexington Books, 1987), pp. 153–184.
2. A discussion of the origins of the new Atlantic-to-the-Urals negotiations will appear in Robert D. Blackwill, "European Security and Conventional Arms Control," James A. Thomson and Uwe Nerlich, eds., *Conventional Arms and the Security of Europe* (Boulder, Colo.: Westview Press, forthcoming.)

*International Security*, Spring 1988 (Vol. 12, No. 4)
© 1988 by the President and Fellows of Harvard College and of the Massachusetts Institute of Technology.

*What Sort of Europe?*

Conventional arms control is sharply distinct from its nuclear counterpart in its potentially historic influence on the political geography of Europe. Nuclear arms control has many avowed and implicit purposes: to reduce the danger of war, to promote better East-West relations, to save money. But even its most avid advocates do not claim that nuclear arms control agreements as presently conceived promise to alter fundamentally the political relationships within and between alliances. Reduce tensions, yes. Change the present political order, no. Conventional arms control in Europe has much wider geopolitical implications.

Roughly six million uniformed members of NATO and the Warsaw Pact military establishments face each other across the East-West dividing line on the continent, with more than two million men in Central Europe alone. These forces manifest the separation of Europe into military blocs and rival political systems. To alter substantially the size and disposition of the two sides' conventional forces is possibly to change the post-war political arrangements themselves.

The Politburo's perspective on this reality is formed by its first principles: the USSR does not intend to be invaded from the West again, ever. The memories of 1941–45 are kept alive in the Soviet Union, precisely to ensure instinctive public support for an enduring Soviet policy that portrays the Federal Republic of Germany as a potential danger to its Eastern neighbors and to the Soviet homeland.

It does seem doubtful that Moscow requires nineteen divisions permanently deployed in the German Democratic Republic (GDR) to be the first line against whatever military threat it believes NATO forces, and especially those of the Federal Republic, pose in Central Europe.[3] One also wonders if a 400,000-strong Soviet force in East Germany is really needed to carry out the Red Army's projection of political intimidation into the Federal Republic and the rest of Western Europe, plus its internal security function, or whether with five or ten divisions less it could perform the same function.

If Gorbachev is sincere when he says he wishes to divert resources from defense to the civilian sector and to address the USSR's severe demographic and labor problems, he could do so by cutting sharply the number of first

---

3. International Institute for Strategic Studies (IISS), *Military Balance 1986–1987* (London: IISS, 1986), p. 42.

line Soviet divisions in East Germany, in the context of an arms control treaty with the West.[4]

But here is the conceptual rub. Apart from the purely military role vis-à-vis NATO of the Group of Soviet Forces Germany, Moscow hardly needs nineteen divisions in East Germany to insure against a reprise of its Nazi nightmare. But the Soviet leadership, at least to this point, seems to think otherwise. That preoccupation with the past will make the Politburo mighty cautious in pulling out many divisions of the Red Army from East Germany, even if several non-German Allied divisions might leave the Federal Republic of Germany (FRG) in return. And West German Chancellor Helmut Kohl's strong talk of German reunification during the September, 1987, visit of East German leader Erich Honecker to the Federal Republic will not make politicians and marshals sleep easier in Moscow.[5]

Apart from its military deployments in the GDR, the Soviet Union manages the rest of its East European empire with five divisions stationed in Czechoslovakia, two in Poland, four in Hungary and none in Bulgaria or Rumania.[6] Here too, at least in theory, there looks like room for Soviet withdrawals. In addition to their power projection capability, one wonders how much of an internal policing function these forces actually carry out. In general, they are kept away from the local population. And if trouble did occur, Moscow would need far more than these troops to put down any serious uprising.

After all, in 1956 the Red Army moved at least six divisions from the USSR into Hungary to crush the rebellion there[7] and in 1968 some fourteen divisions were required to suppress Prague Spring.[8] As for Poland, Moscow watched General Wojciech Jaruzelski crush Solidarity at the end of 1981 with

4. In a February 1987 speech, Gorbachev noted that, "our international policy is more than ever determined by our domestic policy, by our interest in concentrating on constructive endeavors to improve our country. . . . This is where we want to direct our resources, this is where our thoughts are going, on this we intend to spend the intellectual energy of our society." Philip Taubman, "Gorbachev Avows A Need For Peace To Pursue Reform," *New York Times*, February 17, 1987, p. 1.
5. Serge Schmemann, "Bonn Greets East German Leader on Visit That Shakes Old Taboos," *New York Times*, September 8, 1987, p. A8.
6. IISS, *Military Balance 1986–1987*, pp. 42–43.
7. Michel Tatu, "Intervention in Eastern Europe," in Stephen S. Kaplan, *Diplomacy of Power: Soviet Armed Forces as a Political Instrument* (Washington, D.C.: Brookings, 1981), p. 220.
8. Some sources indicate that fourteen Soviet divisions were moved into Czechoslovakia; see Robert Pfaltzgraff, Jr., "The Czechoslovakia Crisis and the Future of the Atlantic Alliance," *Orbis*, Vol. 13, No. 1 (Spring 1969), p. 214. Philip Windsor and Adam Roberts set the figure as high as sixteen Soviet divisions in their book, *Czechoslovakia, 1968: Reform, Repression and Resistance* (New York: Columbia University Press, 1969), p. 108.

no involvement of Soviet regular military forces whatever in the arrests. But had that roundup of dissidents by Polish security services not been successful, the Soviets were ready. They had been exercising hundreds of thousands of troops along the Polish border for months.[9] So it is difficult to see in any of these countries why the Soviet Union should not feel secure with somewhat fewer forces in Eastern Europe than at present.

Nonetheless, this is one place where a Soviet leader does not wish to get it wrong. Gorbachev clearly wants to restructure the Soviet Union's relationship with Eastern Europe. He has lectured the East Europeans on the advantages of *glasnost* and the requirements for reviving the socialist system.[10] There is more political and economic ferment and talk of reform in the region than in many years.[11] That being so, what would be the effect on Eastern European publics, most of whom detest the Soviets, if they turned on their televisions to watch significant withdrawals of the Red Army from Hungary? Or Poland?

No one knows. But Gorbachev could lose his job if he miscalculates in this regard. So Moscow's caution about major reductions in the rest of Eastern Europe, to hedge against turbulence there,[12] reinforces the general Soviet propensity to overcompensate against a resurgent Germany, and to maintain its operational military doctrine which requires large forces forward. Some few divisions might be pulled back across the Soviet border. However, big drawdowns, of more than four to six Soviet divisions, even in the context of an arms control agreement with the West, could, if any part of Eastern Europe erupted, threaten Gorbachev's hold on power in the Kremlin and hand his domestic opponents a powerful political bludgeon. To take such a chance when his most pressing priorities are internal reforms of the Soviet Union would reveal a curious sense of priorities.

NATO's considerations concerning conventional arms control are, like Gorbachev's, complicated by intra-alliance factors. In the West, the issue of the future political geography of Europe is dominated as it has been since 1945

---

9. Serge Schmemann, "Soviet Reports 100,000 on Maneuvers Near Poland," *New York Times*, September 6, 1981, p. 10.
10. Jackson Diehl, "Gorbachev Calls on Eastern Europe to Change But Not to Mimic," *Washington Post*, April 13, 1987, p. A17.
11. For example, John Tagliabue, "Poland Will Raise Prices 40 Percent, Shoppers in Panic," *New York Times*, November 15, 1987, p. 1.
12. A differing view is presented elsewhere in this issue: Jack Snyder, "Limiting Offensive Conventional Forces: Soviet Proposals and Western Options," *International Security*, Vol. 12, No. 4 (Spring 1988), pp. 48–77.

by the future of the Germanies. NATO governments from time to time speak positively about the reunification of Germany. Notwithstanding the negative views of Moscow and Mr. Honecker on German reunification, the idea presupposes the withdrawal of all Soviet divisions now in the German Democratic Republic, after which the citizens of East Germany would presumably freely express their view on the subject. If this outcome were a generally shared long-term objective within NATO, one could imagine a Western conventional arms control proposal which explicitly made that point and enumerated the negotiating stages through which Europe would get from here to there.

It is telling to observe, however, that no prominent politicians in the Federal Republic or elsewhere in Western Europe have linked the withdrawal of Soviet forces from the GDR through conventional arms control to the future status of Germany. Despite the obvious connection between reduced U.S. and Soviet forces in the Germanies and peaceful change in Central Europe, the West remains unready to face up to the long-term possibility of this fundamental transformation of the post-war order on the continent. Much of the West German political elite would like conventional arms control to play a catalytic role regarding closer relations between the two Germanies, but are exceedingly quiet about it. They bury the conceptual cord connecting the technical facets of conventional arms control with the future of Europe deep beneath the surface of the public debate. But it is there. Many Western arms control experts might not understand the connection. Many European politicians do. But can the West want all Soviet troops out of the GDR and at the same time be unprepared to deal with the German question? It would seem so.

This unexpressed linkage, recognized by many West Germans, causes some European nations to defend the status quo vigorously. France leads the way. Although too touchy to be articulated by the French government, an argument frequently heard in France stresses the stability of East-West competition in Europe, and especially its utterly peaceful character since the last Berlin crisis in 1961, without any contribution from arms control. As seen by many in Paris, the familiar European security system, with 42 years free from conflict, looks hard to improve upon fundamentally anytime soon. So French analysts doubt that conventional arms control can or should have a part in reshaping Europe's political landscape. Instead, if the West can avoid foolish concessions to Moscow (which the French worry about), it might at most reduce, to some extent, the immediate Soviet conventional threat to

Europe. But France certainly would not want that to occur at the expense of reopening in a practical way the German question.

Thus, Cartesians would appear to accept, perhaps even secretly welcome, the continued presence in East Germany of at least some divisions of the Red Army. For if Soviet forces were to depart the GDR, Allied divisions might withdraw from the Federal Republic, including the three that are French. France is filled with folks who believe German neutralism and instability would surely follow close behind. Indeed, the political effects in West Germany of the potential withdrawal of a large number of non-indigenous Western divisions from the FRG is a more abiding security concern for some in France than is the level of Soviet forces in the GDR, which are seen as unlikely to attack the West in any event.

These competing but subterranean Western concepts concerning Soviet deployments in the GDR and the future of Germany cannot be reconciled and are therefore not addressed among NATO governments. Instead the Alliance declares, as in its December 11, 1986, "Brussels Declaration on Conventional Arms Control," that its objective is "strengthening stability and security in the whole of Europe, through increased openness and the establishment of a verifiable, comprehensive and stable balance of forces at lower levels." The Alliance cannot get into much trouble with a statement like that. NATO communiqués which require consensus across the Alliance depend on such banalities. But the bedrock differences in objectives among Allies that are hidden by such bland NATO-speak will trouble the West's efforts to produce a conventional arms control proposal that can be supported, both by those in the FRG who want to move along in a measured way towards tangible reaffirmation of the German nation, and those further west who want no such thing.

These long-term political preoccupations in the two alliances will have a decisive effect on the conventional arms control stances of the two sides. Real boldness, as opposed to the rhetorical kind, may be a scarce commodity.

The Warsaw Pact's Budapest Appeal of June, 1986, concerning conventional arms control, would allow Moscow to take its force reductions entirely within the USSR and thus avoid the potential problems with its empire discussed earlier.[13] Even if Moscow were willing to take cuts in Eastern Europe, the substance of the Budapest Appeal appears designed to give the

---

13. Excerpts of the Budapest Appeal are published as, "Address of Warsaw Treaty Member States," *Survival*, Vol. 29, No. 5 (September/October, 1987), p. 463.

Soviet Union sufficient flexibility to ensure that those reductions could be minimal, thereby protecting the geopolitical status quo.[14]

As for the West, gaps between contrary visions of the future of Europe, and the resultant differences in public perceptions in NATO nations on the future of Germany, cannot be narrowed and will not be discussed between governments. Instead, the FRG and France especially will disagree over the philosophy and details of any possible Western proposal. The FRG will wish to use conventional arms control to promote political change in Europe; France will not. The FRG will wish to link conceptually the level of conventional forces on the continent to the nuclear balance in Europe; France will not. The FRG will worry about the negotiability of any Western proposal; France will not. The FRG will accept intensive verification on its soil; France will not. The FRG will easily agree to the collective limitations of a no-increase commitment; France will not. The FRG will be looking aggressively for constraints on the two sides' military forces after the Stockholm agreement of the Conference on Disarmament; France will not. In short, Bonn will want an early and ambitious Western proposal that will fare well in public opinion in the Federal Republic, compared with the Budapest Appeal, and that will propel *Ostpolitik* forward. France will want to proceed with the greatest caution and skepticism.

*What Kind of an American Force in Europe?*

A second conceptual problem relates to the optimum size and makeup of U.S. forces, if any, which ought to be deployed in Europe over the long term, and the relationship of that number to any conventional arms control proposal that the West might put forward. In the early 1950s, when U.S. forces returned to Europe, there was no thought by U.S. decision-makers that these troops would remain in Europe in any numbers for any extended period. As Senator Arthur Vandenberg wrote at the time to a group of constituents concerned with foreign affairs, "I am sure your members will all understand that there is no proposal to put a joint military machine into present physical being . . . except at a planning and equipment level."[15]

---

14. For an analysis of the Budapest Appeal, see Blackwill, "European Security and Conventional Arms Control."
15. Arthur H. Vandenberg, Jr., ed., *The Private Papers of Senator Vandenberg* (Boston: Houghton Mifflin, 1952), p. 419.

In the early days, American nuclear superiority provided the principal guarantee of European security at a time when Soviet nuclear delivery vehicles could not reach the United States. The size of U.S. conventional forces in Europe was less significant in those circumstances than the dominance of the American nuclear deterrent, as long as some U.S. troops were stationed on the continent to serve as a tripwire should the Warsaw Pact attack. When Washington mistakenly concluded in the late 1950s that the Soviets were beginning to catch up in a big way on the nuclear side, the Kennedy administration decided that Eisenhower's "New Look" and threat of massive retaliation were not credible. U.S. forces in Europe were increased from 379,000 to 417,000.[16] During the Vietnam period, the total figure of American troops stationed in Western Europe dropped to 291,000, its lowest since 1950.[17] When that Asian war ended for the United States in 1973, U.S. forces returned to Europe over time and reached their current level of roughly 330,000.[18]

Thus, there has been no clear and consistent notion of what level of U.S. forces is required to make the American contribution to the conventional defense of the continent and to link American military units in Europe to U.S. strategic nuclear forces. The theoretical boundaries on this score stretch from relatively small numbers of U.S. troops in Europe to the present figure. In weighing the right U.S. conventional contribution to the defense of Europe, the following factors are sometimes discussed in the public debate:

—the strategic balance between the two superpowers;
—the respective deployments of nuclear weapons by the two sides in Europe;
—the condition of the conventional balance between NATO and the Warsaw Pact;
—the prevailing judgment about Soviet intentions and the seriousness of the Soviet military threat;
—potential U.S. military obligations outside Europe;
—European assistance in NATO out-of-area problems;
—the relative contribution that West Europeans make to their own defense;
—the trade balance between the United States and Europe, and U.S.-European economic competition in third country markets;

16. Jeffrey Record, *Revising U.S. Military Strategy: Tailoring Means to Ends* (Washington, D.C.: Pergamon-Brassey's, 1984), p. 104.
17. Ibid., p. 104.
18. IISS, *Military Balance, 1986–1987*, p. 30.

—the health of the U.S. economy and the level of resources available for the defense budget; and

—the strength of isolationist and unilateralist tendencies in the United States.

One should now add the relationship between the present level of U.S. forces in Europe, the ideal level (whatever that may be), and the potential role of arms control in equating these two numbers (if they are different). There are analysts and policy-makers on both sides of the Atlantic who argue that virtually no U.S. forces should be withdrawn from Europe as long as the USSR retains a hostile ideology and projects from the Soviet homeland a serious military threat to the West.[19] Thus, notwithstanding whatever cuts Moscow might be willing to accept, anything more than token U.S. troop withdrawals would upset the post-war political balance within Western Europe; compromise American leadership of NATO; undermine extended deterrence; weaken required NATO force-to-space ratios on the Central Front since U.S. troops would not be replaced; exacerbate the Alliance's already serious geographic disadvantages; and result in loss of the withdrawn units from the U.S. force structure for budgetary reasons.

These concerns become ever more salient as the size of proposed U.S. troop cuts in Europe is increased. If one of four U.S. divisions in West Germany can safely be withdrawn in return for adequate compensation from the Soviet Union, what about two out of four? Senator Sam Nunn suggested in Brussels in the spring of 1987 a trade of at least two U.S. divisions for more than thirteen Soviet divisions.[20] But what would happen in such dramatically different circumstances to the political dynamics of NATO and to the U.S. leadership position therein? What reduction in American influence within the Alliance would future administrations find tolerable? It is not obvious that U.S. domestic support for troop deployments in Europe could withstand a significant increase in the number of issues within NATO on which Washington could not get its way. Yet that would surely occur as the United States provided significantly less to NATO defense, whether or not Europeans did more.

---

19. For instance, Caspar Weinberger, "We Need Those Troops in Europe," *Washington Post*, June 22, 1987, p. A19; Elizabeth Pond, "U.S. Envoy to NATO: Alliance Working Well: But Ambassador Abshire Stresses the Need to Beef Up Conventional Forces," *Christian Science Monitor*, December 3, 1986, p. 15; Edward Luttwak, "Entering the Post-Nuclear Age," *New York Times Magazine*, April 5, 1987, pp. 49–51.
20. David Fouquet, "Nunn Urges NATO to Consider 'Bold Innovative' Arms Proposals," *Washington Post*, April 14, 1987, p. A18.

In the wake of an agreement to eliminate intermediate-range nuclear forces (INF), how much U.S. disengagement could occur before Europeans began to conclude that the U.S. nuclear guarantee was no longer credible? Despite U.S. assurances to the contrary, many influential Europeans worry increasingly that the United States has finally begun its long-feared withdrawal from the continent.[21] The sight of sizable numbers of GIs leaving Europe for good would increase that European concern. Which country's forces would replace the U.S. troops? Many Western analysts believe that NATO forces are about as thin along the East-West divide in Europe as they can safely get.[22] But for demographic and budgetary reasons, no NATO ally is likely to take up the slack produced by a U.S. cutback. Could NATO live with a thinner line, given forty years of peace in Europe and the new Soviet leadership?

Further, when American defense spending is decreasing in real terms, could the U.S. afford two sets of equipment for dual-based divisions? Would the U.S. purchase the necessary rapid lift capability to get these divisions back to Europe in a crisis? One certainly wonders, given Army priorities and the budget deficit. Would these withdrawn forces be reconfigured into light divisions for Third World contingencies? How much would that cost? Indeed, would they even remain in active service at all? And if there is a unilateral U.S. move, as Zbigniew Brzezinski recommends, and as Henry Kissinger for several years recommended, to bring home 100,000 or more troops from Europe, where is Moscow's incentive to withdraw its own forces in the context of an arms control treaty?[23]

As the controversy now surrounding the INF zero option has vividly reminded us, these questions should be answered in Washington *before* the U.S. and NATO make a proposal to the Warsaw Pact which Moscow might, again, surprise the West by accepting. For the United States to put aside these troublesome issues in its classified executive and congressional deliberations while inventing simple mechanical formulae calling for American withdrawals from Europe is to invite U.S. confusion and perhaps consternation at a later date.

---

21. "Europe's Braver Colours," *The Economist*, July 11–17, 1987, pp. 11–12.
22. John J. Mearsheimer, "Nuclear Weapons and Deterrence in Europe," *International Security*, Vol. 9, No. 3 (Winter 1984/85), p. 19–46.
23. Zbigniew Brzezinski, *Game Plan: A Geostrategic Framework for the Conduct of the U.S.–Soviet Contest* (Boston: Atlantic Monthly Press, 1986), p. 181. Kissinger has changed his mind and now argues that, "any reduction of conventional forces by the United States would be politically disastrous and must be resisted by any American who believes in the Atlantic Alliance." *Boston Globe*, December 5, 1987, p. 4.

*How to Judge the Conventional Balance?*

The third major conceptual problem of conventional arms control arises from the difficulty of evaluating the present conventional military balance on the continent. If one looks only at the static indicators, the Warsaw Pact clearly enjoys numerical superiority over NATO in men and armaments in Central Europe. There, the East deploys 960,000 ground troops compared to NATO's 790,000 and possesses a 2.4 to 1 advantage in actual combat divisions. It outnumbers the West in fixed wing aircraft, 2,650 to 1,250; in main battle tanks in units, 16,700 to 7,800; in artillery pieces, 9,200 to 3,000; and in crew-served anti-tank missile launchers, 5,000 to 2,000.[24] In the whole of Europe from the Atlantic to the Urals, some of these ratios are better for the West and some are worse, but in no instance does NATO have a numerical advantage. That carries with it unhappy military consequences for the West.

In nuclear arms control since the late 1960s, quantitative disparities have dominated the analytical negotiating framework. Most attention is centered on compiling data bases through national technical means, concerning the ranges of various systems, numbers of launchers, and numbers of warheads on launchers. In the INF negotiations, the effort was to eliminate an entire category of weapons—all land-based missiles with ranges from 500 to 5500 kilometers. At the Strategic Arms Reduction Talks, the two sides have agreed in principle to reduce their respective strategic nuclear forces (those with ranges over 5500 kilometers) by fifty percent. They are discussing how that goal might be applied to achieve lower overall aggregates of launchers and warheads on launchers associated with these systems. In addition, the United States has proposed numerical sub-limits on particularly threatening components of Soviet nuclear forces. In all these cases, it is important to stress that the arms holdings of the two sides can be identified, quantified and to a considerable extent compared. Net assessments may be the stuff of domestic political and analytical debate, but the arguments over these data bases are relatively narrow in character.

In contrast, net assessment of the conventional balance makes these nuclear force comparisons look like the calculations of children manipulating their multiplication tables. First, how does one compare manpower? As Generals Lee and Jackson painfully taught the North in 1861–62, total num-

---

24. These numbers are drawn from the United Kingdom Ministry of Defense, *Statement on Defense Estimates*, 1987.

bers of troops and armaments are often less important than the skill and determination of the individual soldier, relative mobility of opposing forces, and the respective quality of military leadership. The manner in which NATO forces stack up against the East in that regard would surely be crucial to the outcome of war in Europe.

Technology, too, matters a lot. The English use of the longbow against French knights at Crécy in 1346 reminds us that technological advantage can in certain instances make numerical differences between opposing armies trivial.[25] How would the Soviet T-80 tank fare against the American Abrams or the West German Leopard II? The F-16 fighter against the MiG-29?

Measuring to what degree Western technological advantages would compensate for Eastern numerical superiorities is complicated by Moscow's successful efforts in the past decade to narrow the technology gap between the sides.[26] The Soviets have taken the lead in main battle tank modernization, deploying fourth generation T-64B, T-72M and T-80 tanks in the Central Region in numbers that surpass NATO's total tank force. Soviet attack helicopters are now considered roughly equal to those of the West in quality. In factors of air performance, such as range, payload, avionics, and munitions, Eastern aircraft have made considerable strides toward qualitative parity with the West.

How would surprise and sustainability affect the battle? In May of 1940, surprise enabled the German army to march to the English Channel in less than a month and to reach Paris shortly thereafter against a comparatively equal number of French and British forces.[27] Israel's impressive use of surprise against Egypt, Syria and Jordan in June 1967 allowed Israel to seize territory from all three opposing forces.[28]

Sustainability was a critical factor, in 1870, of the Prussian defeat of a French army considered the finest in Europe.[29] And in the American Civil War, the Northern Navy's successful blockade of the Atlantic coast prevented

---

25. On the battle of Crécy see Bernard Brodie and Fawn M. Brodie, *From Crossbow to H-Bomb* (Bloomington: Indiana University Press, 1962), pp. 37–40.
26. The following examples are drawn from Phillip Karber, "Conventional Instabilities in the NATO/Warsaw Pact Balance," unpublished paper for the Aspen Strategy Group, June 15, 1987, pp. 17–26.
27. Richard K. Betts, *Surprise Attack: Lessons for Defense Planning* (Washington, D.C.: Brookings, 1982), pp. 28–34.
28. Ibid., pp. 65–68.
29. William H. McNeill, *The Pursuit of Power: Technology, Armed Force, and Society Since AD 1000* (Chicago: University of Chicago Press, 1982), pp. 250–251.

the South from replenishing its stocks with the European supplies necessary to sustain the war effort.[30] Given the much greater modern rates of lethality and use of ammunition, the two alliances' comparative capacity to keep their war machines going would clearly have a major impact on the outcome of a war in Europe.

Which alliance would have better command and control and intelligence in a war? Which could better depend on its cohesiveness, on the unity of its allies, in crisis and conflict? Would Polish forces be an efficient instrument of Warsaw Pact power projection, or an imminent danger to Soviet lines of communication?[31] Would all conceivable coalition governments of NATO in all conceivable crises really implement Article Five of the North Atlantic Treaty, which states that an attack against one member of the Alliance would be considered an attack against all? Opposing alliances in the War of the Spanish Succession began to shake apart following the initial battle. Savoy, an ally of France, quickly defected to the opposing alliance following the French coalition's losses in Northern Italy.[32] Is NATO entirely immune to Allied governments quickly dropping out of a war that is going badly—or not entering the conflict at all?

Experts reach sharply different conclusions about the impact of all these complicated factors on the conventional balance in Europe.[33] The Soviet Union argues that a rough balance now exists.[34] General Bernard Rogers,

---

30. Ibid., p. 243.
31. This question is examined in Samuel P. Huntington, "Conventional Deterrence and Conventional Retaliation in Europe," *International Security*, Vol. 8, No. 3 (Winter 1983/84), pp. 32–56; and Dale Herspring and Ivan Volgyes, "Political Reliability in the Eastern Warsaw Pact Armies," *Armed Forces and Society*, Vol. 6, No. 2 (Winter 1980), pp. 286–291.
32. B. H. Liddell Hart, *Strategy* (London: Faber and Faber, 1954; second revised ed., New York: New American Library, 1974), p. 74.
33. Somewhat optimistic views of the conventional balance include: William W. Kaufmann, "Nonnuclear Deterrence," in John D. Steinbruner and Leon V. Sigal, eds., *Alliance Security: NATO and the No-First Use Question* (Washington, D.C.: Brookings, 1983), pp. 43–90; William P. Mako, *U.S. Ground Forces and the Defense of Central Europe* (Washington, D.C.: Brookings, 1983); and John J. Mearsheimer, "Why the Soviets Can't Win Quickly in Central Europe," *International Security*, Vol. 7, No. 1 (Summer 1982), pp. 3–39. More pessimistic assessments are found in: Report of the European Security Study (ESECS), *Strengthening Conventional Deterrence in Europe: Proposals for the 1980s* (New York: St. Martins Press, 1983); Nora Slatkin, Congressional Budget Office, *Army Ground Combat Modernization for the 1980s: Potential Cost and Effects for NATO* (Washington, D.C.: U. S. Government Printing Office, November 1982); and chapters by James A. Thomson and Anthony Cordesman in Thomson and Nerlich, *Conventional Arms and the Security of Europe*.
34. *Whence The Threat To Peace*, 4th ed. (Moscow: Military Publishing House, Novosti Press Agency Publishing House, 1987) p. 74. In an interview, Marshal Viktor Kulikov, Commander-in-Chief of the Warsaw Pact forces, argued that "there is no advantage on the part of the Warsaw

recently retired Supreme Allied Commander, asserts that the East possesses clear conventional military superiority in Europe and that, moreover, the trend is getting worse for the West every year. Concerning the political will within the Alliance to redress the imbalance, Rogers has stated that, "if we're not going to let this gap continue to widen—and it does widen every year— every nation's going to have to do more."[35] Although the argument on this vexing subject will continue, it appears difficult if not impossible to factor these largely qualitative factors into a Western arms control methodology that from its beginnings in the 1960s has emphasized numerical standards. At least to this point, neither alliance has managed to figure out how to manage that integration. In the MBFR talks, each side put forward proposals over the years which contained only numerical components.[36] The Warsaw Pact's newest initiative, the Budapest Appeal of June 11, 1986, again emphasizes specific quantitative reductions and constraints on manpower and armaments.

If this conceptual problem of the relationship between arms control and conventional force net assessment was not daunting enough, there is also the geographic factor in this equation. As Soviet negotiators sometimes stress, Moscow cannot be blamed that an ocean separates Western Europe from its primary protector. Nevertheless, the conventional military balance in Europe and the outcome of any war are crucially influenced by NATO's lack of territorial integrity, its minimum strategic depth, and the proximity of Soviet territory and resources to the Central European battlefield, compared to the 6,000 kilometer distance that U.S. forces and material must cross to reach the same area. In such a situation, is even numerical parity in Central Europe a sensible goal for NATO, if the Soviet Union can reintroduce withdrawn forces back into Central Europe much faster than the United States? Or must NATO insist on an agreement with the East which includes Western numerical superiority in the center of the continent to make up for its geographic disadvantages? Here, too, it is hard enough to imagine Western governments reaching a refined consensus on how to factor the operational importance of geography into a conventional arms control proposal, without considering the melancholy fact that the Warsaw Pact does not feel obligated

---

Pact over NATO. There is an approximate balance in conventional weapons between the two alliances." *Danas* (Zagreb), April 14, 1987.
35. Interview, General Bernard Rogers, *Newsweek*, April 27, 1987, p. 27.
36. Prendergast, *Mutual and Balanced Force Reduction*; Keliher, *The Negotiations on Mutual and Balanced Force Reductions*; and Dean, *Watershed in Europe*, pp. 153–184.

to compensate the West for NATO's somewhat awkward political and military shape.

It should be axiomatic that prudent arms control proposals are derived from cautious conclusions about the relevant military balance. Therefore, any sensible Western conventional arms control proposal should proceed logically from judgments about the relative military capabilities of the two sides. But since so much of this determination is based on factors which are subjective or difficult to quantify, proposals are likely to continue to rely for their conceptual basis on simple "bean counting," crude as that approach undoubtedly is. If one could find a way across this particular conceptual abyss, Coronado's Seven Cities of Gold would also probably be within walking distance on the other side.

*Conventional Deterrence?*

Another conceptual impediment to producing a sensible Western conventional arms control initiative has to do with the relationship of deterrence to the conventional balance in Europe. Europeans want NATO's conventional defense to be good enough to forestall early use of nuclear weapons in a conflict, but not so good as to make an extended conventional war on the continent imaginable. Therefore, conventional arms control should not further weaken (and codify) NATO's conventional force posture vis-à-vis the Warsaw Pact, which would increase the likelihood of early Western nuclear use in a war. A European view perhaps less obvious to Americans is that NATO should not construct, through comprehensive conventional parity and deep nuclear reductions on the continent, a nuclear threshold so high that an extended conventional war in Europe could conceivably be fought beneath it. This uncertainty on the part of West Europeans concerning where they want to establish the conventional balance/nuclear threshold confuses the formulation of NATO's long-term objectives in conventional arms control and further complicates the Alliance's search for a comprehensive approach to this subject.

Related to this quintessential NATO dilemma is the nature of deterrence itself. Should West and East succeed, as Reagan and Gorbachev want, in eliminating the role of nuclear weapons in the two alliances' forces, a new military equilibrium would be created that would depend on conventional deterrence to keep the peace. Perhaps this would suffice. After all, conventional deterrence has worked for long periods in the past. The strength of

Persian forces successfully discouraged attacks on their homeland for hundreds of years. The Romans too deterred potential aggressors for centuries. Neither Switzerland nor Sweden have threatened Germany for some time and Mexico has not recently attempted to reclaim Texas by force, despite some occasional temptations to the contrary.

In each of these instances, the massive conventional superiority of one nation appears to have produced a quieting effect on whatever territorial aspirations potential adversaries might have had. One says "might" since it is impossible to be certain why nations refrain from taking certain actions. In these cases, either conventional deterrence held, or these smaller countries had no intention of invading their larger neighbors in the first place. Given the nature of deterrence, causal uncertainty on this matter will always prevail.

Although one can never be certain if conventional deterrence has worked, it is readily apparent when it fails. Wars start. In 431 B.C., Sparta attacked the Athenian empire. In 1980, Iraq invaded Iran. So conventional deterrence is imperfect. Indeed, it has demonstrably collapsed thousands of times in the past twenty-five centuries. And in Europe, it failed in 1812, 1815, 1848, 1870, 1914, and in 1938, 1939, 1940 and 1941. Given this mixed record, the question arises of what risk is acceptable to discover whether conventional deterrence could keep the peace in Europe in the next forty years (and beyond) as perfectly as nuclear deterrence has apparently done since 1945 (assuming Moscow has considered invading Western Europe during this period).

The way this conceptual question is answered will influence one's approach to nuclear weapons deployments on the continent, to the conventional military balance, to the proper level of defense spending, and to the merits of various arms control schemes concerning conventional forces in Europe. The more one worries about the fragility of conventional deterrence, the more cautious one becomes about deep nuclear reductions on the continent and major changes in conventional deployments in Central Europe by the two alliances. Gamblers would want to roll the dice. Those who believe that nuclear weapons in the post-war period have transcended original sin, and thus kept the peace, would be more cautious.

*What Can be Verified?*

A fifth conceptual problem confronting designers of conventional arms control proposals has to do with verification. In view of the constant debates in the past dozen years over the verification of, and compliance with, nuclear arms control agreements, this is hardly a new subject.[37] But the difficulty over the years in verifying various arrangements relating to nuclear forces pales before the challenge of constructing a conventional verification regime which gives the West some hope of uncovering Soviet violations and also has some chance of acceptance by Moscow.

Manpower heads the daunting list. The Warsaw Pact deploys about three million uniformed men full-time in about 200 divisions and over 200 air regiments in Eastern territory west of the Ural Mountains. In its 1986 Budapest Appeal, the Warsaw Pact proposed a cut of 100,000 to 150,000 in each side's forces in one to two years, which would cut three to five per cent of total Eastern manpower. If Moscow decided after those reductions to increase selectively the manning levels among the 190 or so remaining divisions to make up entirely for the required cut, it could do so in a way that would take an act of omniscience for NATO to discover these clandestine force enhancements in a timely way.

This would be the case even if the Soviet Union were to allow unprecedented access to its territory through a regime of dozens of mandatory on-site inspections each year. Should lightning strike and Moscow agree in principle to such numerous challenge inspections, the Soviets could easily, nonetheless, use convoluted modalities to thwart the Western capacity to accumulate accurate information on troop and armament levels. Some of the most obvious means through which the Soviets could confound Western attempts to identify even a minor treaty violation include prolonging the period between inspection request and the arrival of inspectors on the ground, during which forces and weapons could be altered, exchanged or moved; ensuring that inspection teams were too small to do the job; declaring large areas off-limits to Western inspectors; and curtailing inspectors' time on-site and freedom of movement. If Moscow was exceeding its mandated troop or armaments levels, one could expect other creative deceptions from the culture that, after all, invented the Potemkin Village. This is all quite

---

37. See William C. Potter, ed., *Verification and SALT: The Challenge of Strategic Deception* (Boulder, Colo.: Westview, 1980); James A. Schear, "Arms Control Treaty Compliance: Buildup to a Breakdown?" *International Security*, Vol. 10, No. 2 (Fall 1985), pp. 141–182; Jeanette Voas, "The Arms-Control Compliance Debate," *Survival*, Vol. 28, No. 1 (January/February 1986), pp. 8–31; and Albert Carnesale and Richard N. Haass, eds., *Superpower Arms Control: Setting the Record Straight* (Cambridge, Mass.: Ballinger, 1987).

apart from the fact, reflected in the INF and chemical weapons talks, that NATO nations themselves (including the United States) increasingly appreciate the security problems associated with granting frequent and intrusive Eastern inspections on Western territory.[38]

But imagine that such an obligatory inspection at one of the several thousand Warsaw Pact military establishments west of the Urals actually found that a particular division was 500 men above the figure provided NATO by the East. (To assume a comprehensive and detailed data agreement between the two sides on the levels of forces in a zone is a leap to the celestial. And without such a common understanding, as Walter Slocombe has noted, "we can never tell when they give us a piece of data whether it is the correct number, or whether they know we think it is the correct number, or whether it is merely the number they wish us to think is correct.")[39] How would the Alliance decide the relationship of this single overage of 500 men in this single division to the residual Eastern force of almost three million? If one multiplied this disparity in one unit across all divisions in the entire Warsaw Pact, one could assert a violation of about 100,000 men above the residual ceiling. But what Western government would be willing to take that statistical absurdity to its public, especially in a situation in which Moscow was arguing that these extra 500 men were in the inspected division for special training purposes (or because of mumps in their home barracks) and would soon return to their permanent units?

And if, in the exceedingly unlikely event that NATO found a string of such anomalies during a twelve-month period, at what point would Western publics be willing to see their countries withdraw from a solemn treaty with the East because of violations that in total represented a tiny percentage of Warsaw Pact forces? To argue persuasively the military significance of Eastern violations of this kind would test the eloquence of the most defense-minded NATO politician. This had been a major concern of conservative Western analysts throughout MBFR's preoccupation with Warsaw Pact deployments in Central Europe. The problem is so much more serious in the Atlantic-to-the-Urals area, ten times as large as the Warsaw Pact portion of the MBFR

---

38. Michael R. Gordon and Paul Lewis, "The Move to Ban Chemical Weapons: Big Strides and Many More Hurdles," *New York Times*, Nov. 16. 1987, p. A6.
39. Walter Slocombe, "Verification and Negotiation," in Steven E. Miller, ed., *The Nuclear Weapons Freeze and Arms Control* (Cambridge: Harvard University, Center for Science and International Affairs, 1983), p. 85.

zone, that negotiating a verification regime with Moscow that can adequately monitor and thus assess Soviet compliance with manpower limitations seems just about impossible.

To begin to address this problem, a structural approach could be adopted. Units rather than manpower could be used as the primary unit of account in the two alliances' reductions and limitations. Limits on the number of remaining units would allow NATO to identify relatively quickly the introduction of a new unit into the Atlantic-to-the-Urals zone, especially if that unit was moving forward toward the Central Front. But this approach does not deal with increases in either manning or armaments levels in existing units. If an agreement was reached with Moscow, for instance, which saw the removal of six Soviet divisions from Eastern Europe to east of the Urals, with their associated complement of about 1,800 tanks, that would leave a residual ceiling of roughly 49,000 Eastern tanks in the whole of Europe.[40] Given the vast area involved, NATO would have an extraordinarily difficult time in rapidly identifying the reintroduction into the zone of those 1,800 tanks if they were assigned to selected units of the remaining 194 or so Warsaw Pact divisions in the area. On-site inspection would help but would run into similar statistical problems as those associated with manpower limitations. The same goes, with increasing difficulty, for artillery, anti-tank weapons, and so on.

Thus, there is an enormous gap between what NATO would probably ask, in order to acquire some plausible chance of verifying a conventional arms control agreement with the East, and what Gorbachev at his most flexible would likely accept. This discrepancy goes far beyond the nuclear arms control debate in the last two decades, whether verification should be merely "adequate" or, to use the much more stringent term of the Reagan administration, "effective." One of two things would seem to follow. Either verification will become an impenetrable barrier to a conventional arms control treaty between East and West in Europe. Or the United States will have to relax to some extent the strict verification standards which have characterized the Reagan years and to increase its willingness to accept possible undetected violations on the order of tens of thousands of troops and hundreds of tanks, armored personnel carriers and so on.

In that case, bitter arguments about what constituted militarily significant violations could then be expected quickly to follow. This is not an attractive

---

40. United Kingdom, *Statement on Defence Estimates*, 1987, p. 64.

choice for responsible Western political leaders on either side of the Atlantic in a situation in which, especially in the United States, the politics of verification could wash away chances for an agreement or could produce one which could not be reasonably verified.

In 1985, Ronald Reagan told the Congress that, "in order for arms control to have meaning and credibly contribute to national security and to global or regional security, it is essential that all parties to agreements fully comply with them. Strict compliance with all provisions of arms control agreements is fundamental, and this Administration will not accept anything less. To do so would undermine the arms control process and damage the chances for establishing a more constructive U.S.-Soviet leadership."[41]

It is not an exaggeration to say that such a rigorous standard is simply incompatible with conventional force reductions and limitations in the Atlantic-to-the-Urals area.

*Conclusion*

Because of the public affairs pressure coming from Moscow and Gorbachev, NATO nations will pay an increasing penalty with their citizens if they do not respond substantively and soon to the Budapest Appeal of June, 1986. The temptation for individual Western countries and for the Alliance is therefore to develop conventional arms control proposals before thinking through the conceptual questions discussed above.[42] That would be a mistake.

---

41. As quoted in Carnesale and Haass, eds., *Superpower Arms Control*, p. 318.
42. One attempt to integrate these factors is contained in Robert D. Blackwill and James A. Thomson, "A Countdown for Conventional Arms Control," *Los Angeles Times*, October 25, 1987, Part V, p. 1. That piece argues against U.S.-Soviet first-phase reductions and instead calls for a Western conventional arms control proposal that would mandate equal NATO and Warsaw Pact tank and artillery levels both in Central Europe and in the Atlantic-to-the-Urals zone.

# Limiting Offensive Conventional Forces

Jack Snyder

## Soviet Proposals and Western Options

The Soviet-American agreement to ban intermediate-range nuclear forces (INF) throws into high relief the perennial problem of conventional deterrence in Europe. NATO relies on the threat of nuclear escalation as a crucial element in its strategy for deterring an attack by the Warsaw Pact's numerically superior and offensively poised conventional forces. Consequently, as several prominent senators and congressmen have warned, a drift "down the slippery slope toward European denuclearization" would undermine NATO's security unless Soviet capabilities for a conventional offensive were radically reduced at the same time.[1]

Acknowledging this connection between nuclear reductions beyond the INF Treaty and a stabilized conventional balance, the Soviets have proposed mutual reductions in offensive types of conventional weapons, such as tanks and long-range aircraft. According to Soviet arms negotiator Viktor Karpov:

The Soviet position is that armed forces and armaments in Europe should be reduced to such levels as would preclude the possibility of their being used for offensive operations. This could be done first and foremost by scrapping nuclear weapons and by reducing the most dangerous types of arms, which could include tanks, tactical aircraft and strike helicopters.[2]

The Soviets further acknowledge that they enjoy a numerical superiority in tanks and that "the side that is ahead" in a given category of weapons would have to accept asymmetrical cuts.[3]

Among the numerous people who offered helpful suggestions and criticisms, I would particularly like to acknowledge Ted Greenwood, Phillip Karber, Robert Legvold, Barry Posen, and Cynthia Roberts. Hope Harrison provided research assistance, and the National Council for Soviet and East European Research provided financial support.

Jack Snyder is Associate Professor in the Political Science Department and the Harriman Institute for the Advanced Study of the Soviet Union at Columbia University.

1. Representative Les Aspin, "The World after Zero INF," speech delivered to the American Association for the Advancement of Science, Crystal City, Virginia, September 29, 1987, p. 2. See also Senator Sam Nunn, "NATO Challenges and Opportunities: A Three-Track Approach," speech to a North Atlantic Treaty Organization Symposium, Brussels, April 13, 1987.
2. Viktor Karpov, TASS, October 12, 1987; Foreign Broadcast Information Service, Daily Report, Soviet Union (hereinafter FBIS), October 13, 1987, pp. 4–5.
3. Warsaw Pact communique, *Pravda*, May 30, 1987. Gorbachev himself has noted asymmetries

*International Security*, Spring 1988 (Vol. 12, No. 4)
© 1988 by the President and Fellows of Harvard College and of the Massachusetts Institute of Technology.

These are astonishing proposals coming from the Soviets, because they would overturn the main tenets of Soviet military science and eliminate the vast bulk of the Soviets' offensively oriented force posture. One might be excused, therefore, for suspecting that such utopian ideas are intended primarily for their propaganda effect. Indeed, Soviet spokesmen have admitted that "already the very fact of the proclamation of the [defensive conventional] doctrine is having a salutary effect on the climate and the situation in the world."[4]

But public relations is not the whole story. Gorbachev's program of domestic restructuring has created both the need and the possibility for restructuring in the military area as well. Radical conventional arms control is needed to shift investment, manpower, and scarce high-technology resources into the civilian sectors that must thrive if Gorbachev's economic program is to succeed. Conventional restructuring is also needed, Gorbachev believes, because the West's fear of offensive Soviet military power leads it to throw up barriers to increased Soviet participation in the capitalist world market. Such radical changes in military policy may now be possible because the Soviet military is politically weaker now than at any time since 1960.[5]

However, the Soviet military and other potential opponents of conventional restructuring are not utterly supine. While paying lip-service to the idea of a defensive conventional strategy, high-ranking military figures are stressing the need for "counteroffensive" capabilities that would leave the old force posture intact and open the door to a high-technology conventional arms race. Moreover, they are insisting that the Soviet army must not restructure unilaterally. Though some civilian scholars have argued for unilateral cuts, the military is demanding that NATO must reciprocate any reductions in offensive Soviet forces.

NATO may, however, have a hard time identifying forces it could safely give up in exchange for Soviet armor reductions. At present, NATO has not much more than the minimum force needed to man a continuous defense

---

in the conventional force postures of the two alliances "due to history, geography, and other factors," adding that "we are in favor of removing the disparities . . . by reducing their numbers on the side that has a superiority in them." Speech in Prague, April 10, 1987, *Pravda*, April 11, 1987.

4. Vladimir Petrovskii, Deputy Foreign Minister, quoted by TASS, June 22, 1987, cited in FBIS, June 23, p. AA3.

5. For elaboration, see Snyder, "The Gorbachev Revolution: A Waning of Soviet Expansionism?" *International Security*, Vol. 12, No. 3 (Winter 1987/88), pp. 93–131.

line on the Central Front. Even an asymmetric armor-for-armor trade might deplete NATO's defense line beyond the breaking point, leaving it *more* vulnerable to a Pact offensive. Nevertheless, a variety of offensive reductions can be imagined that might enhance the security of both sides. These involve certain kinds of armor-for-armor, airpower-for-airpower, or airpower-for-armor trades. If limitations on the Strategic Defense Initiative (SDI) were negotiated at the same time, the Soviets might be induced to make highly asymmetric conventional cuts, making NATO's problems easier to solve.

The United States has nothing to lose by actively pursuing Gorbachev's proposals for a strictly defensive restructuring of conventional forces. If Gorbachev backs away from his own proposals, propaganda benefits will accrue to the West. Alternatively, if Gorbachev strings the West along in inconclusive talks on offensive force cuts, there is little reason to fear that the West will be lulled into reduced defense spending by the mere act of negotiation. In the past, arms talks have stimulated Western defense efforts (to produce bargaining chips), at least as much as they have lulled the West.[6] If, however, Gorbachev does negotiate in good faith on conventional restructuring, substantial benefits could result. The West would be more secure from Soviet attack, incentives for hair-trigger preemption would be reduced, and—if truly radical conventional restructuring occurred—the path would be cleared for further denuclearization.

In thinking through this issue, I will first discuss Soviet proposals and motivations. What kind of conventional restructuring are the Soviets proposing? How do civilian and military views of conventional restructuring differ? What incentives are leading the Soviets to make these proposals? Are these incentives so strong that the Soviets might reduce their offensive conventional forces unilaterally? What disincentives might hinder a restructuring of the Soviets' conventional force posture?

In the second half of the article, I will discuss possible NATO responses to the Soviet proposals. What criteria should NATO use in evaluating the terms of possible conventional arms control agreements? What weapons should be classified as offensive, and hence subject to limitation? What specific trades might be advantageous to both sides?

---

6. See the detailed, empirical study by Sean M. Lynn-Jones, "Lulling and Stimulating Effects of Arms Control," in Albert Carnesale and Richard N. Haass, *Superpower Arms Control: Setting the Record Straight* (Cambridge, Mass.: Ballinger, 1987), pp. 223–274.

*Soviet Proposals for Non-offensive Conventional Defense*

Soviet proposals have so far addressed only the general principles of conventional restructuring, not its specific content. The touchstone concept, says Gorbachev, is to create "such a structure of the armed forces of a state that they would be sufficient to repulse a possible aggression but would not be sufficient for the conduct of offensive operations."[7] A related aim is to "rule out the possibility of surprise attack. The most dangerous types of offensive arms must be removed from the zone of contact."[8] This would be achieved by the "elimination by mutual agreement of such types of offensive weaponry as tactical long-range bombers, tactical missiles, long-range artillery, large armored formations, etc."[9] Such cuts, the Soviets recognize, would have to be asymmetrical within individual categories of weapons. Thus, the Warsaw Pact has proclaimed its "readiness to rectify in the course of reductions the inequality that has emerged in some elements [of force structure] by way of corresponding cuts on the side that is ahead."[10] In short, the Soviets say, "we are ready for a structure and disposition of our armed forces in zones of contact that would, first, guarantee the other side against sudden attack, and, second, in general exclude the possibility of offensive action against it."[11]

The Warsaw Pact has also announced a unilateral decision to revise the "military-technical" aspects of its doctrine to reflect the principles of non-offensive conventional defense. Previously, the Pact had said that its doctrine was defensive at the "socio-political" level, but offensive on the "military-technical" plane. Military spokesmen, however, have stressed that reductions

---

7. M. S. Gorbachev, "The Reality and Guarantees of a Secure World," *Pravda*, September 17, 1987, pp. 1–2; FBIS, September 17, p. 24.
8. *Pravda*, February 14, 1987; *Current Digest of the Soviet Press* (hereinafter CDSP), Vol. 39, No. 7, p. 23.
9. Comments by Major General Vadim Ivanovich Makarevskii, a retired officer now on the staff of the Institute for World Economy and International Relations, at a roundtable discussion, "Of Reasonable Sufficiency, Precarious Parity, and International Security," *New Times*, No. 27 (July 13, 1987), pp. 18–21, FBIS, July 16, 1987, p. AA5.
10. *Pravda*, May 30, 1987, p. 2.
11. Lt. Gen. Mikhail Abramovich Mil'shtein, in the *New Times* roundtable, FBIS, July 16, 1987, p. AA2. Another formulation specifies the "goal of reorganizing the armed forces of the sides, such that defensive actions would be guaranteed greater success than offensive operations." V. Avakov and V. Baranovskii, "V interesakh sokhraneniia tsivilizatsii," *Mirovaia ekonomika i mezhdunarodnye otnosheniia* (hereinafter MEiMO) No. 4 (1987), p. 30.

in offensive conventional forces will proceed only as part of an agreement with NATO.[12] Sometimes the transition to "non-offensive defense" is also linked to a ban on battlefield nuclear weapons and a NATO no-first-use pledge.[13]

Beyond this, specifics are lacking. "To specify how many rifles, guns, tanks, aircraft and missiles each side should have is impossible at this juncture," says one Soviet commentator. "The concrete parameters will be determined by agreement."[14] It remains unclear, in particular, which kinds of forces the Soviets see as most offensive. They include tanks as prime candidates for reductions and also acknowledge that the Pact must expect to take asymmetrical cuts in this area. Another category that the Soviets normally mention is long-range attack aircraft.[15] Soviet sources state that half of NATO's firepower resides in its air forces,[16] and that NATO enjoys a net superiority in conventional airpower. Thus, demands that NATO take asymmetrical cuts in that area can be expected.[17]

However, nothing so simple as an air-for-armor trade has appeared in Soviet commentary. Rather, there is a tendency to expand the definition of "offensive capability" to cover almost everything. For example, they allege that the West enjoys an advantage in anti-tank weapons and helicopters, implying that the West must take asymmetrical cuts in those categories.[18] Even if this characterization of the balance were true, it would still be puz-

---

12. Colonel-General M. A. Gareev, Deputy Chief of the General Staff, Moscow TV news conference, June 22, 1987, FBIS, June 23, 1987. Colonel-General N. F. Chervov of the General Staff's arms control directorate has said that "one should not expect unilateral steps on the part of the Warsaw Pact. The NATO countries must take practical steps to meet the Warsaw Pact halfway." Ibid., p. AA3.
13. Makarevskii, FBIS, July 16, p. AA5.
14. Mil'shtein, FBIS, July 16, p. AA3.
15. Gareev press conference, FBIS, June 23, 1987, p. AA7. For a discussion of the offensive, first-strike character of NATO's deep-strike air capability, see the interview of Army General A. I. Gribkov, chief of staff of the Warsaw Pact Joint Armed Forces, Krasnaia zvezda, September 25, 1987, pp. 2–3, FBIS, September 30, 1987, p. 5. Thanks to Stephen Meyer for this citation.
16. Christopher N. Donnelly and Phillip A. Petersen, "Soviet Strategists Target Denmark," International Defense Review, Vol. 19, No. 8 (August, 1986), p. 1049, citing Gen. Col. M. Zaytsev, "Organizatsiia PVO," Voyennyi vestnik, No. 2 (1979), p. 23.
17. Major General V. Tatarnikov, "Vienna: Crucial Stage Ahead," Krasnaia zvezda, September 2, 1987, p. 3, FBIS, September 10, 1987, pp. 1–2. A civilian making the same argument is Aleksandr Bessmertnykh, Deputy Minister of Foreign Affairs, Moscow television interview, May 30, 1987, FBIS, June 3, p. CC6.
18. Gareev and Chervov press conference, FBIS, June 23, 1987. These and all other Soviet commentators deny that there is an overall imbalance of conventional forces favoring the Soviet Union.

zling.[19] Anti-tank weapons are hardly offensive, and so should be left alone, according to the principles of non-offensive defense. According to another expansive definition, "the principle of sufficiency [for defensive operations only] also means ending the drive to outstrip the other side in arms development, renouncing the buildup of rapid deployment and other mobile forces, and of enormous facilities for the movement of troops by air and sea."[20]

Another open question is whether the proposed reduction of offensive forces would take place world-wide, "from the Atlantic to the Urals," or primarily in a narrower zone in Central Europe. The Vienna talks on Mutual and Balanced Force Reductions (MBFR) are now being reorganized along the lines of a Soviet proposal for an "Atlantic to the Urals" format. Despite this, Gorbachev continues to stress that "the first step to [wider reductions] could be a controlled withdrawal of nuclear and other offensive weapons from the borders with a subsequent creation along borders of strips of reduced armaments and demilitarized zones."[21] The model provided by the INF Treaty, however, suggests that world-wide limits might be considered for missiles or aircraft. Thus, different geographical zones might be proposed for different types of weapons or for different stages of a phased agreement.

*Civil-Military Divergence on Conventional Defense*

One reason for the vagueness and diversity of Soviet proposals may be that the Soviets disagree among themselves about the proper approach to a defensive conventional strategy. Gorbachev and the civilian defense intellectuals normally talk in terms of making surprise attacks impossible or of enhancing the power of the defense relative to the offense. In this, they draw explicitly on the ideas of the West European left and the Palme Commission report on mutual security in Europe.[22]

---

19. NATO Information Service, *NATO and the Warsaw Pact: Force Comparisons* (Brussels: NATO 1984), shows 18,400 Pact anti-tank guided weapon launchers in or easily deployable to the European theater (35,400 west of the Urals) versus 12,340 for NATO (19,170 including North America). Attack helicopters are counted at 560 (900) for NATO, 1,135 (1,175) for the Pact; unarmed helicopters at 1,900 (6,000) for NATO, 1,180 (1,375) for the Pact.
20. Makarevsky, FBIS, July 16, 1987, p. AA3.
21. *Pravda*, September 17, FBIS, September 17, pp. 24–25.
22. See Avakov and Baranovski, MEiMO, No. 4 (1987), p. 30. For a summary and evaluation of European proposals for a non-offensive defense, see David Gates, "Area Defence Concepts," *Survival*, Vol. 29, No. 4 (July/August 1987), pp. 301–317; and also Jonathan Dean, "Alternative Defense—Answer to NATO's Post INF Problems?" *International Affairs* (London, forthcoming).

Military professionals, however, stress the importance of offensive or counteroffensive capabilities, even in the broader context of a defensive conventional strategy. The Pact's approach to conventional defense must not be "passive," says Army General A. I. Gribkov, the Chief of Staff of the Warsaw Pact Joint Armed Forces.

Gribkov: In the event of an attack taking place, the Warsaw Pact countries' armed forces will operate with exceptional resolve. While repulsing the aggression, they will also conduct counteroffensive operations. This does not contravene the demands of the [defensive] military doctrine, since—as the experience of the Great Patriotic war and local wars shows—such actions are not only possible but necessary within the framework of defensive operations and battles in individual sectors. . . .
Q: Anatoly Ivanovich, if I understand you correctly, it could be claimed that all the most important provisions of the military-technical side of the Warsaw Pact military doctrine are already embodied in the building and training of the Joint Armed Forces. . . .
Gribkov: Yes, that is so. In the past, too, the Warsaw Pact Armed forces trained only to repulse aggressors. Now this process has become even more balanced, purposeful, and coordinated.[23]

In other words, the transition to non-offensive defense would, in Gribkov's view, require little if any fundamental restructuring of Soviet conventional forces.

This reluctance to eliminate offensive capabilities does not mean, however, that the Soviet military sees no merit in a defensive conventional strategy. Even before Gorbachev's discovery of non-offensive defense, authoritative figures on the Soviet General Staff were paying increasing attention to defensive conventional strategies. The former Chief of the General Staff, Nikolai Ogarkov, wrote in 1985 that technological change was undermining the supremacy of the tank on the modern battlefield and the advantage of the attacker over the defender that had allegedly prevailed since World War II. In particular, he saw the development of precision-guided conventional mu-

---

23. Gribkov, FBIS, September 30, 1987, p. 7. For another statement of the view that the defensive doctrine does not mean "passivity," see Rear Admiral G. Kostev, Professor of Military Sciences, "Nasha voennaia doktrina v svete novogo politicheskogo myshleniia," *Kommunist vooruzhennykh sil* (September 1987), pp. 9–15. Similarly, Colonel General V. M. Gordienko argues that "tanks and tank troops are strong not only on the offensive but also in defense. They are capable of quickly becoming an armored shield in the aggressor's way, repulsing the strike by his forces, and moving on to the offensive." Quoted in *Trud*, September 13, 1987, p. 1, FBIS, September 23, p. 70.

nitions as creating new possibilities for both offensive and defensive operations.[24]

Colonel-General M. A. Gareev, a holdover from the Ogarkov era who now
enjoys increased prominence on the General Staff, has laid out the strategic
implications of that view.[25] In the past, says Gareev, Soviet military doctrine
had assumed that there would be plenty of time to mobilize before the
outbreak of war and consequently that Soviet forces would be able to seize
the initiative from the outset of the fighting. But this ignored the possibility
that NATO might attack without warning, or that Soviet political leaders
might be slow in authorizing mobilization and forward deployment out of
the fear that mobilization would inevitably lead to war. Before the Nazi attack,
Gareev notes, Soviet authorities counted on "fighting on the territory of
others," but reluctance to mobilize quickly surrendered the initiative to the
Germans and forced the Soviets to fight on the defensive. "Considering all
of this, the contemporary system of strategic deployment cannot orient itself
exclusively toward one of the contingencies that is most favorable to us, but
should be more flexible and ensure an orderly deployment of forces under
any conditions through which the imperialist aggressors might unleash a
war."[26] In particular, the adoption of a more flexible approach is necessitated
by "the perfection of means of attack by our probable enemies, their counting
on plotting a preemptive blow, and the growing role of the time factor at the
beginning of a war."[27] These conclusions hold "even in battles in which only
conventional arms are used."[28]

However, even if Soviet forces lose the initiative at the outset of the war,
the "defensive" operations that Gareev envisions would be almost indistinguishable from an offensive. Noting a "tendency toward a growing convergence of the forms of action by troops in the attack and on the defense,"
Gareev points out that both the attacker and the defender will be launching

---

24. N. V. Ogarkov, *Istoriia uchit bditel'nosti* (Moscow: Voenizdat, 1985), p. 49.
25. M. A. Gareev, *M. V. Frunze—Voennyi teoretik* (Moscow: Voenizdat, 1985). The following
analysis was spurred in part by the comments of William Burroughs at a conference on Soviet
military policy at the Wilson Center, Washington, D.C., September, 21–23, 1987, though Burroughs should bear no responsibility for the particular interpretation I give here.
26. Ibid., p. 242.
27. Ibid., pp. 242–243. For a recent reassertion of the view that the "surprise factor" is the
"crucial element" in NATO's deep-strike air strategy, see Marshal Viktor Kulikov, commander
in chief of the Warsaw Pact Joint Armed Forces, "NATO: The Threat Remains," *Narodna armiya*
(Sofia), October 13, 1987, FBIS, October 16, p. 3.
28. Gareev, *Frunze*, pp. 243–244.

highly accurate strikes against the "second echelons and reserves" of the opponent.[29] Thus, says Gareev, "contemporary weapons allow . . . great activeness and steadiness of the defense."[30] Gareev's thoughts are therefore not of eliminating offensive weapons, but of using them to shore up the defense and to regain the initiative.

In short, it seems likely that the Soviet military and Soviet civilians are both sincere in considering the merits of defensive conventional strategies, but that they attach nearly opposite meanings to the word "defensive." A somewhat awkward attempt to bridge this gap was a recent article co-authored by Andrei Kokoshin, a deputy director of the U.S.A. and Canada Institute, and V. V. Larionov, a retired military officer who contributed to V. D. Sokolovsky's famous *Military Strategy* in the 1960s.[31] The first two pages reiterate the Warsaw Pact proposal to restructure conventional forces "such that no side, in guaranteeing its own defense, would have the forces for a surprise attack on the other side, or for undertaking offensive operations in general."[32] The bulk of the article, however, describes the battle of Kursk, in which a heavily armored, numerically superior Soviet force launched a massive counterattack after exacting heavy attrition on Germans attacking an impregnable defense line. The authors admit that Kursk has little relevance as an example of "non-provocative defense." Rather, their point was merely to prove that "a pre-positioned defense can resist the powerful onslaught of offensive forces."[33]

It remains to be seen whose definition of conventional defense will prevail, if either does. The civilians could argue that arms control based on the principles of non-provocative defense would obviate the need for the counteroffensive capabilities that the military wants. The persuasiveness of this argument would hinge, presumably, on NATO's willingness to cooperate in such a restructuring and on Gorbachev's political authority vis-à-vis the military.

---

29. Ibid., p. 245.
30. Ibid., p. 246.
31. Andrei Kokoshin and V. V. Larionov, "Kurskaia bitva v svete sovremennoi oboronitel'noi doktriny," MEiMo, No. 8 (August 1987), pp. 32–40.
32. Kokoshin and Larionov, quoting *Pravda*, May 30, 1987, p. 33.
33. Kokoshin and Larionov, MEiMO, No. 8, p. 39. Another important point is their reiteration of Gareev's argument that the problem in June 1941 was not that the Soviets lost the initiative, but rather that the obsessive desire to fight on the territory of others lured them into a deployment that was vulnerable to preemption. Ibid., p. 37.

*Incentives for Change in Soviet Forces and Doctrine*

Gorbachev's motives for proposing a restructuring of conventional forces in Europe are both economic and strategic. Military expenditures have taken a heavy toll on the Soviet economy in usurping a large proportion of funds for industrial investment and in laying priority claim to scarce scientific manpower and high-technology supplies. Conventional forces are the area where big savings might be possible through force reductions.[34] Conventional forces are also an area where a costly high-technology arms race in precision-guided deep-strike weapons is on the horizon. Most interpretations of the ouster of Nikolai Ogarkov as Chief of the General Staff include as a major factor his demands for accelerated investment in this area.[35]

Though Gorbachev's economic reforms are aimed at, among other things, improving Soviet performance in the high-technology sector, big investments in high-technology weaponry in the short run would undermine the needs and logic of Gorbachev's economic plans. Gorbachev is aiming to promote more efficient allocation of productive resources by introducing limited market mechanisms. The military's idea of economic reform has little in common with this. Though military reformers understand that their own programs depend on better performance of the civilian economy, they apparently advocate a somewhat streamlined version of the traditional command economy, which would allow them to retain their traditional leverage in requisitioning

---

34. Sophisticated studies of the effects of restraint in Soviet defense spending have concluded that freezing military outlays at the 1980 level would result in a 0.5 to 1.0 per cent increase in per capita consumption. Abraham Becker, *Sitting on Bayonets: The Soviet Defense Burden and the Slowdown of Soviet Defense Spending* (Santa Monica: RAND/UCLA Center for the Study of International Behavior, JRS-01, December 1985), p. 33, citing Gregory Hildebrandt, "The Dynamic Burden of Soviet Defense Spending," in *The Soviet Economy in the 1980s: Problems and Prospects*, Selected Papers Submitted to the Joint Economic Committee, Congress of the United States, Part 1, pp. 331–350, and Mark Hopkins and Michael Kennedy, *The Tradeoff between Consumption and Military Expenditures for the Soviet Union during the 1980s* (Santa Monica: RAND R-2927, November 1982). These do not address the effects of larger cuts, however, or of defense cuts on investment in civilian high technology sectors. For the argument that "the most critical economic burden of defense expenditures is the preemption of advanced technology and sapping of the economy's innovational energies," see Stanley H. Cohn, "Economic Burden of Soviet Defense Expenditures: Constraints on Productivity," *Studies in Comparative Communism*, Vol. 20, No. 2 (Summer 1987), pp. 145–162.
35. See Bruce Parrott, *The Soviet Union and Ballistic Missile Defense*, SAIS Papers in International Affairs No. 14, (Boulder, Colo.: Westview, 1987); Jeremy R. Azrael, *The Soviet Civilian Leadership and the Military High Command, 1976–1986* (Santa Monica: RAND R-3521-AF, June 1987).

resources through the administrative apparatus.[36] Conventional arms control would help Gorbachev to justify ending this requisitioning system whereby the army gets the good computer chips and everyone else gets the dregs.

In addition to seeking direct economic gains from conventional reductions, Gorbachev also understands that the Soviet military threat to Europe is a barrier to improved political and economic relations with the West. The hope for increased Soviet integration into the world economy plays a significant role in Gorbachev's domestic economic plans. Unlike Brezhnev, he realizes that trade, credits, and technology transfers will be hindered if the Europeans perceive a looming Soviet military threat.[37]

Finally, it is possible that Gorbachev and even Gareev might see significant security benefits in limiting offensive conventional weapons. Especially in light of the Soviet military's evident preoccupation with the threat from NATO's "emerging technologies" of precision-guided, deep-strike attacks, halting such deployments might be seen as a major benefit for which the Soviets might be willing to pay a considerable price. Moreover, conventional arms control would enhance Soviet security by clearing the way towards further denuclearization.

*Barriers to Restructuring Soviet Conventional Forces*

One way to address the question of the barriers to restructuring the Soviet conventional posture is to ask why they embarked on an offensive conventional build-up in the first place. The most persuasive explanation is that the emergence of the offensive "conventional option" in the 1960s was due to the preferences and power of the professional military in the Brezhnev years. Given the steep decline in the military's power and autonomy in the Gorbachev period, this barrier to conventional restructuring has been lowered, though not eliminated.

One possible explanation for the Soviets' offensive inclinations in conventional strategy—the export of revolution to Western Europe by force of

---

36. George Weickhardt, "The Soviet Military-Industrial Complex and Economic Reform," *Soviet Economy*, Vol. 2, No. 3 (July/September 1986), pp. 193–220, esp. pp. 211, 220. For an argument stressing the long-run compatibility of military and civilian economic modernization, see Abraham Becker, "Gorbachev's Program for Economic Modernization and Reform: Some Important Political-Military Implications," (Santa Monica: RAND P-7384, September 1987).
37. See Snyder, "The Gorbachev Revolution: A Waning of Soviet Expansionism?" esp. pp. 115–116.

arms—can be easily ruled out. At least since Stalin's death, "defending the gains of socialism" has been seen as the only legitimate use of Soviet military forces in battle. The *diplomatic* exploitation of Soviet offensive military power did receive some doctrinal sanction under Brezhnev, but as I have argued, Gorbachev now sees the offensive shadow of Soviet military capabilities as more a hindrance than a help to diplomacy.[38]

Purely strategic explanations for the Soviets' offensive conventional stance are also unpersuasive or obsolete. In the late 1940s, an offensive conventional capability might have been desired to hold Western Europe hostage in an era of American atomic monopoly.[39] If so, this function is certainly obsolete in the era of nuclear parity. Also in the late 1940s, the Soviets worried that America would rerun its strategy in World War II: keep a toehold in Eurasia, mobilize its huge economy for war, and use the toehold as a bridgehead for regaining control of Europe.[40] Though no one has discovered direct textual evidence that the Soviets still think that way, Michael MccGwire has argued that the need to eliminate the American toehold in Eurasia at the outset of any conventional war was the main consideration impelling the Soviets to adopt an offensive conventional strategy.[41] However, MccGwire now believes that the Soviets have recently downgraded their estimate of the likelihood of a global conventional war, allowing them to move towards a defensive strategy for Central Europe.[42]

A better explanation for the conventional offensive strategy, as it emerged in the 1960s, is the preferences and power of the professional military. Military authorities and commentators began to argue for a conventional option in 1963, in the face of Khrushchev's demands for extreme cuts in conventional manpower.[43] A defensive conventional option would have

---

38. For elaboration and supporting citations, see ibid.
39. This is argued, with little or no textual evidence, by Thomas W. Wolfe, *Soviet Power and Europe, 1945–1970* (Baltimore: Johns Hopkins University Press, 1970). Notra Trulock and Phillip Petersen, "Soviet Views and Policies toward Theater War in Europe," paper presented at a conference at the Wilson Center, Washington, D.C., September 21–23, 1987, p. 4, have uncovered a rare Soviet statement from 1965 that explicitly asserts that "Europe will remain hostage to the Soviet Army."
40. Raymond L. Garthoff, *Soviet Strategy in the Nuclear Age* (New York: Praeger, 1958), p. 136, citing a 1950 article in *Voennaia mysl'*.
41. Michael K. MccGwire, *Military Objectives in Soviet Foreign Policy* (Washington, D.C.: Brookings, 1987).
42. Michael K. MccGwire, "Soviet Military Objectives," *World Policy Journal*, Vol. 4, No. 4 (Fall 1987), pp. 723–731. In particular, he notes the incentive to stay on the defensive in Europe in the event of a limited war in the Near East.
43. Carl A. Linden, *Khrushchev and the Soviet Leadership, 1957–64* (Baltimore: Johns Hopkins

served their purpose poorly, since defense, being easier than offense, could not justify a large, diversified, modernized conventional military establishment.[44] Khrushchev's policies provoked the disaffection of a whole panoply of conservative vested interests, both civilian and military, and led to his removal. Brezhnev thus learned that these interests, including military interests, had to be accommodated, so he accepted the expensive offensive conventional option, even though its quest for a decisive victory might provoke the very nuclear escalation that it promised to prevent.[45]

Under Gorbachev, Soviet politics works differently, and the power of the military has diminished accordingly. Whereas Brezhnev had, until his final years, appeased the military and other interest groups, the whole logic of Gorbachev's reforms compels him to resist the vested interests. Industrial bureaucrats and orthodox ideologues have come in for the heaviest criticism, but the prestige and practices of the military have also come under fire.[46] Defense Minister Sokolov, removed after hinting that the military was exempt from *perestroika* (restructuring), was replaced by Dmitri Yazov, who jumped over fifty more senior officers to take the post.[47] Yazov, not surprisingly, is a big supporter of Gorbachev's idea of a defensive restructuring of Warsaw Pact force posture.[48]

It should not be concluded, however, that the military is so weak that Gorbachev can force through any military policy he wants. The Chief of the General Staff, Sergei Akhromeev, his key deputy on doctrinal matters, Makhmut Gareev, and the Commander of the Warsaw Pact forces, Viktor Kulikov, are all holdovers from the pre-Gorbachev era. As Gribkov's *Red Star* interview demonstrates, the military is still able to express its own interpretation of what current policy is—or should be.[49] If the military's arguments are con-

University Press, 1966), pp. 191–92; Thomas W. Wolfe, *Soviet Strategy at the Crossroads* (Cambridge: Harvard University Press, 1964), pp. 121–23, 131, 149–152.

44. For theoretical support, see Barry R. Posen, *The Sources of Military Doctrine: France, Britain, and Germany Between the World Wars* (Ithaca: Cornell University Press, 1984), esp. p. 49.

45. For elaboration of this and the following arguments, see Snyder, "The Gorbachev Revolution: A Waning of Soviet Expansionism?" pp. 106–107, 123–124.

46. This is extensively documented by Dale B. Herspring, "On *Perestroyka*: Gorbachev, Yazov, and the Military," *Problems of Communism*, Vol. 36, No. 4 (July–August 1987), pp. 99–107.

47. *New York Times*, May 31, 1987.

48. *Pravda*, July 27, 1987, p. 5.

49. Indeed, it is even conceivable that the authority of the military may already be rebounding from its nadir in June 1987, when then candidate Politburo member Boris Yeltsin charged the military with "smugness, boasting, and complacency." *Krasnaia zvezda*, June 17, 1987. Though pressure for military reforms has been maintained, outright denunciations of this kind have not been repeated.

vincing, they might win adherents among Politburo members who have spoken against precipitous change, like Shcherbitsky and Ligachev—or even among those of Gorbachev's allies, like Lev Zaikov, who have connections to military or military-industrial interests.[50]

In short, Gorbachev has strong economic and security incentives for a defensive restructuring of conventional forces in Europe. Moreover, he has fair prospects for pushing this policy through. The main explanation for the emergence of an offensive conventional option under Brezhnev was the power and preferences of the professional military, but now the power of the military has been significantly curtailed. The independent emergence of an interest in a conventional counteroffensive suggests that military preferences may also be evolving.

*The Prospects for Unilateral Soviet Conventional Cuts*

Despite these favorable circumstances, political conditions and economic incentives for conventional restructuring are not so propitious that the Soviet Union can be expected to do it unilaterally. It is true that a few civilian scholars, fearing that NATO will not respond favorably to Gorbachev's proposals for conventional arms control, have begun to argue for unilateral Soviet moves.[51] Their political arguments for unilateral moves are very sophisticated, following the general logic that Gorbachev has applied to other aspects of East-West diplomacy. The U.S. seeks to wreck the Soviet reforms, they say, by compelling the Soviet Union to run a high-technology arms race in areas of Western comparative advantage, like SDI. Instead of falling into this trap, they argue, the Soviet Union should offset SDI with cheap technical countermeasures. Likewise, it should revive Khrushchev's policy of unilateral troop cuts, which coincided with "a rapid growth of the prestige and influence of the Soviet Union and the gradual improvement of the world situation." Soviet security was not harmed by these unilateral moves, they claim,

---

50. Snyder, "Gorbachev Revolution: A Waning of Soviet Expansionism?" pp. 127–128. A final barrier to conventional arms control, some argue, is the Soviets' need to maintain a large force in Eastern Europe to prevent revolts there. However, none of the reductions in armored forces discussed in this article would prevent the Soviet Union from using light infantry forces to maintain its hegemony in Eastern Europe.
51. Vitaly Zhurkin, deputy director of the U.S.A. and Canada Institute, Sergei Karaganov, a section head at the Institute, and Andrei Kortunov, a senior researcher there, "Reasonable Sufficiency—or How to Break the Vicious Circle," *New Times*, No. 40 (October 12, 1987), pp. 13–15. See also their article in *S.Sh.A.: Ekonomika, Politika, Ideologiia* (December 1987).

because of "a broad peace offensive which made [it] virtually impossible for the West to bring additional military pressure to bear on our country."[52]

However, the success of these advocates of unilateral concessions is doubtful. Even on the issue of responding to SDI, there are signs of some backsliding from Gorbachev's stance in favor of cheap countermeasures. Military calls for emulating SDI, common in earlier years, were taboo during most of 1986 and 1987. Recently, however, Akhromeev has been able to reiterate his earlier view that if the United States were to deploy SDI, "the Soviet Union would also have to equip itself with a nuclear shield."[53] Thus, even in an area where civilian science advisers can offer countervailing expertise, the military is able to put up a rear-guard battle. Its hand is likely to be even stronger in the area of conventional forces, where few if any Soviet civilians can produce detailed operational analyses to challenge the General Staff.[54] The civilians complain that "the absence of reliable information is often used by unscrupulous propaganda agencies for the systematic exaggeration of data and the fabrication of nonexistent 'threats'."[55] According to oral reports, their lack of expertise is hindering the development of detailed proposals for non-offensive conventional defense, though an Academy of Sciences commission headed by Evgenii Velikhov is seeking to develop such proposals.

In short, three competing assessments of Soviet interests in conventional restructuring might be advanced: (1) that they are interested primarily in its propaganda value, (2) that they are so interested in conventional cuts that they will carry them out unilaterally, or (3) that they will make major cuts only if NATO reciprocates through an arms control agreement. Though the first two interpretations cannot be entirely ruled out, the third view seems more plausible. Gorbachev needs and wants a conventional restructuring as

---

52. Zhurkin, et al., "Reasonable Sufficiency," p. 14. They also stress that "the bulk of the costs of the military confrontation is accounted for by the combined arms units and conventional armaments." Ibid., p. 15.
53. *New York Times* interview, October 30, 1987, p. A6. For background on this issue, see Parrott, *The Soviet Union and Ballistic Missile Defense*, chapter 5. Gorbachev continues to call for cheap countermeasures to SDI. See his interview with Tom Brokaw, *New York Times*, December 1, 1987, p. A12.
54. For a discussion of the military's analytical monopoly, see Condoleezza Rice, "The Party, the Military, and Decision Authority in the Soviet Union," *World Politics*, Vol. 40, No. 1 (October 1987), pp. 66–71. For Akhromeev's opposition to unilateral Soviet reductions of conventional forces and to a conventional strategy of "passive defense," see his "Doktrina predotvrashcheniia voiny, zashchity mira i sotsializma," *Problemy mira i sotsializma*, No. 12 (December 1987), pp. 23–28.
55. Zhurkin, et al., "Reasonable Sufficiency," p. 15.

a key element in his economic and security strategy, but it seems probable that he will be able to win the argument against Soviet skeptics only if he can get a reduction in the NATO high-technology threat as a quid pro quo.[56] If so, this raises the question of what the West might safely offer in exchange for a reduction of the Soviet offensive ground-forces threat to Europe.

*Criteria for Conventional Arms Control in Europe*

In evaluating possible conventional arms control deals, the West must keep in view three crucial ratios: (1) the NATO/Warsaw Pact balance of conventional firepower, (2) NATO's force-to-space ratio on the Central Front, and (3) the offense-defense balance.[57] Any deal must be judged by its net effects according to all three criteria. For example, focus solely on reductions in offensive types of forces might actually reduce NATO's security if this led to a thinning-out of NATO's armored forces on the North German plain. Since the firepower balance and the force-to-space ratio are discussed in detail elsewhere in this volume, I will devote greater attention to the offense-defense balance.

### THE NATO/PACT BALANCE

One of the main barriers to conventional arms control in the past has been a disagreement between NATO and the Warsaw Pact about the state of the European conventional balance. While the Soviets deny that they enjoy a net superiority in conventional military power in Europe, Western governments and many independent military analysts contend otherwise. The most sophisticated measures of the ground-forces balance, which express firepower in terms of "Armored Division Equivalents," portray a 1.2:1 Pact advantage at the beginning of the mobilization process. As both sides add reinforce-

---

56. In part, this hinges on one's assessment of how powerful Gorbachev is, not only vis-à-vis the military, but in general. For two quite different assessments, see Thane Gustafson and Dawn Mann, "Gorbachev's Next Gamble," *Problems of Communism*, Vol. 36, No. 4 (July/August 1987), pp. 1–20, and Jerry F. Hough, "Gorbachev Consolidating Power," ibid., pp. 21–43.

57. For a more comprehensive discussion of the factors affecting the conventional balance and NATO's prospects in a conventional war, see John J. Mearsheimer, "Strategy, Numbers, and the European Balance," *International Security*, Vol. 12, No. 4 (Spring 1988), pp. 174–185. Mearsheimer, however, neglects the offense-defense balance.

ments from the rear, the Pact advantage increases to 1.6:1, in the view of some analysts, or perhaps to as much as 2:1, in the view of others.[58]

Some observers contend that this Pact advantage is offset by NATO advantages in airpower and logistics and also by the advantage of defending prepared ground. The logistics advantage has been estimated by Barry Posen to warrant multiplying NATO's firepower score by 1.5.[59] The advantage of the defender, which is greater for tactical engagements on a narrow front than it is for the theater as a whole, has been estimated at anywhere from 1.4:1 to over 3:1.[60] According to purloined lecture notes from the Soviet General Staff Academy, the Soviets hold that attackers need a superiority of 3 or 4:1 in breakthrough sectors, but only 1.0 to 1.5:1 in the theater as a whole.[61] No one has tried to express NATO's advantage in the air as a summary ratio. Though the Pact has more planes and tactical missiles in most categories, most observers contend that NATO's qualitative edge will allow NATO to achieve partial air superiority in the first weeks of the war and then go on to use that air power effectively in the land battle as well.[62]

NATO's official arms control positions have not accepted these more optimistic assessments of the conventional balance. Consequently, at the Vienna talks on Mutual and Balanced Force Reductions, the West has always insisted on asymmetrical Soviet cuts. The Soviets, however, continue to contend that, despite asymmetries in particular types of weapons, there is an overall equality in NATO and Warsaw Pact forces in the European theater.[63] Given official Western views of the balance, this Soviet contention will continue to plague any conventional arms talks.[64] However, if the negotiations are couched in

---

58. For the former estimate, see Barry R. Posen, "Is NATO Decisively Outnumbered?" *International Security*, Vol. 12, No. 4 (Spring 1988) pp.186–202. Somewhat more pessimistic studies are cited in Andrew Hamilton, "Redressing the Conventional Balance: NATO's Reserve Military Manpower," *International Security*, Vol. 10, No. 1 (Summer 1985), pp. 111–136, see esp. Table 3. William P. Mako, *U.S. Ground Forces and the Defense of Central Europe* (Washington, D.C.: Brookings, 1983) offers the fullest explanation of how division equivalents are calculated.
59. Posen, "Is NATO Decisively Outnumbered?" and also "Measuring the European Conventional Balance: Coping with Complexity in Threat Assessment," *International Security*, Vol. 9, No. 3 (Winter 1984/85), pp. 47–88.
60. Hamilton, "Redressing," p. 122, note 7.
61. Donnelly and Peterson, "Soviet Strategists Target Denmark," pp. 1047–1051, figure 5.
62. See, for example, Ted Greenwood, "The Role of Airpower in a NATO-Warsaw Pact Conventional Conflict," in Philip Sabin, ed., *The Future of U.K. Airpower* (London: Brassey's, forthcoming, 1988).
63. Chervov and Gareev press conference, FBIS, June 23, 1987.
64. On this and other barriers to progress in conventional arms control, see Robert D. Blackwill, "Conceptual Problems of Conventional Arms Control," *International Security*, Vol. 12, No. 4 (Spring 1988) pp. 28–47.

terms of reducing offensive forces rather than redressing the alleged NATO/ Pact imbalance *per se*, asymmetrical Soviet cuts might be accepted under the guise of reducing destabilizing armored forces. This would give Gorbachev a fig leaf, allowing him to avoid an explicit acknowledgement that Pact forces had been superior all along.

A related question is whether NATO should worry more about the small imbalance at the beginning of mobilization or about the larger imbalance when forces from the Western USSR arrive at the front. To address the former concern, reductions could be limited to the two Germanies and perhaps Poland and Czechoslovakia. To address the latter, forces throughout Europe from the Atlantic to the Urals—and perhaps world-wide inventories—would have to be limited.

The initial period is of concern because NATO's forward defense line would not be in place until about the fourth day of mobilization.[65] Assuming that the Pact gets a three or four day jump on NATO's mobilization, the Pact might attack before a coherent forward defense line could be formed. As a result, NATO would lose the substantial advantages of a prepared defense. Moreover, the Pact might gamble on completing a lightning victory before NATO could decide to use nuclear weapons.[66] On the other hand, recent intelligence revelations suggest that Soviet forces in Germany are less ready for this kind of "standing start" attack than had previously been believed.[67]

Consequently, some Western analysts worry more about a slow, attritional campaign after several weeks of preparatory mobilization on both sides. However, this would give NATO the advantages of a prepared defense and plenty of time to confer on the use of nuclear weapons. Moreover, John Mearsheimer's historical studies show that modern statesmen have launched conventional wars only when they thought that such a slow, attritional struggle could be avoided.[68]

In conclusion, conventional arms control could contribute to NATO's security by redressing the small imbalance favoring the Pact at the outset of mobilization, and possibly also the somewhat larger imbalance when rein-

---

65. Phillip A. Karber, "In Defense of Forward Defense," *Armed Forces Journal International* (May 1984), pp. 27–50, esp. p. 37.
66. Richard K. Betts, *Surprise Attack: Lessons for Defense Planning* (Washington, D.C.: Brookings, 1982), is the most thorough analysis of this problem. Challenging Betts' view that attempts to achieve surprise almost always succeed at the outset of a war is Ariel Levite, *Intelligence and Strategic Surprises* (New York: Columbia University Press, 1987).
67. Aspin speech, September 29, 1987, p. 12.
68. John J. Mearsheimer, *Conventional Deterrence* (Ithaca: Cornell University Press, 1983).

forcements from the Western USSR arrive. However, even given current force ratios, neither the blitzkrieg nor the attritional scenario looks attractive from the vantage points of the Soviet war planner. Consequently, redressing the alleged NATO/Pact imbalance need not be the dominant consideration in conventional arms talks.

NATO'S FORCE-TO-SPACE RATIO

Of greater concern is the need to maintain a sufficiently thick NATO forward defense line near the inner-German border. A defender's force needs depend as much on the width of the front to be defended as on the size of the attacking force.[69] At Thermopylae, a few good Greeks held off the Persian multitudes by clogging the narrow pass so that the Persians could attack them with only a few men at a time. Armored warfare on a thickly defended front is analogous. The advantage of the attacker is that he can choose the time and place of the engagement, using the initiative to build up a substantial local superiority. However, according to Posen's estimates, an attacker cannot profitably concentrate more than three armored division equivalents (ADEs) on a 50 kilometer section of the front.[70] No matter how many forces the attacker has at his disposal, they will have to be stacked up in reserve, waiting to exploit any breakthrough. If the defender can deploy one ADE in this sector, then the presumed ability of a defender to hold his ground against 3:1 odds should prevent a rapid breakthrough. This should buy sufficient time for the defender to bring reinforcements to the threatened sector. NATO's present posture allows it to deploy one to two ADEs per 50 kilometer sector at the outset of mobilization. By the second week of mobilization, NATO could add eight and one-half ADEs in reserve to stem concentrated breakthrough attempts.[71] Thus, NATO has enough firepower on the ground to provide the minimum acceptable force-to-space ratio.[72]

---

69. Posen, "Measuring the European Conventional Balance," p. 55 and passim; John J. Mearsheimer, "Why the Soviets Can't Win Quickly in Central Europe," *International Security*, Vol. 7, No. 1 (Summer 1982), pp. 3–39, and "Strategy, Numbers, and the European Balance."
70. This discussion is based on Posen, "Measuring the European Conventional Balance," pp. 74–78.
71. This assumes one ADE per 50 km along 500 km of rough terrain and one ADE per 25 km along 250 km of flat terrain, yielding a requirement of twenty ADEs to cover the front with no strategic reserve. NATO has twenty-three or more ADEs on the central front at the outset of mobilization. Calculations are based on Posen, "Is NATO Decisively Outnumbered?" and "Measuring the European Conventional Balance," p. 75.
72. Phillip Karber, using a slightly different method of measurement, reports similar findings. Karber, "Forward Defense," pp. 34–36.

Though NATO's force-to-space ratio is acceptable at present, substantial cuts reducing this force-to-space ratio on likely breakthrough sectors would raise serious questions about the integrity of NATO's forward defense line. This might be true even if the Soviets accepted asymmetrical cuts in armored forces on the Central Front. At Thermopylae, Xerxes would gladly have given up many of his Persians in exchange for a few Greeks. Consequently, NATO should be wary of Soviet assertions that "the threat of offensive operations would naturally become less by sharply cutting the overall numbers of troops."[73]

THE OFFENSE/DEFENSE BALANCE

The third criterion is whether an arms control deal would shift the offense/defense balance in favor of the side that remained on the defensive. By this yardstick, good arms control should ensure that the attacker would suffer disproportionate attrition and that the benefits from striking first would be minimized.[74]

What kinds of forces disproportionately aid the attacker and which aid the defender? Certainly, it is easy to design a strictly defensive force starting with a *tabula rasa*. One might allow fortifications, anti-tank weapons, militia for local defense, and short-range air-defense fighters, while banning everything else. But in the real world the offensive or defensive implications of a particular weapon system depend on the broader context. A fortification can be an offensive weapon if an aggressor uses it to secure his flank or rear, so that he can concentrate overwhelming force against his victim on another front.

This qualification notwithstanding, it is possible to make rough judgments about the relative offensiveness of different weapons.[75] In fact, the U.S. Army

---

73. Viktor Karpov, TASS, October 12, 1987, FBIS, October 13, p. 5.
74. For a theoretical treatment, see Robert Jervis, "Cooperation under the Security Dilemma," *World Politics*, Vol. 30, No. 2 (January 1978), pp. 167–214.
75. It is a widely believed myth that the European powers were unable to define "aggressive armaments" in the 1930s because of the inherent intellectual difficulty of the task. In fact, the powers failed to agree on such a definition because some of them did not want to give up their offensive weapons and because all of them sought to define as "defensive" whatever type of weapon they happened to have in disproportionate quantity. The problem was entirely volitional, not intellectual. Indeed, then as now, serious arms controllers identified tanks, heavy mobile artillery, and long-range ground-attack aircraft as the preeminently offensive weapons. The conclusion is made quite clear in Marion Boggs, *Attempts to Define and Limit "Aggressive" Armament*, University of Missouri Studies, Vol. 16, No. 1 (Columbia, Mo.: University of Missouri, 1941), pp. 41, 48–49, 98–100.

has done so. In calculating Armored Division Equivalents, the U.S. Army gives weapons different scores depending on whether they are to be used in offensive or defensive tactical operations. Tanks and armored personnel carriers are the only categories that are given a higher value in the offensive than on the defensive. Anti-tank weapons, artillery, mortars, and armed helicopters all count more when they are used in a defensive operation. (See Table 1.) Fixed-wing aircraft are not scored in this way by the army, but one civilian analyst boosts by 20% the value of close-air-support planes, like the A-10, when they are used in the defensive.[76]

Some of these classifications are open to debate. It might be argued, for example, that *all* forces, even tanks, are more effective on the defensive, since they can take advantage of terrain cover, whereas their targets must expose themselves during the attack. In relative terms, however, the defender's terrain advantage is more essential for vulnerable anti-tank weapons or for armed helicopters, which must hide behind the tree-line. In contrast, the tank's combination of firepower, maneuverability, and protection diminishes the defender's advantage. This is much less true for lightly-protected armored personnel carriers, the army's scoring notwithstanding. Conversely, many analysts would dispute the army's view that self-propelled artillery is a predominantly defensive weapon, given its role in suppressing anti-tank

**Table 1.   Offensive and Defensive Weapons**

|  | Value in: | |
| --- | --- | --- |
|  | **Offense** | **Defense** |
| Tanks | 64 | 55 |
| Armored personnel carriers | 13 | 6 |
| Anti-tank weapons | 27 | 46 |
| Artillery | 72 | 85 |
| Mortars | 37 | 47 |
| Armed helicopters | 33 | 44 |

SOURCE: William Mako, *U.S. Ground Forces*, appendix tables A-2 through A-14, pp. 114–125. One armored division equivalent equals 47,490 points. Based on U.S. Army figures for 1974.

76. Joshua M. Epstein, *Strategy and Force Planning: The Case of the Persian Gulf* (Washington, D.C.: Brookings, 1987), table D–1, note "r."

defenses during a breakthrough attempt. For this reason, conventional arms control proposals often seek to limit both tanks and artillery.[77]

Tanks represent over two-thirds of the firepower in a Soviet armored division and over one-third of the firepower in a Soviet mechanized division. The comparable figures for an American division are about two-fifths and one-fourth, respectively.[78] Thus, especially in the Soviet case, there is plenty of room for reducing the proportion of offensive firepower.

There is also plenty of room on both sides for increasing the investment in fortifications, which tend to favor the defender. NATO cannot build a Maginot Line because of the Germans' aversion to the symbolic division of their country. However, more limited but still useful measures could be taken to prepare barriers and pill-boxes in key breakthrough sectors. Such defenses were highly successful in the 1973 Arab-Israeli War.[79] One study argues that $5 billion invested in fortifications would have a payoff equal to $25 billion invested in ten additional maneuver divisions.[80] At present, NATO intends to do most of its terrain preparation during the first few days of mobilization. According to one estimate, even this level of fortification and mining, if successfully completed before an attack, might increase the effectiveness of the forces on the forward defense line by as much as one-third.[81] Investing in better terrain preparation does not depend on arms control, of course. It would be desirable even on a unilateral basis. However it might be more palatable to the Germans as part of a conventional arms control package.

Identifying offensive and defensive types of aircraft and missiles is an especially knotty problem. In one view, NATO airpower as a whole should be seen as defensive, in the sense that its job is either to kill offensive Soviet tanks or to destroy Soviet airpower (which exists to hinder the killing of Soviet tanks). This view notwithstanding, some distinctions can be made. Some aircraft are primarily defensive by almost any standard. Specialized air-defense interceptors, like the F-15, are obviously in this category.[82] Simi-

---

77. For example, Robert D. Blackwill, "Conceptual Problems of Conventional Arms Control," proposes common ceilings on tanks and artillery, p. 47. Aspin's September 29 speech, p. 12, stresses "deep reductions and limitations on armored forces—primarily tanks."
78. Mako, *U.S. Ground Forces*, appendix tables A-2 through A-14, pp. 114–125.
79. Major J. B. A. Bailey, Royal Artillery, "The Case for Pre-placed Field Defences," *International Defence Review*, Vol. 17, No. 7 (July, 1984), pp. 887–892.
80. J. F. C. Tillson, "The Forward Defense of Europe," *Military Review*, Vol. 66, No. 5 (May 1981), p. 74. This figure does not include the ten divisions' annual operating costs, which Tillson estimated at $3.5 billion.
81. Phillip Karber interview, September 1987.
82. Because of its long range, the F-15 can also operate in an offensive role, escorting fighter-

larly, close-air-support planes like the A-10 are specialized tank killers, *and* they work best in the tactical defensive.[83] Moreover, their lateral mobility makes them especially valuable for containing unexpected breakthroughs anywhere along the front. In Posen's dynamic model of conventional combat on the Central Front, over half of the attrition exacted against Pact armor in critical breakthrough sectors was caused by close air support.[84] Conventional arms control should not limit such weapons.

Other kinds of planes and missiles are primarily offensive. Many analysts assume, for example, that there is a big first-strike bonus for attacks against airfields, command posts, or air defenses carried out by tactical missiles or long-range fighter-bombers. The side that strikes first and stays on the offensive, it is assumed, can destroy aircraft on the ground, crater runways, and disrupt the coordination of air defense efforts. This might keep enough of the opponents' offensive and defensive aircraft out of the skies for long enough that his force can be destroyed piecemeal.[85] If so, each side would have a strong incentive to attack preemptively at any sign of mobilization by the other.[86]

One might be skeptical about the size of this alleged preemption bonus. Air defenses are always alert, and so would be hard to catch completely by surprise. Aircraft are stored in hardened shelters, which for the most part are not especially vulnerable to air or conventional missile attack. Cratered runways can be repaired in a few hours. Thus, it is not immediately obvious that attackers would impose more meaningful damage than they would suffer. Indeed, in one respect, there is a big first-strike disadvantage. Normally, air-defense fighters cannot use air-to-air missiles beyond visual range

---

bombers in attacks on ground installations behind enemy lines. But if fighter-bombers were banned, then the F-15 would be strictly defensive, except for the F-15E, which has its own ground-attack capability. See Alfred Price, *Air Battle Central Europe* (New York: Free Press, 1986), esp. pp. 37–46, 173–177.

83. Ibid., pp. 92–101.

84. Posen, "Measuring the European Conventional Balance," p. 66.

85. See Greenwood, "Role of Airpower," esp. pp. 16–19; Price, *Air Battle*; and Lt. Col. D. J. Alberts, USAF, *Deterrence in the 1980s: Part II, The Role of Conventional Airpower*, Adelphi Paper No. 193 (London: International Institute for Strategic Studies, 1984).

86. In addition, if NATO were the winner in this duel to destroy the air defenses of the other side, the Soviet Union might lose confidence in its ability to detect and parry nuclear attacks by NATO fighter-bombers flying through the corridors cut during the course of the conventional air war. This could trigger Soviet nuclear preemption out of fear that Soviet *strategic* command and control in Moscow was becoming vulnerable. See Barry Posen, "Inadvertent Nuclear War? Escalation and NATO's Northern Flank," *International Security*, Vol. 7, No. 2 (Fall 1982), pp. 28–54, and his related forthcoming work.

because it is impossible to determine in a reliable way whether the approaching blip is an attacking foe or a friendly craft returning from a bombing mission in the enemy's rear.[87] In the first sortie of the war, however, defenders would know that all the blips were enemies. Despite these factors, however, the belief in a first-strike bonus in a European air battle is widespread, and thus is a problem that arms control should address.

In short, it is possible to distinguish defensive aircraft, like the A-10 and the Soviet Su-25, from offensive air attack weapons, like the F-111, Tornado, Su-24, and Backfire bombers and the SS-21 surface-to-surface missile. Because defensive aircraft kill armor and work best in the tactical defensive, they should not be limited. Offensive air attack weapons, however, combine range, payload, and penetration capability so as to threaten the survival of the command and control and air defense capabilities of the other side.[88] Since they arguably work best in that role when used preemptively, they should be considered candidates for limitation. It goes without saying that strictly defensive interceptor aircraft like the F-15 should not be limited. "Swing" aircraft like the F-16, which can perform either air-to-air or long distance air-to-ground missions, pose a more difficult problem.

TRADE-OFFS AND INTERACTIONS AMONG THE THREE CRITERIA
In some cases, each of these three criteria—the NATO/Pact firepower balance, the force-to-space ratio, and the offense/defense balance—might lead to a different conclusion. Deals that look good according to one criterion might look disadvantageous according to the others. For example, trading ten Pact ADEs for five NATO ADEs would improve the firepower balance, but it would be ruinous from the standpoint of NATO's force-to-space ratio. Similarly, banning long-range fighter-bombers would reduce incentives to preempt in the air war, but it would throw away a NATO advantage without receiving adequate compensation.

Sometimes, however, big advantages by one criterion might offset small disadvantages according to others. Thus, if NATO could trade a small num-

---

87. Price, *Air Battle*, pp. 162–63. The use of IFF (identification friend-or-foe) transponders and pre-designated return corridors are only a partial answer to this problem.
88. Deep-strike aircraft might be retained in small numbers, sufficient to provide a theater nuclear deterrent in the wake of the INF Treaty, but insufficient to mount a significant conventional first strike. For tables summarizing the characteristics and counting the inventories of these weapons, see John M. Collins, *U.S.-Soviet Military Balance, 1980–1985* (Washington, D.C.: Pergamon-Brassey's 1985), esp. pp. 218, 268.

ber of its tanks for a large number of the Pact's, the adverse impact on the force-to-space ratio might be compensated by the overall reduction in the Pact's offensive capability. This would be especially true if NATO reductions could be taken in American forces in southern Germany, where unfavorable terrain makes a Pact attack unlikely to succeed. In short, any proposal must be judged by its overall effect, not by giving veto power to each criterion.

*Some Specific Trading Proposals*

A variety of deals might be advantageous to both sides, involving trades of armor for armor, air for air, air for armor, battlefield nuclear weapons for armor, SDI for armor, or a grand package involving all of the above. As a rule, the more comprehensive the deal, involving more types of weapons, the easier it is to create incentives for both parties to the agreement, but the greater also will be its technical complexity and the time required to negotiate it.

ARMOR FOR ARMOR
The obvious problem with a simple armor-for-armor trade is the asymmetry in the present inventory of the two sides. The Soviets have accepted that the side that is ahead in a given category should give up more, but with the present disparity, any straight armor-for-armor trade would have to be quite asymmetrical to be attractive to NATO.

If Gorbachev wants to cut expensive, forward-deployed Soviet maneuver divisions unilaterally, but needs a token exchange from NATO for domestic political reasons, it would be quite easy to devise arms control formulas that look even but turn out to be highly asymmetric in their effects. For example, Senator Sam Nunn has proposed equal 50% reductions of U.S. and Soviet forces in the MBFR region of Central Europe. Since Soviet ground forces outnumber American ones in this area by about 5 to 1, this trade could eliminate thirteen Soviet divisions (10 from East Germany) in exchange for two American divisions taken from southern Germany, where NATO's force-to-space ratio is more than adequate.[89] This would go far toward eliminating any chance of a Soviet standing start attack. However, it would have no effect on a long, attritional war unless the Soviet units were disbanded and

---

89. Nunn speech, April 13, 1987.

their equipment destroyed rather than just pulled back to the Soviet Union. In fact, it would make the long-war balance worse for the West, since it might be impossible to bring the two American divisions back to Germany.[90]

Even somewhat less uneven trades might still be advantageous to NATO. Assume that the Soviet Union dismantles 4,500 tanks out of a Pact total in the MBFR region of about 17,000. In exchange, the U.S. dismantles 1,500 tanks out of a NATO total there of about 7,000. Translating this into firepower scores, the Soviets would be relinquishing about six ADEs, NATO less than two. At the same time both would be decreasing the proportion of offensive weapons in their force structure. For both reasons, NATO would be more secure against a Pact attack, at least in the early weeks of a war. After such a trade, the Pact/NATO ADE ratio would be 18:24 at the beginning of mobilization, 34:31 after two weeks, and 75:44 after 90 days.[91]

The Soviets might not be interested in such trades unless they are linked to reductions in other forces. Indeed, their discussions of asymmetric armor reductions are always in the context of trades in other categories of weapons, where NATO may enjoy an advantage. Consequently, it is important to consider possible airpower trades as well.

AIR FOR AIR

Devising limits on offensive conventional airpower involves a number of dilemmas. One is its overlap with nuclear missions at one end of the spectrum and air defense missions at the other. Conventional deep-strike forces, like U.S. F-111s and Soviet SS-21s, double as theater nuclear forces. Thus, destroying or withdrawing F-111s from Britain is bound to intensify European complaints that the American nuclear deterrent is being decoupled from NATO. On the other end of the spectrum, scrapping only specialized deep interdiction aircraft would leave intact "swing" aircraft that are also capable,

90. David S. Yost, "Beyond MBFR," *Orbis*, Vol. 31. No. 1 (Spring 1987), pp. 99–134, has a good discussion of the effect of geographical asymmetries on conventional arms control.
91. These calculations are based on Mako, *U.S. Ground Forces*. A widely publicized RAND Corporation study has found that the Pact would have to accept asymmetrical reductions at a ratio of 5:1 (e.g., 20 Pact ADEs for 4 NATO ADEs) for NATO to be able to hold its forward defense line at M+30. The need for this extreme asymmetry is in part due to NATO's force-to-space ratio problem. In part, however, the RAND findings are driven by assumptions about the firepower balance and Pact reinforcement rates that are much more pessimistic than Posen's. See James A. Thomson and Nanette C. Gantz, "Conventional Arms Control Revisited: Objectives in the New Phase" (Santa Monica, RAND N 2697-AF, February, 1988), discussed in *New York Times*, November 12, 1987. Force-to-space deficits resulting from such a trade could be offset by adding fortifications or anti-tank infantry to the front line.

in some measure, of preempting enemy airfields. But scrapping swing air-power would diminish the air defenses of both sides, which are desirable to preserve.

Another problem is the easy return in crisis of aircraft banned from the central region. Limits only in the MBFR region would be attractive because of their simplicity and because they would take first-strike weapons out of each other's range. But it is easy to fly aircraft back into harm's way on short notice.[92] This problem would be solved if the planes were scrapped and covered by global limits, rather than just limits for Central Europe. This, however, could adversely affect air balances against China and Third World states.

A final problem is that the payoff that the Soviets might be most interested in—a ban on high-accuracy, deep-strike "emerging technologies"—might be impossible to verify. Precision-guided munitions would be especially difficult to monitor, since they are small, numerous, easily concealed, and in some cases consist of nothing more than strap-on kits that improve the accuracy of ordinary bombs.[93] Likewise, advances in target acquisition capability by airborne radar are hard to limit, since the same kinds of systems have an indispensable role in air defense. Consequently, the best way to limit "emerging technologies" is to limit their delivery platforms—deep-strike aircraft and surface-to-surface missiles, including such proposed systems as NATO's ATACMs or a follow-on to the Lance missile.

Given all of these difficulties, the simplest solution would be to prohibit deployment of all systems of a given payload within range of the opponent's airfields. This would cover systems like the Soviet SS-21, Backfire, and Fencer, the American F-111, and the European Tornado. A more complicated alternative would be to place low global limits on the number of such systems. Either of these arrangements would hinder Pact preemption of NATO's command and control, theater nuclear forces, and airpower, a mission which has had a high priority in the Soviets' conventional offensive strategy. On the other hand, such limitations on airpower would hinder NATO's ability

---

92. This would even be a problem for a ban on deep-strike weapons from the Atlantic to the Urals.
93. Price, *Air Battle*, especially chapters 4 and 5, describes current "smart" munitions. See also Benjamin Lambeth, "Conventional Forces for NATO," in Joseph Kruzel, ed., *American Defense Annual, 1987–88* (Lexington, Mass.: D. C. Heath, 1987). U.S. Congress, Office of Technology Assessment, *New Technology for NATO: Implementing Follow-On Forces Attack*, OTA-ISC-309 (Washington, D.C.: U.S. Government Printing Office, June, 1987), discusses future systems.

to use its offensive airpower to offset the Pact's advantage in offensive ground forces.

AIR FOR ARMOR

Looking at each of the trades described above separately, the asymmetric armor-for-armor deal would be more attractive to NATO. The air-for-air deal would be more attractive to the Pact. Both sides might perceive benefit in a combination of the two. Indeed, this deal might be quite easy to make, because the Soviets probably rate the threat of the "emerging technologies" more highly than NATO does. Given the urgency of Ogarkov's plea for funds to parry this threat, the Soviets should jump at a chance to curtail it through arms control. Some Western analysts are quite skeptical about the cost-effectiveness of deep interdiction, even with improved weapons.[94] These factors suggest that it would be smart business to trade away goods that are overvalued by the buyer.

BATTLEFIELD NUCLEAR WEAPONS OR SDI FOR ARMOR

Because of the Soviet advantage in conventional forces as a whole, it may turn out to be impossible to strike a deal by limiting conventional forces alone. Indeed, the Soviets strongly imply that battlefield and other tactical nuclear weapons must be included in any restructuring of conventional forces.[95] Perhaps if tanks and artillery were banned from the Atlantic to the Urals, further denuclearization of the European continent would be desirable. But as long as a successful Pact conventional offensive is still a possibility, cuts in battlefield nuclear weapons should be avoided.[96]

An alternative source of bargaining leverage is the Strategic Defense Initiative (SDI). People usually think of SDI as a bargaining chip to be traded for cuts in offensive strategic nuclear forces. But why should the United

---

94. Greenwood, "Role of Airpower," pp. 40–42, argues that interdiction near the battlefield is more effective than deep interdiction, except for attacks on small numbers of high-value fixed targets in the enemy's rear.

95. "No clear boundary exists between conventional weapons and nuclear weapons," says Viktor Karpov, FBIS, October 13, p. 4. For an evaluation of such a proposal, see Joseph S. Nye, "For a 'Triple-Zero' Pact," *New York Times*, October 11, 1987, p. E27. For Soviet insistence on including "dual capable" nuclear systems in conventional arms talks, see Serge Schmemann, "West Rebuffs East on Pact on Europe Troop Cuts," *New York Times*, December 6, 1987, p. 23.

96. For the argument that nuclear first-use options must be retained as a hedge against disaster even if the conventional balance is improved, see Richard K. Betts, "Conventional Deterrence: Predictive Uncertainty and Policy Confidence," *World Politics*, Vol. 37, No. 2 (January 1985), pp. 153–179.

States have to surrender bargaining chips to get the Soviet Union to agree to a symmetrical 50% reduction in offensive strategic forces? Why isn't half of America's nuclear arsenal payment enough for half of Russia's? Rather than paying twice for strategic reductions, America should offer its biggest bargaining chip, SDI, in exchange for steep, asymmetrical reductions in conventional armor.

An overt trade of this kind is unlikely, however, because of the apparent incommensurability of the goods to be exchanged. Moreover, devotees of SDI might portray such an arrangement as forfeiting America's security in favor of Europe's. Nonetheless, as part of a simultaneously negotiated nuclear and conventional package, the prospect of SDI limits would probably pry loose significant Soviet concessions on conventional forces. Such a deal would certainly be attractive to Gorbachev and should be attractive to the U.S. as well. Given its complexity, this package would take time to negotiate and might have to unfold in stages, but getting good agreements that solve real security problems is more important than getting quick, superficial fixes.[97]

*Conclusions and Caveats*

The first rule of arms control is that it should not make a basically stable situation less stable. NATO's conventional forces are already sufficient to make a quick Soviet victory unlikely. Moreover, NATO's nuclear deterrent is credible enough to make any Soviet gamble on such a victory intolerably risky. Consequently, NATO should make sure that its formidable present deterrent is not sacrificed for an arms control will-o'-the-wisp. In particular, NATO should not significantly reduce its force-to-space ratio or scrap its battlefield nuclear weapons unless the Soviets agree to a very radical restructuring of their offensive armored forces.

Nevertheless there are plausible trades that might benefit both sides, increasing the stability of the situation. Especially attractive would be a package that includes asymmetric reductions of armor, either in Central Europe or from the Atlantic to the Urals, and withdrawal of deep-strike missiles and

---

97. SDI is not the West's only "off-agenda" bargaining chip. Warner Schilling reminds me that, insofar as greater integration in the world capitalist economy is one of the indirect goals of Gorbachev's arms control diplomacy, the West might gain bargaining leverage by making this economic linkage explicit.

aircraft from the European theater. By linking this package to a broader agreement including limits on SDI, NATO should be able to extract highly favorable terms.

This optimism hinges on evidence that Gorbachev's proposals for restructuring conventional forces are made in good faith. Gorbachev has powerful economic incentives to desire such restructuring and no good strategic reasons to shun it, provided that NATO reciprocates. The only apparent barrier is the Soviet military's desire to retain "counteroffensive" options as part of any switch to a more defensive conventional strategy. However, Gorbachev probably has the political power to overcome military objections as long as he can show that he is getting valuable concessions from NATO, such as limits on SDI or conventional "emerging technologies."

NATO should aggressively pursue these possibilities for conventional arms control. If Gorbachev is not serious, NATO will expose him and score a propaganda coup. If he is serious, as seems likely, the military security of both sides could be enhanced and a major source of political tensions eliminated.

*Part IV:*
*Projecting American Power*

# Constraints on America's Conduct of Small Wars

*Eliot A. Cohen*

$I$t is the characteristic military dilemma of a world power that it finds itself forced to prepare for two entirely different kinds of wars, large-scale conflicts on the continent of Europe, on the one hand, and lesser battles on its periphery or on other continents, on the other. This difficulty perplexed British statesmen throughout the latter nineteenth and early twentieth centuries; it is now the problem of the United States, Britain's heir as the foremost global power. This article examines the constraints on America's ability to prepare for, wage, and win small wars.

It is often argued that American statesmen will find themselves constrained from using force in the future by public and Congressional repugnance over a repetition of the Vietnam experience. There is some truth in this. What follows, however, will suggest that institutional constraints and to a lesser extent foreign pressures, rather than the vagaries of public opinion, will inhibit American leaders from commencing such wars, and from prosecuting them successfully.

We begin by addressing three questions: What precisely do we mean by the term "small war"? Why is there reason to think that such wars are inevitable? How do the requirements of preparing for such wars differ from the normal military measures of a Great Power?

*The Small War Problem*

At the end of the last century, British strategists defined small wars as conflicts waged against the forces of the lesser powers, to include indigenous guerrilla-type movements.[1] Today, we would include in our definition wars

---

The author is grateful to Robert Blackwill, David Cohen, Judith Cohen, Aaron Friedberg, Samuel Huntington, William Kristol, Arie Ofri, Stephen Rosen, Andrew Ross, Scott Sagan, and Stephen Walt for their comments on earlier drafts of this article.

---

*Eliot A. Cohen is Assistant Professor of Government and Allston Burr Senior Tutor in Quincy House at Harvard University.*

---

1. Definition derived in part from Cyril Falls, *A Hundred Years of War* (New York: Collier, 1953); C.E. Callwell, *Small Wars* (London: HMSO, 1906), pp. 21–24.

---

*International Security*, Fall 1984 (Vol. 9, No. 2) 0162-2889/84/020151-31 $02.50/1
© 1984 by the President and Fellows of Harvard College and of the Massachusetts Institute of Technology.

waged against the proxy forces of other Great Powers. For the British, this type of conflict—"wars of the second or third magnitude"—characterized by "relative unimportance, long duration, or unfavorable climatic conditions" posed the greatest challenge to their military system.[2] They tailored their military establishment and system of high command to cope with this problem, even at the expense of their capacity to intervene in European warfare.

I will use the term "small war" rather than "limited war" here for a number of reasons. First, I thereby exclude the consideration of limited nuclear warfare, which provided the subject matter for many of the first American treatises on limited war in the 1950s (for example, Henry Kissinger's *Nuclear Weapons and Foreign Policy*). Although the possibility (a remote one) of controlled nuclear exchanges between the superpowers exists and should be studied, it must be considered separately from the much more likely contingencies of conventional warfare. Limited nuclear war involves consideration of means (theater and strategic nuclear weapons and advanced command and control technology), ends (above all, avoidance of escalation to cataclysmic levels of destruction), and political conditions (acute anxiety and extremely brief periods of time available for choice) quite different from those of conventional small war.

The term "limited war" also includes the possibility of direct conventional engagement between the superpowers when such conflicts remain regionally contained. In public at least, soldiers and statesmen argue that programs and policies to prepare for conventional war on a less than total scale have as their primary purpose deterrence or containment of Soviet conventional aggression. This has been most noticeably true in the case of the Persian Gulf: policymakers have justified the creation of the Rapid Deployment Force, since its inception, as a measure to counter Soviet conventional threats to the region.[3]

For a variety of political reasons, soldiers and statesmen find it easiest to justify force procurement aimed at deterring, or at least containing, Soviet aggression. The Soviet Union poses the greatest overall threat to American interests and forces, particularly in an age when its capability to project power overseas has grown enormously. On the other hand, the history of the past three decades suggests that armed conflict between the United States

2. Frederick Sleigh Roberts, *Facts and Fallacies* (London: John Murray, 1911), pp. 151–152.
3. See Harold Brown, *Annual Report of the Secretary of Defense, Fiscal Year 1982* (Washington: U.S. Government Printing Office, 1981), pp. 81–83.

and the Soviet Union is the *least* likely contingency America faces. In every postwar crisis which involved potential direct military conflict between the two superpowers—in Iran, Berlin, Korea, Cuba, Vietnam, and the Middle East—both sides have exercised great restraint, hoping to avert all-out war by avoiding the slightest direct hostilities. American troops have actually *fought* only Soviet clients or allies and, occasionally, autonomous but no less hostile powers.

The rules for limited engagement with the Soviets differ from those with lesser powers. In the former case, preemptive deployment of troops to serve as a tripwire may either signal resolve or force on the opponent the onus of unwelcome escalation. In such situations (as during the Cuban missile crisis or as might happen in the Persian Gulf), the successful application of force—military victory—is far less important than the use of military force as a means of communication. In most cases, the highest political leadership will exercise extremely tight control over deployments and actions, even at the expense of militarily sound procedure. A case in point is the shrinkage of the American naval quarantine of Cuba in 1962 to allow the Soviets more time to back down.

The term "low-intensity conflict" has come into vogue more recently to define wars waged against Third World opponents.[4] This too is inaccurate however. From the point of view of the average company commander in Vietnam, there was nothing low in intensity about the conflict, and the heavy casualty rates of the war's peak period compare with those of some World War II battles. Moreover, in the future (particularly in the Persian Gulf), we may expect to see American forces committed against indigenous forces equipped with a variety of modern weapons, from high-performance aircraft to modern main battle tanks. The term "low-intensity warfare" suggests conflicts which can be handled by a few thousand specialists: the reality is that such wars may require the services of tens or even hundreds of thousands of combat and support troops. Thus, where the term "limited war" is too all-inclusive to be useful, the term "low-intensity warfare" excessively narrows the scope of our concern.

The question of terminology is an important one, for the proper term forces us to confront the messy military and political realities small wars embody and the military and political costs they exact. The likelihood of

4. See Sam C. Sarkesian and William L. Scully, eds., *U.S. Policy and Low Intensity Conflict* (New Brunswick: Transaction Books, 1981).

direct U.S.–Soviet conflict is low, but military bureaucracies suffer few political costs in publicly planning to meet such contingencies; such scenarios are, moreover, organizationally congenial to institutions still gripped by the model of World War II. Hence, the public strategic debate has an air of unreality about it. Government officials, experts of various kinds, and politicians talk about the least likely war, and the armed forces prepare for it. When the small war problem does arise, statesmen express the vain hope that such conflicts can be referred to small, specially designed agencies and forces.

Inevitably, the United States will fight small wars, and hence ought to allocate a large proportion of its military resources to preparing to cope with them. More importantly, it must prepare its institutions to fight such wars. Postwar history (Vietnam, Korea, and lesser conflicts such as the Lebanese intervention in 1958, the Dominican Republic affair in 1965, and the Grenada invasion/rescue of 1983) reveals that these are the kinds of wars Americans have fought for over a generation. To be sure, the advent of the Nixon Doctrine has lessened the chances that American troops will find themselves committed to combat before every effort has been made to train and equip local forces. Nonetheless, by treaty and informal agreement the United States has committed itself to the defense of a number of states, all of which could very easily find themselves subject to attack by stronger Third World states: the most prominent examples include South Korea, Thailand, Saudi Arabia, Oman, Sudan, and Honduras. In many cases, American troops are already deployed in these states, either for training or simply as a symbol of American intentions. Nor does the American public, by and large, disapprove of these commitments.

America's need to prepare for small wars flows directly from its role in the postwar world as the preeminent maritime power and the leader of the Western bloc of nations. Such a position requires (as, under similar circumstances, it did of Great Britain) a readiness and a capability to fight small wars to maintain its world position and the global balance of power outside the continent of Europe. The creation of the Rapid Deployment Force (now Central Command) in the late 1970s highlighted one of several major overseas interests of the United States, namely, American interest in the secure and continuous flow of oil to the industrial economies of Western Europe and Japan. In most cases, the United States is the only Western power capable of promptly and substantially reinforcing a Third World state under attack or of sustaining a substantial military commitment should that become necessary. Even the two most important ex-colonial powers, Britain and France, find themselves at least partially dependent on American logistic support for their operations overseas, as the French counterintervention in Zaire in 1978 and the Falklands War of 1982 demonstrated.

During the past decade, American military commitments abroad have, if anything, expanded beyond their 1950 limits. The Carter Doctrine extended American military commitments to the Persian Gulf; turmoil in Central America and the growth of Soviet forces in Cuba have recently forced renewed military attention to that region; the activities of Libya threaten the stability of a number of North African countries, including Chad and Sudan; Libyan airplanes have actually engaged American naval aircraft in the Mediterranean. Even in southeast Asia the potential for a recommitment of American forces remains, as Thailand has come under pressure from a Vietnamese Communist state consolidating its hold on Indochina. In all of these cases, the potential exists for American use of force against hostile minor powers; in many cases, that potential is growing. Three examples of small wars one would imagine the United States fighting in the next decade are: a war to preserve the independence of Honduras, Costa Rica, and Panama; a war to prevent Iranian disruption of Western and Japanese oil supplies; a war to preserve the independence of Thailand.

None of the above should be construed as an argument that small war is anything but a sad necessity; certainly, it is not a foreign policy instrument of choice. Nonetheless, unless one is prepared to advocate a modified form of isolationism—a repudiation of foreign policy commitments outside Europe and Japan, for example—one must confront the need for a small war capability. Small wars present, therefore, a unique military challenge and an inevitable one. Our larger questions remain: What constraints will delay or prevent future American small wars? How will these constraints affect American conduct of such wars once the government embarks on them?

*Public Opinion as a Constraint*

We can distinguish three types of political constraints on the waging of small wars, all of which were intensified by the war in Vietnam. The first of these is public opinion, i.e., public revulsion against any kind of military commitment which could involve American troops in a war such as that which took 50,000 American lives in the jungles of Southeast Asia. It is axiomatic in American politics that the American people want "no more Vietnams"; thus, it is assumed, popular opinion will severely limit the willingness of the American people to support a similar kind of war. Although it is conceivable that an American administration could engage in war despite the vehement disapproval of the American public, few politicians would care to do so, realizing as they must the likely consequences for their chances of future success and reputation.

How would the American public react to a small war in the future? The answer is by no means as simple as the "Vietnam syndrome" argument would suggest. For one thing, it is important to realize the complexity of American public opinion *vis-à-vis* the Vietnam War and its remarkable similarity to that in the Korean War.[5] In both cases, the war received a high degree of initial support, declining steadily but surprisingly slowly as American casualties increased and the prospects of success dimmed. Indeed, in retrospect, it is remarkable that it was not until after three years of combat—in the case of Vietnam, until 1968—that a majority of the American public finally turned against the war.

The experience of the Grenada operation of October 1983 would seem to confirm this: elite disapproval and media skepticism did not prevent the operation from being an extremely popular one. To be sure, the invasion went smoothly and ended very quickly. It took place virtually next door to the United States, had as its avowed purpose the rescue of American citizens (who later appeared grateful for the effort), and received the fervent support of a half dozen small local democracies. If any military operation should have been popular, in fact, it was the invasion (or liberation) of Grenada. The willingness of the American public to tolerate a much more ambiguous, much more distant, and far bloodier military presence in Lebanon was more significant.

Most studies of popular opinion in small wars rely heavily on public opinion polls, which is understandable. Nonetheless, in order to assess the political consequences of public opinion—in other words, its effects on real policy decisions—one must look beyond the polls. Indeed, only if we do so can we understand why Vietnam seemed to contemporary observers to have generated far more antiwar sentiment than Korea, even though both wars exhibit a similar public opinion profile. The political reality of vociferous opposition in the streets played the dominant role in influencing political

5. This is a theme of John E. Mueller, *War, Presidents, and Public Opinion* (New York: John Wiley and Sons, 1973). See in particular pp. 23–66.

leaders, although political leaders were aware of and concerned by the larger slippage in public support revealed in the polls.

The depth of anti-Vietnam sentiment stemmed in part from the length of the war, as John Mueller points out in his comparative study of public opinion in Korea and Vietnam. The antiwar movement, however, drew its strength primarily from the existence of a large, vocal, and politically active group of middle and upper-middle class draft-aged youth. As the coordinator of the Vietnam Moratorium Committee between 1969 and 1970 put it:

[A] fundamental reason for the failure [*sic*] of the antiwar movement was overdependence on upper-middle-class draftable young men. This is a notion I resisted for a long time.[6]

The Korean War draft was much more popular than its Vietnam successor for a number of reasons. Among these was the legitimacy of conscription following World War II (proposals for more radical forms of military service such as Universal Military Training were extremely popular in the polls). The universality of the Korean War draft (over three-quarters of the eligible cohort served in the military) helped contain popular disenchantment with the war. During Vietnam, by way of contrast, the Selective Service draft inducted less than 50 percent of the eligible young men. Whereas in Korea military service was correctly perceived as a virtually inevitable responsibility, by the time of Vietnam it was a burden to be avoided by adroit manipulation of the draft deferment and exemption rules.[7] Paradoxically, a system of selection which offered a good chance of escaping military service fostered more opposition than an all-inclusive draft. More importantly, the initial stages of the Korean War were fought by reservists, most of them World War II veterans recalled for over a year of service. There could be no question thereafter of a twenty-year-old's draft call seeming unusually harsh or unreasonable: rather, he was being asked to make a sacrifice already made in greater degree by older men. Of course, the nature and timing of the war—its beginning with a clear-cut act of aggression and its occurrence at the very opening of the Cold War— made it more acceptable than might otherwise have been the case.

---

6. Anthony Lake, ed., *The Vietnam Legacy* (New York: New York University Press, 1976), p. 124. See also Peter Osnos's similar observations on pp. 69, 112. In addition, see Michael Charlton and Anthony Moncrieff, *Many Reasons Why* (New York: Hill and Wang, 1978), pp. 162–165. For another view from a college student at the time, see Steven Kelman, *Push Comes to Shove* (Boston: Houghton Mifflin, 1970), pp. 117–120.
7. On the Vietnam era draft, see Lawrence M. Baskir and William A. Strauss, *Chance and Circumstance* (New York: Alfred A. Knopf, 1978).

In addition, the nature of antiwar sentiment in the American public varied greatly. As John P. Roche has put it, working class opposition to the Vietnam War could be summed up by a phrase that recurred in letters to the President: "end the —ing war and shoot the —ing draft dodgers."[8] As policymakers knew, much of centrist antiwar sentiment stemmed from a frustrated desire to finish the war victoriously and reasonably quickly. The major reason given in *The Pentagon Papers* for President Johnson's unwillingness to mobilize the reserves to fight the Vietnam War was administration fear that a massive call-up would create pressure to *expand* the war, perhaps to include the use of nuclear weapons.

All of this is not to say that the Vietnam War had no effect on American public support for the use of force overseas: the forbearance shown by the public in 1965–1967 might not reappear in the late 1980s. Opposition to conscription and to military commitments abroad rose after Vietnam, and remains high to this day. A 1975 survey found that a majority of the public would favor U.S. military involvement in a foreign country, including the use of troops, only to defend Canada against invasion. By a narrow margin (41 percent to 39), they opposed the use of troops to defend Western Europe. The same poll, however, conducted again only three years later found a majority willing to fight for Europe; in 1980, majorities were willing to send troops to fight in Europe, the Persian Gulf, Japan, and Pakistan.[9] As the mass (though not necessarily the elite) public reaction to the Iranian hostage crisis of 1980 and the Grenada operation of 1983 (as well as the defense expansion of 1978–1983) indicated, opinion returned to its pre-Vietnam position in favor of a large peacetime military establishment and willingness to use force abroad. Nor has the Vietnam experience created a generational

8. There are numerous studies of public opinion and the Vietnam War. See *inter alia* Hazel Erskine, "The Polls: Is War a Mistake?," *Public Opinion Quarterly*, Vol. 34 (Spring 1970), pp. 134–150; Mueller, *War, Presidents, and Public Opinion*, especially pp. 148–152; Allen H. Barton, "The Columbia Crisis: Campus, Vietnam, and the Ghetto," *Public Opinion Quarterly*, Vol. 32 (Fall 1968), pp. 333–351; Ole R. Holsti and James N. Rosenau, "Vietnam, Consensus, and the Belief Systems of American Leaders," Paper delivered at the 1977 Hendicks Symposium on American Politics and World Order, University of Nebraska, October 6–7, 1977.
9. Compare John E. Rielly, ed., *American Public Opinion and U.S. Foreign Policy, 1975* (Chicago: Chicago Council on Foreign Relations, 1975), p. 18, with a similar table three years later (*American Public Opinion and U.S. Foreign Policy, 1978*, p. 26). Even more bellicosity is revealed in Bruce Russett and Donald R. DeLuca, "'Don't Tread On Me': Public Opinion and Foreign Policy in the Eighties," *Political Science Quarterly*, Vol. 96, No. 3 (Fall 1981), pp. 381–400. The table on p. 387 reveals an across-the-board increase in willingness to fight, i.e., an increase not simply attached to one country or region.

cleavage of major proportions, younger people taking "dovish" and their elders more "hawkish" positions, as some observers had expected it would.[10]

A final lesson can be derived from a study of British public opinion during the Falklands War of 1982. The British fought that war for the sake of some desolate islands that the British Foreign Office had long hoped to cede unobtrusively to Argentina. After the fact, all commentators agreed that it was an enormously popular war, one which enhanced the reputation and stature of the Prime Minister, Margaret Thatcher, who waged it. Yet when the naval task force was initially dispatched to the Falklands (with the approval of 60 percent of the public), less than half the population (44 percent in mid-April) thought the retaking of the Falklands worth a single British serviceman's death. And yet, six weeks later, after heavy fighting by sea and land, 62 percent of the population approved the war despite the human costs. Those who felt the retaking of the Falklands *not* worth loss of life totaled 49 percent of those polled in early April. By the end of May, they made up only 34 percent of the population.[11] This confirms earlier findings from Korea and Vietnam that public support for a war—even a war in a previously unfamiliar or marginal region of the world—increases once troops actually engage in fighting.[12]

All this is not to imply that popular support for small wars is automatic or wholehearted. An important factor in the case of the Falklands was the fact that the islands were British property, not a foreign country. At a deeper level, we find the phenomenon described by Tocqueville in his analysis of democracies at war:

No kind of greatness is more pleasing to the imagination of a democratic people than military greatness which is brilliant and sudden, won without hard work, by risking nothing but one's life.[13]

Small wars (the Falklands might prove an exception) offer few such prospects: they require long and patient efforts and offer little of the dramatic advances and victories which can characterize conventional warfare. Nonetheless, it is more surprising and important that democratic peoples have supported mi-

---

10. Ole R. Holsti and James N. Rosenau, "Does Where You Stand Depend on When You Were Born? The Impact of Generation on Post-Vietnam Foreign Policy Beliefs," *Public Opinion Quarterly*, Vol. 44, No. 1 (Spring 1980), pp. 1–22.
11. See *The Economist*, May 29, 1982.
12. A point made by Mueller in *War, Presidents, and Public Opinion*, p. 53.
13. Alexis de Tocqueville, *Democracy in America*, trans. George Lawrence (New York: Anchor Books, 1969), pp. 657–658.

nor conflicts waged in remote corners of the world and for obscure purposes for years at a time than that they have eventually turned against those wars. Support for Presidential authority, the instinct which leads citizens to rally around the flag in a time of crisis, and above all a sense of national pride (such as that displayed following the Grenada invasion in 1983) will ensure sufficient initial support to allow a President to initiate a small war. Thereafter, support must depend on such variables as the seeming ability to win the war, the justification for it, the President's skill at evoking popular support, and the nature of the burdens (particularly military service) it imposes. The point is not that the Vietnam syndrome does not exist: it does, and will exercise a restraint on American Presidents for some time. However, the effects of a public opinion shaped by the Vietnam War may be less than were originally expected, or at least more predictable.

A President has the power to start a war. The arguments we have examined here suggest that in the opening stages, at least, he will get popular support as well; difficulties will only mount as the war drags on.

*International Politics as a Constraint*

Undoubtedly, the most important change in world politics since 1946 has been the passing of the old colonial order and the associated transformation of the European role in world politics. Most of the small wars of the early postwar period—the Indochina war, the Algerian insurrection, the Malayan insurgency, and the war in Aden—were outgrowths of the decolonization of Africa and Asia. During this period, American policymakers found themselves torn: on the one hand, they were allied to European states which were willing and able to project force overseas and, on the other, they recognized the inevitability, and believed in the desirability, of the collapse of European hegemony outside Europe. The Suez crisis of 1956 revealed this contradiction with exceptional vividness.

By the end of the Vietnam period, the ambivalence had been resolved by external events, and, for the first time in their postwar history, the Americans found themselves uncomfortably isolated in both their willingness and their ability to use force overseas.[14] Where other states had contributed substantial

14. See Alfred Grosser, *The Western Alliance*, trans. Michael Shaw (New York: Vintage Books, 1982), pp. 237–243, for the European reaction to Vietnam.

or symbolic contingents of troops to fight under American command in Korea, Vietnam called forth only mistrust from allies who either feared a misdirection of American resources or simply thought the war an improper and unjust one. Where the problem in the 1950s had been to persuade the Europeans to reduce their military commitments overseas, the difficulty in the 1970s and 1980s was to get them to make appropriate efforts for their own defense and the projection of force overseas. The failure of President Carter's drive for a sustained 3 percent real growth in NATO defense budgets is a case in point.

There were some exceptions to this trend, of course. The Falklands War of 1982 revealed the willingness of the British to engage in military action in defense of their own interests, although the very narrowness of their margin of victory (indeed, the mere fact of the Argentine *coup de main*) revealed how greatly British power had shrunk since the late 1950s. The French continued to maintain a military sphere of influence in North Africa, although following the election of a Socialist President in the mid-1980s they exercised increasing restraint over their troop deployments there. Three European states contributed forces to aid the Lebanese government in 1983. More characteristic, however, was European reaction to the American creation of a Rapid Deployment Force in the late 1970s, and their often and publicly expressed mistrust of its utility as an instrument of policy. Equally striking was the uniformly hostile reaction of America's allies to the invasion of Grenada in 1983.

The character of the likely opponents in a small war, and more importantly the backers of those opponents, has changed as well. China has temporarily disappeared as a source of either military or even substantial ideological threat. Instead, the Soviet Union has emerged as the most likely backer of those states and movements America is likely to fight, and we have also seen the emergence of autonomous but no less anti-Western Third World states—Iran being the most notable example. Additionally, where analysts in the 1960s saw the threat as primarily one of subversion through the mechanism of "wars of national liberation," the 1980s witnessed the use of a mixture of unconventional and conventional means, particularly (but not exclusively) in Africa. This pattern first appeared during the Indochina War: in 1965, American troops engaged a Vietnamese enemy predominantly organized and equipped for guerrilla warfare; in 1972, it helped fight a much more conventionally organized force; and in 1975, its hapless South Vietnamese ally succumbed to a thoroughly conventional invasion, spearheaded by armored columns. These forces were sustained by a Soviet logistical and naval apparatus far greater than that of the 1950s and 1960s, and one comparable (if yet inferior) to that deployed by the United States. Throughout the 1970s and beyond, the Soviet Union displayed repeatedly (in Syria, Ethiopia, and other states) a capacity to transport vast quantities of arms to client states, and to provide proxy troops (Cubans primarily, but East Germans and others as well) to use them. Third World states demonstrated an increasing ability to acquire and use (in some cases, to manufacture) fairly sophisticated modern weaponry. The Iraqi use of indigenously manufactured poison gas in 1984 against Iran offers but one indication of the range of military options open to many Third World states.

The number of potential adversaries (most though not all of them Soviet clients or allies) has increased to include such geographically and culturally diverse states as Vietnam, Syria, Iran, Libya, Cuba, and Nicaragua. Whereas the small wars of the 1950s and the early 1960s were fought primarily against insurgent movements, by the late 1970s and early 1980s the prospect emerged of wars conducted against regional powers such as those listed above. The current crises in Chad, Lebanon, and Central America pose peculiar problems precisely because of their mixed quality and because, in most cases, war would entail a substantial conventional conflict with a regional medium power, coupled with a prolonged campaign of counterinsurgency. Moreover, for the first time since Korea, the increased conventional power of Third World states raises the possibility that, at least in the initial stages of a war, substantial American forces could meet defeat in the field. This possibility never really existed in Vietnam, where North Vietnamese efforts to duplicate the battle of Dienbienphu suffered a gory defeat in the face of overwhelming American firepower. The enormous increase in the quality and quantity of arms in the hands of Third World nations, coupled with increased organizational competence in the handling of such weapons, renders many local conventional balances far more even than before.

A further complicating factor is the role played by regional actors. In Central America, for example, the Contadora group of states (led by Venezuela and Mexico) can exercise influence quite independent of the United States. More importantly, perhaps, a desire to maintain a favorable attitude on the part of these states towards the United States is likely to constrain American Presidents from committing troops overseas. As late as the 1960s, Presidents could commit troops to operations in Latin America with only minimal attention to the wishes and opinions of the Latin American states.[15] This is no longer the case.

The political sensitivities of the regional powers (Egypt and Saudi Arabia, for example) and their real independence will constrain American ability to deploy substantial forces overseas. This trend has been particularly noticeable in the successful efforts of host nations to limit the flexibility of American military bases located in their countries. The European allies' uncooperative attitude towards American military movements during the October 1973 Middle East crisis is indicative of a more general trend.

In short, America is likely to fight its next small war with few and suspicious allies and against well-equipped enemies, some of them supported massively by the Soviet Union or its clients. War diplomacy played a minor role in Korea and Vietnam, but in the next conflict statesmen will have to act from the very beginning to neutralize opponents, woo neutrals, and reassure friends. This task is not an impossible one, as Britain's remarkable diplomatic successes (particularly in Europe) during the Falklands War indicated. It is, nonetheless, a major departure from the foreign policy independence with which American Presidents have been accustomed to operate.

## Congress as a Constraint

From the point of view of each post-Vietnam administration, the most important inhibition on America's small war capabilities has been Congress, which, ever since the late Vietnam period, has attempted to erode Presidential authority to engage American troops in battle without its approval. In particular, after Congress passed the War Powers Act of 1973 over Presidential veto, it seemed to many observers that Presidential war-making power was on the ebb.[16]

We usually assume that greater Congressional involvement in war-making means greater restraint, although cases have occurred in the past (such as

15. See Abraham F. Lowenthal, *The Dominican Intervention* (Cambridge: Harvard University Press, 1972).

16. On the history and meaning of the War Powers Resolution, see: Cecil V. Crabb and Pat M. Holt, *Invitation To Struggle: Congress, the President, and Foreign Policy* (Washington: Congressional Quarterly Press, 1980); Pat M. Holt, *The War Powers Resolution: The Role of Congress in U.S. Armed Intervention* (Washington: American Enterprise Institute, 1978); Edward Keynes, *Undeclared War: Twilight Zone of Constitutional Power* (University Park: Pennsylvania State University Press, 1982); W. Taylor Reveley, *War Powers of the President and Congress* (Charlottesville: University Press of Virginia, 1981).

the Spanish–American War and possibly World War I) in which Congress displayed more interest in going to war than did the President. Nonetheless, the character of the modern Congress and the language of the War Powers Act itself make it likely that Congress will act as a restraining rather than a propelling force on a President bent on making war. The critical provision of the War Powers Act is Section 5(b), which requires that any American troops sent into combat be withdrawn after sixty days (or ninety, if the President declares that to be necessary) unless Congress has authorized the continuance of the commitment.

President Nixon found this paragraph particularly vexing, and said so in his veto of the measure.[17] The other provisions of the War Powers Act—the requirement for prompt reporting to Congress of imminent engagement in hostilities, and Congressional authority to require the withdrawal of troops— added no new powers to Congress and merely confirmed the existence of old ones. In any event, through its control of federal expenditure and military organization, Congress can effectively bring to a halt any military adventure or deployment it cares to. The novelty in Section 5(b) was the automatic brake it imposed on Presidentially inspired military adventures: simply by virtue of inaction, Congress could (in theory) cause a small war to cease.

This, the most potent instrument of the War Powers Act, has recently been called into question by the Supreme Court's striking down of the legislative veto as unconstitutional. Congress therefore must turn to the financial and legislative instruments it has used in the past (for example, the Cooper– Church Amendment of 1970, which prohibited the funding of American operations in Cambodia). The difficulty here is that *positive* Congressional action will always be inhibited in a crisis by the Presidency's inherent advantages—its superior sources of information, its ability to appeal to popular opinion, and above all the fact that it is a unitary actor and Congress a composite of 535 actors. The easy passage of the Tonkin Gulf Resolution in 1964 testified to that imbalance; six long years of warfare passed before Congress summoned up the will to repeal it. More recently, Congress endorsed a Presidential decision to deploy vulnerable American land forces in Lebanon for eighteen months, and to support them with air and naval firepower for that time, despite considerable public and official misgivings over their presence and a hideous loss of life in an attack on the Marine

17. Reveley, *War Powers of the President and Congress,* p. 295.

compound in October 1983. The Marines were subsequently withdrawn well before the year-and-a-half deadline, but more because of the fact that they lacked a useful mission to perform than because of Congressional pressure.

The most important aspect of the War Powers Act lies not in the restrictions it actually imposes on a President, but in its function as a starting point for any debate about military involvement overseas. Whether or not they invoke it, Congressmen and Senators opposing a particular operation can use the War Powers Act to raise the issue of Presidential war-making, and thereby lead the debate beyond a discussion of the merits of any individual military commitment. The mere date of the War Powers Act—almost always included in television newscasts mentioning it—facilitates a comparison of any military involvement overseas with Vietnam, no matter how feeble the true resemblance.

There can be no doubt that Congress (now fortified by a vastly expanded staff and research agencies) can and will exercise its ability to complicate Presidential war-making. Moreover, it is reasonable to think that Presidents will want to assure themselves of Congressional support before embarking on any military adventures, and in any event they will find themselves forced (in part by the War Powers Act) to report periodically to Congress on the progress of such operations. Perhaps most important, future Presidents will bear in mind the effects Vietnam had on two Presidencies, and therefore act cautiously.

*Institutional Inadequacy as a Constraint*

The most substantial constraints on America's ability to conduct small wars result from the resistance of the American defense establishment to the very notion of engaging in such conflicts, and from the unsuitability of that establishment for fighting such wars. One may, as we have noted, debate the merits of any particular military involvement overseas: it is difficult to argue, however, that the United States should not have the capability to enter one.

Before analyzing the American defense establishment's attitudes and capabilities, let us first consider the peculiar military requirements of small war. To understand the peculiar problems of small war, we must understand the differences between it and large war, that is, conventional conflicts such as World War II. Large war, in the current context, means war waged primarily for the domination of Europe, fought side by side with the West

European allies. It means war conducted in developed lands, supported by the infrastructure of modern—and above all, friendly—nation-states. It means war prosecuted with full national economic, psychological, and military mobilization, and fought primarily on familiar kinds of terrain, i.e., the urban and cultivated lands of Central Europe, and in familiar climate.

Small wars, by way of contrast, are often fought in remote corners of the world, devoid of logistical infrastructure, and subject to extreme climatic conditions (the Korean and Falklands Wars are good examples of this). Such wars occur suddenly, without much advance warning. No American statesman would have predicted in 1949 that American troops would soon wage a mountain war in Korea. In 1981, no British statesman would have predicted that Britain would shortly fling the best part of its navy and seven or eight thousand of its best soldiers at bogs and hills of the Falkland Islands. Great Powers usually fight such wars with little or no mobilization (including psychological mobilization on the home front). So far, at least, these have been primarily light infantry wars, fought in mountains or jungles by foot soldiers, although light mechanized forces have also been important in deciding their outcome. The foreign policy context of such wars is also peculiar: where Great Powers wage total war side by side with major allies who must occasionally be appeased or succored, they usually fight small wars on the side of a weak client, with minimal or no help from allies, who may find the cause unattractive or the costs disproportionate.

From the point of view of the Great Power that fights them, small wars are usually wars for a limited political objective, although from the point of view of the minor power this is rarely the case. Even in the Falklands War, the two states had very different stakes in the outcome. On the British side was hurt pride; on the Argentine side, the very essence of national assertion. This disproportion appeared even more clearly in the Vietnam War. By way of contrast, total wars are struggles for survival: there is an equivalent level of commitment and hence of resolve. Because a Great Power will often find itself unwilling to make a full commitment to victory in small war, its opponent will often attempt to drag the war out, in the hope that its enemy will simply lose patience and give up.[18]

These two kinds of wars require very different kinds of military forces and systems of military command, for it is not the case that an army suited for

18. See Andrew J.R. Mack, "Why Big Nations Lose Small Wars: The Politics of Asymmetric Conflict," in Klaus Knorr, ed., *Power, Strategy, and Security: A World Politics Reader* (Princeton: Princeton University Press, 1983), pp. 126–151.

European war can handle all other contingencies with aplomb. This is a particularly important point, often obscured by the habit of defense analysts in speaking of America's "one-and-a-half-war" force posture: small war is not a "half" a war, but rather a completely different kind of conflict.[19] It takes its peculiar coloration from the geopolitical circumstances which call it forth, and hence requires special means for its conduct.

In order to wage small war successfully, a military establishment must meet its requirements in five respects: *expectations* (*vis-à-vis* the foreign and domestic political context of such conflicts), *doctrine, manpower, equipment,* and *organization.*[20] In all respects (though some more than others), the American defense establishment—civilian as well as military—is deficient. In some cases, what is lacking is an understanding of the problem; in others, the ability to implement the solutions.

EXPECTATIONS. The American armed forces' understanding of the domestic political context of small wars has been shaped, and in fact distorted, by the experience of Vietnam. The emotional reaction of the professional officer corps towards its experience in Indochina was one of frustration and shock: frustration, at the American military's seeming inability to crush an opponent inferior in strength and mobility; shock, at the psychological gap that suddenly opened up between American society and the armed forces.[21] Accustomed since World War II to a large measure of popularity and respect, the

---

19. A point made by Stephen P. Rosen in "Vietnam and the American Theory of Limited War," *International Security*, Vol. 7, No. 2 (Fall 1982), pp. 83–113.
20. For the British approach to the problem, see first and foremost the official manual on the subject, Callwell, *Small Wars*, cited above. The literature on this subject is vast, including memoirs (e.g., those of Lord Roberts, cited above) and detailed histories (e.g., Philip Mason's *The Men Who Ruled India*) as well as treatises. Some particularly interesting books are Jay Luvaas, *The Education of an Army: British Military Thought 1815–1940* (Chicago: University of Chicago Press, 1964), and Ian Hamilton, *Compulsory Service* (London: John Murray, 1910). Richard Burdon Haldane, *Army Reform and Other Addresses* (London: T. Fisher Unwin, 1907), gives the views of Britain's great Secretary of State for War. Charles à Court Repington, *Imperial Defense* (London: John Murray, 1906), is also valuable, as is Charles W. Gwynn, *Imperial Policing* (London: Macmillan, 1934). More modern writers include Richard Clutterbuck, Frank Kitson, and Sir Robert Thompson on the insurgency in Malaya. For a good brief summary of the problem, see Major General Sir Edmund Ironside, "Land Warfare (II)," in George Aston, ed., *The Study of War for Statesmen and Citizens* (1927; Port Washington: Kennikat, 1973), pp. 140–147. For the lessons of a recent small war, see Henry Fairlie, "What the Falklands Teaches Us," *The New Republic*, July 12, 1982, pp. 8–12.
21. One gets a good sense of this from Ward Just, *Military Men* (New York: Alfred A. Knopf, 1970). See General Frederick Weyand, "Vietnam Myths and American Realities," *Armor*, September–October 1976, and General Edward Meyer's remarks in Richard Halloran, "U.S. Army Chief Opposes Sending Combat Forces to Aid El Salvador," *The New York Times*, June 10, 1983, p. 1.

armed services found themselves during the Vietnam era the target of criticism and occasional abuse.

Professional officers returning from Vietnam—including the junior and middle-level officers who now run the armed forces—were seared by the experience of public repudiation by large segments of society, including the intellectual elite. Not only (many felt) was appreciation for the heroism and technical competence of the American military lacking; but officers also found themselves pilloried as mass murderers, incompetents, or both.

In reaction to this brutally unfair treatment, the military leadership has determined never again to fight a war without public backing of the fullest kind, a public backing more appropriate to the conditions of world war than small war. One reporter writes of the

deep belief that political leaders in the Vietnam era failed to define their political goals and, instead, gave military commanders shifting objectives. The officers contend they were prevented from winning because strategy and tactics were restrained. They are vehement in asserting that they were left to twist alone in the wind without public support back home.[22]

This craving for popular support, which has translated itself into a profound reluctance to use force and which apparently led the Joint Chiefs of Staff to oppose (initially) even the successful Grenada operation, is at once understandable and unacceptable for a country that must fight small wars. It extends beyond the natural conservatism of military leaders, who are trained to consider the worst possibilities and to plan accordingly.[23] Such military pessimism is probably desirable and in any case inevitable: what is *not* inevitable is the insistence on massive public support for any use of force.

Small wars are, by definition, wars fought under limitations. In order to fight them successfully, a country must limit the resources—material and psychological—it devotes to them. To do otherwise would be to indulge in a disproportionate use of a country's power resources, and to expose itself to premature exhaustion. Small wars are frequently long wars, which require skill and patience to conduct rather than (as in the case of European warfare) the sudden and massive use of power. Even a cursory examination of British

---

22. Richard Halloran, "For Military Leaders, The Shadow of Vietnam," *The New York Times*, March 20, 1984, p. B10. It is instructive that in Secretary of State Alexander Haig's memoirs of the first years of the Reagan Administration, the only two references to the Joint Chiefs of Staff refer (albeit sympathetically) to their opposition to any limited use of force abroad for precisely this reason, i.e., a fear of domestic political isolation.
23. See Harry G. Summers, "Critics Say Pentagon is Dovish: Limited War is Back in Vogue," *The Los Angeles Times*, May 6, 1984, Section IV, p. 2.

history reveals that (with the possible exception of the Boer War) the British government waged war without conjuring up popular efforts on the scale of those summoned forth by the world wars. For that matter, America's three-year-long conflict in the Philippines at the turn of the century was a success despite vocal and persistent dissent (much of it directed at the military per se) back home.

The sad fact is that, with regard to small wars as well as other matters, American civil-military relations are in a state of profound but hidden crisis. Even as portions of the elite (the "military reform" group, for example, but substantial numbers of both liberals and conservatives) have lost operational confidence in the military, the military has developed an acute mistrust of its civilian masters. The military leadership in particular has developed a set of requirements for public support unlikely to be met save in the context of a European war; it has convinced itself that it fought the Vietnam War with "a hand tied behind its back," although the amount of human and material resources poured into the war belies that notion.[24]

Nor is there any evidence that the United States has improved its understanding of how its weaker allies, on whose side a small war might be waged, think and how they should be handled. The curious combination of a reluctance to interfere in "internal politics," so noticeable in the American handling of South Vietnam, with a military desire to operate autonomously again runs counter to the requirements of small war. It is a frequent condition of such conflict that one must build or re-build an allied army, purging a corrupt officer corps while designing organizational structures suitable to both the society and its military predicament. The Indian army and the Arab Legion (the precursor of the modern Jordanian army) stand out as sterling examples of such patiently constructed forces. The American experience—which has a long tradition going back to Stilwell's feuds with Chiang Kai Shek—suggests that American proficiency at imparting technical skills is matched only by American insensitivity to local conditions. The most recent example of this is the apparent failure of U.S. Army trainers (or, more likely, their superiors) to understand the impact of Lebanese politics on the Lebanese army, which disintegrated suddenly in early 1984.[25]

---

24. See Richard Halloran, "For New Commanders, A Key Word is Caution," *The New York Times*, November 16, 1983, p. A22. For an example of the public criticism, some fair, some not, of the operational effectiveness of the military, see Arthur T. Hadley, "America's Broken War Machine," *The New Republic*, May 7, 1984, pp. 18–25.
25. See "The Collapse of Lebanon's Army: U.S. Said to Ignore Factionalism," *The New York Times*, March 11, 1984, p. 1. On the general problem involved here, see Stephen P. Rosen,

Small war almost always involves political interference in the affairs of the country in which it is waged: it is in the very nature of such wars that the military problems are difficult to distinguish from the political ones. The skills of manipulation which successful coalition warfare in such circumstances requires are not only scarce, but in some measure anathema to the American military. The desire of the American military to handle only purely "military" problems is, again, understandable in light of its Vietnam experience, but unrealistic nonetheless.

DOCTRINE. Colonel Harry G. Summers has argued in his fascinating study of the Vietnam War, *On Strategy*, that the model for modern limited war should be that of the Korean conflict. Such, however, was not the assessment of the American high command, which has determined never again to plunge into such a long, low-level war. What this means in practice is that if the military *is* forced to engage in a small war, those who oppose it in the first place will then argue for the largest use of resources to bring it to a close. As Roger Hilsman has pointed out, it was precisely the so-called "Never Again Club" after the Korean War that advocated the most extreme—the most inappropriate and thoughtless—prosecution of the Vietnam War once it had begun.[26]

The American style of war as it evolved in the world wars calls for a vigorous strategic and tactical offensive under conditions of full domestic mobilization, making use of the full array of military assets that the United States can bring to bear. It is a style unsuited, however, to the exigencies of small wars, which often require a strategic defensive and which must be fought under a host of political constraints. Throughout the Vietnam War, the U.S. Army thought primarily in traditional terms, using resources aggressively on a scale appropriate to total war, but unsuited and indeed counterproductive in the context of the war they were fighting (for example, the vast expenditure of artillery and air-delivered munitions for the purposes of "harassment and interdiction"). In the words of one internal critic, there

---

"Brown Soldiers, White Officers: Foreign Military Advisers and Third World Armies," *The Washington Quarterly*, Vol. 5, No. 2 (Spring 1982), pp. 117–130. On the specific problems of the United States Army in El Salvador, see Edward N. Luttwak, "Notes on Low-Intensity Warfare," *Parameters*, Vol. 13, No. 4 (December 1983), pp. 11–18.
26. Roger Hilsman, *To Move A Nation: The Politics of Foreign Policy in the Administration of John F. Kennedy* (New York: Doubleday, 1967), pp. 129, 534. See also his penetrating comments on American inability to adjust to small war, pp. 112–113, 435–444. See also Harry G. Summers, *On Strategy: A Critical Analysis of the Vietnam War* (Novato, Calif.: Presidio, 1982).

is "no evidence of institutional learning in the services" as regards this kind of war, no understanding of the differences between the constraints of small war and America's current "offensive, give-them-everything-you've-got military doctrine."[27] The new AirLand Battle doctrine enshrined in the Army's operational manual, Field Manual 100-5, embodies notions and procedures clearly aimed at European warfare alone, despite lip service to the idea that American forces must prepare to fight virtually anywhere. It is a doctrine which celebrates the kind of offensive aggressiveness so characteristic of the American military style.

Even at a tactical level, American offense-mindedness is occasionally at odds with local realities. The Kissinger Commission Report on Central America makes the following observation:

U.S. tactical doctrine abjures static defense and teaches constant patrolling. But this requires the provision of expensive equipment such as helicopters. In their absence, the Salvadoran military abandon their static defenses for intensive foot patrolling, only to find the strategic objective they had been guarding destroyed in their absence.[28]

In the absence of a serious small war doctrine (there is no treatise comparable to the British army's early twentieth-century manual on the subject by General C.E. Callwell), the American defense establishment, civilian as well as military, has turned to a concept borrowed from nuclear strategy, deterrence. Rather than planning to fight small wars, the defense establishment from the Secretary of Defense on down hopes to intimidate potential opponents and therefore obviate the need for actual fighting. Thus, when Secretary of the Army John O. Marsh Jr. described to Congress the Army's new Light Division, he said, "It is expected that such a force, quickly inserted in the first days of a crisis, could defuse the crisis, thereby precluding the deployment of a much larger force later."[29] The general commanding the Rapid Deployment Force told an audience of sympathetic military men and defense officials, "I do not want you to think that we are an intervention force—because our job is deterrence."[30]

---

27. James A. Bowden, "The RDJTF and Doctrine," *Military Review*, Vol. 62, No. 11 (November 1982), p. 62.
28. *The Report of the President's National Bipartisan Commission on Central America* (New York: Macmillan, 1984), p. 115.
29. Eric C. Ludvigsen, "Elite Light Divisions Among Major Focuses in '85 Army Budget," *Army*, Vol. 34, No. 4 (April 1984), p. 35.
30. Robert C. Kingston, "From RDF to Centcom: New Challenges?," *Journal of the Royal United Services Institute*, Vol. 129, No. 1 (March 1984), p. 17.

The failure to grapple with the difficult task of providing a doctrine for the employment of forces in small war is an old one. A British author writing on the subject in the early 1960s noted that where Britain at the time had "combat forces" for use in the Third World, the United States had "deterrent forces."[31] In the absence of serious doctrine—the kind of doctrine that can only be created by men who expect to fight, not simply deter—one can only expect improvisations like the Grenada operation, in which a tiny island was divided between the Army and the Air Force on one hand, and the Navy and the Marine Corps on the other. To be sure, Grenada was a victory, although that was inevitable given the correlation of forces. It is by no means clear that in the future similar deployments overseas will be equally success-ful, or even nearly so.[32]

MANPOWER. One reason for the success of British small wars has been Britain's development of a military manpower system uniquely suited to such conflicts. In the early nineteenth century, British statesmen created the quasi-tribal regimental system, in which enlisted men and officers (all vol-unteers) served together for long periods of time, alternating between duty overseas and duty at home. It was a system that provided an emotional substitute for the sense of public approbation on which the American military relies: it sustained the fighting spirit of soldiers stationed for years in the remote and alien locations where British power was needed.[33] The United States Army has attempted to create an American regimental system with some success, although such efforts continue to meet the resistance of officers who find such a system administratively inefficient and potentially detri-mental to individual careers.

---

31. Anthony Verrier, "Strategically Mobile Forces—U.S. Theory and British Practice," *Journal of the Royal United Services Institute,* Number 624 (November 1961), pp. 479–485.
32. It is instructive to consider the American intervention in Lebanon in 1958 in this regard. One semi-official study suggests that had that intervention been opposed, disaster could well have resulted from the lack of a common approach to the operation. By implication, the difficulties remain. Roger J. Spiller, "'Not War But Like War': The American Intervention in Lebanon," *Leavenworth Papers,* Number 3 (Fort Leavenworth: U.S. Army Command and General Staff College Combat Studies Institute, 1981).
33. On the regimental system, particularly as it relates to small war, see John Keegan, "Regi-mental Ideology," in Geoffrey Best and Andrew Wheatcroft, eds., *War, Economy, and the Military Mind* (London: Croom Helm, 1976), pp. 3–17; G.F.R. Henderson, *The Science of War* (London: Longmans Green, 1913), pp. 365–434. For a recent assessment, see Jeremy J.J. Phipps, "Unit Cohesion: A Prerequisite for Combat Effectiveness," *National Security Affairs Issue Paper,* Number 82-3 (Washington: National Defense University, 1982).

The renewal of the regimental system in the United States, plus efforts at unit as opposed to individual rotation policies, enhances American abilities to conduct small wars. The reliance on a standby draft in the event of any sizable conflict and, even more importantly, the Army's dependence upon reservists are as detrimental, however, as the reforms mentioned above are useful. A major reason for the success of British small wars has been Britain's near-exclusive reliance on volunteer professional soldiers rather than draftees or reservists. Not only are such soldiers more adept at the difficult kinds of operations mandated by small war: their use also involves fewer domestic political complications, since it does not raise the issue of sending unwilling men to fight obscure and protracted wars.

The American armed forces today, volunteer though they may be, could not conduct any major operation (save a brief defense of Europe) without a reserve mobilization. Many Army units require reserve forces for up to a third of their front-line combat strength, and the Army as a whole relies heavily on reserve tactical support forces. Even the Rapid Deployment Force depends for about one-third of its manpower and most of its combat support on the National Guard and Reserves. Moreover, it is important to realize that a mobilization would inevitably require, in the interests of equity, a resumption of conscription. As the hue and cry over the 1961 mobilization of reservists demonstrated, it is far harder to uproot civilians with jobs and families to support than to draft eighteen-year-olds: to do the one without the other would be virtually unthinkable. Thus, the so-called All Volunteer Force is merely a peacetime construct, unsustainable in any but the most minor of military conflicts. The leaders of the military do not necessarily object to this, however, because they see dependence upon reserve mobilization and conscription as guarantees of the public support for war discussed above. In reality, however, dependence on reserves is only a formidable brake on the government's ability to conduct small wars *successfully*. It is inevitable that most army reserve units would perform their missions less well, and at far greater cost in casualties (some resulting from sheer physical stress) than the active duty units might.[34] Small wars frequently entail fast deployments to extreme climates (e.g., the Persian Gulf), and it is absurd to think that reservists can be as physically hardened to such challenges as their

---

34. See Philip Gold, "What the Reserves Can—and Can't—Do," *The Public Interest*, No. 75 (Spring 1984), pp. 47–61.

active duty counterparts, or that they can be equally practiced in their individual and group skills.

A small war may require both a swift intervention and a long period of consolidation. This pattern—a sudden beginning and a protracted sequel—occurred even in the 1983 Grenada operation, a petty conflict to be sure, but an instructive one. Instead of the invasion force remaining only a few weeks, as the White House first announced, the force remained two months, not merely to mop up resistance, but to stabilize a nation suddenly deprived of all orderly administration. (Indeed, if one considers the presence of several hundred military police, who are in fact combat troops, the follow-up lasted well over six months.) Since most small wars consist of high-intensity conventional phases (e.g., Korea in 1950–1951, and Vietnam in 1965–1966) and low-intensity insurgency operations, the manpower system must be suited to both.

Draftees, however, are not well suited to the protracted counterinsurgency phase of a small war, for both narrow military and broader political reasons. For the sake of equity, a draft-based army will minimize the length of tours in the theater of war, thereby obstructing unit cohesion and the development of familiarity with the environment. Politically, the use of draftees presents domestic difficulties in maintaining public support for a war, and indeed in maintaining the morale of the army in the field. Small wonder, then, that both the British and the French, with one or two notable exceptions, fought both the high and low intensity phases of their small wars with volunteer professional soldiers. Similarly, America's successful campaigns in the Philippines in 1899–1902 and in the Caribbean and Central America during the first third of this century made use only of volunteer professional armed forces.

EQUIPMENT. Small war often requires unique types of equipment and technology, types that may have no utility in large or all-out warfare. This was true even in the nineteenth century: the heliograph and light mountain pack howitzer are only two examples of technological innovations which met the peculiar requirements of small war but had no larger applications.[35] As military establishments have become increasingly specialized, this is even more true than before.

---

35. See V.G. Kiernan, *From Conquest to Collapse: European Empires From 1815 to 1960* (New York: Pantheon, 1982), pp. 123–128.

The United States armed forces have begun to acquire some of the specialized equipment they will need for warfare in the extreme climates where they can expect to fight—mobile water purification plants, for example, and hospital ships to treat casualties. In other respects, however, virtually no headway has been made, for example, in the Army's attempt to procure a light tank, which would be easily transportable by air.[36] Despite the oft-declared need for vastly increased airlift and sealift to transport American forces to non-European theaters of war, spending on such needs has remained low. In 1983, the United States Air Force had precisely as many C-5A heavy transport aircraft (the mainstay for airlifting "outsized" cargo such as tanks and helicopters over long distances) as it did in 1976; it had only thirty more short-range transports (the aging C-130 Hercules) than it did seven years earlier (294 vs. 262). A bias towards pre-positioning of equipment detracts from the flexibility of American forces, as well as presenting attractive targets for preemptive attacks, although some compensating advantages also exist.[37]

In some cases, service rivalries prevent the acquisition of suitable small war equipment. A case in point is "ARAPAHO," a relatively cheap set of prefabricated modules that can be used to convert a merchant vessel into a mini-aircraft carrier. On the basis of their experience in the Falklands (where improvised helicopter and Very Short Take-Off and Landing aircraft landing pads were of great use), the Royal Navy has demonstrated an interest in procuring ARAPAHO. The U.S. Army is interested in ARAPAHO as a means of suddenly improvising support vessels in off-shore operations, but the United States Navy has little interest in the program.[38]

ORGANIZATION. On the face of it, the United States has available a large force suited to the waging of small wars. In addition to the Marine Corps (which, until the postwar period, traditionally fought such conflicts), numbering three divisions plus combat support, the United States has an airborne and an airmobile division, a light infantry division (the 9th Division, also

---

36. For a discussion of the long-standing utility of light tanks in certain kinds of mountain warfare, see D.A.L. Mackenzie, "Operations in the Lower Khaisora Valley, Waziristan, in 1937," *Journal of the Royal United Services Institute*, Number 528 (November 1937), pp. 805–822.
37. On these and other RDF-related issues, see Congressional Budget Office, "Rapid Deployment Forces: Policy and Budgetary Implications" (Washington: CBO, 1983). See also Richard Halloran, "Poised for the Persian Gulf," *The New York Times Magazine*, April 1, 1984, p. 38 ff.
38. Millard Barger, "USN Abandons Arapaho; British Employ It; US Army Considers It," *Armed Forces Journal International*, April 1984, pp. 22, 27.

known as the High Technology Test Bed), two (soon to be three) Ranger battalions, several Special Forces Groups (soon to be expanded and placed under a separate command), and other infantry units currently dedicated to Third World missions (the 2nd Infantry Division in Korea and the 25th Division in Hawaii), plus, in the future, two more light divisions, the 7th (currently an understrength unit in California) and a new one to be created in 1985.

On paper, this force would seem both substantial and diverse enough to meet any contingency. Yet much of this strength is deceptive, not only because of the deficiencies alluded to above, but because of organizational difficulties. The Marine Corps, for example, is spread over the globe, and must prepare for its traditional mission of amphibious warfare (which it holds exclusively) in such diverse locales as Southeast Asia, the northern flank of NATO (Norway and Denmark), and the Mediterranean. It is primarily an infantry force and hence lacks the mechanized punch to cope with serious armored forces. The 82nd Airborne and 101st Airmobile Divisions are not merely small war forces, but part of America's overall strategic reserve, and hence have multiple missions, including European ones. Similarly, the 2nd Division is stationed in and the 25th Division is committed to the reinforcement of South Korea; and the 24th Mechanized Division, the Army's most powerful contribution to the Rapid Deployment Force, is committed to European tasks as well. The 9th Division is, and for one or two years will remain, in the throes of continual reequipment and innovation because of its role as the test division for future light divisions.

The incredibly varied locales of small wars require specially trained and acclimatized troops. The United States lacks the specialized units—mountain and jungle divisions, for example—trained in such unique environments and suited to operations in them. Since the very first years of World War II, the U.S. Army has resolutely opposed the creation of specially adapted divisions, in contrast to the practice of other countries.

These problems are compounded by the anomalous setup of the avowed small war force of the United States, the Rapid Deployment Force. The RDF consists of forces from the four major services, none of which, however, comes under the peacetime control of Central Command, which would control their use in a war in the Persian Gulf. No command or other exercises can provide the intimate cooperation and mutual understanding necessary for rapid deployment missions: thus, the separation between peacetime and wartime command is a serious deficiency. In addition, the limitation of

Central Command to the Persian Gulf precludes sustained work on joint deployments in other areas. The problems of cooperation became manifest in the Grenada operation, in the course of which a tiny island was divided in half, the Air Force and the Army in the south, the Navy and the Marine Corps in the north. In matters ranging from communications to coordination of attacks, failures of service cooperation were revealed. Similar chain-of-command and coordination difficulties appeared in the deployment of American Marines to Lebanon in 1983, and may have been partly responsible for the disastrous lack of security at the Marine compound in Beirut.[39]

At a higher level, there is no evidence that lessons have been learned from either Vietnam or the Falklands concerning the higher organization of government for small war. The need for the unity of command under central civilian control (as in Malaya, where one official controlled both military and civic operations) has been ignored. Similarly, no provisions have been made to centralize a war's strategic and diplomatic coordination in the hands of a full-time civil servant or political appointee, a practice often urged in Vietnam but never implemented there, but a practice which the British adopted and which contributed to their military and diplomatic victory in the Falklands.[40]

*Conclusions*

Of all the constraints on the conduct of small wars by the American government, the most important is the institutional one, and in particular the difficulties created by the unsuitability of the American national security apparatus to conduct small wars. The other factors constraining the conduct of small wars—public opinion, foreign pressures, and Congressional struggles for control over war powers—will vary with the particular crisis and the way it is handled. The reluctance of the armed services to prepare suitably for such wars and the inability of the United States' higher command to conduct such wars with the finesse they require are deeper, more permanent, and more dangerous problems.

---

39. See Samuel P. Huntington, "Defense Organization and Military Strategy," *The Public Interest,* No. 75 (Spring 1984), pp. 20–46, especially pp. 41–45.

40. See Robert W. Komer, *Bureaucracy Does Its Thing: Institutional Constraints on U.S.–G.V.N. Performance in Vietnam,* R-967-ARPA 1972 (Santa Monica: Rand, 1973), pp. 75–105; and Summers, *On Strategy,* pp. 141–150. The work of Sir Michael Palliser's small coordinating committee of senior civil servants and military men was particularly important (communications with senior British officials).

The institutional deficiencies of the United States defense establishment regarding small wars result from a number of causes: the ineptitude of some civilian and military leaders, Congressional micro-management of various procurement and organizational policies, and the understandable psychological trauma of the American officer corps consequent upon the Vietnam War. It would be neither just nor profitable to condemn one group or the other: rather, it would be desirable to begin thinking about means of redressing American weaknesses in this area.

The first and most important measure is a search for a sound theoretical understanding of the problems and perplexities of small wars, because unlike the British, Americans cannot assume the existence of institutions adapted to this challenge. However, it is not simply the case that more study is required. Rather, what is needed is a willingness to publicly acknowledge the implications of what we already know. The American defense establishment must cure itself of an obsession with European warfare, and the officer corps must be weaned from its understandable but pernicious belief in the need for public support of the kind it had during World War II. Additionally, American force structure, including emphasis on airlift, percentage of forces dedicated to European missions, and organization for rapid deployment, must reflect the realities of where American forces are likely to fight.

Two options have been advanced as possible solutions to the small war dilemma: one, that small war missions be devolved upon the Marine Corps; the other, that American strategists contrive to make such wars as short as possible.[41] There is something to be said for each policy, but neither separately nor together can these solve the problem. Service rivalries preclude the exclusive assignment of such an important mission to the Marines, and, as we have noted above, the Marines are already thinly stretched and are not equipped to handle certain contingencies (for example, those requiring mechanized or airborne forces). There is room for improved utilization of the Marine Corps, however, most importantly by relieving it of responsibility for the *conduct* of all amphibious operations. During World War II, after all, the

---

41. The former seems to me to be implicit in the position of Colonel Summers's book on Vietnam; the latter is put forward by Samuel P. Huntington in his edited work, *The Strategic Imperative: New Policies for American Security* (Cambridge: Ballinger, 1982), p. 49. On the Marine contribution to the Rapid Deployment Force, see David A. Quinlan, "The Role of the Marine Corps in Rapid Deployment Forces," *National Security Essay*, Number 83-3 (Washington: National Defense University, 1983).

Army conducted more amphibious operations than did the Marine Corps. In the future, the Marine Corps could continue to prepare the *doctrine* for such operations, while it concentrated more closely on small war missions outside Europe.[42]

Although speed is of the essence in all military operations, it may be particularly important in small wars—hence the importance of substantial airlift capabilities, even though air transport is a highly uneconomic means of moving men and materiel. Nonetheless, it is in the nature of small wars that they frequently require sustained commitments of forces to stabilize a country following an initial victory. Hence, the attractive notion of a violent but brief conflict is chimerical. Even in the Falklands, where a victory seemed fairly swift and complete, the war led the British armed forces to deploy several thousand troops plus air and naval forces in a region hitherto guarded by a cutter and fewer than a hundred marines. To take but one example, it is hard to envision a war fought to protect small Persian Gulf states against Iran which would not involve prolonged deployments of American armed forces overseas. As we have noted above, it is in the nature of small wars that they alternate between high- and low-intensity phases.

The United States cannot fashion a small war capability from an instrument prepared mainly for all-out war in Europe, a replay of World War II except with more advanced technology and conducted against the Soviets rather than the Germans. The lessons of the Grenada micro-war are instructive, for in it admittedly conservative military planners underestimated both the intensity and the duration of the operation. Initially, planners committed some 4,000 paratroops, Marines, and Rangers in two waves: within a few days 5,000 paratroops were flown in to replace the initial 2,000-man assault force. Invasion forces peaked at over 7,000 men, or nearly twice the force originally envisioned. As I have pointed out above, the invasion entailed a far longer commitment than that originally envisioned. A further lesson from the Grenada operation concerns its unfortuitous timing. Even as American troops fought in the Caribbean, others began to recover from a far bloodier debacle in Lebanon; indeed, the Marines who fought in Grenada were on their way to replace the Marine contingent there. Small wars do not necessarily occur

---

42. Such was the Marine Corps role in World War II. See Jeter A. Isely and Philip A. Crowl, *The U.S. Marines and Amphibious War: Its Theory, and Its Practice in the Pacific* (Princeton: Princeton University Press, 1951), especially pp. 3–71, 580–590.

one at a time. Indeed, they are as or more likely to occur simultaneously, and hence no single small war "fire brigade" can hope to cover all contingencies.

A public and institutional acknowledgment of the small war problem is but the first step in dealing with it. An intellectual comprehension of the demands of small war does not necessarily translate itself into implementation of the policies required to wage it successfully, a point on which Robert Komer's study of the Vietnam era bureaucracy is eloquent.[43] One necessary step is surely the procurement of the proper kinds of equipment to deal with small war. More importantly, the United States should consider reorganizing its forces to cope with it. Here, the manpower problems alluded to above become particularly sharp. If, as has been argued above, a small war expeditionary force should consist exclusively of professional or at least volunteer active-duty soldiers, the force structure of the Army in particular will need to be changed. One possibility might be the creation of, in effect, two armies: a self-contained professional expeditionary force consisting of seven or eight specialized divisions (plus the Marines), and a Europe-oriented draft-based army. By executive declaration or law, it could be established that no draftees could be dispatched overseas, except to Europe, without a Congressional declaration of war. Even in such a case, it might be necessary to reduce U.S. standing forces in Europe somewhat while increasing U.S. commitment to European reinforcement late in a conflict.

There is ample precedent for this kind of institutional arrangement in the case of France, the only Great Power to have sustained both European and overseas commitments for well over a century. From the late nineteenth century until the present, with the exception of the Algerian war, French law and policy have prohibited the use of conscripts overseas. Partly as a result of this wise policy, France sustains even today effective forces in such contested countries as Chad and Djibouti, as well as a substantial Europe-oriented conventional force.

The two most probable loci for American small wars are in the Persian Gulf and Central America, yet paradoxically Central Command and Southern Command have the fewest forces assigned to their peacetime control for training and operations. Certainly, both Commands should have adequate forces under their peacetime control for at least the first stages of any fore-

---

43. Komer, *Bureaucracy Does Its Thing.*

seeable small war. This would further help reduce the mismatch between the types of forces the United States has and the locations where it is likely to use them.

American participation in small wars remains an inevitable concomitant of America's world role. Civilians and soldiers cannot avoid the problem by simply refusing to believe that they will again send soldiers into obscure corners of the world to fight for limited political objectives against a hostile non-European power. If they are sincere in this disbelief, they must accept the consequences for American foreign policy. Such a disbelief put into practice would mean a unilateral American rejection of its status as a world power, a status held to with enormous benefit for this country and others since 1945.

The choice, then, is between being ready to fight well when it is necessary to fight and fighting badly. The costs in the latter case include the loss of American and foreign lives and failures in American foreign and security policy. The best way to reduce the likelihood of small wars is to be well prepared for them, but it is a delusion to think that they are escapable through conventional deterrence, any more than they were in the late 1950s through a policy of massive nuclear retaliation. The first task, therefore, is to acknowledge the problem and study it. At the moment, however, one must concur regretfully with the judgment of Lieutenant General Wallace H. Nutting, former commander of U.S. forces in Central and Latin America, who recently said of small war, "As a nation we don't understand it and as a government we are not prepared to deal with it."[44]

---

44. Quoted in *Newsweek*, June 6, 1983, p. 24.

# Soviet Vulnerabilities in Iran and the RDF Deterrent

*Joshua M. Epstein*

**I**t is difficult to imagine a region at once so vital economically and so volatile politically as the Persian Gulf today. To its economic importance, the Arab oil embargo of 1973 was, for many, the first rude awakening. Since then, a stormy sequence of events has underlined its political instability. The Iranian revolution, the fall of the Shah, and the bitter ordeal of the hostages were, for many Americans, a shocking demonstration of that fact; the seizure of the Great Mosque at Mecca and the Iraq–Iran War, part of its grim and continuing confirmation.

Concurrent with these stark realizations, the West saw Soviet foreign policy enter a particularly adventurist phase, one in which regional instabilities—in Angola, in Ethiopia, and in South Yemen—were made targets of military opportunity. The possibility that a crumbling order in the Gulf would present the Soviets with even more attractive opportunities was lost on a very few.

And when the Soviets invaded Afghanistan, the West's worst fears suddenly seemed ominously at hand. Jolted by the alarming convergence of events, former President Carter threw down the gauntlet, warning in his 1980 State of the Union Address that "an attempt by any outside force to gain control of the Persian Gulf region—will be repelled by any means necessary, including military force." [1]

Today, few would deny the claim of former CIA Director, Admiral Stansfield Turner that ". . . the most demanding need for military force in the region would be to oppose a direct thrust by the Soviets into Iran." [2] Indeed, this contingency, under the Carter Doctrine has served as a principal basis for planning of the Rapid Deployment Joint Task Force (RDF).

---

While the author bears sole responsibility for all views expressed here, he is grateful to William W. Kaufmann, Barry Posen, Steven Miller, and Ted Greenwood for their suggestions.

---

*Joshua Epstein is a Research Fellow at Harvard's Center for Science and International Affairs, and a consultant to the Rand Corporation.*

---

1. U.S., Congress, Senate, Committee on Foreign Relations, "U.S. Security Interests and Policies in Southwest Asia," Hearings Before the Subcommittee on Near Eastern and South Asian Affairs, Ninety-Sixth Congress, second session, February–March 1980, p. 350.
2. Admiral Stansfield Turner (USN–Ret.), "Toward a New Defense Strategy," *New York Times Magazine*, May 10, 1981, p. 16.

---

*International Security*, Fall 1981 (Vol. 6, No. 2) 0162-2889/81/020126-33 $02.50/0
© 1981 by the President and Fellows of Harvard College and the Massachusetts Institute of Technology.

Given the exceedingly grave consequences that would attend its successful execution, and the uncertainty surrounding Soviet intentions in the region, it is a contingency which no responsible analyst can ignore. And, of the numerous Persian Gulf contingencies of interest, a Soviet drive for the oil of Khuzestan is the threat to be examined here.

The prevailing view of American deterrent capabilities is frighteningly pessimistic. In peacetime, there are twenty-four Soviet divisions in the region, while the RDF's ground complement is assumed to number around four divisions.[3] The Soviets enjoy proximity. They share a border with Iran while the bulk of the U.S. force is thousands of miles away. It is widely assumed in addition that simultaneous contingencies pose far more serious problems for the United States than they do for the Soviets.

As a consequence, there is a general consensus that without using nuclear weapons, the United States would stand little chance of handling an all-out invasion of Iran, and that in no event can there be a feasible defense without a dramatic expansion of American basing in the region.

Columnist Jack Anderson reports Government testimony to the effect that "the Rapid Deployment Force would be no more than a 'trip wire' against the Soviets. The contingency plan calls for a nuclear strike to stop the Soviets from annihilating the force."[4] Defense Secretary Weinberger himself has warned that "the U.S., at present, is incapable of stopping an assault on Western oil supplies,"[5] while prominent analysts have gone so far as to say that Iran "may be inherently indefensible."[6]

The military situation, however, has not received the close examination that it deserves. In divisions, the Soviets outweigh the RDF, and the larger force is the closer to Iran; those are undeniable facts. But the conclusions drawn from them are unwarranted.

If planned and postured according to the strategy proposed in this essay, the RDF can present an imposing deterrent to Soviet aggression. Further-

3. James Wooten, *Rapid Deployment Forces, Issue Brief Number IB80027* (Washington, D.C.: The Library of Congress Congressional Research Service, 1980), p. 4 and Sir John Hackett, "Protecting Oil Supplies: The Military Requirements," Paper presented to the International Institute For Strategic Studies, Twenty-Second Annual Conference, Stresa, Italy, September 1980, pp. 9–10.
4. Jack Anderson, "Frightening Facts on the Persian Gulf," *The Washington Post*, February 3, 1981, p. 18.
5. Robert S. Dudney, "The Defense Gap that Worries the President," *U.S. News and World Report*, February 16, 1981.
6. Jeffrey Record, "Disneyland Planning for Persian Gulf Oil Defense," *The Washington Star*, Friday, March 20, 1981, p. 17.

more, under such a strategy, tactical nuclear employment would be not only unnecessary, but ill-advised. Contrary to the prevailing view, moreover, the constraint of simultaneous contingencies weighs at least as heavily upon the Soviets as it does on the United States.

The essential features of that strategy are the abandonment of forward defense and the exploitation of warning time. But first, two issues must be addressed: the Soviet overland threat to Iran and the prospects for Soviet airlifted assaults. Each must be appreciated if Soviet tactics combining them are to be assessed.

*The Soviet Overland Threat*

As a consequence of the terrain (see map), this may be divided into three successive phases:

*Phase I:* The advance through northern Iran, over the mountains south to the Tehran line.

One might postulate the seizure of Qazvin and/or Tehran as Phase I goals. These might then be seen as the main bases of operation for

*Phase II:* The advance south through central Iran for a build-up at Dezful (or some other appropriate area at the southern base of the Zagros Mountains).

*Phase III:* The final thrust south to drive the RDF out of Khuzestan, securing Soviet control of Iran's principal oil and shipping facilities.

This plan closely resembles that set forth in the *Soviet Command Study of Iran* (1941).[7] There, the Soviet General Staff wrote,

After the capture of Tehran and Qazvin, an advance in a straight line on to Hamadan and on to the Persian Gulf along the Southern leg of the Trans-Iranian railroad will be possible. Here is where the entire supply of weapons and munitions for Iran [read the RDF] will probably be concentrated. This line leads most directly to the center of Iran's oil industry.[8]

The objective, given this not entirely hypothetical plan, is to delay and wear down the Soviets' southern advance in such a way that an adequate coun-

---

7. *Soviet Command Study of Iran (Moscow 1941): Draft Translation and Brief Analysis*, Gerold Guensberg (trans.) (Arlington, Virginia: SRI International, January 1980).
8. *Soviet Command Study*, p. 160.

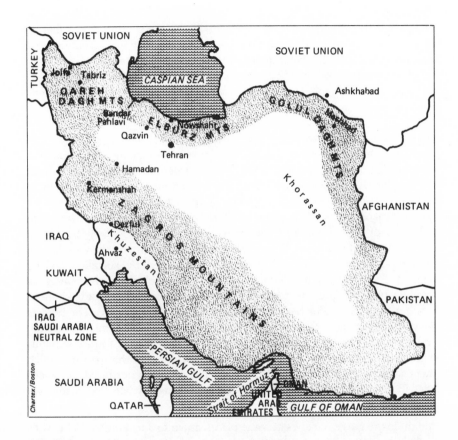

terpose can be inserted for the Battle of Khuzestan, as it were. Accordingly, the RDF strategy proposed here falls into three phases corresponding to those of the threat itself.

*Phase I:* Delay the advance into northern Iran while constructing a defense perimeter in Khuzestan.

*Phase II:* Delay and attrit the advance over the Zagros Mountains while building up for the ground war in Khuzestan.

*Phase III:* Battle of Khuzestan. (This would be a combined arms conflict including ground, air, and naval forces.)

The goal of this strategy is to deter aggression by the credible threat that its object—the oil—will be denied. Whether or not the RDF is adequate to that deterrent mission is the basic question to be addressed here.

Let us examine each of these phases in turn. It will become evident that the defensive plan exploits many of the vulnerabilities stressed in the Soviets' own *Command Study*.

### PHASE I: DELAYING ACTION IN THE NORTH

There are three axes from the Soviet Union into Iran by land: from the Caspian Sea directly, and across the Soviet borders to the East and West of the Caspian. All three axes suffer a number of common problems. First, there is a very limited transportation system along each axis: there are roughly a dozen surface arteries from the Soviet Union to Tehran.[9] Moreover, each (rail or road) must pass over formidable mountain ranges, notably the Qareh Dagh in the northwest, the Elburz south of the Caspian, and the Golul Dagh in the northeast. Third, each artery is punctuated by so-called "choke points." These are points at which a) destruction or blockage of the artery is feasible; b) bypassing the resultant obstacle is not feasible; and where c) clearing the blockage or restoring the route is time-consuming. The Soviets were, and doubtless are, very well aware of the vulnerability this represents, and especially, as the *Command Study* emphasized, of each route's vulnerability to air interdiction. Consider their commentary on the road (of which there remains essentially one) from Ashkhabad, in the northeast, to Mashhad. In reference to the Dash Arasy gorge, through which that road must pass, the Soviets wrote,

At km-25 the gorge narrows at some places down to 3 to 4 meters. The walls of rock on both sides reach heights of 200 to 300 m. The gorge can be easily destroyed which would seriously impede traffic.

---

9. This, and all subsequent statements concerning the number, length, or condition of surface arteries in the various sectors of Iran are derived primarily from *Map of Iran*, Central Intelligence Agency, 1977 and *Road Map of Iran*, Sahab Geographic and Drafting Institute (Tehran, Iran, 1977). A careful attempt has been made to compare the Soviets' 1941 discussion to the current transportation system. The match remains very close in the sectors of interest. While certain arteries have doubtless been upgraded for commercial use, this need not entail any reduction in vulnerability to military attack. Lightweight construction materials, for example, may be efficient from the point of view of economic growth while representing no enhancement in hardness or reduction in susceptibility to structural attacks. Moreover, even where arteries have been upgraded in the latter respect since 1941, so have air-to-ground munitions grown in effectiveness. In the view of experts interviewed by the author, the net effect of these developments has not been to reduce the vulnerability of the Iranian transportation system significantly. Indeed, some feel that it is more vulnerable (to modern ordnance) than it was in 1941.

In general, the Soviets stressed that

The road—along its entire stretch—is easily attackable from the air. Mountain sides and the narrow width of the plain (15–20 km) provide cover and allow divebomber attacks with ease. [10]

In each of the successive mountain chains of the northern Khorassan, the Soviets enumerated "narrow gorges which can be easily blocked." [11] Roads are very scarce and vulnerable, as they were in 1941. For these reasons, it is difficult not to concur in the Soviets' own view that the mountain range of the northeast

constitutes a mighty frontier protection which makes very difficult an invasion from the north into the Khorassan interior. [12]

Looking westward to the Caspian approaches, the Soviets wrote of the Elburz mountains that

they simplify considerably the defense of the important central areas of Iran against an enemy who has landed along the southern shores of the Caspian Sea. [13]

Why? Because, of the roughly five roads over the Elburz to Tehran or Qazvin, all must cross bridges over precipitous faults thousands of meters in the mountains, or must pass through narrow gorges. [14] So concerned were the Soviets that the few available arteries would be closed off, that they took an inventory of all draught animals (horses, donkeys, mules, and camels) in Iran, anticipating that air interdiction might force them to advance over the pack animal tracks that lace this craggy terrain. [15]

There is one railroad from the Caspian to Tehran, the trans-Iranian railroad. It is the only railroad from Tehran south to Dezful. It traverses the above terrain first in the Elburz and again south in the Zagros Mountains. Of the passage over the Elburz, the Soviets wrote that the line "can be easily

---

10. *Soviet Command Study*, pp. 218–219, and 220.
11. *Ibid.*
12. *Ibid.*, pp. 20–21.
13. *Ibid.*, p. 164.
14. From the coastal city of Now Shahr, south of the main port of Pahlavi, for example, the meticulous Soviet planners noted that "the more deeply the path penetrates the gorge (up to km. 20) the more difficult becomes the traffic. A dynamiting of the rocks or the destruction of the road or the bridges would greatly slow down the movement of troops. . . . Bypassing the road in the event of destruction is nearly impossible. The traffic can be resumed only after the road has been repaired." *Ibid.*, p. 176.
15. *Ibid.*, p. 100.

attacked from the air." [16] Even in the lowlands near Tehran, they cautioned that "the entire section is observable from the air and it can be easily attacked." [17]

Finally, in the northwest, the Iranian Azerbaidjan, the same vulnerabilities prevail. There is a single road from Jolfa (just across the Soviet border in Iran) to the first main city, Tabriz. Of that crucial artery, the detailed *Command Study* records:

At km 22 from Dshulfa [Jolfa] begins the Daradis gorge which is 7 km long. The advance of troops through this small and narrow pass can be most difficult. The movement of troops can be made even more difficult if the enemy employs roadblocks or attacks from the air. [18]

Again, bypass is virtually infeasible. The shoulders of the gorge are walls of boulder. Detonations creating rockslides would severely hamper troop movement, and could be cleared only with extensive military engineering efforts.

NUCLEAR VS. CONVENTIONAL WEAPONS. The first phase of the defensive plan is to delay the advance of Soviet units by choking off this transportation system. This mission could be accomplished with nuclear weapons or with conventional forces.

As to the feasibility of nuclear interdiction, a study conducted for the Office of the Assistant Secretary of Defense for Program Analysis and Evaluation (PA&E) concluded that "ADM [Atomic Demolition Munitions] alone could quickly seal all avenues of approach into Iran." [19]

It is far from clear, however, that nuclear employment is necessary, despite claims to the contrary. [20] Those claims generally fail to draw a critical distinction. They begin by noting that the RDF is, among other things, designed to *protect* the West's "oil lifeline"; this is located in *southern* Iran. In the same breath, however, recourse to nuclear weapons is deemed necessary, for lack

---

16. *Ibid.*, p. 201.
17. *Ibid.*
18. *Ibid.*, p. 127.
19. Captain Henry Leonard and Mr. Jeffrey Scott, *Methodology For Estimating Movement Rates of Ground Forces in Mountainous Terrain With and Without Defensive Obstacles: First Draft* (Washington: Study for the Office of Assistant Secretary of Defense, Program Analysis and Evaluation, October 12, 1979), p. 3.8.
20. While at *The New York Times*, now Director of the State Department's Bureau of Politico-Military Affairs Richard Burt related that:
"A Defense Department report on the military situation in the Persian Gulf region has concluded that American forces could not stop a Soviet thrust into northern Iran and that the

of other means, to *blunt* a Soviet violation of *northern* Iran. The prevailing assumption that the use of nuclear weapons is necessary therefore rests critically upon the premise that a forward defense of the northern Iranian border is required to prevent Soviet control of Khuzestan's oil riches. But why should it be? The oil lies roughly a thousand kilometers and two formidable mountain chains south of the "inviolable" border.

If, by a series of conventional delaying operations, enough time can be bought to permit the emplacement of an adequate American defense force there, Soviet control of Khuzestan could be denied. In the final analysis, the RDF's problem is time. To be sure, nuclear weapons would buy more time, and more quickly, for a Western build-up in the south than would conventional munitions. But if *enough* time can be bought conventionally, that, for a host of reasons, is surely the approach to be preferred.[21] And it *is* a feasible approach.

---

United States should therefore consider using 'tactical' nuclear weapons in any conflict there." Richard Burt, "Study Says a Soviet Move in Iran Might Require U.S. Atom Arms," *The New York Times*, February 2, 1980, p. 1.
Columnist Jack Anderson reported in *The Washington Post* that
"President Carter established the far-flung, multi-service Rapid Deployment Force to protect our oil lifeline. Yet top military hands warn that it . . . could never be a match for the Soviet juggernaut across the Iranian border." Jack Anderson, "Frightening Facts on the Persian Gulf."
21. In addition to being adequate to the deterrent goal, denial, conventional operations would avoid those externalities which could attend nuclear employment. Assume for the moment that in the face of American nuclear use the Soviets did not respond in kind, but for example, simply "threw in the towel" and withdrew their surviving troops. The entire world would be watching. The event would have provided it a graphic example of the military utility of nuclear weapons and could thus be a positive stimulant to nuclear proliferation. The United States would be hard pressed, having successfully relied upon them, to argue their superfluity to, for example, the Saudis, Pakistanis, South Koreans, even the Iranians themselves.
In the latter regard, it might be noted that collateral nuclear damage to Iran and the untoward consequences for its northern populations could eventuate in such bitter and enduring enmity toward the United States and its Allies as to produce economic consequences indistinguishable in their gravity from those the employment was intended to avert.
As for Europe, such a demonstration of U.S. willingness to use nuclear weapons in a forward defense could reinforce whatever preemptive inclinations the Soviets may harbor toward NATO's vulnerable land-based theater nuclear weapons; "the Americans used them first to buy mobilization time in Iran and they'd use them first to buy mobilization time in central Europe." The implications of this altogether natural train of thought for "Euro-strategic crisis stability" should be obvious.
All of these perfectly plausible and very unfortunate consequences—for Western energy, for proliferation, and for European security—could attend the "best case" in which the Soviets fail to respond in kind. And there is always the grave risk of Soviet escalation itself, a risk which is certainly associated with any use of nuclear weapons. If, in closing roads, ground bursts were

The first step is to delay the Soviets' advance through northern Iran.

To do this, the major units with forces available to the RDF are impressive, and include the following:

*Army*

82d Airborne Division

101st Airborne Division (Air Assault)

24th Infantry Division (Mechanized)

194th Armored Brigade

6th Combat Brigade (Air Cavalry)

Various Ranger and Special Forces units

*Air Force*

27th Tactical Fighter Wing (F-111)

49th Tactical Fighter Wing (F-15)

347th Tactical Fighter Wing (F-4)

354th Tactical Fighter Wing (A-10)

366th Tactical Fighter Wing (F-111)

552nd Airborne Warning and Control Wing (E-3A)

150th Tactical Fighter Group, Air National Guard (A-7)

---

the *modus operandi*, then, depending upon the prevailing winds, the Soviet Union (which "enjoys" proximity) could be subjected to substantial fallout.

While seeking to avoid unnecessary risks of escalation by one's adversary, it is equally important to avoid imposing escalatory pressures upon oneself. Casualties are, of course, to be minimized on humane grounds. But they should be minimized for this less immediate reason as well. As one's casualties mount, so may the pressure to prosecute the war to an extent, or in a manner, not called for by its original, limited objectives. That is, if the human "sunk costs" quickly come to outstrip the original objectives, since the former cannot be reclaimed, the latter may be raised to ensure that death was not in vain. Ill-considered expansions of war goals, and an ever-increasing commitment of troops may follow.

While the risk of Soviet escalation is associated with a nuclear defense, these considerations would counsel against airborne and in favor of air power as the conventional instrument in Phase I; first, because transport of airborne (dropped) troops into the northern mountains of Iran would be quite vulnerable to Soviet-based fighters. Even assuming that a sufficiently large contingent of airborne troops could be securely delivered, are they to be recovered or left to "fend for themselves"? To pick them up would require the use of vulnerable helicopters or fixed-wing aircraft, while to resupply them for a sustained defense would be equally demanding. To lose them and/or the forces engaged in either their recovery or resupply, could be escalatory.

The classic method of dealing with the vulnerability of airdropped forces would, of course, be to press an advance north, expanding one's perimeter until the airborne forces were within it. Aside from being totally inconsistent with all of America's expressed aims in Iran, this tactic— essentially an occupation—would subject the U.S. to all those vulnerabilities upon whose exploitation its strategy should be based.

For all of these reasons, then, conventional air forces seem the most intelligent instruments in the first delay phase.

188th Tactical Fighter Group, Air National Guard (A-7)
Reconnaissance squadrons
Tactical airlift squadrons
Conventional Strategic Projection Force
Various other units
*Navy*
   3 Aircraft carrier battle groups
   1 Surface action group
   5 Squadrons of antisubmarine warfare patrol aircraft
   6 Amphibious ships
   7 Near-term prepositioning ships (NTPS)
*Marine Corps*
   Marine amphibious force (division + wing)
   7th Marine Amphibious Brigade (NTPS MAB)[22]

While the regional basing currently available is inadequate to accommodate so large an air arm, that does not warrant fatalism regarding the first delay phase. Its limited goal, recall, is to bound the Soviets' rate of advance sufficiently to ensure enough time to mount an adequate combined arms defense in Khuzestan. As will become evident, if the interdiction campaign were to ensure a month in transit from the Soviets' bases to the point at which the second delay phase is conducted (in the southern Zagros), that should be adequate (as always, on the assumption that warning time is exploited).

The on-road distances involved are all on the order of 1000 kilometers at least. To ask that the RDF's air operation yield a month in transit is therefore merely to require that it limit the Soviets' overall (repair plus movement) rate to no more than roughly 33⅓ km/day. But that, history records, would be a remarkable pace. It would exceed that achieved by Hitler's armies in their blitz of Flanders in 1940 (31 km/day) and in Operation Barbarossa the following year (29 km/day). The Normandy Breakout of 1944 saw a rate of 28 km/day, while 13 km/day was logged by the North Koreans in their offensive of 1950. The Israeli's victories on the West Bank and the Golan in 1967 were achieved under advance rates of 27 and 18 km/day respectively.[23] Notwithstanding the myriad differences between each of the above and the Soviet

22. *Fact Sheet*, Public Affairs Office, HQ Rapid Deployment Joint Task Force, April 1981, pp. 2–3.
23. Colonel T. N. Dupuy, *Numbers, Predictions and War*, (Indianapolis: The Bobbs–Merrill Company, Inc., 1979), p. 16.

advance as posited here, 33⅓ km/day is a very spirited clip. And in none of these historical cases was the cited rate sustained over so great a distance as that facing a Soviet "drive for oil."

In short, the Soviets would be operating in truly forbidding terrain, over northern Iran's limited and vulnerable transportation system—a system so constricted that at its narrowest points, the mere disabling of lead elements would bring whole columns to a standstill; it is a network dotted with severe choke points. Under such conditions, to hold the Soviets down to one of the highest advance rates in history must be seen as a modest goal. And although more ambitious goals may fall within its grasp should the RDF's regional basing expand, current resources should be capable of holding a Soviet advance to that rate or lower. Indeed, an array of options present themselves.

The less stringent is one's demand for time urgency, the less demanding the interdiction operation becomes. And there is no compelling military reason, if the United States exploits warning time, either to strike every lucrative choke point in a single day or to conduct the operation solely with tactical air. In one of the most innovative moves of recent years, twenty-eight B-52Hs (in North Dakota) "have been organized into a quick-response outfit called the Strategic Projection Force, or *Spif*." [24] Designed specifically for conventional bombing operations in the Gulf region, *Spif*'s "war plans call for the bombers to strike at night at low level." As of this writing, *Spif* planners report that "training for Persian Gulf missions has reached the point that a full-dress exercise will be conducted soon."

While feasible from the continental United States, such conventional B-52 operations could also be staged from bases in Guam, Australia, Clark Field in the Philippines and elsewhere. Diego Garcia will shortly be capable of accommodating the B-52s. It can be hoped, as SAC Commander General Ellis notes, that

sending B-52s to the trouble spot in the first hours of a crisis might be enough to freeze the Soviet military. Bombs might not have to be dropped at all, as long as the will and ability to do so were demonstrated . . . [25]

If deterrence fails, however, the RDF could initially create the northernmost tier of choke points, working south only as reconnaissance dictates, relying primarily on the bombers, and phasing in air from the Khuzestan perimeter

---

24. George C. Wilson, "'Anytime Anywhere:' A New Conventional Role for B-52 Bombers," *The Washington Post*, March 31, 1981, p. 6.
25. *Ibid.*

as it becomes available. This "tiered interdiction" could effectively deny Soviet engineering units any opportunity to restore routes before the main columns arrive. Aircraft from the two carriers now on station in the region could, from the Gulf of Oman, be used to provide escort for the bombers or, if they were aerially refuelled, to conduct a portion of the interdiction operation. The carriers' classical mission, however, would be to provide tactical air cover (power projection) for the Marine beachhead in Khuzestan, cover which could be augmented by offshore support (if necessary) from smaller surface combatants inside the Persian Gulf. As the Marine perimeter expands and establishes its air defense, the carriers can be withdrawn while, from within the perimeter, Air Force and/or Marine aircraft take over the continuing air interdiction campaign from the bombers. The latter could then be withheld as an intra-war deterrent or could strike targets in central Iran, Afghanistan, or elsewhere. With the establishment of a perimeter air defense, carrier air, arrayed from the Gulf of Oman to the Arabian Sea, could be flexibly employed in a variety of ways, including fleet defense, power projection, and Sea Line of Communication (SLOC) protection. With warning, the RDF's third carrier could supplement aerial refuelling and air defense of the two on-station carriers, used in any of the above capacities.

This particular scheme is not the only one possible. The range of tactical combinations and employment schedules is wide. It is one of many alternatives to carrier operations, however brief, inside the Persian Gulf. Although further regional basing—particularly Turkish, Omani, or Saudi— would simplify it, the RDF's northern interdiction campaign is feasible and, while limited in scope, it would form an effective spearhead to an imposing deterrent posture.

PHASE II: DELAYING ACTION IN THE ZAGROS

Phase II is conducted in the Zagros Mountains from within the southern perimeter by highly mobile (heliborne) special forces. The tactics are similar to those used by the Finns in the Soviet–Finnish Winter War, in which ambush and "hit and run" tactics figured prominently. Termed *"motti"* tactics, their employment by the vastly outnumbered defenders thoroughly frustrated the Soviets' continuing attempts to penetrate the waist of Finland.

The Soviets' overland passage through the Zagros would be as difficult as in the north; there are again very few arteries. In every case, choke points abound, and they may be selected to maximize defensive opportunity. Of the countless gorges through the parallel chains which are the Zagros, the

Soviets wrote, ". . . with the use of obstacles or roadblocks, these can be turned into excellent defensive positions."[26]

The RDF would have two objectives in Phase II: delay and attrition. Both can be made quite severe with surprising economy. Regarding attrition, the above-mentioned study for PA&E concludes that,

The mission of light forces in the delay phase should be to inflict losses on the invader without becoming decisively engaged. . . . Airmobile infantry forces employed in small-unit (company or even platoon) ambushes can seriously harass heavier enemy forces for very short periods without risking severe losses or entrapment. . . . Our forces could choose the time and place of the ambush, and enjoy, briefly, the advantage of surprise.[27]

Indeed,

gaming of a five-minute engagement between a U.S. light infantry company and the point of a Soviet mechanized column . . . indicates that the U.S. unit would incur minor losses while practically wiping out the opposing force.[28]

Finally, and consistent with the Soviets' own observations:

The use of a small expedient obstacle such as a point minefield would make the engagement even more lopsided, as it would provide the ambush force with stationary targets from the onset of the fighting . . . Ideally, the ambush force would be positioned only a short time before the enemy column came into range. It would be withdrawn immediately after the ambush. Given adequate helicopter transportation and ammunition, a light infantry company could conduct three or four such ambushes per day for a period of time. . . . A battalion of 3 companies could impose practically constant attrition and harassment on enemy columns . . .[29]

It is difficult to say precisely how severe the attrition exacted by these measures would be. There seems little doubt, however, that it could significantly reduce the force that the RDF would face in Khuzestan, and the same campaign affords the United States still more time to expand its force there.

In addition to the delay imposed by the Phase I air interdiction campaign, one can use the study's "planning guideline of two days' delay per engineer platoon day of effort"[30] to gauge the extent of further delay imposed upon

---

26. *Soviet Command Study*, p. 190.
27. Leonard and Scott, *Methodology For Estimating Movement Rates*, p. 4.1.
28. *Ibid.*
29. *Ibid.*, p. 4.3.
30. *Ibid.*, p. 4.5. This planning factor is given in connection with Zagros operations specifically.

Soviet troops in the Zagros. Bearing in mind that a platoon is one eighty-first ($1/81$) of a division,[31] the economies available are quickly evident.

There are literally two roads over the Zagros directly onto Dezful. The trans-Iranian railroad is a third avenue, assuming it has survived the air campaign in the north. The two roads which descend on Dezful from Kermanshah bring the total to roughly five arteries. From the above planning factor, it follows that a force of six platoons could, with two weeks of effort, close each of those approaches for thirty-four days.[32]

Time is the name of this game. And under reasonable assumptions, the Phase I air interdiction operation should have ensured thirty days of mobilization and deployment time for the battle of Khuzestan, while these Phase II *motti*-like tactics should raise the Soviets' time in transit (movement plus repair time) to Dezful by roughly another month. As far as the Soviet overland advance is concerned, then, sixty days does not seem overly optimistic as an estimate of the time the Soviets would require to emerge at the base of the Zagros. Is that all the time the RDF would have for mobilization and deployment for the final pitched battle in Khuzestan? It seems unlikely that it is. The RDF would have warning time as well. The question is, how much?

SOVIET READINESS, U.S. WARNING, AND DECISION TIME. The 1968 invasion of Czechoslovakia was preceded by a three-month build-up of which Western intelligence was aware. The invasion of Afghanistan was also preceded by three months of warning.[33] Should the Soviets invade Poland, that move will, in retrospect, have been preceded by at least three months of warning.

Of the roughly 24 divisions stationed in peacetime in the Southern Military Districts of the Soviet Union (North Caucasus, Transcaucasus, and Turkestan), none are accounted as Category I.[34] Indeed, over eighty percent are rated as Category III divisions.[35] To ready these forces for combat, the Soviets

---

31. A standard U.S. division structure is: 3 platoons/company; 3 companies/battalion; 3 battalions/brigade; 3 brigades/division.

32. Needless to say, the planning factor is a linear approximation of a more complicated relationship. However, even if it overestimates the effectiveness of such tactics by a significant margin, the effort involved in imposing the same delay would remain very modest. Some of the demolition responsibilities could also be assumed by tactical air.

33. See Jiri Valenta, "From Prague to Kabul: The Soviet Style of Invasion," *International Security*, Volume 5, Number 2 (Fall 1980).

34. *The Military Balance 1980–81* (London: The International Institute for Strategic Studies, 1980), p. 10–11. Soviet divisions have three degrees of combat readiness: Category I, between three-quarters and full strength, with complete equipment; Category II, between half and three-quarters strength, complete with fighting vehicles; Category III, about one-quarter strength, possibly complete with fighting vehicles (some obsolescent).

35. Henry Stanhope, "New Threat—or Old Fears?" in Derek Leebaert (ed.) *European Security: Prospects for the 1980s* (Lexington, MA: Lexington Books, 1979), p. 49.

would have to call up manpower and train or refresh much of it. Petroleum, oil, lubricants, spares, water, ammunition, and other supplies would have to be marshalled and loaded. The shipment of combat equipment into the area would be required while backlogged maintenance and, in some cases, final assembly of equipment would be performed. If the current mobilization for Poland is any indication, a great many trucks would be impressed from diverse quarters.

All of this activity takes time, and much of it would be visible to the West. Recent reports do indicate that, since the invasion of Afghanistan, the readiness of these forces has increased somewhat.[36] There is no indication, however, that Category I levels have been widely attained, while even those would credit the Soviets with as little as seventy-five percent of their full wartime manpower.

The standard category ranking of forces is, moreover, a static indicator. The "readiness" of forces depends on the missions facing them. One should not think of forces as "ready," but as "ready *for*" something; something specific.

In Czechoslovakia, resistance was essentially passive while in Afghanistan it, while tenacious, has lacked the sophisticated air force or the ground firepower that today's Soviet planner must anticipate in Iran. Thus, while granting some increase in "static readiness," if you will, to the Soviet units of interest, one must also assume that the Soviet planner recognizes the vast difference between the resistance of the Czechs and Afghans and that for which his forces must be "ready" in Iran. For all of these reasons, it is perfectly plausible that warning time would stay in the neighborhood of the usual three months. But let us be conservative and assume only one month of warning. The entire mobilization and deployment (M&D) time available to the main ground force of the RDF would thus appear to be 90 days.

| | |
|---|---|
| Warning Time | 1 month |
| Phase I Delay (air) | 1 month |
| Phase II Delay (special forces) | 1 month |
| **Total M & D Time** | **3 months** |

It must be stressed that warning time, in this military sense, and decision time among political figures are radically different entities. A great deal can

36. William W. Kaufmann, "Defense Policy," in Joseph A. Pechman (ed.), *Setting National Priorities: Agenda for the 1980s* (Washington D.C.: The Brookings Institution, 1980), p. 305.

be done with warning time: to broadcast one's cognizance of developments, to enhance the credibility of one's deterrent commitments, as well as to ready one's forces.[37] The availability of warning time, however, does not ensure that it will be used. Among the most important peacetime goals for the United States is to ensure that it *is* used, through procedural agreements with U.S. intelligence services and forces, and through diplomatic understandings with countries in the region. Time bought with warning is cheaper than time bought with force. Indeed, if it is utilized in the communication of one's military readiness and political determination, warning time may, by deterrence, avoid the conflict. If war *should* come, however, the Soviets would have little basis for confidence.

PHASE III: THE BATTLE OF KHUZESTAN
There are three basic issues concerning the ground balance. First, how many divisions could the Soviets support south of the Zagros? Second, in the time available (total M & D time), what is a conservative estimate of the U.S. build-up in Khuzestan? And finally, what confidence could the Soviets have of defeating that force in battle?

As to the second question, a range of estimates has appeared regarding the size of the RDF that could be brought to bear in sixty days. There is a well-founded consensus, however, that in addition to a Marine contingent of three brigades, three divisions and their initial support increments could be deployed to Khuzestan in roughly that time.[38] Since ninety, rather than sixty days of mobilization and deployment time would likely be available to all but the very spearhead of the force, the four division figure may even be conservative. A force considerably larger than this might be brought to bear if equipment and stocks were pre-positioned at, for example, Australian facilities, Clark Field, and Subic Bay in addition to Diego Garcia, particularly if warning time were exploited in a pre-arranged commitment of allied commercial shipping to the RDF's sea line of communication. This valuable

---

37. For example, load cargo, fuel-up for the lift, pre-deploy certain materiel, increase reconnaissance densities, move further Marine units into position, marshal allied commercial shipping, stand down and perform backlogged maintenance, and increase NATO alerts.
38. See for example, Sir John Hackett, "Protecting Oil Supplies," p. 14, and *U.S. Airlift Forces: Enhancement Alternatives for NATO and Non-NATO Contingencies* (Washington: The Congressional Budget Office, April 1979), pp. 23, 55. Relevant force weights, airlift planning factors, and computational methods are provided in that study and in *U.S. Projection Forces: Requirements, Scenarios, and Options* (Washington D.C.: The Congressional Budget Office, April 1978).

contribution would be a clear signal of allied involvement without being a commitment of allied troops to combat.

SIMULTANEOUS CONTINGENCIES. It is true that, at present, the 4-division figure assumes use of the full fleet of 77 C-5As,[39] the only U.S. aircraft capable of lifting outsized cargo. This represents a compromise in the U.S. ability to reinforce other theaters simultaneously. Maturation of the RDF's near- and long-term maritime pre-positioning programs, however, will relieve the outsized constraint, while oversized and bulk cargo capacities will rise with the C-141 "stretch" and aerial refuelling programs. Procurement of SL-7 fast sealift ships would further loosen these logistical constraints. Eight alone would allow the movement of "a mechanized infantry division from the East Coast to the Persian Gulf in about three weeks."[40] Commitment of U.S., Japanese, and European commercial air and shipping to logistical support would add a further measure of confidence to the sustainability of combat operations.

Since a Soviet attack on Iran would raise the specter of nuclear war, the Strategic Air Command would probably rank high in the pecking order for tanker support. While this is not a crippling constraint, either through procurement of additional long-range tankers, or by other measures, it is one that must be addressed.

Finally, third parties, such as North Korea, could take a superpower conflict in Iran as the occasion to settle vendettas of their own. Were such contingencies to coincide with wars in Central Europe and Iran, current U.S. strategic mobility and *active duty* forces might be stretched far too thin for comfort. That problem, however, is not irremediable.[41]

The United States faces challenges in the area of simultaneity. But those facing the Soviets are no less severe. The only Soviet aircraft with an outsized capability is the Antonov-22, of which there are reported to be but 75.[42] And, in reference to a statement by Defense Secretary Weinberger, the *New York*

---

39. Jeffrey Record, *The Rapid Deployment Force and U.S. Military Intervention in the Persian Gulf* (Cambridge, MA: Institute for Foreign Policy Analysis, 1981), p. 50.
40. RDJTF Fact Sheet, p. 7.
41. For a detailed discussion of U.S. corrective options, and their relative merits and costs, see William W. Kaufmann, "The Defense Budget," in Joseph Pechman (ed.), *Setting National Priorities, The 1982 Budget* (Washington D.C.: The Brookings Institution, 1981).
42. Robert P. Berman, *Soviet Airpower in Transition* (Washington D.C.: The Brookings Institution, 1978), p. 35. Berman notes that "about two-thirds of their fleet of seventy-five is in operation at any one time."

*Times* has reported that, "The airlift capacity of the Soviet Union was said to be unable to cope with two large operations at one time." [43]

Thus, while the lift to Iran would initially tie up the U.S. C-5A fleet, any comparable lift on the Soviets' part would similarly strain their outsized airlift capacity. (The vulnerability of Soviet airlift is discussed below). Moreover, with China, NATO, the Poles and Afghanistan, Iran would be, not their third, but rather, the Soviets' *fifth* contingency—one which could severely hamper their capability elsewhere.

The force with which a four-division RDF would have to contend, over a thousand kilometers south of the Soviet border, depends upon other factors which have not been widely appreciated. While the peacetime deployment of twenty-four divisions in the southern Soviet Union has been publicized, the pertinent questions have not been raised. Over what duration of conflict could the Soviets *support* a field force of a given size? To provide a force with the consumables required to sustain combat at the distances facing the Soviets is a major logistical challenge, and one they have never faced before. Indeed, they have addressed far less challenging logistical problems with something less than virtuosity.

For example, in the invasion of Czechoslovakia, the Soviets met little resistance.

No bridges were destroyed, no road blocks erected, and no minefields were planted in the invaders' path. Under such conditions, there was no reason to expect anything other than a brilliant performance by the Soviet Army.

Yet,

Short of organic transport, the armored and mechanized divisions were left without basic supplies on the third day of occupation. Under actual combat conditions, they would have lacked many essential items after the first 24 hours. [44]

Although the Soviets appear to have expanded their organic transport somewhat, logistics remains among the weakest links in the Soviet military machine.

At daily consumption rates (of ammunition, spare parts, petroleum, oil, and lubricants) consistent with a high offensive lethality (discussed below),

---

43. Richard Halloran, "U.S. Is Weighing Aid to China If Soviet Acts Against Poles," *The New York Times*, April 5, 1981, p. 6.

44. Leo Heiman, "Soviet Invasion Weaknesses," *Military Review*, August 1969, p. 39 and p. 43.

it is implausible that the Soviets could sustain a combat force of more than about seven divisions in Khuzestan without degrading their European, Far Eastern, or Afghanistan capabilities. Beyond that level, the requirement in logistics trucks alone grows at so disproportionate a rate that to sustain the full 24-division[45] "threat" could dictate a draw-down (from other theaters) on the order of 55 Category I divisions' worth of trucks.[46] This would exceed the supply available from the sum of Soviet forces deployed opposite China (46 divisions) and in Afghanistan (6 divisions), even if those forces were all Category I. And since they are not all Category I, a 24-division force in Khuzestan would, in fact, denude an even greater number of divisions.

The calculation underlying these assertions, moreover, is quite conservative. It assumes *no* attrition of Soviet trucks and that *none* suffer mechanical breakdown. It leaves out of account *all* limitations on road capacity, a factor which alone could limit the Soviet force to the same low level. In calculating the Soviets' combat tonnage requirement, such necessities as food and water were excluded, again to be conservative.

Giving the Soviets the benefit of some rather serious doubts, then, and assuming that a seven-division combat force could be supported for a Battle of Khuzestan, what confidence would that force have of defeating an RDF of four divisions?

LETHALITY, DEFENSIVE ADVANTAGE, AND THE GROUND BATTLE IN KHUZESTAN. Although the RDF would not be grossly outnumbered, history in fact records innumerable cases in which even the vastly outnumbered defender staves off aggression. The defense, for example, may enjoy the advantage of operation from prepared, or even fortified, positions while an attacker must come out into the open to advance, exposing himself to fire.

If he is not to increase his vulnerability further by halting, the attacker must locate the more concealed target and fire on it while in motion; but

---

45. The 24 divisions facing Iran are those of the Southern Soviet Military Districts (Northern Caucasus, Transcaucasus, and Turkestan). For conservatism's sake, let us add the six divisions of the Central Military Districts (Urals and Volga). From this theater total, subtract again six, the force now in Afghanistan. The remaining 24 divisions is then the theater pool with which we are concerned. All other forces are either deployed to the Sino–Soviet border, to Eastern Europe or to the latter's reinforcement in the Military Districts of the European USSR. Requirements beyond those organic to the theater pool of 24 divisions must therefore be seen as draw-downs from these other contingencies, and thus as representing sacrifices in the Soviets' capacity to undertake them simultaneously. *The Military Balance, 1980–1981,* pp. 10–11.

46. These calculations are presented in Joshua M. Epstein, *The Soviet Threat to Iran and the Deterrent Adequacy of U.S. Rapid Deployment Forces,* (Paper presented to the Oil and Security Roundtable, July 23–24, 1981, Harvard University).

motion generally reduces accuracy. In this case, moreover, the defender (the RDF) is agreed to retain a significant technological edge in the areas of target acquisition, battlefield reconnaissance, and its processing.

Where these defensive advantages apply, military experience has handed down the general planning factor that a defender should be able to hold the front essentially stable so long as the attacker enjoys no more than a 2 to 1 advantage in lethality.[47] More conservative planning factors (1.5 to 1) and less conservative ones (3 to 1) are available, as are more or less demanding tactics than holding the front stationary. But, even under the most conservative tactics and planning factors, an RDF of four divisions should be expected to fare rather well.

Such judgments, of course, are based on some measure of relative lethality, a difficult entity to gauge. By the crudest of indices, the division count, the 4-division RDF balances the Soviet 7-division threat, at the above-cited Army planning factor of 2 to 1. However, the more refined is one's measure of lethality, the more powerful grows the RDF in relation to the Soviets. For example, under the Army's WEI/WUV scoring, a U.S. armored division on the defensive is rated as being 50 percent stronger than a Soviet tank division on the offensive; a Soviet tank division, that is, represents 0.67 U.S. Armored Division Equivalents (ADEs).[48] At relative lethalities in this range, the 7-division Soviet force is the equivalent of 4.69 U.S. divisions of the same class; the lethality ratio falls thus to $4.69/4 = 1.17$, well within the more conservative planning factor of 1.5 to 1. But, the WEI/WUV scoring considers only the assets of the division and, in leaving support and non-divisional (corps) assets out of account, attributes disproportionate weight to the Soviet divi-

---

47. U.S. Army Field Manual FM 105-5, *Maneuver Control* (Department of the Army, 1967), p. 212.
48. In the WEI/WUV system, the U.S. armored division is assigned the value of 1.0. In relation to the U.S. armored division, the lethality of any other force may be gauged by a weighted aggregation of the strength of its component units. By a combination of test range data and military operational judgment, the components are assigned weapon effectiveness indices (WEIs). These are then added up to obtain the weighted unit values (WUVs), expressed in U.S. Armored Division Equivalents. The procedure differs from the older firepower scoring in "working down," as it were, from the U.S. armored division rather than "working up" to a firepower score in M-16 rifle equivalents. The WEI/WUV system also incorporates accuracy and other factors not embodied in the firepower scoring. Remarkably enough, the systems do not differ notably in their estimates of the relative lethality of U.S. and Soviet units. Given their comparable valuations, since it embodies factors, such as accuracy, in which the U.S. is generally agreed to enjoy an edge, the WEI/WUV system may be considered the more conservative of the two. The methodology is fully elaborated in *Final Report: Weapon Effectiveness Indices/Weighted Unit Values: Volume I, Executive Summary*, Prepared by The War Gaming Directorate, U.S. Army Concepts Analysis Agency (Study Report CAA–ST–73–18) Bethesda, Maryland, April 1974.

sion's front end, or "teeth," as it were. Not only should the United States be able to position *corps* assets in the region, but the second delay phase has, as one of its primary functions, the attrition of precisely those teeth which weigh so heavily on the WEI/WUV scale. In addition, at these distances from the Soviet Union, the RDF would have a clear advantage in close air support, another factor not embraced by the 1.17 ratio derived above. When all these factors are considered, parity, the most conservative planning factor of all, seems altogether plausible.

DYNAMIC FACTORS AND THE BATTLE OF KHUZESTAN. Division counts and these more refined measures—indeed all static indicators—ignore a host of factors which may prove decisive in war. For this reason, over-reliance on such approaches is ill-advised. Morale, mobility, logistics, and coordination— factors not reflected in such static measures—have often tipped the balance. Granted. But where, in any of these less tangible and perhaps decisive areas, would the Soviets enjoy a relative advantage?

The least tangible, morale, is by far the most difficult to assess. But, descriptions of the Allied resupply of Russia through the Persian Corridor may suggest the type of fatigue these routes would exact.

Mile after mile of washboard roads took toll on men as well as vehicles. As an anonymous military scribe put it, vibration "shook the trucks to pieces . . . and pounded the men's kidneys to jelly."[49]

Though an open question, such physical stress, when compounded by the trauma of surprise ambush day and night in the Zagros, would hardly seem to contribute to the élan of Soviet troops.

Even were such punishment to galvanize the steely invaders, the Soviets would not enjoy the advantage of mobility, canalized as their descent would be, into a very few corridors onto Dezful. The RDF would not be so channeled, operating from the relatively open lowlands south of the Zagros. Moreover, insofar as Soviet training consists in refining the advance in broad echelons, that training and that tactic are wholly inappropriate to this terrain.

As for relative sustainability, in Khuzestan it is the RDF which could avail itself of a shorter and more secure line of communication certainly for the first few weeks, after which time the RDF's reliance on long-distance sea-lift

---

49. T. H. Vail Motter, *The Persian Corridor and Aid to Russia*, (Washington D.C.: Office of The Chief of Military History, Department of The Army, 1952), p. 327. More historical information on aid to Russia through the Persian Gulf may be found in Richard M. Leighton and Robert W. Coakley, *Global Logistics and Strategy 1940–1943* (Washington D.C.: Office of the Chief of Military History, Department of The Army, 1955).

would grow. And, while there is debate concerning the interdiction which that sea line of communication might suffer, it is hard to see it as being any *more* vulnerable than Soviet lines, strung out as they would be over hundreds of miles of vulnerable terrain. Nor, as we shall see, would the Soviets be likely to enjoy any advantage in the aerial resupply of forces.

More important, perhaps, than questions of morale, mobility, training, or sustainability is that of coordination. In particular, even the quite acceptable WEI/WUV estimate of a 1.17 to 1 lethality ratio was predicated on the assumption that all of the Soviet divisions emerge from the Zagros *at the same time* and instantaneously constitute themselves as a seven-division fighting force. If they come through two divisions or three divisions at a time, they can be taken on piecemeal and, by such measures as those above, would be grossly outweighed by the RDF. Indeed, at anything less than a simultaneous arrival, the Soviet forces would be unlikely to achieve parity with the RDF.

The coordination problem was not lost on the thorough Soviet planners, who wrote,

As a result of the mountainous terrain structure and because of the few roads, the combat engagements will be carried out mostly with mixed units which, at times, must operate completely independently. For this reason, the coordination of individual separate columns . . . is of exceptional importance.[50]

To recognize the problem is one thing. To solve it is another. And there is no neat way for the Soviets to circumvent it. Concentration (reducing the number of advance axes) in the interest of simultaneous arrival merely raises the value of each choke point while reducing their number, thus simplifying the RDF's delaying operations. On the other hand, dispersion (raising the number of advance axes), while forcing the United States to spread its resources over a greater (but still very small) number of choke points, exacerbates the coordination problem, possibly reducing the land threat with which the RDF would ultimately contend in Khuzestan. Neither alternative should be especially attractive to the Soviets.

The above points are summarized in Table 1.

While the more refined WEI/WUV ratio falls well within the conservative defensive criterion of 1.5 to 1, elimination of the WEI/WUV's pro-Soviet bias, and inclusion of close air and other factors would reduce the actual ratio to

---

50. *Soviet Command Study*, pp. 240–241.

**Table 1. Relative Capabilities: Battle of Khuzestan**

| Measure | Soviets | RDF | Lethality Ratio |
|---|---|---|---|
| Divisions | 7 | 4 | 1.75 |
| U.S. Division Equivalents | 4.69 | 4 | 1.17 |
| **Other Factors** | | | **Effect on Ratio** |
| Morale | ? | ? | ? |
| WEI/WUV Bias | − | + | reduces |
| Close Air Support | − | + | reduces |
| Battlefield Mobility | − | + | reduces |
| Coordination | − | + | reduces |

still less than the quite acceptable 1.17. Indeed, without virtually perfect coordination, the Soviets would be unlikely to achieve more than parity with the RDF.

A DRIVE FROM AFGHANISTAN? It might be added that an overland drive from Afghanistan, which would be extremely difficult in its own right, would merely exacerbate the coordination problem if attempted as the eastern axis of a grand envelopment. The distances to Khuzestan from Afghanistan are considerably greater than those from the Soviet Union. This alone would make a simultaneous arrival difficult. In addition, there are no surfaced roads directly across the intervening desert of the Khorassan. There, the Soviets tell us,

During summer the temperature is so high that the inhabitants of the cities withdraw to the so-called "Sirisamin" (cellar) and along the caravan routes, the caravans usually do not continue travel during the day.[51]

Water sources are confined to a few oases. In addition to sending up clouds of dust to advertise its position, a summer blitz across this terrain would ensure a very high mechanical breakdown rate. Roads south of the desert either terminate in the difficult Zagros or traverse them. On the other hand, the "end run" above the Khorassan (which reduces to a single road along the base of the Golul Dagh Mountains.) would force a crossing of the Zagros from the north, over the same limited and vulnerable system of roads already glutted by the advance from the Soviet Union. To pull any significant

---

51. *Ibid.*, p. 42.

force from Afghanistan would require a reinforcement of Soviet efforts there, thus entailing a draw-down from other theaters.

While summer is surely the worst time in the Khorassan, winter finds the mountain passes of northern Iran snowed in. In the spring thaw, lowlands, particularly those of the Caspian basin, are transformed into a swampy morass, precluding off-road traffic.[52] Finally, fall, though probably the best season in general, is the rainy season in the northwest, opposite which the bulk of Soviet forces are deployed. During that time, the main rivers of the Azerbaidjan become unfordable torrents, making indispensible what few bridges exist. In any season, an attempt to coordinate the simultaneous advance of forces along all of these axes would be, in short, a logistician's nightmare.

For all these reasons and by any measure—static or dynamic—a pure overland advance would be exceedingly risky for the Soviets. Thus, one may expect them to consider airlifted assault. Airlift, however, would face vulnerabilities which are just as severe.

*Airlifted Assault*

The Soviets have developed a considerable airlifted power projection capability, as demonstrated in the October War, Angola, Ethiopia, and Afghanistan. However, none of these lifts was opposed by anything even remotely resembling the kind of airpower the Soviets would face in Iran. Their problem is not one of lift capability *per se;* rather it is fighter escort for the lift. Without the protection provided by that escort, the Soviets' chances for an airborne insertion and aerial resupply of forces would be slim. If the United States exploited warning, the Soviets' prospects would be very slight indeed.

Recognizing the importance of fighter escort, it is important to note that, despite strides since Khrushchev's ouster, the Soviets remain outclassed in the air-to-air combat arena.

In addition to the technological edge,[53] U.S. pilot skill exceeds that of the Soviets. Soviet pilot training is far more routine and is far less realistic than

52. In fact, the main port of Pahlavi is situated in an area called the "Gilan," meaning "swampy, muddy place." *Ibid.,* p. 161.
53. While the very sophistication of U.S. systems has created serious problems in areas of support, notably those of sortie generation and sustainability, it is far from clear that the Soviets have avoided the same problems. There is every reason to believe, in fact, that while Soviet air systems are by some measures, simpler than those of the United States, the Soviet ground

American.[54] Furthermore, the U.S. pilot flies roughly twice as much as his Soviet counterpart.[55] American non-flying hours are spent, in part, on very sophisticated simulators, of which the Soviets are reported to possess nothing comparable. Finally, U.S. training has built on a great deal of combat experience gained since World War II, in Korea and in Vietnam, far more than the Soviets. Given these advantages—more realistic training, and more of it, in addition to the benefits of far more combat experience—it is difficult to imagine the United States enjoying anything less than a significant margin in pilot skill, the importance of which cannot be overemphasized. Essentially alone, it accounted for the exchange ratios of 12.5 to 1 recorded in Indochina (F-4 *vs.* MiG-21). And when combined with a technological advantage, it goes a long way toward explaining the extraordinarily high exchange rates logged by the Israelis in 1967 and 1973 (20 to 1 and 40 to 1 respectively).[56] Thus, even if this conflict presented a classical air-to-air combat situation, the Soviets would have little basis for confidence that they would enjoy air superiority. That being the case, under the highly *non*-classical conditions of Iran, the RDF would enjoy a number of pronounced advantages.

For one, the exchange ratios of the Korean and Vietnam conflicts, as well as the remarkable Israeli ratios, were kills of *fighters* by other fighters. In opposing a Soviet airlift, however, U.S. pilots would be attempting to shoot down Soviet *transports*—very sluggish, easily acquired, and highly vulnerable

---

support (maintenance, logistics) system is so much less efficient than the American that, in the net, the Soviets find their advanced systems to be no more supportable than the U.S. finds its own to be. In turn, it can be argued that, due to the inefficiency of their ground support environment, the Soviets face equally severe problems in sortie generation and sustainability. Joshua M. Epstein, *Political Impediments to Military Effectiveness: The Case of Soviet Frontal Aviation* (doctoral dissertation, MIT, 1980).

54. The Soviet military literature is full of high-ranking commentary attesting both to the routinized character of Soviet pilot training and to its adverse effect on flexibility. Characteristic examples are: Pavlov, General–Lieutenant G., "Inexhaustible Reserve," *Krasnaya Zvezda,* August 4, 1976 (April 1977); Konstantinov, General–Colonel Anatoliy Ustinovich, "Thorough Knowledge of Affairs," *Krasnaya Zvezda,* March 13, 1977 (June 1977); or Babayev, General–Colonel Aleksandr Ivanovich, "Flight and the Combat Maneuver," *Krasnaya Kvezeda,* December 23, 1976 (April 1977). For these and all subsequent Russian citations, the parenthesized date is for the English language version appearing in *Soviet Press Selected Translations,* Directorate of Soviet Affairs, Air Force Intelligence Service.
55. Robert P. Berman, *Soviet Air Power in Transition,* p. 57.
56. All of these data are given in Steven J. Rosen, "What a Fifth Arab–Israeli War Might Look Like," *International Security,* Volume 2, Number 4 (Spring 1978), p. 160. See, in general, Peter de Leon, *The Peacetime Evaluation of the Pilot Skill Factor in Air-to-Air Combat R–2070–Pr* (Santa Monica, CA: The Rand Corporation, January 1977).

targets. The situation then is highly preferential to the defense. Khuzestan, moreover, is simply out of range of virtually all Soviet tactical fighters, based either in Afghanistan or the Soviet Union.[57] The direct airlift to Khuzestan, for these reasons, would be vulnerable in the extreme.

Much of central Iran is also out of range for all but late model Soviet fighters (whose adaptibility to the local basing system must be considered an open question).

Even where central Iran is within range of those aircraft, it may be well out of range of Soviet ground control.[58] Under Soviet ground-controlled intercept (GCI), target acquisition, vectoring, and other critical intercept instructions are transmitted from stations on the ground. If not actually out of range of Soviet-based GCI, then fighter operations in much of central Iran and all of southern Iran could be at ranges where the GCI link is highly susceptible to jamming by, for example, carrier-based EA-6B (4 per carrier) electronic warfare aircraft. However rigidly the Soviet pilot is trained to fight under ground control, he is virtually untrained to fight without it.[59]

The problem, from the Soviets' perspective, is how to get the GCI south of the northern mountains. Overland, as we've seen, would not be promising and would certainly be slow. So, if the GCI is to be established with any dispatch, it must be airlifted in. In order to airlift it in however, fighter escort would be essential. But the escort cannot be run effectively until the GCI is in place! There is the rub.

Even if airlanded in central Iran, the GCI radars and other components would be highly vulnerable to low-altitude attack by U.S. aircraft, especially if, with forward-looking infra red (FLIR) technology, the strikes were conducted under cover of darkness. And, while Soviet airborne reconnaissance of low-level attack is progressing, it is generally agreed that, even in daylight,

---

57. The possibility of re-equipping the longer-range SU-24 advanced ground attack aircraft for air-to-air combat is unpromising. First, it is an open question whether rudimentary Afghan bases could accommodate the system. But more important is the fact that the SU-24 pilot, rigidly drilled in his ground attack mission, cannot easily be converted to a master of air-to-air combat, even if his aircraft could be so adapted. Similarly, air-to-air pilots are unlikely ever to have flown the SU-24 and would be ill-prepared to substitute for its usual operators.
58. Soviet problems in maintaining the integrity of the ground control data link as range increases are discussed in Colonel V. A. Uryzhnikov, "In a Complex Situation," *Krasnaya Zvezda*, January 7, 1977 (April 1977).
59. *Soviet Aerospace Handbook AF Pamphlet 200–21* (Washington D.C.: Department of the Air Force, May 1978), p. 45.

Soviet fighters do not possess a sophisticated look-down/shoot-down capability.[60] These factors support the assessment of General David Jones, Chairman of the Joint Chiefs of Staff, who in June of 1980,

> told the Senate Armed Services Committee that "a few AWACS (Airborne Warning and Control Aircraft) and a few fighters could just devastate an airborne operation," if the Soviet Armed Forces sought to seize oil fields in the Persian Gulf region.[61]

Thus, while the Soviet overland invasion is highly vulnerable, the airlifted assault would not be any less so.

It is implicit in such assessments that warning time is exploited and that the decision to use force be taken. Otherwise, the West's significant advantages could erode and her promising defensive avenues could quickly close.

*Carrier Vulnerability*

In a Soviet invasion of Iran, the "worst case" scenario would posit the simultaneous initiation of airlifted and overland assaults, coordinated with a massed Soviet bomber attack on the carriers. In discussing that threat, certain points should be stressed.

First, the strategy proposed here has four basic elements: two delay phases against the overland threat, the interdiction of Soviet airlift, and a build-up and combined arms defense in Khuzestan. *This*, and not the carriers, *per se*, is what the Soviets must overcome to secure control of Khuzestan's oil. After all, even to sink the carriers would not, in and of itself, transport a single Russian to Khuzestan. Nor would it guarantee that the United States would be incapable of carrying out its own strategy. If the carriers can survive long enough to ensure that the four basic operations are executed, they will have performed their war mission.

Just as carrier interdiction is not, *per se*, the Soviets' war goal, so, carrier survival is not, *per se*, the RDF's goal; that is to deny Soviet control of Khuzestan. And if American interests in the area are vital, then the United States should be willing to run the risk that carriers will be lost. The carriers, after all, were bought to fight. And while their vulnerability can and should be minimized, in a fight, they may be destroyed.

---

60. *Ibid.*, p. 66.
61. John M. Collins, *U.S.–Soviet Military Balance, Concepts and Capabilities 1960–1980* (New York: McGraw-Hill, 1980), footnote, p. 394.

The carriers are at their most vulnerable only in the initial period, when the northern tier of Iranian choke points is being struck and the Marine perimeter in Khuzestan is being established. But even in that period, as noted above, the carriers can be employed in a way that avoids their passage into the Persian Gulf, leaves them substantial resources for air defense, and allows for their timely and rapid withdrawal to the Arabian Sea area. And while all is not lost even if the carriers are lost, there is no particular reason that they should be.[62]

THE SOVIET BOMBER THREAT. Of the two Soviet bomber forces, Long-Range Aviation (LRA) and Naval Aviation, the former is deployed solely to the European Soviet Union (2 Air Armies) and the Far East (1 Air Army).[63] A significant diversion of LRA's bomber resources would clearly represent a sacrifice in the Soviets' capacity to execute either the Sino–Soviet or NATO contingencies at the same time, not to mention those strategic nuclear missions for which LRA might be withheld. Particularly in the European theater, the presence of LRA and of Naval Aviation's Northern and Baltic Fleet bomber forces would be critical, if the Soviets are to credibly threaten the execution of their short-war doctrine, or the achievement of their vaunted preemption there.

Accordingly, unless we assume the Soviets are willing to free up forces otherwise earmarked to cope with those threats to Europe, our attention should first be directed to the Black Sea and Pacific Fleets of Naval Aviation. However, were the entire Pacific Fleet force reallocated to the Gulf, the Soviets would have sacrificed maritime strike operations in defense of critical facilities in the Vladivostok area. Similarly, a full redeployment of the Black Sea fleet would free U.S. forces in the Eastern Mediterranean from the threat of bomber attack. While these considerations could militate against such wholesale Soviet redeployments, even if they were attempted, one may doubt the basing capacity of the southern Soviet Union to accommodate them. Finally, the *total* Backfire inventory of Naval Aviation's *four* fleets is

---

62. Of course, should the carriers be destroyed by nuclear means, a U.S. nuclear response on the northern transportation system would still deny the Soviets their posited objective, as would the clearly more provocative nuclear response on division bases, rail lines, air fields, supply dumps, or other conventional military facilities in the southern USSR. For an insightful discussion of the latter action and its possible implications, see Thomas C. Schelling, *Arms and Influence* (New Haven, CT: Yale University Press, 1966), pp. 160–162.
63. *The Military Balance 1980–1981*, p. 9.

reported to be 70.[64] Thus, even on the questionable assumption that a size-able portion of *two* (Black Sea and Pacific) Fleet bomber forces were allocated to this mission, the number of Backfires involved could be even more limited.

As for warning of such an attack, the Soviets would need a certain amount of time to ready their forces. They might succeed in doing so under cover of deception. But if, as postulated, the bomber attack is to take place simulta-neously with the overland drive, it must wait until the Soviet ground forces are mobilized. And of that activity, the United States would have warning. It would certainly be odd for the Soviets to maximize surprise in the bomber attack by launching it a month before the ground forces were ready to exploit it. In short, the United States *would* have warning time in which to ready its resistance.

"LAYERED" CARRIER DEFENSES. Although there are uncertainties, when the above factors are taken into account, the bomber threat facing the carriers' multiple defensive "layers" does not seem unmanageable.

Assets for the so-called "outer air battle," in the words of the Chief of Naval Operations Admiral Hayward,

consist primarily of the E-2 B/C airborne early warning aircraft used to detect and track incoming aircraft and missiles, the F-14 variable-geometry fighter which is capable of launching and tracking as many as six AIM-54A long-range PHOENIX air intercept missiles, and the F-4 fighter aircraft capable of launching the AIM-7 SPARROW all-aspect air intercept missile.[65]

Secretary of the Navy Claytor has testified, moreover, that the F-14 "can go out and shoot down the Russian's Backfire out of range of its ability to launch a missile."[66]

Soviet bombers surviving that first layer, while remaining susceptible to further counterair (air-to-air) resistance and jamming, would pass into the second ring of carrier defenses. Again, the current debate presents an image of carriers operating alone. But the carrier, albeit a prima donna, is a social animal whose coterie of guided missile escorts is designed to provide it with a tough area defense.[67]

---

64. *Ibid.*, p. 11.
65. U.S., Congress, House, Committee on Appropriations, *Department of Defense Appropriations For 1980, Hearings before the Subcommittee on the Department of Defense*, Ninety-Sixth Congress, First Session, Part 2, p. 266.
66. *Ibid.*, p. 277.
67. *Ibid.*, p. 266.

Finally, the Soviet bombers would encounter the carrier battle group's so-called "self-defense." Here,

. . . we look at two types of "kills"—the "hard kill" in which we destroy the inbound missile and the "soft kill" in which we deceive the missile so that it misses the target.[68]

In addition, it should be borne in mind that the closer the Soviet bomber gets to the carriers, the thinner becomes its fighter escort. And, over a broad perimeter around the carriers, it would be likely to lack any fighter protection. Essentially the same very serious vulnerability would then prevail as in the case of Soviet airlift.

If the bomber survives to launch its missiles, and against the carrier battle group's layered defenses, the missiles are neither intercepted nor deceived, there still remains the question of accuracy. One may assume hit probabilities greater than fifty percent if one chooses, but it would be irresponsible not to raise those assumed on the RDF's side correspondingly. And to do so would allow the RDF's northern interdiction campaign (Phase I) to be conducted more quickly.

Finally, even a hit is not necessarily a kill. Carriers can be rather durable entities.

During training exercises in 1969, the nuclear carrier ENTERPRISE endured explosions of nine major caliber bombs (equivalent in explosive weight to 6 anti-ship cruise missiles) on the flight deck. All essential ship systems remained operable, effective damage control contained the effects of the fire, and the ship could have resumed flight operations within hours.[69]

While the remark applies to ship- and submarine-launched cruise missiles as well, the carrier's cruise missile defense is likewise one layered in depth, terminating in "rings of long- and medium-range surface to air missiles (SAM), close-in SAMs, and aircraft."[70] The F-14 is reported to have demonstrated a capacity to engage, again, six.[71] The tactical ASW system of the carrier task force is organized along the same principals and might be visualized as an inverted, underwater variation on its anti-air warfare rings.

These capabilities give the carrier battle group a more than fighting chance in the Gulf region; an area in which the limited Soviet surface fleet would

---

68. *Ibid.*
69. *Ibid.*, p. 268.
70. *Ibid.*, p. 282.
71. *Ibid.*, p. 264.

lack comparable defensive avenues and logistical support, i.e., underway replenishment. Indeed, Washington officials have stated that "even if they bring in the Minsk (V/STOL Carrier), it would be no contest."[72]

Destruction of the carriers would, *per se*, be a formidable task. Moreover, in order to frustrate the larger four-point RDF strategy proposed here, the Soviets would have to destroy them *very* fast. And, if the United States uses its warning time to ready the carriers' imposing defenses, then even focusing the bombers on their destruction, it is hard to imagine great Soviet confidence of success. And that allocation is questionable.

DIVERSION OF SOVIET BOMBERS. For the Soviets to focus the full bomber threat on the carriers would leave them virtually no resources with which to harass the Marine landing in Khuzestan. As noted above, the preponderance of Soviet *tactical* air effectively lacks either the range to attack the Khuzestan landing or the capacity to operate from the crude Afghan bases which might be within range.[73]

Diego Garcia, which the United States already controls, will shortly be capable of accommodating the B-52s. Given its importance as a maritime staging area generally, Diego Garcia would be yet another target to which the Soviets might be forced to divert bombers.

In short, the Soviets face a target system considerably more complicated than the two carriers. And this contributes to the carriers' already substantial survivability by forcing some dispersion of Soviet bomber resources.

If, during the warning time which should be available, a third carrier were brought on line, the RDF's interdiction and landing operations might be conducted even more rapidly. In that case, the Soviets would have a) yet more targets to destroy, b) an even denser air defense to overcome in doing so, and c) even less time in which to accomplish the task.

*Conclusions*

While facing a redundant, flexible, and in fact rather dispersed resistance, the Soviets possess only two viable modes of advance into Iran: airlifted and

---

72. "Soviet Naval Presence Doubles in Indian Ocean, Lacks Support," *Aviation Week and Space Technology*, April 6, 1981, p. 60.
73. If we are to assume that from Afghanistan, the BEAR can penetrate the F–14 net to attack U.S. carriers in the Persian Gulf or Gulf of Oman, then the B-52H should certainly be assumed capable of penetrating the MiG-21 (or MiG-23) net to attack Afghan bases. *Spif*'s B-52H night-low altitude mission is specifically designed to exploit the weakness of Soviet look-down/shoot-down capabilities. George C. Wilson, ". . . New Conventional Role for B-52 Bombers," pp. 6–7.

overland. In exploiting the Soviets' numerous vulnerabilities, the RDF's essential missions are four: to delay, in two successive phases, the overland advance and to interdict Soviet airlift, while building up a combined arms defense in Khuzestan. If the Soviets' goal is control of Iran's oil, this strategy, rather than a forward defense is appropriate. And if warning time is exploited, U.S. forces should be able to execute the plan conventionally. In the pitched battle of Khuzestan, that is, the Soviet force which could be supported without penalizing their capacity to handle simultaneous contingencies would be unlikely to enjoy any meaningful superiority over an RDF assembled under the same strategic constraint. And if the deep problem of Soviet coordination were exploited, it is questionable whether the Soviet force would even achieve parity with that RDF.

The Europeans can contribute significantly to the defense of Western interests in the Gulf by maintaining Central Front forces in sufficient readiness that the Soviets are sternly reminded of their simultaneous contingencies.

To argue the feasibility of a conventional defense is not to deny that the RDF has substantial work ahead of it. It does, particularly in the areas of logistics, training, command and control, and in basic detailed planning for the employment of its forces, some of which must be tailored very precisely to the tactics contemplated here. However, while stressing that the RDF faces challenges, the current situation warrants neither the kind of pessimism that has been heaped upon it nor an ill-considered "drive for bases" which may flow from overassessments of the Soviet threat.

Militarily, the RDF is clearly better off with more regional basing than it is without it. And there is no reason for the United States to abandon its efforts to negotiate suitable arrangements in the event of crisis. In doing so, however, the United States can afford to bargain from a position of strength, eschewing entanglements with regimes less worthy of American political support than military relationships may suggest; regimes whose stability (as Iran should have taught) may be far more tenuous than Americans might wish to believe; regimes which, in the final analysis, may acquire political interests quite inimical to those of the United States and to those of its proven ally, Israel.

No one has found a way to predict with *certainty* the outcome of any given conflict. But the invasion of Iran would be an exceedingly *low confidence* affair for the Soviets—a fact which I believe they've known for roughly 40 years. Indeed, it can be argued that they now regard it as far less attractive even than their *Command Study* of 1941 portrayed it as being. While, to be sure, Soviet military capabilities have evolved very significantly since that time, so have those of the United States and, more importantly, so have the Soviets' military commitments and deterrent needs. Certainly to cover three contingencies simultaneously would strain the United States. But beyond China, NATO, the Poles, and Afghanistan, an invasion of Iran would be the Soviets' fifth contingency. And it is one which, as we've seen, could severely hamper their capability elsewhere.

The Soviets face the grave threat that the military cost of a move on Iran would vastly outweigh its potential benefits—indeed, the risk that all such benefits would be decisively denied. It can only be assumed, therefore, that the Soviets would prefer to secure their ends in the Gulf by other means, by coercive measures short of direct intervention. All of those measures find their underpinning, finally, in the appearance of crushing Soviet military power and in the perception that the Soviets are prepared to use it to get what they want, and are confident of doing so with success. The fundamental question, and it is a political one, is this: by overdrawing the direct Soviet threat to Iran—or to any country—do we not aid the Soviets in their diplomacy of coercion?

By presenting the United States as if it alone suffers simultaneous contingency problems, and by presenting the Soviets as if they enjoyed some clear superiority in the Gulf, we do. In the final analysis that is not "getting tough" with the Soviets.

One "gets tough" with an adversary by credibly threatening to exploit his military vulnerabilities, not by refusing to admit that any exist, as is the general practice among so-called "hard-liners." Such talk, however, is not "hard" on the Soviets. On the contrary, the rhetoric of an invincible Soviet threat, while alienating those whose cooperation we seek and/or exposing them to the coercion we fear, merely discredits the larger cause it purports to champion—management of the global competition and deterrence of war. These are feasible goals. In the case of the Gulf, forces exist which can and should be postured to communicate that fact. While they are not invincible, the Soviets are attentive. They will get the message.